GLOBAL CIVIL SOCIETY
2005/6

Marlies Glasius, Mary Kaldor, Helmut Anheier, editors-in-chief

Fiona Holland, managing editor

SAGE Publications
London • Thousand Oaks • New Delhi

First published 2006

SAGE Publications Ltd
1 Oliver's Yard
55 City Road
London EC1Y 1SP

SAGE Publications Inc.
2455 Teller Road
Thousand Oaks, California 91320

SAGE Publications India Pvt Ltd
B-42, Panchsheel Enclave
Post Box 4109
New Delhi 110 017

British Library Cataloguing in Publication data

A catalogue record for this book is available from the British Library

ISBN 1-4129-1192-3
ISBN 1-4129-1193-1 (pbk)

Library of Congress Control Number: 2005926720

Typeset by People, Design Consultants
Printed in Great Britain by Cromwell Press, Trowbridge, Wilts
Printed on paper from sustainable resources

MISSION STATEMENT

Global civil society is diverse, creative and chaotic. That's what makes it always interesting, often unpredictable and sometimes very powerful. Studying global civil society is a way of understanding globalisation, which is all too often seen as a predominantly economic phenomenon. The reality of globalisation is more complex. Globalisation is about individual autonomy, responsibility and participation. It embodies a growing global consciousness and emerging sphere of shared values and ideas.

We are interested in how individuals try to take control of global processes rather than being overwhelmed by them. Citizens around the world, their values and identities, communities and forms of political participation, help to shape and, in turn, are shaped by globalisation – in ways that are poorly documented and little understood.

Global Civil Society is an attempt to fill this gap in our knowledge – a gap that could become politically dangerous and socially damaging in a global era full of tensions, anxieties and uncertainties. Bringing together leading thinkers in the social sciences, as well as activists and practitioners in civil societies around the world, the Yearbook seeks to chart and analyse the nature and terrain of global civil society.

The term 'global civil society' is highly contested. Many meanings have been proposed and while some adopt the term enthusiastically, others question the validity of the concept. The ambiguity surrounding global civil society might seem problematic for a Yearbook such as this. But far from being an obstacle, we see the terminological tangle that envelops the concept as an opportunity. Debate about its meaning is part of what global civil society is all about. We offer a simple working definition of global civil society as the realm of non-coercive collective action around shared interests and values that operates beyond the boundaries of nation states.

But this is just one view. As the idea spreads around the globe, is variously manifested and continuously debated, new interpretations will continue to emerge. The Yearbook offers a platform for such debate, the background to key issues and actors, and an exploration of the building blocks of global civil society.

Each edition of *Global Civil Society* is organised as follows:

Part 1 Concepts: is dedicated to ongoing conceptual discussions about the different facets and meanings of global civil society.

Part 2 Issues: explores the role of global civil society in debating and influencing specific global issues. These case studies, built upon original research by experts in relevant fields, offer a different perspective on global issues: 'globalisation from below'.

Part 3 Infrastructure: explores both the political and practical preconditions for global civil society to operate. Political preconditions include, for example, peace and security and freedom of association. Practical considerations include funding, technology, and human resources. Some chapters in this section examine the infrastructure of particular sectors of global civil society, for example the trade union movement or peasants' movements.

Part 4 Records: offers a statistical overview, via tables, maps and diagrams, of global civil society's dimensions and contours. The chronology, gathered by individuals around the world, provides an insight into the myriad protests, conferences and campaigns that are the sinews of global civil society. Integral to this section is a methodological chapter that presents alternative social science approaches and methods of analysis. We believe that conventional nation-state-centred methodology is ill-equipped to understand global civil society and, to that end, we are laying the foundations for a social science 'without borders'.

Global Civil Society is intended for a broad audience: theorists, activists, journalists, policy-makers, students… in fact anyone interested in how groups and individuals in civil society are influencing global processes. Perhaps its most important aim is simply this: to stimulate thinking and encourage debate among a range of actors and scholars at global and local levels. In doing so, the Yearbook is part of global civil society itself.

ACKNOWLEDGEMENTS

The production of the Yearbook depends on the support, advice and contributions of numerous individuals and organisations. We endeavour to acknowledge them all in these pages. The final publication of course remains the responsibility of the editors.

Editorial Committee

Helmut Anheier, Olaf Corry, Meghnad Desai, Marlies Glasius, David Held, Fiona Holland (managing editor), Jude Howell, Armine Ishkanian, Mary Kaldor, Hagai Katz (data and maps editor), Mathias Koenig-Archibugi, Denisa Kostovicova, Ebenezer Obadare, Iavor Rangelov, Yahia Said, Hakan Seckinelgin, Sabine Selchow, Sally Stares, Jill Timms (chronology).

Consultations

Gender and Civil Society, 7 October 2004 and 3 February 2005. Input for chapter 1

Bakin Babajanian, Christine Chinkin, Judy El-Bushra, Khadijah Fancy, Marlies Glasius, Armine Ishkanian, Ruth Jacobson, Mary Kaldor, Ulla-Brit Lilleaas, Nisrine Mansour, Diane Perrons, Hakan Seckinelgin, Victor Seidler, Purna Sen, Judith Squires, and Karen Wright.

Other input

Special contributions

Guest boxes: Guiseppe Caruso, Olaf Corry, Nitin Desai, Dana R Fisher, Stefanie Grant, Stuart Hodkinson, Nicholas Howen, Ruth Jacobson, Adriana Jimenez-Cuen, Ana Jordan, Jeff Juris, Ruth Kattumuri, Brenden Kuerbis, Alex Leveringhaus, Nisrine Mansour, Jennifer Mosley, Milton Mueller, Ebenezer Obadare, Christiane Page, Oscar Reyes.

Correspondents: input on chronology

Marcelo Batalha, Baris Gencer Baykan, Andrew Bolgar, Guiseppe Caruso, Joabe Cavalcanti, Hyo-Je Cho, Andrew Davey, Bernard Dreano, Heba Raouf Ezzat, Louise Fraser, Iuliana Gavril, Martin Gurch, Stuart Hodkinson, Vicky Holland, Kadi Jumu, Yung Law, Silke Lechner, Otilia Mihai, Selma Muhic, Richard Nagle, Tim Nagle, Alejandro Natal, Beatriz Marti-n Nieto, Katarina Sehm Patomaki, Mario Pianta, Oscar Reyes, Asthriesslav Rocuts, Ineke Roose, Thomas Ruddy, Mohamed El-Sayed Said, Kate Townsend, Lilian Outtes Wanderley, Caroline Watt, Sébastien Ziegler.

Others who provided input or support

Tricia Coyle, Howard Davies, Elaine Fleming, Judith Higgin, Anthony Judge, Nadia McLaren, Mary Robinson, Jessica Roman, Saskia Sassen, Adele Simmons, Gus Stewart, Jess Winterstein.

Research and editorial assistance

Rachel Bishop (proof reader), Olaf Corry, Clarisse Cunha, Chris Dance (indexer), Michael James (copy editor), Chiara Jasson (translation), Adriana Jimenez-Cuen, Marcus Lam, Peter Lenny (translation), Gwen Litvak, Jennifer Mosley, Anamaria Sanchez, Sabine Selchow, Sally Stares (data programe), Jill Timms (chronology).

Design and production

People, Design Consultants; Andrew Harrison, Lisa Hicks.

Photography

Sourcing: David Arnott, Adrian Evans, Zoe Slotover, Teresa Wolowiec (Panos Pictures); Elena Gerebizza (Tavola Della Pace); Calliste Lelliott (Friends of the Earth).
Photographers: Foto Belfiore, Pep Bonet, Pietro Cenini, Matias Costa, Steve Forrest, Pablo García, Mark Henley, Alvaro Leiva, Paul Lowe, Claire Martin, Frits Meyst, Eric Miller, Richard Nagle, Mikkel Ostergaard, Caroline Penn, Marcus Rose, Tim Sander, Marc Schlossman, Dean Sewell, Qilai Shen, Clive Shirley, Tim Smith, Trygve Sorvaag, Chris Stowers, Dieter Telemans, Jill Timms, Sven Torfinn, Ami Vitale, Teun Voeten, Petterik Wiggers.

Administrative support

Jocelyn Guihama, Jennifer Otoadese, Davina Rodriques, Laurie Spivak.

Financial support

We gratefully acknowledge the financial support of the following organisations:

Aventis Foundation
Robert Bosch Foundation
Compagnia di San Paolo
Victor Phillip Dahdaleh
Ford Foundation
LSE
Charles Stewart Mott Foundation
Rockefeller Foundation
The Atlantic Philanthropies
UCLA School of Public Affairs

CONTENTS

Boxes

Figures

Maps

Tables

Records

CONTRIBUTORS

Helmut Anheier is Professor of Public Policy and Social Welfare at the University of California, Los Angeles (UCLA), and Director of the Center for Civil Society, and the Center for Globalization and Policy Research at UCLA. He is also a Centennial Professor at the Centre for the Study of Global Governance, London School of Economics (LSE). His work has focused on civil society, the non-profit sector, organisational studies and policy analysis, and comparative methodology. He is a founding editor of *The Journal of Civil Society* and author of over 250 publications in several languages. His present research examines the emergence of new organisational forms in global civil society, the role of foundations, and methodological aspects of social science research on globalisation.

Bernard Cassen is a member of the International Council of the World Social Forum, journalist and Director General of *Le Monde Diplomatique*, and Honorary President of ATTAC France. He is author of many books including *Tout a commencé à Porto Alegre* (Editions 1001 Nuits 2003), which was updated and translated into Portuguese, *Tudo começou em Porto Alegre* (Campo da comunicação 2005).

Manuel Castells holds the Wallis Annenberg Chair in Communication Technology and Society at the Annenberg School for Communication, University of Southern California, Los Angeles. He is Research Professor at the Open University of Catalonia in Barcelona, and Professor Emeritus of Sociology and of City and Regional Planning at the University of California, Berkeley. He is the author of 21 books and editor or co-author of 15 additional books, as well as over 100 articles in academic journals. His trilogy, *The Information Age: Economy, Society, and Culture* (Blackwell 2000-2003), has been translated into Spanish, French, Portuguese, Chinese, Russian, Swedish, German, Italian, Croatian, Bulgarian, Romanian, Danish, Korean, Japanese, Parsi, Arabic, Lithuanian, and Catalan. His most recent books include: *The Internet Galaxy* (Oxford University Press 2001), *The Information Society and the Welfare State: The Finnish Model* (Oxford University Press 2002), with Pekka Himanen, and *The Network Society: A Cross-Cultural Perspective* (Edward Elgar 2004), as editor and co-author.

Meghnad Desai was created Lord Desai of St Clement Danes in 1991 and is active in the House of Lords. He was founder and Director of the Centre for the Study of Global Governance at LSE, 1991-2003. He is author of numerous publications, among the most recent: *Money, Macroeconomics and Keynes, Essays in Honour of Victoria Chick* (2 Vols) edited with P Arestis and S Dow (Routledge 2002), *Marx's Revenge: The Resurgence of Capitalism and the Death of Statist Socialism* (Verso 2002), *Development and Nationhood: Essays in the Political Economy of South Asia* (Oxford University Press 2004) and *Why is India a Democracy?* (Roli Books 2005).

Richard Falk is Professor of International Law Emeritus at Princeton University, and since 2002, Visiting Professor of Global Studies at the Unviersity of California, Santa Barbara. He is chair of the Board of the Nuclear Age Peace Foundation. His recent books include *The Declining World Order: America's Imperial Geopolitics* (Routledge 2004) and, with Howard Friel, *The Record of the Paper: How The New York Times Misreports American Foreign Policy* (Verso 2004).

Marlies Glasius is Lecturer in NGO management at the Centre for Civil Society, and a Research Fellow at the Centre for the Study of Global Governance, LSE. In 1999 she published *Foreign Policy on Human Rights: Its Influence on Indonesia under Soeharto* (Intersentia). She was managing editor of the Global Civil Society Yearbook 2000-2003, and recently published another sole-authored book, T*he International Criminal Court: A Global Civil Society Achievement* (Routledge 2005). She also co-edited *Exploring Civil Society: Political and Cultural Contexts*, with David Lewis and Hakan Seckinelgin (Routledge 2004) and *A Human Security Doctrine for Europe: Project, Principles, Practicalities*, with Mary Kaldor (Routledge 2005). Her present interests include global civil society, social forums, economic and social rights, and human security.

Jude Howell is Director of the Centre for Civil Society, LSE and Director of the Economic and Social Science Research Council Research Programme on Non-Governmental Public Action. She has written extensively on issues of governance, gender and civil society. Her recent books include *Gender and Civil Society. Transcending Boundaries*, co-edited with Diane Mulligan (Routledge 2005), *Governance in China* (Rowman and Littlefield 2004), *Civil Society and Development* co-authored with Jenny Pearce, (Lynne Rienner Inc 2002). She has also published numerous articles and book chapters on civil society and development, gender and civil society, trade unions and labour organisation in China and India, women's organising in China, and organising around marginalised interests. Her current research includes a project on the effects of the global war on terror on civil society.

Mary Kaldor is Professor of Global Governance at LSE and Director of the Centre for the Study of Global Governance, LSE. She has written widely on security issues and on democracy and civil society. Her recent books include *Global Civil Society: An Answer to War* (Polity Press 2003) and *New and Old Wars: Organised Violence in a Global Era* (1999). She was a founder member of European Nuclear Disarmament (END), founder and Co-Chair on the Helsinki Citizen's Assembly, and is currently a governor of the Westminster Foundation for Democracy. She is convenor of the Study Group on European Security Capabilities established at the request of Javier Solana.

Hagai Katz is Lecturer at the Department of Business Administration at the School of Management at Ben Gurion University of the Negev in Beersheba, Israel, and a Research Associate at the Israeli Center for Third-sector Research and the UCLA Centre for Civil Society. He has published extensively on the non-profit sector in Israel and on global civil society. Hagai Katz is editor of the Yearbook's Data Programme.

Peter Newell is Senior Research Fellow at the Centre for the Study of Globalisation and Regionalisation, University of Warwick. Prior to this he held posts as Fellow at the Institute of Development Studies, University of Sussex, Visiting Researcher at FLACSO Argentina, Lecturer in International Studies at the University of Warwick, and researcher and lobbyist for Climate Network Europe in Brussels. He is author of *Climate for Change: Non-State Actors and the Global Politics of the Greenhouse* (CUP 2000), co-author of *The Effectiveness of EU Environmental Policy* (MacMillan 2000), co-editor of *Development and the Challenge of Globalisation* (ITDG 2002), *The Business of Global Environmental Governance* (MIT Press 2005) and *Rights, Resources and the Politics of Accountability* (Zed Books, forthcoming). He has also conducted consultancy and policy advisory work for the Department for International Development and the Cabinet Office (UK), the Ministry of Foreign Affairs (Sweden), the Global Environment Facility and UNDP.

Boaventura de Sousa Santos is Professor of Sociology at the School of Economics, Coimbra University, and Distinguished Legal Scholar at the Law School, University of Wisconsin-Madison. He is author of many books published in Portuguese, English, Spanish and French. His most recent books in English include *Toward a New Legal Common Sense* (Butterworths 2002), *Democratizing Democracy* (Verso 2005), *The World Social Forum: A User's Manual* (Zed Books, forthcoming) and, as editor with Cesar Rodríguez, *Law and Globalization from Below: Towards a Cosmopolitan Legality* (Cambridge University Press 2005).

Jill Timms is a Visiting Lecturer at Queen Mary University of London and research assistant at the Centre for the Study of Global Governance, LSE. She is currently completing her doctorate research on corporate social responsibility at the Department of Sociology, LSE. Her research interests include corporate citizenship, anti-corporate groups, labour activism and social forums. Her publications include 'Trade Union Internationalism and a Global Civil Society in the Making', co-authored with Peter Waterman, in *Global Civil Society 2004/5* (Sage 2005) and 'Corporate Citizenship: a social role for corporations in a globalising world?' in Sociological Research Online (forthcoming). She is also coordinator of the Chronology of global civil society events for the Yearbook.

Chico Whitaker (Francisco Whitaker Ferreira) has been active in various social movements since the 1950s. As an urban and regional planner, he worked on agrarian reform in Brazil. After the military coup in Brazil in 1964, he was exiled to France and Chile for 15 years, where he taught the methodology of research for regional planning, and worked for the United Nations. Chico Whitaker has been a municipal councillor in São Paulo twice, after which he became executive secretary of the Brazilian Justice and Peace Commission (of the National Catholic Bishops' Conference), in which capacity he sat on the Organizing Committee of the World Social Forum (and now on the WSF International Council). He has written many articles and several books on his political experiences and *The World Social Forum Challenge* (Zed Books, forthcoming).

INTRODUCTION

Marlies Glasius, Mary Kaldor and Helmut Anheier

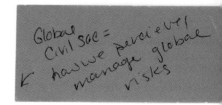

'This is a show about risk', said the steward in a hard yellow hat. She was telling people where to stand for a firework show that was part of a cultural festival in Brighton. 'Are you a risk-taker?', she asked. Illuminated above the heads of the crowd was a giant figure sitting in an armchair underneath a standard lamp. As the show began, flares and sparks whistled across the sky and a disembodied voice read extracts from the UK government's pamphlet, sent to every household in the country, about what to do in the event of a terrorist attack. 'Go in, stay in, tune in', the voice boomed as the fireworks gathered pace and the giant figure exploded in a cascade of fire. A circular wall of fireworks surrounded the risk-takers in the park – giant Catherine wheels, Roman candles, and green flames. A lone violinist rose to the sky playing a mournful tune on a platform of silver fountains and sparklers. And when the show ended after a magnificent gold and silver, pink, green and blue display of stars and sparkles and rockets, the disembodied voice could be heard saying, 'This can happen to anyone, anytime, anywhere.'

This is a Yearbook about risk. What do climate change, migration, the tsunami of 26 December 2004, the terrorist threat and the fall in the dollar have in common? Ulrich Beck, one of the foremost theorists of risk, would say 'world risk society'. Beck argues that the calculation and management of risk was part of the 'master narrative' of the first phase of modernity, the construction of nation-states and modern industry. The modern state was designed to protect and insure citizens against risk – the dangers posed by nature, personal risks of ill health and unemployment, as well as threats posed by foreign enemies. Civic preparedness programmes, military defence, and the welfare state are the results of the state's response to collective risk.

Yet, as Beck and others have argued, the challenges of risk in terms of policy and risk management have changed, and no longer fit the policy blueprints of state modernity. For Beck, 'world risk society does not mean that life has generally become more dangerous. It is not a matter of the *increase*, but rather of the *de-bounding* of uncontrollable risks. This de-bounding is three-dimensional: spatial, temporal and social' (Beck 2002: 41). In other words, risks cross borders; they may be far into the future; and they are increasingly the cumulative outcome of the actions of many individuals.

Global civil society can be conceived as the medium through which consciousness and perceptions of risk are shaped and new methods of protection are pro-moted. The Brighton festival, like media stories and performances, demonstrations and protests, or meetings and conferences in other parts of the world, are all ways in which we become aware of and argue about risk, and through which we develop the global politics of risk. According to Beck, it is these new unbounded risks that give rise to new pressures for global cooperation. Some risks are real – everyday dangers faced especially by those who live on the margins of existence. Some are imagined, constructed for the purpose of political mobilisation. Global civil society is the arena where risks are enunciated, exaggerated, discounted, debunked, assessed and debated. It is an arena that encompasses information, expert knowledge and reasoned deduction as well as fear, prejudice and superstition. And it provides a forum, albeit uneven and unequal, for expressing and communicating differential knowledge about risk.

For understanding what has changed, it is useful to review developments around risk in the context of the nation state, and then explore how it differs for world risk society. We then describe the differential ways in which consciousness of risk is purveyed through global civil society. In a following section we consider the mechanisms that constitute global civil society, through which individuals have an opportunity to join in global politics and influence decision-making, and how they are relating to governmental institutions at different levels. In conclusion, we ask whether a form of global protection against risk is beginning to develop as a result of growing consciousness as well as direct pressures.

The precautionary principle and world risk society

The precautionary principle

The modern, state-centred concept of risk assumed its most developed expression in what has become known as the precautionary principle of policy-making (Lofstedt 2003; European Commission 2000). In its simplest formulation, taken from the 1992 Rio Declaration, the principle states, 'where there are threats of serious or irreversible damage, lack of full scientific certainty shall not be used as a reason for postponing cost-effective measures to prevent environmental degradation.' Subsequently, the application of the precautionary principle spread to other fields such as the chemical industry, pharmaceuticals, climate change, and even the threat of terrorism, although the term is largely used in relation to environmental risk. Indeed, it can be argued that the state's responsibility for physical and material security – for protecting people against risks which range from nuclear war to poverty – was always an expression of the precautionary principle within the boundaries of the nation-state.

In practice, different versions of the principle have emerged, promoted by national preferences and reflecting their political cultures. According to Wiener and Rogers (2002: 230–1), there are three major versions:

Version 1: Uncertainty does not justify inaction...

Version 2: Uncertainty justifies action...

*Version 3: Uncertainty requires shifting the
             burden and standard of proof...*

The first version of the principle permits regulation in the absence of complete evidence about the particular risk scenario. The US Clean Air and Water Pollution Act of 1970 is an example of such policy-making, as is much of the Kyoto Agreement. The second version of the precautionary principle is a more aggressive approach, and demands policy action, which is reflected in the decision of some countries in the 1990s to phase out nuclear energy and the approach of the Bush administration to fighting terrorism. The third version is more far-reaching yet. It states that uncertain risk requires forbidding the potentially risky activity until the producer of the activity demonstrates that it poses no unacceptable risk. EU policy making, as suggested

in *Strategy for a Future Chemicals Policy* (European Commission 2001: 8) is of this nature: 'The Commission proposes to shift responsibility to enterprises for generating and assessing data and assessing the risks of the use of substances. The enterprises should also provide adequate information to downstream users.'

The precautionary principle, whose goal as a policy blueprint was to help manage risk, had a number of effects that went beyond the purpose of specific policies. It changed the relationships among stakeholders, including the general public, bringing about a new politics of risk management at the national and increasingly the regional and global levels. Importantly, it paved the way for civil society organisations to assume a greater role in the identification, handling and oversight of risk-related aspects of policy concerns such as the environment, human rights, industrial safety or transnational crime.

First, the principle generated a big increase in the amount of information about risk. Aided by advances in technology and, later, a greater use of the internet, access to information about 'the who, the why, the how and the for what' of risky activities by government and industry became widely available. In many cases, it revealed uncertainties and the influence of money and power in situations where the public previously may have assumed greater certainty, more neutral reasoning and less politicking. As a result, awareness about risk increased, as did public uncertainties about risk assessments. This pattern began in countries where the precautionary principle was in place first, such as the US, Germany or Sweden, but soon spread to other parts of the world.

Second, more information implied a greater likelihood that faults and bad behaviours of all sorts, large and small, would become known and publicised. The greater transparency in effect decreased rather than increased public trust in regulators and industry, and, ultimately, even in science itself. The fate of the nuclear industry in the 1970s and the genetically modified food (GM) debacle in the 1990s are cases in point that show a decline in confidence in institutions entrusted with risk assessment and risk management. Industrial disasters such as Contergan in Germany, Bhopal in India and Chernobyl in the former Soviet Union, and the role of transnational corporations like Nestlé in Africa, Shell in Nigeria or the tobacco industry in general, added to the decline in trust in institutions responsible for assessing and managing risk.

Third, as citizens and stakeholders increasingly began to question the motives and performance of governments and industry in relation to risk, other actors entered the policy arena, in particular NGOs such as Greenpeace, the World Wide Fund for Nature, and Friends of the Earth. They benefited from the confidence gap that emerged between citizens and the conventional risk management community. They pressed for the precautionary principle to be applied to ever more policy fields, and they also became important watchdogs of policy formulation, implementation and performance.

In particular, as we argued in *Global Civil Society 2003*, the last 20 years witnessed the institutionalisation of a social movement industry (McAdam, Tarrow and Tilly 2001; Smith 1997; Kaldor 2003). Indeed, environmental NGOs now make up 1,781, or 4 per cent, of the over 50,000 INGOs reported by the Union of International Associations in Brussels. In 1980, there were about 200 and in 1924 just one. In recent years, their number has been growing between 3 and 5 per cent annually (Kaldor, Anheier and Glasius 2003). The new social movements, and the NGOs they spawned, provide the institutional connection between the drop in confidence in conventional, nation-state institutions and the growth of global civil society. In the environmental and other fields, they helped fill and, in cases like Brent Spar, expanded the confidence gap.

The de-bounding of risk

NGOs usually pushed for the second and third versions of the precautionary principle, which turned out to be more complex as it became clear that many risks at the global and transnational levels were of a different quality. Whereas the principle sought to establish an explicit – if typically under-specified and yet unproven – link between cause and effect, the risks of world society are of a qualitatively different nature.

The bounding efforts the precautionary principle was designed to achieve are more likely to fail in a world risk society than in national or regional risk societies and communities. Risks have become less controllable and manageable from a policy perspective even when efforts are made to build risk-management strategies on government-industry-NGO coalitions, based on principles of trust and institutional confidence. For one thing, the precautionary principle implied that those responsible for and affected by risk would have similar perceptions, interpretations or at least similar world views about it. The pioneering work by Mary Douglas (1992; Douglas and Wildavsky 1983) has shown just how much ideas about risk differ across and within cultures.

It also assumed that those exposed to risk would have equal voice to those producing it. Clearly, as the examples of industrial accidents, such as Bhopal or Exxon Valdez, corporations like Nestlé, governments deregulating pensions, and episodes like 'mad cow disease' or SARS, amply demonstrate, this is often not the case, particularly in developing countries.

There is a further implication of the world risk society and the de-bounding process. Risk communities, framed largely in national and regional policy contexts, are becoming increasingly linked in ways that are frequently unknown and ill-understood. Sometimes, these risk communities are latent and defined by the possibility of a highly unlikely catastrophic event, such as afflicted the fishermen, the hotel service workers and the tourists in Thai coastal resorts in 2004 when the 26 December tsunami hit. In such cases, global civil society creates a sphere of awareness and action for the (now) manifest risk communities.

In other cases, the risks may be better understood and attributable in terms of benefits and costs, even across boundaries, time and social class, but the framework for policy action either lacks regulatory capacity in the first place or has incomplete and ineffective enforcement mechanisms. Such scenarios make the application of the precautionary principle more difficult, if not impossible. Environmental laws, the law of the sea, the Genocide Convention and a range of human rights instruments are examples that come to mind. Of course, this is precisely where risk policies confront the typical problems of a deficient global governance system.

Global civil society and the world risk society

According to Beck (2005: 17), the 'theory of world risk society can throw considerable light on the emergence of transnational public spaces… Global risks release an element of reflexion and communication… Acknowledged risks force people to build communicative bridges where none or almost none existed before: between monologic arenas and sectoral publics, across systemic and linguistic boundaries, beyond conflicts of opinion, interest, class, nation and denomination.'

But the process through which this happens varies according to region, culture, class and gender. Beck himself points to the gulf in risk perception between Europe and America. He argues that, in Europe, trans-

Box I.1: **Tsunami relief effort**

On the morning of 26 December 2004, giant tsunami waves tore across the Indian Ocean as a result of a massive 9.3 earthquake near Sumatra. They left in their wake approximately 200,000 people dead, many more injured, and millions displaced in 12 countries, with Indonesia, Thailand, India, Sri Lanka, Malaysia, and the Maldives among the hardest hit. In Indonesia alone, more than 128,000 people died and 500,000 became homeless; and in the severely affected Aceh province approximately 44 per cent of the population lost their fishing- and agriculture-related livelihoods (*BBC News* 2005).

The response to the tragedy was immediate and global in nature. United Nations agencies like the World Food Program and the World Health Organization, took the lead along with major NGOs such as Oxfam and the International Federation of Red Cross/Red Crescent Societies. According to Reuters, six months after the tsunami struck, governments had contributed approximately US$4.2 billion, and NGOs had raised an additional $2.7 billion. Private donations are harder to calculate and different numbers abound. The Reuters Foundation reports that private donations have topped $5 billion (Large 2005), although the United Nations has only counted $2.5 billion of that (OCHA 2005).

While the early response necessarily focused on emergency relief, long-term recovery plans are much more complex. The United Nations estimates that it will take between 5 and 12 years and $9 billion for all affected areas to fully recover from the damage. Infrastructure needs, such as the rebuilding of schools, hospitals and roads, are extensive. Adding to the challenges are the high poverty and poor communication facilities found in these mostly rural regions which make access difficult and costly. Planned giving and a coordinated international effort are also required for prevention of future tsunami-related disasters. Work on an early warning system for the Indian Ocean region is now under way, to be completed in 2006, with coordination and funding provided mainly by UNESCO and the International Red Crescent (Kettlewell 2005).

The UN flash appeal

The UN response has been extensive, involving most of the UN related organisations, and high-profile – for example, Bill Clinton was named Special Envoy for Tsunami-affected Countries by the UN in March 2005 and he has travelled widely in an effort to 'sustain international interest' (UNSG 2005; UN News Centre 2005). To coordinate efforts, on 6 January, a flash appeal was issued by the UN Office for the Coordination of Humanitarian Affairs (OCHA). A flash appeal is more than an appeal for funds; rather, it is a coordinated strategic planning process and a platform to publicise what is being done and where needs are greatest, representing the work of not just the UN but a variety of NGOs.

The flash appeal raised over US$1 billion from 54 countries and 32 NGOs and inter-governmental organisations, not counting the UN agencies themselves. As of 13 July, more than $335 million has been spent, almost a third of that by the World Food Program. The largest amounts were given by the countries of North America and Western Europe, along with Japan, China, Australia, and New Zealand. Japan stands out as by far the most generous nation, giving over $225 million, more than the United States, the United Kingdom, Germany, France and Australia combined. NGOs contributing most to the flash appeal were the American Red Cross, the International Organization for Migration, Helen Keller International, the International Rescue Committee, CARE, and Islamic Relief. Of course, many other NGOs chose to raise money for their own projects, rather than working through the flash appeal process.

Other philanthropic efforts

The timing of the tsunami so close to Christmas, the involvement of foreign tourists (particularly from northern Europe), the growing popularity of giving over the internet with the corresponding shift from in-kind giving to cash, and the increasing visibility of international NGO work has resulted in one of the most generous global responses to a natural disaster ever seen. In fact, the overwhelming response to the tsunami disaster has led OCHA to publicise a campaign highlighting 'Forgotten and Neglected Disasters' comparing the outpouring of wealth for tsunami victims with the generally ignored crises in Niger, the Democratic Republic of Congo and the Central African Republic.

Of the major disaster relief NGOs, the International Federation of Red Cross/Red Crescent Societies has played the most significant role in the tsunami relief effort. It currently has over $248 million in pledges from private donors and government bodies. A major success of the tsunami relief effort was the swift response of the Red Cross/Red Crescent, preventing any significant outbreaks of water-borne diseases or other epidemics.

Although most individual donors gave to the most prominent disaster relief organisations, such as the Red Cross/Red Crescent, even small and medium-sized relief agencies found themselves flooded with contributions in the days after the tsunami. For example, the US arm of Action Against Hunger, an INGO with higher name recognition in Europe, raised $418,000 in the first ten days after the tsunami struck through the internet alone, compared with $466,000 for the whole of 2004 (Aitchison 2005).

Some organisations even found themselves in the unusual position of having more money donated than they could reasonably plan to spend on their efforts in the region. Recalling the American Red Cross controversy after the 11 September 2001 terrorist attacks, when many donors became upset that some of the money donated was going to overheads or being diverted to general funds, many NGOs were anxious to be clear with donors regarding where and how their money would be spent. For example, on 4 January 2005 Médecins Sans Frontières (MSF) posted a notice on its website urging prospective donors to give to the organisation's general Emergency Relief Fund, stating that it had 'received sufficient funds' for its tsunami relief activities (MSF 2005). However, organisations engaging in long-term reconstruction had funding needs much greater than MSF's, and some criticised this action, fearing it could put off future donors whose contributions were desperately needed for other projects.

Criticism of the response to the tsunami

Although the global response to the tragedy of 26 December has been generous, it is not without critics. Many have expressed the fear that the outpouring of wealth around the tsunami will threaten smaller domestic charities that may see donations to their causes decline. Anecdotal evidence, however, indicates that while some charities feel overlooked (Souccar 2005) others have actually seen increases in donations (Wallack 2005). Another criticism is that smaller NGOs arrived on the scene without the necessary skills or expertise to lend effective help, leading some to call for a UN accreditation system (Associated Press 2005). Others, such as Oxfam, have noted that much of the aid is going to businesses and landowners, while many of the poor are still stranded in refugee camps (Oxfam International 2005b).

There are also inevitable controversies over how money is spent now that it has been given, such as the construction of mud sea walls around villages in the Andaman Islands. The government now has the money to build them, but environmental experts say that not only will they do nothing to stop the force of a tsunami-strength wave, they will be harmful both to the recovery of saline-soaked farmlands and to the coral reefs surrounding the islands, which are vital to the area's fishing economy (Bhaumik 2005).

Finally, it has been noted that after many humanitarian disasters like the 2004 tsunami, the actual aid received by affected countries is often much lower than that pledged originally. An example of this is the 2003 Bam earthquake in Iran, for which only about a fifth of the more than US$1 billion pledged has been received. It remains to be seen if the response to the tsunami will be an exception, but according to Reuters all of the top donors, with the exception of fully paid Japan, have major contributions outstanding. A worrisome example is that, as of mid-May, neither Australia ($602 million outstanding) nor Germany ($517 million outstanding) had paid even a quarter of its stated commitments. Norway, the United States and the United Kingdom, on the other hand, have each paid more than 85 per cent of their intended contributions already (Large 2005).

Jennifer Mosley, Center for Civil Society, UCLA

Map I.1: Tsunami relief

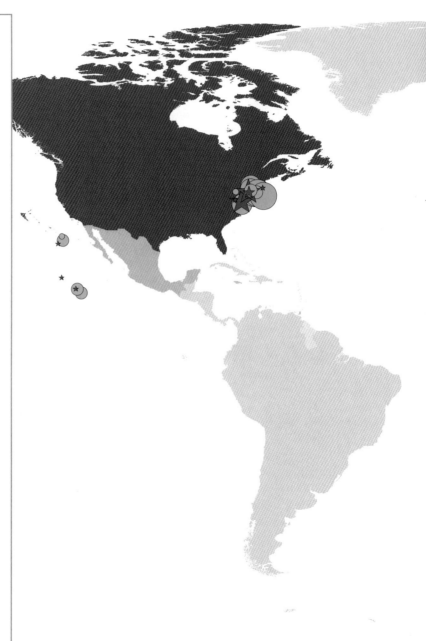

Aid flows, in US$
(Total: $1,021 Million)

Donor countries

	10,000 - 198,826
	198,827 - 1,933,176
	1,933,177 - 15,476,621
	15,476,622 - 228,900,000

Organisational donors

★	3,000 - 636,000
★	636,001 - 3,071,049
★	3,071,050 - 18,995,929
★	18,995,930 - 299,557,122

Channel agencies*

●	3,000 - 636,000
●	636,001 - 3,071,049
●	3,071,050 - 18,995,929
●	18,995,930 - 299,557,122

Recipient countries

	1,200,000 - 3,670,000
	3,670,001 - 8,023,603
	8,023,604 - 90,085,630
	90,085,631 - 177,353,898

▲	Epicenter

*Unspecified NGO and
UN channels US $14.5 million

In this map, shading represents level of funds donated to each country in the disaster area. Green shades represent the 'flash appeal' contributions from donor nations, darker shades indicating greater contributions. Yellow/brown shades indicate contributions received by disaster area countries, darker shades representing greater receipts. The red stars represent agencies acting as donors, and the blue circles those acting as channels for flash appeal contributions, responsible for raising funds and transferring them to the disaster area.

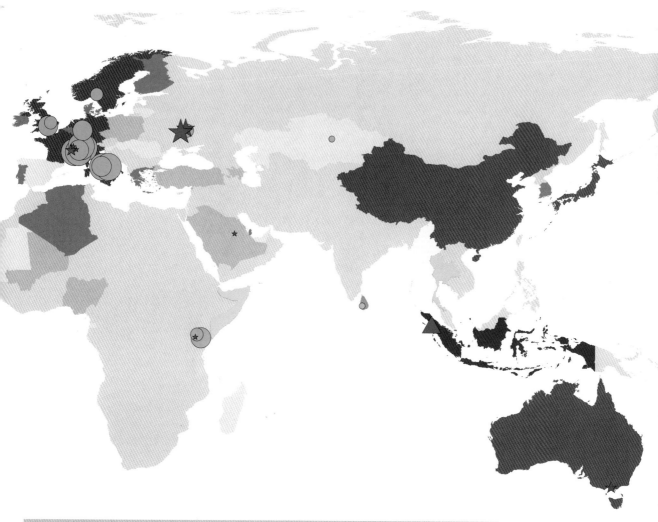

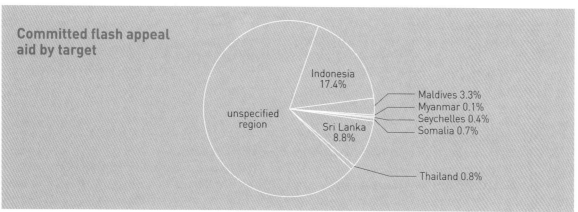

**Committed flash appeal
aid by target**

unspecified
region

Indonesia
17.4%

Maldives 3.3%
Myanmar 0.1%
Seychelles 0.4%
Somalia 0.7%

Sri Lanka
8.8%

Thailand 0.8%

national campaigning groups play much a larger role in staging 'the cultural symbols that raise the latent threat to the level of consciousness'. In America, he argues, it is the state that 'plays the role of staging the terrorist risk in the mass media' (2005:18). Beck also suggests that Europeans tend to be more worried about climate change whereas Americans fear the terrorist threat more (2005: 9-10). But it may be rather that Europeans and Americans worry about these risks in very different ways. According to Lofstedt (2003), Europe and the US are drifting apart in their use and interpretation of the precautionary principle when applied to environmental risk. The European Commission is the main proponent trying to maintain and strengthen it, while the current US Bush administration attempts to undermine and discredit it both domestically and internationally. Likewise, fear of terrorism in the US is used as an argument for the 'war on terror' whereas, in Europe, the 'war on terror' is often opposed on the grounds that it could actually increase the terrorist threat.

The role that global civil society plays as the medium through which consciousness of risk is increased and risk protection is promoted also, of course , varies widely between rich and poor regions. Risk experienced in the poorer parts of the world is much more pervasive and less amenable to control than risks in the richer parts of the world. Indeed, authors like Douglas (1992: 38–54) and Luhmann (1993: 22–3) draw a distinction between risk and danger, between uncertainties that might be averted through alternative human decision-making and immediate threats to one's daily survival. It could therefore be argued that worrying about risk is a luxury of privileged Northerners. People in conflict zones or at the margins of survival do not attend festival performances with a 'risk' theme. Yet it is the privileged Northerners who dominate global civil society and who therefore have the biggest say in determining what counts as global risk.

Finally, global civil society is uneven and unequal in the gendering of risk perceptions. As Jude Howell shows in Chapter 1, the gendered nature of global civil society is ambiguous. On the one hand, civil society may be a sphere more permeable to women than the market and the state due to its roots in charity and voluntarism. On the other hand, civil society is seen by some feminists as a 'public' and hence historically exclusively male domain. As Howell points out, the theorists and activists who reinvigorated the concept did not problematise this heritage. Hence, risk framing in global civil society

is likely to be male-dominated. Despite the campaigns on violence against women, a universal but 'private' risk such as rape is not likely to get the same consideration as climate change or terrorism.

One response to world risk society is the demand for a re-bounding of risk, applying the precautionary principle in national terms, and the rebuilding of protective walls around nation-states or particular groups. This is the argument for Israel's new wall designed to exclude Palestinian suicide bombers. A different version of such attempts at re-bounding is efforts to establish quasi-markets for transnational goods and bads, such as pollutions rights and credits, even though their regulatory framework and enforceability remain unclear ((Kaul, Conceicao, Le Goulven and Mendoza 2003).

Likewise, re-bounding is the goal of a myriad of ethnic, religious or tribal groups that try to re-establish exclusive control over territory, or of the growing political factions in rich countries that call for tighter controls over immigration. And it is the belief in re-bounding that explains the new American global unilateralism designed to keep the terrorist threat at bay. But, of course, there are others who press for new policies at a global level – global regulations and global public goods designed to minimise, overcome or manage global risk. Current preoccupations with, for example, reform of the United Nations or a new European constitution have to do with this universalist interpretation of risk.

Consciousness of global risk

The 2004 tsunami, global poverty and Darfur

According to one set of authors, 'the essence of risk is not that it is happening, but that it might be happening'. Moreover, most turn-of-the-century literature focuses on risk as 'manufactured, not only through the application of technologies, but also in the making of sense' (Adam and van Loon 2000: 2). In this sense, the tsunami that swept the Indian Ocean on 26 December 2004 had nothing to do with risk. It had not been manufactured either in the technological sense or in the discursive sense. Instead, it came as a complete surprise, and afterwards it was no longer a risk but a reality.

Nonetheless, it bears a relation to risk in the way it entered the global collective imagination. Many people across the globe knew one or more people who might be affected, and so the brief period of uncertainty and information-seeking that usually follows a disaster affected millions rather than thousands of people. Moreover, there was a real sense that this particular disaster could have happened to each and any of us. It was felt from Somalia and the Maldives to Burma and Indonesia, and emotionally felt far beyond the Indian Ocean.

The disaster itself was indiscriminate, hitting poor fishermen and rich holidaymakers alike, but the responses to it were more complicated. From the outset, there was a disproportionate attention in the Western media to the plight of the relatively small number of tourists who had been affected, particularly in Thailand. But, paradoxically, this attention to the 'recognisable' victim may have increased the sense of a 'global imagined community', and consequently contributed to the huge sums of money raised for the tsunami victims.

On one reading, the unprecedented response to the tsunami could be considered as proof of a greater global connectedness, global solidarity, global civil society in the twenty-first century

---

The tsunami will live on in the global collective consciousness in many ways. For the direct victims and to a lesser extent for others, it will live on as a risk, something that 'might happen again'. Governments have also gone into classic risk-management mode, designing monitoring and warning systems after the event, while squabbling over coordination (Tarrant 2005; Cumming-Bruce 2005; IOC URL). For some of those who have given money, especially people who do not usually make donations to international causes, it may foster a more lasting interest in the regions where their money is being spent. On one reading, the unprecedented response to the tsunami could be considered as proof of a greater global connectedness, global solidarity, global civil society in the twenty-first century.

In this light, many global civil society actors saw it as an opportunity. In the first place, it was a financial opportunity. Large international NGOs saw their coffers filled beyond their capacity to spend in the disaster-stricken areas, and had to find ethically acceptable ways of diverting the money to more structural problems. Local groups sprang up or changed gear to take part in the tsunami bonanza (Frerks and Klem 2005: 20–2; Box I.1). But the tsunami effect was appropriated in other ways, too.

In response to the public outpouring of generosity, the Paris Club of major donors offered to suspend payments from the countries affected. But some, such as Thailand, did not take up the offer because it would turn their country into 'a credit risk', and NGOs characterised the step as inadequate (Oxfam 2005; Jubilee Debt Campaign and World Development Movement 2005). Thus, the tsunami has helped to reopen the discussion on debt relief.

'Other tsunamis' were discovered in the form of the war in Iraq (Monbiot 2005), the AIDS/HIV epidemic, the '24,000 deaths every day from poverty and debt and division that are the products of a supercult called neoliberalism' (Pilger 2005), and the consequences of climate change (*Guardian* 2004; *Christian Today* 2005), which would leave some of the coastal areas affected by the tsunami permanently submerged. These attempts to apply the successful 'tsunami risk frame' to other areas did not always succeed in galvanising the global imagination.

On the one hand, according to British journalist Andrew Gilligan, the tsunami 'lowered the bar to get development stories on TV' (Gilligan 2005). The Global Call to Action Against Poverty (GCAP), initiated at the World Social Forum in Porto Alegre in January 2005, built up a rapid momentum in the first six months of the year, with groups in more than 60 countries calling for the implementation of the Millennium Development Goals. The focus was the G8 meeting in Scotland. The Make Poverty History campaign, with the Live 8 concerts and the white armbands, mobilised millions of people around the slogan 'Justice not Charity' (see Box I.2). On the other hand, the situation in Darfur, where tens of thousands have died as a result of violence, hunger or disease, has not entered the global imagination as something that could happen to any of us or as something we can all help alleviate. It may spark feelings of compassion but also alienation and apathy. This is happening only to them, and will probably continue to do so.

The responses to the tsunami and to Darfur would suggest that shared risk perceptions on a global scale are possible, but only in very particular circumstances. Literally, the tsunami was a danger, not a risk, but the response to it has been to that of a risk: imaginable to us all, and fixable at least in its consequences by human agency. The Darfur crisis, on the other hand, was and is conceived as a danger: deplorable, inevitable, but not something we can internalise as a risk to us all that we must try to avert. This response is all the more

Box I.2: Mainstreaming Africa

In 2005 Africans found themselves the centre of attention around the globe. A convergence of international summits and presidencies, research reports and civil society mobilisations hoisted Africa, poverty and, to a lesser degree, the plight of developing countries generally, high on the political agenda, both on the global stage and within many countries. Three events were pivotal in this plethora of anti-poverty activities: the G8 Summit in Gleneagles in July, the UN Millennium +5 Summit in September in New York and the World Trade Organization (WTO) meeting in December in Hong Kong.

An impression of Africa entered people's imagination, particularly in Britain, in a way that the continent has not done before: while the focus was on poverty and how to tackle it, attention was not directed towards any specific famine, and the appeal was not for money but for justice.

Campaigning for such a concept presents a challenge and a risk: not only are the means to achieve it disputed, but the very nature of justice is a subject of fierce debate that poses fundamental questions about the relationship between the rich industrialised world and developing countries.

This debate would continue behind the key messages, celebrity endorsements and clever marketing of the Global Call to Action Against Poverty (GCAP), billed as the world's largest anti-poverty alliance, which unites some 150 million people in 72 countries. Under the symbolic white band, national GCAP coalitions organised their own series of events and campaign slogans – among them: 'Plus d' Excuse' in France, 'You promised – Act Now' in Zambia and 'Poverty is an enemy to Humanity' in Palestine. These campaigns coalesced on 1 July 2005, the First International White Band Day, when demonstrators wore them and pubic buildings were wrapped in them, as a reminder to world leaders to fulfil their commitments to trade justice, debt cancellation, and more and better aid.

Around the world there were demonstrations, petitions, debates, pop concerts and media campaigns. In Africa GCAP campaigners and celebrities launched Thumbs Down 2 Poverty, via Africa Snaps, a series of television adverts featuring Youssour N'Dour, Ladysmith Black Mambazo and Seun Anikulapo Kuti, which were seen by an estimated 20 million people in 15 African countries. In Britain, it was the 'click films' – the clicking fingers of Kate Moss, Kylie Minogue, Brad Pitt and others, symbolising the death of a child every three seconds; 30,000 deaths from poverty each day. Such simple statistics and the endorsing celebrities were compelling; among them Archbishop Desmond Tutu, Nelson Mandela, Bono, Scarlett Johansson, Claudia Schiffer and Sir Bob Geldof.

The celebrity sheen of the campaigns was one spark in the fierce debate about how to tackle poverty, which was played out both between rich and poor worlds and within them. Focus on the Global South (URL) and Jubilee South (URL) were among the groups refusing to sign up to GCAP, arguing that it was a Northern-dominated campaign that had failed to work or consult with those it purported to represent (Hodkinson 2005). Others argued that even to engage with Western NGOs and the G8 was a mistake. Firoze Manji, editor of Pambazuka News, a web-based forum, says:

The western media and western 'development' agencies feed us with a diet that makes us think that 'poverty' is the problem. But poverty is not the problem. It is the looting, theft and frank exploitation that forces Africa's people into destitution, that impoverishes them, and prevents millions from realising their full potential as humans... Let's end this charade about 'fighting poverty': turn instead to fighting those who caused the profit and impoverishment. (Manji 2005)

Divergences within civil society were to resurface in Britain too, where Make Poverty History (URL) arguably honed its message most finely of all the national GCAP coalitions. Comprising hundreds of NGOs, faith groups, trade unions and networks, Make Poverty History attracted more than 225,000 people to the Edinburgh demonstration on 2 July, four days before the G8 meeting. Its effectiveness in mobilising more than double the numbers expected – and selling millions of white bands in the process – should perhaps be no surprise, given those behind it. Film-maker Richard Curtis, a friend of Britain's Chancellor of the Exchequer Gordon Brown, played a leading role in bringing NGOs together, encouraging celebrities to take part (Hodkinson 2005) and devising marketing gems such as the 'click' films (Rampton 2005).

The Make Poverty History campaign supported the report of the Commission for Africa, which had been set up by Prime Minister Tony Blair with 17 commissioners, including himself, Brown and Geldof. Only a few weeks before the G8, Geldof was persuaded to stage Live 8 – ten concerts, one if each of the G8 countries, one in South Africa and a second hastily arranged UK concert featuring African musicians at the Eden Project. These concerts, beamed around the world on 2 July, took place almost exactly 20 years after the original LiveAid. Unlike LiveAid, in which Geldof memorably told the audience to 'Give us yer fokkin money', Live 8 called for justice. The musicians' messages might have been mixed but their lure was undeniable – an estimated one million attended the ten concerts and almost 30 million people watched them on television at some point during 2 July.

Given this momentum and the diversity of expectations around the world, perhaps the G8 was bound to disappoint. The final communiqué pledged US$48 billion in aid by 2010 and cancellation of some of the debts of the most heavily indebted poor countries. The G8 also promised to provide treatment for HIV/AIDS to all those who need it by 2010. Progress on trade was negligible; no timetable was set for phasing out export subsidies, and detailed negotiations were left to the WTO meeting in December. Make Poverty History was downbeat, estimating that only around US$20 billion of the promised aid was new money, and that the debt relief deal would provide only one billion of the estimated US$10 billion a year of debt cancellation needed to eradicate extreme poverty.

African civil society campaigners said the G8 had simply reaffirmed existing decisions on debt relief and aid, and the deals were still attached to harmful policy conditionality. 'The message from Gleneagles is clear to us in Africa. We will intensify our call to our Governments that have not secured debate cancellation to strongly consider repudiating their unjust and odious external debt,' said Justice Egware of the Civil Society Action Coalition on Education for All in Nigeria (GCAP 2005).

Those that had criticised the Commission for Africa report for its reliance on a free-market approach to development were more vociferous in their condemnation of the G8. The World Development Movement said the outcome was a disaster for the world's poor and an insult to the thousands of campaigners who had genuinely believed the G8 was committed to change. According to WDM head of policy, Peter Hardstaff, 'These tiny sums of money are nothing more than a sticking plaster over the deep wounds the G8 are inflicting by forcing failed economic policies such as privatisation, free trade and corporate deregulation, on Africa.' (Hardstaff 2005)

Others argued that, in any case, the focus of NGOs and the British government on reducing subsidies and trade barriers was misdirected. According to Matthew Lockwood, former head of policy and campaigns at ActionAid UK, the real problem for African countries is how to diversify out of primary commodity exports, especially when faced with competitors such as China. Not only has Africa become marginalised from world trade, unable to share in the boom in high-value manufactured products, but it has seen the prices of its primary commodities fall (Lockwood 2005).

The breadth of global mobilisation – some 30 million text messages were sent urging G8 leaders to act – was hailed by many, such as Kumi Naidoo (2005), as a 'victory for civil society.' Jamie Drummond, executive director of Data, the campaign group set up by Bono of U2, argues that the involvement of celebrities and the campaign tactics of Make Poverty History has had a democratising effect on development policy and poverty alleviation: 'Bob and Bono are doing something far more significant and strategic: making these issues massive and mainstream so power must come to the people, and not the other way around' (Drummond 2005).

What impact has all of this activity and debate had on people's attitudes towards Africa? As Tidjane Thiam, a member of the Commission for Africa, has pointed out, challenging perceptions is crucial to combating Afro-pessimism. 'I think it's very important to win the battle of public opinion ....and be able to kill forever a number of ideas that have been very, very detrimental – all African leaders are corrupt, everything ends up

Box I.2 continued

in war anyway, they cannot get their act together – if I go further they're lazy, why put money there and so on and so forth' (Thiam 2005).

Indeed, in Britain the 'Public Perceptions of Poverty' research programme for Comic Relief* (Darnton 2005) suggests that many people are deterred from taking action by what they perceive as the hopeless state of Africa – which has been dubbed the 'Live Aid Legacy' (VSO 2002). In the 2003 Office for National Statistics Omnibus survey for Britain's Department for International Development (DFID), people expressed concern about poverty but their understanding of its underlying causes was low; they cited 'internal' issues such as war, famine and corruption, rather than the international trade system, for example (Dawe 2003). In 2005, the second wave of Public Perceptions of Poverty (conducted 25 March-5 April) found that trade justice was the least understood method of tackling poverty, with 47 per cent saying they knew nothing about it (Darnton 2005). However, initial findings from the third wave of this research, conducted 15-19 July 2005 in the wake of the G8, indicate significantly increased awareness of trade justice (57 per cent) and of Make Poverty History (87 per cent) (Darnton 2005), which may be linked to the rise in media coverage of Africa in the UK and elsewhere (see Table I.1). The British government's support for such attitudinal research suggests it believes that increasing awareness and empathy can stimulate political action – which may explain its role in kindling campaigns such as Make Poverty History and the establishment of the Commission for Africa.

Table I.1: Media coverage of Africa, 2002–2005**

LexisNexis category	2005	2004	2003	2002
Major world newspapers	853	39	65	82
Global newswires	578	93	115	147
UK news	840	30	46	70
Asia Pacific news	243	31	49	68
US news	574	52	107	59

With the use of the LexisNexis database of media, the terms poverty w/p africa and end! (that is, poverty and africa in the same paragraph, narrowed down with end/ending/ended) were searched for the period 10 June–10 July in 2005, 2004, 2003 and 2002. The table indicates the numbers of articles mentioning these search words. The search was conducted on 16 July 2005.

While assessing African perceptions of this year's anti-poverty initiatives is stymied by lack of research and the limitations of media search engines, African experiences of poverty and views on the future have been captured. Afrobarometer surveys conducted in 15 countries between June 2002 and October 2003 demonstrate that many Africa[...]perate lives', with significant numbers experiencing frequent shortages of basic necessities and [...] research also finds an inspiring sense of optimism. 'Yet as Africans endure the imp[...]nt adjustment, they do not conclude simply and cynically that "t[...] their children will lead better lives than themselves' (Afrobarometer [...]

* Public Perceptions of Pover[...]me for Comic Relief, funded by DFID, which aims to explore the media's role in shaping public awarenes[...]riers and drivers to public empathy, understanding, optimism and action in relation to poverty and development issue[...]

** With thanks to Olaf Corry, Hagai Katz and Lucy Shaikh for advice.

Fiona Holland, Centre for the Study of Global Goverance, LSE

paradoxical because in fact the Darfur crisis was man-made, whereas the tsunami was the natural disaster. It would suggest that the tsunami was a 'one-off' in global empathy, and in fact global civil society has a long way to go in representing environmental destruction, conflicts, hunger and disease as 'other tsunamis' or 'global risks' that could even hypothetically affect us all.

Climate change

One of Ulrich Beck's major theses about the risk society, or world risk society, is that it has superseded the class society. In his seminal *Risk Society: Towards a New Modernity* (1992), Beck predicted that the problematic of scarcity and distribution would increasingly give way to that of risk and safety. In 2000, Ruth Levitas still confirmed that, in her students' annual essays on utopia 'The question of safety (and hence of risk) has been increasingly present ... and the question of economic equality less so' (Levitas 2000: 203).

But there was always a tension between the global aspirations of the 'risk society' as proclaimed by Beck (1992) and Giddens (1990), and the recognition that the shift from class to risk preoccupations would occur only 'where and to the extent that *genuine material need* can be objectively reduced and socially isolated through the development of human and technological productivity, as well as through legal and welfare state protections and regulations' (Beck 1992: 19). Hence one of their friendly critics warned that 'as the fault lines of risk expand, we must not lose sight of society's oldest burden, the crushing weight of poverty' (Mythen 2004: 185).

The research in this series would suggest that, after the advent of the anti-capitalist movement, the idea that equality discourse has been replaced by risk discourse is no longer tenable. Instead, the two are increasingly linked by global civil society actors. New connections are being made, with class framed in a new, more global way that focuses on gender and ethnic dimensions as much as income distribution.

To begin with, various critics have pointed out that Beck's 'democratisation of risk' is predicated on a reliance on 'worst case scenarios': disasters of at least the magnitude and globalising tendency of the tsunami. More conventional risks of famines, war or even pollution continue to affect people unevenly according to class (Scott 2000). The worst-case effects of climate change would presumably be in the 'ultimate catastrophe' category.

But Peter Newell shows in Chapter 3 in this Yearbook that, in fact, global civil society actors are now busy reconnecting class to risk even with respect to climate change, not just between but within societies. Since 2002, a self-styled 'climate justice' movement has joined the more conventional Northern-based environmental NGOs. It is not just more global and more radical, but also more holistic in its analysis than the old actors, who would not have connected greenhouse effects to either social justice or human rights.

Newell also cites the recent foundation, in the US, of the Environmental Justice and Climate Change Initiative, which advocates 'the fair treatment of people of all races, tribes and economic groups in the implementation and enforcement of environmental protection laws' in the light of the 'disproportionate impacts from climate change (which) might accrue to these groups because, for example, 80 per cent of people of colour and indigenous people in the US live in coastal regions.' In response, a coal lobby group has published a report arguing that ratification of the Kyoto Protocol would 'disproportionately threaten the well-being of Blacks and Hispanics in the United States' (Newell, Chapter 3).

Similar social justice arguments are being made in other classic 'risk' domains, such as GM foods. In Europe the debate has focused mainly on whether the risks are acceptable. But in the developing world there are further divisions between those, such as International Service for the Acquisition of Agri-biotech (ISAAA URL) and the Biotechnology Information Centres (BIC URL; MABIC URL; Safetybio URL), which argue that, if carefully managed, biotechnology can be helpful to poor farmers, and those, including GRAIN (URL) and Pesticide Action Network (URL), which consider the global experiment with GM technology a risk to food and income security for the poor because the power concentration involved means that small farmers are at risk of being driven out of business by transnational agribusiness corporations.

The Bhopal campaign has also been revitalised as it lends itself very well to a holistic analysis, having environmental, social justice and human rights aspects as well as a corporate villain (Jain 2003). In 2004, the campaign made various advances in both Indian and US courts, it presented its case in workshops at the World Social Forum, and two core campaigners won the prestigious Goldman Prize (Kuruganthi 2004).

Terrorism

At a meeting organised by the Club of Madrid, the club of 140 former presidents and prime ministers, on the first anniversary of the 2004 Madrid bombings, Kofi Annan, the UN Secretary-General, called for a more active role for global civil society in countering terrorism:

Not only political leaders, but civil society and religious leaders should clearly denounce terrorist tactics as criminal and inexcusable. Civil society has already conducted magnificent campaigns against landmines, against the recruitment of children as soldiers, and against allowing war crimes to go unpunished. I should like to see an equally strong global campaign against terrorism... We must pay more attention to the victims of terrorism, and make sure their voices can be heard. (Annan 2005)

As Figure I.1 shows, deaths and injuries from terrorist incidents have greatly increased since 2000. But the way in which terrorism is perceived varies greatly in different regions. Indeed, perhaps more than any other risk, terrorism is subject to manipulation, instrumentalisation, and reinterpretation. The figures in the chart, which comes from a US funded source, refer only to non-state terrorism. This reflects the dominant perception in the US, where terrorism is seen as a threat to the US, akin to a foreign enemy like the Soviet Union or Germany. This is partly to be explained by the shock of 9/11, when more people were killed than at Pearl Harbour in 1941, which marked the start of US involvement in the Second World War. But it can also be understood in terms of the way this perception of terrorism chimes with a narrative about the role of the US in promoting and defending freedom – a narrative that is deeply embedded in the structures of government and is narrative, moreover, widely purveyed by the American media.

In fact, the majority of incidents included in Figure I.1 took place in the Middle East. There, more civilian deaths have resulted from state violence than from non-state violence. In other words, the figure shows only a minority of civilian deaths resulting from political violence. In Iraq, the best estimates suggest that around 25,000 civilians have been killed since the beginning of the war in March 2003; the majority are the result of American attacks, even though in recent months the share claimed by insurgent incidents has been increasing[1]. In Palestine, more Palestinian civilians

have been killed by Israeli forces than Israeli civilians killed by Palestinian suicide bombers[2]. In much of the Middle East and beyond, it is the policies of the United States and Israel that are seen as the major threat. Although the majority condemn jihadists or suicide bombers, especially in Iraq, these are seen as lesser or equal evils.

Indeed, in much of the world the word 'terrorism' is rejected because of the way it has been politicised and captured by the rhetoric of the Bush administration and its allies. The word seems to be used to emphasise threats to Western citizens and to downplay the kind of political, criminal or just senseless violence that is the daily experience of many Colombian or Congolese citizens, for instance.

In Europe, the perception that terrorism is a crime that has no political rationality competes with the perception that the risk of terrorism has increased as a result of Western foreign policies. In Spain, it was the latter perception that predominated. The Madrid bombings of 11 March 2005 led to a popular mobilisation because the government had tried to attribute responsibility for the bombings to Basque separatists, in the knowledge that the attacks would be linked to Spain's involvement in Iraq. The government was subsequently defeated at a general election, and Spain immediately announced its withdrawal from Iraq.

---

1 *These figures come from Iraqbodycount.org. The other source is the painstaking study reported in the British medical journal The Lancet. This study was based on sampling of clusters of households in all the governorates of Iraq. Excluding the Fallujah cluster, which had much higher casualties than elsewhere (accounting for two-thirds of violent deaths) the study found the rate of casualties much higher than actually reported to the press. The study estimated an additional 98,000 deaths, excluding Fallujah, throughout Iraq, compared with a similar period before the war. The biggest cause of death was violent incidents accounting for some 24 per cent of the total; of these the majority were caused by American air strikes. See Roberts et al. (2004).*

2 *According to the Israeli human rights organisation B'Tselem (Human Rights Watch 2005), between the beginning of the Intifada and the end of November 2004, 3,040 Palestinians were killed by Israeli security forces, including 606 children, in the Occupied Palestinian Territories. According to their investigations at least 1,661 of those killed (including 531 children under the age of 18) were not involved in hostilities when they were killed. According to the Israeli-based International Policy Institute for Counter Terrorism (URL), between the start of the Al-Aqsa Intifada and May 2003, Palestinians had been responsible for the deaths of 700 Israelis, 546 of whom were non-combatants. According to the Palestinian Red Crescent Society (URL), which does not distinguish between combatants and civilians, between 29 September 2000 and 13 May 2005, 3,607 Palestinians had died and 28,695 been injured.*

A year later, the bombings in London on 7 and 21 July were universally condemned, as in Madrid. Initially, it was the former perception that terrorism is a crime with no political rationality that predominated. The attacks were seen as a crime not against Britain but against multicultural London. According to London's Mayor, Ken Livingstone:

This was not a terrorist attack against the mighty and the powerful. It was not aimed at Presidents or Prime Ministers. It was aimed at ordinary, working-class Londoners, black and white, Muslim and Christian, Hindu and Jew, young and old. It was an indiscriminate attempt to slaughter, irrespective of any considerations for age, for class, for religion, or whatever. That isn't an ideology, it isn't even a perverted faith – it is just an indiscriminate attempt at mass murder. (London Homepage 2005)

But it was not long before the issue of the war in Iraq began to be raised. The bombastic Respect MP George Galloway was widely criticised for blaming Britain's involvement in the war in Iraq in the immediate aftermath of the attacks. But the criticism was as much about the tasteless timing as about the content of the argument. Members of the Muslim Community condemned the attacks but nevertheless insisted that the war in Iraq, and the double standards vis-à-vis Israel, has alienated many young Muslims. The Mayor of London made a similar argument, and a poll undertaken by the *Guardian* newspaper showed that two-thirds of the British public felt the government had some responsibility for the attacks because of the war in Iraq. An even stronger report from the Royal Institute for International Affairs (2005) published shortly after the attacks suggested that the war in Iraq had increased the risk of terrorism. The government, of course, strongly denied any link, arguing that the attackers were under the sway of an 'evil ideology' that long predated Iraq.

One constant that tends to be shared among these different perceptions is the growing recognition of the importance of the social justice argument. As with other risk domains like climate change and GM foods, the risk of terrorism is increasingly used to bolster the case for social justice. In ministries of development and in the various reports discussed below, the link between poverty and insecurity has received considerable attention. While many would argue that terrorism cannot be explained or rationalised in terms of inequality or poverty, the readiness of the Bush administration and the G8 to respond to civil society pressure in the new global climate of fear is evidence that they recognise some kind of connection.

The debate about the meaning and nature of terrorism is only just beginning. It is clear that terrorism is a global risk – indeed, it epitomises the de-bounding of risk. At the same time, the risk is played out in local circumstances, involving local players with very specific local impacts. The fact that the London bombers were British citizens, far removed from the culture of violence experienced in the 'black holes' of conflict in other parts of the world, was particularly shocking. The narrative of the terrorists was global. The jihadist ideology, to which the bombers presumably subscribed, centres on a Muslim community under siege in different parts of the world. The 7 July attacks took place in the same week as the tenth anniversary of Srebrenica, where 8,000 Bosnian men and boys were killed by Serb militants, and in a week when some 150 Iraqis were also killed by suicide bombers. The attacks showed that the West can no longer insulate itself from what happens in the rest of the world, that Western citizens nowadays have multiple identities, and that dangers in the rest of the world are translated into risks experienced in rich countries. But the political and social climate in which terrorists operate, whether in London, Madrid or Istanbul, is local. The attacks on London were also viewed as a reflection of the alienation of young Muslim men living in urban areas in Britain.

The bombers may have emphasised their Muslim identity. But they failed to respect human identity. Some may condemn the bombers for being more Muslim than British – this is evidently the implication of the government's preoccupation with dialogue with Muslim leaders. But while globalisation may throw up new transnational exclusive identities in place of territorially bound identities, it also offers the possibility for greater solidarity with other human beings, whether they are Muslim, British, American, Iraqi, Palestinian or Spanish.

In world risk society, citizens cannot rely only on states to protect them from risk (even though the response to the London bombings demonstrated how efficiently public services can operate). They are agents and not just victims. This is why Kofi Annan's proposal is so timely.

Figure I.1: Deaths and injuries from terrorism 2000–2005

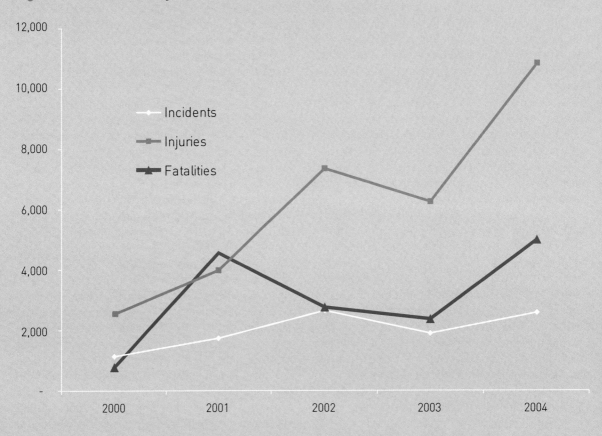

Source: The National Memorial Institute for the Prevention of Terrorism (MIPT), Terrorism Knowledge Base, http://www.tkb.org

Region	2000			2001			2002		
	Incidents	Injuries	Fatalities	Incidents	Injuries	Fatalities	Incidents	Injuries	Fatalities
Africa	28	139	37	27	239	289	29	183	129
East & Central Asia				23	23	13	12	3	3
Eastern Europe	27	234	65	104	259	70	215	1236	375
Latin America	225	176	198	163	306	307	477	757	298
Middle East/Persian Gulf	309	190	60	508	1267	257	627	1914	564
North America	9	0	0	39	11	2987	16	3	3
South Asia	96	1043	297	197	1171	440	836	2169	1021
Southeast Asia & Oceania	72	601	87	122	494	161	96	975	351
Western Europe	372	153	33	550	213	31	342	104	15
World	**1138**	**2536**	**777**	**1733**	**3983**	**4555**	**2650**	**7344**	**2759**

Region	2003			2004			2005 (to July 24)		
	Incidents	Injuries	Fatalities	Incidents	Injuries	Fatalities	Incidents	Injuries	Fatalities
Africa	29	51	109	36	424	390	18	139	53
East & Central Asia	13	1	21	15	43	26	5	10	4
Eastern Europe	125	689	266	167	1232	536	64	91	24
Latin America	199	473	185	102	238	146	32	66	39
Middle East/Persian Gulf	496	3205	907	1287	4901	2600	1535	4939	2943
North America	18	0	0	6	0	0	2	0	0
South Asia	613	1326	803	643	2936	895	474	1367	436
Southeast Asia & Oceania	30	394	72	51	408	202	37	235	68
Western Europe	372	114	6	271	653	194	146	286	56
World	**1895**	**6253**	**2369**	**2578**	**10835**	**4989**	**2313**	**7133**	**3623**

World	1998	1999	2000	2001	2002	2003	2004	2005 (to July 28)
Incidents	1274	1159	1138	1733	2650	1895	2578	2313
Injuries	8184	2333	2536	3983	7344	6253	10835	7133
Fatalities	2242	849	777	4555	2759	2369	4989	3623

Migration

Ulrich Beck (1992; much less in 2002) sees an important democratising potential in the notion of the world risk society, which he believes to be capable of transforming global politics. Late modern technology has slipped beyond the grasp of the technologists who create it. This may lead to disasters, but it also means that the technologists can no longer claim a privileged understanding of the technologies, so that – in contrast to the modern era – any interested members of the public can challenge the claims of the technocrats and take part in ethical debates about the risks, in which there is space both for fact-based calculation and for emotional or ethical arguments. This optimism may be based on the experiences of the green movement, especially in Germany, and more recently the Europe-wide debates on GMOs (Beck 2000; Mythen 2004).

Some authors have doubted whether this potential is actually being fulfilled, pointing out that 'subpolitical groups are susceptible to engulfment by the formal process' (Mythen 2004: 173), and further that 'discourses about risk are socially constructed narratives' (Culpitt 1999: 13) which can be used for hegemonic as much as for counter-hegemonic projects.

The lack of voice on the issue of migration reflects what seems to be an increasing divergence between social justice and civil liberties

---

This becomes more obvious as one moves beyond the field of late modern technology, on which most risk theorists focus, to review discourses which relate to globalisation more generally (see also Beck 2005). In the case of technology, it is easy to paint a picture of David-like social movement activists armed with emotional and moral arguments pitted against the Goliath of corporate and state-led technologists armed with outdated rationality models. But when one surveys the debates on migration, the picture becomes more mixed.

It is often the case that those who are attracted to extremist ideologies that are associated with terrorism are migrants, either from countryside to town or across borders (see Kaldor and Muro 2003). In Chapter 4, Meghnad Desai discusses how old social-democratic concerns with welfare and distribution combine messily with communitarian cultural arguments about identity, security obsessions and racism to portray immigration as a risk to host societies, while neo-liberal economic arguments combine with a celebration of cultural diversity and support for the human right to move in favour of immigration. Both sides use combinations of economic reasoning and moral and emotional appeals. In the sending societies, concerns about heavy brain drain, and again human rights concerns relating to the treatment of migrants, compete with the advantages of remittances in public discourse and government policy. Desai argues that anti-immigration lobbies have dominated the debate within global civil society and that those who favour the right to free movement need to be less defensive and to put their reasonable case to the test of public debate. In particular, the anti-capitalist movement has not been vocal on this issue, and advocacy of the pro-migrant position within anti-capitalist circles has been largely confined to a few peripheral anarchist and human rights groups.

The lack of voice on the issue of migration reflects what seems to be an increasing divergence between social justice and civil liberties. Security fears tend to be used to marginalise the case for civil liberties but they often help the case for social justice. During the cold war, civil liberties were often curtailed but pro-social justice groups were much stronger. Then in the 1990s, a period of neo-liberalism, the human rights movement was able to strengthen the global human rights regime in significant ways. In the aftermath of 9/11 the social justice agenda seems to have acquired a new lease of life but terrorism is being used to legitimise all kinds of restrictions on civil liberties. The debate about migration may be a casualty of this trend. Security and domestic welfare concerns have been allowed to override the human rights and global welfare case for migration.

Democratisation and instrumentalisation

Where are the spaces in which global civil society communicates and argues about risk? How are individual concerns about risk translated into political decision making? In this Yearbook we discuss four such forms. First of all, for many people the national level remains important. National governments are key participants in global negotiations and are often the first target of civil society action. To an extent that was hardly thinkable during the first phase of modernity, civil society activists can use global links to expand the space for democratic participation. The latest wave of democratisation in post-Soviet republics and in the

Middle East illustrates this global dynamic of democratisation. Second, international organisations are under increasing pressure to make more meaningful arrangements for citizen participation. In Chapter 5, Richard Falk discusses the UN's efforts to come to terms with the challenge of opening up access for global civil society. We suggest below that the series of 'no's' to the European Union's draft constitution may also be related to issues of access and participation. Third, the new phenomenon of social forums is, at least in aspirational terms, about creating new mechanisms for political participation. And finally, a new medium for global civil society is the rash of reports, study groups, and commissions initiated by global leaders and carried out by independent experts.

Mobilisation for democracy

In the opening chapter of *Global Civil Society 2004/5*, we noticed a trend of renewed civil society interest in mobilising for national elections. We and others had earlier noted a shift in the recent decades away from public participation in political parties and from civil society interest in national politics. Since the turn of the century, however, there appears to be a renewed interest in national politics, but not in the form of renewed political party activism. Instead, civil society mobilises on a more occasional basis against authoritarianism, rigged elections, lying politicians, and corruption.

Chapter 8, by Castells et al., brings out how these forms of mobilisation are different from older forms of national mobilisation. First, and most eye-catchingly, there is the use of new information and communications technology (ICT). Where earlier work by Castells and others has concentrated on the transformative features of the internet, Chapter 8 focuses on mobilisation by mobile phone. Like the internet, it can have the function of breaking into information oligarchies. New ICTs became so important in the Korean, the Spanish, and perhaps also the Philippine cases because the old media was, for whatever reason, on the side of the establishment. But the speed with which mobile phones can spread information greatly surpasses that of the internet, although, as the authors point out, texting is great for mobilisation but much less so for deliberation.

Second, while all the case studies describe national politics, none of the mobilisations was exclusively national in its concerns. Iraq binds the Spanish, the US and to some extent the Korean cases together as a global preoccupation impinging on national politics.

In the Spanish case global communications technology provided a clear anti-censorship factor in the sense that, astoundingly after 30 years of democracy, people went to foreign websites for trustworthy information. In the Philippines case the 'global element' was more ambiguous as the wealthy diaspora helped to replace a populist with a neo-liberal regime.

The trend for civil society mobilisation to democratise national politics seems to be continuing in 2005, making inroads into remaining bastions of authoritarianism in the former Soviet Union (Ukraine, Kyrgyzstan) and the Middle East (Lebanon). While the first two were about election-rigging, Lebanon uniquely concerned foreign occupation (see Box I.3). The Ukrainian and Lebanese events in particular show very similar features, and raise similar questions, to those described in Chapter 8.

In both the Ukrainian and the Lebanese revolutions, text messaging again played an important role in mobilising especially young people (Koprowski 2004; Quilty 2005). There seems to be clear evidence of transnational contagion and imitation in these 'colour-coordinated' revolutions. While the Ukrainian revolution looked the most heroic in braving the bitter cold, the Lebanese one put on the best display:

> *Pieces of cardboard (coloured red, white or green on one side and black on the other) were distributed to the 10,000 people assembled in the adjacent Martyrs' Square. On cue, the demonstrators flipped their cardboard to form a 3,800-square-metre flag (when the speaker demanded to know the truth about Hariri's killing) or a black rectangle of the same size (in reference to the opposition's enemies).* (Quilty 2005)

But it has been questioned whether the global element in all these revolutions was just a matter of horizontal contagion or whether there was deliberate foreign manipulation. Both the Bush administration and the financier-philanthropist George Soros have been named as fomenters of the revolution, usually with sinister intent. Soros did indeed quite openly support the democratic revolutions in Serbia, Georgia and Ukraine, financially and strategically, and the Bush administration has welcomed all the recent mobilisations, and may also have given prior support – although it must be pointed out that is due to Soros's attempts at regime change.

The confluence of local people's movements and foreign interests should be no surprise in a globalised world. It may be that the US administration's change of tack on democracy in the Middle East has provided a space for the 'cedar revolution' (a brand name courtesy of the US administration), which might not otherwise have been allowed to exist. But to attribute weeks of demonstrations by hundreds of thousands of Ukrainian and Lebanese individuals to Soros or Bush is to deny agency, to deny the possibility that Ukrainians and Lebanese, like Spaniards or Koreans, could act on their own initiative to express their disaffection with politics-as-usual.

Another question the recent revolutions raise is the extent to which they will actually succeed in bringing about lasting social change

---

A more problematic element, related to the use of mobile phones, is that of class. In most of the world, as in the Philippines, mobiles are still a luxury and will continue to be unavailable to those living on a few dollars a day. Therefore, in most parts of the world any mobile phone mobilisation could be only a middle-class mobilisation. Castells writes in Chapter 8 that 'Estrada had overwhelming support in the countryside and among the poor, as shown in his landslide victory in the 1998 election'. Mobile phones were not a feature of the subsequent Poor People Power mobilisation: 'Unlike those who had gathered there during People Power II, the crowd in what came to be billed as the 'Poor People Power' was trucked in by Estrada's political operatives from the slums and nearby provinces and provided with money, food, and, on at least certain occasions, alcohol' (Rafael, quoted in Castells et al. in Chapter 8).

Very similar dynamics operated in Ukraine and in Lebanon. In Lebanon, Jim Quilty (2005) writes of a smaller counter-demonstration by Hizbollah:

the most striking difference between these demonstrators and the 70,000 or so anti-regime activists who gathered at Martyrs' Square the night before was class. Though sometimes evident in matters of dress or manner, this difference was mostly registered in means of transportation – Hezbollah supporters travelling by bus or foot rather than the fleets of Mercedes, SUVs and Hummers used by opposition supporters. There was a very

strong sense that the Martyrs' Square rallies were demonstrations of privilege whereas this was one of the dispossessed – albeit a dispossessed being instrumentalised by Hezbollah.

There are various ways of interpreting these reports, none of which is comfortable from a global civil society perspective. The first would be that the middle classes are in cahoots with American or global neo-liberal interests, while the poor are manipulated by populists, authoritarians and Islamists. The second would be that only the middle classes are capable of exercising their own judgement with respect to the democratic credentials of their politicians, while the poor and uneducated are subject to instrumentalisation. The third would be that both groups are capable of exercising their own judgement, and are mobilising of their own volition, but have fundamentally different concerns and interests. Only the middle classes are concerned with abstract and 'bourgeois' concerns about democracy, while the poor are concerned with social justice – even if the politicians in whom they put their faith do not necessarily deliver it. The reality is undoubtedly more complex and more determined by local and historical factors than any of these interpretations allows. Still, the idea that the recent revolutions are evidence of an unproblematic global trajectory towards democracy, transparency and justice should be treated with some scepticism.

Another question the recent revolutions raise is the extent to which they will actually succeed in bringing about lasting social change. In Georgia, a new post-cold war generation has entered politics. In Lebanon, Syrian troops have been forced to leave, but the political parties seem to have returned to their usual sectarian bickering (see Box I.3). In Ukraine and Kyrgyzstan, the result of the 'revolutions' was one of intra-elite accommodation, as former ministers who had had a spell in opposition returned to government. Nonetheless, the confident assert that the Kyrgyz 'revolutionary uprising… set an example for neighbouring peoples and governments' (Sari and Yigit 2005). No one knows how far bloodless revolutions will extend in either the former Soviet Union or the Arab world. The bloody confrontation in Andijan, Uzbekistan, suggests that there may be setbacks. Our next Yearbook may be in a position to discuss the implications of further challenges to Central-Asian and Middle Eastern authoritarianism.

Government reform and civil society: the risk of instrumentalisation

Not all encounters between civil society and the state are dramatic tales of miraculous victory or bloody defeat. Global civil society also faces more conventional risks, such as being instrumentalised by governments and international organisations. For example, heads of state at the Sixth Global Forum in Reinventing Government[3], held in Seoul, 23–27 May 2005, and attended by several thousand representatives from 140 countries, made repeated calls for governments to work with civil society in meeting the growing gap between social needs and public resources. In an address delivered by Undersecretary Moreno, Kofi Annan called for a global government-civil society consensus on development as part of a 'system-wide exercise'; the Prime Minister of Korea stressed the link between civil society and governmental reform and accountability; the President of Brazil emphasised that civil society and engaged citizens were at the centre of policy action locally as well as globally; and leading government officials from countries and organisations as diverse as Tanzania, Thailand, Iran, Tajikistan, Tunisia, Italy, South Africa, the European Union and the OECD stressed the role of civil society in forging efficient systems of public-private partnerships in service delivery, the contribution of civil society to greater transparency and accountability, and greater social inclusion. While many scholars are beginning to problematise the idea of civil society as a panacea (Chandhoke 2005), diverse government leaders continue to be all the more enamoured of the concept.

The change in terminology that has occurred over recent years is remarkable. Whereas until the late 1990s 'NGO' was the term most commonly used in such international gatherings, the term 'civil society' has gained much currency. Increasingly, 'NGOs' and 'civil society' are being used interchangeably, and civil society has become reified as an actor similar to 'the state' and 'the market'. For one thing, that policy makers have begun to ascribe agency to civil society reflects a limited understanding of its nature and function, transforms civil society into an organisational, even sectoral, phenomenon, and paints over diversity and complexity in favour of finding a convenient 'conceptual handle' on a par with 'the state' and 'the market'.

Equating NGOs and non-profit organisations with civil society is also part of a process of instrumentalisation by national governments and international organisations that are in search of greater legitimacy, and eager to try out seemingly new ways towards overdue public sector reform. The statements and proceedings of the Sixth Global Forum on Reinventing Government, mentioned above, the UN's High Level Panel on Civil Society (see below), the World Bank's projects on social accountability and civic engagement, or the EU's attempts to 'reach out to civil society', are examples of this instrumentalisation.

Top-down views of the functions of civil society include three broad perspectives that have become prominent in recent years. First, NGOs have become part of new public management and mixed 'economies of welfare', which involve public and private providers. New public management approaches see NGOs as closely linked to welfare state reform or welfare state alternatives. Second, civil society is seen as central to 'civil society-social capital' approaches, specifically the neo-Tocquevillian emphasis on the nexus between social capital and participation in voluntary associations of many kinds. Third, from a wider social accountability perspective, civil society is an instrument for achieving greater transparency, heightened accountability and improved governance of public institutions. The 'other genealogy' of civil society, that which describes its functions in terms of counter-hegemony and contestation (Howell and Pearce 2002: 18–31; Kaldor 2003), is left firmly out of the picture.

Apart from the discounting of more confrontational notions, civil society is also 'domesticated' in another sense. Quite against the recent history of actually existing organisations, movements and networks, much government rhetoric (less so that of international institutions) treats civil society as a national phenomenon. As such, it can conveniently be cast in a role of 'junior partner' to government. Such typecasting masks the fact that it is precisely the transcending of boundaries that has made global civil society a force to be reckoned with (whether governments like it or not).

The first of the three approaches set out above sees NGOs as service providers within public-private partnerships under the rubric of new public management and the rise of markets and quasi-markets in areas that have hitherto been part of the welfare state. The

---

3 The forum goes back to a Clinton-Gore initiative for government reform. The first forum was held at the White House in 1999, and has since then emerged as the major international meeting on governmental modernisation and innovation.

Box I.3: Lebanon's 'Independence 05': from a moment to a movement?

Since 14 February 2005, and the assassination of former Prime Minister Rafiq Hariri, Lebanon has captured the attention of the international community. The murder of Hariri, a powerful international businessman and major player in Lebanon's reconstruction and peace process, sparked an immense and unexpected reaction from ordinary people. Winds of civic change seemed to be blowing from Kiev to Beirut and Cairo, legitimising and reinstating the role of popular democratic practices in changing the course of politics and challenging incumbent regimes. The intensity of this popular response enhanced the prospects of a coherent and enduring civic movement that would impose new standards of participatory democracy and break the hold of a sectarian political leadership. This review of the period between 14 February and 30 April 2005 – 'Independence 05' – attempts to trace the continuity of the movement.

The assassination of Hariri concluded the post-war period since 1990, which had seen Syria's role as Lebanon's guarantor strengthen in response to the Israeli occupation of South Lebanon between 1978 and 2000. Since 1990 the influence of Syrian and collaborating Lebanese security services nurtured political and economic corruption in a clientelist sectarian political system. Political tension had increased in the wake of a Syrian-induced constitutional change in October 2004, which extended President Emile Lahoud's term. Hariri led the opposition to the pro-Lahoud government, reshuffling political alliances into pro- and anti-Syrian camps. His assassination provoked outrage from politicians and ordinary people. A 'Opposition' bloc was formed, which denounced the assassination as an unacceptable breach of the rules of the Lebanese political game. Citizens of all ages – led by youth groups – poured on to the streets for a protest that lasted more than ten weeks. The minister of interior's attempt to ban the protest met with defiance from protesters. Instead of violence, the demonstrations were commemorative, marked by sports events, human chains and thousands of people collectively forming the Lebanese flag. Protesters offered flowers to the armed forces, portraying and emphasising the 'civilised' nature of the movement.

In its formative phase, this civic action was inspired by personal and emotional responses, and evolved in four steps: an emotional reaction to the assassination of Hariri, his public funeral, the youth-led protests and the transformation of his grave into a shrine. The brutal assassination of such a powerful man destroyed his invincible image, which had been part of Lebanon's collective consciousness. People responded from many diverse motives: grief at the death of a great enabler of reconstruction and peace-building, fear of violent retribution and recurrence of civil war, or simply anger at the sabotage of the political process. Hundreds of thousands of citizens from all over the country attended his funeral and burial in Beirut's Martyrs' Square, which was renamed 'Freedom Square' by opposition youth groups staging sit-ins.

In the consolidation phase of this civic movement, the personal amalgamated with the political. Opposition leaders demanded that the assassins be brought to justice. A blue ribbon and pin of Hariri that said simply 'the truth', became the slogan of the campaign. Opposition leaders' demands for justice and accountability sealed popular support. It contrasted with dozens of unresolved political assassinations and a frustrating end-of-war amnesty granted to warlords. A shift in gendered political roles also boosted the momentum. In a coordinated division of labour, Hariri's wife and daughters represented the 'feminine' and 'private' image of sorrow, with moving broadcasts of their visits to the grave. MP Bahia Hariri, sister of the late Hariri, stepped into a 'masculine' and 'public' political role while maintaining a 'feminine' appearance of mourning and insisting she be called the 'Martyr's sister'. Her speech in the parliamentary session, broadcast live to the weeping nation, was key to the government's resignation two weeks after the assassination. Her resolute and frequent public appearances enhanced her potential as the successor of her brother. Other women opposition politicians joined the solidarity front, including two widows of former presidents who had also been assassinated.

The confrontation phase focused on gaining politicised popular support. Momentum was built by strengthening the concept of national identity against an external enemy. 'Lebaneseness' was promoted as civilised solidarity of all faiths facing barbaric terrorism. Legitimisation of the movement's demands relied on the adoption of international (Western) standards of democracy, exemplified by French and US support for the cause. The external enemy was Syria, blamed for masterminding the assassination, and already unpopular because of the political and economic advantages the country's presence in Lebanon afforded it. Loyalists tried to counter-attack taking a legalistic-technical approach to the assassination, denying its terrorist nature, and hastily naming bogus culprits. They also tried to legitimise Syria's presence based on historic ties, and blamed foreign powers for supporting opposition groups and weakening state institutions. In an attempt to co-opt the growing opposition, loyalists called for a massive 'one-million' demonstration on 8 March 2005. Hundreds of thousands of demonstrators gathered including, in addition to some pro-Syrian political groups, an overwhelming number of members of one sectarian community mainly coming from disadvantaged areas. The tensions between the pro- and anti-Syrian camps assumed a new sectarian and socio-economic dimension.

In a resounding political rebuff to loyalists, the Opposition also called for a 'one-million' demonstration, on 14 March. In an unprecedented effort, civil society groups, political parties and economic institutions collaborated on this memorable civic march, which encapsulated the spirit of the 'Independence 05 uprising'. In addition to television stations providing continuous live transmission (especially the Hariri-owned channel), leading advertising agencies created popular political slogans and paraphernalia, and many singers joined in solidarity songs. Many large firms, from banks to private hospitals, arranged for their employees to participate in the demonstration. As a result, leaders of political parties and youth groups marched alongside individuals, families, neighbourhood associations and rural groups in the streets of downtown Beirut. More than a million demonstrators gathered – the largest demonstration in Lebanon. Protesters' demands included an international inquiry into Hariri's assassination, the resignation of the president, the resignation and detention of the heads of the five main security services, the immediate withdrawal of Syrian troops and security services, and the holding of elections by the end of May, in accordance with the constitution. In the following weeks Syrian troops and security forces withdrew after a 30-year presence in Lebanon, and four out of the five heads of the Lebanese security forces stepped down.

The UN response was in two stages. Ten days after the assassination, a UN mission of inquiry flew to Lebanon, examined the crime scene and presented a report to the Security Council. On 7 April 2005, following a unanimous UN Security Council decision, a UN independent investigation commission flew to Lebanon to investigate Hariri's death, and is still working on the case at the time of writing. General elections were scheduled for 29 May–19 June 2005.

The concluding phase was not as glorious. Less then three months after Independence 05, the temporality of national solidarity, civic engagement and political reform was clear. Once the Opposition's demands had been fulfilled, cracks started to appear. The final days of the youth sit-in reflected this tension before it was hastily called off. The sectarian-based political system and electoral competition have proven to be the most difficult challenge facing any reformist civic movement. Opposition leaders fell out over diverging electoral interests and began mobilising support by playing on clientelistic sectarian loyalties. As the loyalist camp atrophied, many loyalists dropped their pro-Syrian stand and took up a polarised sectarian discourse. With electoral alliances reuniting Opposition and Loyalist candidates, new sectarian-based grievances have been created. Many citizens from the '14 March' have aligned themselves with their leaders' political and sectarian swings. This realignment restored gendered political roles as Hariri's sister was sidelined and his son inherited the family's political leadership. Also, the leaders of most youth groups were excluded from representation in electoral coalitions by traditional candidates. Promises of an opposition reunion and reform have been set for the post-election period and are again backed by international players such as France and the US. The 'Independence 05' civic movement will probably have to wait for another moment to be revived.

Nisrine Mansour, Social Policy Department, LSE

assumption is that NGOs are more efficient providers than governments. The second approach – the discovery of civil society as a source of social capital – is based on the growing awareness among policy-makers and scholars that the very social fabric of society is changing. The assumption here is that civil society is key to social trust and cohesion. In the developed world, the decline of traditional membership organisations such as unions, political parties and churches, alleged erosions in social capital and interpersonal as well as institutional trust, and other factors, bring with them a profound awareness of uncertainty and a concern about social stability. In the developing world, debate about social exclusion, failing states and social disintegration raises similar expectations whereby civil society is to serve as the panacea to counteract social isolation and the negative impact of individualism on social cohesion.

The third approach – social accountability – sees governance as a combined effort that includes civil society actors and business as well as government. The assumption in this case is that civil society enhances accountability and transparency. It is about affirming and operationalising directly accountable relationships between citizens and the state. It includes efforts by citizens and civil society organisations to hold the state to account as well as actions on the part of government, civil society, the media and other actors to promote or facilitate greater accountability.

The combination of these three, somewhat contra-dictory, perspectives could be seen as a kind of merger of neo-liberal policies of welfare state reform with 'third way' approaches. Whereas neo-liberal policies stress smaller governments overall, greater fiscal account-ability and individual responsibility, the third way calls for decentralised forms of government based on transparency and accountability, efficient administration, more opportunities for direct democracy, social inclusion, and an environmentally friendly economy.

There was always a technocratic overlap between new public management and decentralisation; but they differed in terms of civil engagement and empowerment. Initially, the third way foresaw a re-organisation of the state that required an activation of civil society and social participation, the encouragement of social entrepreneurship, and new approaches to public-private partnerships in the provision of public goods and services. Specifically, the framework involved a renewal of political institutions to encourage greater

citizen participation; a new relationship between government and civil society with an engaged gov-ernment and a vibrant set of voluntary associations of many kinds; a wider role for businesses as socially and environmentally responsible institutions; and a structural reform of the welfare state away from 'entitlement' towards risk management (Giddens 1998; 2000; The White House 1999).

Yet, in the course of less than a decade, the ideological foundations of a renewal of government have been cleansed of the ideology of empowerment in favour of technocratic approaches that essentially incorporate NGOs in the project to achieve greater public sector efficiency. New public management and not civic renewal dominates, and the government-civil society dialogue is increasingly top-down, paying lip service to social accountability and self-organisation.

Instrumentalisation of civil society rhetoric for essentially neo-liberal policies has allowed govern-ments with very different political ideologies and varied human rights backgrounds to make claims on what they term 'civil society' but mean privatised governmental functions under state tutelage. And yet the rhetoric of civil society, which has proved surprisingly durable since the early 1990s, opens opportunities for civil society leaders to respond to the apolitical and top-down view of civil society, and to correct both terminology and agenda by engaging the new public management dialogue more forcefully. The UN's recent interest in civil society may offer a platform in this respect for what we see as a need to counteract the top-down and instrumentalist view of government organisations vis-à-vis civil society. More doubtfully, the rejection of the European Union's draft constitution in a series of referenda may also offer such an opportunity.

The UN and global civil society

In 2004/5 we wrote that 'if key decisions are taken at the global level, there have to be mechanisms for increasing the responsiveness of global institutions to the demands of individual citizens' (Kaldor, Anheier and Glasius 2005: 16). This question has taken centre stage at the United Nations in 2005, as Secretary-General Kofi Annan commissioned two high-level panels to advise on the UN's relation with global civil society on the one hand, and its arrangements on governance of global security on the other hand. As Richard Falk describes in Chapter 5, both panels have made some useful practical suggestions, but neither lives up to the Secretary-General's dramatic announcement that the UN has reached 'a fork in the road' and needs 'a hard look at fundamental issues', leading to 'structural changes' (see Chapter 5).

The Panel of Eminent Persons on United Nations-Civil Society Relations stakes a major claim for global civil society by titling its report *We the Peoples: the United Nations, Civil Society and Global Governance* (UN 2004a). It has often been remarked that the United Nations does not in fact represent 'peoples' or 'nations', but states. By its choice of title, the panel appears to suggest that civil society represents 'the peoples' instead. It draws inspiration from ideas about participatory or deliberative democracy to argue that, through the mediation of global civil society, 'anyone can enter the debates that most interest them, through advocacy, protest, and in other ways' (UN 2004a: para 13). These are radical claims, which are valid in principle but are extremely difficult to apply in practice (see also Glasius 2005; Kaldor 2003). But the panel's concrete recommendations are hardly in keeping with such an optimistic view of civil society's role in global governance. As Richard Falk notes in Chapter 5, the report engages in 'soft advocacy', proposing primarily to maintain the concessions global civil society has won over the decades through sustained pressure, rather than to specify a structural role for civic participation.

Moreover, the panel appears to show a tendency to want to 'streamline' and homogenise civil society views. To this end, it proposes 'disciplined networking and peer review processes of the constituencies' (UN 2004a: para 26). But does not this run counter to the aspiration of democratising the United Nations through global civil society participation? As Iris Marion Young (1997: 401) puts it, deliberative democracy should not be 'a comfortable place of conversation among those who share language, assumptions, and ways of looking at issues'. The emphasis on 'disciplined networking and peer review' could have the effect of brushing out differences within global civil society. This may make 'consultation' more convenient and speedy for international institutions, but it has negative consequences for the legitimacy and creativity of global civil society, and hence for its influence in the long term. It would also be a strategic mistake for the United Nations. Procedures to invite and manage different and even opposing perspectives are not only a requirement for having serious democratic debate. It would be a victory for the United Nations and for multilateralism if groups which are sceptical and suspicious of international institutions devote energy to participating in its debates, rather than fighting the organisation from the outside.

Despite the caution of the panel, Falk predicts that 'a campaign on behalf of some institutional presence for global civil society within the structure of the United Nations is likely to build momentum and generate worldwide excitement' (Chapter 5). There are various developments that would back up this forecast: the self-styled 'World Forum of Civil Society Networks' Ubuntu launched a campaign to reform international institutions, beginning with the United Nations, in 2002 (Reform Campaign URL), and the Italian Tavola della Pace followed suit with an ambitious event in Padua in 2004 (Tavola della Pace URL).

---

representation in the elective sense is not what global civil society does

---

At the World Social Forum, where the interest in international institutions has steadily risen (see Marlies Glasius and Jill Timms, Chapter 6), the 2005 seminars on UN reform have generated a network backed by 140 organisations and a host of global celebrities. An appeal, again in the name of 'we the people', calls for 'a constituent process involving all possible actors in civil society, local authorities and parliaments. Priority must be given to ensure due representation of region, race, class, gender and all social pluralities in this process'. A 'Global Day of Mobilisation For a New World Order Against Poverty, War and Unilateralism' has been proclaimed for 10 September (September 10 URL). But the details of the proposed reforms are not (yet?) worked out.

Many proposals for UN reform go in the direction of some kind of global civil society assembly, sometimes alongside an assembly of parliamentarians, to supplement or replace the existing General Assembly (Falk Chapter 5; Van Rooy 2004: 134). But the fundamental flaw of all these proposals is that they try to push civil society into the straitjacket of representative democracy. As we and others have argued before, representation in the elective sense is not what global civil society does (Edwards 2003; Van Rooy 2004: 62–76; Anderson and Rieff 2004/5: 29–31). We believe the claims, and hence also the structures, for democratising the United Nations through global civil society should be more imaginative.

Civil society participation can aid the transparency of decision-making through calling states to account and monitoring state behaviour. It can contribute – although not inevitably – to levelling the playing field between states. It can introduce new viewpoints into discussions and spark more substantial deliberation, not just predicated on putative state interest. And it can inject arguments based on (contestable) ethical claims regarding the global common good (Glasius 2005; Van Rooy 2004; Scholte 2001). Thinking about how such 'supplementary democracy' (Van Rooy 2004: 137) through global civil society can be strengthened is both more creative and more realistic than proposals that would make a set of international NGOs represent global civil society, which would in turn represent the global demos.

Even so, the upsurge of interest within global civil society to radically democratise the United Nations and other international institutions, not incrementally, but as a campaign in itself, may revitalise a rather tired debate. As Hagai Katz and Helmut Anheier write in Chapter 7, 'in light of the deepening weakness of the UN system ...global governance actors lack any motivation to act and often prefer to free ride', and, as Falk discusses at length in Chapter 5, there are many barriers to innovation. A new campaign may put sufficient pressure on states and on the institution itself to accept some changes. At least, it may help to prevent a simultaneous rollback of the power of global civil society within international institutions, and of international institutions within global governance.

The EU constitution and citizen participation

The European project is in trouble as the EU's draft constitution is the subject of a series of referenda. At the time of writing, Spain and Luxembourg have voted 'yes', the former with a record low turnout, whereas France and the Netherlands have voted 'no'; and it is not clear whether other planned referenda in the Czech Republic, Denmark, Ireland, Poland, Portugal and the United Kingdom will go ahead. Some of these countries are expected to be Euro-sceptic, but how did the citizens of two of the founding members of the EU, with a history of Euro-enthusiasm, come to turn against the constitution?

In both the Netherlands and France, there has emerged in recent years a general mood of distrust of establishment politicians, as evidenced by the break-

through of Jean-Marie Le Pen, leader of the National Front, to the final round of the 2002 French presidential elections and the spectacular, if short-lived, success of the Pim Fortuyn List in the 2002 Dutch parliamentary election. Part of the reason for the 'no' vote clearly lay in the desire to punish the main parties (including in both cases the socialist opposition), which advocated a 'yes' vote.

> the rejection of the constitution reflected the growing distance between the European political class and the citizens. For the 'man in the street' interviewed on television, the rejection was a chance to express disaffection with the political process

But there was a wider problem with the way in which the constitution had come about and the way it was communicated to the European public. A constitution is an emotive document, and could be considered as nothing less than a covenant between a community of citizens, establishing not just the rules of how they are to be governed but also the values they share. The US Constitution is a prime example of such a text, but even the Charter of Principles of the World Social Forum could be considered akin to constitutions as a foundational statement (Glasius and Timms Chapter 6). But the European Constitution is a bureaucratic document, negotiated between politicians and former politicians, with little attempt at resonance with the people of Europe. Indeed, politicians did not make sufficient effort to explain what was in the constitution and why it was important. In the Netherlands, 'lack of information' was one of the main reasons for voting no (De Volkskrant 2005). The same explanation was given for the abstention by many Spanish voters, where the vote was 'yes', but with a turnout of only 42 per cent (Shields 2005).

Thus, the rejection of the constitution reflected the growing distance between the European political class and the citizens. For the 'man in the street' interviewed on television, the rejection was a chance to express disaffection with the political process. It was a response to decades of decision-making by the European elites behind closed doors. There is no 'face' of Europe, no obvious address to which requests, objections, ideas, or proposals can be sent. Yet Europe is often used as an excuse for not responding to requests, objections, ideas and proposals sent to a national address. Europe seems to most people to be a set of buildings in Brussels. The constitution became a symbol of distrust and frustration with the opaque character of decision-making in a global era.

Opposition to the constitution came from both Left and Right. The Left voted against the content of the constitution, particularly the neo-liberalism of the constitution, the clauses incorporating wholesale the Thatcher-era provisions for the single market originally contained in the Maastricht Treaty. The Right were voting against Europe. It was both a debate about what kind of Europe and a debate about the French and Dutch relationships to Europe. And this was one of the big problems with the referenda. Because they took place in separate countries, they became pro- or anti-Europe debates, debates about national identity, debates about 'in' or 'out', rather than debates about the future of Europe.

There is no question that EU reform is necessary, and many of the provisions in the constitution would have made the organisation more effective, particularly in the area of foreign policy. But the rejection could be taken by the politicians of Europe as an opportunity to rectify the mistake they made in foisting a 'constitution' upon their citizens without consulting them. This could be a chance to have really open Union-wide discussions about what people like, and dislike, about 'being European'; whether they feel in need of a constitution; and what should be in it. In such a process, which could include town hall meetings, school assemblies and online discussion forums, the people of Europe could define for themselves to what extent they actually have a common identity. If a real constitution can be forged out of such discussions and consultations, the process and text itself could actually be drivers of a common European spirit, as defined by the people themselves.

Social forums and interconnectedness

Two chapters in this Yearbook discuss directly the matter of global civil society's infrastructure: how global it is in terms of actual on-the-ground presence and connectedness rather than rhetoric. The conclusions of Katz and Anheier's chapter on international NGOs give a bleak response to this question. While international NGOs are nearly all connected to each other in one huge inclusive network, there is a 'pronounced centre-periphery structure'. Moreover,

the biggest clusters of INGOs mirror the centres of corporate and governmental power: New York, London, Washington DC and Brussels. Hence, the network reproduces rather than counteracts the amplification of Northern over Southern voices.

Glasius and Timms, in their chapter on social forums, come to rather different conclusions. The decision to hold the first World Social Forum in Brazil (albeit in the relatively wealthy south of the country) was a conscious attempt to get away from the self-reinforcing dynamic described by Katz and Anheier. Social forums have since organised primarily around a South-American/European axis, more recently and more problematically also including the Indian subcontinent and Africa (see Glasius and Timms, Chapter 6). Europe is undoubtedly still over-represented, but social forum organisation in North America is very weak. But beyond the geography of the social forums, the most important thing about them from a global civil society infrastructure perspective is the way they have focused on horizontal networking across cultures and issues, and experimenting with participatory forms of organising, as values in themselves.

The debate in Chapter 2, between three thinkers deeply invested in the World Social Forum (WSF), including two of its founder members, focuses on the difference between a movement and a space. For Chico Whitaker, the WSF is a space where myriad individuals and organisations can come together to meet, debate, argue, and plan campaigns. Such a space can stimulate campaigns or movements; indeed, the march against the war in Iraq on 15 February 2003 and the Global Call to Action Against Poverty, which came out of the 2005 WSF, are two such examples. But to be effective in developing and purveying shared bottom-up analyses of global risks and injustices, the Forum needs to retain its horizontal networking character. In contrast, Bernard Cassen and Boaventura de Sousa Santos warn against the 'tyranny of structurelessness' and argue that the WSF needs more transparent organisational rules in order to be able to build on its strength to put forward concrete proposals for opposing neo-liberalism. They find the social forums too amorphous, and hark back to earlier movements with more clearly circumscribed mandates and a clear leadership. In particular, they defend the 'Manifesto of Porto Alegre', launched in 2005 with very little fanfare. Among the young activists of the social forums, however, the Whitaker view seems to be in the ascendant.

Box I.4: Key reports and strategies of 2004/5

A More Secure World: Our Shared Responsibility

Report of the High-Level Panel on Threats, Challenges and Change
Established by UN Secretary-General Kofi Annan under the chairmanship of Anand Panyarachun, former Prime Minister of Thailand, this panel reconsidered the role of the UN with regard to peace and security in an era of globalisation when 'a threat to one is a threat to all'. Tasked with generating new ideas about the policies and institutions needed for the UN to be effective in the twenty-first century, the panel outlines the rationale for the concept and system of 'collective security'. It endorses the notion of 'a collective international responsibility to protect', exercisable by the Security Council authorising military intervention, in the case of genocide, ethnic cleansing or serious violations of international law, when states are unable or unwilling to act. In contrast to the past failure of member states to agree on a definition of terrorism, the report provides a clear definition, arguing that terrorism can never be justified, and urges the General Assembly to conclude a comprehensive convention on terrorism. In addition to revitalising the Commission on Human Rights and creating a Peacebuilding Commission, the report offers two models for reform of the Security Council that, by broadening the states represented, would increase its credibility and effectiveness.
www.un.org/secureworld/

We the Peoples: Civil Society, the UN and Global Governance

Panel of Eminent Persons on UN-Civil Society Relations
Acknowledging that public opinion had become a key factor 'influencing intergovernmental and governmental policies and actions', this panel is based on the premise that 'civil society is now so vital to the UN that engaging with it well is a necessity, not an option'. Chaired by Fernando Henrique Cardoso, former President of Brazil, the panel report makes 30 recommendations, based on four paradigms: that the UN become a more outward-looking organisation, embrace a plurality of constituencies, connect the local with the global, and help strengthen democracy.
www.un.org/reform/pdfs/cardosopaper13june.htm

In Larger Freedom: Towards Development, Security and Human Rights for All

Report of the Secretary-General
This report embraces the recommendations of the High-Level Panel on Threats, Challenges and Change, and the Panel of Eminent Persons on Civil Society-UN Relations. In articulating priority areas for action by members states under the principle of freedom – from want, from fear and to live in dignity – the report emphasises the necessity, challenge and capability of meeting the Millennium Development Goals (MDGs) by 2015. This encapsulates the ethos of the Millennium Project Report to the UN Secretary General (see below). In Larger Freedom also outlines the changes needed to reform the structure and culture of the UN. The report concludes with an annex listing specific actions on which heads of state will decide at the Millennium +5 Summit in New York in September 2005.
www.un.org/largerfreedom/

Our Common Interest

The Commission for Africa

This report by the Commission for Africa, set up by UK Prime Minister Tony Blair in March 2004 with 17 commissioners, proposes a 'coherent package for Africa' based on 'a new kind of partnership' between the continent and the developed world. Arguing that many African countries have been making progress in governance and growth, the report outlines recommendations in six key areas: governance and capacity building, peace and security, investing in people, growth and poverty reduction, more and fairer trade, and resources. On trade, the report recommends that industrialised nations should dismantle the tariffs and subsidies that give them an unfair advantage over African producers. Africa has to make changes internally to improve the transport network, and reduce bureaucracy and tariffs system. Among proposals for financing, the recommendations include an additional US$25 billion per year in aid by 2010 (and a further $25 billion per year by 2015), a commitment from rich countries to give 0.7 per cent of their GDP in aid, and debt cancellation for the poorest countries in sub-Saharan Africa.
www.commissionforafrica.org/english/report/introduction.html

Investing in Development: A Practical Plan to Achieve the Millennium Development Goals

UN Millennium Project

This report is the outcome of research by the ten task forces of the UN Millennium Project, an independent advisory body to the Secretary-General, led by Professor Jeffrey Sachs. The report's ten recommendations comprise practical actions designed to speed up progress towards achieving the MDGs by 2015. Based on the current rate of progress many countries, particularly in Africa, will fail to meet these eight targets designed to tackle the worst offences of poverty, which were enshrined in the 2000 Millennium Declaration.

   The first recommendation urges developing countries to have in place by 2006 poverty reduction strategies that are radical enough to meet the MDGs by 2015. These strategies should scale up public investments and provide a framework for strengthening governance. Another recommendation is the 'Quick Win actions', launched in 2005, which include free mass distribution of malaria nets and medicines for children, expansion of provision of anti-retroviral medicines to people living with HIV/AIDS, ending fees for primary schools and health services, and replenishing soil nutrients for small farmers. Among the proposals aimed at high-income countries are increases in development assistance, opening markets to developing country exports, and increased support for and investment in scientific research in health, agriculture, environmental management and climate.
www.unmillenniumproject.org/reports/index.htm

A Human Security Doctrine for Europe

The Barcelona Report of the Study Group on Europe's Security Capabilities

The report, commissioned by EU High Representative for Common Foreign and Security Policy Javier Solana, argues for a fundamental rethink of Europe's approach to security – not only within its borders but beyond. With terrorism, the changing nature of warfare, and ripple effects of state collapse, Europe cannot ignore the growing insecurity around the globe. A bottom-up approach, predicated on human rather than nation-state security, should be at the heart of European policy, the report argues. Instead of defeating enemies or pacifying warring parties, EU missions should focus on protecting civilians through law enforcement and, if necessary, the use of military force. To carry out such missions, the report proposes an integrated civil-military force of 15,000 personnel, a third of whom would be civilians with various professional skills and experiences. The Study Group developed seven principles for Europe's security policy which apply to prevention, conflict and post-conflict contexts alike, and which are intended to guide the actions of high-level EU officials, politicians in the member states, diplomats, and soldiers and civilians in the field, as well as a new legal framework governing such operations.
www.lse.ac.uk/Depts/global/Publications/HumanSecurityDoctrine.pdf

An optimistic conclusion from these chapters could therefore be that an INGO contingent within global civil society, focused on lobbying work in the corridors of power, is complemented by a more dispersed, more militant as well as more self-reflexive contingent of social forums. But the question arises to what extent and in what manner the get-on-with-it culture of the relatively powerful INGOs interacts with the more contentious, chaotic and creative social forum culture. Further research might provide a fuller picture of whether these two worlds are fairly separate or intimately linked, and whether relations are cordial, antagonistic, or creatively contentious.

The year of the reports

Starting with the Brandt Commission in 1980, a phenomenon that has become an important component of global civil society is the plethora of commissions, study groups and task forces set up by governments or international institutions to bring together expert opinion on specific global issues. The reports of these international bodies can be viewed as a sort of filter between civil society groups and the institutions of global governance. They are a way of drawing attention to global issues, both for the public and for decision-makers. They can be both 'top-down', in the sense that they are generally commissioned by political institutions and are often regarded as mechanisms for mobilisation, and at the same time 'bottom-up', in so far as they take evidence from citizens and civil society groups and offer a form of access. Whether they represent democratisation or instrumentalisation, therefore, remains a question to be researched.

The past year has been the year of reports (see Box I.4), particularly for the United Nations and the European Union. A number of reports were commissioned in the aftermath of the crises in both institutions as a result of the war in Iraq. The profound divisions over the war immobilised the institutions and represented a profound crisis of multilateralism and global governance. The reports can be viewed as proposals for overcoming these crises and reinvigorating efforts to apply the precautionary principle at a global level. The key conclusions of some of these reports are listed in Box I.4, with further discussion of some in Richard Falk's chapter.

The central concerns of the 2005 reports are poverty and security. Perhaps the most significant idea that comes out of the all the reports is the connection between poverty and security, between – to use the language of this introduction – dangers and risks. Terrorism and weapons of mass destruction are presented, in these reports, as 'other tsunami' in the sense that they are represented as a potential risk to us all. As in the case of climate change, connections are made between terrorism and inequality. But here the dominant argument is not that terrorism would hit the poor harder, but rather that inequality itself increases the risk of terrorism. Thus, the connection becomes one of self-interest, and is not the preserve of a radical social justice movement. It has become common ground, at least in the rhetoric if not in the policy of Western states, and expressed in these reports, that poverty and inequality are security risks, and poverty alleviation can therefore be a form of anti-terrorist policy.

This year's reports have engendered a mixed response. Within decision-making circles, the reports have been welcomed as bringing together and taking forward a range of proposals on the global and European agenda. Among campaigning groups and NGOs, many have expressed scepticism that the reports are too moderate and that, by focusing on what is perceived to be politically possible, they have failed to shift the global consensus in a more radical direction. Reports are, of course, a form of deliberation. The question is whether the proposals contained in a report can be translated into global decision-making, whether moderation was the appropriate strategy or whether action requires more widespread pressure.

> The past year has been a roller coaster year for global civil society. Events like the tsunami or the London bombings have exposed the meaning of world risk society

At the 2005 World Economic Forum meeting in Davos, French President Jacques Chirac endorsed the idea of an 'international solidarity levy' to fight HIV/AIDS; British Prime Minister Tony Blair proposed a doubling of aid to Africa and debt relief; and German Chancellor Gerhard Schröder called for an end to 'developed world agriculture and export subsidies, punitive customs and excise duties' (WEF 2005). It is uncertain to what extent this increased social justice agenda can be attributed to the activities of the re-styled global social justice movement or to the desire to assuage the 'global rancour' of potential future terrorists. Nor is it yet clear whether any of these proposals will make it to the implementation stage. The G8 summit has been predictably modest in its decisions, but at least it was discussing issues such as trade subsidies or climate change, which would not previously have been on its agenda.

The G8 campaigners have pledged to maintain the pressure on political leaders, who will meet again at the UN Millennium + 5 Summit in New York in September 2005, to review progress on the eight Millennium Development Goals, which were intended to address the worst offences of poverty by 2015. As Kofi Annan said at a public event in London's St Paul's Cathedral on the eve of the G8: 'We cannot win overnight. Success will require sustained action across the entire decade between now and the deadline (2015)... This is why the mass mobilization we are seeing now is so important' (UNIS 2005).

Conclusion: risk and human security

The past year has been a roller coaster year for global civil society. Events like the tsunami or the London bombings have exposed the meaning of world risk society. Global civil society action, ranging from respectable reports to anarchic demonstrations, can be understood as attempts to portray both everyday dangers faced by millions of people in the poorer and more violent parts of the world and their translation into risks faced by people living in the richer, supposedly more secure parts of the world.

One concept that brings together many of these concerns is that of 'human security'. The term has been popularised by yet another report, that of the Commission on Human Security (2003), and is applied in the Secretary-General's High-Level Panel on Threats, Challenges and Change (UN 2004b). But although the term is beginning to be used in development discourse, its potential may not yet be fully realised. It is a term with which global civil society activists can confront the current preoccupation of governments and public opinion with terrorism, entering the security debate with strategies that go beyond repression. This could be more realistic and productive than just lamenting the current security paradigm.

On the one hand, it involves accepting that security is not just an obsession of controlling governments, it is a deeply felt concern by people all over the world. On the other hand, the term 'human security' suggests that security policies must go well beyond securing metro-politan populations against terrorist attacks. Everyone has a right to feel secure, which means to be free from fear and free from want. Yet, as the Commission on Human Security makes clear, it is not a good that can be delivered to passive subjects; it also involves an element of emancipation.

Finally, the concept refers to the security of individuals and communities rather than states, whether we are talking about state borders or the protection of the state apparatus, and is thus connected to human rights as well as human development, civil liberties as well as social justice. In the case of security, this is particularly important because it strips it from its historic connection with the state, and the state's prerogative to decide what constitutes a threat to security and what does not. The human security frame acknowledges that the security of citizens is not always bound up with the security of the state; sometimes it is the state itself that most threatens its citizens. On the other hand, it also acknowledges that in the twenty-first century the state may not always be able to keep its citizens secure, and other actors, at the local, regional and global levels, should share responsibility for human security.

This is where global civil society comes in. The idea of human security can connect many of the global civil society activities described in this introduction, from social justice and climate change campaigns to disaster relief and campaigns against political violence. Because the concept applies to the community of human beings, it offers the potential for expressing a global precautionary principle. In *Global Civil Society 2004/5* we redefined global civil society as the medium through which one or more social contracts are negotiated by individual citizens and the various institutions of global governance (national, international and local) (Kaldor, Anheier and Glasius, 2004/5:2; Held 2004). This is an ongoing process involving debate, argument, campaigning, struggle, pressure, information, and a wide range of groups and individuals. One scenario is the further instrumentalisation of global civil society as a partner in a top-down effort to contain risk. The alternative scenario is a combined effort to confront everyday dangers of poverty, insecurity and environmental degradation. Human security could be a powerful framework for global civil society in framing these risks in transformative ways.

REFERENCES

Adam, B. and van Loon, J. (2000). 'Introduction: Repositioning Risk: The Challenges for Social Theory', in B. Adam, U. Beck and J. van Loon (eds.), *The Risk Society and Beyond: Critical Issues for Social Theory*. London: Sage.

Afrobarometer (2004) 'Lived Poverty in Africa: Desperation, Hope and Patience.' Briefing Paper No. 11, April. www.afrobarometer.org/AfrobriefNo11.pdf (consulted 28 July 2005).

Aitchison, T. (2005) 'Internet Is Boon to Smaller Nonprofits Providing Tsunami Disaster Relief', *Convio*, 17 January. www.convio.com/site/News2?JServSessionIdr006=tw4nugxw g1.app7b&abbr=news_&page=NewsArticle&id=2602066 (consulted 29 July 2005).

Anderson, K. and Rieff, D. (2004) 'Global Civil Society: A Sceptical View'. in H. Anheier, M. Glasius and M. Kaldor (eds.), *Global Civil Society 2004/5*. London: Sage.

Annan, K. (2005) 'A Global Strategy for Fighting Terrorism'. Keynote address to the Closing Plenary of the International Summit on Democracy, Terrorism and Security, Club of Madrid. Madrid, 10 March. http://english.safe-democracy.org/keynotes/a-global-strategy-for-fighting-terrorism.html (consulted 27 July 2005).

Associated Press (2005) 'Tsunami Charities Said to Lack Experience.' 26 January. www.wjla.com/news/stories/0105/202897.html (consulted 28 July 2005).

BBC News (2005) 'At-a-glance: Countries hit', 22 June. http://news.bbc.co.uk/1/hi/world/asia-pacific/4126019.stm (consulted 28 July 2005).

Beck, U. (1992) *Risk Society: Towards a New Modernity*. London: Sage.

– (2000) 'The Risk Society Revisited: Theory, Politics and Research Programmes', in B. Adam, U. Beck and J. van Loon (eds.), T*he Risk Society and Beyond: Critical Issues for Social Theory*. London : Sage.

– (2002) 'The Terrorist Threat: World Risk Society Revisited', *Theory, Culture & Society*, 19 (4): 39–55.

– (forthcoming 2005) 'World Risk Society and the Changing Foundations of Transnational Politics', in E. Grande and L. Pauly (eds.), *Complex Sovereignty: Reconstituting Political Authority in the Twenty-First Century*. Toronto: University of Toronto Press.

Bhaumik, S. (2005) 'Questions over Andaman Tsunami Aid.' *BBC News*, 22 June. http://news.bbc.co.uk/1/hi/world/south_asia/4119374.stm (consulted 28 July 2005).

BIC (Biotechonology Information Center) (URL) www.searca.org/~bic/ (consulted 28 July 2005).

Chandhoke, N. (2005). 'What the Hell is Civil Society?' *openDemocracy*, 17 March. www.opendemocracy.net/debates/article-3-122-2375.jsp (consulted 28 July 2005).

Christian Today (2005) 'Church Leaders say Tsunami Disaster warns of Climate Change', 4 January. http://www.christiantoday.com/news/church/church.leaders. say.tsunami.disaster.warns.of.climate.change/311.htm (consulted 28 July 2005).

Commission on Human Security (2003). *Human Security Now*. New York: United Nations: http://www.humansecurity-chs.org/finalreport/English/FinalReport.pdf (consulted 28 July 2005).

Culpitt, I. (1999). Social Policy and Risk. London: Sage.

Cumming-Bruce, N. (2005). 'Thais Open Center for Tsunami Warnings', *International Herald Tribune*, 1 June.

Darnton, A. (2005) 'Public Awareness – Understanding International Development Issues', *Bond*. www.bond.org.uk/networker/may05/devissues.htm (consulted 29 July and 5 August 2005).

Dawe, F. (2003) *Public Attitudes Towards Development*. London: Social and Vital Statistics, Office for National Statistics. www.dfid.gov.uk/pubs/files/omnibus2003.pdf (consulted 29 July 2005).

Douglas, M. (1992) *Risk and Blame: Essays in Cultural Theory*. London: Routledge.

– and Wildavsky, A. (1983) *Risk and Culture: An Essay on the Selection of Technical and Environmental Dangers*. Berkeley: University of California Press.

Drummond, J. (2005) 'Bob, Bono and Africa'. Letter to *The Guardian*, 27 June. http://society.guardian.co.uk/aid/comment/0,14178,1515562, 00.html (consulted 29 July 2005).

Edwards, M. (2003) 'NGO Legitimacy: Voice or Vote?', *BOND Networker*, February.

European Commission (2000) *Communication from the Commission on the precautionary principle*. COM 2001-1. Brussels: European Commission.

– (2001) *Strategy for a Future Chemicals Policy*. COM 2001-88. Brussels: European Commission.

Frerks, G. and Klem, B. (2005) *Tsunami Response in Sri Lanka: Report on a Field Visit From 6–20 February 2005*. Wageningen and The Hague: Disaster Studies Conflict Research Unit, Wageningen University and Clingendael Institute.

Focus on the Global South (URL) www.focusweb.org (consulted 28 July 2005).

GCAP (Global Call to Action Against Poverty) (2005) 'Joint Statement from African Civil Society', 8 July. www.whiteband.org/specialIssues/G8/gcapnews.2005-07-13.0208823378/en?set_language=ar&cl=ar (consulted 29 July 2005).

Giddens, A. (1990) *The Consequences of Modernity*. Cambridge: Polity.

– (1998) *The Third Way*. Cambridge: Polity Press.

– (1999) *The Third Way: The Renewal of Social Democracy*. Cambridge: Polity Press.

– (2000) *The Third Way and its Critics*. Cambridge: Polity Press.

Gilligan, A. (2005) 'The Media after Tsunami: What Hope is There for the 'Forgotten' Emergencies?', *Reuters Foundation Panel Debate*, 10 May.

Glasius, M. (2005) *The International Criminal Court: A Global Civil Society Achievement*. Oxford: Routledge.

Global Call to Action Against Poverty (URL) http://www.whiteband.org (consulted 28 July 2005).

GRAIN (URL) http://www.grain.org/front/ (consulted 28 July 2005).

The Guardian (2004) 'Tsunami Highlights Climate Change Risk, Says Scientist', 31 December.

Held, D. (2004) *Global Covenant*. Cambridge: Polity Press

Hodkinson, S. (2005) 'Inside the Murky World of the UK's Make Poverty History Campaign.' www.focusweb.org/main/html/modules.php?op=modload&name=NMake Poverty Hoistoryews&file=article&sid=626 (consulted 28 July 2005).

Howell, J. and Pearce, J. (2002) *Civil Society and Development: A Critical Interrogation*. Boulder, CO: Lynne Rienner Publishers.

Human Rights Watch (2005) 'Publications Summary', June http://hrw.org/reports/2005/iopt0605/1.htm#_ftn8 (consulted 6 August 2005).

IOC (Intergovernmental Oceanographic Commission) (URL) *Towards Tsunami Warning and Mitigation System for the Indian Ocean*. http://ioc.unesco.org/indotsunami/ (consulted 28 July 2005).

ISAAA (International Service for the Acquisition of Agri-biotech Applications) (URL) http://www.isaaa.org (consulted 28 July 2005).

International Policy Institute for Counter Terrorism (URL) www.ict.org.il/ (consulted 5 August 2005).

Jain, T. (2003) 'Bhopal: A New Momentum'. *India Together*. December. www.indiatogether.org/2003/dec/hrt-bhopal03.htm (consulted 28 July 2005).

Jubilee Debt Campaign and World Development Movement (2005). 'Campaigners Say Brown Tsunami Debt Plan Welcome but Inadequate.' Joint Press Release, 5 January. *World Development Movement News*. www.wdm.org.uk/news/presrel/current/tsunami.htm (consulted 28 July 2005).

Jubilee South (URL) www.jubileesouth.org (consulted 29 July 2005).

Kaldor, M. (2003) *Global Civil Society: An Answer to War*. Polity Press, Cambridge.

–, Anheier, H. and Glasius, M. (2005) 'Introduction', in H. Anheier, M. Glasius and M. Kaldor (eds.), *Global Civil Society 2004/5*. London: Sage.

Kaul, I., Conceicao, P., Le Goulven, K. and Mendoza, R. (eds.) (2003) *Providing Global Public Goods*. New York: Oxford University Press.

Kettlewell, J. (2005) 'Tsunami Alert System Takes Shape', *BBC News*, 24 June. http://news.bbc.co.uk/1/hi/sci/tech/4619069.stm (consulted 28 July 2005).

Koprowski, G. (2004). 'Wireless World: The "Orange Revolution", *United Press International*. 27 December. www.upi.com/view.cfm?StoryID=20041223-015351-8440r (consulted 28 July 2005).

Kuruganthi, K. (2004). 'Persistent and Tenacious Struggle'. *India Together*. December. http://www.indiatogether.org/2004/dec/hrt-bhopal04.htm (consulted 28 July 2005).

Large, T. (2005) 'Big Tsunami Donors Rank Poorly in Generosity League.' *Reuters AlertNet*, 23 June. www.alertnet.org/thefacts/reliefresources/111954000778.htm (consulted 28 July 2005).

Levitas, R. (2000) 'Discourses of Risk and Utopia', in B. Adam, U. Beck and J. van Loon (eds.), *The Risk Society and Beyond: Critical Issues for Social Theory*. London: Sage.

Lockwood, M. (2005) *The State They're In: An Agenda for International Action on Poverty in Africa*. London: ITDG.

Lofstedt, R. (2003) 'The Precautionary Principle: Risk, Regulation and Politics', *Trans IchemE*, 81(B): 36–43.

London Homepage (2005) 'Text of statement delivered by Ken Livingstone', 7 July. http://www.urban75.org/london/livingstone.html (consulted 27 July 2005).

Luhmann, N. (1993) *Risk: A Sociological Theory*. New York: de Gruyter.

MABIC (Malaysian Biotechnology Information Centre) (URL) www.bic.org.my (consulted 28 July 2005).

Make Poverty History (URL) www.makepovertyhistory.org (consulted 29 July 2005).

Manji, F. (2005) 'Make Looting History', *Pambazuka News*, 7 July. www.pambazuka.org/index.php?id=28865 (consulted 29 July 2005).

McAdam, D., Tarrow, S. and Tilly, C. (2001) *Dynamics of Contention*. Cambridge: Cambridge University Press.

Monbiot, G. (2005) 'The Victims of the Tsunami Pay the Price of War on Iraq', *The Guardian*, 4 January.

MSF (Médecins Sans Frontières) (2005) 'MSF Clarifies Donations for Asian Tsunami Disaster Relief.' Press release, 4 January. www.msf.org/msfinternational/invoke.cfm?component=pressrelease&objectid=1F31BDDD-6840-4368-AC061BF061867501&method=full_html (consulted 29 July 2005).

Mythen, G. (2004) *Ulrich Beck: A Critical Introduction to the Risk Society*. London: Pluto.

Naidoo, K. (2005) 'Reflections on the G8 Summit', Global Call to Action Against Poverty, 13 July. www.whiteband.org/specialIssues/G8/gcapnews.2005-07-14.5388032995/en (consulted 28 July 2005).

OCHA (UN Office for the Coordination of Humanitarian Affairs) (2005) 'Total Humanitarian Assistance per Donor'. http://ocha.unog.ch/fts/reports/daily/ocha_R24_A669___05072521.pdf (consulted 29 July 2005).

Oxfam International (2005a) 'Debt Mustn't Stand in the way of Recovery'. Press Release , 11 January. http://www.oxfam.org/eng/pr050111_tsunami.htm (consulted 28 July 2005).

– (2005b) *Targeting Poor People: Rebuilding Lives After the Tsunami*. Oxfam Briefing Note, 25 June. www.oxfam.org/eng/pdfs/bn050625_tsunami_targetingthepoor.pdf (consulted 28 July 2005).

Palestinian Red Crescent Society (URL) www.palestinercs.org (consulted 5 August 2005)

Pesticide Action Network (URL) www.pan-international.org (consulted 28 July 2005).

Pilger, J. (2005) 'The Other Tsunami'. *New Statesman*, 10 January. www.newstatesman.com/Economy/200501100003 (consulted 28 July 2005).

Quilty, J. (2005) 'Lebanon: Talking About a Revolution?', *Socialist Review*. April. www.socialistreview.org.uk/article.php?articlenumber=9336 (consulted 28 July 2005).

Rampton, J. (2005) 'Politics and Passion', *The Independent*, 17 June.

Reform Campaign (URL) http://www.reformcampaign.net/# (consulted 28 July 2005).

Roberts, L., Lafta, R., Garfield, R., Khudhairi, J. and Burnham, G. (2004) 'Mortality before and after the 2003 Invasion of Iraq: Cluster Sample Survey', *The Lancet*, 364 (9448): 1854–64.

Royal Institute for International Affairs (2005) *Security, Terrorism and the UK*. ISP/NCS Briefing Paper 05/01, July. London: RIIA. www.chathamhouse.org.uk/pdf/research/niis/BPsecurity.pdf (consulted 27 July 2005).

Sari, Y. and Yigit, S. (2005) 'Kyrgyzstan: Revolution or Not?', *openDemocracy*, 4 April. http://opendemocracy.net/content/articles/PDF/2404.pdf (consulted 28 July 2005).

Safetybio (Biotechnology and Biosafety Information Centre) (URL). http://www.safetybio.com/ (consulted 28 July 2005).

Scholte, J. (2001) *Civil Society and Democracy in Global Governance* (Working Paper No. 65/01). Coventry: Centre for the Study of Globalisation and Regionalisation, Warwick University.

Scott, A. 'Risk Society or Angst Society: Two Views of Risk, Consciousness and Community', in B. Adam, U. Beck and J. van Loon (eds.), *The Risk Society and Beyond: Critical Issues for Social Theory*. London: Sage.

September 10 (URL) www.sept10.org/ (consulted 28 July 2005).

Shields, E. (2005). 'Spain's Mixed EU Signals'. *BBC News*, Madrid, 21 February. http://news.bbc.co.uk/1/hi/world/europe/4284607.stm (consulted 28 July 2005).

Smith, J. (ed.) (1997) *Transnational Social Movements and World Politics: Solidarity Beyond the State*. Syracuse, NY: Syracuse University Press.

Souccar, M. (2005) 'NY Nonprofits See Drought As Funds Go To Asia.' *Crain's New York Business*, 17 January. www.baileyhouse.org/news2.asp?id=33&theType=news (consulted 28 July 2005).

Tarrant, Bill (2005) 'Interim Indian Ocean Tsunami Warning System by Oct.' *Reuters*, 19 May. www.alertnet.org/thenews/newsdesk/B248010.htm (consulted 1 June 2005).

Tavola della Pace (URL). www.tavoladellapace.org (consulted 28 July 2005).

Thiam, T. (2005) 'Our Common Interest: Supporting Africa's Resurgence.' Public lecture, London School of Economics, 9 May. www.commissionforafrica.org/english/about/documents/09-05-05_ev_lse_transcription.pdf (consulted 29 July 2005).

UN (United Nations) (2004a) *We the Peoples: Civil Society, the United Nations and Global Governance*. Report of the Panel of Eminent Persons on United Nations–Civil Society Relations (Cardoso Report). UN Doc. A/58/817 www.un-ngls.org/Final%20report%20-%20HLP.doc (consulted 28 July 2005).

– (2004b) *A More Secure World: Our Shared Responsibility*. Report of the Security-General's High-Level Panel on threats, challenges and change. New York: United Nations

UNIS (United Nations Information Service) (2005) 'Millennium Development Goals Have Unprecedented Political Support, Secretary-General Says at London Event', 6 July. www.unis.unvienna.org/unis/pressrels/2005/sgsm9984.html (comsulted 27 July 2005).

UN News Centre (2005) 'Tsunami Envoy Clinton Urges UN to Keep Up Momentum on Relief Effort.' 14 July. www.un.org/apps/news/story.asp?NewsID=15023&Cr=tsunami&Cr1= (consulted 28 July 2005).

UNSG (United Nations Secretary-General) (2005) 'Secretary-General Kofi Annan and his Special Envoy for Tsunami-affected countries, former U.S. President Bill Clinton, at press conference at UN headquarters', 13 April. www.un.org/apps/sg/offthecuff.asp?nid=714 (consulted 28 July 2005).

Van Rooy, A. (2004) *The Global Legitimacy Game: Civil Society, Globalization, and Protest*. Basingstoke: Palgrave Macmillan.

De Volkskrant (2005) 'Infografiek: Door kiezers genoemde redenen om voor of tegen te stemmen' [Info graphic: Reasons quoted for voting for or against], 2 June.

VSO (Voluntary Service Overseas) (2002) *The Live Aid Legacy: The Developing World Through British Eyes*. London: VSO.

Wallack, T. (2005) 'Charities Riding Out Tsunami: Contributions to Nonprofits Haven't Slowed', *San Francisco Chronicle*, 11 January. www.aegis.com/news/sc/2005/SC050105.html (consulted 29 July 2005).

WDM (World Development Movement) (2005) 'G8 Condemn Africa to Miss Millennium Development Goals.' Press release, 8 July. www.wdm.org.uk/news/presrel/current/g82005final.htm (consulted 29 July 2005).

WEF (World Economic Forum) (2005) 'Chancellor Schröder outlines Germany's development vision'. Annual Meeting. www.weforum.org/site/homepublic.nsf/Content/Annual+Meeting+2005#11 (consulted 27 July 2005).

The White House (1999). The Third Way: Progressive Governance for the 21st Century. Remarks by the President and Other Participants in Democratic Leadership Forum. Washington, DC. (April 25). http://clinton6.nara.gov/1999/04/1999-04-25-remarks-by-the-president-and-nato-leaders-in-dlc-roundtable.html (consulted 28 July 2005).

Wiener, J. and Rogers, M. 2002. 'Comparing Precaution in the United States and Europe', *Journal of Risk Research*, 5: 317–49.

World Development Movement (URL) www.wdm.org.uk (consulted 6 August 2005).

Young, I. (1997) 'Difference as a Resource for Democratic Communication', in: J. Bohman and W. Rehg (eds.), *Deliberative Democracy: Essays on Reason and Politics*. Cambridge, MA: MIT Press.

CHAPTER 1

GENDER AND CIVIL SOCIETY
Jude Howell

Introduction

When Eastern European intellectuals such as Václav Havel and Adam Michnik seized upon the vocabulary of civil society to articulate their dissent from overbearing Leninist regimes, they could not have known how much political and intellectual interest in the notion of non-governmental public action their choice of concept would generate. Appropriated for diverse and often discordant ideological ends, and used empirically to refer to an array of referents, the concept of civil society has been subject to ongoing assault, with criticisms ranging from its apparent vagueness to its historico-cultural specificity. Nevertheless, politicians, activists, government bureaucrats, and intellectuals across the globe continue to embrace the discourse of civil society to explain and justify their differing visions of the world and their courses of action.

The revival of the concept of civil society has promoted further study in the fields of political science and sociology of the changing forms of collective action, the politics of the non-governmental, the emergence of new democracies and the changing contours of state–society relations. In social policy, the term has provided a lens through which to analyse welfare services provision, social exclusion and volunteerism. In development theory, policy and practice, the resurgence of interest in civil society has contributed to a paradigmatic shift in thinking away from a dualistic, ideologically informed fixation with the state versus the market towards a new triadic paradigm embracing civil society, the state and the market (Howell and Pearce 2001). This triadic model in turn has not only informed debate around governance, poverty reduction, participation, and policy influence but has also led to the creation of specific programmes aimed at fostering civil society in aid-recipient contexts, with the effect of gradually depoliticising the term[1]. For law academics and practitioners, the resurgence of interest in civil society has focused attention on the legal and regulatory regimes shaping state relations with non-governmental actors. In international relations, the arrival of the idea of civil society and the growing presence of global non-governmental actors have undermined the dominant focus on nation-states, multilateral institutions and international regimes, and prised open the concept of global governance (Kaldor 2003).

Nevertheless, it is curious that there has been so little interrogation of the relationship between gender and civil society, within either feminist or civil society theories[2]. This is surprising not only because each set of theories would have much to gain from the other in terms of theorisation and practical knowledge, but also because organising around gender relations can constitute in different historical and cultural contexts a significant part of actually existing civil societies. This chapter addresses this lacuna. It begins by laying out the reasons for promoting a closer encounter between gender and civil society theory. It then explores what this would mean for the way in which civil society and gender are theorised and conceptualised. In particular, it develops a framework for conceptualising gender and civil society that highlights the interconnectedness of sites of power and the constant flow of socially con-structed male and female bodies through a circuit of gender relations. Finally, it maps out the practical and theoretical issues that deserve further investigation and action.

I am very grateful for the immensely helpful discussion of earlier drafts of this chapter at two workshops on gender and civil society held at the LSE, in November 2004 and February 2005. Participants at this workshop included Bakin Babajanian, Christine Chinkin, Judy El-Bushra, Marlies Glasius, Khadijah Fancy, Armine Ishkanian, Ruth Jacobson, Mary Kaldor, Ulla-Brit Lilleaas, Nisrine Mansour, Diane Perrons, Hakan Seckinelgin, Victor Seidler, Purna Sen, Judith Squires, and Karen Wright. Their lively and reflective engagement with earlier drafts and their insightful comments have helped to move this chapter forwards.

Time for gender and civil society theorists to tango

There are many reasons why it is time to interrogate more closely the relationship between gender and civil society. The first and perhaps most obvious reason for feminist theorists and practitioners is that women have been significant actors in the theatres of civil societies across the world. Often excluded from state institutions and male-dominated politics, women in different historical and cultural contexts have found it easier to become active at the local level through, for example, community organisations, self-help groups, traders' associations, faith-based organisations, mothers' groups, or campaigning. It is on this terrain that women activists, including feminists[3], have articulated their demands, mobilised around issues such as the right to vote, dowry, land rights and domestic violence, and created networks of solidarity. The spaces and institutions within civil society can exclude women, but they also have an emancipatory potential, which feminists can and do make use of.

Given the centrality of civil society to feminists as a space for association, for the articulation of interests, and for ideological contestation, it is important that we theorise these spaces from a feminist perspective, and the language of civil society can be useful in this endeavour. In the past, feminist theorists have used the diverse languages of social movements, struggle, rights, equality and emancipation to frame their understanding of women's activism. As a result, there is a rich, empirical treasury of historical, structural and analytic accounts of the rise of women's movements in a diversity of contexts. Feminist researchers focused on women's movements apart from the broader context of civil society, while civil society theorists referred to women's activism to illustrate the dynamism and vibrancy of actual civil societies. Yet there are surprisingly few studies of how such movements and forms of collective action impinge more generally upon the spaces, organisations and regulatory frameworks governing civil society, nor of how the regulatory frameworks governing civil society, the organisational composition and forms of civil society, and the range of issues and values espoused by civil society actors in turn affect the way women organise. In what ways, if at all, do women organise differently from men in civil society? As civil society is a broader concept than social movements, it allows for the possibility of exploring these larger questions about how spaces for collective action are used, how they become politicised, and how they are gendered.

Second, drawing attention to how women and gender relations have been absent in the work of many civil society researchers is important for enriching empirical analysis. However, it is also of interest how, why and when men organise in the spaces of civil society, and how such action in turn shapes the possibilities for women's participation. In this way, we can begin to ask whether men and women organise differently, whether the styles of leadership and mobilisation are different, whether the organisational forms are distinct, whether the issues addressed, the language expressed and the type of activities engaged in differ between male and female bodies. Although much discussion of civil society ignores the gendered nature of organising, the emergence of a field of study around men and masculinities has much to offer in understanding men's engagement in civil society[4]. Moreover, this would provide an opening to develop a more nuanced approach to men's organising, that takes on board competing notions of masculinity and diverse identities and solidarities. The differences between various types of men's organising such as the military, working men's clubs, gay movements, anti-feminist men's groups, and Fathers 4 Justice could then be explored and comparisons drawn with women's organising.

Third, civil society is a double-edged sword for feminists. It can provide a site for organising around feminist issues, for articulating counter-hegemonic discourses, for experimenting with alternative lifestyles and for envisioning other less sexist and more just worlds. With its organisations of self-support,

---

1. For a critique of these processes see Howell and Pearce (2001), Ottaway and Carothers (2000), Carothers (1999), Biekart (1999), and Van Rooy (1998).
2. Researchers who have tried to engender the discussion of civil society and the public sphere include Beckwith (2000), Fraser (1992; 1997), Howell (1998), Howell and Mulligan (2003; 2004), Landes (1988), Phillips (2002), and Rabo (1996). It should be noted that a similar vacuum relates in relation to the concept of social capital, as exposed forcefully by Molyneux (2002).
3. We distinguish here between the broad term 'women activists', which embraces activism by women informed by diverse ideological positions and who do not necessarily describe themselves as 'feminists', and the term 'feminist activists', which refers to women who envision a world where gender differences are not a source of oppression and inequality. The visions of feminist activists are in turn shaped by analyses of gender premised on liberal, socialist and radical perspectives.
4. See, for example, Carver (1995), Connell (1995), Ruxton (2004), and Seidler (1991).

Civil society can be a double-edged sword for feminists ©Caroline Penn/Panos Pictures

community action, and voluntary care, it can foster solidarity, promote mutual support and prioritise values of care, respect and equality. Yet it can also be an arena where gendered behaviours, norms and practices are acted out and reproduced. As Anne Phillips (2002: 80) warns, the associations of civil society are relatively unregulated when compared with the state and therefore vulnerable to sexist and other discriminatory practices[5]. Civil society can be the terrain of conservative ideologies that foster women's dependency in the constricted space of the family as well as of emancipatory ideologies that aspire to gender equality. It offers fertile soil not only to liberal, socialist and radical feminists, gay and lesbian movements, and progressive men's groups, but also to conservative women activists, anti-gay lobbies and patriarchal and misogynistic male groups.

We need therefore to interrogate the positioning of women in civil society. Why is it that women form the mainstay of volunteers in many countries? Why are they more visible in community and neighbourhood organisations than in political parties, trade unions and state institutions? What are the barriers of entry to women in civil society? In what ways does civil society exclude women along the lines of gender, class and ethnicity? Why is it that some associations are dominated by one or another sex? Through what discourses, ideologies and practices are women excluded from certain activities and organising?

Fourth, the discourse of civil society has been appropriated across the ideological spectrum to propel particular political agendas and positions. Feminists need to be particularly cautious when the language of civil society is used in debates about state deregulation, user choice and community provision of welfare services. There is the danger that the language of civil society and related concepts of community and social capital becomes an ideological device for justifying a particular vision of the state, which entails the return of welfare services to the

---

5 Anne Phillips qualifies this in her chapter by both noting the gap between government regulations and actual practice, and pointing out that voluntary associations do fall under some form of national legislation in the United Kingdom that requires them to act with probity and comply with broad legislation on discrimination.

family, and in practice to the unpaid and undervalued female carer[6].

Finally, because of their own experiences and their analytic emphasis on issues of oppression and emancipation, feminists are well placed to take up issues of subordination, domination and power in civil society and to problematise the notion of civil society as a harmonious unity, as a comfortable and benign field of diversity and plurality or as the site of peace and justice. Through their past focus on exposing the complex ways in which the gendered relations of the family become reproduced in the economy and state, feminist thinkers have developed conceptual and theoretical frameworks and methodological approaches that can be readily deployed in interrogating the gendered interconnections between the family and civil society[7]. Similarly, researchers and male activists working in the fields of men and masculinities, queer theory and sexuality possess analytic frameworks and tools for addressing the gender contours of civil society.

After this outline of several reasons for fostering a closer and livelier engagement between civil society and gender research, the next section traces the way each of these fields has dealt with the other and explores the theoretical and conceptual implications of closer engagement.

The uneasy encounter between gender and civil society theories

Civil society theories and the family

Civil society theorists have taken but a cursory interest in the relationship between gender and civil society. The main axis of engagement around gender and civil society has centred on whether the family or household is part of civil society, although this is not an issue that has aroused great passion. While some theorists conceptualise the family or household as outside of and separate from civil society and the state, others include the family within civil society.

Enlightenment and post-Enlightenment thinkers in the eighteenth and nineteenth centuries, such as Rousseau, Ferguson, Paine, and de Tocqueville, counterposed civil society not only to the state but also to the family, although they paid little attention to the latter. In their conceptualisations of individual rights, freedom and civil society, they operated with a gendered notion of the public based on the abstract individual male. For Hegel, the (patriarchal) family and the state form the two hierarchical poles between which civil society is located. As economic relations are integral to civil society, civil society is defined as both non-state and non-family. Hegel excludes the family from civil society not only because the family is the first context in which the abstract legal person is situated but also because the family is assumed to be a unity, based on love, without any conflict between its members, and from which its (male) head enters the world of civil society (Cohen and Arato 1995: 628–31, n. 48). Among contemporary writers on civil society the Hegelian distinction between family and civil society is, whether implicit or explicit, commonplace[8] (see, for example, Carothers 1999: 207; Diamond 1994: 5; White 1994: 379; Hawthorn 2001: 269–86; Van Rooy 1998: 6–30).

One of the few contemporary writers to engage more systematically with the family in relation to civil society, public spheres and the state is Juergen Habermas. In his discussion of the transformation of the eighteenth-century bourgeois public sphere, Habermas distinguishes the family from civil society (understood as the realm of commodity exchange and social labour) and state. For Habermas (1989: 46–7) the family is both a precursor to civil society and a site of intimacy that maintains the illusion of autonomy, voluntariness and humanity despite its embeddedness in the market economy and its role in reproducing social norms and values and patriarchal authority. In tracing the decline of the bourgeois public sphere through the processes of urbanisation, the rise of the welfare state and mass democracy, Habermas (1989: 154–5) paints a picture of a weakening, income-dependent and consumerist family that loses its functions of social internalisation and welfare protection, and becomes increasingly disengaged from social production.

---

6 Molyneux (2002: 172) also draws attention to communitarian interpretations of social capital, which not only idealise community but also gloss over the power relations, including gender relations, that permeate localities and communities.

7 See, for example, the work of Butler and Scott (1992), Catagay (2003), Elson (1998; 1995), MacKinnon (1989), Mies (1983), Okin (1979), Pateman (1988a; 1989), Kabeer (1994), Perrons (2002; 2003), Phillips (1991; 1998) to name but a few.

8 However, most writers often depart from this in positioning the economy as separate from civil society, which is conceived as the realm of voluntary association around shared concerns. Furthermore, it should be noted that most writers are so centred on the relationship between civil society and the state that they do not even mention the boundary with the family.

Box 1.1: Organising around transsexuality: India's hijra community

In recent years, activism by and for hijra, the transsexual community in India, has increased in response to discrimination and violence, concerns about HIV and AIDS, and changes to traditions that until recently allowed hijra to earn a living performing at weddings, ceremonies and festivals.

Hijra is an Urdu word meaning 'hermaphrodite' (intersexed) and its closest English translation is 'eunuch', which is taken to represent transsexuality (Nag 1996; Nanda 1990). 'Hermaphrodite' refers to a person whose genitals are ambiguously male-like, while eunuchs are castrated males. Both are associated with impotence. In India 'hijra' connotes a cultural, institutionalised third gender, and impotence is a necessary but not sufficient condition. According to Nag (1996), only a small proportion of hijra are hermaphrodites, and there might be some who are neither castrated nor hermaphrodites but identify themselves as hijra. Sometimes women who failed to develop secondary female sexual characteristics (breasts and menarche) at puberty also became hijra (see also Nanda 1990). The exact number of hijra in India is not known because they are counted as women in the census, but unofficial estimates suggest between 50,000 and one million (Beary 2003; Nag 1996). There are also hijra communities in Bangladesh and Pakistan.

Traditionally, hijra are believed to be bearers of divine power bestowed on them by a female deity, Bahuchara Mata, who transforms their impotence into the power of fertility (Nanda 1990). They are paid to perform at weddings, the birth of a male child and other functions, where they sing, dance and bestow blessings of prosperity, health and fertility. Hijra are concentrated in north Indian cities, but their traditional role is not as significant in south India, where they are derided with derogatory names such as 'kojja' in Telugu (the native language in Andhra Pradesh) and 'pottai', 'ali', or 'onbadu' in Tamil (the native language in Tamil Nadu).

Their status has varied over time and is the subject of dispute by scholars. According to Nanda (1990), Hinduism has accorded hijra a special place in Indian society as a 'third gender': 'Hinduism...has always been more able to accommodate gender variation, ambiguity and contradictions.' Western labels such as 'gay' are misleading in the Indian context, according to Shivananda Khan (2001), founder of the Naz Foundation. Indeed, Maya Indira Ganesh (2003) says that, 'The Indian sexual canvas is vast and poorly documented and thanks to pioneers like Khan spaces for indigenous masculine sexualities, desires and gender-bending exist. Thus there are not just Indian gay men, but Kothis, Parikhs/Panthis, Dublis, Hijras, Ackua Kothis as well.' Of course, gender orientation is just one layer in multiple and overlapping identities that contribute to the expression of an individual's personality and politics.

If in the past the activism of Western gays and lesbians has been contrasted with the absence of such public identity politics in India, that is beginning to change. Motivated by marginalisation, discrimination and violence – not to mention the desire for a safe means of earning a living – hijra have begun to organise. A key focus has been HIV and AIDS, particularly because one of the main ways hijra earn a living is through commercial sex. NGOs working on this issue with the hijra community include All India Hijra Kalyan Sabha, Network of Indian Male Sexworkers, Sexual Health Resource Centre, Urban Health and Training Institute, and Solidarity and Action Against the HIV Infection in India. When it comes to promoting safe sex, in some ways the hijra household and culture is more receptive to such messages than are female sex workers. Hijra are able to exercise safe sex practices also because they enjoy greater autonomy through their community network.

But their campaigns are not restricted to sexual health. Increasingly, hijra are speaking out about discrimination and violence. Their experiences are being documented by organisations that have adopted a rights-based approach. In 2003, the People's Union for Civil Liberties (PUCL-K), in collaboration with a range of NGOs, published a report, *Human Rights Violations Against the Transgender Community*, which detailed widespread harassment, beating and sexual abuse of hijras and kothis at the hands of police, security guards, businessmen and tourists.

Sangama (URL) is one of the campaign groups that collaborate with the PUCL-K. It runs an outreach programme for hijra, kothi and other transgender identities in Bangalore, and was instrumental in the creation of the Coalition for Sexual Minorities' Rights to fight against police harassment. Sangama has been active in promoting the voices of sexual minorities, facilitating the formation of Vividha, an independent collective,

Hijra dance at a wedding celebration in Puri, Orissa, India ©Mark Henley/Panos Pictures

which in December 2002 organised a rally attended by more than 100 hijra, kothis and other sexual minorities who came out publicly for the first time. Vividha's charter calls for the repeal of section 377 of the Indian Penal Code, which criminalises homosexuality, and of the Immoral Trafficking and Prevention Act, which campaigners say is used to harass and abuse sex workers (Narrain 2003). The collective also demands that hijra be recognised as women, given equal opportunities and be entitled to housing, employment benefits and travel concessions.

Similarly, the Dai Welfare Society, established in Bombay by several hijras, actively campaigns for equality. 'All we want is to be treated as human beings,' says Shabeena Joseph, the group's president. 'We want to open bank accounts, possess a passport and find jobs' (Ganguly 2000).

Through their community and political activities and media support, hijra are increasingly gaining confidence in demanding their rights (Beary 2003). The new option, 'E' for 'eunuch', which has been available in web-based applications for passports since March 2005, is the first official recognition of a third gender in India. The desire to be part of mainstream society and to have the right to vote with their chosen gender identity has been growing in the hijra community. In 1993, the Election Commission directed officials to include eunuchs on the electoral roll. Although they had never been banned (the Constitution forbids discrimination on the basis of gender), most hijras were overlooked in the counting; they had to register as 'female', often against their wishes, or they were too embarrassed to go to the booths where derisory comments would be made about their sexual identity (*The Telegraph* 2005).

Hijra have entered the public consciousness in other ways. At the annual festival at Koothandavar temple in Koovakam near Villupuram, Tamil Nadu, thousands of hijra and other sexual minorities take part in beauty pageants and dance contests (George 2004; *The Hindu* 2002).

Some hijra have entered formal party politics (Wikipedia 2005). Shabnam Mausi, a hijra whose life has been made into film, was elected to the Legislative Assembly in Madhya Pradesh in 1999. In November 2000, Asha Devi was elected mayor of the city of Gorakhpur in Utter Pradesh. Asha Devi has done great things for the town, eclipsing her predecessors and avoiding much of the corruption typical of Indian office bearers. Consequently, some of the major political parties in India are trying to recruit hijra to stand for them in elections (*The Green Man* 2003). However, there have been legal challenges to the right of hijras to hold public office.

Ruth Kattumuri, LSE

GENDER

43

Although the family forms an important element in Habermas's account of the transformation of the public sphere, so distinguishing Habermas from many contemporary writers on civil society, feminist thinkers such as Joan Landes, Mary Ryan and Nancy Fraser have challenged the normative ideal of a (bourgeois) public sphere as open and accessible to all. Joan Landes (1988) argues that gender became the main axis of exclusion in the new republican sphere in France through discursive practices that belittled women's participation in political life. Mary Ryan (1998: 195–222) challenges Habermas's depiction of a decline of the bourgeois public sphere by documenting the movement of North American women into politics from the early nineteenth century onwards. In doing so she subverts the masculinist, bourgeois concept of a single public sphere and highlights the profusion of counter-publics that were neither liberal, nor bourgeois, nor necessarily male. In defence of the normative concept of public spheres in actually existing democracies, Nancy Fraser (1997:136–7) argues that any adequate conception of the public sphere has not only to bracket social differences such as gender but also to eliminate social inequality.

Some contemporary political theorists view the family as an integral part of civil society. Jean Cohen (1998: 37), for instance, places the family within civil society, which she in turn distinguishes from the economy and state[9]. In their discussion of Hegel's exclusion of the family from civil society, Cohen and Arato (1995: 631, n 48) argue that the family should be included in civil society as 'its first association'. By being conceived of in egalitarian terms, the family then offers a primary experience of the principles of 'horizontal solidarity, collective identity and equal participation' that form the basis of other forms of civil society association and, more broadly, political life. Such a portrayal of the family, however, ignores the power relations and hierarchies prevalent within families, often along gender and intergenerational lines, and overlooks the problems of exploitation, violence and abuse within families.

Yet political theorists have not been overly concerned with the conceptual difficulties of marking the divide between family and civil society. The debate about whether the family is part of civil society is conducted at the most superficial level. Once a line is drawn, the theorist enquires no further as to what this might mean for the way civil society is constructed in gender

terms. On the contrary, the prime interest has been in defining sharply the boundaries between civil society and other key conceptual categories, in particular the state and market, whereby the family is a defining but uninteresting boundary. Indeed, in many discussions of civil society and the state, the family is not even mentioned. By treating the family as of only residual interest in the pursuit of understanding the more important and higher-level relations between state, civil society and market, civil society theorists have failed to grasp the engendering effects of conceptual categories and of civil society in particular.

The lack of interest among political theorists in the family as a variable affecting the nature of civil society leads in turn to a failure to problematise the concept of the family. Writers on civil society often use the terms 'family' and 'household' interchangeably. However, in gender, women's and feminist studies, development studies and anthropology, the concepts are seen as overlapping but distinct. While 'household' refers more specifically to those 'eating from the same pot', the term 'family' is a much broader notion of a 'private domain' that is centred around intimate blood relations and embraces also a broader set of blood-related ties. The boundaries between household and family vary considerably across historical periods and cultural contexts. Feminist writers and anthropologists have explored in depth the cultural specificities of the scope and the social, economic and political significance of the family and household. Given the different forms that families can assume over time and space, we need then also to ask how the gendered identities circulating within families in turn shape the way women and men, boys and girls, participate in civil society, and how such participation in turn reproduces and reaffirms gendered norms and practices within families and households.

One reason, perhaps, for the failure to problematise the notion of family and to keep the family out of the definition of civil society relates to its conceptualisation as a 'modern' phenomenon. Many writers, including Hegel, Gellner, de Tocqueville, and Marx argued that the space and organisational forms of civil society emerged in the context of capitalist indus-

9 Jean Cohen (1998: 37) states, 'I understand civil society as a sphere of social interaction distinct from economy and state, composed above all of associations (including the family) and publics'.

trialisation. Relationships that are bound by place, blood and ethnicity are thereby viewed as 'traditional' and destined to weaken as societies modernise. By characterising civil society as a modern category beyond the intimate ties of family, civil society theorists not only contribute to the reification of the particular spheres of state, civil society and family but also fail to investigate the way these spheres are intertwined through blood-bound social relations, cultural norms and values.

A second reason why contemporary civil society theorists have not engaged with the gender dimension lies also in the legitimisation of the discourse of civil society by reference to the past[10]. As the concept of civil society had fallen out of use in contemporary social sciences (Keane 1998), reintroducing the notion as an analytically useful tool required intellectual justification. Where else to look but to the past? But in doing so, civil society theorists in general also fell into the trap of their predecessors by assuming the family to be separate from the state and civil society, and irrelevant to the relations within and between the state and civil society. By casting aside the family as an arena worthy of investigation, they also bypassed the concept of gender and the related field of knowledge that has developed around

it over the last 30 years.

A third reason for the absence of any discussion of issues of family and gender in mainstream civil society theory relates to the alarming failure in political theory more generally to take into account the vast body of feminist work that has exposed the gendered assumptions underpinning political theory over the last three centuries[11]. One exception here is perhaps Steven DeLue's survey (1997) of political theory and civil society, which includes a chapter on feminist responses to civil society[12]. The feminist political theorist, Anne Phillips, for example, draws attention to the seemingly innocent but highly gendered view of the public and the private apparent in Hegel's work. In

10 *I am grateful to Mary Kaldor for drawing my attention to this point.*

11 *See, in particular, the work of Carol Pateman (1988a; 1989), Jean Bethke Elshtain (1981), Susan Moller Okin (1979), and Catherine MacKinnon (1989), Squires (1999) to name but a few.*

12 *This is an interesting and valuable chapter but it details the positions of feminists on political theory, and in particular the gendered nature of the public–private divide, rather than specifically interrogating the concept civil society from a feminist perspective. In his review of three books on global civil society, Waterman (2003: 304) comments on the remarkable lack of engagement of international relations theory with feminist writing on globalisation and international relations.*

Box 1.2: Confrontations over 'gender' at the global level: the ICC negotiations

While confrontations between women and patriarchal power-holders are as old as the hills, national policy debates about sexuality and birth control in particular emerged in the West with the second generation of women's movements in the 1960s and 1970s. The issue of abortion became the prime matter of controversy, especially in the United States. But at the global level, within United Nations fora, feminist women's groups still tend to be collectively considered as the sole representatives of women's concerns. Some 'pro-family groups' explicitly question this notion. Realistic Active for Life (REAL) Women of Canada, for instance, argues:

No one organization or ideology can represent the views of all women any more than any one organization can represent the views of all men. Until the formation of REAL Women of Canada, there was no voice to represent the views of those many thousands of women who take a different point of view from that of the established feminist groups. (REAL Women URL).

Transnational debates over feminist priorities, and the eventual convergence of many women's groups around the issue of violence against women, have received ample academic consideration. Less attention has been paid to the fact that pro-family groups, both Protestant and Catholic but always supported by a globally oriented Catholic Church, have also come to form a transnational movement, which confronts the women's movement at every UN forum that has any relevance to sexual issues. (Some attention is paid to this movement in Kulczycki 1999: 25–8, and Keck and Sikkink 1998: 189–91.)

At the International Criminal Court (ICC) negotiations, the Women's Caucus for Gender Justice was formed in 1997 on the initiative of a small group of women's rights activists who realised that, without a much greater effort, gender concerns were not going to be adequately represented in the negotiations. The caucus quickly grew to be a coalition within a coalition, with hundreds of member organisations by the time of the Rome conference. The Women's Caucus was highly visible in Rome: it had between 12 and 15 people at Rome at all times. The delegation, moreover, included women from all parts of the world, including grassroots activists as well as experts on the 'hard-core legal stuff'.

A pro-family group called the Catholic Family and Human Rights Institute (C-FAM), which has a permanent office at the UN in New York and keeps a close eye on all UN processes that touch on its concerns, warned like-minded organisations in late 1997 that 'the strong presence of many feminist NGOs in the preparation for the upcoming ICC conference' should be of concern to pro-family activists (C-FAM 1997).

Relations between the two groups of activists present at the final ICC negotiations in Rome in June/July 1998 can be described as hostile, even vitriolic. Members of the Women's Caucus have described the involvement of the opposition as an 'intense and sustained attack by an alliance of religious fundamentalists and conservative organisations' (Oosterveld 1999: 39), 'intent on undermining the Court's ability to appropriately address sexual and gender crimes', by making 'misleading linkages' (Bedont and Hall Martinez 1999: 67). The pro-family groups usually referred to the opposition simply as 'feminists' or 'radical feminists' (probably a swearword in their circles), but occasionally they became more venomous: one article, for instance, claimed that a Canadian Women's Caucus member was being referred to as 'the snake' behind her back (REAL Women of Canada 1998), while another referred to the women's groups as the 'anti-life, anti-family movement'.

The Women's Caucus had very good relations with Australia, Bosnia, Canada, Costa Rica, Mexico, the Netherlands, Sweden, European countries generally, and South Africa. This list is particularly formidable because it includes the two countries chairing the negotiations (first the Netherlands and later Canada) and the country chairing the special negotiations on gender issues (Australia). One person from the Women's Caucus (the 'snake') became a member of the Canadian state delegation; another went on the delegation of Costa Rica. All this suggests that there was a strong overlap in values and aspirations between the Women's Caucus and the so-called Like-Minded Group of states that drove the negotiations. The pro-family groups, in contrast, were tolerated by states and NGOs, but not exactly welcomed. Most NGOs and many state delegates greeted them with irritation and hostility. The Australian delegate who chaired negotiations on gender issues, for instance, called their lobbying an 'unfortunate departure from the generally constructive role played by NGOs throughout the Conference' (Steains 1999: 368). However, they also had some very strong state allies, particularly in the Vatican and to a lesser extent other Catholic and Arab countries.

Gender

One of the battlefields between the two movements was the term 'gender' itself. The Women's Caucus argued that '(i)t is precisely because the vast majority of laws, legal instruments and institutions have been created without a gender perspective that the everyday violations of women's human rights are invisible to the law and the most atrocious violations have been rendered trivial' (Facio: 1997). Pro-family groups objected to the use of the term 'gender' anywhere in the Statute because it might 'provide protection for "other genders" including homosexuals, lesbians, bisexuals, transgendered, etc' (REAL Women of Canada 1998).

After protracted negotiations, the following definition of gender was agreed: 'the term gender refers to the two sexes, male and female, within the context of society. The term gender does not indicate any meaning different from the above.' The Australian coordinator of these negotiations later wrote:

While the Statute's definition of 'gender' appears, on its face, to be rather unusual (with the tautological second part of the definition), it represents the culmination of hard-fought negotiations that managed to produce language acceptable to delegations on both sides of the debate. At the end of the day, it was the only definition of 'gender' to which the Arab states and others were willing to agree. At the same time, the reference to 'within the context of society' satisfied those delegations that wanted the definition to encapsulate the broader sociological aspects of the term, along the lines of earlier definitions. (Steains 1999: 374–5)

Forced pregnancy

The second, even more contentious, issue was whether to criminalise 'forced pregnancy': the practice, which first emerged in Bosnia, of raping a woman with a view to impregnating her, and then forcing her to carry the baby to full term. Pro-family groups joined the Vatican in voicing objections to the inclusion of forced pregnancy as a war crime, calling it a 'code word for criminalizing any denial of access to abortion' (C-FAM 1998). Proponents of the clause, including many Western states, but also conflict states like Bosnia and Rwanda and Muslim states such as Azerbaijan and Turkey, argued that it was meant to codify a terrible crime, such as witnessed in Bosnia, and had nothing to do with viewpoints on abortion (Steains 1999: 366). The definition that came out of these negotiations in the final week of the conference was as follows: 'the unlawful confinement of a woman forcibly made pregnant, with the intent of affecting the ethnic composition of any population or carrying out other grave violations of international law. This definition shall not in any way be interpreted as affecting national laws relating to pregnancy.' The second sentence was clearly inserted to protect the anti-abortion laws of the objecting countries (Steains 1999: 366–8)

Conclusion

As a result of the compromises reached on the definition of gender and on forced pregnancy, the Women's Caucus and the pro-family groups could both claim victory. A few conclusions can be drawn from this case study. First of all, it has demonstrated that, despite the poisonous relations between the two groups, it was actually possible for the confrontation between different understandings of gender to produce mutually satisfactory outcomes.

Second, there is a pervading sense in the women's movement generally that those who work on gender concerns are necessarily disadvantaged and marginalised. This sense of being the underdog, undoubtedly justified in many local, national and international settings, should not be assumed to be applicable to every situation. The Women's Caucus did not, in fact, meet with intense opposition from many representatives; it met with intense opposition from very few representatives. Despite their close links with the Vatican, it was, in fact, the pro-family groups that were marginalised at this particular forum.

Finally, it suggests that excluding 'conservatives' and 'fundamentalists' from global decision-making forums is short-sighted from both a moral and a strategic perspective. Global civil society should not be understood as the exclusive domain of 'progressive' human rights, environmental, social justice and women's rights activists. It is a space shared with conservatives, anti-abortionists, and religious fundamentalists. Global civil society is populated by actors with strongly held values, but these strongly held values are not all the same. Plurality and even discord are part and parcel of global civil society. The United Nations, although more in some parts than in others, has, in recent years, explicitly embraced the notion that civil society participation is one of the elements of its legitimacy. But if we believe that there is such a right to participate or interact, then excluding certain types of groups from participation would infringe this right. If women's groups have a right to be active at fora such as the ICC negotiations, and they have fought hard for that right, then so do pro-family groups.

See Glasius (2004; 2005) for a more extensive treatment of the gender component of the negotiations on the Statute for an International Criminal Court.

Marlies Glasius, Centre for the Study of Global Governance, and Centre for Civil Society, LSE

the *Philosophy of Right* (1821) Hegel depicts women as having their 'substantive destiny' in the family, while men's lives were played out in the state and civil society (section 166, cited in Phillips 2002: 72). Carole Pateman (1988b: 114) exposes the patriarchal underpinnings in the works of contract theorists such as Locke and Rousseau, who, in Pateman's words, see women as 'unable to transcend their bodily natures in the manner required of individuals who are to ...uphold the universal laws of civil society'[13].

Although political correctness might inhibit many civil society theorists from expressing such an explicit view on gender and the public–private distinction today, the silence on gender and civil society suggests a more pervasive hegemonic framing that acquiesces in rather than challenges the gendered relations of civil society. Civil society is discussed as though gender is irrelevant[14], even though 'gender' is now a globalised concept, appropriated in the discourses of both international and national state institutions. Civil society theorists continue their debates oblivious to the gender content of the UN Millennium Development Goals or global treaties such as the Convention on the Elimination of Discrimination against Women (CEDAW). Such a perspective implicitly reinforces the notion that the public is the natural domain of the male and the family that of the female. Similarly, the inclusion of economic relations within civil society in the writings of eighteenth- and nineteenth-century political thinkers such as Ferguson, de Tocqueville, Hegel and Marx in turn discursively reinforced the separation of the political economy (and later classical and neo-classical economics) from the household economy, thereby masking the structural interrelations between the domestic sphere, civil society and capitalist economy. In challenging these gendered dichotomies, feminist thinkers have also criticised the narrow and dominant understanding of politics that excludes the private domestic world. Instead, they have argued for a broader conceptualisation of politics that extends beyond the study of formal political institutions to include all aspects of social life (McClure 1992: 346).

Had civil society theorists engaged more with the feminist problematisation of the public–private divide, they might have been better equipped conceptually to explore how the family shapes norms and practices in the sphere of civil society and how gendered power relations pervade the spheres of state, market, civil society and family. This might have led civil society

theorists to lavish more attention on issues of power and subordination within the realm of civil society, thereby introducing caution into debates that portray civil society as the realm of the benign, virtuous and harmonious, in contrast to the venal, oppressive state. Moreover, it might have steered civil society theory and discussion away from definitional marathons towards a more productive focus on the interconnectedness, fluidity and permeability of spheres.

Feminist political theory and civil society

If civil society theorists have not scrutinised civil society from a gender perspective, feminist theorists, too, have not engaged to any great extent with theoretical debates about civil society[15]. This is not least because, as Anne Phillips (2002: 72) puts it, 'Civil society is not a significant organising category for feminists, and rarely figures in the feminist taxonomy'. For feminist thinkers, the key conceptual divide lies between the public (state, market and civil society) and the private (family). Yet, given the ambiguity in political theory around public and private, this dichotomy could have provided an opportunity for feminist and civil society theorists to engage in a common dialogue. In political theory, as Susan Moller Okin (1979: 68–70) points out, the dichotomy is laden with ambiguities in its points of reference and meanings. In one rendering, the dichotomy is between state and society, as in the familiar public and private property divide; in another rendering, it is between the domestic and the non-domestic (see also Pateman 1988b: 102 for further discussion). These different interpretations in turn have implications for the

---

13 *Another reason for the failure of civil society theorists to engage with the household lies in their emphasis on the voluntary nature of civil society, which contrasts with the ascriptive nature of relations within the family.*

14 *In his review of three recent contributions on global civil society, Waterman (2003: 303) laments the lack of engagement with women's movements and feminisms, even though, in his words, 'the dramatic presence alone of women and feminists at the parallel events of UN Conferences surely deserves better than this'.*

15 *This is interesting given that there has been some interrogation of the gender dimensions of social capital. See, for example, Edwards, Franklin and Holland (2003), Molyneux (2002), and Goulbourne and Solomos (2003). I am grateful to Karen Wright for drawing my attention to this literature. However, in the practical world of development, Molyneux (2002:169) notes the parallel development of work on social capital and that on gender, as reflected in the absence of any discussion of social capital in the World Bank's report* Engendering Development *(2001).*

Ambiguity surrounds the public–private divide °*Qilai Shen/Panos Pictures*

positioning of civil society. In the first rendering civil society is understood as part of the private, while in the second interpretation it is part of the public. As Jonathan Hearn (2001: 342) notes, civil society 'is sometimes treated as primarily a matter of private interactions, especially in regard to the market, and sometimes as primarily a matter of publicness and the formation of collective identities and agendas'.

Although in feminist theory the public–private divide is a significant organising category, there are as diverse a range of positions on whether the family is or is not part of civil society as among civil society theorists. For some feminists, the public world of civil society is as excluding to women as the concept and institutions of the state. The dominant framing of civil society as in opposition to the state and the subsequent discussions around the definitional boundaries between civil society, state and market appear irrelevant and uninteresting to many feminists, for whom the family figures larger in importance than the public (state, civil society and market). Moreover, for many feminists, it is not the demarcation of boundaries that is analytically important or interesting, but understanding how the relations between males and females in the family shape the norms, practices and behaviours in the public realm, that is, in state, civil society and market institutions (Phillips 2002: 73–5).

For others, though, the family does form an integral part of civil society. Carole Pateman (1989: 132–3, quoted in Phillips 2002: 88), for example, views the sphere of domestic life as 'at the heart of civil society rather than apart or separate from it'. Drude Dahlerup (1994) likewise includes the family within civil society, but gives no justification for her position. However, whether the family constitutes part of civil society has not been a prime focus of analytic interest within feminist theory.

Although feminist theorists have not paid much attention to the relationship between civil society and the family, it can be argued that conceptualising the family as inside or outside civil society has consequences for the way we theorise civil society and gender, and indeed for practical strategies around gender eman-cipation. Arguing, as Pateman does, that the family is 'at the heart of civil society' challenges modernist and voluntarist views of civil society, which posit civil-society-type organisations as free of clan and familial ties and obligations. Taking the family as crucial calls for a gender analysis of civil society and state institutions. It thus strengthens the idea that civil society discourses,

GENDER

Institutions such as schools and religious organisations influence gender identities °*Mark Henley/Panos Pictures*

spaces and organisations, as well as state organisations and practices, are shaped by, and in turn reproduce, particular configurations of gender relations. Moreover, it places organisations based on ethnicity or blood ties within the scope of analysis by civil society researchers, a dilemma that has been captured in the works of researchers in Africa.

Keeping the family out of civil society, however, reifies the family as a distinct sphere with clear boundaries between the state and civil society. By implying that the family is independent from state and civil society, it removes the question of how the engendering of male and female bodies shapes these other spheres and contributes to the false impression that state and civil society are free of gender relations. However, whether the family is conceptualised as within or outside civil society will not alone determine whether the gendered nature of civil society is problematised. This depends much more on power relations within society that find their expression in academic, political and practical discourses.

Developing a conceptual framework

In her insightful and novel analysis of the organi-sation of production, Diane Elson (1998: 197) argues cogently for a model of political economy that includes the domestic. Using a tripartite model of the private, public and domestic sectors, she demonstrates how the circuits of the market (through which goods, services, money and labour flow), of taxes and benefits (through which income transfers and public goods flow) and of communications (through which information, rumours, ideas, values and meanings flow) connect these sectors and channel the flows between them. At the same time, the sectors feed into these channels. To illustrate, the market feeds commercial values through the communications network, the state transmits regulatory values, and the domestic feeds provisioning values. These values in turn can have positive as well as negative dimensions. Thus, the domestic sector may feed in values of caring and giving as well as of patriarchy (Elson 1998: 197).

Elson argues that both the sectors and the circuits are gendered. Hence the domestic sector constitutes, and is constituted by, the circuits of the market, of taxes and benefits and of communications. To illustrate, the market relies on a labour force that is reproduced daily and across generations in the domestic sector using unpaid labour. Market transactions are frequently gendered to the disadvantage of women, as reflected in the exclusion of women from contracts or certain marketplaces. The tax and benefit system is often based upon an implicit assumption that women are dependent on men. Essential to the communications network are communicative people, and the primary locus for producing such people is the domestic sector (1998: 197).

Elson's model provides a useful starting point for conceptualising gender and civil society. We develop this model in two ways. First, we introduce the 'forgotten site' of civil society, which receives no mention in Elson's model. This is partly because Elson's analysis is concerned with the discourse of macroeconomics rather than politics and partly because, like other feminist theorists, she subsumes civil society within the public. Hence in Elson's model, the domestic stands in contrast to the private (enterprises) and the state. In the discourse of politics, the domestic is presented as the private and contrasted with the public sphere of government, trade unions, factories and clubs, a depiction of the public that blends the governmental and non-governmental. As Elson rightly claims, in both the macroeconomic and political discourses, the domestic is taken for granted and not deemed worthy of further analysis.

Like the public and domestic 'sites', civil society, too, is made up of a diversity of associational forms, varying in their size, purpose, duration, values, ideologies, degree of formality, and interconnections with the market and state. These can range from burial societies to single mothers' groups, trades unions, animal rights' groups, football clubs, business associations, global social movements, and world social forums. What unites these diverse units is the dynamic of voluntary solidarity[16]. For civil society to sustain itself, people need to be able to associate voluntarily (in contrast to the ascriptive ties of the family) and to have a common reason to associate. We prefer here the concept of 'sites' to sectors, as the term allows for more fuzzy, porous and evolving boundaries than the more compartmentalised, legalistic and rigid image that 'sector' evokes. Furthermore, we conceptualise these sites as concentrations of power galvanised by distinct dynamics – in the case of the state, the dynamic of

coercion and regulation; in the case of the market, the dynamic of profit and accumulation; in the case of the household, the dynamic of material and affective provisioning; and in the case of civil society, the dynamic of voluntary solidarity.

By separating civil society from the state, we can explore the interconnections between civil society and the household. While the communications network provides a channel through which civil society can transmit ideas about solidarity, trust, citizenship and the values of association, it is in the household that people have their first experience of association. It is here that they develop a sense of empathy towards others, trust in 'strangers', a sense of citizenship and responsibility towards those beyond their immediate household or family unit. Just as the market depends on the unpaid work of the household in regenerating its labour force, so too civil society depends on the unpaid work of the household, such as the care of dependents, child-rearing, and other household activities, to free its participants to commit time and energy to its causes. Given that in most societies it is women who take the main responsibility for these household activities, participation in civil society that requires at least time becomes a gendered activity.

Second, we put forward a circuit of gender relations, comprising male and female bodies, and culturally specific roles, identities, norms and values that delineate male and female bodies as socially distinct beings[17]. This circuit of gender relations flows between, and connects the sites of, market, state, household and civil society. By conceptualising gender relations as a circuit, we free it from any essentially given location. Thus, it recognises not only that the household is the primary site in which young

---

16 This builds upon but diverges from Elson's analysis in some respects. Thus, with the concern of politics with association, the dynamic of the state includes both coercion and regulation. Although the term 'provisioning' used by Elson refers to those activities concerned with 'supplying people with what they need to thrive, including care and concern as well as material goods' (1998: 207), here we highlight the distinct affective nature of association in the household as compared with the market or state. Of course, this is not to say that affective relations also do not exist in the sites of the market, state or civil society or that households are never devoid of affection, but merely that affection and intimacy feature more prominently in the household.

17 In Elson's analysis (1998), the mode of operation of the sectors and circuits is constructed upon the 'prevailing gender order'. Elson does not develop further the idea of the 'gender order'; here we propose instead a circuit of gender relations.

In the international arena, organising around gender issues takes on new meanings ©Eric Miller/Panos Pictures

bodies become impregnated, from the moment of birth, with gendered identities, values, norms and roles that make up the gender order of any particular society, but also that other sites of power such as the market, state, and civil society can also create, reaffirm, usurp and destabilise any gender order. Furthermore, this conceptualisation allows the disaggregation of the household so that the hidden gender relations can surface and be analysed. This avoids the trap that most civil society theorists fall into: that is, after deploying the household as a boundary-marking device, they dispense with it as analytically irrelevant for understanding civil society and the state and fail to interrogate its internal relations, which are constituted in part through gender relations. The circuit of gender relations also allows us to take into account the gendered socialising effects of different institutions such as schools and faith-based organisations.

In Elson's model, the private, public and domestic sectors pass different messages through the circuit of communications, which reflect the organising dynamics of these sectors. If we take the organising dynamic of civil society to be voluntary solidarity, civil society then transmits the values of voluntariness, common cause and solidarity, which contain both positive (generosity, sociability) and negative dimensions (exclusion, prejudice). Similarly, the sites of civil society, state, market and household also transmit through the gender relations circuit different messages reflecting their organisational dynamic. Gendered norms and values distribute male and female bodies across the sites of state, market, civil society and household in different ways. Gendered hierarchies prevail in the state, where male bodies inhabit most positions of leadership and authority, while gendered divisions of labour characterise certain markets (textiles are often dominated by female workers in many countries and the steel industry by male workers, for example). The site of civil society not only is constituted by the gender relations circuit, but also shapes this in diverse and sometimes contradictory ways. When nationalist movements deploy the symbol of motherhood to depict the nation, they promote an image of gender relations that draws on women's reproductive role. Or, when civil society associations exclude women, either implicitly through gendered norms or explicitly through regulations, as with working men's clubs, then male and female bodies become distributed unevenly across the terrain of civil society.

It should be noted that the circuit of gender relations is concerned with a diversity of gender identities, norms and values, and thereby includes within its analytic vision transsexuality, homosexuality, and diverse masculine and feminine identities. In this way, it becomes possible to investigate gender-issue organisational forms in civil society such as global transsexual activism, chauvinistic male organising, feminist men's groups, or pro-life groups (see Box 1.2). Furthermore, the idea of a circuit of gender relations allows the study not only of gender-issue groups, but also of how forms of organising in civil society become gendered, regardless of their ultimate purpose.

This framework for analysing civil society and gender involves some further interrogation of the concepts of global, public, and autonomy.

Thinking globally

Civil society as a sphere of articulation and organisation separate from the state, and the study thereof, emerged in the eighteenth century. As such, the concept has been rooted in the historical processes of industrialisation and capitalist development in Western Europe and North America. Such origins have led critics to question the universality of the concept and its applicability to non-Western concepts. Nevertheless, following the revitalisation of the idea of civil society from the late 1980s onwards in Eastern Europe, the concept has been appropriated across the world to articulate a plethora of ideological aspirations and to describe a range of collective forms of action. In addition, the increasing linkages between civil society organisations in different countries and the formation of cross-border networks, alliances, and movements suggest that any conceptualisation of civil society must look beyond national boundaries.

The model posited above applies across the levels of the global, national and local. Markets are increasingly globalised as financial and capital flows pay little heed to national boundaries. Households are consumers and producers of global goods and services, and their savings are invested through various insurance and pension schemes in global operations. The power of nation-states is increasingly tempered by the need to negotiate and abide by rules and regulations in international governing institutions. Civil society, too, is increasingly bound up in global networks, as local organisations forge international links and campaigns are targeted at international bodies such as the UN.

Any model of gender and civil society has thus to incorporate global networks, institutions, influences and ideas. This then poses the challenge of moving beyond the nation-state as the unit of analysis. Comparative work on gender relations and on civil society tends to start from the national context and seeks points of commonality and difference. Trying to understand international organising around gender and the continuities between this and national–local forms of activism calls for a different approach that is less framed, or maybe not at all framed, within the notion of territory. Given the plurality of norms and identities circulating in international contexts, the relative significance of the national is potentially questioned.

However, current analyses of global civil society pay little attention to its gender aspects, and thereby assume away the mediation of global organising through gendered power relations. For global civil society theorists, the key boundary markers have been global institutions of governance on the one hand and nation-states on the other. In such a framework family, household and gender relations all disappear from view. As a result, a range of questions concerning gender, civil society, state, and market are left unaddressed. How are global markets gendered and how are gender values and norms distributed through the circuit of the market across the local, national and global levels? If, as feminist political theorists have shown, the nation-state is a highly gendered institution, with complex gender ideologies, male domination of leadership positions and of particular arms of the state such as the military, then how does this impinge upon the gender formation of multilateral institutions?

Similarly, how does the gender composition of national and local civil society organisations feed into the way men and women are positioned in cross-border, global organising? How are diverse cultural and ideological interpretations of gender and feminism played out in the global arena? What mechanisms exist at the international level to resolve differences over gender values, a case in point being

Box 1.3: The costs and risks of being 'out of place'

The expansion in the scale and impact of civil society activism to improve women's status at the global level is beyond dispute. The year 2005 marks the tenth anniversary of the UN Women's Conference in Beijing. As Mary Kaldor (2003: 96) notes, the conference was grounded in intensive and preparatory research and reflection at the global, regional, national and local levels. Another milestone at the global level has been the 2000 UN Security Council Resolution 1325 on the necessity of integrating gender concerns into the entire range of peacekeeping operations, peace negotiations, and their aftermath. These are just some examples of the unprecedented level of activity of global civic networks working together towards an emancipatory transformation of women's status. The activity encompasses and cuts across the fields of academic research, political activism, policy formulation, socio-economic development, humanitarian action, conflict analysis, peacekeeping and peace building.

In the face of these achievements, it becomes increasingly difficult to deny women the capacity for significant agency in their own right rather than as dependents of men, and this is correctly represented in current accounts. However, there remain some underdeveloped areas. Some literature on women's campaigns tends to emphasise their transformational content while overlooking the costs and risks incurred by the participants. As the present chapter demonstrates, feminist political scholarship about the public–private divide has produced substantial evidence that the parameters of 'the public' have always been gendered in the West. The public sphere is represented as the sphere of rationality and intellect while the domestic sphere has been designated a sphere of emotion, passion, non-rationality and nature. Historically, 'women's place' has been confined to the private/family sphere, and attempts to claim public space, such as the suffrage movement, met with ridicule and sometimes harsher measures.

Women's entry into waged labour and formal political representation in the 'developed' world and some areas of the former 'Third World' have indisputably shifted the public–private boundaries significantly, but not to the extent of making gender irrelevant. Time-use surveys in both industrial and developing societies consistently find that women continue to bear a heavier proportion of the burden of domestic and caring work regardless of other wage/income earning activities. As a result, when women participate in civil society initiatives, they incur time costs. These kinds of cost may be particularly demanding in the post-colonial nations of the global South where the withdrawal of state services has confined the rich collective activities of indigenous women's organisations to a narrower area of service delivery.

Research from the field also points out the significance of local gender orders – that is, the dynamic process of symbolic and material representations of gender relations institutionalised through practices at the micro, meso and macro levels of the political economy and reproduction. In some settings, this gender order operates strong social sanctions to maintain the boundaries around 'women's place'. Evaluators of a community-based water project in Angola observed that there was a majority of women on the Water Committee, but:

We asked these women during the meeting whether they wanted to add anything to what the male members had said on their behalf. They replied that they agreed with everything that had been said and that they didn't think it was necessary to repeat information which had been correctly presented by the men. On the occasions when the soba (the local traditional leader) was present at these meetings, the timidity and modesty with which the women made any contribution was noticeable, which was the contrary of what happened when meetings were made up only of women. (Jacobson and Perreira 2001)

Other projects in Angola set out to make a space for women and men of different generations that would allow the less powerful to speak about community priorities. Older women chose a song to convey their views, which condemned husbands who spent women's hard-earned money on alcohol, gambling and women. Younger women began to speak out against domestic violence and control over their movements. Men fought back, accusing the younger women of washing dirty linen in public. In a review eight months later, women declared their pride at gaining greater access to legal representation in cases of domestic violence, maintenance of children and inheritance. Men, however, spoke of women's violation of cultural taboos by bringing 'private' issues into the public domain. There had been a backlash and younger wives had taken the brunt; women had been beaten as a direct result of spending their time in meetings rather than on domestic work. The divorce rate had increased as a consequence.

Gender orders also impose costs and risks on men. This is most evident in homophobic violence, but there can be other strong social pressures. NGOs working on health and reproduction with men in Latin America note that:

> *Peers are often reported to be an obstacle to change. A man who is changing his life is a threat to other men, who will criticise or ridicule him as unmanly, as dominated by his wife ('his chicken orders him around') or a sissy... this occurs with problems like alcoholism or violence, and also in the reproductive decision making around vasectomy... (De Keijzer 2004: 38)*

It is evident from the continuing levels of activism that these risks are negotiable – the Angolan women did not withdraw from the organisation, and the Latin America men drew on humour to defuse the criticism. Nevertheless, a gendered approach to civil society activism demands that costs and risks are taken into account, both conceptually in policy and in implementation.

Ruth Jacobson, Peace Studies, Bradford University

the contradictions between pro-family and feminist groups at the International Criminal Court (see Box 1.2). Why is it that women's human rights organisations take up gender issues but human rights NGOs are resistant to doing so? Why have global movements around social justice, anti-capitalism, and anti-globalisation been so resistant to gender justice? (Obando 2005). How do global institutions, international development agencies and international NGOs shape debates around gender and civil society? How does the circuit of gender relations fuse the global and the local? For example, in post-Soviet states such as Armenia, the creation of NGOs through a combination of domestic and external factors has enabled women to remain in the public sphere (Ishkanian 2004). In other contexts such as Chile, donor support to new NGOs has contributed to the de-radicalisation of women's movements (Stevenson 2004). In brief, our four-site model cannot thus be confined to the territorial boundaries of nation-states, and therefore self-consciously deploys a global frame.

Revisiting the public and the private

As demonstrated above, feminist theorists have not seen civil society as an organising category. Instead, the key axis of analysis has been the public–private divide, where the private refers to the household and the public to the state. At the same time, civil society theorists have portrayed the family as the sphere of the private and the intimate in contrast to the public arena of the state and civil society. Feminist political theorists have challenged mainstream political theory for its limited view of politics and argued forcefully that relationships within the family are also political, as captured in the maxim 'the personal is political'. Yet, in exploring the boundaries between public and private, feminist scholars have focused on the interplay between the state, gender and family, exploring issues such as marriage laws, domestic violence, rape within marriage, and welfare policy. Feminist economists, on the other hand, have deployed the language of the domestic sector to distinguish this from the private sector of production and the public world of the state. By drawing the domestic into their economic analyses, they also have left civil society hidden, absorbed within the concept of public sector.

The above model overcomes these limitations by positing a four-site model incorporating the household, state, market and civil society. The notion of the 'public' is broken down here into the two constituent elements of the state and civil society. This then allows feminist analysts of gender and civil society to distinguish the different organising dynamics of the state and civil society, namely, regulation and voluntary solidarity, and to analyse the connection of these sites through, *inter alia*, the gender relations circuit. As argued above, all this needs to be situated within a global frame that takes the circuits of market, communications and gender relations (and increasingly tax and benefits[18]) to flow across national and local boundaries. Furthermore, the discussion of the public–private divide needs to go beyond the limitations of the nation-state to embrace global institutions, global civil society and the global economy.

Autonomy

By highlighting the idea of the interconnectedness of sites, the model undermines the hegemony of autonomy. The notion of sectors, the prevalence of negative (and reductive) definitions of civil society organisations as non-profit and non-governmental, and the dominance of the 'civil society versus state' debate have all contributed to the definition of these sites within rigid boundaries. Civil society theorists have deployed the concept of autonomy as a distinguishing feature of civil-society-type associations. Some liberal and neo-liberal theories of the state assume its autonomy from social relations. This focus on autonomy makes it difficult to analyse the flow of ideas, values and norms between sectors. Where such influences penetrate, they are interpreted as diverging from an ideal type. In contrast, an analysis that focuses on the flows of bodies, norms and values through relatively fixed, though fungible, sites of power can illuminate the complex mechanisms by which gendered power relations are produced and reproduced. Such an approach implies a more diffuse notion of power that is rarely a zero-sum process. In this way, we can begin to understand how particular gendered norms, ideologies, practices and values work their way through the power sites of the state, civil society, market and family and position male and female bodies in different ways, and why particular gender patterns become congealed at certain

---

18 *The circuit of taxes and benefits is becoming increasingly internationalised as migration complicates citizenship and obligations, reflected, for example, in cross-border flows of remittances and rules about residency and entitlements.*

©Chris Stowers/Panos Pictures

points and moments. Recognising this fluidity makes it harder at the conceptual and practical levels to ignore the influence of gender relations in apparently separate domains such as the state and civil society, or in apparently non-gender specific issues such as architecture, health and the environment, or the cross-cutting of gender relations with other organisers of identity such as class, religion, sexuality and ethnicity. Furthermore, it also gives us scope to examine the blockages in flows, and, in particular, flows of male and female bodies between sites of power. This in turn draws attention to the risks involved in moving between sites and the gendered nature thereof (see Box 1.4).

History

As a final point, it should be emphasised that any model of gender and civil society relations needs also to be placed in an historical context. Our purpose here is not to look towards the past to justify the present, but to deepen our understanding of contemporary processes of social change. Thinking historically about civil society gender relations will ensure that the analysis of contemporary civil society gender relations draws out the continuities with the past and identifies key watersheds of conceptual formation, activism, and gender practices. Such analysis therefore requires seeing the nation-state as an historically bounded concept that has been shaken from the mid-twentieth century onwards by the growing force of global interconnections. It also permits a broader understanding of how conceptual shifts across time both reflect and reframe the way we think about the state, civil society, household, market and gender.

Box 1.4: **Men's activism in global civil society**

Men's activism in global civil society has arisen as a response to global women's movements. Just as women's activism has manifested itself in a wide variety of forms, articulating distinct perspectives and campaigning for diverse objectives, the range of men's groups is broad and each presents different and often conflicting discourses and agendas. The literature on masculinities and men's movements emphasises this diversity and suggests various typologies for distinguishing between groups. Clatterbaugh (1997) identifies eight major perspectives exemplifying distinct views on men's actual status in contemporary society and on the nature of masculine social roles in North America: conservative groups, pro-feminist perspectives, men's rights movements, the Mythopoetic perspective, socialist groups, gay male activism, African American men's perspectives and the evangelical Christian men's movement. Others use alternative categories such as anti-machismo groups, or point to other focuses for men's activism, including men's health and father's rights groups (Wadham 2001; Russell 2001). The plethora of labels and classifications highlights the illusion of a cohesive perspective implied by umbrella terms such as 'The Men's Movement', and suggests that it is more accurate to use the plural, eschew capitals, and refer instead to 'men's movements'.

However, men's activism as a category does suggest some unifying characteristics across men's groups. Perhaps because the discourse of gender as a legitimate and salient nexus for coordination in civil society was created by feminist movements, one feature that men's movements can be said to have in common is that all articulate a standpoint on feminism – whether negative or positive. Attitudes towards feminism depend on the perception of what 'feminism' is and how it has affected men's status, as well as assumptions about ideal gender roles. Conservative activists and some elements of the Mythopoetic movement, for example, see feminism as threatening to a traditional (Western) form of masculinity and aim to correct what they perceive as the increasing feminisation of men and men's roles in contemporary society. By contrast, pro-feminist and some gay male movements have a benign conception of feminism as here the hegemonic forms of masculinity celebrated by anti-feminist groups are seen as damaging to men as well as women, such that it is in men's interests to act alongside feminist women to undermine restrictive gender roles (Clatterbaugh 1997: 9-14). Women's movements similarly express different viewpoints on the nature of gender roles and vary as to whether they describe themselves as feminist or reject feminist perspectives. A further common attribute of men's movements is that all perceive masculinity or maleness to be politically significant in some respect, and their activism is aimed at supporting men and addressing issues that are seen as peculiarly the concern of men. Again, this mirrors women's movements where gender is the organising principle, and certain issues are perceived as fundamentally women's issues.

Case studies of men's groups:

Pro-feminist groups

- *The White Ribbon Campaign (WRC)*. The WRC was founded in Canada in 1991 as a response to the murder of 14 women in Montreal. The movement asks men to wear a white ribbon for a week to demonstrate their opposition to men's violence against women and to develop local responses to support abused women and challenge men's violence (Kimmel 2001: 34). The founders of the group were motivated by a feeling of responsibility for violence against women – men's silence allows violence to continue. According to this view, violence damages both men and women and can only be halted through men's commitment to change themselves and others. They also aim to allow men to redefine traditional ways of working together and promote unity rather than the competition characterising most male-dominated organisations (Kaufman 2001: 47).

  Local men's groups challenging violence against women include Men Against Sexual Assault (MASA) in Australia, Asosiaun Mane Kontra Violensia (Men's Association Against Violence or AMKV) in East Timor, and the Group of Men Against Violence (GMAV) in Managua, Nicaragua.

Men's rights movements

- *Fathers 4 Justice (F4J)*. Fathers 4 Justice is a British Father's Rights Group founded in 2002, which campaigns for changes to current family law. It sees men as unfairly discriminated against in gaining access to their children after divorce, claiming that the will of parliament has not been enacted with regard to the 1989 Children's Act, which states that the welfare of children is best served by maintaining as good a relationship as possible with both parents. In practice, however, F4J say that children often live with their mother and lose contact with their father, even where court orders are issued legally obliging mothers to allow fathers time with their children. They also wish to establish a legal presumption of contact between children and parents and grandchildren and grandparents.

  The group uses what they describe as a 'humorous' approach, involving publicity stunts in order to make 'injustice visible'. Members of the 'Dad's Army' have famously made a habit of dressing up as superheroes, and alongside more peaceful protests, have perpetrated several acts of civil disobedience such as the incident in May 2004 when condoms filled with purple flour were thrown at Prime Minister Tony Blair in the House of Commons. Such actions have been seen by many as irresponsible and inconsistent with F4J's claim to be a peaceful pressure group. The organisation uses a discourse of equal rights and justice – the use of the colour purple, for example, is said to be significant as it represents the international colour of equality and was used by the Suffragettes.

Mythopoetic perspective

- *Robert Bly*. The Mythopoetic perspective arose from the writings and workshops of poet Robert Bly (URL) in the 1980s and 1990s. It was founded on a neo-Jungian view, which states that masculinities derive from deep unconscious patterns or archetypes that can be revealed through a tradition of stories, myths and rituals. Men-only workshops involve reading poetry, drumming and speaking of emotional and psychic wounds. Men and women are seen as essentially different beings with different needs. Bly argues that the feminist movement has tapped into women's unconscious minds and found a way to unleash women's energy positively, but that men have found no such release. According to Bly, feminism harms men as it promotes a spiritualism that is antagonistic to the 'deep masculine' and has been responsible for modern men becoming overly feminised (Clatterbaugh 1997).

- *John Rowan*. Another branch of the Mythopoetic movement, also based on neo-Jungian thought, represents a challenge to Bly's position. Figures such as John Rowan state that men have been cut off from a feminine understanding of themselves, and that they should look to the Wicca tradition for remedy. The Wicca tradition is a pre-Christian pagan religion that centers on an earth goddess and several lesser deities, teaching that the deep masculine should be controlled by the 'Great Goddess'. In this view, then, masculinity is suffering from a lack of feminisation (Clatterbaugh 1997).

Ana Jordan, University of Bristol

Looking ahead

The failure of researchers in the fields of civil society and gender to engage in a serious dialogue with one another, for all the reasons given above, has affected the development of theory, the formation of concepts, the state of empirical knowledge, and the design of practical strategies of emancipation. Much remains to be done. Armed with a sharper set of conceptual tools, we start to identify an agenda for future research, debate and critical reflection.

First, there is a huge gap in the literature concerning the gendered composition of civil society, the gendered norms and practices prevailing among civil society organisations, and the barriers to the participation of not only women in civil society but also some men. There is no systematic, comprehensive disaggregated data available on the gendered make-up of civil society. How many male-dominated or female-dominated associations are there, and what kinds of issues, sectors or activities are these associated with? What do we mean by a gender-based organisation? What is the gender distribution of different kinds of formal and informal organisation? What percentage of volunteers and employees are women, and how does this vary across time, country context and sector? How do we explain the predominance of men or women in particular types of groups? What proportion of directors, trustees and managers of civil society organisations are male, and why are women under- or over-represented in different country contexts or at the global level? How has this changed over time? What legal or regulatory mechanisms facilitate the exclusion or inclusion of many women and some men from participating in civil society? Through what gendered norms and practices, such as the lack of childcare facilities or the times of meetings, are women effectively excluded from taking part in different civil society groups? How do gender relations within the household affect the way women participate and organise, be it in women's organisations or other kinds of civil society groups? Although some of these questions have been broached in relation to state institutions and formal politics, their application to the realm of civil society requires systematic attention and research.

Second, there is a need for further empirical studies and theoretical work to describe and explain the distinctiveness of men's and women's organising. In what ways does women's organising differ from men's?

How does organising by women around women's rights differ from that of human rights groups, business associations, trades unions, or professional associations? What unique material, psychological and discursive resources do men and women deploy to promote their agendas? What kinds of organisational forms are best disposed to advance gender issues in state policy? To what extent are the internal ways of organising and leadership different in women's organisations from men's organisations and other civil society organisations? Do women do politics differently from men and, if so, in what ways and with what effects? (See Box 1.4.)

Third, there is a need to theorise further the interconnectedness of different spheres and the flow of gendered discourses, practices and norms within and between spheres. Why is it that activism in local civil societies and social movements tends to provide a springboard for men into formal politics but less so for women? How does state policy on gender alter gender relations in civil society, and why is it that the state has proved better than civil society at absorbing demands for and the language of gender equality, as reflected in the UN Millennium Development Goals and CEDAW? How do gendered norms and practices within the family reverberate through state institutions and civil society? To what extent do theories of power or gender relations or civil society illuminate these processes?

Fourth, the concept of civil society needs to be disaggregated into not only different types of organisations with divergent ideological and political predilections, but also into individuals, structured by societal divisions such as class, gender, and ethnicity. The focus within civil society studies on organisations[19] as well as the tendency to reduce 'civil society' to a singular actor and voice has analytically steered the gaze away from the constituent individuals who come together in the spaces of civil society. Similarly, although many feminist theorists cautiously refer to 'feminisms', in the plural, there is still a tendency to work with aggregate notions of 'the women's movement', which can mask rather than reveal the ideological nuances among women's groups.

---

19 I am grateful to Karen Wright for this observation about the focus on organisations.

Fifth, at the theoretical level, there is work to be done on reviewing the gendered nature of the concept of civil society as used in Western political thought, and similar concepts used in other traditions, to unmask the gendered assumptions underlying the distinction between family and civil society, and to query the boundedness and autonomy of spheres and concepts.

> the start of a dialogue between civil society and feminist theories should not only enrich knowledge in both fields but strengthen the effectiveness of practical feminist strategies to bring about changes in gender relations

Sixth, accounts of women's organising need to take on board the increasingly global set of players engaging with national and local civil societies. In particular, there is room for further research into the role of international donor agencies, global networks and international women's coalitions on the development of women's organisations in different contexts. To what extent do international donor agencies reproduce 'Western' understandings of the public–private divide[20], of civil society and of gender relations in their support to women's groups in aid-recipient contexts? What is the impact of major international events such as UN conferences on women, on discourses, agendas, frameworks and practices in different contexts? In what ways do global women's coalitions and organisations set gender agendas, contribute to processes of change at global and national levels, and frame debates on issues such as domestic violence and genital mutilation?

Finally, at the practical level, a number of challenges need to be addressed in creative and productive ways. How do we evaluate the professionalisation or NGO-isation of women's organising and gender issues in post-transition contexts? How do we deal with contestation among groups of women with different gender ideologies, values and politics? Who should mediate these struggles and how? How can feminist activists bring men into debates around gender relations, and where should a deeper engagement begin? Where should feminists seek allies among men's organisations, and how should they analyse these? What kind of global organising by women around gender issues is most effective, and why? How can groups concerned about gender issues persuade other actors in civil society who perceive gender to be marginal to their primary interests to reflect critically upon gender issues both within their organisations and in relation to the issues they are battling for? And how can we reduce the risks to women and to subaltern gender identities of traversing the four interconnected sites of power?

This may be an ambitious agenda. However, the start of a dialogue between civil society and feminist theorists should not only enrich knowledge in both fields but also strengthen the effectiveness of practical feminist strategies to bring about changes in gender relations. For civil society activists, too, there is a need for a moment of reflection and probing if the arena of civil society is to serve as an emancipatory terrain for both men and women.

---

20 I am grateful to Hakan Seckinelgin for this comment on donors and the public–private divide.

REFERENCES

Beary, H. (2003) 'India's Eunuchs Demand Rights',
BBC News, 4 September.
http://news.bbc.co.uk/2/hi/south_asia/3080116.stm
(consulted 28 June 2005).

Beckwith, K. (2000) 'Beyond Compare? Women's Movements
in Comparative Perspective', *European Journal of Political
Research*, 37: 431–68.

Bedont, B. and Hall Martinez, K. (1999) 'Ending Impunity for
Gender Crimes under the International Criminal Court',
Brown Journal of World Affairs, 6(1): 65–85.

Biekart, K. (1999) *The Politics of Civil Society Building: European
Private Aid Agencies and Democratic Transitions in Central
America*. Amsterdam: Utrecht International Books and the
Transnational Institute.

Bly, Robert (URL) www.robertbly.com (consulted 14 June 2005).

Butler, J. and Scott, J. W. (eds) (1992) *Feminists Theorise the
Political*. New York and London: Routledge.

Carothers, T. (1999) *Aiding Democracy Abroad: The Learning Curve*.
Washington, DC: Carnegie Endowment for International Peace.

Carver, Terrell (1995) *Gender is Not a Synonym for Woman*.
Boulder, CO: Lynne Rienner.

Catagay, N. (2003) 'Gender Budgets and Beyond: Feminist
Fiscal Policy in the Context of Globalisation', *Gender and
Development*, 11(1): 15–24.

C-FAM (Catholic Family and Human Rights Institute) (1997)
'Rome Makes Urgent Call for Life and Family Voices at UN
Conferences', *Friday Fax*, 1(9). 21 November.
– (1998) 'Rome Conference Ends Without Consensus For Creating
International Criminal Court', *Friday Fax*, 1(40). 18 July.

Clatterbaugh, K. (1997) *Contemporary Perspectives on
Masculinity: Men, Women and Politics in Modern Society*.
Boulder, CO: Westview Press.

Cohen, J. (1998) 'Interpreting the Notion of Civil Society', in M.
Walzer (ed.), *Toward a Global Civil Society*. New York:
Berghahn Books.
– and Arato, A. (1995) *Civil Society and Political Theory*.
Cambridge, MA: MIT Press.

Connell, R. (1995) *Masculinities*. Cambridge: Polity Press.

Dahlerup, D. (1994) 'Learning to Live with the State. State,
Market and Civil Society: Women's Need for State
Interventions in East and West', *Women's Studies
International Forum*, 17(2/3): 117–27.

De Keijzer, B. (2004) 'Masculinities: Resistance and Change',
in S. Ruxton (ed.), *Gender, Equality and Men: Learning from
Practice*. Oxford: Oxfam.

DeLue, S. (1997) *Political Thinking, Political Theory and Civil
Society*. Boston: Allyn and Bacon.

Diamond, L. (1994) 'Rethinking Civil Society. Toward
Democratic Consolidation', *Journal of Democracy*, 5(3): 4–17.

Edwards, R., Franklin, J. and Holland, J. (2003) *Families and
Social Capital: Exploring the Issues* (Working Paper).
London: ESRC Families and Social Capital Research Group.

Elshtain, J. (1981) *Public Man, Private Woman: Women in Social
and Political Thought*. Oxford: Martin Robertson.

Elson, D. (1995) 'Male Bias in Macro-Economics:
The Case of Structural Adjustment', in D. Elson (ed.),
Male Bias in the Development Process. Manchester:
Manchester University Press.
– (1998) 'The Economic, the Political and the Domestic:
Businesses, States and Households in the Organisation
of Production', *New Political Economy*, 3(2): 189–209.

Facio, A. (1997) 'A Word (or Two) about Gender',
The International Criminal Court Monitor, Issue 6: 5.

Fathers 4 Justice (URL) www.fathers-4-justice.org (consulted
14 June 2005).

Fraser, N. (1992) 'Rethinking the Public Sphere: A Contribution
to the Critique of Actually Existing Democracy', in C.
Calhoun (ed.), *Habermas and the Public Sphere*.
Cambridge, MA: MIT Press.
– (1997) *Justice Interruptus: Critical Reflections on the
'Post-Socialist' Condition*. New York: Routledge.

Ganesh, M. (2003) 'HIV, Sexuality and Identity in India',
InfoChange Analysis, October.
www.infochangeindia.org/analysis06.jsp
(consulted 10 June 2005).

Ganguly, M. (2000) 'In from the Outside', *TimeAsia*,
156(11), 18 September.
www.time.com/time/asia/magazine/2000/0918/india.eunuchs.html
(consulted 4 July 2005).

George, J. (2004) 'In search of an Identity', *Sunday Herald*, 16 May.
www.deccanherald.com/deccanherald/may162004/sh1.asp
(consulted 9 July 2005).

Glasius, M. (2004) 'Who is the Real Civil Society? Women's
Groups versus Pro-Family Groups at the International
Criminal Court Negotiations', in J. Howell and D. Mulligan
(eds), *Gender and Civil Society*. London: Routledge.
– (2005). *The International Criminal Court: A Global Civil Society
Achievement*. Oxford: Routledge.

Goulbourne, H. and Solomos, J. (2003) 'Families, Ethnicity and
Social Capital', *Social Policy and Society*, 2: 329–38.

The Green Man (2003) 'Flash Mob', 30 August.
http://thegreenman.net.au/mt/archives/2003_08.html
(consulted 28 June 2005).

The Hindu (2002) 'When Appearance Does Matter', 6 June.
www.hindu.com/thehindu/mp/2002/06/06/stories/
2002060600110100.htm (consulted 9 July 2005).

Habermas, J. (1989) *The Structural Transformation of the
Public Sphere*. Cambridge, MA: MIT Press.

Hawthorn, G. (2001) 'The Promise of "Civil Society" in the South',
in S. Kaviraj and S. Khilnani (eds), *Civil Society: History and
Possibilities*. Cambridge: Cambridge University Press

Hearn, J. (2001) 'Taking Liberties: Contesting Visions of the
Civil Society Project', *Critique of Anthropology*, 21(4): 339–60.

Howell, Jude (1998) 'Gender, Civil Society and the
State in China', in G. Waylen and V. Randall (eds),
Gender, Politics and the State. London: Routledge.
– and Mulligan, D. (2004) *Gender and Civil Society:
Transcending Boundaries*. London: Routledge.
– (2003) 'Editorial', *International Feminist Journal of Politics*,
5(2): 157–62.
– and Pearce, J. (2001) *Civil Society and Development:
A Critical Exploration*. Boulder, CO: Lynne Rienner.

Ishkanian, A. (2004) 'Working at the Global-Local Intersection:
The Challenges Facing Women in Armenia's NGO Sector',
in C. Nechemias and K. Kuehnast (eds), *Post-Soviet Women
Encountering Transition: Nation-Building, Economic Survival,
and Civic Activism*. Baltimore, MD/Washington, DC: Johns
Hopkins University Press/Woodrow Wilson Center Press.

Jacobson, R. and Pereirra, A. (2001) 'Briefing study for Oxfam
International on the relationship between gender violence
and Oxfam's development aims in Angola' (unpublished).
Oxford: Oxfam International.

Kabeer, N. (1994) *Reversed Realities: Gender Hierarchies in
Development Thought*. London and New York: Verso Books.

Kaldor, M. (2003) *Global Civil Society: An Answer to War*.
Cambridge: Polity Press.

Kaufman, M. (2001) 'The White Ribbon Campaign: Involving
Men and Boys in Ending Global Violence Against Women',
in B. Pease and K. Pringle (eds), *A Man's World: Changing
Men's Practices in a Globalized World*. London: Zed Books.

Keane, J. (1998), *Civil Society. Old Images, New Visions*. Cambridge: Polity Press.

Keck, M. and Sikkink, K. (1998) 'Transnational Networks on Violence against Women', in M. Keck and K. Sikkink (eds), *Activists beyond Borders; Advocacy Networks in International Politics*. Ithaca, NY: Cornell University Press.

Khan, S. (2001). 'Culture, Sexualities, and Identities: Men Who Have Sex With Men in India', *Journal of Homosexuality*, 40(3/4): 99–115.

Kimmel, M. S. (2001) 'Global Masculinities: Restoration and Resistance', in B. Pease and K. Pringle (eds), *A Man's World: Changing Men's Practices in a Globalized World*. London: Zed Books.

Kulczycki, A. (1999) *The Abortion Debate in the World Arena*. Basingstoke: Macmillan.

Landes, J. B. (1988) *Women and the Public Sphere in the Age of the French Revolution*. Ithaca, NY: Cornell University Press.

McClure, K. (1992) 'The Issue of Foundations: Scientized Politics, Politicized Science and Feminist Critical Practice', in J. Butler and J. W. Scott (eds), *Feminists Theorise the Political*. London: Routledge.

MacKinnon, C. (1989) *Towards a Feminist Theory of the State*. Cambridge, MA: Harvard University Press.

Mies, M. (1983) 'Towards a Methodology for Feminist Research' in G. Bowles and R. Duelli Klein (eds), *Theories of Women's Studies*. London: Routledge.

Molyneux, M. (2002) 'Gender and the Silences of Social Capital: Lessons from Latin America', *Development and Change*, 33(2): 167–89.

Nag, M. (1996) *Sexual Behaviour and AIDS in India*. New Delhi: Vikas Publishing House.

Nanda, S. (1990) *Neither Man nor Woman: The Hijras of India*. Wadsworth, Belmont CA.

Narrain, S. (2003) 'Being a Eunuch', *Countercurrents.org*, 14 October. www.countercurrents.org/gen-narrain141003.htm (consulted 11 July 2005).

Obando, Ana Elena (2005). 'Sexism in the World Social Forum: Is Another World Possible?'. WHRnet Issue www.whrnet.org/docs/issue-sexism_wsf.html (Consulted 18 July 2005)

Okin, S. M. (1979) *Women in Western Political Thought*. Princeton, NJ: Princeton University Press.

Oosterveld, V. (1999) 'The Making of a Gender-Sensitive International Criminal Court', *International Law FORUM du droit international*, 1(1): 38–41.

Ottaway, M. and Carothers, T. (eds) (2000) *Funding Virtue: Civil Society Aid and Democracy Promotion*. Washington, DC: Carnegie Endowment for International Peace.

Pateman, C. (1988a) *The Sexual Contract*. Cambridge: Polity Press.

– (1988b) 'The Fraternal Social Contract', in J. Keane (ed.), *Civil Society and the State: New European Perspectives*. London: Verso.

– (1989) *The Disorder of Women: Democracy, Feminism and Political Theory*. Cambridge: Polity Press.

Perrons, D. (2002) 'Gendered Divisions in the New Economy: Risks and Opportunities', *Geojournal*, 56: 271–80.

– (2003) 'The New Economy, Labour Market Inequalities and the Work Life Balance', in R. Martin and P. Morrison (eds), *Geographies of Labour Market Inequality*. London: Routledge.

Phillips, A. (1991) *Engendering Democracy*. Cambridge: Polity Press.

– (ed.) (1998) *Feminism and Politics*. Oxford: Oxford University Press.

– (2002) 'Does Feminism Need a Conception of Civil Society?', in S. Chambers and W. Kymlicka (eds), *Alternative Conceptions of Civil Society*. Princeton, NJ: Princeton University Press.

PUCL-K (People's Union for Civil Liberties) (2003) *Human Rights Violations against the Transgender Community: A Study of Kothi and Hijra Sex Workers in Bangalore, India*. PUCL-K. http://ai.eecs.umich.edu/people/conway/TS/PUCL/ PUCL%20Report.pdf (consulted 7 July 2005).

Rabo, A. (1996) 'Gender, State and Civil Society in Jordan and Syria', in C. Hann and E. Dunn (eds), *Civil Society: Challenging Western Models*. London: Routledge.

REAL Women of Canada (URL) www.realwomenca.com (consulted 4 July 2005).

– (1998) 'Canada Courts Disaster With World Court', *REALity Newsletter*, 17 (10).

Rowan, John (URL) www.johnrowan.org.uk (consulted 14 June 2005).

Russell, G. (2001) 'Adopting a Global Perspective on Fatherhood', in B. Pease and K. Pringle (eds), A Man's World: *Changing Men's Practices in a Globalized World*. London: Zed Books.

Ruxton, S. (ed.) (2004) *Gender Equality and Men: Learning from Practice*. Oxford: Oxfam.

Ryan, M. (1998) 'Gender and Public Access: Women's Politics in Nineteenth-Century America', in J. B. Landes (ed.), *Feminism, the Public and the Private*. Oxford: Oxford University Press.

Sangama (URL) www.sangamaonline.org/aboutsangama.htm (consulted 7 July 2005).

Seidler, V. (ed.) (1991) *Achilles Heel Reader: Men, Sexual Politics and Socialism*. London: Routledge.

Squires, J. (1999) *Gender in Political Theory*. Cambridge: Polity Press.

Steains, C. (1999). 'Gender Issues', in Roy S. Lee (ed.), *The International Criminal Court: The Making of the Rome Statute; Issues, Negotiations, Results*. The Hague: Kluwer Law International.

Stevenson, L. (2004) 'The Impact of Feminist Civil Society and Political Alliances on Gender Policies in Mexico' chapter 8: 163-195 in Howell, Jude and Mulligan, Diane, (2004) *Gender and Civil Society. Transcending Boundaries*. Abingdon and New York: Routledge.

The Telegraph (2005) 'M,F, E or More?', 12 March. www.telegraphindia.com/1050312/asp/opinion/story_4481301.asp (consulted 28 June 2005).

Van Rooy, A. (ed.) (1998) *Civil Society and the Aid Industry*. London: Earthscan.

Wadham, B. (2001) 'Global Men's Health and the Crisis of Western Masculinity', in B. Pease and K. Pringle (eds), *A Man's World: Changing Men's Practices in a Globalized World*. London: Zed Books.

Waterman, P. (2003) 'Review Essay. Women, Workers, the World Social Forum and the World Wide Web in the Civilizing of Global Society', *International Feminist Journal of Politics*, 5: 301–9.

White, G. (1994) 'Civil Society, Democratisation and Development (I): Clearing the Analytical Ground', *Democratisation*, 1: 375–90.

White Ribbon Campaign (URL) www.whiteribbon.ca (consulted 14 June 2005).

Wikipedia (2005) 'Hijra (India)'. http://en.wikipedia.org/wiki/Hijra_(India) (consulted 28 June 2005).

World Bank (2001) *Engendering Development Through Gender Equality in Rights, Resources, and Voice*. Washington, DC: World Bank.

CHAPTER 2

THE WORLD SOCIAL FORUM:
WHERE DO WE STAND AND WHERE ARE WE GOING?

This chapter seeks to portray different perspectives on the nature, evolution and future of the World Social Forum. We invited contributions from three people who have played a significant role in the origins and development of the World Social Forum. Their contributions are timely: the Porto Alegre Manifesto, a platform of proposals launched at the 5th World Social Forum in Porto Alegre in 2005, sparked a debate that we would like to continue in the Global Civil Society Yearbook. Key issues include the appropriateness of such a manifesto and its implications for the nature of the World Social Forum, including, for example, the discussion about whether it is a space for debate or a campaigning movement.

The manifesto was signed by 19 people, among them Bernard Cassen and Boaventura de Sousa Santos. Chico Whitaker did not sign the manifesto. Unlike Chapter 6, which analyses the social forum phenomenon from an empirical perspective, this chapter offers personal reflections.

Chico Whitaker is a member of the Brazilian Justice and Peace Commission (of the Catholic Bishops' Conference) and of the International Council of the World Social Forum. He is author of *The World Social Forum Challenge* (Zed Books, forthcoming).

Boaventura de Sousa Santos is professor of Sociology at the School of Economics, Coimbra University, and distinguished legal scholar at the Law School, University of Wisconsin-Madison. He is author of many books including *Democratizing Democracy* (Verso 2005) and *The World Social Forum: A User's Manual* (Zed Books, forthcoming).

Bernard Cassen is a member of the International Council of the World Social Forum, journalist and director general of *Le Monde Diplomatique* and honorary president of ATTAC* France. He is author of many books including *Tout a commencé à Porto Alegre* (Editions 1001 Nuits 2003).

*Originally, the Association for the Taxation of Financial Transactions for the Aid of Citizens.

Chico Whitaker

Introduction

Where does the World Social Forum (WSF URL) process stand today? After the success of the 2005 event, which drew 150,000 participants to Porto Alegre, many of those engaged in organising forums are worried. Where is this process heading? What is the WSF actually intended to achieve? How effective is it in promoting the necessary political changes? Is it running out of steam? Is it not at risk of causing a great deal of frustration – with all the accompanying ill effects – by announcing that 'Another World Is Possible' and thus raising expectations that are difficult to meet given the resurgence of wars and terrorism and the increasingly visible likelihood of irreversible ecological disasters?

Indeed, it is becoming increasingly necessary and urgent to analyse the Forum itself in greater depth. For that very reason, at its meeting in Utrecht, the Netherlands, in late March 2005, the WSF International Council decided to set aside a day and a half at its June 2005 meeting in Barcelona to consider all that was happening in the world today, to assess the ground gained or lost towards the 'other possible world' and to examine in depth the Forum's role in that overall context.

Some thoughts on the World Social Forum itself

A collective effort to think about the role and the nature of the Forum began in October 2002, when an email discussion list titled 'WSFitself' was formed. This was proposed by Brazilian and French participants who, after the success of the second Forum, foresaw the likelihood of growth and felt the need to clarify the meaning of the whole endeavour. At the 2003 Forum, that discussion list gave rise to a workshop on proposed innovations in the form and principles underlying its organisation. In 2004, at the Mumbai WSF, two significant events took place: a seminar on the subject 'Forum: open space?' and a plenary on the future of the WSF. Mumbai also saw the release of an anthology of essays on the World Social Forum as a challenge to the Empires (Sen et al 2004). Also in 2005, a number of activities addressed this issue from various perspectives and at least two books discussing the Forum were published (Santos 2004; Whitaker 2005).

However, underlying thinking and discussions about the nature of the Forum and its position in the array of forces present in the world today there linger thought-provoking questions stemming from an assertion that shapes way the Forums are organised: in order for the struggle against triumphalist turn-of-the-century neo-liberalism to be effective, it must go beyond the paradigms of political action that prevailed throughout the twentieth century. That really is a bold assertion. Is such a paradigm change really necessary? If so, is the present method of organising the Forums the best way to bring about that change?

Horizontal networked organisation

The method adopted to date is indeed designed to permit both Forum organisers and participants to experiment practically with a new way of organising and acting politically. From the outset, the organisers of Forums have referred to themselves as 'facilitators', never as 'coordinators', far less as 'leaders'. Such vocabulary is extremely important because it reflects the pursuit of a new political culture marked by horizontal relations among actors, in place of the vertical ones that have predominated to date both in capitalist authoritarianism and Western bureaucratic culture and in the actions of their left-wing adversaries.

The argument is that such horizontal relations, with actors organised into networks, are actually much more efficient than vertical and pyramidal relations, as they make it possible to build a collective power, sharing responsibility and therefore becoming stronger. Networks function on the logic that action is taken not because someone issues an order or directive but because people believe it is necessary and take it upon themselves as active subjects. In any case, in pyramidal organisations directives do not always filter down, and managers do not always know what is happening among

The author is grateful to Peter Lenny for his translation of this chapter.

those they manage, which tends to set up a barrier between them. In addition, as power is concentrated at different levels within the pyramid, struggles emerge for control of that power which, instead of uniting those involved, divide and so weaken them.

In fact, experimentation of this kind – which is essentially participatory in nature – is not new. It reinstates the teachings of a tradition of social struggle worldwide against authoritarianism of various kinds, starting with the mobilisations of 1968. In the decades that followed, networks were proposed and consolidated as a different organisational structure in many political undertakings that innovated ways of waging political struggles. For instance, some invented a collegiate structure of direction. The landmark event in this process took place at the end of the twentieth century during the 1999 World Trade Organization (WTO) conference in Seattle – and thus well before the first World Social Forum. These protests were of such proportions and so effective in blocking the anti-democratic measures planned for the occasion by the WTO that they surprised even those who – in their enormous diversity of immediate aims – had thrown themselves into the effort.

The Forum's Charter of Principles

Immediately following the success of the first Forum, its organisers drafted a Charter of Principles (WSF 2001; see also Box 6.1), explicitly adopting horizontal relationships. Believing that these relationships were the key to the success of the first Forum, the organisers wanted to ensure that such experimentation would continue and be extended to other events held at the world or the regional level. The charter embodies a set of guidelines completely at variance with current political practices, such as not drawing up final documents at the forums, guaranteeing that participants would be completely at liberty to organise their own activities at these events[1], pledging that the organisers would not direct such activities or any collaboration among them, and not designating spokespeople or representatives of the Forum.

The basic conception of the Forum, as expressed in the charter, is that it is an open space designed to facilitate an interchange of concrete experiences and an ongoing process of increasing links among participants. With this in mind, the organisers included in the charter certain rules – here they really are rules and not the usual empty rhetoric – such as respect for diversity and the pledge to seek effective democracy in

both the preparation and the functioning of the events, with the intention of surmounting the barriers and prejudices that today divide the various types of organisations and sectors that believe that 'Another World Is Possible'. Respecting diversity is in fact a core principle of the WSF, and not only in relation to the organisation of events. It is grounded in the conviction that it is one of the fundamental characteristics of the other world – or, as we say, of the 'other possible worlds' – that we intend to build.

Then, after the third World Social Forum, the charter leveraged another strikingly effective episode in worldwide mobilisation, based on the same logic of networked organisation that had proved so successful at Seattle. On 15 February 2003, protests brought 15 million people onto the streets, in a great number of countries, to demonstrate for peace and against the invasion of Iraq. The proposal to hold these demonstrations was presented and discussed during the Forums in November 2002 (in Florence, the first European Social Forum) and January 2003 (the WSF in Porto Alegre). Under its Charter of Principles, however, the Forum is not an organisation but a 'space'; it has no leaders and cannot call for demonstrations from the top down. The 15 February protests were thus convened by the multiple networks that participated in the Forum or that then started working together, drawing freely – as had happened at Seattle – on an extremely powerful tool for horizontal communication, namely, the internet. The calls that went out for the 2003 demonstrations far exceeded whatever ability the Forum itself may have had to mobilise for action. However, it probably was decisive to the process that the Forum made an open meeting space available, under the terms of its charter, for proposals to be presented and discussed, and for the planning and coordination necessary to carry them out.

Nevertheless, and notwithstanding the success of these demonstrations, some would have preferred to mobilise through a call from the Forum as a way of introducing and reinforcing the forums as a new political actor, with its own initiatives. This points to an important, and perhaps the main, question about the nature of the Forum that is continuously debated: is it a space

---

1 *This principle, combined with the priority that came to be given to the activities planned by participants, meant that, from one Forum to the next, such activities grew in number, while the number of activities planned by the organisers decreased. Indeed, in 2005, the Forum was completely self-managed.*

or a movement? How we answer this question will determine the organisation and process of the forums, as well as their future. I have discussed previously, in an article that appears in several publications[2], why the 'space' conception is preferable to that of a movement, and how some were trying to imbue the Forum with the characteristics of a movement.

How does a space differ from a movement?[3]

A movement and a space are completely different things. Without Manichaeistic simplifications, we can't be both things. One doesn't exclude the other, which means they can coexist. They are also not opposites, which means that they do not neutralise each other, and can even be additive. But you can't be both things at the same time, not even be a part of each – this would cause prejudice to one and to the other. A movement and a space can have the same general objectives, but each does so in its own way, aiming for specific objectives.

A movement assembles people. Its militants, like the militants of a party, decide to organise themselves to accomplish certain aims collectively. Its formation and existence require that, to attain these objectives, strategies must be defined, action programmes formulated and responsibilities distributed among the movement's members, including that concerning the direction of the movement. Whoever assumes this function will lead the militants of the movement, getting each of them – with authoritarian or democratic methods, according to the choice made by the founders – to perform a part of the collective action. A movement's structure is necessarily pyramidal, even when the internal processes for reaching decisions and choosing decision makers at the different levels are very democratic. But its effectiveness depends on how explicit and precise its specific objectives are, and thus on how delimited they are in time and place.

A space, by contrast, has no leaders. It is just a place, basically horizontal, like the earth's surface, although undulating. Like a square, it has no owner – if the square has an owner other than those who use it, it becomes a private territory. Squares are generally open spaces that can be visited by all those with any kind of interest in using them. They have no other function than the function of squares, offering a specific kind of service to those who frequent them. The longer they last as squares, the better for those who make use of them to achieve their respective aims.

Even when a square contains trees and small hills, it is a socially horizontal space. Whoever climbs the trees or the hills cannot aspire, from high up, to command, either entirely or partially, those who are in the square. The least that can happen to climbers is to be considered ridiculous by the others in the square. If they become too insistent and troublesome, speaking for nobody, the visitors leave the square – or even come back with 'public authorities' empowered to stop them, and return peace and tranquillity to the public square.

Like a square, the Forum is an open space, as specified in the Charter of Principles. But unlike a public square it is not a neutral space. The Forum opens up from time to time in different parts of the world with one key objective: to allow as many people, organisations and movements as possible that oppose neo-liberalism to get together freely, to listen to each other, to learn from the experiences and struggles of others, to discuss proposals for action and to become linked to new networks and organisations that aim to challenge the present process of globalisation dominated by large international corporations and financial interests. Thus, it is a space created to serve the common aim of all those who converge on the Forum, and it functions horizontally like a public square, without leaders or pyramids of power. All those who come to the Forum accept this, and participants are therefore required to agree to abide by the Charter of Principles.

In fact, the Forum works as an 'ideas factory' or an incubator, whereby it is hoped that many new initiatives will emerge for constructing another world, one that we all consider possible, necessary and urgent. It is thus to be expected that a plethora of movements will emerge – large or small, combative or quiescent – each with its own aims and strategies in the same struggle, the struggle the square stands for. Another advantage of the 'Forum-space', or a 'square with no owner', is that it creates a feeling of mutual responsibility more readily than a movement.

2 See n 3.
3 The paragraphs of this section are taken from Whitaker (2004). This article (originally published in 2003 under the title 'Notes for the Debate on the World Social Forum') is available in three languages on the Forum website (www.forumsocialmundial.org.br). It has been published in French on the ATTAC movement website (www.france.attac.org), in Spanish by Revista de Fomento Social (Cordoba, Spain), in English in Sen et al (2004), and in German. It should also soon be published in Italian by the organisation Transform.

The slow pace of cultural change

This conception of the Forum as a space, not a movement, is based on the assumption that it is not the Forum that can change the world but the social movements and organisations engaged in that struggle.

But the new avenues the Forum is designed to open up to become effective in the struggle to surpass neo-liberalism raise two related problems. First, paradigm change, like all cultural change, is necessarily slow, especially in view of the fact that throughout the twentieth century, the Left was shaped and trained according to paradigms deriving from the need for vanguards to conduct the struggle – exactly what is being called into question at the Forum. Second, new paradigms require that countless practices, concepts and values be revised, along with the very concepts of democracy and representation. To complicate things still further, they also entail changes within ourselves, in our personal behaviour and attitudes. It may thus be a long time before the effects of this whole process can be seen in terms of concrete political results.

That difficulty is compounded by our anguish about the intensity and speed with which the world situation is deteriorating, which demands urgent action. Not to mention that with every passing day, more and more people die for lack of food, medicines or basic sanitation, while the incessant quest for profit at any price continues to dominate economic activities in countries rich and poor. The dialectic of action and reaction set up by the present government of the United States in its war on terrorism is, in turn, driving insecurity worldwide. To make the situation even more serious, the same government – as if its threatened 'preventive wars' were not enough – is ringing China with military bases, signalling in that way the new enemy it intends to confront to maintain US hegemony. In addition, accepted and completely feasible measures to address the ecological risks facing humankind are being adopted at an extremely slow rate, and social irresponsibility on the part of business and government continues to prevail over efforts to control the harmful environmental effects of many systems of economic production and activity. In short, the prospects we face are little short of terrifying.

How then can the gradual, bottom-up reconstruction of paradigms of political action be effective? Why reject the action of mainstream powerful political forces or even charismatic leaders that could lead humankind towards other horizons?

This debate heightens existing tensions among the Forum's participants and organisers. Shaped as we have been by theories and practices based on vertical conceptions of the exercise of power, of militant disciplines, of politics as the struggle for hegemony, we do not always manage to divest ourselves of them – 'to learn to unlearn' (Whitaker 2005) – or to go on to adopt the proposals for horizontal, non-directive freedom that is the shared experience of the Forum. Realising the Forum's power to mobilise, many are unable to resist the temptation to turn it as quickly as possible into an extremely powerful new instrument, a kind of 'movement of movements', finally capable of confronting and overthrowing the capitalist monster – and not without entertaining the idea of putting themselves forward to lead it.

But, as I have indicated before, if the Forum does become a 'movement of movements', none of these movements would be in a position to open up this space and marshal all the others to accept its invitation without conditions. Meeting with others would be restricted by the need to build another structure to unify – with all the rules necessary to make that possible – within which competition would again arise, and with it division, as a result of the fight to win space, to set directions, and to define the objectives of the new movement.

The saviours

One very concrete example of the temptation to turn the WSF into a movement was an initiative launched at the 2005 Forum by a group of personalities, among them two Nobel laureates. As intellectuals enjoying worldwide recognition, they publicised a manifesto in which they presented 12 themes of the struggle that, in their opinion, all the Forum's participants could agree on: the 'Porto Alegre Consensus', in contrast to the 'Washington Consensus' (see Box 2.1). In practice, it amounted to a new 'right thinking', mimicking the 'one truth' of those who command imperial domination. They successfully invited much of the international press present at Porto Alegre to the launch of the manifesto, which was, however, presented with the proviso that it was not a 'final document' of the Forum: otherwise it would have run counter to the Charter of Principles. Nonetheless, the intention to draw up a conclusive, consensual synthesis, the stature of its signatories and the solemnity with which it was presented necessarily left a certain ambiguity in the air.

Of course, the manifesto did not have the effect that its sponsors may have desired. It did not become a single banner hoisted collectively by the Forum's 150,000 participants. Very few of them – besides the journalists – attended the launch, which was held outside the Forum territory, in the press room of the most important hotel in town. Most participants found out about the manifesto the following day in the newspapers. As they had not been even remotely consulted on the content of the 12 items, there was no lack of criticism of their incompleteness and of the formulation and presentation of the manifesto as a top-down initiative, calling into question the very nature of the WSF.

When questioned by journalists about the nature of this initiative, the Forum's organisers had no choice but to point out that it was simply one of the 353 proposals for action presented at the Forum. They took the opportunity to emphasise that the Forum's Charter of Principles ruled out any 'final' document, which would necessarily be so reductionist and impoverished as to end up winning active support from no one; rather, instead of any single such document, hundreds or thousands of final documents should emerge, one from each activity carried out at the Forum, and each of them fully supported by those who signed it.

Actually, using the freedom of initiative that is assured to all its participants, the manifesto continued, within the Forum itself, the tradition of the great leaders that mobilise the masses. The initiative, or the 'manifesto', like other attempts to marshal the strength of the Forum for specific ends[4], reveals the challenges we have to overcome to change current political behaviour – the Forum being, in fact, a school of new practices.

Participation by political parties

Another area where the provisions of the Charter of Principles are being frequently called into question relates to political parties: the charter prohibits them from engaging in activities at the Forums in the way that other civil society movements and organisations do, and from participating in organising the Forums. A similar prohibition on governments and 'military' organisations is more easily accepted, since the Forum defines itself as a civil society space, independent of governments, and its participants completely reject violence as a method of political action. The prohibition on political parties, which have traditionally been considered the only route to participation in political

action, is questioned repeatedly. The purpose of this prohibition was to prevent the Forum being penetrated by inter-party strife, which derives from the goal, proper to political parties, of gaining political power. It was believed that parties would all, quite naturally, compete to 'control' the Forums as a new tool for mobilising support, and seek to make them political party instruments.

The hope is that no one will seek to turn the Forum space into an instrument for political party aims

---

Of course, people who are members of political parties have every right to take part in the Forums, individually or through whatever other organisations they may belong to. It would not be practical to identify and prevent members of political parties from participating; indeed, many of the Forum's organisers are affiliated to political parties. The hope is that no one will seek to turn the Forum space into an instrument for party political aims. As for the parties themselves, it is hoped they will take the opportunity – while resisting the temptation to win converts – to listen to what is proposed at the Forums. Later, at their own meetings, they will be able to discuss the ideas garnered in this way, decide whether or not to incorporate them into their own programmes and even associate with or collaborate in activities in the struggle proposed by Forum participants. Without a doubt, this would help them perform their own role – which is different from that of civil society as such – and at the same time rebuild their links with the grass roots.

The grass roots are indeed becoming more remote from political parties, and at the Forums they find a place to engage in political activities that are broader than purely party politics. In fact, it is much more in parties' interest to maintain the Forum as it is, with its independence from governments and parties, instead of absorbing it into their own natural contradictions, thus finally destroying it.

---

4 *The presence of President Lula of Brazil and President Chavez of Venezuela at the 2005 Forum could be seen as one of these attempts, taking the form of reciprocal manipulation: of the presidents by the organisations, which by their own initiative arranged for them to be present, and of those organisations by the presidents, who took advantage of the opportunity for visibility that the Forum offered them. It remains to be seen whether the Forum gained or lost from those initiatives.*

A more flexible Charter of Principles?

Another question that arises repeatedly among the Forum's organisers and participants is this: should the Forum's initiators and the supporters of the Forum-space concept adopt such an unyielding stance and not permit any move towards a more flexible Charter of Principles? The answer is not easy, given the logic and coherence of the principles. Where should there be greater flexibility?

In practice, some of the groups that organise the Forums do treat the charter more flexibly, without much concern for the consequences. Only the world forums held so far have strictly abided by the Charter of Principles; the same cannot be said of all the regional, national or local forums. There are cases, for example, of forums that have ended with final documents, been presented as organisations, and had spokespeople or coordinators. Others are not really 'open spaces' but rather events taken over by particular political forces. Others are organised from the top down only, as if they were seminars. One of the most flagrant cases of breach of the charter had to do precisely with party and government participation. According to the reports of participants, the Socialist Workers' Party and Ken Livingstone, Mayor of London, played central roles in the organisation of the European Social Forum held in London in October 2004.

Denouncing such breaches does not always persuade the perpetrators to change their behaviour because they may not fully understand the rationale behind the Charter of Principles. For that very reason, there must be wide-ranging and in-depth discussion about the nature of the Forum so that it does not self-destruct – that was the thinking behind the workshop held at the 2003 Forum, inspired by the WSF discussion list itself.

In order to understand the logic of the Charter of Principles, it is useful to situate the Forum in recent history. Its characteristics and principles are rooted in the moment when it came into being. This was marked by a build-up of frustrations and disappointments with the kind of political action hitherto undertaken until then to confront an economic and political system that had brought humankind to the difficulties it faces today. For those who initiated the Forum and those who joined them at that time, there was nothing to suggest that good results would come from continuing with the old methods, practices and strategies of the century that had just ended. Why then continue down that path?

The Forum proposed trying new avenues, which today are proving more worthwhile. One of the initial motivations was precisely that the former type of mobilisation, limited to protests pure and simple, which had multiplied after Seattle, had reached a stalemate and participants were already showing signs of exhaustion. When the Forum was proposed as a counterpoint to the thinking of Davos, it was insisted that it should table proposals of its own. It had to combine mobilisation with proposals and proposals with mobilisation.

For that very reason, two types of concern arose as the process developed, and the methodology employed in organising the Forums made every effort to deal with them: the need to encourage the formulation of more new initiatives to effect change in the world and the need to get the participating organisations to collaborate at the global level, before, during and after the Forums, in order to strengthen their actions. It was for this reason that a Mural of Proposals for Action was created during the 2005 Forum. It was to be the centrepiece of the final closing event, where all the participants would come together in all their diversity of actions and strategies and their overall unity of final aims. Because of organisational shortcomings, this did not happen. However, the mural remained as the product of debates and collaborations that had occurred during the Forum, and its 353 proposals were posted on the Forum's website, available to both participants and non-participants, forming the basis for further collaboration.

The 'Map of Action Towards Building a New World'

Building on the mural, which was designed to make everyone's proposals visible and to facilitate meshing and collaboration among them with a view to their implementation, a further proposal to serve the Forum as a whole was presented in the Utrecht meeting of the International Council. This was to draw up a 'Map of Action Towards Building a New World'.

The purpose of this map was to provide participating organisations with a special programme on the internet, a kind of permanent Mural of Proposals, where initiatives and information on action in progress could be added continually. Using this programme, interested parties could organise groups to discuss or act on the subjects and proposals that concerned them; they could contact other groups and invite them to consider issues or proposals in greater depth, to hold encounters and meetings, and to organise demonstrations or other kinds of concrete action.

The system would function independently of the Forum events, but would be interconnected with them because the Forums would figure as special opportunities for in-person encounters and for furthering understanding and action, and thus would foster quality leaps in the effectiveness of any action proposed. Set free of the events themselves, the World Social Forum process would advance much more quickly in building an ever larger number of local, national, regional and world networks, thus empowering global civil society to achieve concrete objectives in changing the world.

...new types of relationship, which are more cooperative than competitive, are being constructed

---

Such an instrument could also work to the benefit of the approach adopted in the WSF International Council's decision to make polycentric the 2006 World Social Forum. Some events will parallel Davos, and others will follow in various regions of the world, all resting on the same participatory approach, characteristic of the process as a whole. The challenge now is to ensure coordination and articulation among them all, so that the whole is not fragmented but rather advances with increasing unity towards the World Social Forum to be held in Africa in 2007.

'Old world' versus 'new world'

Among the various ways of seeing the Forum, supporters of the 'open space' proposal see the tensions indicated above as a confrontation between what they call 'old world' and 'new world' practices. In fact, these tensions are present throughout the meetings, proposals and decisions about the organisational arrangements of the Forum process, from the local to the world level, however much their members declare and believe they are building a 'new world'. Nonetheless, it can be said with optimism that new types of relationship, which are more cooperative than competitive, are being constructed among the individuals and organisations in the Forum's various set-ups; and now, as we head towards the polycentric Forum of 2006, these advances are visible. The conception of the Forum as a movement reappears regularly in proposals and practices, but without doubt, it is the Forum as an open space, along with the other provisions of the charter, that is asserting

itself increasingly.

This is shown by the remarks of some North American participants drafted after the 2005 Forum (Foltz, Moodiliar and Pramas 2005):

The Social Forum should not be seen as the answer to the challenges of our time; it should be seen as a valuable part of the answer(s) with a very distinctive contribution. Other sites for action, for campaigning, for taking decisions are necessary for the global progressive movement; the Social Forum is an important space for incubating these; those who want action (the authors included) should get on with it and organize those actions, making as best use of the Forum as possible!

Whether or not the Forum will continue as a process in the way it has been to date depends on the orientation adopted by its organisers. In fact, we face a dual challenge. The first is not necessarily easy: to ensure that, in the events that are held and the new instruments that are created, the Forum is not swallowed up by the errors of the past that led to its emergence, and that it can continue its endeavours towards the new world that is to be built. The second is as difficult as it is urgent: to expand and entrench this process all over the planet, as quickly as possible. This expansion does not seek to assert the positions of one or another political force, but is designed to make more and more people and organisations join in the hope that the Forum holds out, and participate in the change-making initiatives that are being proposed.

The intention is that increasing numbers of citizens around the world exercise actively and in solidarity – through networks – the enormous power at their disposal as workers and as consumers, and thus contribute to changing the world. At the same time, the expectation is that, as voters, they will elect and increasingly monitor governments to ensure that they defend and promote the interests of people and not capital, in a real commitment to peace, development and social justice.

In confronting the hegemony of top-down political action dependent on enlightened leaders, the Forum can play a decisive role in preventing the defeat of humanisation in the world. If it retreats within the borders of the 'old world', it will certainly disappear. In that case, we will be left watching the dream fade. The right moment will not yet have arrived to change paradigms.

Boaventura de Sousa Santos

Introduction

In order to understand the debates that take place within the World Social Forum (WSF), it is necessary to analyse the ways in which, at the beginning of the twenty-first century, utopian thinking interacts with political activism. In my conception, 'utopia' means exploring new modes of human possibility and styles of will, and using the imagination to confront the apparent inevitability of whatever exists with something radically better that is worth fighting for, and to which humankind is fully entitled (see Santos 1995: 479). The conceptions of and aspirations to a better life and society, ever present in human history, vary in their form and content over time and space. They express the tendencies and latencies of a given epoch and a given society. They constitute an anticipatory consciousness that manifests itself by enlarging the signs or traces of emerging realities.

The hegemonic conception of our age is that of linear time (the idea of progress) that presents itself as a post-linear time–space (the idea of globalisation). Whatever is currently dominant in social and political terms is infinitely expansive, thereby encompassing all future possibilities. The total control over the current state of affairs is deemed to be possible by means of extremely efficient powers and knowledges. Herein lies the radical denial of alternatives to present-day reality. This is the context underlying the utopian dimension of the WSF, which consists of asserting the existence of alternatives to neoliberal globalisation. The specificity of this utopian content, when compared with that of other utopias prevailing at the end of the nineteenth century and beginning of the twentieth century, thus becomes clear: rather than choosing from different alternatives, as happened in the past, it simply claims the possibility of alternatives, that is, the possibility of counter-hegemonic forms of globalisation. Hence the open nature, vague if you will, of the utopian dimension of the WSF. In a context of radical denial of alternatives, it is more important to affirm the possibility of alternatives than to define them. In other words, the utopia of the WSF asserts itself more as a negative (the

definition of what it critiques) than as a positive (the definition of that to which it aspires).

The specificity of the utopian dimension of the WSF has one more explanation. It aims to break with the tradition of the utopias of Western modernity, many of which turned into radical denials of alternatives: beginning by asserting utopian alternatives, they ended up denying alternatives under the excuse that the realisation of utopia was under way. The openness of the utopian dimension of the WSF corresponds to the latter's attempt to escape this perversion. For the WSF, both the form of the affirmation of alternatives and the content of the alternatives are plural. The affirmation of alternatives goes hand in hand with the affirmation that there are alternatives to the alternatives. The other possible world is a utopian aspiration that comprises several possible worlds. The other possible world may be many things, but never a world with no alternative.

The utopia of the WSF is a radically democratic utopia. This utopian design – grounded on the denial of the present rather than the definition of the future focused on the processes of intercourse among the movements rather than providing an assessment of the movements' political content – is the major cohesive force of the WSF. It helps to maximise what unites and to minimise what divides, to celebrate intercourse rather than to dispute power, to be a strong presence rather than an agenda. This utopian design, which is also an ethical design, privileges the ethical discourse, quite evident in the WSF's Charter of Principles, aimed at gathering consensus beyond the ideological and political cleavages among the movements and organisations that compose it. The movements and organisations bracket the cleavages that divide them as much as is necessary to affirm the possibility of a counter-hegemonic globalisation.

The nature of this utopia has been the most adequate for the initial objective of the WSF: to affirm the existence of a counter-hegemonic globalisation. Far from being vague, it is as concrete as it is adequate for this phase of the construction of a counter-hegemonic globalisation. It remains to be seen whether the nature of this utopia is the most adequate one to guide the next steps. Once counter-hegemonic globalisation is consolidated, and hence the idea that another world is possible is made credible, will it be possible to fulfil this idea with the same level of radical democracy that helped formulate it?

To answer this question, the articulation between the WSF's utopian dimension and the political activism it has been giving rise to must be brought into the picture.

Utopia meets politics

The newness of the WSF's utopian dimension in Left thinking in Western capitalist modernity can only be problematic as it translates into strategic planning and political action. These are marked by the historical trajectory of the political Left throughout the twentieth century. The translation of utopia into politics is not, in this case, merely the translation of the long range into the medium and short range. It is also the translation of the new into the old. This means that divergences about concrete political options are often mixed up with divergences about the codes and languages of political options.

It should be stressed, however, that the novelty of the utopia has managed so far to overcome the emergence of severe political divergences. At this juncture, it is adequate to distinguish between high-intensity cleavages and low-intensity cleavages. The former are the cleavages where radical discursive differences translate into some form of factionalism, be it collective splits and abandonment of the political organisation or organised tendencies inside the organisation; the latter, by contrast, are those in which the discursive differences, no matter how radical, do not preclude continued participation in the organisation. So far, the divergences or cleavages within the WSF have been of the low-intensity kind. Contrary to what happened in the thinking and practice of the Left in Western capitalist modernity throughout the twentieth century, the WSF managed to create a style and an atmosphere of inclusion of and respect for divergences that made it very difficult for the different political factions to exclude themselves from the start with the excuse that they were being excluded. The WSF's 'minimalist' programme, stated in its Charter of Principles, contributed decisively to this effect: emphatic assertion of respect for diversity; access denied only to movements or groups that advocate political violence; no voting or deliberations at the Forum as such; no representative entity to speak for the Forum. It is almost

like a tabula rasa where all forms of struggle against neoliberalism and for a more just society may have their place. Confronted with such openness, those who choose to exclude themselves find it difficult to define what exactly they are excluding themselves from.

All this has contributed to making the WSF's power of attraction greater than its capacity to repel. Even the movements that are most severely critical of the WSF, such as the anarchists or the revolutionary Left political parties, have not been absent. There is definitely something new in the air, something that is chaotic, messy, ambiguous, and indefinite enough to deserve the benefit of the doubt. For all these reasons, the desire to highlight what the movements and organisations have in common has prevailed over the desire to underscore what separates them. The manifestation of tensions or cleavages has been relatively tenuous and, above all, has not resulted in mutual exclusions. It remains to be seen for how long this will to convergence and this chaotic sharing of differences will last.

...is it possible to link up the different peoples of the WSF as an embryonic form of a counter-hegemonic civil society?

This does not mean that there are no strong disagreements. There are, and they have become louder and louder in recent years. This raises several issues. First of all, is it possible to link up the different peoples of the WSF as an embryonic form of a counter-hegemonic civil society? Second, how to transform the areas of widely shared consensuses into calls for collective action? Third, how better to explore the implications of both the agreements and the disagreements? For instance, should disagreements be the object of specific discussions in the WSF? Fourth, how to conceive of the relationship between participants and organisers (the International Council, (IC), and the International Secretariat, (IS)? Fifth, how to articulate such diversity with the common core upon which the WSF builds its identity and eventually develops its capacity to act?

These questions lurk behind most formulations of most cleavages manifested inside the WSF. Elsewhere, I have identified the following main strategic cleavages: reform or revolution; socialism or social emancipation; the state as enemy or as ally (potentially, at least); priority to be given to national or to global struggles;

direct action or institutional action or relations between them; priority to be given to the principle of equality or to the principle of respect for difference; the WSF as a space or as a movement (Santos 2004). In this contribution, I will focus on the last of these. But before doing so, I would like to stress that, except for the last one in the above list, the cleavages are not specific to the WSF. They in fact belong to the historical legacy of the social forces that for the past 200 years have struggled against the status quo for a better society. The specificity of the WSF resides in the fact that the different cleavages are important in different ways for the different movements and organisations, and none of them is present in the practices or discourses of all the movements and organisations. When cleavages are acknowledged, the different movements and organisations distribute themselves among them in a non-linear way. Movements that oppose one another in a given cleavage may well be on the same side in another cleavage. Thus, the different strategic alliances or common actions featured by each movement tend to have different partners. But, on the whole, all the movements and organisations have room for action and discourse in which to agree with all the other movements or organisations, whatever the cleavages among them. In this way, the accumulation and strengthening of divergences that could result from the alignment of the movements in multiple cleavages are precluded. The cleavages end up neutralising or disempowering one another. At the same time as they tend towards factionalism, they liberate the potential for consensus. Herein has lain, in the last instance, the WSF's aggregating power.

The WSF as a space or as a movement

The cleavage over whether the WSF should be a space or a movement occurs at a different level from the others. Rather than the political differences between movements and NGOs inside the WSF, it concerns their differences about the political nature of the WSF itself. Indeed, this cleavage runs through all the others, since differences about strategic goals and forms of action often boil down to differences about the role of the WSF in those goals and actions.

This cleavage has been present from the outset. It led, for instance, to some scarcely known clashes within the organising committee of the first edition of the WSF. But it was within and after the third WSF that this cleavage gained notoriety and involved a large number of participants. The sheer size of the WSF 2003 and the organisational problems it raised prompted the discussion about the future of the WSF. It soon became clear to the broader public of the WSF that the discussion was not about organisational issues but rather about the political role and nature of the WSF. The cleavages in this debate deepened after the fourth (2004, Mumbai) and the fifth (2005, Porto Alegre) editions of the WSF.

> In order to be enabling, diversity must have an organisational and political core capable of deciding and carrying out collective actions in the name of the WSF

Two extreme positions can be identified in this debate, and between them a whole range of intermediate positions. On one side is the conception of the WSF as a 'movement of movements'. This conception has been expounded almost from the very beginning by influential members of the global network of social movements, whose general assembly meets in parallel with the WSF. The idea behind this conception is that, unless the WSF becomes a political actor in its own right, it will soon be discredited as a talking shop, and the anti-capitalist energy that it has generated will be wasted. If left alone, the celebration of diversity, however praiseworthy, will have a paralysing effect, and become vulnerable to capitalist domination. In order to be enabling, diversity must have an organisational and political core capable of deciding and carrying out collective actions in the name of the WSF. Such decisions should be stated in a final declaration of each edition of the WSF. With this in mind, the Charter of Principles must be revised. Horizontal organisation based on consensus should be replaced by (or at least articulated with) a democratic command authorised to act in the name of the WSF.

On the other side, there is the conception of the WSF as a space, a meeting ground in which no one can be or feel excluded. This does not mean that the WSF is a neutral space. Its objective is to allow the largest possible number of people, organisations and movements opposing neoliberalism to get together freely. Once together, they can listen to each other, learn from the experience and struggles of others, discuss proposals for action, and become linked in new networks and organisations without being interfered with by leaders, commands or programmes. The extreme version of this conception has been expounded by Chico Whitaker, one of the founders of the WSF and an influential member of the IS and the IC. He argues in this chapter that the nature of the WSF as an open space (he uses the metaphor of the public square) based on the power of free horizontal articulation should be preserved at all cost. After counterposing the organisational structure of a space and of a movement, he lashes out against the 'so-called social movements' that want to transform the WSF into a movement:

(T)those who want to transform it (the WSF) into a movement will end up, if they succeed, by working against our common cause, whether they are aware or not of what they are doing, whether they are movements or political parties, and however important, strategically urgent and legitimate their objectives might be. They will be effectively acting against themselves and against all of us. They will be hindering and suffocating its own source of life – stemming from those articulations and initiatives born in the Forum – or at least destroying an enormous instrument that is available for them to expand and to enlarge their presence in the struggle we are all engaged in. (Whitaker 2003)

The second conception is by far the dominant one in the IS and is also prevalent in the IC, but it is rarely defended in terms of Whitaker's extreme version[1]. For instance, Candido Grzybowski, another founder of the WSF whose NGO, Brazilian Institute of Social and Economic Analysis (IBASE), is a very influential member of the IS, wrote in the first issue of the journal of the Forum, *Terraviva* (2003):

To try to eliminate contradictions at the core of the WSF and turn it into a more homogeneous space and process for confronting neoliberalism is the aim of certain forces, inspired by the classic political partisanship of the left. I would even say that this struggle within the Forum is legitimate and deserves respect, given its visions and values. But it destroys innovation of the WSF, what it possesses in terms of potential to feed a broad and diverse movement of the global citizenry in building another world.

Another intermediate position in this cleavage, but closer to the movement position, has been adopted by Teivo Teivainen (2004), member of the IC, representing the National Institute for Global Democracy (NIGD):

We have to move beyond rigid movement/space dichotomies if we want to understand the role of the WSF. The WSF can play and has played a role in facilitating radical social action. One example is the fact that the massive antiwar protests of 15 February 2003 were to a significant extent initiated and organized from within the WSF process. We should use this example more consciously to counter the claims that the WSF is politically useless. We should also use it as a learning experience, to build more effective channels for concrete action without building a traditional movement (of movements)... The WSF should not be turned into a political party or a new International. It should, however, have better mechanisms for exchanging, disseminating and debating strategies of radical transformation. More explicit mechanisms and procedures mean more possibilities for getting things done.

More than any other, this cleavage, however intensely fought among some leading figures in the WSF, does not resonate among the social base of the Forum. The vast majority of the movements and NGOs come to the WSF to exchange experiences, learn about relevant issues and look for possible alliances that may strengthen the struggles in which they are already involved. The contacts made at the WSF may lead them into new struggles or courses of action, but only if they choose to do so.

This cleavage surfaced with some intensity in the WSF 2005 and afterwards in the aftermath of the presentation by some high-profile participants in the WSF of a declaration entitled 'Manifesto of Porto Alegre' (see Box 2.1), to which I now turn.

---

1 *During the WSF 2003 there were severe tensions within the OC and between the OC and the assembly of the social movements over the fact that, by being held on the last day of the WSF and ending with a final document or declaration, the assembly was allegedly trying to present its declaration to the participants and international media as the final declaration of the WSF.*

To manifest or not to manifest?

The idea of drafting a document that would synthesise the major points of agreement among the movements and NGOs participating in the WSF dates back to the second WSF, in 2002. Impressed by the enthusiasm with which so many organisations across the world responded to the call of the WSF and the atmosphere of general consensus on major global issues expressed in so many meetings convened by so many different organisations, some intellectual activists started discussing the idea of putting together the main points of agreement in a document. The document would have the twofold purpose of providing the participants with an overview of the diversity of the WSF and showing the outside world that such diversity was neither chaotic nor devoid of concrete orientations for collective global action. The success of the third WSF (2003) was interpreted as providing further justification for the idea of a document in light of the immense range of topics discussed and the generalised view that the lively debates were not being used to generate concrete proposals for action against neoliberal globalisation. In the WSF held in Mumbai (2004), Bernard Cassen, founder of ATTAC, was particularly insistent on the idea that the growing strength of the WSF demanded that the alternative provided by the WSF to the World Economic Forum of Davos be sharpened and made visible worldwide. If the WEF had been for many years the think tank of hegemonic globalisation and the legitimating amplifier for the Washington Consensus, the WSF should present itself to the world as being the major manifestation of a counter-hegemonic globalisation and the bearer of an alternative global consensus, the Consensus of Porto Alegre. How to accomplish this, having in mind the informal and horizontal structure of the WSF and the terms of the Charter of Principles? The idea of a manifesto of the WSF was ruled out by the charter. The charter, however, did not prevent the participants from drafting manifestos and from presenting them as expressing the political will of the signers. The political weight of the manifesto would depend on the number of participants willing to sign it. The manifesto was finally drafted during the fifth WSF, signed by 19 well-known participants[2], and presented to the media outside the World Social Territory (the grounds where the WSF was convened) as a document opened to the subscription of all participants in the WSF. The focus of the document was on concrete proposals, 'twelve proposals for another possible world'.

The document met with strong criticism. Two major types of criticisms can be identified: methodological and substantive. The methodological criticism stated that the manifesto either violated the Charter of Principles or came close to doing so. By presenting their document as the Manifesto of Porto Alegre, the signers induced the media wrongly to take the terms of the document as an authoritative interpretation of the political will of the WSF. The WSF does not provide for any mechanism by means of which such a political will may be determined, for the simple reason that such determination is ruled out by the spirit and the letter of the charter. In other words, the document violated the idea that the WSF is an open space where different political wills can be formulated. As might be expected, Francisco Whitaker was the most vocal critic, minimising the importance of the manifesto by viewing it as one among hundreds (if not thousands) of proposals being presented at the Forum. When the signers responded that that was precisely what they had tried to do (to present as a proposal a document to be signed by whoever agreed with its terms), Whitaker argued that, such being the case, they should not have used such an ambiguously all-encompassing title, the 'Manifesto of Porto Alegre'.

The second, substantive, kind of criticism focused on the content of the document. Two criticisms should be mentioned, both of them emphasising the reductionist view of the 'consensus' presented, which allegedly suppressed the diversity and the pluralism present at the Forum. One of the criticisms, originating in the feminist movements and organisations, stated that the document had been drafted and signed by 18 white men and one African woman. Not surprisingly, it was argued, sexual discrimination was mentioned in only one of the proposals (number 8), among many other forms of discrimination, and there was no trace of a gender perspective in the rest of the document. The other criticism, originating in the radical Leftist groups, alleged that the manifesto was a reformist or neo-reformist document, drafted by a small group of intellectuals (the same old types). Most proposals, even

---

2 The first signers were Adolfo Pérez Esquivel, Aminata Traoré, Eduardo Galeano, José Saramago, François Houtart, Armand Matellart, Roberto Sávio, Ignácio Ramonet, Ricardo Petrella, Bernard Cassen, Samuel Luis Garcia, Tariq Ali, Frei Betto, Emir Sader, Samir Amin, Atílio Borón, Walden Bello, Immanuel Wallerstein, and the author.

if correct, were limited in scope, so the argument ran, thus contributing to the illusion that imperialism may be successfully confronted by non-radical measures and struggles.

> My guess is that most people did not know about or read the manifesto, and that those few who did found it obvious, neither dangerous nor important

As one of the signers of the document, I would like to respond to these criticisms. Starting with the substantive criticisms, and in a kind of voluntary self-criticism, I fully accept the feminist critique. As for the anti-reformist criticism, I start from the assumption that social revolution is not on the political agenda (for the time being, at least) of short-term or medium-term social transformation. If we bear this in mind, the proposals formulated in the manifesto, both individually and taken together, are very radical indeed. Concerning the methodological criticism, I see a point in Whitaker's stance, since I fully share his idea that the strength of the WSF lies in the rich diversity of the participants and in the celebration of pluralism and horizontality. But I would like to add the following comments. First, the strength of the WSF may become its weakness if more and more groups reach the conclusion that the costs of getting involved in the WSF are too high when compared with the real impact of the WSF in making the world less comfortable for global capitalism. The danger of being prey to factionalism is as real as the danger of being dismissed as irrelevant. The manifesto was aimed at addressing the latter danger, even if, as I admit, it was not carried out in a consistent and correct way. Rather than being dismissed, it should be recovered and carried out with a new and more participatory and democratic methodology. The second comment is that the idea that nobody and no group owns the WSF is our most precious heritage. But it applies both to those who try to write a manifesto that may be taken as binding to all of us, and to those who criticise the initiative on the basis of the seemingly sole authorised and authoritative interpretation of the Charter of Principles. The commitment to horizontality may end up a dogmatism like any other.

The 'incident' of the manifesto highlighted the cleavage between those who conceive of the WSF as a social space and those who conceive of it as the embryo of a global civil society, constituted by a wide range of global or globally linked social actors. But, as I said above, this cleavage was confined to a group of high-profile participants. My guess is that most people did not know about or read the manifesto, and that those few who did found it obvious, neither dangerous nor important.

Conclusion

The WSF is a power space. The opposite claim – that the WSF is a totally open space, with no centre and no hierarchies, and potentially all-inclusive (within the limits set by the Charter of Principles) – seems to be a bit far-fetched. It is true that many of the concrete limits of inclusion are not the responsibility of the organisers. Nonetheless, crucial organisational options are decided by the IS and by the IC, and they condition the types of events that will take place, the themes that will be discussed and the ambit of the discussion. It is, therefore, wise to recognise the existence of power relations and submit them to the same criteria we want to see applied in society at large: transparency in the operation of such relations and their submission to the mechanisms of participatory democracy. Herein lies the new strength of the WSF, a strength that is necessary to confront the new challenges as the WSF moves to ever more efficient ways of making the world less and less comfortable for neoliberal globalisation, that is, for global capitalism as we know it.

Bernard Cassen

Unlike with the four editions held in Porto Alegre, Brazil and the 2004 sessions in Mumbai, India, the World Social Forum (WSF) will not convene in a single annual meeting in 2006. While a sixth annual Forum will be held in Africa in 2007, the WSF International Council unanimously agreed to hold meetings in several countries in 2006. Such gatherings will fit into the broader framework of a 'Polycentric World Social Forum'. The most important one will be held in Caracas, Venezuela, 24–29 January, and the other two will take place in Karachi, Pakistan and Bamako, Mali. The Caracas event will also serve as the second edition of the Social Forum of the Americas.

The dates selected for the Venezuela meeting parallel those of the Davos World Economic Forum (WEF) so as to prevent world leaders from marking the beginning of each year by dominating the media's agenda with the unchallenged expression of their vision for the planet's future. Past experience has shown that the simultaneity of these two events is an important asset. This had been acknowledged by Klaus Schwab, founder and chairman of the WEF who, addressing journalists in Buenos Aires on 21 March 2001 (two months after the first WSF), argued that the World Social Forum had affected the WEF's reputation in a negative way: 'Very smartly, place your name next to another, globally known one, and you become famous'. In other words, Schwab's statement was effectively saying, 'Without Davos, nobody would have ever heard of Porto Alegre'. While this claim is certainly exaggerated, one has to recognise that we have indeed been able to make the most out of the concurrence of these two events.

After the first meeting of the WSF in 2001, it became clear that the city of Porto Alegre alone would not suffice to host, on a yearly basis, the entire resistance movment that is committed to finding alternatives to corporate-led globalisation. During the closing session of the first WSF, which reconfirmed the Rio Grande do Sul State capital as the 2002 host city, it was also agreed that the Forum needed to undergo geographic globalisation. Such expansion did not actually begin until the following year, with the appearance of the Thematic and Continental (or Regional in some parts of the world) Social Forums, in particular the European Social Forums of Florence (2002), Paris and Saint-Denis (2003) and London (2004). These were also complemented by numerous national and local forums – not mentioned here because the list would be too long.

Heads of multinational companies, bankers and political leaders have the opportunity to meet informally throughout the year at the WEF in Davos, the Trilateral Commission, the European Round Table of Industrialists, the Transatlantic Business Dialogue, the World Business Council for Sustainable Development, the Bilderberg Group, and many other symposiums organised by US and European foundations. Within these conclaves, political and business leaders discuss the state of neoliberal globalisation and the potential threats against it, as well as the strength of its opponents and ways to contain them. No official reports are published; information and strategies circulate by word of mouth, building very strong personal ties among the parties involved. Echoes of these meetings' proceedings are found in selected journals, in working documents with restricted circulation, and in the accounts of the hand-picked journalists who manage to attend these discrete encounters.

Nothing of the sort existed on the social movements' side. Of course, through their international structures, innumerable campaign activists, as well as religious, academic, humanitarian, NGO and trade-union networks did meet periodically. Nonetheless, experience has shown that these single-issue meetings rarely resulted in concrete global action, precisely because of their very specificity. What was missing was a space where the greatest number of social players, geographically isolated and usually lacking funds, could meet to articulate and exchange their views and their experience of political struggles.

In June 1999, the international gathering organised by ATTAC France (of which I was president at the time)

With thanks to Chiara Jasson for the translation of this chapter.

in Saint-Denis represented the first attempt at creating such space. In my opening remarks, I explained that:

One of this meeting's objectives is to give individual struggles a global visibility, showing their coherence and convergence. Throughout the course of these three days, we are going to analyse, share our respective experiences, and devise plans of action for the forthcoming months and years. Equally importantly, we are going to get to know each other within and among our countries and continents. We are going to build bridges connecting one another.

At the time, I could not anticipate that, out of this original ambition, less than two years later and on a much larger scale, the World Social Forum would come into existence. The WSF represented a forum that would allow for debate, agreements and disagreements, as well as for the gradual building of consensus among all sorts of movements. Such a space was to fulfil the crucial role of defining common strategies.

The World Social Forum was radically innovative in its ability to shift from a 'no'-oriented culture, which had spectacularly manifested itself in Seattle in 1999 and in other subsequent protest demonstrations, to a 'yes' culture implied in the slogan, 'Another World is Possible'. The novelty of WSF lay too in its ability and willingness to find viable alternatives, outlining the boundaries of national, continental and global coalitions. Moreover, it has succeeded in bringing together actors and social movements whose logic and views did not always spontaneously converge. These include trade unions and voluntary organisations, churches, small and medium-sized firms, as well as national or local elected representatives.

According to its first statements and to the reference document known as the Porto Alegre Charter of Principles, adopted in 2001 in order to frame the structure of future forums, the WSF represents both a 'space' and a 'process' rather than an 'entity'. In fact, since Porto Alegre I (January 2001) the WSF has been about facilitating dialogue and exchanges, elaborating proposals and strategies for action, as well as forming coalitions among all social players opposing neoliberal globalisation – such opposition being the sine qua non condition for their participation. It must be noted that participating in the WSF does not necessarily imply a commitment to all or any of these initiatives. They only commit those wishing to get involved.

As underlined by Chico Whitaker in his contribution to this chapter, the WSF does not take a political stance, as such. There is no such thing as a final statement. While there are documents adopted in the course of the WSF, there are no official WSF texts other than those defining the 'rules of the game'.

This is also true for the majority of its continental offspring (such as the European Social Forums) and for its guiding structure, the International Council. This peculiar status still has not been fully understood by numerous observers, who fail to understand why the WSF should end without official statements and proposals. This has led many to accuse us of backing away from our plans when faced with reality. Yet, had they wandered through the WSF's hundreds of workshops and seminars between 2001 and 2005, they might have realised that proposals were certainly not lacking.

It seems to me that the World Social Forum process represents a double historical turning point: first, through the continuing elaboration, at the local, national and global levels, of a growing body of analyses and proposals widely shared by social players committed to finding viable alternatives to neoliberal policies; and second, through the geographic multiplicity of its forces and actors. This is clearly expressed in its choice of a Brazilian city, a city of the South, as its symbolic headquarters.

The question constantly asked by delegates and observers is: what are the main conclusions of these global or European meetings, and what can they lead to in concrete terms?

Another positive aspect of these forums, somewhat underestimated by the vast majority of social movements as well as by the International Secretariat and the International Council (in which the topic was never seriously discussed), is the involvement of elected representatives in this process. The relationship between social movements and the political sphere has been addressed in countless theoretical and practical debates, whose terms vary significantly from one country to another. For my part, I have always thought that excessive distance in talking to political parties and representatives was unnecessary if mutual respect was shown and a few working rules were obeyed.

The Charter of Principles makes clear that 'representatives of political parties and military organisations are not allowed to take part in the Forum. Nonetheless, political representatives and parliamentarians endorsing the fundamental principles of this Charter may be invited to attend'. Some observers have seen a discrepancy between such principles and the publicised attendance of ministers and political representatives during the previous five World Social Forums. Their presence can be partially explained by the meetings of the Parliamentarians 'Forum and of the Local' Authorities Forum, held one or two days before the opening of nearly every World Social Forum.

In these two specialised Forums, deputies, senators and ministers speak in their official capacities but in an informal manner. They are then free to attend WSF seminars and workshops as observers. This has allowed the inclusion of elected and government representatives in the broader WSF movement. Moreover, it has facilitated contact between such politicians, trade unions and NGO activists. For instance, the fact that Paris Mayor Bertrand Delanoé and Saint-Denis Mayor Patrick Braouzec were sitting a few tables away from me at the Hotel Plaza São Rafael bar during the 2002 WSF allowed me to obtain their agreement to host jointly the 2003 European Social Forum (ESF).

Another positive development lies in the final statements of the Local Authorities', and Parliamentarians', Forums. These documents signal a clearer involvement of elected political representatives in the struggle against neoliberal globalisation and, in the case of parliamentarians, in support for the Tobin tax as well as other global taxes, opposition to the war in Iraq and to the General Agreement on Trade in Services (GATS) of the World Trade Organization (WTO), among other issues.

The decision not to hold a full-scale WSF annual meeting in 2006 is not only due to the need to allow Africa to prepare itself to host it in 2007. It has also to do with the fact that, even though it has been partly revamped in 2005 at Porto Alegre, notably by taking the demands and priorities of social grassroots movements more into account when drafting the programme, the original format inaugurated in 2001 has somewhat run out of steam. The question constantly asked by delegates and observers is: what are the main conclusions of these global or European meetings, and what can they lead to in concrete terms? Several possible and different indicators can be used to measure the success they have had so far.

- *The number of participants.* The mass presence recorded since the first WSF, culminating in the attendance of 150,000 participants in 2005, has shown that, while numbers are important, they are not necessarily meaningful. Clearly, more and more delegates could attend every year. But so what?
- *The broadening of the WSF's social base and the increasingly wide spectrum of organisations seeking 'a different kind of world'.* From this viewpoint, the number of participants has been an important element in that it has encouraged reluctant organisations (such as trade unions) to make the most of a highly visible forum and to adopt, albeit temporarily, an anti-globalisation stance. However, the involvement of many organisations stops there; it does not extend to further initiatives. Fortunately, the present situation is constantly moving.
- *The incorporation of the host country or continent's social forces in the anti-globalisation movement.* This was one of Porto Alegre's great achievements. Holding the WSF in Brazil has made Latin America a crucial player in the movement against neoliberal globalisation, previously led by European and North American groups. The 2004 Mumbai Forum was a historic event in so far as South (and to a lesser extent East) Asia became the world movement's fourth component.
- *The public projection of proposals elaborated within the WSFs and their injection into national, continental and international politics.* That's where the shoe pinches: for ordinary citizens, the World Social Forums essentially remain a sort of itinerant activists' fair with both positive (such as the internationalist 'all together' feeling) and negative elements. We are at pains to explain what exactly 'came out' of a Forum. Calls from 'social movements' assemblies' held during the Forums cannot fulfil this role, not least because of the disparity between the number of organisations drafting and adopting them and the total number of those taking part in the Forums. Such ratios range, at best, between 1:20 and 1:50. While all this is important, it does not yet result in prospects for change achievable in a foreseeable future.

And exactly what change are we referring to? The anti-globalisation movement states that 'a different world' is possible, but what kind of world? We are faced with a paradox: numerous proposals are being put forth within the Forums, but these officially remain invisible. This has prevented an adequate circulation of information and increased the chance of repetition from one meeting to the next. Hence the frustration of many participants, who expect conclusions in terms of a minimal political programme.

In this respect, the making of a collective 'memory' of the Social Forums (be they local, national, continental or global), as exhaustive and thorough as possible, has become a priority. Such a memory implies the use of different media: books, articles, databases, films and videos, exhibitions, and so on. We need to inform the general public of our discussions and conclusions so as to fuel our struggles and debates. This ongoing endeavour has been updated and coordinated at the international level after the Paris/Saint-Denis ESF, partly thanks to a surplus of funds remaining after this meeting. We can therefore hope that, in the foreseeable future, an operational memory of the World Social Forums will be available.

A second and more sensitive priority is the drafting of clearly legible 'sets' of proposals resulting from the Forums, designed not only for the participating organisations but as a means of mobilising others at the national, continental and global levels. It is clear that neoliberalism functions as a system, and cannot be challenged only by random, single-issue responses. In order to capture the attention of wider audiences and sectors, as well as to neutralise its adversaries who accuse it of 'not proposing' viable alternatives, the WSF movement must put forth sets of coherent measures serving both as a system and as an official public manifesto. In order to succeed in this complex task, two major pitfalls must be avoided: first, that of generalised concepts contained in verbal form in the programmes of governments and parties; and second, that of over-specification, potentially appealing only to the most radical factions of the movement. Here, the objective should be the creation of a new paradigm divergent from the neoliberal one, while leaving enough doors open to respect the diversity of the movement's participants and preserve all prospects for enlargement.

Such 'platforms' would enhance the meaning of the term 'anti-globalisation'. In fact, we would propose a new system, thus laying the foundations of a different

world. Without this, we risk running around in circles and perpetuating the very political impotence that makes our adversaries and some of our self-proclaimed 'friends' happy. In fact, their greatest fear would be that of facing an emancipatory project benefiting from mass support and endorsed at the local or global level.

> Activists are no longer satisfied with mere debate. They want to move on to action in order to change the world, with a certain number of shared objectives

This was the situation after the London European Social Forum of October 2004, three months before the 2005 session of the WSF in Porto Alegre. The London ESF had been criticised in so far as its three core objectives – the confrontation of ideas, the elaboration of proposals, and common plans of action – had not been equally achieved. Such confrontations had actually occurred during the preparatory stages of the ESF.

A significant proportion of participants succeeded in shifting the themes of 'war' and 'racism' to the top of the agenda. While these issues were certainly very important, they ended up dominating the meeting at the expense of other topics such as social issues and the future of the European Union. For instance, while all EU Member States were facing the problem of the ratification of the proposed European Constitution, this issue remained marginalised throughout the ESF which failed to provide any new ideas capable of creating a common European 'platform'. The only proposals came from existing networks, in particular that of the European ATTACs, which had been working closely together and for which the London meeting represented one of the many scheduled in their agenda.

In many respects, for these networks, the WSF plays the same role as the ESF, but on a global scale. In the case of ATTAC, which has chapters in about 50 countries, its represents the annual opportunity to bring together members from Chile, France, Quebec, Burkina Faso, Japan and so forth. Throughout the rest of the year, meetings are bilateral, except in Europe, where they occur nearly every six weeks. In the meantime, internet and conference calls ensure that regular contact is maintained.

It can be said that, after five WSFs, three ESFs and several other forums held in Latin America and elsewhere, we have in mind a comprehensive list of current and potential alliances between the social movements of Europe and the Americas. We have a fairly precise 'map' of forces likely to be 'mobilised'. However, in spite of Mumbai, much remains to be done in Asia, Africa and the Near East. These parts of the world are fertile ground for the anti-globalisation movement. This, among other considerations, justifies the decision to hold forthcoming World Social Forums in or close to these regions.

While not yet universal, the anti-globalisation movement's current maturity provides an additional reason to make the most of its achievements by developing the platforms of proposals mentioned earlier. The Porto Alegre Manifesto proposed at the 2005 WSF represents a first concrete step in this process (see Box 2.1). Chico Whitaker is right to describe this initiative as one of the 353 resulting from the Forum. Its signatories have said it themselves. This manifesto, endorsed by individuals whose commitment to the anti-globalisation movement is undeniable, has generated such a wide array of comments as well as occasional criticism that we are led to believe it is a little different from the other 352 initiatives. In fact, it marks a turning point in the history of the WSF, and its consequences have not yet fully worked themselves out. First, it does not conflict with the Porto Alegre Charter of Principles. Second, it is not an attempt by intellectuals to proclaim themselves 'leaders' of the anti-globalisation movement. None of its signatories has such an ambition, which would not only be laughable but also bound to fail.

Their objective was to provide a first answer to widespread aspirations that, if not taken into account, will progressively empty the WSFs of their most active members. One must be aware that this process has already begun, at both the European and the global levels, where several organisations feel that they are wasting their time and limited financial resources in repetitive discussions. Activists are no longer satisfied with mere debate. They want to move on to action in order to change the world, with a certain number of shared objectives. The body of proposals resulting from past Forums is extensive enough to draft largely consensual platforms and challenge political parties, governments and multilateral organisations. While this first manifesto is not frozen, and remains open to amendments, it does represent a starting point.

It is for this reason that, in my view, the organisers

of future WSFs should take into account the following imperatives:

1. Preserve, in full respect of the Charter, the WSF status as an open process and space.
2. Reinforce the visibility and coherence of the key sector-based proposals. Producing 353 of them, as happened at the 2005 WSF, without setting priorities, may be intellectually appealing but lacks political feasibility at a time when this is exactly what is expected from the Forums.
3. Give top priority to the debates on ongoing world or continental campaigns: Third World debt, tax havens, global taxes, the WTO and GATS, free-trade agreements, US wars, genetically modified organisms, common goods, access to water, and so on. I would tentatively go as far as saying that the Social Forums could be built exclusively on these ongoing campaigns, to which could be added a few others already prepared within ad hoc networks.
4. Within the framework of these Forums, discuss and enrich the platforms of proposals outlining global projects. How? By drawing on campaign proposals and gradually expanding the number of organisations supporting them; the Porto Alegre Manifesto is the first but not the only building block in this construction.
5. Articulate the activities of Social Forums with those of the Local Authorities', Trade Unions', and Parliamentarians' Forums. Until now, these activities have not been coordinated. We can no longer afford the luxury of preserving a wall between elected representatives and social movements if they share the same global objectives of resisting neoliberalism. With due respect for the autonomy of the parties involved, such wide cooperation should become a central objective of the Forums.

Around the world there are millions of citizens wanting radical change. If the Forums are unable to play host not only to discussion and debate but also to the ways and means to put proposals into practice, other structures will replace them. The Forums will run the risk of becoming empty shells, progressively deserted by social actors. Fortunately, we are still able to prevent this development.

Box 2.1: The Porto Alegre Manifesto: twelve proposals for a different, achievable world

Since the first World Social Forum held in Porto Alegre in January 2001, the phenomenon of Social Forums has spread to all continents, and to all levels: national and local. It has created a global sense of citizenship and a worldwide public arena for campaigns. It has permitted the elaboration of political proposals presenting an alternative to the tyranny of neoliberal globalisation driven by financial markets and transnational corporations, and supported by the imperial power of the United States. Through its diversity, and the solidarity between the actors and the social movements which together constitute it, the alternative global movement is now a significant force on a worldwide level.

An abundance of proposalsis emerging from these Forums, of which a great many seem to attract strong support from social movements. The signatories of the Porto Alegre Manifesto, who express themselves here in a purely personal capacity and do not claim to speak for the Forum, have identified twelve of these proposals that, together, provide both a strategy and a design for the construction of a different, and achievable, world. Should they be applied, they would at last allow citizens to act together in order to start taking charge of their future.

This minimum set of proposals is subject to the approval of actors and social movements in every country. It will be up to them, on all levels – global, continental, national and local – to engage in the necessary struggles in order for it to become a reality. We hold no illusions about the desire of governments and international institutions to put these proposals willingly into practice, even if, through sheer opportunism, they borrow phrases from them.

I – A different, achievable world must respect every human being's right to life with new economic rules. It is therefore necessary:

1. to cancel Third World debt, which has already been paid several times over, and which constitutes, for the creditor states, banks and financial institutions, the privileged means of placing the greater part of mankind under their control and keeping it poor. This measure must be accompanied by returning the huge sums of money that corrupt leaders have stripped from their people.

2. to introduce global taxes on financial transactions (in particular the Tobin tax on currency speculation), on direct investments abroad, on the consolidated profits of transnational corporations, on the sale of weapons and on activities producing large quantities of greenhouse gases. Added to public aid to development, which must reach 0.7% of the GDP of developed countries, the resources from these taxes should be used to fight against widespread pandemics (such as AIDS) and to ensure that the whole of mankind has access to drinking water, accommodation, energy, healthcare and medicine, education and social services.

3. To dismantle progressively all forms of tax, judicial and financial havens, which are lairs for organised crime, corruption, all kinds of traffic, fraud and tax evasion, and criminal operations by large companies and governments. These tax havens are not only certain states acting outside the remit of international law; they also include legislation in certain developed countries. Initially it would be appropriate to tax heavily the flows of capital entering or leaving these 'havens', as well as the institutions and actors, financial or otherwise, which make such large-scale embezzlement possible.

4. to make imperative in public policy, as much national as international, the right of every inhabitant of this planet to a job, social protection and a pension, with respect for gender equality.

5. – to promote all forms of fair trade by rejecting the free-trade regulations of the World Trade Organization and by creating mechanisms that, in the production of goods and services, foster an upwards harmonisation of social (as written in the International Labour Organization conventions) and environmental norms.
   – to exclude education, health, social services and culture from the ambit of the WTO's General Agreement on Trade in Services (GATS). The Convention on cultural diversity, currently under negotiation at UNESCO, must explicitly give precedence to the right to culture, and to public policies in support of culture, over trade law.

6. to guarantee each country's, or grouping of countries', right to food safety and sovereignty through the promotion of small-scale farming. This should lead to the complete suppression of export subsidies on agricultural products, most notably by the United States and the European Union, and the possibility to tax imports in order to prevent dumping practices. Likewise, each country or group of countries must be able to decide independently whether to prohibit the production and importation of genetically modified organisms for alimentary purposes.

7. to prohibit all forms of knowledge and life patenting (of humans and animals as well as plants), and any privatisation of public common goods, water in particular.

II – A different, achievable world must promote 'living together' in peace and justice for all mankind. It is therefore necessary:

8. – to fight, initially through new public policies, against all forms of discrimination, sexism, xenophobia, racism and anti-semitism.
   – to recognise fully political, cultural and economic rights (including the control of their natural resources) of indigenous peoples.

9. – to take urgent measures to put an end to the destruction of the environment, and to the threat of major climate change due to greenhouse gases, mainly the result of the proliferation of transport and of the careless use of non-renewable energy.
   – to demand the implementation of existing agreements, conventions and treaties, even if they are insufficient.
   – to initiate a different kind of development based upon the moderate use of energy and the democratic control of natural resources, in particular drinking water, at a global level.

10. to demand the dismantling of foreign military bases and the removal of all foreign troops, except those with a direct mandate from the UN, starting with Iraq and Palestine.

III – A different, achievable world must promote local and global democracy. It is therefore necessary:

11. – to guarantee through legislation the right to information and the right to inform citizens.
    – to put an end to the concentration of the media within groups owned by communication conglomerates.
    – to guarantee the independence of journalists in relation to shareholders.
    – to favour the non-profit press, notably alternative and community media.

    Respecting these rights implies the building of citizens' counterpowers, in particular in the form of voluntary international and national media watch organisations.

12. to reform and further democratise international organisations, making human, economic, social and cultural rights a priority, through the extension of the Universal Declaration on Human Rights. This implies the incorporation of the World Bank, the International Monetary Fund, and the WTO into the United Nations decision-making mechanisms. In the event of continued violations of international law by the United States, it will be necessary to transfer the United Nations headquarters from New York to another country, preferably in the South.

Porto Alegre, 29 January 2005
Translation: Victoria Roberts
Source: www.mondialisations.org/php/public/art.php?id=16995&lan=EN (consulted 11 July 2005)

Tariq Ali (Pakistan), Samir Amin (Egypt), Walden Bello (Philippines), Frei Betto (Brazil), Atilio Boron (Argentina), Bernard Cassen (France), Eduardo Galeano (Uruguay), François Houtart (Belgium), Armand Mattelart (Belgium), Adolfo Pérez Esquivel (Argentina), Riccardo Petrella (Italy), Ignacio Ramonet (Spain), Samuel Ruiz Garcia (Mexico), Emir Sader (Brazil), José Saramago (Portugal), Roberto Savio (Italy), Boaventura de Sousa Santos (Portugal), Aminata Traoré (Mali), Immanuel Wallerstein (United States).

REFERENCES

Fisher, W. and Ponniah, T. (eds) (2003) *Another World is Possible: Popular Alternatives to Globalization at the World Social Forum*. London and New York: Zed Books.

Foltz, K., Moodiliar, S. and Pramas, J. (2005) 'The Future of the World Social Forum Process – Modest Reforms Needed', *Znet*, 9 February. www.zmag.org/content/showarticle.cfm?SectionID=1&ItemID=7207 (consulted 2 June 2005).

Grzybowski, C. (2003) 'Por que pensar o Fórum Social Mundial?', *Terraviva*, 17 January.

Santos, Boaventura de Sousa (1995) *Toward a New Common Sense: Law, Science and Politics in the Paradigmatic Transition*. New York: Routledge.

– (2004) *The World Social Forum: A User's Manual*. www.ces.fe.uc.pt/bss/documentos/fsm_eng.pdf (consulted 1 July 2005) also London: Zed Books (forthcoming).

Sen, J., Arnand, A., Escobar, A. and Waterman, P. (eds) (2004) *World Social Forum: Challenging Empires*. New Delhi: Viveka Foundation (German and Spanish editions have also been published.)

Teivainen, T. (2004) *Twenty-Two Theses on the Problems of Democracy in the World Social Forum*. www.forumsocialmundial.org.br/dinamic.php?pagina=bib_teivo_fsm2004_in (consulted 1 July 2005).

Whitaker, F. (2003) *Notes about the World Social Forum*. São Paulo: Brazilian Peace and Justice Commission, 17 March. www.cbjp.org.br/artigos/chicowitaker/avalia%E7%E3o_fsm2003_ingl_rev.htm (consulted 1 July 2005).

Whitaker, C. (2004) 'The WSF as Open Space', in J. Sen et al. (eds), *World Social Forum: Challenging Empires*. New Delhi: The Viveka Foundation.

– (2005) *O Desafio do Fórum Social Mundial – Um modo de ver*. São Paulo: Editoras Perseu Abramo e Loyola.

WSF (World Social Forum) (2001) *World Social Forum Charter of Principles*, 10 June. www.nycsocialforum.org/about_wsf/wsf_charter (consulted 2 June 2005).

– (URL) www.forumsocialmundial.org.br (consulted 1 June 2005).

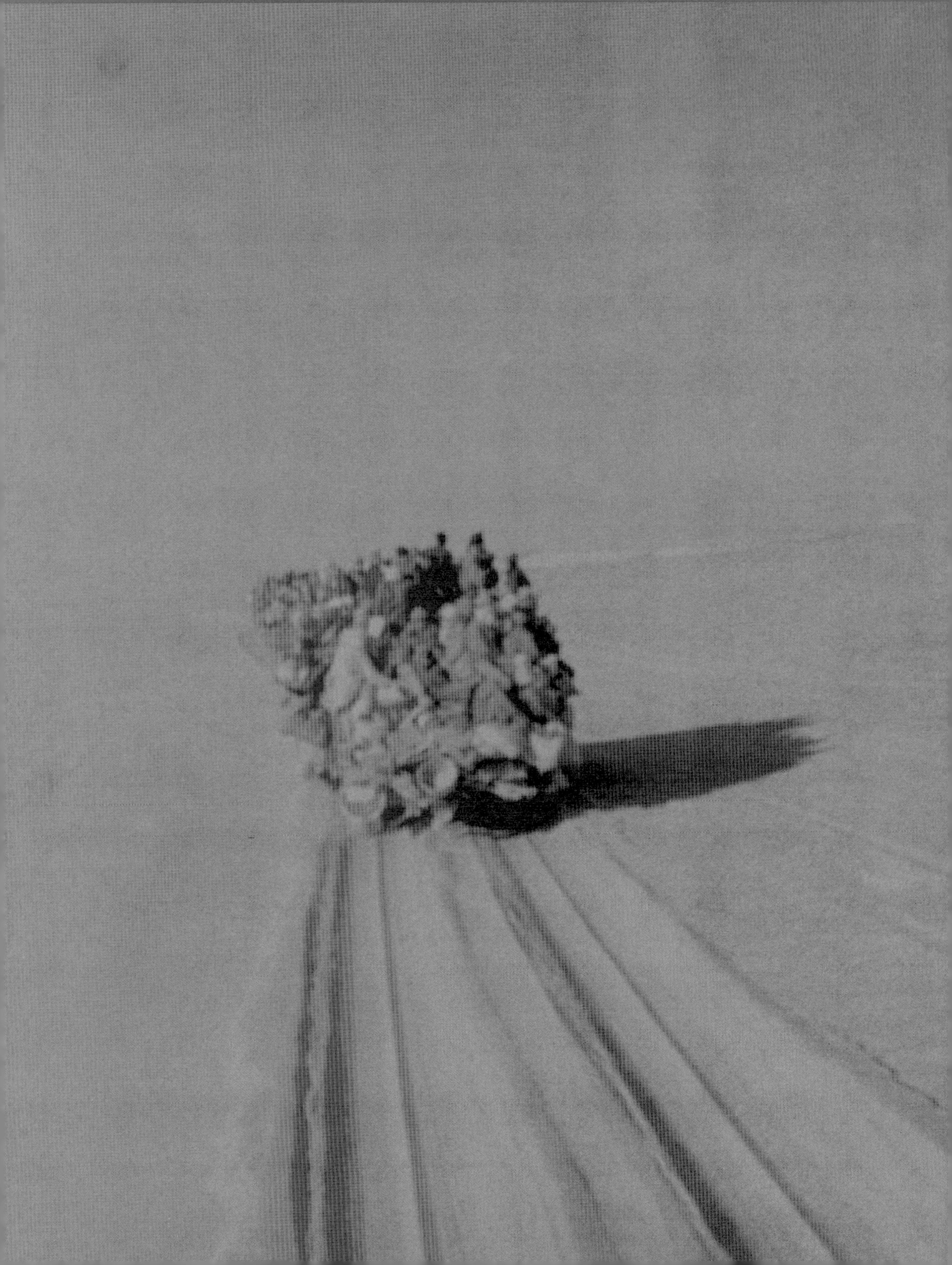

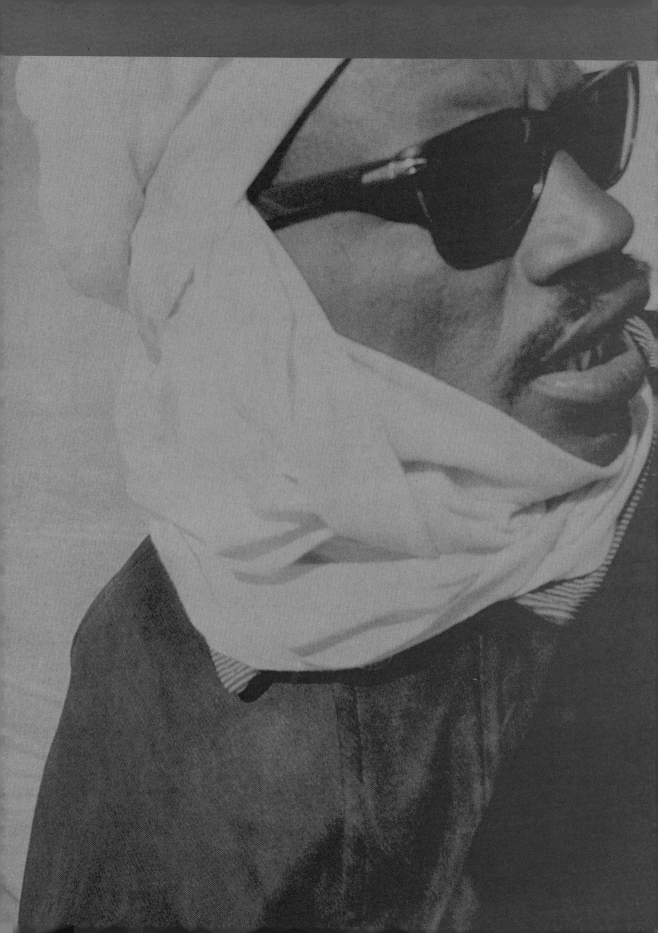

CHAPTER 3

CLIMATE FOR CHANGE?
CIVIL SOCIETY AND THE POLITICS OF GLOBAL WARMING
Peter Newell

Introduction

Climate change is increasingly recognised as one of the most serious environmental threats facing humankind. The rapidly growing consensus about the severity of the issue is at odds with the slow rate of progress to date in addressing the problem through international cooperation. The re-election of President Bush in 2004 in the United States did nothing to stem the tide of concern about the fate of the Kyoto Protocol, the key pillar of the global political architecture for tackling climate change, despite the agreement's recent entry into force as a result of its ratification by the Russian Duma (UNFCCC 2004)[1]. Against this background, Pettit (2004: 102) cites a climate activist who suggests that 'The chances of our getting anywhere near where we need to be with international diplomacy are grim'. Other activists, though increasingly frustrated at the low returns from continued engagement with the negotiations, see Kyoto as the only game in town and are unwilling to give up on an agreement they worked so hard to secure. Stalemate continues to prevail over the extent to which, and the ways in which, developing countries should assume commitments to reduce their own emissions. This, and other key issues regarding the mechanisms for delivering the goals of Kyoto, and the UN Framework Convention on Climate Change (UNFCC) before it, have served to create divisions within the environmental movement, mirroring those which continue to cause fissures within the broader international community.

The scale of the challenge this implies for concerned civil society should not be underestimated. Aligned against action are not only the most powerful country and simultaneously the world's largest polluter, but a strong and well-organised front of the world's most important companies in strategically key sectors such as oil. These industries have been active from the earliest stages of the debate about how the international community should respond to the threat of climate change, questioning the case for action through bodies such as the Global Climate Coalition and Climate Council, representing broad sectors of industry at the international level. This is in addition to national media campaigns against the Kyoto Protocol, for example, and more localised types of organising in the form of industry-funded environmental front groups such as the Information Council for the Environment[2], disseminating information materials that challenge the prevailing consensus about the severity of the problem (Newell and Paterson 1998; Newell 2000; Levy 2005). Through the provision of funding for the work of scientists sceptical about the Intergovernmental Panel on Climate Change (IPCC) consensus, industry groups have been able to find allies in the scientific community able to validate their doubts regarding the science and lend legitimacy to claims that might otherwise be dismissed as based on nothing more than self-interest. Prominent figures who have performed this role include Fred Singer (George Mason University), Richard Lindzen (Massachusetts Institue of Technology) and, more recently, the controversial Bjørn Lomborg, whose widely publicised critique of the assumptions behind many environmental threats has been enthusiastically endorsed by industry groups (Lomborg 2001; see Box 3.1).

These challenges merely add, then, to the generic barriers environmentalists must overcome in promoting action on environmental issues, including classic problems of scientific uncertainty that allow politicians to claim that more time and research are required before action can be justified, and intergenerational issues whereby benefits of action will be felt in years to come but sacrifices have to be made now. Politically, imposing costs on current electorates to tackle problems that are seen as long term is often unpalatable. Finally, the fact that environmental problems, perhaps especially climate change, are

---

1 The ratification was significant because the Protocol must be ratified by 55 Parties to the Convention, including developed countries whose combined 1990 emissions of carbon dioxide exceed 55% of that group's total. With the US and Australia not intending to ratify, the 55% threshold can be met only with the participation of Russia.
2 The Information Council for the Environment receives funding, for example, from the US National Coal Association and the Western Fuels Association.

Business as usual: Bangladeshis are used to flooding ©*Dieter Telemans/Panos Pictures*

created by everyday patterns of consumption means asking people to forgo luxuries they either already have or aspire to having. This makes the agenda that many, though certainly not all, environmental groups are seeking to advance, both politically controversial and unpopular at a societal level.

Despite this, a wide variety of groups across the world have sought to deploy a range of strategies to promote action on climate change, engaging state and non-state actors in the public and private sectors and employing a range of levers to enhance their influence. This chapter surveys some of these strategies and seeks to provide an account of the degree of influence they appear to have on the contemporary course of public–political debate on this key global environmental challenge.

The chapter is structured in four main sections. The first section briefly summarises the politics of climate change and the negotiations to date by way of understanding the landscape of power and coalition building within which civil society organisations operate. The second section explores the diverse strategies that groups have adopted, with a particular emphasis on the ways in which strategies have evolved over time and continue to adapt to the changing realities of global climate politics. The third section looks at the key issue of the internal politics of civil society mobilisation: issues of representation and the differences that have emerged between groups over specific aspects of the climate change debate. The final section draws out some of the main insights from the chapter and suggests future challenges for civil society in promoting effective action on climate change.

CLIMATE CHANGE

Box 3.1: **The sceptics**

Not all civil society actors support action against climate change – particularly not through reductions in CO_2 emissions as envisaged in the Kyoto Protocol. Some of the most outspoken criticism of action on climate change comes from think tanks, largely of a free-market persuasion, as well as from individuals and organisations linked to the scientific community. Examples of such groups and individuals who challenge the science of climate change and/or the tactics of its mitigation are outlined below, and their strategies summarised.

Anti-environmentalist civil society

Most sceptical groups are based or originate in the United States, but anti-environmentalist or 'wise use' organisations can be found in other countries – especially where there is a strong environmental movement. Overall, three kinds of anti-environmentalist civil society can be identified. First, established think tanks and policy institutes have adopted stances against climate change environmentalism. Mostly, these are free-market think tanks such as the US-based Cato Institute and Heartland.org, which continue to campaign actively against the Kyoto Protocol and the 'scare tactics' of environmentalists by advocating an 'evidence-based' and 'balanced' environmental policy. Likewise, the Competitive Enterprise Institute promotes 'free-market environmentalism' arguing that 'Although global warming has been described as the greatest threat facing mankind, the policies designed to address global warming actually pose a greater threat' (CEI URL).

Second, elements of the scientific community have been active in the dispute about global warming. Individual scientists have organised petitions (see below) and the George C Marshall Institute, a non-profit organisation set up to 'preserve the integrity of science' in policy making, suggests that actions concerning climate change 'should flow from the state of knowledge, should be related to a long-term strategy and objectives and should be capable of being adjusted – one way or the other – as the understanding of human influence improves' (George C Marshall Institute URL). Richard Lindzen, of MIT, argues that global warming may dry out the troposphere, reducing water vapour and thereby dampening the greenhouse effect. This 'negative feedback', which could cancel out the positive feedbacks that would amplify warming, has not been factored into climate change predictions, he argues (Pearce 2005).

Third, engaged individuals have sometimes made significant impacts on the policy debate. Bjørn Lomborg, author of *The Skeptical Environmentalist* (2001), became a virtual one-man pressure group, first in his native Denmark and then globally. Originally disputing evidence of man-made global warming, he later switched his focus to the costs of mitigation and especially the Kyoto Protocol. Lomborg was listed in *Time Magazine*'s 100 most influential people in 2004 after he organised the Copenhagen Consensus, which sought to assess the relative costs and benefits of tackling various global problems, including global warming. Similarly, British botanist David Bellamy argues that:

> Global warming is a largely natural phenomenon. The world is wasting stupendous amounts of money
> on trying to fix something that can't be fixed... The climate change people have no proof for their claims.
> They have computer models which do not prove anything. (Leake 2005).

Civil society or corporate interests?

Some would question whether anti-environmentalism even qualifies as 'civil society', due to the support and involvement of business interests. Most notoriously, the Global Climate Coalition (URL), now defunct, was set up in 1989 by various US business associations to 'coordinate business participation in the international policy debate on the issue of global climate change and global warming'. Other organisations rely on a combination of corporate and private funding, such as the Greening Earth Society (URL), which according to its website is 'a not-for-profit membership organization comprised of rural electric cooperatives and municipal electric utilities, their fuel suppliers, and thousands of individuals'. The oil corporation ExxonMobil funds several think tanks and research programmes that question the science behind global warming or challenge the viability of mitigation strategies. Recipients of ExxonMobil funds include the Marshall Institute, the Competitive Enterprise Institute, and the Joint Program on the Science and Policy of Climate Change at the Massachusetts Institute of Technology (Mooney 2005).

However, funding civil society groups is different from direct business sector lobbying and some in the scientific community have acted entirely without support or promptings from corporate interests. Furthermore, the strategies pursued have been typical of those normally associated with civil society.

Anti-environmentalist strategies

Strategies of sceptical civil society actors include disputing the science of climate change and questioning the economics of climate change mitigation. First, some groups contest the reality or scale of global warming, challenging the notion of a scientific consensus on climate change. Various petitions have been organised by scientists including the so-called Oregon Petition organised by Frederick Seitz, professor emeritus at Rockefeller University, which has gathered over 18,000 signatories (though their authenticity has been the subject of controversy). Organisers claim that signatories are predominantly fellow scientists who subscribe to the petition's view that:

> There is no convincing scientific evidence that human release of carbon dioxide, methane, or other greenhouse gasses is causing or will, in the foreseeable future, cause catastrophic heating of the Earth's atmosphere and disruption of the Earth's climate. Moreover, there is substantial scientific evidence that increases in atmospheric carbon dioxide produce many beneficial effects upon the natural plant and animal environments of the Earth. (Petition Project URL)

Likewise, the Leipzig Declaration on Climate Change (URL) garnered signatures in support of the position that 'drastic emission control policies deriving from the Kyoto conference' lack credible support from the underlying science and are therefore 'ill-advised and premature'. The declaration was first drafted in 1995 by Fred Singer (an atmospheric physicist who also started the anti-environmentalist organisation The Science and Environmental Policy Project), and then revised it in 1997.

A second strategy employed is to concede that global warming is happening but to dispute the idea that this is exclusively a negative thing (or assert at least that it is not as catastrophic as many environmentalists claim). For instance, www.CO2andClimate.org is used to disseminate debate and research that casts doubt on the gravity of the situation, suggesting, for example, that human activity may have averted or postponed the arrival of the next ice age (see for example Ruddiman, Vavrus and Kutzbach 2005).

Third, a related stance is to accept the reality of man-made global warming but question the way in which future scenarios have been arrived at and the economic logic of pursuing CO_2 reductions. This is largely the position of the Danish Environmental Assessment Institute, set up by the Danish government at the suggestion of Bjørn Lomborg, who became its first director.

A final strategy is to challenge the philosophical basis of environmentalism that underpins the arguments in favour of climate change mitigation. Anti-environmentalism often fuses belief in free markets, anthropocentrism (according humans sovereign rights over other animals and nature) and a belief in 'evidence-based' policy making. For example, the Environmental Conservation Organisation (URL) argues that:

> the environment includes human beings who prosper or perish as the result of their stewardship of natural resources. We reject the notion that the environment is 'fragile' and must be protected from human use by massive federal and international regulations.

This view tends to value the environment in terms of human welfare – resources available to humans – and is critical of those who view nature as intrinsically valuable or as qualitatively different from other 'factors of production' or 'welfare goods'. Thus, climate change is reframed in terms of market solutions rather than government intervention, an exclusive focus on human welfare supported by cost-benefit studies of measures to mitigate climate change, and arguments about 'sound science', rather than the precautionary principle, as the basis for action. In historical terms, the battle within civil society concerning climate change policy echoes earlier skirmishes between environmentalists and 'wise use' movements that see exploitation of resources and wilderness as the 'manifest destiny' of human beings (Brulle 2000). The argument is not only about the science of climate change, but about the rights of individuals and the right of the human species to make fundamental changes to nature.

Olaf Corry, University of Copenhagen

Background

In many ways, the threat of human-induced climate change represents a classic collective action problem. It is a problem that affects everyone and that, to different degrees, is caused by everyone. The scale of international cooperation that is required is in many ways without precedent. The sources of the problem are widespread and ingrained in the everyday practices of production and consumption. The problem spans from the global to the local level and therefore requires changes at all levels of human activity from the household upwards. This presents an enormous challenge for effective interventions. As Geoffrey Heal (1999: 222–3) notes, carbon dioxide is produced as a result of 'billions of decentralised and independent decisions by private households for heating and transportation and by corporations for these and other needs, all outside the government sphere. The government can influence these decisions, but only indirectly through regulations or incentives.'

There is also a clear North–South dimension, both in terms of vulnerability to the effects of climate change (particularly sea-level rise and changes to agricultural systems) and in terms of responsibility. This dynamic affects the success of any attempt to provide global public goods in this area. Industrialised countries have historically contributed to the problem far more than developing countries. Nevertheless, larger developing countries such as China, India and Brazil, experiencing rapid industrialisation, are seeing their emissions of greenhouse gases (GHG) rise significantly. Given this, there is an ongoing debate about whether, and if so in what form, developing countries should take on their own emission reduction commitments. There is a perception among some in the North that newly industrialised countries, in particular, will be able to free-ride on the sacrifices made by European and North American countries. The related concern is that industries will uproot and relocate to areas of the world not covered by the provisions of the Kyoto Protocol, resulting in 'carbon leakage' (Barrett 1999: 207). In the meantime, technology transfer, climate aid and private sector investments in carbon abatement initiatives will play a central role in inducing parties to the agreements to meet their existing commitments. If a degree of 'leap-frogging' for developing countries is to be achieved, enabling a transition from pollution-intensive forms of production to energy-efficient and energy-conserving modes of production, fresh sources of finance and new institutional mechanisms will be required to create the right sets of incentives and disincentives to steer government and market actors towards a climate-benign development path.

Climate change clearly also has a strong inter-generational element in that the current generation is being asked to bear the costs of a problem that was also created by previous generations but whose most severe impacts will be felt by future generations. This creates an important political obstacle to action, or 'incentive gap', in that those being asked to make sacrifices now are not likely to reap the benefits of that action. The scientific uncertainties that also characterise climate change lend support to those that argue that the costs of action outweigh the benefits of protecting ourselves from a threat that may not turn out to be as serious as we currently predict. Attempting to address the problem of climate change is ridden with such dilemmas, which involve trade-offs with enormous implications for the future of humankind.

The response of the international community to the threat of climate change dates back to the 1980s, when the scientific community was organised to provide state-of-the-art reviews of the science of climate change to policy makers. Assessments of the latest under-standings of the climate change problem produced in 1990, 1995 and 2001 have repeatedly underscored the need for immediate action justified by the latest scientific thinking. The negotiations towards the UNFCCC began in 1991 and ended with the conclusion of the convention at the Rio Summit in 1992. With scientific assessments of the severity of climate change becoming increasingly common, and a growing awareness of the inadequacy of existing policy responses, momentum built for a follow-up to the convention. Negotiations thus began towards a protocol that would set legally binding targets to reduce GHG emissions, unlike the UNFCC, which requires parties only to 'aim' towards stabilising their emissions at their 1990 levels by the year 2000[3]. The Kyoto Protocol, concluded in 1997, sets differentiated targets for industrialised countries while setting in train a process to further elaborate joint implementation schemes, set up an emissions trading scheme and to create a Clean Development Mechanism (see Box 3.2).

---

3 For detailed histories of the negotiations see Paterson (1996), Newell (1998; 2000), and Mintzer and Leonard (1994).

Box 3.2: The Kyoto Protocol in brief

Commitments:

- Industrialised countries will reduce their collective emissions of GHG by an average of 5.2 per cent below 1990 levels in the commitment period 2008–12. Parties are expected to have demonstrated progress in reaching this target by the year 2005. Cuts in the three important gases (CO_2, NH_4 and NO_2) will be calculated against a base year of 1990, and cuts in the long-lived industrial gases (hydroflurocarbons, perflurocarbons and sulphur hexafluroide) can be measured against a base year of either 1990 or 1995.

- The US has to reduce its emissions by an average of 7 per cent, Japan by an average of 6 per cent, and the EU by an average of 8 per cent. Other industrialised countries are permitted small increases while yet others are obliged only to freeze their emissions.

- Developed countries are obliged to provide:

  - *new and additional financial resources to meet the agreed full costs incurred by developing country Parties in advancing the implementation of existing commitments.*

  - *such financial resources, including transfer of technology, needed by the developing country parties to meet the agreed and full incremental costs of advancing the implementation of existing commitments*

  - *financial resources for the implementation of Article 10, through bilateral, regional and other multilateral channels 'which developing country parties can avail of'.*

Instruments:

- *Clean Development Mechanism (CDM)*. The aim of this body is to assist developing countries in 'achieving sustainable development' and at the same time to help developed countries 'in achieving compliance with their quantified emission limitation and reduction commitments'. In effect, its purpose is to oversee the implementation of projects funded by developed states wanting to accrue credits for emissions achieved overseas. Participation is voluntary and procedures and modalities for auditing and verifying projects are in the process of being worked out in the negotiations. Reduction credits will be certified by the CDM to ensure that projects add value to savings that would have been made in their absence (Article 12). Importantly from the point of view of financing, 'a share of the proceeds from the certified activities is used to cover administrative expenses as well as to assist the developing country parties that are particularly vulnerable to the effects of climate change to meet the costs of adaptation'.

- *Joint Implementation*. Actions implemented jointly have to be 'additional to any that would otherwise occur' and 'supplemental to domestic actions'. Scope is provided to include 'verifiable changes in stocks of sinks' in parties' assessment of their net GHG emissions (Article 6). Such projects will be certified under the CDM.

- *Emissions Trading* (the modalities of which have yet to be worked out) (Article 17).

- *Implementation* will be via national reports overseen by teams of experts nominated by the parties.

Source: United Nations (1997)

Despite the recent entry into force of the Kyoto Protocol with its ratification by the Russian Duma, the future of the Kyoto Protocol is currently in serious doubt given the ongoing non-cooperation of the largest single contributor to the problem: the United States. Arguably, the greatest single challenge to the further elaboration and effective implementation of the protocol continues to be the refusal of the US to sign the agreement. On being elected US President in 2000, one of George Bush's first moves was to make clear that he had no intention of signing the Kyoto Protocol. His rationale was that, unless developing countries also sign the agreement, which they are currently unwilling or unable to do, the protocol will have a damaging effect on the competitiveness of US firms. The withdrawal of US support for the protocol has leant urgency to the search for alternative ways of providing and financing action on climate change, given that many of the key actors currently involved in the financing of climate change action rely upon the financial support of the US (these include the World Bank and the Global Environment Facility (GEF) most notably).

We should recognise at the outset that many of the world's most important political and economic actors benefit enormously from the processes and practices that create climate change. Most systems of large-scale industrial production and energy provision are based on the use of fossil fuels that contribute to climate change. To the extent that climate change highlights the unsustainability of the fossil-fuelled growth trajectory that underpins the contemporary global economy, it focuses scrutiny on the economic growth strategies promoted by the world's leading global economic institutions, most notably the World Bank and the International Monetary Fund. Because of the enormous global climate footprint that results from the increased movement of goods transported around the world as a result of lower trade barriers, the World Trade Organization (WTO) and the governments that created and sustain it, necessarily also enter the spotlight. Internalising the externality of dangerous climate change amounts to demanding that the richest and most powerful economies of the world transform the economic structures that have brought them their economic wealth (the abundant supply and exploitation of cheap reserves of fossil fuels). We should not underestimate the political obstacles to doing this. The threat that action on climate change poses to traditional patterns of

economic production and energy consumption is evident in the response of the Bush administration in the US to the Kyoto Protocol.

While in theory, therefore, no one can be excluded either from the public bad of global warming or from the public good of measures to protect the climate, some populations are affected more than others and some stand to gain more from action to combat climate change than others. In the political negotiations on climate change, for example, the Alliance of Small Island States (AOSIS), those most vulnerable to sea-level rise, have consistently argued for tougher action to combat climate change, while other countries have not only been reluctant to reduce their emissions and therefore their contribution to the problem, but have argued, on occasion, that some global warming may actually be beneficial to regions with colder climates. Countries are also differently placed in terms of their ability to adapt to the climate change that most scientists now feel is inevitable. While wealthier countries can build sea defences, for example, to protect themselves from sea-level rise, poorer low-lying countries that have contributed very little to the problem are likely to suffer loss of land and livelihood as a result of the same process. This is what makes climate change first and foremost an issue of equity and social justice.

Despite a significant degree of consensus on the causes and proposed solutions to the problem, the science that underpins the problem has been subject to repeated challenge by those claiming that global warming is not a problem at all, or not as serious a problem as many suggest, or that it may actually be beneficial. Hence, consensus about the level of political action that is appropriate to address the threat of climate change or the funding that it requires is unlikely to come from greater scientific consensus about the scale and impacts of climate change. Experience to date suggests that we already have the political tools to tackle the problem: it is political will to use them that is missing.

Mapping the role of civil society

By the time negotiations towards an international agreement on climate change began in 1991, there had already been almost 20 years of institutional activity, albeit mainly in the scientific realm. Scientific programmes such as the International Biosphere Programme had been running since the 1970s,

©Claire Martin/Friends of the Earth

helping to consolidate an international network of scientific institutions working on the different dimensions of global climate change. Although such groups should also be considered part of civil society, the focus here is environmental pressure groups, and particularly those groups that have evolved strategies aimed at influencing and shaping international policy on climate change.

Some of the most significant actors in global civil society have been active on the climate change issue, particularly from the 1980s onwards, coinciding with growing interest in global threats such as ozone depletion and climate change, and rising appreciation of the global sources and impacts of threats facing the human race. World Wide Fund for Nature (WWF), Greenpeace and Friends of the Earth have been among the most active groups on this issue. By the time of the Sixth Conference of the Parties to the UNFCCC in the Hague in November 2000, however, participants from 323 intergovernmental and non-governmental organisations were present (Yamin 2001). In order to bring about a measure of coordination of their activities, pooling of resources and expertise, civil society groups have organised themselves into coalitions such as the Climate Action Network (CAN).

Created in 1989 by 63 NGOs from 22 countries,

under the initial guidance of Greenpeace International and the then Environmental Defense Fund (now Environmental Defense), CAN now operates as a global network of 365 environmental NGOs working to promote action on climate change (Durban Declaration 2004). CAN seeks to coordinate the strategies of its members on the climate change issue, exchanging information and attempting to develop joint position papers to be presented at key international meetings. CAN brings together a broad church of groups working on various aspects of the climate issue and with different positions on many of the key negotiating issues discussed below. It has a number of separate working groups reflecting the breadth of their expertise and serving to consolidate a division of labour across the spectrum of issue areas on which they work. Gulbrandsen and Andresen (2004: 61) suggest:

Although CAN is more important for the less resource-rich groups than for the major ones, the CAN network is usually an effective way of communicating NGO positions with one voice during the climate negotiations.

It maintains regional offices in Latin America, Europe, Africa and South and South-East Asia. Many of the groups discussed in the following sections belong to the network.

Moving targets: changing strategies, shifting goals

The strategies adopted by civil society groups shift over time and reflect their understanding of where change is most likely to come from. Their mobilisations in many ways adapt to changes in the locus of decision making authority as this regionalises, transnationalises and, in some cases, decentralises. This helps to explain the degree of attention paid by European groups to the institutions of the EU, for example (Grant, Matthews and Newell 2000). Key decisions continue to be made at the international level, however, through the ongoing negotiations on the procedures and details for the implementation of the Kyoto Protocol, despite the recent stalemate. The following section looks at the efforts of groups to engage with this process from agenda setting to implementation and enforcement.

The international policy process

In order to understand the role of civil society groups in the international negotiations on climate change, a policy cycle is described, from agenda setting to implementation and enforcement, each stage of which implies a different opportunity structure for NGOs to be able to exert influence. The key dynamic is between policy making at the national and international levels, although the stages described in practice occur simultaneously and are rarely sequential.

There is also a sense in which influence waxes and wanes over time, consistent with 'issue-attention cycles' (Downs 1972) as environmental issues compete for policy space with other pressing economic and security issues, for example. There are also, of course, 'movement cycles' whereby outside and critical voices often set policy agendas and are then drawn or co-opted by various means into the policy process. Groups move into and out of the process over time. Strategies of engagement also appear to reflect shifting thinking among NGOs about how to affect change, manifested in differing degrees of engagement with international negotiations based on judgements about expected returns from costs (finance and personnel) incurred and assessments of competing priorities within the organisation (Charnovitz 1997). For example, Yamin (2001: 161) notes:

amidst signs of increasing US isolationism given by the Bush administration, many NGOs are privately asking whether it is time to prioritize other channels of influence to achieve results

These other possible channels of influence are discussed further below in the section on new targets.

As noted in the introduction to this chapter, despite growing cynicism about the returns from continued engagement with the international negotiations on climate change, many groups remain committed to using those channels available to them to influence the future of the Kyoto Protocol. This choice takes place against a background of growing emphasis under international law, from the Rio declaration to the Aarhus Convention, on the importance of public participation (see Box 3.3). Agenda 21, for example, calls upon intergovernmental organisations to provide regular channels for NGOs 'to contribute to policy design, decision-making, implementation and evaluation of IGO activities' (United Nations 1992a).

At the same time, we have to recognise at the outset that only a fraction of global civil society organisations actively participate in these processes. Southern-based groups are under-represented in international negotiating processes because they lack the resources required to attend and meaningfully participate in international meetings held all around the world, and which place a high premium on legal, scientific and other forms of expertise that Northern elites tend to have in greater abundance. The international reach of some groups derives from their access to the decision making process within powerful states. The influence of groups such as Natural Resources Defense Council (NRDC) and Environmental Defense (ED) on the Environmental Protection Agency (EPA) and their ability to change the course of votes in the US Congress have provided key leverage in achieving positive environmental outcomes in the past (O'Brien et al 2000). At the same time, such leverage ensures that the groups' voice and influence is out of all proportion to the numbers they represent, generating concerns among governments. It accounts for the resistance of some developing country delegates to moves to open up regional and international policy processes to further participation from civil society. The argument is that well-resourced groups have an opportunity both to influence their own government at national level and to make their voice heard regionally

Box 3.3: Commitments in regional and multilateral environmental agreements

The notion that public participation in environmental decision making is important to policy success has been underscored in numerous international policy instruments, including the Rio declaration, principle 10 of which declares:

Environmental issues are best handled with the participation of all concerned citizens, at the relevant level. At the national level each individual shall have appropriate *access to information* concerning the environment ...and the *opportunity to participate* in decision making processes. States shall *facilitate and encourage public awareness and participation* by making information widely available. Effective *access to judicial and administrative proceedings, including redress and remedy*, shall be provided. (United Nations 1992b, emphasis added)

Similarly, Article 1 of the Convention of 1998 on Access to Information, Public Participation in Decision Making and Access to Justice in Environmental Matters (Aarhus Convention) states that: 'each Party shall guarantee the rights of access to information, public participation in decision making and access to justice in environmental matters in accordance with the provisions of this Convention'. (UNECE 1998).

The Convention contains provisions on access to information, access to justice and public participation in decision making.

– allowing them 'two bites at the apple' – in a way that is not possible for other less well-resourced groups.

In many ways, it is these better-resourced groups that are able to contribute to each stage of the international policy process described below. Some, such as WWF, have a more global reach, by virtue of having country offices across the world. This puts them in a better position to push for domestic ratification, since they can pool resources and channel them through country offices in the ratification process. Though generally considered under-resourced, total finances available to NGOs participating in these processes easily exceed the amount available, for example, to the United Nations Environment Programme. For example, WWF has around 5 million members worldwide with a combined income of around SwFr470 million ($US391 million); Greenpeace International has more than 2.5 million members in 158 countries with an annual budget in the region of $US30 million; and Friends of the Earth has over a million members in 58 countries (Yamin 2001: 151). Resources on this scale are not available to many other groups, of course, and of themselves explain to only a limited degree the types of influence that groups have been able to exert.

Various models have been employed to account for the influence of these groups (Arts 1998; Betsill and Correll 2001; Newell 2000). Though malleable and shifting, the distinction between groups that might be considered 'insiders' and those that are characterised more by their exclusion from the centres of decision making as 'outsiders' does help to highlight important divisions among those groups engaged in the climate change debate. Groups move between these categories over time depending on which strategies they adopt; and the insider–outsider distinction describes, in reality, a spectrum of access and influence rather than a hard-and-fast dichotomy. It is, nevertheless, the case that some groups, by virtue of their resources, expertise and connections to key government officials, are in a position to exert a much greater direct influence upon the decision-making process than groups whose campaigning agendas, lack of resources and choice of strategy serve to exclude them from the centres of decision making power.

Sometimes it is the strategies themselves, rather than the groups, that might be considered 'inside' or 'outside'. Table 3.1 (see page 114) provides a loose typology of groups and strategies that seeks to distinguish more conservative 'inside-insider' groups, which employ traditional patterns of lobbying and interest representation, from 'inside-outsider' groups, which are involved in the formal policy process but adopt more confrontational strategies to influence it, reflecting different ideologies regarding market mechanisms and the role of the private sector, for example. The final category identified is 'outside-outsiders', which covers the position and strategy of those groups that are not involved in the formal policy negotiations on climate change, but rather seek to draw attention to the impacts of the problem on existing patterns of inequality and social injustice through a variety of campaigning tools and technologies of protest. As with any typology, the classification does not hold in all cases, nor does it imply that groups do not move between categories and strategies, as, on occasion, they clearly do. The point is to highlight points of comparison which help to explain the diversity of aims, strategies and ideologies that characterise civil society organising around this complex theme.

Agenda setting

Agenda setting refers to the earliest stages of the policy, when a problem is being defined and policy makers contemplate appropriate and viable courses of action. It is in this context of uncertainty and political turbulence, particularly in the light of a (perceived) crisis or amid high expectations of a policy response, that an opportunity is created for well-thought-through and politically acceptable solutions. When interests are unclear, there is scope for well-organised groups to attempt to define the dimensions of a problem, reflecting, of course, their own preferences and agendas. They can generate demand for action when policy positions are being developed, when policy responses are being defined, expertise sought and the need for international action discussed. Besides drawing on research and policy advocacy to present scenarios and options and to build the case for a particular course of action, other strategies include drawing attention to work within the scientific community, and operating as knowledge brokers in its translation into popular and politically digestible and palatable forms by working through the media and engaging in popular education. Politically, an important strategy is to help build support for constituencies favouring action within government, where departments may look to other actors to bolster their bureaucratic negotiating position.

The ability of groups to do this is affected by a number of variables. It is important not to under-estimate the significance of party politics and the nature of the administration in office. For example,

though environmental NGOs in the US enjoyed frequent pre-negotiation meetings with the delegation before key meetings, 'following the change of administration (to G W Bush) environmental NGOs no longer enjoy the same access to governments and have had to adopt other tactics to pursue their agenda' (Gulbrandsen and Andresen 2004: 61). Levels of access are also affected by whether groups enjoy 'insider' or 'outsider' status. Such distinctions transgress North–South divides, as groups such as The Energy and Resource Institute (TERI), Centre for Science and Environment (CSE) from India or the Bangladesh Centre for Advanced Studies (BCAS) have established channels of access to their governments reflecting the unique forms of knowledge they can bring to government decision making. As Yamin (2000: 150) notes:

The ability of NGOs to influence substantive developments was (and still remains) underpinned by the fact that scientific and environmental associations possess the technical expertise that is so often needed to ground international environmental policy-making processes.

Knowledge brokers, research-based institutions such as the World Resources Institute, Union of Concerned Scientists, WorldWatch Institute, TERI and Foundation for International Environmental Law and Development (FIELD) are in many ways part of the epistemic communities that operate as conduits between the world of research and the world of policy (Gough and Shackley 2001). By providing, packaging and disseminating key findings of use to policy makers, such actors perform key roles as knowledge-brokers, agenda setting within the international negotiations, as we will see below. As Yamin (2001: 157) notes:

By publishing reports and providing information to states through briefing papers, and in many cases behind the scenes discussions with policy-makers about the implications of latest research before this has been published in peer-reviewed journals, such groups add enormously to government capacity to undertake international negotiations on an informed basis.

Yet even well-informed research-oriented NGOs may not be welcome partners to governments unaccustomed to, suspicious of, or downright hostile towards collaboration with NGOs. Many groups from business and the NGO community complain about the lack of opportunities made available to them for consultation and discussion by the Chinese government, for example. Clearly, then, different state attitudes towards participation condition opportunities for influence, as do the broader dynamics of degrees and forms of democratisation, shaping possibilities of media work and the degree of respect for fundamental political freedoms. As noted above, however, participation does not equate with influence. If access is confined to weaker parts of government, it is less likely that groups will be able to influence the overall direction of policy. For example, good ties with environment ministries come to nothing if trade and finance ministries get to exercise a final veto over policy initiatives.

Negotiation–bargaining

Once international meetings actually begin, there is a perception among NGOs that national capitals exercise strong control over the negotiating space of their teams, and that, as a result, the scope for meaningful shifts in positions during negotiating meetings is often fairly minimal. In addition, NGOs do not have legal rights to put items formally on the agenda. They may be represented at Conference of the Parties (COP) meetings as observers, however, if parties agree, on the proviso that they are qualified in matters covered by the convention. Opportunities to intervene in meetings are normally restricted to opening or closing plenary sessions. NGOs' ability to make interventions is subject to the discretion of the chairperson of the meeting and ultimately rests with the parties to the convention. Spaces are provided, nevertheless, for position statements to be heard in the plenary sessions from groups claiming to represent different elements of civil society, such that in the past CAN has spoken on behalf of assembled NGOs, and the International Chamber of Commerce has made an intervention on behalf of industry.

It is increasingly true also that the formal legal rules assigning NGOs a peripheral role in global environmental governance are at odds with overwhelming evidence of the multiple and diverse ways in which NGOs are shaping policy and strengthening the effectiveness of institutions through their day-to-day activities. Nevertheless, some aspects of the negotiating process are effectively off-limits for NGOs. The more high level the meeting, the less access NGOs tends to have. As Yamin (2001: 158) notes, 'Parties often cite

concerns that last minute trade-offs and compromises are more difficult to make if each step is being watched by a large group of observers.' Informal-informals are sometimes organised whereby a member of the secretariat brings together leaders of different negotiating blocs currently experiencing stalemate to try to agree on the basic contours of a negotiating package. These are off-limits for NGOs, unless they have managed to secure for themselves a senior role on a leading delegation. Despite the existence of these mechanisms by which civil society involvement can be restricted, Yamin (2001: 58) notes how communication technologies and mobile phones make it increasingly difficult to exclude groups in practice:

In the last few hours of negotiations of the failed Hague climate change summit in November 2000, the 'big' NGOs were able to 'number crunch' the figures and submit their analysis via phones more or less in 'real time'. Because some of the deals being struck were made in the corridors outside the ministerial meeting, some of these NGOs were actually more in touch with what was going on than developing country negotiators in discussion with President Pronk. What counted was who was an 'insider' not who was physically outside.

Membership of delegations remains the most direct way in which NGOs are able to participate in the negotiating process and to attempt to influence government positions. Following this logic, those with access to the most powerful delegations, see their influence extend further. As Raustiala (1996: 56) notes, 'many US based NGOs, because of their size, expertise and influence on the government of the US were particularly influential'. At the same time, groups also play key roles in bolstering the negotiating capacity of delegations with fewer resources and personnel and less voice in the negotiations. The use of non-national technical or legal experts to assist delegations in complex negotiations, in the way FIELD lawyers have assisted representatives of AOSIS, is now commonplace. (Yamin 2001: 157) argues:

The provision of NGO analysis and recommendation of policy options is, of course, not new - it is indeed the hallmark of their lobbying efforts - but the degree to which it appears to be relied upon by many governments, without further checks, may be far more widespread than previously seems to have been the case.

The ability of groups to play this role is enhanced by the negotiations fatigue experienced by many delegations, but particularly those with fewer resources, who find themselves over stretched. Diplomats from developing countries and countries-in-transition in particular 'rush from meeting to meeting, often only reading the paperwork on flights, and becoming increasingly reliant on the briefings provided by their favoured NGOs in the hope that these will provide them with a sufficient analysis of the issues at stake and the stance they should take' (Yamin 2001: 157).

> 'the pledge and review' proposal...was dubbed by NGOs as a 'hedge and retreat' strategy, and governments fearful of a continued negative reaction quickly dropped the idea

Performing this sort of role is not a benign act on the part of NGOs; it provides a position of leverage and a platform from which to launch proposals. Working with supportive delegations can provide a transmission belt for ideas and proposals, even if direct presence on the negotiating team is not possible. The example of the AOSIS Protocol, thought to have been heavily drafted by FIELD lawyers, is an oft-cited example of such direct influence (Newell 2000). Identifying states that will potentially serve as collaborative partners, however small or seemingly peripheral to the negotiations, is a way of greatly influencing the debate, given that every state has an automatic right of access to committees and working groups from which NGOs are excluded.

Besides seeking to affect directly the course of the negotiations and to be present when final trade-offs are being made, attending the meetings also serves a valuable function for NGOs from countries, often but not exclusively developing ones, where access to key ministries is difficult in a national setting. Opportunities for formal meetings and informal lobbying are potentially multiplied at international occasions, where bureaucrats are absent from their normal duties and competing demands for up to two weeks at a time.

International meetings also provide an opportunity to attempt to influence the domestic debate on climate change. Stunts, press conferences and press releases

have been used to this end in the past. Business groups sought to undermine positions in favour of binding emission reductions adopted by the Clinton administration by hosting press conferences with senators vowing to veto ratification of any agreement not containing emission reduction commitments from developing countries. Likewise, NGOs supportive of action have made use of the press to expose recalcitrant positions or to maintain support for positions they approve of. A recent example would be the 'Fossil of the day awards' presented at the COP 10 meeting in Buenos Aires in December 2004, where, for example, the Netherlands was targeted, as reigning European Union President, for making too many concessions to the US in order to bring it back into the negotiating process. NGO interventions can also help governments to foresee domestic reactions to proposals; to gauge whether they will be acceptable to the public and whether NGOs will support or ridicule them 'back home'. An example would be the 'pledge and review' proposal suggested by several delegations during the negotiations towards the UNFCCC. This voluntary process of self-set targets was dubbed by NGOs as a 'hedge and retreat' strategy, and governments fearful of a continued negative reaction quickly dropped the idea. According to Susskind (1994: 127), such interventions:

can help even the most powerful leader anticipate national and international reactions and gauge the acceptability of various negotiating postures more effectively before public pronouncements are made.

NGOs can also help to break deadlocks in the process. In 1995, at the COP1, CAN helped to mobilise the support of China and India for a protocol, bringing them into the 'green group' that it had been constructing. Grubb (1995: 4) notes:

NGOs probably played a significant role in persuading Indian and Brazilian delegates to make moves that broke the impasse and that led ultimately to the developing countries' 'green paper' and thence to the Berlin mandate.

It is also important not to underestimate the power of a saleable idea at an opportune moment in the process. Amid debates about whether or which way to take the Kyoto Protocol forward, the Global Commons Institute (GCI) has successfully promoted the idea of 'contraction and convergence' among key developing countries and even some developed countries seeking a leadership position on the climate change issue. The concept implies a contraction of emissions from developed countries in order to create ecological space for an increase in the emissions of developing countries, towards an agreed international benchmark of per capita entitlements. In addition to support from key developing countries such as India, within the UK government Geoff Mulgan and David Miliband, former heads of the Prime Minister's No 10 Policy Unit, have both highlighted the idea publicly. More explicit support for the idea has come from Sir John Harman, chairman of the Environment Agency; Sir John Houghton, the eminent UK climatologist; and the parliamentary environmental audit and international development committee (Lynas 2004). Earlier in the negotiations, GCI was also able to contest the use of cost-benefit analysis in IPCC Working Group 3's reports and, in so doing, challenge a 'given' of environmental decision making. Masood and Ochert (1995) claim:

> *GCI persuaded those responsible for the summary for policy-makers to erase references to damage estimates and include phrases such as 'the literature on the subject is controversial', mention of the 'value of life' and reference to the fact that the 'loss of unique cultures cannot be quantified'.*

York, Britain: flooding is increasingly common in developed countries ©*Trygve Sorvaag/Panos Pictures*

Careful lobbying and appeals to persuasive moral claims can, on occasion, trump routinised practices of decision making.

In sum, direct and unambiguously attributable influence of NGOs is almost impossible to identify if measured in terms of its impact on the text of agreements that are generally hammered out in negotiating rooms to which NGOs are denied access. It is more easily discernible in the process whereby agreements come into being, the issues they do and do not tackle, and the ways in which those issues are framed and ultimately acted upon.

Enforcement–implementation

The vagueness of commitments agreed at the international level leaves enormous scope for national discretion in priority setting and policy making. NGOs rely once again on nationally oriented strategies and networks of influence described above in the subsection on agenda setting. At this stage of the process, they

can bear witness to governments' commitments, use whistle-blowing when commitments are being violated and use 'naming and shaming' strategies to expose those most guilty of failing to implement their commitments. One recent strategy in this respect has centred on shaming parties that buy 'hot air' quotas from Russia and other Central and Eastern European countries in order to meet their commitments under Kyoto (Gulbrandsen and Andresen 2004: 70). To dissuade parties from exploiting these loopholes, Greenpeace developed a computer 'loophole analysis' which highlights the country-specific consequences of exploiting the loopholes. As noted below, however, despite the efforts of groups such as SinksWatch and CDM Watch, monitoring the multiplicity of private transactions that may be undertaken under the purview of the Clean Development Mechanism and its associated mechanisms presents a formidable task for groups wanting to assess the extent of countries' commitments to genuine emissions reductions.

Besides such strategies of public exposure, NGOs have also undertaken detailed analysis of national communications, highlighting gaps in data and silences in reports, particularly relating to policies and programmes that might offset projected gains. Groups from the CAN network have also produced their own reviews of countries' policies and commitments and whether these are on course to be met. These have been widely distributed at the international meetings. To some extent, as Arts (1998) notes, testimony to the influence of NGO evaluations is found in the fact that they are widely referenced in governments' own policy documents.

We note below how NGOs have involved themselves in post-Kyoto debates about institutions and mechanisms. They have played an ongoing role, however, in debates about arrangements that exist within the UNFCCC regarding aid and technology transfers to help non-annex I (principally developing) countries meet their commitments. Channels of access are available to recognised NGOs with bodies such as GEF responsible for overseeing these transfers; for example, the Ad Hoc Working Group on Global Warming and Energy under the Scientific and Technical Advisory Panel of the GEF. The patterns of access and influence reflect familiar structures of insider–outsider NGO participation. As noted above, this includes the disproportionate influence of US groups in general, as a result of the reliance of those institutions upon funding from the US that has to be approved by Congress, where the largest Washington-based environmental groups, or the 'big 10' as they are often referred to, have channels of access and good networks of influence (Newell 2000).

The text of the Kyoto agreement having been secured, the key battleground for many NGOs has become the rules and mechanisms for realising the commitments contained in the agreement. Debates between governments, as well as within civil society, about compliance have focused on the rules for sinks[4] and the ways in which the flexibility mechanisms contained within Kyoto can and should be used. What Gulbrandsen and Andresen (2004) call 'advisory organisations', such as the Centre for International Environmental Law (CIEL) and FIELD, have played a key role on many of the technical issues concerning benchmarking and measurement of activities for which credits are claimed against commitments. The authors contrast such groups with activist organisations

that derive their legitimacy from a wide membership and a popular base of support.

The final negotiations on the compliance procedure for the Kyoto Protocol were conducted behind closed doors. Some NGOs nevertheless belonged to networks of experts on compliance that were able to access the discussions. Others managed to secure participation on government delegations. For example, Gulbrandsen and Andresen (2004: 60) cite the case of Samoa acting as co-chair of the Joint Working Group on Compliance while having a US lawyer from FIELD on its delegation 'who is said to have played an important role in the compliance negotiations and in the G77 discussions'. The fact that questions of sinks and flexibility mechanisms attracted most attention, at the expense of time on compliance, at least until the final stages of negotiations, provided an opportunity for research-oriented organisations with these types of legal and technical competence. They operated as intellectual leaders as a result of their ability to frame the compliance issue in a novel and constructive way. To some extent, this also reflects the sort of division of labour discussed above, allowing CIEL and WWF to focus on these issues, with less involvement from more activist groups such as Friends of the Earth and Greenpeace. In particular, knowledge gaps on the issue and the lack of priority given to it by most delegations meant that the persistence and experience of these groups was important in forging the compliance regime. In this regard, Gulbrandsen and Andresen (2004: 68) note:

their capacity to influence the way the issue was framed appears to have been quite substantial when compliance was coined in more technical and politically neutral terms in the early phase. As positions polarised towards the end of the negotiations, their influence was substantially reduced.

Attitudes of states towards civil society participation continue to be key to the settlement of these issues. NGOs were united in their desire for openness and public participation, against the opposition of countries like Russia that firmly rejected an open compliance regime to which NGOs would be able to submit information.

---

4 'Sinks' are carbon sinks, principally forests, that absorb CO_2. Those countries with significant forest land cover are seeking credit for preserving forests in the interests of climate protection.

NGOs were successful in ensuring that in their capacity as observers they could attend enforcement branch deliberations and hearings, unless the branch decided otherwise. NGOs could also submit technical or factual information to the facilitative and enforcement branch, even if these bodies were required to accept information only from 'official' sources.

> some 850 local authorities in Europe are now jointly implementing local climate protection initiatives, while in Japan more than 50 municipalities are setting local environmental targets

One strategy adopted by groups at the national level to force mandates for government action involves filing legal suits. Twelve US states, several cities and over a dozen environmental groups[5] joined forces to challenge an administrative ruling denying the EPA authority to control greenhouse gases on the grounds that these gases do not meet the Clean Air Act's definition of 'pollutant' (ICTA 2003). The plaintiffs challenged the EPA decision in the Court of Appeals for the DC Circuit. Joseph Mendelson, Legal Director of the International Center for Technology Assessment, said of the case:

The Bush administration can try to ignore the science behind the causes of global warming, but it can't hide from the law. If it takes lawsuit after lawsuit to force the Bush administration to accept its responsibilities and pursue good public policy on this issue, then that's what it will face. (ICTA 2003)

A key rationale behind the use of legal suits is that they help to focus public attention on a particular instance of government inaction. Yet it should be noted that many of the strategies of awareness-raising and public education that are adopted at earlier stages of the policy process have less traction at this stage. Put bluntly, 'the questions of verification and monitoring are extremely complex and boring for the media and the public' (Gulbrandsen and Andresen 2004: 70).

At this stage of the process in general, environmental NGOs find it harder to bring the weight of public pressure to bear on governments, as such pressure is more easily dissipated by the lethargy and complexity of bureaucracy and by the realisation of the costs associated with policy options designed to meet international obligations. Frustration with the slow pace of implementation has led some groups to pressure local councils to set their own greenhouse gas reduction targets. In persuading local authorities to make commitments, NGOs have played a facilitating role in exchanging information about how other towns and cities have managed to reduce emissions. For example, some 850 local authorities in Europe are now jointly implementing local climate protection initiatives, while in Japan more than 50 municipalities are setting local environmental targets. The International Council for Local Environmental Initiatives (ICLEI) has brought together more than 400 municipalities to reduce emissions in cities in Central and Eastern Europe (ICLEI 2004).

We find further evidence in the following section of the ways in which both frustrations with existing channels of participation or perceptions of opportunities to press for change drive civil society organisations to pursue fresh strategies with new actors in order to achieve their goals more effectively.

New targets and strategic alliances

Targeting the multilateral development banks

The World Bank has the potential to finance a number of important climate protection initiatives, as well as reduce the climate-changing impact of other leading development actors. In addition to being an implementing agency of the GEF, the World Bank has a separate Climate Change Programme made up of three components: Climate Change Overlays Programme; World Bank Activities Implemented Jointly (AIJ) Programme and the Global Carbon Initiative. The Bank also has a Clean Coal Initiative intended to encourage the use of 'environmentally-friendly' coal technologies.

Yet a number of factors prevent the World Bank from making a greater contribution to the action on climate change. One of the most serious is its failure to integrate effectively and systematically the goals of climate change protection into mainstream lending activities. Others are its 'market-fixated' approach,

---

5 Besides groups that have an established track record of working on climate change, such as Sierra Club, Greenpeace, NRDC, Environmental Defense and Friends of the Earth, groups such as Centre for Food Safety, Centre for Biological Diversity and US Public Interest Research Group also joined the challenge (ICTA 2003).

Box 3.4: **When global citizen action works**

Brown and Fox (2001) suggest that groups able to do some the following may have a longer-lasting impact:
- Make the campaign fit the target by using the right tactics, coalitions and resources to bring about a particular type of change. Reflecting on International Financial Institution (IFI) campaigns, Nelson (2001: 69) suggests: 'NGO influence is focused on a handful of policy issues and their victories have come in carefully, strategically chosen campaigns.'
- Open up cracks in the system by engaging with allies within the system who may also be looking for support for their own positions.
- Recognise that impact takes different forms and that definitions of success change over time. Campaigns that do not succeed with direct influence may still be considered to have had significant impact when measured by more indirect indicators.
- Create footholds for others to follow, creating institutional openings and changes that will allow other groups to shape change in the future from the earliest stages of the policy process.
- Address their own accountability to those they claim to represent.
- Address power and communication gaps to build trust and enable quick and cohesive responses to changing circumstances.
- Key individuals and organisations, acting as bridges in a global network, can have influence wildly disproportionate to their wealth or formal power.

which prevents direct support for energy efficiency and renewable energy, and the way it calculates the costs and benefits of projects, which, because it eschews life-cycle analysis, puts energy efficiency technologies at a disadvantage[6]. The Power Failure report produced by Natural Resources Defense Council and Environmental Defense in March 1994 found that World Bank task managers are currently not subject to incentives or requirements to give end-use energy efficiency a high priority in power loans, and that few loans incorporate demand-side management or address energy efficiency other than through price increases (EDF and NRDC 1994). As noted above, the more research-oriented and conservative NGOs are currently working with the World Bank to reduce its contribution to climate change, through mechanisms such as the Ad Hoc Working Group on Global Warming and Energy under the Scientific and Technical Advisory Panel of the GEF. They face an enormous challenge, however, in pushing a reform agenda within a bank which, through a combination of ideological imperatives, bureaucratic inertia and material necessity, systematically favours projects and forms of energy production that contribute to climate change.

Alongside those seeking to engage the World Bank, there is a vocal army of critics such as the Bretton Woods project and many other like-minded environment and development NGOs that celebrated the World Bank's 50th anniversary by declaring that '50 years is enough!' There is now a rich history of social movements organising around the activities of the leading multilateral development banks that should yield some important lessons for groups mobilising around the climate footprint of these actors. Some of the key reflections from previous struggles are summarised in Box 3.4.

Targeting the corporate sector

Although much of the civil society activity described so far in this chapter is oriented towards the state, not all groups are concerned with policy reform. There has been a growing recognition that sources of resistance and therefore, simultaneously, potential drivers of change are to be found among the business actors, who often operate as the 'street-level bureaucrats' of climate policy because of their command of the capital, technology and expertise that is central to change at the level of corporate strategy (Levy and Newell 2005).

Among some groups, this recognition has produced a form of positive engagement with like-minded elements within the business community. In this respect, there has been an important role for organisations like the

---

6 *This is because these technologies are relatively expensive to install but save money over the course of their lifetime.*

Pew Centre on Climate Change, whose 'Partnership for Climate Change' has acted as a catalyst in bringing together reform-minded elements of the business community to support the science of climate change and commit themselves to meaningful action. This has undermined the ability of those industry coalitions that dispute the need to fund action on climate action to present themselves as the voice of industry. Eileen Claussen, a former US Assistant Secretary of State for Environmental Affairs and negotiator at the climate negotiations, formed the Pew Centre on Global Climate Change in April 1998. According to Levy (2005: 92), it serves both to legitimise a position that favours action on climate change and to create a channel of policy influence for member companies.

Pursuing the same strategy of forming links to like-minded elements within the business community, some groups have sought to work with the insurance industry, forging alliances with insurance companies and banks and encouraging them to shift their lending away from fossil fuels into renewables (Paterson 1999). The aim is to mobilise the financial sector to bring about the shifts in industry necessary to promote more sustainable and climate-benign forms of energy production. The political weight of the sector is not lost on those environmentalists seeking to engage it. As Greenpeace Business (1993: 4) notes, 'the government is fully aware that the London insurance world is a major employer and contributes handsomely to the UK's invisible earnings'. The insurance industry has a particular stake in promoting these changes given that it has suffered in the past and will continue to suffer huge losses from pay-outs following climate-related damage to properties that they have insured. For example, by 1995, 'leading insurers from all the world's main insurance centres had spoken of the threat of bankruptcy from unmanageable catastrophe losses' (Jeremy Leggett cited in Paterson 1999: 25). This came on the back of hurricane Andrew in 1992, which cost the insurance industry $US20 billion in pay-outs on weather-related damage. The fragile alliance between environmentalists and sections of the financial community provides one example of the type of strategic political coalition that environmentalists are seeking to construct to advance a proactive agenda on climate change.

Other alliances between NGOs and sectors that stand to gain more directly from efforts to combat climate change include Greenpeace's connections with clean energy companies and trade associations such as the European Association for the Conservation of Energy (EUROACE) and the European Wind Energy Association. At regional level, the umbrella coalition Climate Network Europe also enjoys close relations with the European Association for the Promotion of Co-generation (COGEN), the corporate umbrella group promoting the interests of the co-generation industries, and has supported the group's efforts to promote this form of energy within the EU. NGOs have also been supportive of the positions of groups such as the Business Council for Sustainable Energy, representing insulation manufacturers and the renewable energy sector, but increasingly also larger companies from the gas sector such as Enron (Levy 2005: 92).

Alongside these strategies of engagement and collaboration, a range of civil society groups seek to challenge the power of fossil fuel companies in the climate change debate in more confrontational ways. Groups such as Corporate Watch, for example, aim at exposing the machinations of power that enable fossil fuel companies to exercise what they perceive to be excessive influence in the climate change debate. One company that has come under particular fire in this regard is the oil company ExxonMobil (Esso in Europe). The 'StopEsso' campaign has sought to encourage consumers to boycott Esso and lobby the company to reverse its strident opposition to the Kyoto agreement, manifested through extensive media work, funding for the Bush administration, and the use of corporate lobbyists to slow progress in the climate negotiations. Exxon has been targeted in particular because it is the oil company that makes the largest contribution to the Bush campaign coffers ($US1.376 million to the Republicans in the 2000 campaign) and has been the most active and high profile of the companies opposed to Kyoto (StopEsso 2005). The campaign forms part of a broader 'boycott Bush' initiative launched by the *Ethical Consumer* magazine in the UK in 2001, with the aim of encouraging consumers to boycott leading companies that contribute to Republican Party funds, including other high-street names such as Microsoft and Budweiser beer, and to let those companies know why they were boycotting their products (Boycott Bush URL).

The cumulative effect of these actions may have been to bring about a shift in strategy on the part of leading firms. Levy (2005: 91) cites an interview with a Ford executive suggesting learning on the part of the

Executive director of Friends of the Earth, Tony Juniper, explains the dangers of cheap fuel ©Tim Sander/Friends of the Earth

company from confrontations with NGOs. The company official reflects:

We lost the first round of battles. We are now trying to be more positive with the science, while still pointing to the high cost of precipitate action before scientific uncertainties are resolved. Our actions will be less strident in the future.

There is clearly a key role, therefore, for NGOs in pushing businesses to commit more resources to combating climate change and in disseminating evidence of the economic gains to be made from 'win–win' investment opportunities. Shareholders and institutional investors have also attracted attention because of the leverage they have with firms to re-orient investment choices towards sustainable energy.

The extent to which NGO pressure is effective in altering company practice appears to depend upon the company in question. Some companies are far more vulnerable and susceptible to civil society pressure on climate change than others. While Shell has a long-term scenario called 'People power' that looks at the

risk of significant public pressure on environmental issues, companies such as ExxonMobil take a very different view. An official from the company said:

If we appear more green, it might get us a better seat at the table, but the real question is whether it would improve our access to resources and markets. BP and Shell actually attract counter-pressure for talking green but not doing enough. There is a Norwegian saying that the spouting whale gets harpooned. (Levy 2005: 85)

Levy suggests there is evidence of a general trend in this respect whereby European managers express far more concern for their legitimacy and image than do managers of US oil firms.

Strategies of civil regulation of the sort described above suggest evidence, according to Yamin (2001: 161), of 'NGO acceptance of the fact that traditional NGO techniques are, on their own, inadequate ways of instigating significant, real changes'. As Gulbrandsen and Andresen (2004: 57) put it:

As long as the Kyoto Protocol has not entered into force and as long as most states have not yet established forceful domestic climate policies, strategies aimed at influencing industry directly are potentially important parts of the activist repertoire. This is likely to continue when and if the Protocol enters into force as behaviour change by target groups is ultimately the only way to reduce GHG emissions.

Many of the key changes necessary to fund climate protection and deter activities that accelerate climate change will come not from more international cooperation alone but from changes in industry itself, and in this case from pressure from stakeholders with a clear self-interest in promoting action.

Targeting consumers

Many of the changes in company policy are also consumer driven, and we should not underestimate the importance of consumer choice and consumer pressure in driving private sector action on climate change. As we have seen, this can be manifested in a confrontational manner, with consumers boycotting firms that continue to oppose the Kyoto Protocol and using their purchasing power to register their disapproval with companies' obstruction of international action on climate change. But it can also take the form of deliberate individual and collective consumer choices aimed at reducing the climate impact of everyday consumption.

In this sense, consumers themselves are being asked to internalise the externalities that they impose on the environment through their consumer choices. As Panayotou (1994: 6) notes, 'consumers are indeed the ultimate polluters since without demand the polluting products would not be produced'. One way they can use this power to positive effect is by supporting markets for climate-benign products, as well as changing their own patterns of consumption in relation to energy use, transportation and the like. Many NGOs belonging to the CAN network have sought to supplement government efforts to persuade consumers to use energy more efficiently by providing booklets and other information materials on how savings can be made from changing simple household practices. Better insulation and longer-lasting energy-efficient light bulbs are examples of 'win–win' measures that activists have pointed to where there is a demonstrable economic and environmental benefit from taking a simple action.

Beyond such short-term remedies, however, tackling climate change implies persuading people to make more significant sacrifices and potentially substantial changes to their patterns of material consumption. The protests against fuel taxes in the UK in 2000, or the resistance to the introduction of the congestion charge in central London, give an indication of the unpopularity of certain measures that help to tackle climate change, even if governments do not often promote them in those terms. It is difficult for campaigners to package measures to address climate change in appealing and attractive terms where there are perceived threats to people's standard of living or freedom of choice (regarding transport options, for example). Groups such as Reclaim the Streets have made the case for car-free city centres through appeals to notions of the liveable city and the enhanced safety that results from pedestrianised spaces, rather than relying on more abstract claims about climate change. The political sensitivity of the climate change issue can be contrasted, therefore, with an issue such as ozone depletion, whereby consumers were asked merely to select brands that did not contain ozone-depleting chlorofluorocarbons (CFCs), or with campaigns on biotechnology, where activists encouraged consumers simply to avoid buying products containing genetically-modified (GM) ingredients, rather than make more difficult adjustments to their lifestyles.

Within civil society: alliances, fissures and the politics of consensus building

In the North, civil society has concentrated on climate change more exclusively as an environmental issue by environmental NGOs and researchers and has focussed on scientific and technical solutions such as emissions controls and carbon credits. In the South, however, climate change emerged primarily as a sustainable development issue, whose solutions are seen as inseparable from larger issues of poverty, trade and globalisation. (Pettit 2004: 102)

The ways in which civil society groups have sought to engage and work with one another have changed over the course of the international community's response to the threat of climate change. Early episodes of conflict and misunderstanding, often resulting from

Climate-change-induced drought adds to the burden of women and children in developing countries °Sven Torfinn/Panos Pictures

insensitivities borne of inequities between groups, partly though not exclusively along North–South lines, have given way to more inclusive decision making and organisational arrangements characterised by the CAN network. As noted above, structural inequalities such as the under-representation of Southern groups at international meetings, which means that their voices are effectively screened out of global debates by resource barriers, as well as institutional structures that privilege organised inputs from civil society, continue to be important. Many of the conflicts over policy agendas and preferences transgress these divides, however, and are explored in more detail below.

Current conflicts

Just as in the international negotiations themselves, so too within civil society there is significant debate and friction regarding the role of developing countries and, more specifically, the issue of whether and at what point they should assume emission reduction commitments. Conflict over this issue of commitments transgresses the North–South divide, with the G8

Climate Action Group[7] opposing developing country commitments at this stage, while more conservative environmental groups are pushing for commitments from developing countries on the basis that this is increasingly a pre-requisite for US (re)-engagement with the Kyoto regime.

A second divisive issue for organised civil society is the role of market mechanisms and carbon sinks, where again the 'big 10' Washington-based groups are aligned against more critical groups such as Carbon Trade Watch, CDM watch and SinksWatch. While the former see important potential in market mechanisms to achieve much-needed emissions reductions, the latter view them as a distraction from the need for the largest polluters, primarily in the North, to reduce their own emissions through actions at home rather than projects sponsored in developing countries. Many of these groups attend the executive board meetings of the CDM, and seek to monitor

---

7 *This includes Greenpeace, Friends of the Earth, New Economics Foundation, Rising Tide and People and Planet.*

sinks projects as well as challenge the use of finance for 'clean coal' and nuclear projects which they do not regard as viable or sustainable alternatives to fossil fuels. While it may be difficult to influence the board directly – and it will certainly be difficult to keep track of all CDM projects in practice – the prospect of NGO shaming may serve to prevent some projects that NGOs would want to oppose from being funded.

NGOs generally oppose market mechanisms because they distract attention from the need for tough domestic action to reduce emissions. Groups such as Forests and the European Union Resource Network (FERN) and Climate Trade Watch have been particularly critical of the delays caused by attempts to construct a carbon market, including trading in carbon sinks (Climate Trade Watch 2005; FERN 2005). The Durban Declaration on Carbon Trading, produced at a meeting on this issue in October 2004 that brought together a number of environmental groups associated with the climate justice movement (see below), stated, 'As representatives of peoples' movements and independent organisations, we reject the claim that carbon trading will halt the climate crisis'. Groups such as Carbon Trade Watch (part of the Transnational Institute) have lodged complaints over the carbon-neutral claims of companies and wealthy individuals. There has been a proliferation of organisations such as Future Forests and Climate Care, claiming that their work on tree planting, for example, can 'neutralise' CO_2 emissions (Future Forests 2005; Climate Care 2005). They offer clients, such as internationally acclaimed rock groups Simply Red and Coldplay, CarbonNeutral flights, driving and homes. Carbon Trade Watch, however, have challenged what it considers to be the 'scientifically dubious practice of planting trees to compensate for pollution'. Their critique is informed by a broader position adopted by many environmental NGOs on this issue that such practices 'distract attention away from the fundamental changes urgently necessary if we are to achieve a more sustainable and just future' (CTW 2004).

Campaigning on very similar themes is the group SinksWatch which has been critical of the booming carbon market and its principal beneficiaries, the financial services industry and organisations such as the International Petroleum Exchange. SinksWatch has also been active in monitoring and contesting the role of the World Bank's Prototype Carbon Fund as a mechanism for reducing GHG emissions. For example,

it lobbied for the bank to drop from its portfolio projects such as the Plantar monoculture plantation project in Brazil on grounds of its high social costs for the rural poor and relatively modest environmental returns compared with other possible investments (SinksWatch 2004). Key dissenters from this oppositional consensus include Environmental Defense (ED), a steadfast proponent of a market-based approach to environmental policy. In part, this commitment stems from its role as one of the principal architects of the US SO_2 tradable permit system. Gulbrandsen and Andresen (2004: 65) suggest: 'Considering its expertise, close connections with the US administration and its political clout, there is reason to believe that it has had an effect on the design of the Kyoto mechanisms – mainly a US brainchild.'

Another key divisive issue is whether there should be restrictions on the use of such mechanisms as a supplement to domestic action. ED was opposed to a cap to encourage maximum flexibility. Differences on this and other issues between groups in Europe, as opposed to the US, to some extent mirror the different regulatory approaches adopted by governments in those regions. The compatibility of the position of groups like ED, in particular, with the position of the US government generated some suspicion towards the group among other NGOs. ED was one of the few environmental NGOs supporting the position of the previous US administration on the possibility of claiming carbon credits for carbon stored in forests and soils. This issue, in particular, created tension within CAN, which suspended ED's membership during the Hague meeting (though it was reinstated later). On the issue of compliance mechanisms, ED sided with the US government and against the majority view within the environmental community that was in favour of stricter penalties for non-compliance.

The outsiders cohere

If these are some of the conflicts and divisions that characterise those groups closely involved in tracking and seeking to shape the negotiations, another set of groups approach the issue from a very different angle. Their focus is on the relationship between rights, environmental injustice and climate inequality. These links are manifested in the relationship between climate change and the struggles pursued by broader social movements such as the environmental justice movement and the anti-globalisation movement. Destruction of the world's climate increasingly features

Box 3.5: Climate change activism and the law

Frustrated by the slow progress and limitations of Kyoto, around the world activists and NGOs are turning to the law in order to combat climate change. According to the Climate Justice Programme (URL), a collaboration between lawyers, scientists and NGOs, existing international and domestic laws can be powerful tools, with the potential to force emission reductions and make perpetrators liable for the climate consequences of their actions. Using various legal principles including human rights, product liability, public nuisance, pollution and harm to other states, civil society actors, often collaborating with state or city authorities, are bringing pressure to bear on governments and companies to reduce emissions. Current legal actions on climate change, grouped by legal category, include:

Public law

A coalition of 12 US states, several cities and a host of environmental groups are suing the Environmental Protection Agency (EPA) for its failure to regulate greenhouse gas emissions under the Clean Air Act. The EPA has argued that it does not have the authority to regulate greenhouse gases for climate change purposes under this legislation. The EPA is supported by the Alliance of Automobile Manufacturers, the American Petroleum Institute, the National Association of Convenience Stores, the US Chamber of Commerce and 11 states. The plaintiffs are challenging the EPA's decision. **www.climatelaw.org/media/states.challenge.bush**

Elsewhere in the US, Greenpeace, Friends of the Earth, individual citizens and the city governments of Boulder, Oakland and Arcata are suing export credit agencies for funding fossil fuel projects under the National Environmental Policy Act (NEPA). According to the plaintiffs, the Export-Import Bank of the United States and Overseas Private Investment Corporation has provided US $32 billion in financing and insurance for oil fields, pipelines and coal-fired plants over the last ten years without assessing their contribution to global warming, which is required by NEPA. **www.climatelawsuit.org/**

In Australia, the Australian Conservation Foundation, WWF Australia, Environment Victoria and Climate Action Network Australia challenged the Minister of Planning's direction to a planning committee to exclude the impact of greenhouse gas emissions from its consideration of a proposal for the expansion of a coal power plant. In October 2004, the judicial review found that such emissions were relevant and should be considered. **www.austlii.edu.au/au/cases/vic/VCAT/2004/2029.html**

Germanwatch and BUND (Friends of the Earth Germany) are taking legal action to force the German government to disclose contributions to support fossil fuel projects through its export credit agency Euler Hermes AG. **www.climatelaw.org/media/german.suit**

Civil law

In July 2004, in New York City, eight US states and a group of NGOs filed a civil law suit against the five biggest US power companies, arguing that emissions are a public nuisance and the court should order their reduction. **www.pawalaw.com/html**

Human rights

In support of the Inuit people's rights, the Inuit Circumpolar Conference is developing a case against the Bush administration at the Inter-American Human Rights Commission, based on the impacts in the Artic of human-induced climate change. **www.inuit.org/index.asp?lang=eng&num=244**

Public international law

An alliance of individuals and NGOs including the Belize Institute of Environmental Law and Policy, Foro Ecologico del Peru and Pro Public (Friends of the Earth Nepal), submitted petitions to the World Heritage Committee to place the Belize Barrier Reef, Huarascan National Park and Sagarmatha National Park on the List of World Heritage in Danger, as a result of climate change. Danger listing is a mechanism under the UNESCO World Heritage Convention requiring an increased level of protection. The petitions argue that the committee must address both the causes and impacts of climate change when drawing up protection measures, in order to ensure the legal duty of states to comply with Article 4 of the convention to transmit World Heritage Sites to future generations. **www.climatelaw.org/media/UNESCO.petitions.release**

in broader critiques of neoliberalism, testimony for which is the profile the issue has received in European and World Social Forums.

These movements have made links to unjust North–South relations, globalisation and long-standing traditions of environmental justice campaigning centred on the disproportionate exposure of poorer communities, often of colour, to pollution. In the latter regard, groups have sought to contest their role as the 'social sinks' for the externalisation of environmental costs. More generally, Pettit (2004: 103) notes, 'By and large, the framing of "climate justice" reflects the same social and economic rights perspectives voiced by global movements on debt, trade and globalisation'. The Durban Declaration on Carbon Trading produced by the climate justice movement, for example, makes explicit links between current attempts to turn the earth's 'carbon-cycling capacity into property to be bought and sold in a global market' and historical 'attempts to commodify land, food, labour, forests, water, genes and ideas' (Durban Declaration 2004). Groups signing up to the declaration claim:

Through this process of creating a new commodity – carbon – the Earth's ability and capacity to support a climate conducive to life and human societies is now passing into the same corporate hands that are destroying the climate. (Durban Declaration 2004)

In terms of strategy, groups belonging to the climate justice movement, such as Rising Tide, have opted for public education strategies and training (campaigning and public speaking workshops), and the production of materials (videos, fact sheets, CD-ROMs, comic books) alongside strategies directly critical of the current course of the policy debate and continued financing of new oil and gas development, for example (Rising Tide 2004). Groups working on the impacts of climate change on specific social groups have also begun to organise themselves. Genanet, which describes itself as a focal point for gender justice and sustainability, would be one example of a group drawing attention to the differential role of women with regard to the impacts and perceived risks associated with climate change, as well as their lack of participation in decision making to date (Genanet (URL)). Similarly, the Environmental Justice and Climate Change Initiative is a coalition of dozens of religious and civil rights organisations advocating 'the fair treatment

of people of all races, tribes and economic groups in the implementation and enforcement of environmental protection laws' (EJCCI 2002). Disproportionate impacts from climate change might accrue to these groups because, for example, 80 per cent of people of colour and indigenous people in the US live in coastal regions.

The Inuit people of Canada and Alaska (the Inuit Circumpolar Conference) have adopted a strategy of litigation, threatening, alongside CIEL, to file a petition with the Inter-American Commission on Human Rights in 2005 against the Bush administration for posing a climate-related threat to their survival. A briefing circulated at COP10 in Buenos Aires stated: 'It is not an exaggeration to say that the impacts are of such a magnitude that they ultimately could destroy the ancient Inuit culture' (EarthJustice and CIEL 2004). Responsible for approximately 25 per cent of global emissions, the US is targeted because of its failure to reduce emissions that have contributed substantially to the impacts felt by indigenous communities (see Box 3.5).

Although not as able to influence opinion or mobilise as effectively as its counterparts within the mainstream environmental movement, the climate justice movement has nevertheless been very active. The groups adopting more critical positions under the umbrella of climate justice held a summit by this name at the COP8 in 2002 in Delhi. The event was attended by hundreds of activists from throughout India, including farmers, fisherfolk, indigenous people and groups representing the urban poor. The Delhi Climate Justice Declaration reveals the essence of these groups' concerns with climate change and the current nature of policy responses to the threat:

We affirm that climate change is a rights issue – it affects our livelihoods, our health, our children and our natural resources. We will build alliances across states and borders to oppose climate change inducing patterns and advocate for and practice sustainable development. We reject the market based principles that guide the current negotiations to solve the climate crisis: Our World is Not for Sale! (India Climate Justice Forum 2002)

Before this, the Climate Justice Summit was held in 2000 in the Hague, paralleling the COP6 negotiations. It was attended by a delegation of Hispanic, black and indigenous leaders from the environmental justice movement in North America, who also held their own

Table 3.1: Typology of groups and their strategies

	Inside-insiders	Inside-outsiders	Outside-outsiders
Examples	• WWF • ED • NRDC • FIELD	• Friends of the Earth • Greenpeace • SinksWatch	• Climate justice movement • Indigenous peoples activists • Rising Tide
Aims	• To advance action on climate change within existing frameworks • To gain access to government decision making • To directly influence the negotiations	• To advance more drastic action on climate change • To question more fundamentally how the issue is currently being addressed (adequacy of goals and the means for achieving them)	• To question the current framing of the climate change debate • To raise popular awareness about the impact of climate change on the poor
Strategies	• Access to delegations • Research (scientific and economic studies) • Provision of legal advice • Support to like-minded delegations • Diplomatic lobbying	• Research for public audiences • Use of media • More confrontational styles of lobbying and exposure	• Protest, demonstrations • Parallel actions and side events • Cross-movement mobilisation • Litigation • Popular education
Focus of influence	• Governments • Regional and international institutions • Private sector (collaboratively)	• Governments (including local councils) • Regional and international institutions • Private sector (critical approach)	• Governments • The public • Other movements (anti-globalisation movement)
Ideologies	• Generally benign view of the market • Critical view of command and control approaches but faith in governments and international institutions to respond effectively to the issue	• Critical view of market mechanisms • Residual faith in international and regional institutions to deliver action and belief in the primacy of legal-based approaches to regulation	• Failure to act on climate change seen as part of broader failing of globalisation • Critical view of the willingness or ability of governments and international institutions to deliver environmental justice because of their ties to the corporate sector.

forum. They expressed scepticism about the technical nature of the UN negotiations and the role of corporate lobbyists and emission brokers therein, claiming:

In the end, the impetus will not likely come from within government. It is a sure bet not to come from the polluting industry. Climate justice will likely take root from meetings like the Climate Justice Summit where those most affected share their common experiences and decide to take collective action. Waiting for governments may be too deadly for communities of color and the planet. (Bullard 2000)

The challenge, as Pettit (2004: 104) describes it, is that 'Climate justice needs to evolve from a parallel noise maker into a genuine pincer that cannot be ignored and into a strategic force that can have a direct impact.'

In an attempt to co-opt the environmental justice agenda, some business and labour groups rejecting the Kyoto Protocol produced a report in July 2004 titled 'Refusing to Repeat Past Mistakes: How the Kyoto Climate Change Protocol Would Disproportionately Threaten the Economic Well-Being of Blacks and Hispanics in the United States' (Pettit 2004:104). The Centre for Energy and Economic Development, a coal lobby group, was responsible for the report, invoking links between race and environmental protection measures by arguing that the Kyoto Protocol would disproportionately threaten the well-being of blacks and Hispanics in the US. Attempts to co-opt and distort the intent of critical agendas have a long history in climate politics. Business groups have, in the past, established 'astro-turf' organisations – industry-funded environmental groups that provide public information on environmental issues that reflects industry viewpoints. Their use by industry groups indicates the importance of public opinion as a battle-ground for legitimising positions on climate policy.

Reflections on the evolving role of civil society in the climate change debate

This chapter has illustrated a number of overarching themes relating to civil society engagement with the climate change issue.

1. *Influence operates over multiple levels.* We have seen how groups are active from the local level up to the global, depending on the types of change they are seeking to achieve and the resources they have at their disposal to bring that change about. Political opportunity structures significantly shape the possibilities for influence, but at the same time groups contest and re-negotiate the spaces available to them. This is true at the national, international and increasingly also the regional level.

2. *Influence is only possible for some groups, some of the time.* Insider–outsider dynamics are important here, implying different degrees of access and ability to take advantage of those political opportunity structures that do exist and contingent on their location within policy networks and expertise, among other things. Strategies for achieving change both evolve and are affected by the stage of the policy cycle, such that some groups can move from the inside to the outside (and vice versa), and often it is the strategy rather than group itself which should be considered 'inside' or 'outside'.

3. *Creating spaces for civil society participation is not enough without the capacity to make use of those spaces.* The climate case would suggest that, without attention to inequalities within civil society, new mechanisms of participation and representation may merely serve to reproduce those inequalities. This issue was raised in the discussion about the disproportionate influence of better-resourced groups and the opportunities they have for 'two bites at the apple', exercising voice at both the national and the international level.

4. *There are patterns of divergence as well as convergence among civil society groups working on climate change.* Although there is evidence of a basic unity of purpose among those groups examined here seeking further action on the issue of climate change, this broad overarching objective conceals enormous diversity in agendas and strategies. Although, at times, this (sometimes rightly) gives an impression of conflict and incoherence, diversity can also be considered a strength of the NGOs and social movements working on climate change. This is true in part because of the broad spectrum of actors and policy processes that have to be engaged with in the climate change debate. But diverse strategies can also reinforce one another in productive and mutually-supportive ways. Here I refer to arguments rehearsed elsewhere (Audley 1997), and in other contexts, about the way in which 'good cop–bad cop' strategies can serve to reinforce one another, or how combinations of cooperative and confrontational

Drought and heat create menacing bush fires in Australia ©*Dean Sewell/Panos Pictures*

approaches provide both carrots (incentives) and sticks (sanctions) to induce state action. Pettit (2004: 105) nevertheless cautions that 'The "insider–outsider" approach can only work if there are elements of a common vision and objective, but not if the campaigns are working at cross purposes or worse, attacking each other'.

5. *Limits are imposed by the problem-structure of climate change.* A recurring theme throughout the chapter has been the ways in which the nature of climate change creates unique challenges for NGOs seeking to influence the policy debate. The close association of the issue with contemporary forms of energy production and consumption, and the ties that exist to issues of security of supply and the geopolitical implications this entails, make climate change an intrinsically more politically sensitive issue than many other global environmental issues. This stronger sense of high politics also means that climate change touches more directly the interests of powerful and well-organised sectors of the global economy, such as oil, the energy sector in general, and the chemical and automotive industries.

In this sense, many of the lessons from other environmental campaigns do not apply to climate change. In the case of ozone depletion, for example, with which climate change is often compared, alternative technologies (CFC substitutes) were available, regulation needed only to address a relatively small number of producers in a small number of countries (mainly in the North) and the scientific consensus on the issue was in many ways more robust. The issue of climate change, despite a catalogue of recent extreme weather events that resemble effects associated with climate change, has less of the immediacy or moral outrage associated with issues such as toxic wastes and whaling. This negatively affects the prospects for short-term action on the problem.

Implications for future strategy

Amid the diversity of mobilising and organising strategies described above, it is impossible to foresee in precise terms the future course of civil society engagement with the climate change issue. In general terms, however, we can expect to see the proliferation of new constellations of state and industry coalitions: both continued lobbying of states to implement the terms of the Kyoto Protocol and renewed efforts to target the largest polluters and foot-draggers directly through a variety of strategies of civil regulation. There is also growing interest in the possibility of forging links with other elements of civil society, including non-traditional allies such as trade union organisations (Obach 2004). Building popular awareness about the issue and strengthening the case for action may also imply an expansion of public education work by civil society organisations, important strategically for leveraging pressure on governments and companies. Such public education and shaming strategies exist alongside the creation of strategic links to other sectors and policy issues in order to improve the salience of the climate change issue. This has taken the form of efforts to draw into proactive coalitions those sectors most likely to be detrimentally affected by climate change, as we saw above. As in the case of the insurance industry, there is an important supportive role that can be performed by international organisations such as the United Nations Environment Programme (UNEP url) in catalysing and providing a platform for these coalitions.

Environmental groups have also sought to mobilise counterparts in other movements, such as groups working with indigenous peoples and development NGOs, where there is an increasing coalescence of interests. The development community, in particular, has been relatively silent on the climate change issue, until recently. Moves are now afoot to engage donors in a conversation about the need to mainstream climate change objectives in aid programming in order to avoid exposing the poor to enhanced vulnerability as a result of climate change. The challenge is to urge international development actors to 'recognise climate change as one of the greatest risks to poor people – a force capable of literally "undoing" decades of development' (Pettit 2004: 102). Despite the ongoing reluctance of donors to engage seriously with the issue, one indication of change has been a recent report by donors on Poverty and Climate Change, which calls for 'steps towards mainstreaming climate issues into all national, sub-national and sectoral planning processes such as Poverty Reduction Strategies or national strategies for sustainable development' (World Bank Group 2003: xi). Groups have been more successful in raising awareness among development NGOs that have become more involved as evidence mounts of the impacts of climate change on the poor in the form of floods, droughts and other 'natural' disasters. Groups such as the UK-based Christian Aid and Tear Fund have made their voices heard, issuing reports and statements at the climate meetings (Tear Fund 2004).

Given the rapidly changing contours of global climate policy, those groups that are flexible in their approach to the issue and that show themselves willing to engage with new actors in order to construct imaginative and diverse coalitions of interest are likely to be more successful in the long term. A reading of where power lies in the climate debate suggests that attention increasingly needs to turn to the power brokers in the global political economy. Pension funds, export credit-rating agencies, banks, as well of course as the larger multilateral development banks that oversee the allocation and use of significant sums of aid money, are central actors in day-to-day decision making, in direct and indirect ways, about whether resources are channelled into activities that benefit or undermine the goal of climate protection. Groups with more access to the legal and scientific expertise necessary to meaningfully engage the international negotiations on climate change appear to enjoy the most influence on climate policy, as traditionally understood. Yet ultimately, the real agents of change may be those groups that are able to alter the behaviour of economic and corporate actors whose decisions chart the climate footprint of the global economy in more direct and immediate ways than the governments that continue to attract most attention from civil society activists.

It is to be expected then that civil society strategies for mobilising government, corporate and consumer action on the issue of climate change will react to, and at the same time seek to change, the continually evolving strategies of each of these actors. Strategies will need to work simultaneously across the material, institutional and discursive spheres that constitute the terrain of contestation between competing actors, interests and discourses in the battle to define future policy on what is increasingly regarded as one of the most serious threats facing humankind.

As more actors enter the climate change debate, bringing with them a plurality of perspectives, ideologies and priorities, we can expect a more complex, but perhaps more nuanced, form of politics to emerge – one which views climate change not as a discrete environmental problem, but which identifies it more squarely as a function of broader processes of economic development and social exclusion. A focus up on the role of those key global economic actors that are contributing to climate change, while at the same time professing to serve the poor, as well as upon the social impacts of further climate change, may contribute to the development of such a politics. Increased emphasis on climate change as a question of social justice and, at the same time, a manifestation of global injustice, may serve to re-energise efforts to tackle the problem in a prevailing context of pessimism about the prospects of a post-Kyoto settlement.

Arts, B. (1998) The Political Influence of Global NGOs: *Case Studies on the Climate and Biodiversity Conventions.* Utrecht: International Books.

Audley, John (1997) *Green Politics and Global Trade: NAFTA and the Future of Environmental Politics.* Washington DC: Georgetown University Press.

Barrett, S. (1999) 'Montreal versus Kyoto: International Cooperation on the Global Environment', in I. Kaul, I. Grunberg and M. Stern (eds), *Global Public Goods: International Cooperation in the Twenty-first Century.* New York: Oxford University Press.

Betsill, M. and Correll, E. (2001) 'NGO Influence in International Environmental Negotiations: A Framework for Analysis', *Global Environmental Politics*, 1(4): 65–85.

Boycott Bush (URL) www.boycottbush.net (consulted 19 November 2004).

Brown, D. L. and Fox, J., (2001) 'Transnational Civil Society Coalitions and the World Bank: Lessons from Project and Policy Influence Campaigns', in M. Edwards and J. Gaventa (eds), *Global Citizen Action.* Boulder, CO: Lynne Rienner Press.

Brulle, R. J. (2000) 'Environmental Discourse and Social Movement Organizations: a Historical and Rhetorical Perspective on the Development of U.S. Environmental Organizations', in R. Scott Frey (ed.), *The Environment and Society Reader.* Toronto: Allyn and Bacon.

Bullard, R. (2000) 'Climate Justice and People of Color'. Atlanta, GA: Environmental Justice Resource Centre, Clark Atlanta University. www.ejrc.cau.edu (consulted 18 November 2004).

CEI (Competitive Enterprise Institute) (URL) 'About Global Warming'. www.cei.org/sections/subsection.cfm?section=3 (consulted 22 June 2005).

Charnovitz, S. (1997) 'Two Centuries of Participation: NGOs and International Governance', *Michigan Journal of International Law*, 18(2): 183–286.

Climate Care (2005) www.climatecare.org (consulted 27 April 2005).

Climate Justice Programme (URL) www.climatelaw.org (consulted 5 May 2005)

Climate Trade Watch (2005) www.tni.org/ctw/ (consulted 27 April 2005).

CTW (Carbon Trade Watch) (2004) 'Environmentalists Cry Foul at Rock Stars Polluting Companies Carbon-Neutral Claims' (press release, 6 May). www.tni.org/ctw (consulted 19 November 2004).

Downs, A. (1972) 'Up and Down with Ecology: The Issue Attention Cycle', *Public Interest*, 28: 38–50.

Durban Declaration (2004) 'Climate Justice Now! The Durban Declaration on Carbon Trading', signed 10 October, Glenmore Centre, Durban, South Africa. www.climnet.org/resources/docs_interest.htm (consulted 19 November 2004)

EarthJustice and CIEL (Center for International Environmental Law) (2004) 'An Inuit Petition to the Inter-American Commission on Human Rights for Dangerous Impacts of Climate Change' (circulated at COP10 Buenos Aires).

EDF (Environmental Defense Fund) and NRDC (Natural Resources Defense Council) (1994) *Power Failure: A Review of the World Bank's Implementation of its New Energy Policy.* Washington, DC: EDF and NRDC.

EJCCI (Environmental Justice and Climate Change Initiative) (2002) 'About Us', www.ejcc.org/aboutus. html, and 'Climate Change and Environmental Justice Fact Sheet' (press briefing, 28 January). www.ejcc.org/releases/020128fact.html (consulted 11 November 2004).

Environmental Conservation Organisation (URL) www.eco.freedom.org (consulted 22 June 2005).

FERN (Forests and the European Union Resource Network) (2005) www.fern.org (consulted 27 April 2005).

Future Forests (2005) www.futureforests.com (consulted 27 April 2005).

Genanet (URL) 'A Healthy Climate? Gender Justice and Climate Protection'. Frankfurt: Genanet. www.wecf.de/cms/download/Healthy_climate_english.pdf; (consulted 17 December 2004).

– 'A Powerful Connection: Gender and Renewables'. Frankfurt: Genanet. www.genanet.de/uploads/media/leaflet__gender__and__renewables_01.pdf (consulted 17 December 2004).

George C. Marshall Institute (URL) 'Climate Change'. www.marshall.org/subcategory.php?id=9 (consulted 22 June 2005).

Global Climate Coalition (URL) 'What Is the GCC?' www.globalclimate.org/aboutus.htm (consulted 22 June 2005).

Gough, C. and Shackley, S. (2001) 'The Respectable Politics of Climate Change: The Epistemic Communities and NGOs', *International Affairs*, 77(2): 329–45.

Grant, W., Matthews, D. and Newell, P. (2000) *The Effectiveness of EU Environmental Policy.* Basingstoke: Macmillan.

Greening Earth Society (URL) 'About Us'. www.greeningearthsociety.org/about.html (consulted 22 June 2005).

Greenpeace Business (1993) 'Insurance Industry Taking Climate Change Seriously'. London: Greenpeace UK.

Grubb, M. (1995) 'The Berlin Climate Conference: Outcome and Implications' (Briefing Paper No. 21). London: Royal Institute of International Affairs.

Gulbrandsen, L. and Andresen, S. (2004) 'NGO Influence in the Implementation of The Kyoto Protocol: Compliance, Flexibility Mechanisms and Sinks', *Global Environmental Politics*, 4(4): 54–75.

Heal, G. (1999) 'New Strategies for the Provision of Global Public Goods: Learning From International Environmental Challenges', in I. Kaul, I. Grunberg and M. Stern (eds), *Global Public Goods: International Cooperation in the Twenty-first Century.* New York: Oxford University Press.

ICLEI (The International Council for Local Environmental Initiatives) (2004) 'Reducing the City's Footprint'. www.iclei.org/projserv.htm (consulted 11 December 2004).

ICTA (International Center for Technology Assessment) (2003) 'States, Environmental Groups Challenge Bush on Global Warming'. Washington, DC: ICTA, 23 October. www.climatelaw.org/media/states.challenge.bush (consulted 8 November 2004).

India Climate Justice Forum (2002) 'Delhi Climate Justice Declaration'. Delhi: India Resource Centre, 28 October. www.indiaresource.org/issues/energycc/2003/delhicjdeclare.html (consulted 12 November 2004).

Leake, J. (2005) 'Wildlife Groups Axe Bellamy as Global Warming "Heretic"'. *Sunday Times*, 15 May. www.timesonline.co.uk/article/0,,2087-1612958,00.html (consulted 22 June 2005).

Leipzig Declaration on Climate Change (URL) www.sepp.org/leipzig.html (consulted 22 June 2005).

Levy, D. (2005) 'Business and the Evolution of the Climate Regime: The Dynamics of Corporate Strategies', in D. Levy and P. Newell (eds), *The Business of Global Environmental Governance*. Cambridge, MA: MIT Press.

– and Newell, P. (eds) (2005) *The Business of Global Environmental Governance*. Cambridge, MA: MIT Press.

Lomborg, B. (2001) *The Skeptical Environmentalist: Measuring the Real State of the World*. Cambridge: Cambridge University Press.

Lynas, M. (2004) 'Give Blair Another Chance', *New Statesman*, 2 April. www.newstatesman.com (consulted 1 December 2004).

Masood, E. and Ochert, K. (1995) 'UN Climate Change Report Turns Up the Heat', *Nature*, 378: 119.

Mintzer, I. and Leonard, J. (eds) (1994) *Negotiating Climate Change*. Cambridge: Cambridge University Press.

Mooney, C. (2005) 'Some Like it Hot', *Mother Jones*, May/June. www.motherjones.com/news/feature/2005/05/some_like_it_hot.html (consulted 22 June 2005).

Nelson, P. (2001) 'Information, Location and Legitimacy: The Changing Bases of Civil Society Involvement in International Economic Policy', in M. Edwards and J. Gaventa (eds) *Global Citizen Action*. Boulder, CO: Lynne Rienner Press.

Newell, P. (1998) 'Who CoPed Out at Kyoto? An Assessment of the Third Conference of the Parties to the Framework Convention on Climate Change', *Environmental Politics*, 7(2): 153–60.

– (2000) *Climate for Change: Non-State Actors and the Global Politics of the Greenhouse*. Cambridge: Cambridge University Press.

– and Paterson, M. (1998) 'Climate for Business: Global Warming, the State and Capital', *Review of International Political Economy*, 5(4): 679–704.

Obach, B. (2004) *Labor and the Environmental Movement: The Quest for Common Ground*. Cambridge, MA: MIT Press.

O'Brien, R. et al. (eds) (2000) *Contesting Global Governance*. Cambridge: Cambridge University Press.

Panayotou, T. (1994) *Economic Instruments for Environmental Management and Sustainable Development*. Nairobi: UNEP Environment and Economics Unit.

Paterson, M. (1996) *Global Warming, Global Politics*. London: Routledge.

– (1999) 'Global Finance and Environmental Politics: The Insurance Industry and Climate Change', *IDS Bulletin*, 30(3): 25–30.

Pearce, F. (2005) 'Climate Change? Menace or Myth?', *NewScientist.com* 12 February. www.newscientist.com/article.ns?id=mg18524861.400 (consulted 22 June 2005).

Petition Project (URL) 'Global Warming Petition'. www.oism.org/pproject/s33p37.htm (consulted 22 June 2005).

Pettit, J. (2004) 'Climate Justice: A New Social Movement for Atmospheric Rights', *IDS Bulletin* (Climate Change and Development special issue), 35(3): 102–06.

Raustiala, K. (1996) 'Non-state Actors', in D. Sprinz and U. Luterbacher (eds), *International Relations and Global Climate Change* (PIK report No. 21). Potsdam: Potsdam Institute.

Rising Tide (2004) 'Rising Tide: Supporting the Grassroots Movement Against Climate Change'. London: Rising Tide. www.risingtide.org.uk (consulted 1 May 2005).

Ruddiman, W. F., Vavrus, S. J. and Kutzbach, J. E., 2005. 'A Test of the Overdue-Glaciation Hypothesis', *Quaternary Science Reviews*, 24: 1–10.

SinksWatch (2004) www.sinkswatch.org (consulted 19 November 2004).

StopEsso (2005) www.stopesso.com (consulted 10 May 2005).

Susskind, L. (1994) *Environmental Diplomacy: Negotiating More Effective Global Agreements*. Oxford: Oxford University Press.

Tear Fund (2004) 'Climate Change and Poverty' (Public Policy Briefing CoP10, 6–17 December). Buenos Aires: Tear Fund.

UNECE (United Nations Economic Commission for Europe) (1998) *Convention on Access to Information, Public Participation in Decision-Making and Access to Justice in Environmental Matters* (Aarhus Convention). Geneva: UNECE. www.unece.org/env/pp/treatytext.htm (consulted 9 May 2005)

UNEP (United Nations Environment Programme) (URL) 'Statement of Environmental Commitment by the Insurance Industry'. Geneva: UNEP. www.unepfi.org/signatories/statements/ii (consulted 12 April 2003).

UNFCCC (United Nations Framework Convention on Climate Change) (2004) 'Russian Decision on Ratification: Major Step Towards Entry into Force of Kyoto Protocol' (press release, 7 October). Bonn: UNFCCC.

United Nations (1992a) *Agenda* 21. New York: United Nations. www.un.org/esa/sustdev/documents/agenda21/english/agenda21toc.htm (consulted 10 May 2005).

– (1992b) *Rio Declaration on Environment and Development*. New York: United Nations. www.un.org/documents/ga/conf151/aconf15126-annex1.htm (consulted 10 May 2005).

– (1997) *Kyoto Protocol to the UN Framework Convention on Climate Change*. New York: United Nations. http://unfccc.int/essential_background/kyoto_protocol/items/1678.php (consulted 10 May 2005).

World Bank Group (2003) *Poverty and Climate Change: Reducing the Vulnerability of the Poor through Adaptation*. Washington, DC: World Bank Group.

Yamin, F. (2001) 'NGOs and International Environmental Law: A Critical Evaluation of their Roles and Responsibilities', *RECIEL* (Review of European Community and International Environmental Law), 10(2): 149–62.

CHAPTER 4

THE MOVEMENT OF LABOUR AND GLOBAL CIVIL SOCIETY
Meghnad Desai with Fiona Holland and Mary Kaldor

Introduction

On 1 April 2005, around 100 people occupied the office of the International Organization for Migration (IOM) in Paris, in protest at the oppression of migrants and against 'Fortress Europe' (Noborder 2005). This was just one of many demonstrations, part of the second European Day of Action for the Freedom of Movement and Right to Stay, which saw anti-capitalist networks, faith associations, migrant support groups, organisations for asylum seekers and refugees, and anti-racist groups demonstrate in cities across the continent. One of many organisations participating in the 1,000-strong London march on 2 April 2005, was the No border network, which campaigns for 'freedom of movement, for the freedom for all to stay in the place which they have chosen, against repression and the many controls which multiply the borders everywhere in all countries' (Noborder URL).

In wealthy industrialised countries, civil society campaigns for open borders have been much less vocal than those lobbying against migration. Typical of the latter is CitizensLobby.com (URL), a US-based grassroots organisation, which campaigns for stronger border security, revamped immigration controls and the scaling back of guest worker quotas, arguing that migrants, whether legal or illegal, risk Americans' jobs and threaten national security and 'traditional values'.

Attitudes towards migration are polarised in sending countries too, with diverse responses by civil society. For many years Mexicans living in the US have maintained links and invested in development projects in their home country via hundreds of hometown associations, a trend that has inspired the Mexican government to facilitate remittance flows through initiatives such as the Programme for Mexican Communities Living Abroad (see Box 4.1). By contrast, civil society in some African countries has become increasingly alarmed by the exodus of massive numbers of medical staff to countries that can afford to pay higher wages and offer professional development opportunities. The outflow means that, for example, Ghana has nine doctors for every 100,000 patients. In response, the Ghana Medical Association has lobbied its government to improve conditions of service and professional training in order to encourage doctors and nurses to remain at home (IRIN 2003).

These diverse responses indicate the complex causes and effects of the movement of labour, an increasingly significant feature of globalisation, the extent and impact of which civil society, nation states and institutions of regional and global governance have begun to consider in recent years (Klein Solomon and Bartsch 2003; Aleinikoff 2002).

Globalisation is often thought of in predominantly economic terms – the movement of goods, services and capital around the world – but it also involves other flows, of culture, crime, ideas and people. However, the globalisation of trade and finance has not been matched by the free movement of labour.

This chapter focuses on legal voluntary migration, which involves both skilled and unskilled labour, typically from South to North. Migration can be within national boundaries – rural-urban migration, for example – or across national boundaries. The focus here is on international migration. The chapter explores the economists' argument for the freer movement of labour which, unlike the freer movement capital, has found few champions. Unlike flows of other resources, such as goods and finance, labour migration is not only about economics but encompasses human rights, issues of identity and concerns about security. The post-9/11 context has injected a new dimension into the debate about migration, encouraged the emergence of new civil society groups, polarised political parties, and seen immigration rise on the political agenda in developed countries. This chapter outlines the ways in which these different arguments are represented by organisations and groups within global civil society.

The authors would like to thank Clarisse Cunha, Adriana Jimenez-Cuen, Anamaria Sanchez and Sabine Selchow for research assistance.

Background

There has been large-scale migration throughout human history. The many forms migration takes comprise rural-urban migration within a country, country-to-country migration and some collectivities such as the Roma, who are perennially moving and have no fixed territory. In war-torn countries there are also displaced persons who have been moved involuntarily. Much of the literature and in contemporary politics focuses on inter-country migration and especially migration from the poor countries to the rich countries.

> After the First World War, economic migration was much reduced compared with the previous hundred years... since the resurgence of globalisation in the late twentieth century, migration has again become a topic of debate

Of course, the very notion of a country with settled borders is a recent one; in the past, land-based empires such as the Ottoman or Hapsburg comprised large territories that subsequently broke up into separate countries. What was intra-empire migration then became inter-country migration. To some extent the same was true of maritime empires, but they straddled what we now call the First World and the Third World. All people living in these empires were treated as subjects (the British Empire) or citizens (the French Empire from the Third Republic onwards), and they had the right to move across the empire, although there was a racial distinction between the white and the non-white subjects/citizens despite the rhetoric of equal treatment.

After the First World War, economic migration was much reduced compared with the previous hundred years. Trans-border movements were most often involuntary movements of political refugees displaced by war or persecution. Legal movements of voluntary migrants faced new difficulties. National boundaries became fixed and a system of passports and visas came into being. But since the resurgence of globalisation in the late-twentieth century, migration has again become a topic of debate.

Migrations in the modern era

In the modern era starting from the Iberian expansion in late fifteenth century, migrations became much faster and took place over longer distances. There were three waves of such migration:

- The first wave took black slaves from Africa to the Americas from the sixteenth to mid-nineteenth centuries.
- A second wave took Indian migrants to Africa, south-east Asia and the Americas, especially the Caribbean, and the Chinese to America and Australia, in the nineteenth and early twentieth centuries.
- A third wave took poor white people from Europe to North America and the Antipodes, also in the nineteenth and early twentieth centuries.

Of course, there were other migrations; slaves also travelled within Africa and from Africa to Asia. Wars often led to captive populations being displaced over long distances. There was slavery across Asia when slaves travelled within and between countries. Since national boundaries were not yet fixed and sanctioned by international law, the distinction between within-country or between-country migration is a later systemisation of the data we have on human movement. There have also been seasonal migrations: for example, transhumance, where large groups moved back and forth in search of livelihoods every year (Braudel 1972/1996).

The most notable of these migrations were the involuntary slave migrations from Africa to North and South America. Angus Maddison (2001) estimates that between 1500 and 1870 nine million African slaves crossed the Atlantic, the bulk of those going to South America and the Caribbean, and about 400,000 to North America. After slavery was made illegal across the British Empire, the Royal Navy policed the seas to prevent the slave trade, whereupon labour migrations took other forms. Imports of slaves stopped in North America; and, after the American civil war, slaves attained the status of free labourers. Their condition remained one of near servitude, with few rights and opportunities to improve their position. Most of them worked as sharecroppers (Blackburn 1997).

In the British territories of South America and the Caribbean islands, indentured labourers from the Indian subcontinent were recruited to replace slaves who used to work in sugar cane fields. They had contracts to work for fixed periods in conditions of near slavery, after

Box 4.1: The role of remittances

If labour migration is driven by a human need to secure a better life back home, are remittances a compelling ground for allowing access to new labour markets? The movement of thousands of people around the world, results in thousands of dollars in remittance flows. Certainly the rapid increase in remittances in recent years is revolutionising attitudes towards labour migration among governments, international organisations, civil society groups and academic circles, which are debating the extent to which the import of capital in the form of remittances justifies the export of people.

The numbers are convincing. The remittances market nearly reached US$126 billion in 2004, according to the World Bank (2005). The volume of remittances has quadrupled in little more than ten years. In 1990 remittance flows represented less than $30 billion (UNDP 2004). However, official figures are underestimates because remittances often flow through informal channels rather than via banks or money transfer companies.

Remittances can be defined as sums of money that migrant workers send back home from their country of employment. They can also be seen, especially in poor countries, as part of a family contract whereby one or more members agree to migrate in order to sustain financially those who remain at home. In many countries remittances play a significant role, sometimes even exceeding the amount of international trade and official development assistance (ODA). In Ecuador, for example, according to the Inter-American Development Bank (IADB 2005), the total received from remittances in 2004 exceeded the gross domestic product (GDP).

In 2004 Mexico was the biggest receiver of remittances, with an estimated $16.6 billion, followed by India, Pakistan, Egypt and Morocco. The biggest senders of remittances were the US, Saudi Arabia, Germany, Malaysia and France (World Bank 2003). In terms of regions, Latin America is the biggest single destination of remittances in the world. According to the IADB, economic migrants from Latin America and the Caribbean sent home $45.8 billion in 2004, 20 per cent more than in 2003. However, if calculated as a share of GDP, lower middle-income and low-income countries in south-east Asia and sub-Saharan Africa are also significant recipients of remittances. In Jordan, Lesotho and Vanuatu remittances make up more than 25 per cent of GDP (Migration Policy Institute 2003).

Recently, the benefits of remittances have attracted much attention. Research shows that remittance transfers appear to be a more stable and steady form of external funding than capital flows for development in poor countries. Moreover, as remittance flows reach people directly in their home country without passing through governments, NGOs or businesses, many argue that they are more effective than overseas aid in sustaining and developing societies (Ratha 2003).

In particular, the increase in remittances and their economic and social impacts have begun to change the attitudes of sending countries towards labour migration. Countries such as Mexico, the Philippines and Sri Lanka have focused on intensifying ties with their diasporas and strengthening patriotic sentiments, while others have created policies and institutions to encourage and assist their nationals to invest at home. For example, the Philippines operates one of the most advanced labour migration strategies, run since 1982 by the Philippine Overseas Employer Administration (POEA). In 2004, a total of 933,588 legal overseas Filipino workers were deployed to 190 countries worldwide, sending home $8.5 billion in remittances (Gonzales 2005).

Mexico offers an interesting case study. In 2003 Mexico became the largest recipient of remittances in the world, receiving more than $16 billion from migrants in the US. In 2004 remittances flows rose by 24 per cent above the 2003 level, surpassing foreign tourism and becoming the country's second-largest source of foreign income after oil exports. This growth is attributed to various factors, including better monitoring by banks, reductions in transfer charges, improvements to the US economy and the steady growth of Mexican emigration. There are approximately 23 million people of Mexican origin living in the US, many of whom crossed the northern border with the intention of remitting money to their families back home. Wage differentials are the lure: the average hourly wage of a migrant in the US is estimated to be six times higher than in Mexico (OECD). Even when Mexico's economy has struggled, for instance during the Peso crisis of 1995, 'migra-dollars' have offset difficult times at home.

Jose Guadalupe, a Mexican immigrant, working on a cotton gin in Missouri ©Alvaro Leiva/Panos Pictures

For many years, hundreds of Mexican hometown associations in the US, apart from fostering cultural and social links between migrants and their places of origin, have also been investing in development projects back home. According to the OECD (2003), between 1993 and 2000 429 projects were initiated in the state of Zacatecas, with a total value of $17 million. In another prominent migrant-sending state, Guanajuato, an initiative called 'mi community', co-financed equally by migrants and the government, created 14 maquiladoras (export assembly plants).

Since the 1990s the Mexican government has undertaken several initiatives to support migrants' money flows. Among the most successful have been identity documents known as 'matriculas consulares', granted by Mexican consulates to enable illegal immigrants in the US to open bank accounts and send money home by more secure and cheaper means. The Mexican government also created the Programme for Mexican Communities living Abroad (PCME) to promote the formation of migrant associations and help them develop collective social and economic projects in their communities of origin.

Given that the economic impact of remittances in Mexico is concentrated in the poorer states, the Mexican government (at state and federal level) has also worked with hometown associations to channel 'collective' remittances into productive investment in places of origin. In 1993 a state funding programme in Zacatecas known as 'Dos por Uno' ('Two for One') matched every dollar raised by a US-based hometown club. This initiative spread to other states and became 'Three for One'. In less than a decade, the programme had raised some $4.5 million for hundreds of projects that provide water and build schools and other facilities.

It is perhaps no surprise that for some developing countries the benefits of remittances can counteract the negative effects of the 'brain drain' – the phenomenon whereby developing countries lose between 10 and 30 per cent of their skilled manpower (ILO 2002). Another debate is whether migrants' money flows cover only consumption back home or lead to development, reducing in turn the incentives to migrate in the long term. Some argue that remittances raise income inequalities in poor countries and tend to decline in the long term (Tanner 2005). Others view remittances as the new development finance, funding relatives' education and health care, which improves the country's human capital. According to a World Bank report, a 10 per cent increase in the share of international migrants in a country will lead to 1.6 per cent decline in the poverty headcount (Adams and Page 2003).

Adriana Jimenez-Cuen, Department of Government, LSE

On the move: migration predates the era of globalisation ©*Matias Costa*

which they could settle down or return to their homes. Most chose to stay. A lot of Indian workers went also to South Africa and to the rubber plantations of Malaya. This migration was quasi-voluntary and the conditions of work were more akin to servitude than free labour. The movement was from one part of the periphery of the metropolitan empire to other peripheral parts. The practice of indenture was abolished within the British Empire in 1920 (Tinker 1974).

A big wave of European migration to North America and the Antipodes took place in the nineteenth century. This was migration within the First World or from the Second World to the First World. England alone lost 12 million people between 1820 and 1913. A third of Europe's population migrated to the US, which received 21 million people between 1820 and 1913. These migration waves were voluntary, although a result of the push factor of poverty and often pogroms in Europe, and the pull of the promise of prosperity in the US. This third type of migration was the largest in the four centuries up to the beginning of the twentieth century.

It was during the years following the First World War and even more so after 1945 that migration became difficult. The reason was the rise of the nation (terri-torial) state in Europe and later Asia and Africa (the Americas remained open to migration). As a result partly of the war effort and partly of the growth of the mass franchise, the state had to promise to look after the well-being of its citizens (in return for the obligation to be conscripted). This historical shift in the nature of the international system set up obstacles to the free movement of people. Passports were not usual for international travel until then, and much of the British Empire allowed free movement. (South Africa, especially after the Boer War, was an exception; Australia also switched to a whites-only immigration policy when the federation was set up at the beginning of the twentieth century). Territorial states made distinctions between citizens and aliens. Citizens were entitled to the benefits that the state accorded them, had the right to vote, and could reside in the country. But resident aliens were not entitled to benefits, although they had to pay taxes and abide by the law. They had also no franchise. Immigrants and refugees became legal categories denoting people with restricted right of abode. The territorial state con-tinues to restrict outmigration as much as in-migration, although here again the US is an exception in having a half-open door to immigrants (Harris 1995).

In the quarter century following the end of the Second World War, Keynesian policies guaranteed full employment in developed countries, and soon there was a shortage of labour. The old imperial countries attracted labour from their former colonies, and a Third World diaspora began to grow in Britain, France, and the Netherlands. Turkish workers migrated to West Germany as guest workers. Since the OPEC oil shocks of the 1970s, migration has again speeded up but changed its character. Very much as in the case of the sugar colonies of the early nineteenth century, the oil-exporting Arab countries of the Middle East have absorbed migrant labour from South Asia and North Africa, although as temporary workers rather than long-term proto-citizens. A lot of the movement to Europe was of unskilled and semi-skilled workers who took up low-paid, hard and unsafe jobs spurned by native Europeans. Health workers too were imported into the UK by the National Health Service from the New Commonwealth. Middle Eastern countries also absorbed workers at all levels except the top professional categories (Sassen 1998).

Western Europe lost 3.6 million people during 1914–49. Immigration into Western Europe resumed in the post-war period; between 1950 and 1975, 9.4 million people migrated into Western Europe, and 11 million in the next quarter-century (Maddison 2004: 128). If we examine this trend further, it is Europe, North America and Oceania that have experienced the biggest migrant stock as a percentage of population; respectively 7.7 per cent, 13.0 per cent and 19.1 per cent. Asia, Africa and Latin America are all below the global average of 2.9 per cent in 2000. The exception in Asia is, of course, in Middle Eastern oil-exporting countries and the faster growing 'Asian Tigers'. Thus, Saudi Arabia and Kuwait attracted migrants in the 1990s, so that by 1999 57 per cent of the total labour force in Saudi Arabia was foreign and 82 per cent in Kuwait. By 1999, there were 10 million expatriates in the Gulf region. The proportions were not as high but still noticeable in Singapore (28 per cent), and Malaysia (18 per cent). In terms of growth of the migrant population, South Korea's was 28 per cent per annum between 1990 and 1999, and Japan's 9 per cent.

Yet migration in this recent phase of globalisation has not reached the share of the total population that it attained in the nineteenth century episode, when the global population was smaller, and territorial states were fewer, and did not subscribe to the idea that they

could or should manage their economies. Migrants have constituted 2–3 per cent of the total population in the years since 1965 at a global level (IOM 2003). Today, while capital moves relatively freely, labour movements are restricted by the separate jurisdictions of territorial states. Only movements of refugees and asylum seekers are subject to an international treaty regime. Wars and civil wars, especially in Africa, have also generated massive movements of people but these are distress movements and do not have economic significance. Thus, in 2000 around 175 million migrant workers, permanent immigrants and refugees, and their families, were living outside their home countries (ILO 2004).

Economic theory of movements in goods and people

In economic theory, both classical and neo-classical, labour is categorised as free labour, that is, free to move about and free to enter into contracts. In classical economics, labour was seen as a class comparable to capitalists and landlords. In neo-classical economics a labourer is anyone willing to supply labour services. Karl Marx added a historical dimension to this definition. He said that under previous modes of production, such as ancient (slavery) and feudalism (serfdom), workers had access to the means of production – land, tools, and so on, but no freedom to move and no right to contract out their labour services. With the advent of capitalism, workers were separated from the means of production and therefore had to sell their labour power, their capacity to work, on a periodic basis. They were thus free in the double sense of being divested of any means of production and free to move and enter into contracts (Marx 1867/1887).

In matters of internal migration, typically from the country to the city, economists have seen migrating labour as a source of surplus transferred from one part of the economy to another. Marx considered the dispossession of farmers due to the enclosure movements in Britain to be the seed from which grew the preconditions for capitalist accumulation by driving labourers into the towns, where they were forced to work for low wages, ready for exploitation by the new machine-owning capitalists. W. Arthur Lewis developed this insight in a seminal article in modern development theory, in which surplus – low-productivity – labour is transferred to urban areas for employment, taking with itself, as it were, its food rations. The employment of the surplus labour in urban areas creates profits, which sets off a development process (Lewis 1954). In neo-classical economics, migration is a matter of choice on the part of the migrant, based on a calculation of costs and benefits, attitudes towards risks and the uncertainties of getting employment.

There is no reason why these insights cannot be transferred to global, inter-country migration. But in economic theory, classical as well as neo-classical, international trade has always been treated differently from internal trade. In international trade, the assumption is that factors of production – labour and capital – do not move, but goods produced by these factors do move (land, the third factor, is of course immobile). Ricardo's theory of comparative advantage stipulates what each country should specialise in given that it could produce many if not all commodities. The criterion is comparative labour costs, and the theory leads to a policy prescription of specialisation even when a country can make everything more cheaply than its rivals. It still pays it to confine itself to those commodities where its comparative advantage is greatest. This was the theory that economists held to throughout much of the nineteenth and twenteith centuries.

Swedish economists Eli Heckscher (1919/1949) and Bertil Ohlin (1933/1966) refined this theory in the inter-war period by saying that, given that different countries have different endowments of labour and capital while the set of technological possibilities is the same for all, countries will specialise in commodities best suited to their factor intensity. Thus, a capital-rich but labour-scarce country will export capital-intensive products and import labour-intensive ones. Trade in goods then has the effect of compensating for relative factor scarcity and for equalising, or at least leading to a convergence of, the prices of traded goods across the world. Hence, the price of scarce labour in the first country declines relative to what it would have been in the absence of trade, and the price of capital comes down in the scarce capital-abundant labour country that imports capital-intensive goods. Thus, over the long run the differences between factor prices – real wages, for example – will diminish.

Although economists are aware that the 'long run' is a conceptual and not a calendar time notion, the prediction of the narrowing of factor price differentials between countries over time is a powerful weapon in the economists' armour in defending free trade. As yet, this does not allow for factor movements despite the empirical facts known to economists that throughout the nineteenth and twenteith centuries capital as well as labour moved across boundaries. Scholars have used data on the nineteenth century migrations across the Atlantic to test the predictions of the Heckscher/Ohlin model. The results do not refute their predictions (Hatton and Williamson 1994).

> lately, even more 'liberal' opinion has begun to ask whether a community can be preserved if its diversity is too great

With the transport and telecommunications revolution, two things have happened that enhance the economists' optimism. First, many goods which were non-tradeable, such as services, have become tradeable. This is what is behind outsourcing. Thus, the standard conclusions of Heckscher/Ohlin are applicable to a larger portion of the economy. Second, migration has speeded up despite many restrictions. Some developed countries – the UK and Germany, for instance – are pursuing a positive policy of attracting skilled workers from abroad. Since travel is cheaper and information about entry restrictions is available on websites, individuals can take their own decision to migrate and bear the risk.

The effect of these movements is a rising number of legal and illegal migrants and a growing political debate about the limits of migration in host societies. An influx of labour would obviously impact on the remuneration that labour of all skill levels receives, and hence trade unions are wary of migration flows (as they are of freer commodity trade, as the agitation against China's entry into the World Trade Organization, at the Seattle meeting in 1999 showed, both inside and outside the conference halls; see Desai and Said 2001). The cultural diversity between locals and incomers has also raised problems of adaptation and assimilation, and of threats to the identities of both. This issue of how to deal with diversity was traditionally treated in a hostile, often racist, way by political fringe groups; lately, even more 'liberal' opinion has begun to ask whether a 'community' can be preserved if its diversity is too great (Goodhart 2004). This difficulty of social adaptation raises the question of whether the idea of labour as a commodity is too simplistic. Is the ideal of free world-wide movement of labour utopian?

Is labour just a commodity?

In economic theory, labour is just a factor of production along with capital and land. Thus, if free movement of capital is allowed, so free movement of labour should be. Against this is the view of Karl Polanyi in *The Great Transformation* that labour is more than a factor of production and that the reaction against laissez-faire in late nineteenth century Britain was an attempt to contain in the market for labour within certain safety nets (Polanyi 1944). Marx (along with classical and neo-classical economists) and Polanyi represent two extremes of attitudes towards labour. One holds that labour power is a commodity and hence should have as much freedom of contract as does capital (though for Marx, but not the classical or the neo-classical economists, it does so in a condition of class inequality). The other holds that protection of workers from the worst effects of commodification defines the essence of the revolt against free markets. These rival perspectives on labour are useful as markers for judging attitudes towards migration.

The classical, Marxian and neo-classical perspective has always been one of 'cosmopolitical economy', as Friederich List, a formidable opponent of free trade

and of classical economists, recognised (List 1837/56). Polanyi's perspective is that of a national political economy. He regards free markets in commodities, but especially labour, as a liberal dystopia:

Nineteenth century civilisation has collapsed. The key to the institutional system of the nineteenth century lay in the laws governing market economy. Our thesis is that the idea of a self-adjusting market implied a stark utopia. Such an institution could not exist for any length of time without annihilating the human and natural substance of society; it would have physically destroyed man and transformed his surroundings into a wilderness. Inevitably society took measures to protect itself but whatever measures it took impaired the self-regulation of the market, disorganised industrial life, and thus endangered society in yet another way. (Polanyi 1944: 3–4)

The reform of the British Poor Law in the 1840s was based on the notion that able-bodied workers should be encouraged to move around for jobs and not be granted relief. But the extension of the franchise in the 1860s and 1880s brought the lower-middle and upper-working classes into the political arena. These forces began a programme of intervention in the labour market to correct the imbalance of economic power between labour and capital. Polanyi saw the Great Depression of the 1930s as the final collapse of liberal capitalism. The arrival of Keynes-Beveridge welfare capitalism soon after the Second World War vindicated his thesis in the eyes of many. Yet his argument is very Anglo-centric. Thus, the US, despite the New Deal, had a very different trajectory from the UK as far as its welfare state is concerned (Desai 2002: 211–14). What is more, by the final quarter of the twenteith century, that is, within 40 years of Polanyi's *The Great Transformation*, liberal forces reappeared. However, Polanyi remains, a powerful tool in the armoury of the anti-globalisers. He would of course be hostile to the migration of labour and take a nationalistic view of well-being, much as List did about manufacturing and wealth creation.

Concepts and categories

Two classifications may be useful in theorising about migration. One is the distinction between voluntary and involuntary migration. The other is that between legal and illegal migration. This schema will be helpful in understanding migration. Thus slaves moved involuntarily, although, until the abolition of slavery, legally. Of course, some voluntary migration is illegal as it runs into legal barriers set up by host states. Illegal but voluntary migration constitutes a major problem for many developed countries. The US and Spain announce periodic amnesties for illegal migrants, which *ex post facto* legalises them. The categories of legal-involuntary and illegal-involuntary migration involve criminal behaviour and are matters for international policing authorities to control. The latter is not the focus of this chapter, which explores the movement of labour that is voluntary and legal. However, this distinction often becomes blurred in public debate and civil society responses to migration, which tend to conflate or ignore the differences between legal migrant worker, asylum seeker, refugee and 'irregular' or undocumented migrant. Also, what is discussed rarely in the public debate about migration is the fact that the right to move is enshrined in the Universal Declaration of Human Rights. It could be argued that legal barriers to voluntary migration should be progressively removed in a world where capital migration is so prized. This is an extreme liberal viewpoint and remains highly controversial; indeed, barriers to migration are increasing,

fuelled by fears about national security and identity in the post-9/11 era, as well as by concerns about jobs, social security and health provision.

> Just as people differ about the benefits of freer trade or freer movement of capital, they disagree about the benefits of freer movement of labour

One consequence of the growing gap between the numbers of migrants and their ability to enter countries of employment lawfully is an increase in irregular migration and trafficking, and heightened vulnerability of all migrants to human rights abuses. This situation has stimulated efforts to create an effective international framework to protect the rights of migrants and better manage the flow of people around the world. The International Convention on the Protection of the Rights of All Migrant Workers and Their Families (ICMW), which was established in 1990, brings together in a single treaty the jigsaw of rights and responsibilities that governments had already agreed to, via various international laws and treaties (see Box 4.2). As Stefanie Grant argues, in addition to uniting these rights and duties, the significance of the convention lies in the set of principles it enshrines, which should guide policy making at national and international levels. The fact that relatively few host governments have ratified the convention illustrates a wariness about adopting a rights-based approach to migration, discussed further below.

The debate about labour migration within global civil society

The issue of freer – voluntary, legal – migration remains controversial. Just as people differ about the benefits of freer trade or freer movement of capital, they disagree about the benefits of freer movement of labour. It is helpful to think of the various NGOs distributed among the four cells of the matrix presented in Figure 4.1. The vertical axis represents the distinction between cosmopolitan and nationalist perspectives. The horizontal axis represents a spectrum of views on capitalism, from pro-capitalist through reformist (but pro-capitalist) to anti-capitalist. The matrix contains the vital distinction between anti-capitalist and pro-capitalist nationalists. The former are at the bottom xenophobic, if not racist, while the latter are liberal-minded but

Figure 4.1 Civil society positions on migration

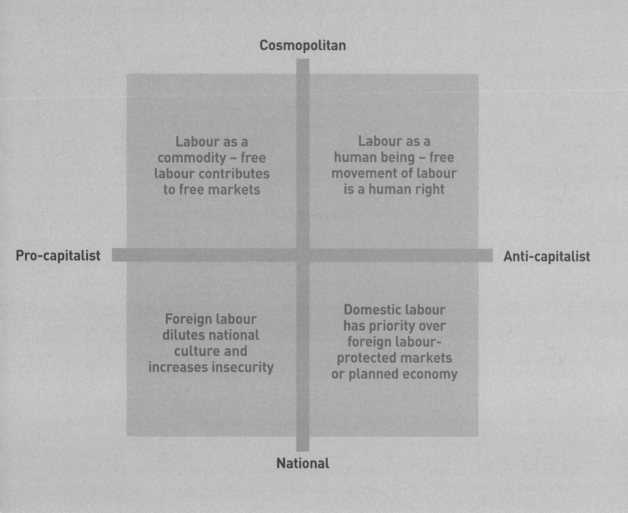

may still have reservations about immigration. This particular division is not an easy one to draw and lines of demarcation can become fuzzy.

Thus, to use the language of previous Yearbooks, Supporters are those who favour the free movement of labour, while Reformers favour fewer restrictions on the movement of labour (Kaldor, Anheier and Glasius 2003). They include pro-capitalists who are pro-economic liberalisation, such as free-market think tanks and economists who support the free movement of labour in order to promote economic development, and who view labour as a commodity. And they include those in the anti-capitalist movement who believe in the free movement of labour as a basic human right.

Rejectionists are against the free movement of labour, while Regressives favour controlled immigration to meet domestic economic needs but are wary of wider migration (or asylum seekers), who are perceived as a threat to both the social security and the culture or identity of a nation. The former favour domestic labour over foreign labour, while the latter are more fearful about national security. Both Rejectionists and Regressive globalisers share the notion of what Ulrich Beck (2004) describes as a 'container culture', which is bounded by, in this case, national boundaries, and not influenced by 'external' influences.

A broad range of civil society actors are involved in the debate about migration, from business lobbies,

Box 4.2: Migrants' human rights: legal protection and rights-based policy making

The globalisation of goods, services and capital has not been accompanied by free movement of workers. This has led to an acute discordance between the numbers of international migrants and their opportunities to enter countries of employment lawfully. It has fuelled irregular migration, encouraged trafficking and smuggling, and sharply increased the vulnerability of all migrants to human rights abuse. It has made more urgent the task of creating an effective international legal regime to protect migrants' rights.

International law has defined refugees, children and women as vulnerable groups with special protection needs, and their rights are protected through special treaties (such as the Convention on the Status of Refugees, the Convention on the Rights of the Child, and the Convention on the Elimination of all forms of Discrimination against Women), which have been widely ratified by states. The need for a treaty to protect migrants as a vulnerable group was recognised in 1990, when the General Assembly adopted the International Convention on the Protection of the Rights of All Migrant Workers and Their Families (ICMW), which had been ratified by 29 states by 1 June 2005. The ICMW protects the human rights of all those working outside their countries of nationality, but it has not yet been widely ratified by states.

Historically, migrants' rights have been protected under different branches of international law, but because the protections were never consolidated and remained dispersed – in human rights law, labour law, consular law and criminal law – there has been no single legal source of migrants' rights, but only a 'giant, unassembled juridical jigsaw' (Lillich 1984).

The ICMW was drafted to consolidate these different protections in a single treaty that would cover all migrant workers and their families. The convention protects basic rights: against forced labour, torture, inhuman or degrading treatment or punishment, and collective expulsion; and the rights to life, due process, freedom of religion, thought and opinion, privacy, liberty and security of the person, trade union membership, and emergency medical care. It gives additional rights to regular migrant workers, and requires the host state to facilitate family reunification.

The ICMW does not bestow any right to enter another country, nor does it give migrants who may have entered or remained illegally any right to regularise their immigration status. It requires states to cooperate to promote 'sound, equitable, humane and lawful conditions for the international migration of workers, and also to collaborate 'with a view to preventing and eliminating illegal or clandestine' migration (Article 68 ICMW/URL).

The ICMW is important on the one hand as a compilation of rights and duties which governments have already agreed through different treaty-making processes, and on the other hand, as a set of principles which should guide policy making at the national and international levels.

The ICMW came into effect in 2003, and the relatively few governments that have ratified it thus far tend to be those of 'sending' and not 'receiving' countries. Some industrialised states object that the Convention recognises and protects the rights not only of regular migrants but also of those who are not lawfully in the country. Nonetheless, although the inclusion of irregular migrants may make the treaty politically controversial to some states, in legal terms it merely reflects the basic principle that the act of entering a country in violation of national immigration laws does not deprive a migrant of his or her fundamental human rights. Nor does it nullify the obligation of the host state to protect a migrant's rights, regardless of his or her legal status.

This political objection also overlooks the degree to which migrants' rights are already protected under general human rights law – for example, the Convention on the Rights of the Child (CRC) and the International Covenant on Civil and Political Rights (ICCPR) – which most states (including all EU members) have already ratified.* Although the treaties seldom refer explicitly to migrants, they nonetheless protect migrants because they are universal in scope, and apply to 'everyone', 'all persons', and 'all individuals', including those who are not citizens.

The fundamental principle of equality of treatment between aliens (including migrants) and citizens was clearly articulated by the House of Lords, the highest UK court, in a case brought by foreign nationals who had been detained on grounds of national security. They challenged UK legislation which allowed their indefinite detention without trial, arguing that it was discriminatory because it applied only to foreign nationals and not to British nationals. The court agreed, ruling that, while the rights of these two groups might differ in an immigration context, international human rights law does not permit a state to discriminate between its own citizens and aliens in their rights to liberty, even in such a sensitive area as national security.**

The urgent need today is for all governments to ratify the ICMW and adopt a 'rights-based approach' to migration, and for the integration of human rights principles and labour standards into national policy-making. Over the last decade, rights-based approaches have been developed in policy making on issues as diverse as, for example, children, health, and poverty reduction. Many believe that a similar approach should be used in developing migration policies. Such an approach would use human rights commitments voluntarily entered into by states – whether of origin, destination or transit – when they ratified the treaty as a tool to protect migrants' rights and prevent serious human rights violations during the migration cycle. Human rights should become an integral part of any migration-related procedure, and the provisions of the ICMW should act as guiding principles in migration policy making.

The value of a rights-based approach lies in its ability to identify and rectify at an early stage laws, policies and practices that could lead to abuse of migrants' rights. Such a policy approach would include these elements:

- Before a new national law, policy or practice is introduced, it should be reviewed to ensure its consistency with the state's national and international legal obligations, including those relating to human rights and international labour standards.
- Data should be systematically collected and disaggregated by, for example, sex, geographic origin, age and ethnicity, to enable discrimination or potential discrimination to be identified.
- Existing national laws should be reviewed to ensure that they protect migrants and citizens equally.
- Employment contracts made under bilateral agreements should reflect labour and human rights; this should also be the case for workers moving for temporary employment under GATS Mode 4 agreements.

*A total of 192 states had ratified the CRC and 154 the ICCPR as of 1 June 2005.

** A(FC) and others (FC) (Appellants) v. SSHD (Respondents), (2004) UKHL 56.

Stefanie Grant, partner, Harrison Grant Solicitors

Poles apart no longer: Polish labourers in Britain °Caroline Penn/Panos Pictures

trade unions, think tanks, migrant support groups and anti-capitalist networks. Academics, the media and research institutions also play a role in framing perceptions and influencing policy. As discussed, the focus of this chapter is legal/voluntary migration, and so the civil society organisations and individuals whose attitudes and impacts we analyse tend to focus on this flow. However, there is a tendency among all groups to blur the distinctions between different legal categories of migrant.

The mobility of qualified workers, and to a lesser extent unskilled workers, which has increased since the 1990s in the wake of the end of communism, the expansion of the EU and continued effects of economic globalisation, has thrown the spotlight on laws and policies regulating the national, regional and global flow of migrants. However, policy-makers are still grappling with the contradictions of nation states attempting to regulate a phenomenon that is global or at least regional.

The perspectives of civil society groups on migration stretch the boundaries of these positions on globalisa-tion and throw up some interesting paradoxes (see Table 4.1, page 144). In exploring the movement of labour, which currently flows mostly from South to North, the focus of this chapter is on civil society actors in the industrialised countries and, to a lesser extent, those in developing countries.

Supporters and Reformers

Supporters and Reformers tend to share the belief that in a globalised world, where information, goods, currency and cultures are mobile, the movement of people and labour is increasingly difficult to resist. Supporters and Reformers encompass a very broad range of civil society actors, from trade unions and migrant support groups to think tanks and anti-capitalist networks, which favour varying degrees of control over the migration flows they advocate.

Opening the borders

Just as previous research revealed few out and out supporters of globalisation, so very few people or organ-isations support entirely open borders. A few exceptions

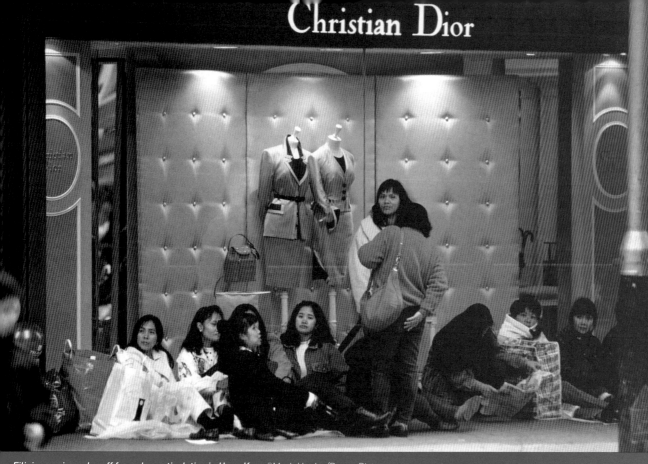

Filipinos enjoy a day off from domestic duties in Hong Kong ©*Mark Henley/Panos Pictures*

– for example, the economist Jagdish Bhagwati and the British think tank Demos (URL) – have proposed radical alternatives to the current and, they argue, futile attempts by nation states to curtail immigration via passports, border controls and quota systems. But even their proposals include mechanisms and institutions to manage the flow of migrants. According to Bhagwati:

> The reality is that borders are beyond control and little can be done to really cut down on immigration. The societies of developed countries will simply not allow it. The less developed countries also seem overwhelmed by forces propelling emigration. Thus, there must be a seismic shift in the way migration is addressed: governments must reorient their policies from attempting to curtail migration to coping and working with it to seek benefits for all. (Bhagwati 2003)

Bhagwati proposes a 'diaspora model' that captures the benefits of migration for sending and receiving countries via remittance schemes, the facilitation of dual nationality, and loyalty schemes. His proposed World Migration Organisation would highlight best practice in managing migration among member nations and fill the gap in the international institutional framework with regard to flows of people across borders. Unlike the International Monetary Fund (IMF) for finance, World Health Organization (WHO) for health, and World Bank for aid, responsibility for migration is splintered between various bodies, including the International Labour Organization for workers, the World Trade Organization for service flows, and the International Organization for Migration, which lacks authority in the international arena (Bhagwati 2003). More radical is the approach of Demos, which is based on the concept of people flow management. In this system, outlined in the 2003 report *People Flow*, all migrants would be treated equally, removing the incentive for false asylum claims. International transit centres and mobility service points would be established to offer shelter and services to migrants, including visas allowing travel throughout Europe (Bentley, Buonfino and Veenkamp 2003).

Managing migration

Think tanks, research institutes and trade unions such as the Global Commission on International Migration (GCIM), the ILO and Britain's Trades Union Congress (TUC) and Institute for Public Policy Research (IPPR) support migration (which they see as simply another facet of globalisation) because it benefits migrants, their countries and host nations – if it is properly managed. These organisations believe that the benefits of migration have not been sufficiently promoted and are often subsumed by the disadvantages aired in the media by politicians and civil society. The GCIM sees migration as a major global policy issue that is likely to become increasingly important as globalisation accelerates. It says:

> ...while the issue of international migration receives extensive media coverage, it is often discussed in an unsatisfactory manner. Distorted images of migrants and migration are often conveyed in the popular press and other media. And the important linkages between international migration and other global issues are not adequately explored. (GCIM 2004)

Established with the support of the UN Secretary-General Kofi Annan to review the extent and implications of migration flows and policies for better managing them, the GCIM will publish its report in October 2005.

The benefits of migrant workers

Many civil society actors who fall into the Reformers category cite the ill-informed public debate about migration as the reason for their promotion of its benefits. But even they tread a fine line between highlighting the beneficial role of migrants in host economies and protecting the interests of indigenous workers.

According to IPPR (2004), the UK has had more than half a million unfilled job vacancies since 1999. Its research into the health sector in the UK found that one in three doctors working in the National Health Service had received qualifications overseas (IPPR 2005). The effect of this brain drain on sending countries has galvanised calls for an end to, or at the very least controls on, the recruitment of medical staff from developing countries, which are investing resources in human capital but reaping few of the rewards (see Box 4.3). But ethical recruitment policies, such as that established by Britain's Department of Health, which stipulates countries from which medical staff should not be hired, may not be enough. The solution, according to the British Medical Association (URL), is for rich countries like the UK to expand training to make themselves self-sufficient in doctors and nurses (Johnson 2005). The response of developing countries to migration varies. As discussed in Box 4.1, the growing significance of remittances for some sending countries is altering their perspective.

---

at a social forum on migration
600 participants from 35 countries discussed the notion of 'universal citizenship'

In addition to civil society organisations with a strong advocacy focus, a raft of research institutes, including the Centre on Migration, Policy and Society (COMPAS) at Oxford University (URL), explores global mobility and evaluates migration policy in order to disseminate best practice and new ideas. Similarly, the Washington-based Migration Policy Institute (URL), which runs the web-based Migration Information Source, 'seeks to assist governments and civil society organisations to develop solutions to international migration'. The International Organization for Migration (URL) also seeks to increase understanding of migration and meet the 'growing operational challenges of managing migration'. While their advocacy of better management makes their focus predominantly legal migration, many Reformist groups also work on illegal migration and forced labour.

Supporting migrants

Among Supporters and Reformers are vocal migrants' support groups, established in host countries wherever a significant migrant worker population exists, which lobby for the rights of migrant and/or undocumented workers. The particular focus of these groups depends on the situation, skills and experience of their constituents. The US-based Farm Labor Organizing Committee (FLOC URL), whose motto is 'As capital is free to move, workers should be free to move. Hasta la Victoria!', campaigns vigorously for permanent residency and labour rights for farm workers. The Chinese Staff and Workers' Association (URL), founded in New York in 1979, supports its mostly low-income garment, restaurant and construction workers by challenging the sweatshop system, racism and sexism. The Association

The human right to move is often overlooked in the debate about immigration ©*Sven Torfinn/Panos Pictures*

des Travailleurs Maghrébins en France (URL) fights for the rights of immigrants from the Maghreb region. In Hong Kong the Mission for Filipino Migrant Workers (URL) assists the 100,000 Filipinos who mostly work as domestic helpers under a controlled flow agreed by the respective governments. This organisation has helped its constituents to seek legal redress in cases of physical abuse, and lobbies the Special Administrative Region Government of Hong Kong on the minimum wage for domestic helpers.

In sending countries, there are migrants' rights groups that fall into the Reformers category as well. Brazil's Servico Pastoral dos Migrantes (SPM URL) holds an annual forum, as part of the Bishops' National Conference, to promote respect for migrants' rights and raise awareness about the challenges they face. At a social forum on migration held in January 2005, a few days before the fifth World Social Forum in Porto Alegre, 600 participants from 35 countries discussed the notion of 'universal citizenship' and how migrants might use it to stand up for their rights (SPM 2005).

Migration and human rights

In host countries, among the prominent anti-capitalist groups and networks that campaign against the policies and prescriptions of neo-liberal economics, in particular the free flow of capital and goods around the world, very little attention is paid to the movement of labour. For example, it is not a policy focus for groups such as the World Development Movement (URL), Our World is Not for Sale (URL), and 50 Years is Enough (URL). Those groups that do take a stance, such as ATTAC (URL) and the San Francisco-based CorpWatch (URL), tend to focus on the rights of migrants, with campaigns against discrimination and racism. Across Europe a host of networks and organisations campaign against discrimination and racism, and for migrants rights. These include the Italian anti-capitalist group Lunaria (URL) which, as well as mounting anti-racism campaigns, lobbies for migrants rights' as citizens and against detention centres. Similarly, Aktion Courage (URL), a German NGO, campaigns against racism and for equal opportunities for migrants. In Spain, a host of left-

Box 4.3: The brain drain

In May 2005 the British High Commission in Lagos made a much-criticised decision to ban visa applications by Nigerians between the ages of 18 and 30 years. Coming in the thick of an election campaign in the UK, in which Michael Howard, the Conservative Party leader, had made immigration an issue ('Are you thinking what we are thinking?'), the British High Commission's decision was a timely reminder of what is arguably the most important sociological phenomenon in Africa over the past decade and more: the compulsive emigration from the continent to various Western destinations of young and, in many cases, highly skilled professionals. This persistent human haemorrhage contrasts sharply with the picture just over a decade ago when, as Jeffrey Herbst, a distinguished Africanist scholar, rightly observes, human traffic in the continent was essentially internal and economically motivated, and as such 'to some degree under the control of governments' (Herbst 1990: 202).

Since then, such has been the rapidity and seriousness of the human flight from African countries that, for the severely affected countries (for example, Nigeria) the establishment of an office for Diaspora affairs has become de rigueur. To be sure, this trend is not Africa-specific; the entire globe is seemingly held in thrall to the dynamics of 'flows', to use Appadurai's (1996) famous imagery. According to Harris (2002), more than 200 million people migrate annually, a figure that is bound to increase as the uneven consequences of globalisation affect societies in different parts of the world, and particularly in the global South (Held, McGrew, Goldblatt and Perraton 1999).

Relevant scholarship and policy discourses have so far failed to agree on what Africa stands to gain and/or lose as a result of this profound (and continuing) demographic shift. Even the earlier wisdom on the assumed positive impact of monetary remittances by migrants has come under increasing scrutiny. Ironically, this rethink is in large part due to the massive increase in the volume of such remittances. While, as of the late 1980s, remittances worldwide were greater than the total foreign aid dispensed by all the various governmental agencies around the world (Sowell 1996: 22), today they constitute the fastest-growing and most stable capital flow to developing countries. Relative to GDP (and if we allow for the fact that figures for the subcontinent are usually either under-reported or incomplete), sub-Saharan Africa is the third largest recipient of global remittances (Sander 2003).

Such an influx of capital must necessarily have an impact on the recipient societies, especially given the economic depression and social instability for which such polities have become infamous. Remittances are literally saving lives in the context of state dereliction, thus fulfilling their primary role as a form of insurance where its institutional expression is glaringly absent. But that is not the whole story. Currently, doubts are being expressed, legitimately, about their consequences for social citizenship, particularly as an increasing percentage of the population are starting to regard the 'Western Union' as an alternative to a failed state.

The question of citizenship raised by what is clearly a case of 'remittance dependency' in many African countries is an important one, pointing as it does to the very origins of the crisis of emigration itself. If, indeed, the pattern of human movement in Africa less than 20 years ago was, as Herbst notes, essentially internal, this was due in no small part to the relative institutional coherence of the African state, the comparable solidity of the existing state-society compact, and the sanctity of citizenship regimes. However, the African crises of the 1980s, most significantly the economic travails occasioned by structural adjustment, considerably weakened the welfare delivery capacity of African states, making them unable to meet their traditional obligations, and consequently their forced retrenchment from those areas of civic life where institutional intervention is most needed. This was the immediate sociological background to the exodus from Africa, a process facilitated by the global permeability of national boundaries as a result of the revolution in telecommunications technology.

Whether a swelling African diaspora is able to reverse the obvious momentum towards decay, or whether the process of emigration itself will ultimately benefit Africa is, as noted earlier, difficult to say. The obvious benefits from remittances to the economy of recipient countries must be regarded as dubious if such monies, as is generally the case, end up largely nourishing conspicuous consumption and a sybaritic lifestyle to the detriment of actual and sustainable productivity.

This is not to oversimplify what is admittedly a complex and rapidly evolving situation. After all, the totality of North-South relations, into which explosive matrix the reality of emigration, remittances, and so on, must be located, is itself historical and rich in twists and turns. This leads to a related point about how the current global formation, of which emigration to the North is an increasingly significant part, is believed to reify the subaltern position of the South, especially Africa, in relation to the developed North. For those who subscribe to this view, the process of emigration to the North by Africans ultimately serves an existing Western hegemonic agenda, according to which Africa will be stripped of both its human resources and cultural identity.

Developments in the sporting arena, particularly what Simms and Rendell (2004) have described as the 'global trade in muscle', appear to lend credence to this claim, although it must be said that these developments also show vividly the inherent ambiguities of the migration process. For to the extent to which the contemporary 'brawn drain' from Africa is a product of a discernible social process, that dynamic is the inseparable concourse of state negligence, individual (the athlete's) necessity, and foreign cynicism. Thus, no student of African history, particularly of the still unfolding post-colonial moment, can miss the sad irony of the parallel between the current wave of 'exit' from the continent, which is by and large voluntary, and the forced dislocation which characterised the colonial era.

Ebenezer Obadare, Centre for Civil Society, LSE

leaning groups provide legal advice for immigrants and advocate greater tolerance, including SOS RACISMO (URL) and the Movement against Intolerance (URL).

These initiatives tend not to distinguish between legal migrant workers, refugees and asylum seekers. Indeed, a rights-based approach enshrines the fundamental principle of equality of treatment, regardless of the legal status of an individual. As Stefanie Grant points out in Box 4.2, applying such an approach to migration should prevent laws, policies and practices that would lead to the abuse of migrants' rights.

However, very few civil society groups grapple with the fundamental human right to move, which is often overlooked in the debate about migration. Yet a section of anti-capitalist and anti-racist civil society is active, vocal and dynamic on the issue. For example, the No border network, No One is Illegal Group UK, and Abolishing the Borders from Below, campaign for freedom of movement, arguing that to move is a human right and that global immigration controls are inherently racist, authoritarian, and therefore unjust. Such groups ignore the distinction between legal workers, undocumented migrants, refugees and asylum seekers, arguing that these are the constructed and meaningless concepts of an unjust capitalist system. Freedom of movement is at the heart of other issues on which these groups campaign, including housing, women's emancipation, workers' rights, and against racism.

If freedom of movement is a human right, there should be no management of migration; accordingly, these groups campaign against the organisations, structures, and practices that they see as an inherent part of the neo-liberal economic system. No border network (URL), a European coalition of grassroots organisations and activists established in 1999, is against the International Migration Organization, which it argues is fundamentally flawed:

Their basic policy is not concerned with the well being of people but the well being of economies. Secondly, their ideology is based on racist principles of homogeneous ethnic states and xenophobic concepts of 'home'...In an era of globalisation migration appears as a major social movement against the imperialist concept of zones of differentiated reproduction cost. The IOM has been best prepared to implement concepts of enforcing the borders necessary to uphold such a regime and to conform to new forms of neoliberal migration management.

Airlines that fly deported people home are also targeted by the No border network, via its spoof discount airline website www.deportation-class.com. No One is Illegal UK (URL) campaigns against what it calls the 'new gulag archipelago' – detention camps on EU borders – which it sees as part of the managed migration system it abhors: 'We support the unfettered right of entry of the feckless, the unemployable and the uncultured. We assert No One is Illegal.' The groups cited above were among those taking part in the European Day of Action on 2 April 2005, which saw demonstrations in several cities, including London, Athens, Vienna, Paris and Helsinki (Global Project URL).

The perceived threat posed by immigration to notions of national identity and historical continuity is increasingly commonly voiced in industrialised societies

---

Some groups have sprung up to defend migrants from voluntary forces patrolling borders, described below. And, as a consequence of the demonisation of some minorities, particularly post-9/11, community representatives have become more vocal. These individuals and groups tend to be Reformers. For example, in the US, the Border Action Network (URL) was formed to protect the rights of people living along the Arizona-Mexico border. Representing 'mostly people of colour, women and young people under the age of 30', the grassroots organisation campaigns against what it sees as racist vigilante border patrols.

Regressives and Rejectionists

The arguments used by Rejectionists and Regressives against migration are based on economic considerations and concerns about identity, culture and security. Often these two strands are interwoven. Just as Reformers argue that the public debate about migration is skewed by selective and partial use of information (IPPR 2005), so too Rejectionists and Regressives decry misinformation and failure to debate the issue openly (Migrationwatch UK URL).

Identity and security concerns

The perceived threat posed by immigration to notions of national identity and historical continuity is increasingly commonly voiced in industrialised societies. For example, while accepting that 'immigration on a modest scale brings benefits in the form of diversity and new ideas', professor Robert Rowthorn of Cambridge University argues that 'the pace of the present transformation in Europe worries me. I believe it to be a recipe for conflict.' This is related not to the personal qualities of immigrants, he stresses, but to the sheer numbers. 'Rapid changes in the ethnic or cultural composition of a society may cause widespread disorientation, resentment and conflict' (Rowthorn 2003: 71).

The rise of Regressive and Rejectionist civil society groups may have been influenced by right-wing political parties in Europe that are strident in their nationalism and anti-immigration stance. During the 1990s some parties, such as Le Pen's National Front, the British National Party and Pim Fortuyn's LPF, achieved electoral success (Kaldor and Muro 2003). Civil society groups and political parties that are anti-immigration deny they are racist. However, emboldened by the post-9/11 context, their rhetoric has hardened and their public profile has been enhanced. Rowthorn (2003: 63) argues that these concerns should not be dismissed lightly:

> It is not surprising that the political parties most hostile to immigration are normally the most hostile to economic globalisation and to supra-national institutions. They are raising, albeit in xenophobic form, issues of community, identity and self-determination that should be of concern to all democrats.

Immigrant culture: recipe for conflict or peaceful cohabitation?
©Tim Smith/Panos Pictures

A common refrain among Regressives is that they are not opposed to immigration in principle, but few give many arguments in favour. Migrationwatch UK, a think tank chaired by Sir Andrew Green, former Ambassador to Saudia Arabia, is 'not opposed to immigration that is moderate or managed' but argues that 'such massive immigration (to Britain) is contrary to the interests of all sections of our community'. Apart from arguing that the economic benefits of immigration have been exaggerated, Migrationwatch has concerns about the social impact, citing statistics about the age profile of immigrants, the birth rate of foreign-born mothers and the ethnic mix of particular British cities.

> The very high proportion of births to foreign-born mothers in some English cities together with the outflow of city dwellers to the regions explains the very rapid changes taking place in parts of our cities. It again raises the question of how satisfactory integration can be achieved in areas where British culture itself is already diminishing. (Migrationwatch UK 2005)

David Goodhart, editor of Britain's *Prospect* magazine, makes an explicit link between the extent of ethnic diversity – or what he calls 'de-homogenisation' as a

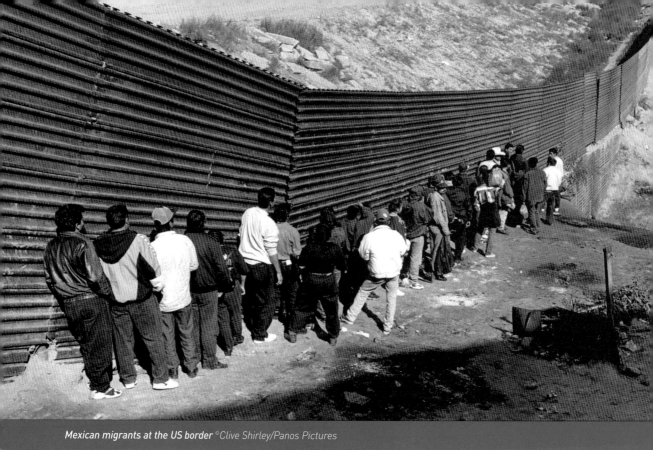

Mexican migrants at the US border ©*Clive Shirley/Panos Pictures*

result of the many impacts of globalisation (including immigration) – and people's willingness to pay taxes, and faith in government efforts to combat inequality (Goodhart 2005). Governments must take seriously people's concerns about 'security and identity issues', he says, arguing that the diversity of British society is so great that shared values are no longer a unifying force. Instead, what is needed is a 'progressive nationalism' based on 'a new myth of Britishness' that would counter social fragmentation.

The Rejectionists and Regressives base their position on the argument that citizenship in any country should be awarded only if the citizen behaves responsibly (this requires cooperating and cohering with one's neighbours, doing more than just earning money and remitting it back home); that communities are defined by a number of shared values and that too much diversity in a country, although a sign of openness, can undermine tolerance. The contention is not an economic one about jobs, social security or housing. The position is basically liberal but points to the conflict between a liberal society and the degree to which it can uncritically admit people who do not share the values of the liberal society.

Post-9/11

Another argument, very much post-9/11, has been made by Samuel Huntington (2004) to the effect that one can be never sure of the immigrant's loyalty to the culture he or she has decided to co-habit with. Even an immigrant country like America has limits to its capacity to assimilate, and thus cohesion requires limits on immigration. There is a tension here between tolerance of other cultures and the dangers of leaving the door open for citizens of countries who may harbour feelings of enmity towards the host country. This is the argument about national security and the fear of 'the enemy within' (see Box 4.4) A plethora of civil society groups in the US unite concerns about immigration (both legal and illegal) for job security, social cohesion and security of Americans. CitizensLobby.com (URL) campaigns for troops on the border, an end to amnesties for illegal immigrants and a scaling back of guest worker quotas. Its 'America first' foreign and trade policy also lobbies for a boycott of Chinese-made products and the abolition of 'wasteful government programs like foreign aid'.

While previously the dominant concern of many of these groups was the threat immigration posed to

American jobs, fear of terrorism and other forms of criminality has become a key strand in their rhetoric. Immigrationshumancosts.org (URL), CitizensLobby.com, Deport Aliens (URL) and Americans for Immigration Control (URL) are vocal in their belief that immigration to the US, whether legal or illegal, is increasingly out of control and threatens to have serious consequences. According to CitizensLobby.com (URL):

Our weak borders and lax immigration laws allowed thousands of terrorists, suspected terrorists and 'sleeper agents' to sneak into our country to commit acts of war against US citizens.

In response to the perceived failure of US government border patrols, a group of citizens has even established a volunteer border watch. The Official Minuteman Civil Defense Corps (URL) deploys volunteers to 'observe, report and protect the US from illegal immigration in all southern border states'.

Our effort will be tangibly effective in supporting the defenders of our border, the patriotic men and women of the U.S. Border Patrol. You will offer your assistance and become force-multipliers to assist their monumental task of turning back the tidal wave of people entering our country illegally.

For some civil society organisations that fall into the Rejectionist and Regressive category, threats to identity and security are more important than threats to jobs (see Box 4.4). Post-9/11, the antagonism is directed towards not only new arrivals but established ethnic communities, diasporas that may have experienced discrimination decades earlier.

One half-way house in this difficult area has been to suggest that immigrants who arrive to work should be given a temporary status short of full citizenship (similar to the American Green Card). With this status the immigrant will not qualify for welfare benefits, although an exception has to be made for children and for acute health care. After a period of, say, five years, the immigrant could qualify for full citizenship. This passage of time softens the (often false) claim that immigrants who have not paid taxes are claiming benefits, and it also allows time for families to assimilate. In this assimilation, civil society groups such as churches, schools and residents associations can be of immense help.

Economic arguments against migration

Where Regressives differ from Rejectionists is in their readiness to accept some immigration where it is beneficial for the domestic economy. The typical Regressive globaliser on migration is a pro-capitalist business lobby or sector-specific organisation with the interests of employers in mind. The Institute of Economic Affairs (IEA URL), a British free-market think tank, argues for more flexible, managed migration that would take account of Britain's changing skill needs. While the IEA and similar lobbies in the industrialised world stress the need for more skilled migrants, business or sector-specific organisations, such as the Western Growers Association (WGA) in the US, lobby for unskilled migrants to meet seasonal needs for farm labour. According to its President, Tom Nassif, of the top ten issues that matter to WGA's 3,000 members in 2005, farm labour is number one. The organisation made the headlines in March 2005 when it said that, because of the clampdown on legal seasonal labour, its members could not survive without illegal immigrants to work in the fields. Nassif went as far as saying that US Border Patrol should stop manning highway checkpoints during the lettuce season, when thousands of 'lechugeros' (lettuce people) descend on the region, dubbed the 'winter salad bowl'. While many labourers migrate from California to Arizona, others illegally cross the border at the beginning of the season and leave when it ends (Jordan 2005).

The pensions pot debate

Shortage of skills and prevention of a 'pensions crisis' are often cited by Reformers and Supporters in support of freer migration. For example, think tanks such as the National Foundation for American Policy (NFAP URL) believes the movement of goods and people is key to prosperity and warns that reducing legal migration 'would worsen the solvency of Social Security, harm taxpayers, and increase the size of the long-range actuarial deficit of the Social Security trust fund'. Leading newspapers, including *The Economist* and the *Financial Times*, also cite pension provision in their support of controlled migration. But the idea that taxes paid by skilled migrants can contribute to the pensions pot of developed countries, many of which have a declining ratio of workers to retired people, is disputed. Migrationwatch UK (URL) says the pensions crisis will be fuelled, not solved, by migrants, who like everyone else grow old, an argument with which economists such as professor David Coleman (2003) concur.

Box 4.4: **Migration, 9/11 and the US 'home front'**

The terrorist attacks of 11 September 2001 on the US were quickly perceived as a watershed for the world. A distinction was established between a 'before' and 'after', and attempts at 're-ordering the world' began (Leonard 2002). Immigration is one of the issues that was 're-ordered' after 9/11, both through legislation and in public and political discourse about immigration. This is not true of every country in the world, but it is true of Western countries in general and of the US in particular. The Bush administration interpreted the events of 9/11 as attacks on the US and launched the international 'war on terror' as well as the 'battle' over its 'home front', as Paul Wolfowitz, then Deputy Director of Defense, announced in 2002:

> Fifty years ago, when we said, 'home front,' we were referring to citizens back home doing their part to support the war front. Since last September, however, the home front has become a battlefront every bit as real as any we've known before.

On this 'battlefront' immigration has become one of the most prominent issues. Only a few days after the terrorist attacks, a regulation was amended to allow the detention of aliens without charge for 48 hours (or further for a 'reasonable time') (ColorLines URL 2005), followed, most significantly, by the USA PATRIOT Act* of October 2001. The Immigration and Naturalization Service (INS) was abolished and replaced in 2002 by the Department of Homeland Security (DHS), with its newly created division of US Citizenship and Immigration Services. (For an extensive timeline of policies and events affecting US immigrants and civil liberties see ColorLines URL).

Although the economic and especially welfare arguments that used to dominate the debate about immigration are still significant, they are no longer the central rhetorical focus of debates about immigration in the US. Both conservative and liberal critics, including Robert S. Leiken (2004) of The Nixon Centre (URL), and Deborah Waller Meyers and Demetrios G. Papademetriou (2002) of the Washington-based Migration Policy Institute (URL), argue that 'the most significant change is that immigration... is now viewed through a security lens'.

Opinion polls still show that large numbers of Americans favour immigration, but opposition is growing. Although various polls show different outcomes,** and despite the fact that the attacks of 9/11 were not committed by immigrants, let alone illegal immigrants (those responsible entered the US as 'visitors', mainly on student visas), what is clear is that terrorism and immigration are unquestionably linked in political discourse and public debate. The White House (URL) lists information and speeches on immigration under the issue of 'national security' and a significant number of civil society groups have focused their efforts 'to secure America' on the issue of immigration, mainly concentrating on illegal immigrants.

What these groups have in common is an understanding, articulated most explicitly by the 9/11 Families for a Secure America (URL), 'that the problems of open borders, illegal immigration and terrorism are inextricably linked'. Some of these groups focus on very specific issues, others on more general concerns. For example, the Coalition of Secure Driver's License (URL) argues that '(f)or would-be terrorists, a driver's license can be a license to kill' (Walsh 2004), and lobbies for a tightening of requirements for (illegal) immigrants. Meanwhile numerous think tanks, such as the Center for Immigration Studies (URL) and groups such as Americans For Legal Immigration (URL) and Americans For Better Immigration (URL), lobby more generally for immigration reform.

While these groups campaign for tighter legal restrictions on immigration generally, for example opposing President Bush's 'Fair and Secure Immigration Reform' plan (2004), others take Wolfowitz's notion of the 'real battlefront' more literally. Grassroots organisations such as the American Border Patrol (URL) and The Official Minuteman Civil Defense Corps (URL), are active on the US-Mexican border, observing and reporting illegal migrants to the authorities. The Minutemanhq.com (URL) invites volunteers thus:

You are reading this because you believe that you can actively participate in one of the most important, socially responsible and peaceful movements for justice since the civil rights movement of the 1960s...Our effort will be tangibly effective in supporting the defenders of our border, the patriotic men and women of the U.S. Border Patrol. You will offer your assistance and become force-multipliers to assist their monumental task of turning back the tidal wave of people entering our country illegally.

Their critics call them vigilantes, but Minuteman defends its actions by reference to the threat of 'criminals and potential terrorists'. Indeed, in harking back to the original 'Minutemen' of the eighteenth century who defended New England against the British, these self-styled 'American heroes' of the twenty-first century make an explicit link to external enemies:

In recent times, the legacy of the Minutemen has been honoured by Americans who share a concern for homeland defense...Since the infamous terrorist attacks of September 11 2001, the term has also applied to groups of volunteers that seek to protect America's borders from unwelcome intruders.

* Uniting and Strengthening America by Providing Appropriate Tools Required to Intercept and Obstruct Terrorism.

** In a 2002 US poll conducted by Hamilton College, 57 per cent of respondents expressed the belief that immigrants enhance US society and 41 per cent favoured a decrease in immigration (Hagstrom 2002). In contrast, a 2005 Gallup poll suggested that 52 per cent of Americans favoured a decrease in immigration, in comparison with 45 per cent pre-9/11 and 58 per cent in January 2002 (Gallup Poll News Service 2005).

Sabine Selchow, Centre for the Study of Global Governance, LSE

Table 4.1: Civil society positions on labour migration

	Supporter	Reformer	Regressive	Rejectionist
	For open borders	Pro-migration but opinions diverge on how free migrant flows should be	For managed immigration of highly skilled workers for domestic economic needs, but wary of wider migration because it threatens perceived national interests	Anti-migration because it undermines national interests – economic, cultural and environmental. Fear of terrorism has injected a new dimension and vigour into groups taking this position
Academic	Jagdish Bhagwhati		Robert Rowthorn David Coleman David Goodhart	Samuel Huntingdon
Think tank/ Institute	Demos	Global Commission on International Migration Institute for Public Policy Research Centre on Migration, Policy and Society Migration Policy Institute		Migrationwatch UK
Business lobby		Farm Labor Organising Committee National Foundation for American Policy	Institute of Economic Affairs Western Growers Association	
NGO/ network	Abolishing the Borders from Below No One is Illegal Group UK No Border Network	Lunaria ATTAC Border Action Network CorpWatch National Council of La Reza SOS Racismo Association des Travailleurs Magrébins en France Mission for Filipino Migrant Workers Chinese Staff and Workers Association Servico Pastoral dos Migrantes		Americans for Immigration Control Immigrationshumancost.org CitizensLobby.com The Official Minuteman Civil Defense Corps Deport Aliens Californians for Population Stablization 9/11 Families for a Secure America American Border Patrol
International organisation		ILO OIM		
Media			*Financial Times* *Wall Street Journal* *The Economist*	

Conclusion

The debate about migration is currently dominated by Regressive and Rejectionist groups. Supporters of migration are very few in number – largely a handful of anarchist, anti-racist and human rights groups that believe in the right to move. Reformers, who have a powerful economic case, often find themselves on the defensive. Moreover, most of the anti-capitalist groups described in previous editions of the Yearbook are uncharacteristically quiet when it comes to the issue of migration. The free movement of labour tends to be opposed not on economic but on security and identity grounds. Although some fear the loss of jobs to lower-paid workers and the erosion of welfare benefits, the hue and cry over immigration is largely the result of perceived fears about the dilution of an imagined idea of nation, and the spread of terrorism and organised crime, especially after 9/11.

But it can be argued that the benefits to the global economy and to global emancipation that would flow from the freer movement of labour could negate security fears. Free movement of labour would contribute to prosperity and welfare in both rich and poor countries. The former would benefit from the increased availability of young skilled workers, in terms of both pensions and economic growth. The latter would benefit from remittances and, hopefully, compensation for the brain drain. Just as both Europe and America benefited from migration in the nineteenth century, so both North and South could benefit today. Such a virtuous circle could turn out to be the best way to minimise security fears. Criminals and terrorists can always circumvent borders. Indeed, the more that borders are fortified, the more this encourages illegal trafficking. The best way to deal with criminals and terrorists is to marginalise the informal economy and the economic sources of insecurity in which they thrive.

As for the argument about the dilution of national culture, this has to be answered head-on. Do we celebrate the cultural diversity that accompanies globalisation? Or do we retreat into insecure, imaginary concepts of cultural containment?

Adams, R. and Page, J. (2003) *The Impact of International Migration and Remittances on Poverty*. Washington, DC: Poverty Reduction Group, World Bank.

Abolishing the Borders from Below (URL) www.abb.hardcore.lt/index.htm (consulted 5 August 2005).

Aktion Courage (URL) www.aktioncourage.org (consulted 5 August 2005).

Aleinikoff, T. (2002) *International Legal Norms and Migration: An Analysis*, International Dialogue on Migration No. 3. Geneva: IOM.

American Border Patrol (URL) www.americanborderpatrol.com (consulted 23 July 2005).

Americans For Better Immigration (URL) www.betterimmigration.org (consulted 23 July 2005).

Americans For Legal Immigration (URL) www.alipac.us (consulted 23 July 2005).

Americans for Immigration Control (URL) http://immigrationcontrol.com/ (consulted 30 June 2005).

Appadurai, A. (1996) *Modernity at Large: Cultural Dimensions of Globalization*. Minneapolis: University of Minnesota.

Association des Travailleurs Maghrébins en France (URL) www.atmf.ras.eu.org/rubrique.php3?id_rubrique=1 (consulted 5 August 2005).

ATTAC (URL) www.attac.org/indexfla.htm

Beck, U. (2004) 'Cosmopolitan Realism: Towards a Cosmopolitan Social Science.' Public lecture, London School of Economics, 19 February.

Bentley, T., Buonfino, A. and Veenkamp, T. (2003) *People Flow: Managing Migration in a New European Commonwealth*. London: Demos.

Bhagwati, J. (2003) 'Borders Beyond Control', *Foreign Affairs*, 82(1): 96–104. www.cfr.org/publication.php?id=5356.xml (consulted 5 August 2005).

Blackburn, R. (1997) *The Making of New World Slavery: from Baroque to the Modern* 1492-1800. London: Verso.

Border Action Network (URL) www.borderaction.org/index.php (consulted 30 June 2005)

Braudel, F. (1972/1996) *The Mediterranean and the Mediterranean World in the Age of Philip II*. Berkeley and Los Angeles: University of California.

Center for Immigration Studies (URL) www.cis.org (consulted 23 July 2005).

Chinese Staff and Workers' Association (URL) www.cswa.org (consulted 5 August 2005).

CitizensLobby.com (URL) www.citizenslobby.com/index.htm (consulted 30 June 2005).

Coalition For Secure Driver's License (URL) www.securelicense.org (consulted 5 August 2005).

Coleman, D. (2003) 'Demographic, Economic and Social Consequences of UK Migration', in H. Disney (ed.), *Work in Progress: Migration, Integration and the European Labour Market*. London: Civitas: Institute for Civil Society. www.civitas.org.uk/pdf/WorkInProgress.pdf (consulted 5 August 2005).

ColorLines Magazine (2001). '2001–2004: A Timeline of Major Events and Policies Affecting Immigrants and Civil Liberties.' www.arc.org/C_Lines/CLArchive/timeline.shtml, (consulted 23 July 2005).

Centre on Migration, Policy and Society (COMPAS) (URL) www.compas.ox.ac.uk (consulted 17 June 2005).

Corpwatch (URL) www.corpwatch.org/index.php (consulted 5 August 2005).

Demos (URL) www.demos.co.uk (consulted 5 August 2005).

Deport Aliens (URL) www.deportaliens.com (consulted 19 July 2005).

Desai, M. (2002) *Marx's Revenge*. London: Verso.

– and Said, Y. (2001) 'The New Anti-capitalist Movement: Money and Global Civil Society', in H. Anheier, M. Glasius and M. Kaldor (eds.), *Global Civil Society 2001*. Oxford: Oxford University Press.

Fair and Secure Immigration Reform (2004) www.whitehouse.gov/news/releases/2004/01/20040107-1.html (consulted 27 July 2005).

The Farm Labor Organizing Committee AFL-CIO (FLOC) US (URL) http://www.floc.com (consulted 30 July 2005)

50 Years is Enough network (URL) www.50years.org (consulted 23 July 2005).

Gallup Poll News Service (2005) 'Gallup Poll on Immigration'. www.amren.com/mtnews/archives/2005/02/gallup_poll_on.php (consulted 5 August 2005).

Ghana Medical Association (URL) www.ghanamedassn.org/gma3.htm (consulted 29 July 2005).

Global Commission on International Migration (URL) www.gcim.org (consulted 20 March 2005).

Global Project (URL) www.globalproject.info/art-4103.html (consulted 19 July 2005).

Gonzales, R. (2005) 'DoLE aims to generate 65,000 jobs for OFWs', *The Manila Bulletin Online*, 7 April. www.mb.com.ph/issues/2005/04/08/BSNS2005040832200.html (consulted 5 August 2005).

Goodhart, D. (2004) 'Too Much Diversity?', *Prospect*, No. 95 (February).

– (2005) 'The New Egalitarianism.' Public lecture, London School of Economics, 29 June.

Hagstrom, P. (2002) *The Hamilton College Immigration Opinion Poll*. www.hamilton.edu/levitt/surveys/immigration/immigration.pdf (consulted 24 July 2005)

Harris, N. (1995) *The New Untouchables: Immigration and the New World Worker*. London: I. B. Tauris.

Hatton, T. and Williamson, J. (1994) *Migration and the International Labour Market 1850–1939*. London: Routledge.

Heckscher, E. (1919/1949) 'The Effect of Foreign Trade on the Distribution of Income', in H. Ellis and L. Metzler (eds), *Readings in the Theory of International Trade*. Philadelphia: Blakiston for the American Economic Association.

Held, D., McGrew, A., Goldblatt, D. and Perraton, J. (1999). *Global Transformations: Politics, Economics and Culture*. Cambridge: Polity Press.

Herbst, J. (1990) 'Migration, the Politics of Protest, and State Consolidation in Africa', *African Affairs*, 89 (355), 183–203.

Huntingdon, S. (2002) *The Clash of Civilizations*. New York: Free Press.

– (2004) *Who Are We? The Challenges to America's National Identity*. New York: Simon & Schuster.

ImmigrationsHumanCost.org (URL) www.immigrationshumancost.org (consulted 5 August 2005).

Indymedia (URL)
  http://paris.indymedia.org/article.php3?id_article=34682
  (consulted 19 July 2005).
Institute of Economic Affairs (URL) wwwiea.org.uk
  (consulted 10 March 2005).
Institute for Public Policy Research (2005) *Migration and Health
  in the UK*. London: IPPR .
– (2004) *Labour Migration to the UK*. London: IPPR.
Inter-American Development Bank's Multilateral Investment
  Fund (MIF) (2005) *Remittances 2004: Transforming Labour
  Markets and Promoting Financial Democracies*.
  Washington, DC: International Labour Organization.
International Labour Organization (ILO) (2004) 'Facts on
  Migrant Labour' June. www.ilo.org/migrant
International Migration Policy Programme (2003) 'Migrant
  Remittances – Country of Origin Experiences : Strategies,
  Policies, Challenges, and Concerns', paper prepared for
  International Migration Policy Program conference on
  Migrant Remittances: Developmental Impact and Future
  Prospects, London, 9-10 October.
  www.livelihoods.org/hot_topics/docs/REMITPAPER.doc
  (consulted 5 August 2005).
International Organization for Migration (URL) www.iom.int
  (consulted 17 June 2005).
– (2003) *World Migration 2003: Managing Migration – Challenges
  and Responses for People on the Move*. Geneva: International
  Organisation for Migration. Graph 1.1, p 5.
  www.iom.int//DOCUMENTS/PUBLICATION/EN/chap01p1_24.pdf
  (consulted 5 August 2005).
IRIN (2003) 'The Brain Drain in Healthcare in Ghana:
  An Interview', 6 October. CBCFHealth.org.
  www.cbcfhealth.org/content/contentID/2264
  (consulted 5 August 2005).
Johnson, J. (2005) 'Stopping Africa's Medical Brain Drain',
  British Medical Journal, 331 (7507, 2 July): 2–3.
Jordan, M. (2005) 'A Job Americans Won't Do', *Wall Street Journal*,
  11 March. www.smfws.com/art3112005.htm
  (consulted 5 August 2005).
Kaldor, M. and Muro, D. (2003) 'Religious and Militant
  Nationalist Groups' in M. Kaldor, H. Anheier and M. Glasius
  (eds) *Global Civil Society 2003*. Oxford: OUP
Klein Solomon, M. and Bartsch, K. (2003) 'The Berne Initiative:
  Toward the Development of an International Policy
  Framework on Migration', Migration Policy Initiative, 1 April.
  www.migrationinformation.org/Feature/print.cfm?ID=114
  (consulted 14 March 2005).
Leiken, R. (2004). *Bearers of Global Jihad? Immigration and
  National Security after 9/11*. Washington, DC: The Nixon Center.
  www.nixoncenter.org/publications/monographs/Leiken_Bear
  ers_of_Global_Jihad.pdf (consulted 5 August 2005).
Leonard, M. (ed.) (2002) *Re-Ordering the World: The Long-Term
  Implications of 11 September*. London: Foreign Policy Centre.
Lewis, W.A. (1954) 'Economic Development with Unlimited
  Supplies of Labour', *Manchester School*, 22: 139–90.
Lillich, R. (1984) *The Human Rights of Aliens in Contemporary
  International Law*. Manchester: Manchester University Press.
List, F. (1837/1956) *The National System of Political Economy*,
  trans. S. Lloyd. London: Longmans Green.

Lowell, B. Lindsay and Findlay, A. (2002) *Migration of Highly
  Skilled Persons from Developing Countries – Impact and Policy
  Responses. Synthesis Report*. International Migration Paper
  No. 44. Geneva: ILO.
  www.ilo.org/public/english/protection/migrant/download/im
  p/imp44.pdf (consulted 5 August 2005).
Lunaria (URL) www.lunaria.org (consulted 19 July 2005).
Maddison, A. (2001) *The World Economy: A Millennial
  Perspective*. Paris: OECD.
Marx, K. (1867/1887) *Das Capital, Volume 1: Capitalist
  Production*. Trans. S. Moore and W. Aveling.
  London: Swan Sonnenschein, Lowry and Co.
Meyers, D. and Papademetriou, D. (2002) 'The US-Mexico
  Immigration Relationship: Operating in a New Context',
  Foreign Affairs en Español, 2(1).
  www.migrationpolicy.org/pubs/foreign_affairs.php
  (consulted 5 August 2005).
Migration Policy Institute (URL)
  www.migrationpolicy.org/research/index
  (consulted 17 June 2005).
Migration Policy Institute (2003) 'Migration Information source
  Remittance Data'.
  www.migrationinformation.com/USfocus/display.cfm?ID=137
  (consulted 5 August 2005).
Migrationwatch UK (URL) www.migrationwatchuk.org
  (consulted 20 March 2005).
Mission for Filipino Migrant Workers (Hong Kong) (URL)
  www.migrants.net (consulted 5 August 2005).
The Movement against Intolerance (URL)
  http://www.movimientocontralaintolerancia.com
  (consulted 6 August 2005).
National Foundation for American Policy (URL) www.nfap.net
  (consulted 5 August 2005).
9/11 Families for a Secure America (URL) www.911fsa.org
  (consulted 23 July 2005).
The Nixon Centre (URL) www.nixoncenter.org
  (consulted 23 July 2005).
No border network (URL) www.noborder.org/news_index.php
  (consulted 19 July 2005).
OECD (2004) OECD *Economic Surveys: Mexico 2003*. Paris: OECD.
No One Is Illegal UK (URL) http://noii.trick.ca
  (consulted 30 June 2005).
The Official Minuteman Civil Defense Corps (URL)
  www.minutemanhq.com/hq/aboutus.php
  (consulted 30 July 2005).
Ohlin, B. (1933/1966) *Interregional Trade and International Trade*.
  Cambridge, MA: Harvard University Press.
Our World is Not for Sale (URL) www.ourworldisnotforsale.org
  (consulted 5 August 2005).
Polanyi, K. (1944) *The Great Transformation*. New York: Farrar
  and Reinhart.
Ratha, D. (2003) *Global Development Finance 2003*.
  Washington, DC: World Bank.
Rowthorn, R. (2003) 'Numbers and National Identity', in H.
  Disney (ed.), *Work in Progress: Migration, Integration and the
  European Labour Market*. London: Civitas: Institute for Civil
  Society. www.civitas.org.uk/pdf/WorkInProgress.pdf
  (consulted 5 August 2005).

Sander, C. (2003) *Migrant Remittances to Developing Countries. A Scoping Study: Overview and Introduction to Issues for Pro-poor Financial Services. Report prepared for UK Department of International Development (DFID)*. London: Bannock Consulting.

Sassen, S. (1998) *Globalization and its Discontents: Essays on the Mobility of People and Money*. New York: The New Press

Servico Pastoral dos Migrantes (SPM) (URL) www.migracoes.com.br/eventos.html (consulted 17 June 2005).

Simms, A. and Rendell, M. (2004) 'The Global Trade in Muscle', *New Statesman*, 9 August. www.newstatesman.com/200408090017 (consulted 9 August 2005).

SOS RACISMO (URL) www.sosracismo.org/index.php (consulted 5 August 2005).

Sowell, T. (1996) *Migrations and Cultures: A World View*. New York: Basic Books.

Tanner, A. (2005) B*rain Drain and Beyond: Returns and Remittances of Highly Skilled Migrants*. Global Migration Perspectives No. 24. Washington, DC: Global Commission on International Migration. www.gcim.org/gmp/Global%20Migration%20Perspectives%20No%2024.pdf (consulted 5 August 2005).

Tinker, H. (1974) *A New System of Slavery: The Expert of Indian Labour Overseas*, 1830–1920. London: Oxford University Press for the Institute of Race Relations.

United Nations Development Program (2004) Human Development Report (2004) *Cultural Liberty in Today's Diverse World*. New York: UNDP http://hdr.undp.org/reports/global/2004 (consulted 5 August 2005).

UNGA (United Nations General Assembly) (1990) *International Convention on the Protection of the Rights of All Migrant Workers and Members of Their Families*. Resolution 45/158 of 18 December. New York: UNGA. www.ohchr.org/english/law/cmw.htm (consulted 2 August 2005).

Walsh, E. (2004) 'Driver's License a Vehicle for Terrorism', *Daily News*, 30 March. www.nydailynews.com (consulted 26 July 2005).

Western Growers (URL) www.wga.com/public/index.php (consulted 19 July 2005).

The White House (URL) Immigration issues on the White House website. www.whitehouse.gov/infocus/index.html (consulted 5 August 2005).

Wolfowitz, P. (2002) 'Standup of U.S. Northern Command: Remarks as Prepared for Delivery by Deputy Secretary of Defense Paul Wolfowitz, Petersen AFB, Colorado Springs, CO, Tuesday, October 1, 2002.' U.S. Department of Defence. www.defenselink.mil/speeches/2002/s20021001-depsecdef1.html (consulted 5 August 2005).

World Development Movement (URL) www.wdm.org.uk (accessed 5 August 2005).

CHAPTER 5

REFORMING THE UNITED NATIONS:
GLOBAL CIVIL SOCIETY PERSPECTIVES AND INITIATIVES

Richard Falk

... the UN must undergo the most sweeping overhaul of its 60-year history. World leaders must recapture the spirit of San Francisco and forge a new compact to advance the cause of larger freedom.

Kofi Annan (2005)

Introduction

The subject of the reform of the United Nations, the embattled target of neoconservative wrath that has been given a new intensity by UN Secretary-General Kofi Annan's criticism of the Iraq war, is bound to be a site of struggle in the current period. On the one side are these efforts, led by the United States and given a sharp edge by the designation of John Bolton, a leading critic of the UN, as its representative, to marginalise the UN generally, but especially in relation to peace and security and the work of the specialised agencies dealing with poverty, health, and children. On the other side are the great majority of UN members, led by moderate governments, receptive to the outlook of Kofi Annan, who seek to bring the UN into the twenty-first century in a manner that is consistent with humanitarian values, development and democratisation priorities, and security concerns, exhibiting sensitivity to the problems and interests of weak and strong members alike. Representatives of global civil society have much at stake in this debate over the future of the United Nations. Although it has been assumed that civil society actors have been generally perceived as supporters of a strong UN, and could be expected to stand shoulder to shoulder with Annan and his governmental allies, it is also true that influential NGOs in the United States (including the American Enterprise Institute, the Heritage Foundation, and, less visibly, Move America Forward) have long had the UN in their sights, and regard the Bush presidency and the UN oil-for-food scandal as an opportune moment to promote vigorously their anti-UN agenda.

Of course, among supporters of the UN there are also crucial divisions among liberals, Third World advocates, and radical transformers. The liberal position, typified by most national chapters of the United Nations Association, draws heavily on the leadership of internationally minded establishment figures, especially former diplomats, and seeks to reconcile an important role for the United Nations with a pragmatic understanding of world politics. This includes an acceptance of the special influence of leading states within and outside the organisation that trumps the sovereignty mantra of 'the equality of states'. The Third World outlook, which may be grasped by reference to the activities and policy prescriptions of the Third World Network, pays less attention to the UN as a whole than to the policies and role of the International Monetary Fund (IMF) and World Bank, as well as to the development dialogue and debate about world economic policy that goes on within the General Assembly and elsewhere in the United Nations. And then there are radical peace groups, possibly best illustrated by Tavola Della Pace, which perceive the United Nations as currently dominated by geopolitics and the manipulations of Washington and Davos. Such groups seek to shift control over UN operations with respect to such issues as war and peace, self-determination (for the Palestinians, for example), and development from the dominant states to popular democratic forces and to the guidance of the rule of law and the dictates of global equity; just such a shift is the goal of their campaign provocatively called Reclaiming the United Nations. Tavola Della Pace also organised every second year in Perugia 'A United Nations of the Peoples' that gives voice to grassroots views on global issues from NGO representatives and citizens from around the world, a contrasting atmosphere and agenda to the statist show put on at UN headquarters in New York City, or even in Geneva.

There are also a large number of civil society actors around the world with issue-oriented agendas, especially in relation to environment and human rights. These actors make use of the United Nations to the extent relevant to their substantive preoccupations. EarthAction, World Wide Fund for Nature, and Greenpeace are environmental NGOs that push their causes at the UN whenever it seems useful. Human

Rights Watch and Amnesty International do the same with respect to human rights. One of the oldest and most widely respected organisations, Women's International League for Peace and Freedom (WILPF), has been active especially at the Geneva end of UN operations, but also in UN conferences around the world, particularly if the subject matter bears on feminist concerns or disarmament. WILPF has a civil society presence and possesses a strong internationalist identity that long antedates the establishment of the United Nations. The role and activism of WILPF prefigures in many respects the emergent reality of global civil society.

> the essential agenda of UN reform runs far deeper and is far wider than an expanded membership for the Security Council

It is in these ideological and historical circumstances that this chapter considers the issue of UN reform from the perspective of global civil society. It begins by presenting the debate on reform as emerging out of a swirl of conflicting political projects, and then proceeds to discuss how reform has accompanied the evolution of the UN. Because changes in the Charter of the United Nations are often impossible to achieve by formal amendment, the story of reform is often mainly told in terms of shifting patterns of practice, especially in the Security Council and Secretariat, which adapt the UN to changing values and imperatives, and amount to what might be described as 'reform from within'. This discussion is followed by a consideration of three important reports addressing UN reform produced on the initiative of the Secretary-General. This is essentially a state-friendly approach to UN reform that can be understood as 'reform from above'. A further section considers some prominent initiatives that emanate from global civil society and enjoy widespread support in the more radical reformist domains, and can be understood as 'reform from below' (and without), although on occasion with crucial collaborative support from coalitions of governments. It is this pattern of political action that successfully brought the International Criminal Court into being despite intense opposition from leading geopolitical actors. That is, this kind of globalism is a new form of diplomacy that should not be regarded as either traditionally statist in

character or a postmodern instance of non-state transnationalism. It is really a diplomatic hybrid that could be tentatively identified as the 'new globalism'.

Why this sudden interest in reform? The recent flurry of activity related to UN reform arises at this time for a cluster of reasons: the upcoming 60th anniversary of the UN, the expectation that the goals set for the UN at its Millennium Special Session of the General Assembly is scheduled for review in 2005, the frustrations associated with the failure to agree on some plan to make the Security Council more representative of the twenty-first century, and the restless insistence by the United States that making the UN useful requires drastic reform that will make the organisation more responsive to geopolitical realities (UNGA 2004).

The background of UN reform

As portrayed in the media, the issue of UN reform is often reduced in public discussion to this one issue of the enlargement of the permanent membership of the Security Council, to make it more representative of the power structure of states in the world as of 2005. There is no doubt that this issue has a significant substantive and symbolic importance in showing the capacity of the UN to adjust to changes in the relations among states, and especially to give states that were either defeated in the Second World War or situated in then colonised Third World regions a proper place at the head table of the United Nations. This persisting preoccupation also illustrates the disturbing inability of the membership to agree upon a solution to the challenge of reform despite a major push in the period leading up to the millennium, and now again five years later. These difficulties apply even to basic reforms that were almost universally accepted as necessary. More recently, it has been recognised that the essential agenda of UN reform runs far deeper and is far wider than an expanded membership for the Security Council, and poses decisive challenges to and opportunities for global civil society in these early years of the twenty-first century.

Of course, the United Nations is used to designate a complex assemblage or system of distinct actors, organisations, and programmes, and a wide range of undertakings. It is a complex system, and has grown more complex during its existence as additional goals and functions have been adopted (see Figure 5.1). The meaning of 'reform of the United Nations' is rather

Figure 5.1: The UN system

Principal Organs

Trusteeship Council	Security Council	General Assembly

Subsidiary Bodies

Military Staff Committee

Standing Committee and ad hoc bodies

International Criminal Tribunal for the
Former Yugoslavia

International Criminal Tribunal for Rwanda

UN Monitoring, Verification and Inspection
Commission (Iraq)

United Nations Compensation Commission

Peacekeeping Operations and Missions

Subsidiary Bodies

Main committees

Other sessional committees

Standing committees and ad hoc bodies

Other subsidiary organs

Programmes and Funds

UNCTAD United Nations Conference
on Trade and Development

ITC International Trade Centre
(UNCTAD/WTO)

UNDCP United Nations Drug
Control Programme[a]

UNEP United Nations
Environment Programme

UNICEF United Nations
Children's Fund

UNDP United Nations
Development Programme

UNIFEM United Nations Development
Fund for Women

UNV United Nations Volunteers

UNCDF United Nations Capital
Development Fund

UNFPA United Nations
Population Fund

UNHCR Office of the United Nations
High Commissioner for Refugees

WFP World Food Programme

UNRWA[b] United Nations Relief
and Works Agency for Palestine
Refugees in the Near East

UN-HABITAT United Nations
Human Settlements
Programme (UNHSP)

Research and Training Institutes

UNICRI United Nations Interregional
Crime and Justice Research Institute

UNITAR United Nations Institute for
Training and Research

UNRISD United Nations Research
Institute for Social Development

UNIDIR[b] United Nations Institute
for Disarmament Research

INSTRAW International Research
and Training Institute for the
Advancement of Women

Other UN Entities

OHCHR Office of the
United Nations High
Commissioner for
Human Rights

UNOPS United
Nations Office for
Project Services

UNU United
Nations University

UNSSC United
Nations System
Staff College

UNAIDS Joint United
Nations Programme
on HIV/AIDS

NOTES: Solid lines from a Principal Organ indicate a direct reporting relationship; dashes indicate a nonsubsidiary relationship.
[a]The UN Drug Control Programme is part of the UN Office on Drugs and Crime. [b]UNRWA and UNIDIR report onl y to the GA.
[c]The World Trade Organization and World Tourism Organization use the same acronym. [d]IAEA reports to the Security Council
and the General Assembly (GA). [e]The CTBTO Prep.Com and OPCW report to the GA. [f]Specialized agencies are autonomous
organizations working with the UN and each other through the coordinating machinery of the ECOSOC at the intergovernmental
level, and through the Chief Executives Board for coordination (CEB) at the inter-secretariat level.

Economic and Social Council

International Court of Justice

Secretariat

Functional Commissions

Commissions on:
    Human Rights
    Narcotic Drugs
    Crime Prevention and Criminal
      Justice
    Science and Technology for
      Development
    Sustainable Development
    Status of Women
    Population and Development
    Commission for Social
      Development
    Statistical Commission

Regional Commissions

Economic Commission for
    Africa (ECA)
Economic Commission for Europe
    (ECE)
Economic Commission for Latin
    America and the Caribbean
    (ECLAC)
Economic and Social Commission
    for Asia and the Pacific (ESCAP)
Economic and Social Commission
    for Western Asia (ESCWA)

Other Bodies

Permanent Forum on Indigenous
    Issues (PFII)
United Nations Forum on Forests
Sessional and standing committees
Expert, ad hoc and related bodies

Related Organizations

WTO[c] World Trade Organization

IAEA[d] International Atomic
Energy Agency

CTBTO Prep.com[e] PrepCom
for the Nuclear-Test-Ban-Treaty
Organization

OPCW[e] Organization for the
Prohibition of Chemical Weapons

Specialized Agencies[f]

ILO International Labour
Organization

FAO Food and Agriculture
Organization of the United Nations

UNESCO United Nations
Educational, Scientific and Cultural
Organization

WHO World Health Organization

World Bank Group

IBRD International Bank for
Reconstruction and Development

IDA International
Development Association

IFC International Finance
Corporation

MIGA Multilateral Investment
Guarantee Agency

ICSID International Centre for
Settlement of Investment Disputes

IMF International Monetary Fund

ICAO International Civil
Aviation Organization

IMO International Maritime
Organization

ITU International
Telecommunication Union

UPU Universal Postal Union

WMO World Meterological
Organization

WIPO World Intellectual
Property Organization

IFAD International Fund for
Agricultural Development

UNIDO United Nations Industrial
Development Organization

WTO[c] World Tourism
Organization

Departments and Offices

OSG Office of the
Secretary-General

OIOS Office of Internal
Oversight Services

OLA Office of Legal Affairs

DPA Department of
Political Affairs

DDA Department for
Disarmament Affairs

DPKO Department of
Peacekeeping Operations

OCHA Office for the Coordination
of Humanitarian Affairs

DESA Department of Economic
and Social Affairs

DGACM Department for General
Assembly and Conference
Management

DPI Department of Public
Information

DM Department of Management

OHRLLS Office of the
High Representative for the
Least Developed Countries,
Landlocked Developing
Countries and Small Island
Developing States

UNSECOORD Office of
the United Nations
Security Coordinator

UNODC United Nations Office
on Drugs and Crime

UNOG UN Office at Geneva

UNOV UN Office at Vienna

UNON UN Office at Nairobi

*Published by the UN Department of
Public Information DPI/2342, March 2004*

The United Nations headquarters, New York ©*Pietro Cenini/Panos Pictures*

ambiguous. In this chapter, 'reform' is understood to refer to basic adjustments needed to achieve a revitalised relevance to the global problematique. But reform can also be properly understood as pertaining to changes throughout the UN system, including with regard to the activities of the various specialised agencies and the organisational interplay of the various actors. Rethinking the role of the Secretary-General and of leadership within the United Nations, as well as of the principal organs – the Security Council and the General Assembly – is a daunting task, and has many aspects. The full agenda of UN reform can be touched upon only impressionistically, and in light of the apparent priorities of global civil society, which centre more and more on the democratisation of global political spaces. This means access, participation, accountability, transparency, and respect for international law.

Perceptions and representations

There is also the highly contested terrain of representation as it pertains to the United Nations. The UN is represented variously by its most ardent supporters as offering by far the straightest road to peace, justice, and global governance. The UN is generally represented by its fiercest critics as a dream palace of illusion, as 'a dangerous place' where 'irresponsible majorities' rule the roost, and as an irrelevant talking shop when it comes to the critical challenges of global security

and the world economy. Richard Perle, an influential neoconservative, and Dore Gold, a leading Israeli diplomat, illustrate how far this hostility to the United Nations can be carried (Perle 2003; Gold 2004). This spectrum of representations explains why it seems often impossible to achieve a consensus on the content and character of global reform. Both clusters of representations, the favorable and the critical, tend to proceed from the premise that the UN is the boldest global experiment ever in establishing a normative framework and an institutional authority that challenge the primacy of the sovereign state. Such talk about the UN seems inflated, even grandiose. It overlooks the extent to which the boldest and most consequential organisational initiatives on an international level, at least with respect to overriding sovereignty, can be more convincingly associated with either the European Union or the triad of international financial institutions – the IMF, the World Bank and the World Trade Organization (WTO) – rather than with the UN (Falk 2004: ch 3). The IMF and World Bank are nominally linked to the UN but are operationally autonomous, while the WTO was deliberately established with no formal link to the UN. At this stage of history, even governmental critics treat the UN as a sufficiently important arena for achieving the legitimisation and implementation of policies that they rarely advocate the policy option of withdrawal. But acknowledging this importance is not the same as a shared commitment to a stronger or more effective organisation in relation to the Charter (the goal of genuine UN reform, as distinct from the United States' geopolitical or hegemonic understanding of effectiveness). It is this encounter in the realm of representation, and related imaginaries of world order, that has made previous reformist efforts in the UN setting so often founder. Such a realisation of these difficulties erodes commitments to reform and suggests the need for a politics of reform for the UN on the part of those who believe that the UN has the potential to contribute more to peace, justice, equity, and sustainability in the world.

The profound character of the reformist imperative was most dramatically articulated by Kofi Annan when, in a September 2003 speech to the General Assembly, he said:

> We have come to a fork in the road. This may be a moment no less decisive than 1945 itself, when the United Nations was founded... I believe the time is ripe for a hard look at fundamental issues, and at the structural changes that may be needed in order to strengthen (the Organisation). History is a harsh judge: it will not forgive us if we let this moment pass. (BBC News 2003)

In effect, the Secretary-General was saying that the UN must change to survive and flourish as the institutional centrepiece of hope for a better world. His call was made in the shadow of the controversial Iraq war, undertaken by its leading member without the benefit of a mandate from the Security Council, and in a manner so defiant of the UN Charter that Annan himself publicly declared it 'illegal'. The invasion of Iraq violates the core conception of the United Nations as an organisation dedicated, above all, to the prevention of war (allowing only a narrow exception for wars of self-defence), based on an unconditional prohibition of unilateral recourse to war. The UN was also in the related, somewhat earlier dark shadow cast by the obvious implications of the 9/11 attacks on the United States, indicating the menacing rise of non-state political actors and the related inability, already acknowledged in the 1990s, to treat crises internal to states as beyond the purview of the UN. Such developments raised fundamental questions about contested uses of international force under the Charter and the nature of wars supposedly undertaken in self-defence. Such a realisation of the need for fundamental adjustment in doctrine and practice was also

reinforced by the rise of international human rights as a challenge to the territorial supremacy of the sovereign state. Additionally, on several earlier occasions, most notably in the course of talks given at the World Economic Forum at Davos, Annan had insisted on the importance to the United Nations of finding ways to make its structure and operations more receptive to the participation of both global market forces and civil society actors, thereby acknowledging that the 1945 image of world order as constituted by sovereign states was no longer adequate as the basis for UN constitutionalism in an era of multidimensional globalisation. And so there was little doubt that the Secretary-General's arresting words about a fork in the road were a timely acknowledgement that the UN needed substantial reforms if it were to adapt to the changing needs of the twenty-first century, as well as fulfil its potential to contribute to the widely demanded democratic forms of global governance (Held 2004).

Civil society and the UN

The relation of civil society actors to the United Nations has been complex and problematic from the time of its founding. There is no doubt that the peoples of the world and their associations and representatives, who hoped for a more peaceful, orderly, and humane world, looked upon the establishment of the United Nations as a historic positive step, and believed that over time it would encourage the emergence of a disarmed and warless world governed by the rule of law, thereby eliminating the use of force to resolve international disputes. The UN was seen in 1945 by its champions as an idealist dream coming true, offering the best prospect ever of governing the international behaviour of sovereign states. The long strategic and ideological conflict associated with the cold war often resulted in stalemates within the organisation, and suggested to many observers that the important developments in the area of peace and security were still being promoted by traditional modes of statecraft. It also became painfully clear that the voices of civil society, although given nominal access in the limited setting of the Economic and Social Council[1] (itself a marginal actor within the

---

1 Article 71 of Chapter X of the UN Charter states: 'The Economic and Social Council may make suitable arrangements for consultation with non-governmental organizations which are concerned with matters within its competence. Such arrangements may be made with international organizations and, where appropriate, with national organizations after consultation with the Member of the United Nations concerned'.

Box 5.1: UN conferences/summits and civil society

It is noteworthy that the Economic and Social Council (ECOSOC) is the only organ of the UN that allows for consultation with non-governmental organisations (see footnote 1 of the present chapter). This provision simply reflects a spillover from the experience of the pre-Second World War League of Nations with social and humanitarian work in which NGOs had played an important role. The exclusion of political, security and disarmament questions from the formal part of the UN–NGO relationship means that the strong global movements for decolonisation and nuclear disarmament do not have a direct voice in UN deliberations on these matters.

Several hundred NGOs were accredited and quite a few worked diligently in the meetings of the ECOSOC and its bodies from the very beginning. But until the 1990s, there was no qualitative change from the way this relationship had functioned in the days of the League. Even the new area of human rights operated in a low key, perhaps even more so than minority rights in the League.

The situation changed substantially in the 1990s, particularly after the Conference on Environment and Development (UNCED) in Rio, which engaged with NGOs on an unprecedented scale. Every UN conference after that involved large-scale NGO participation in parallel conferences and meetings, as accredited bodies influencing the intergovernmental process and as members of official delegations. A stakeholder culture emerged with like-minded NGOs forming caucuses of women or youth or faith-based groups and the like. The North–South divide manifested itself with the emergence of a Southern caucus (although there was no counterpart Northern caucus) and regional caucuses for Africa, Caribbean, Latin America, and elsewhere.

The crucial steps were taken at an early stage in the preparations for the 'Rio Conference', and, more specifically, at the preparatory meeting in Nairobi in August 1990. The General Assembly resolution setting up the conference spoke of the involvement only of NGOs in consultative status with ECOSOC. This would have excluded quite a few environmental NGOs, and there was pressure to broaden eligibility so as to cover all NGOs who wished to participate. A long and difficult negotiation ended with an agreement to open the door to NGOs that did not have any established status with the UN, but with a provision for prior scrutiny of eligibility.

The Rio Conference was at least partly a product of pressure from NGOs, some of which wanted a negotiating role. But there was little support for this, and a provision for closed meetings was written into the decision.

The Rio Conference precedent was used in later conferences, but each of them marked some further advance. At the Cairo Conference on Population and the Beijing Conference on Women and Development, NGOs played a larger role in shaping the outcome than ever before. In the Copenhagen Conference on Social Development, they won the right to be present in negotiations even if they were not given an active role. In the Istanbul Conference on Human Settlements, local authorities, normally treated as NGOs, had a formal committee to contribute to the outcome. At the Johannesburg Summit on Sustainable Development, where the focus was on implementation rather than on policy development, the whole idea of multi-stakeholder partnerships was promoted.

The outcome of the UN conferences of the 1990s was a formal agreement among governments. But, because the intergovernmental process was opened to NGO participation, the outcome also had to take NGOs' views into account. NGOs also became more skilled as lobbyists, suggesting precise changes in negotiating texts, using their media contacts to raise the alarm when crucial positions, for instance on women's rights, were under threat, and generally dominating the more public parts of the conference process. The impact has been greatest in the conferences where women's rights were being discussed and least in the ones where core economic interests were at stake.

The conferences helped the NGOs, particularly those whose primary aim was to lobby political processes. Several global networks of NGOs, like the Women's Environment and Development Organisation (WEDO), developed on the strength of the resources mobilised for their work on these conferences. Even those that had a substantive programme outside the UN found the conferences useful for strengthening their international networks. In some ways, the UN conferences of the 1990s helped to provide global civil society with a space where it could be visible and where its various parts could connect with one another.

Governments have questioned the symbiotic relationship between the UN and NGOs, typically on the ground that it is not clear whom NGOs represent. But the subtext here is really their concern that dissident groups in their countries will find a voice in international forums. Many NGOs also question the wisdom of being 'part of the system'. This can be seen in the World Social Forum and in the demonstrations outside the meeting halls at conferences of the IMF, the World Bank, and G8. The UN has been exempt from these because most NGOs continue to see some merit in its aims, if not in its actual practice or its effectiveness.

Where do we go from here? One route is that of more formal arrangements like a People's Assembly. Others, like the Johannesburg partnership initiatives, seek to bring NGOs into the implementation process. In a few cases, the UN is trying to put together structured multi-stakeholder groups involving governments, corporations and NGOs. But in all of this, the central role of civil society is clear – it is to bring into inter-country negotiations a point of view that is informed by principles that cut across national interests.

Nitin Desai, former Under-Secretary General for Economic and Social Affairs, United Nations

UN Secretary-General Kofi Annan in Darfur, Sudan
©*Petterik Wiggers/Panos Pictures*

most powerful states and their friends and allies. Such a constitutional limit on authority was both a reassurance that sovereign rights would not be brushed aside by an attempt of a major state to establish a global tyranny under UN auspices, and a warning to weak states that they could not count on the UN to uphold their vital interests, including their self-defence. This realist image of the UN sat uncomfortably over the years with lingering idealist expectations, accounting for both disappointments about the failures to implement the Charter, especially in the setting of collective security, and continuing demands by peace and justice forces that all members, including the veto powers, live within the four corners of Charter restraints. At the same time, geopolitical architects are for ever complaining that the irresponsible use of the veto to block the policies of the United States is making the UN again, as during the cold war, of marginal relevance.

Throughout the period of the cold war, civil society actors increasingly disregarded the United Nations, concentrating their energies on issues such as human rights, environment, and social justice, or they shaped movements opposing the Vietnam War or building the worldwide anti-apartheid campaign. In the 1970s and the 1980s, civil society energies led to the emergence of both robust anti-nuclear movements and anti-authoritarian networks that proclaimed their belief in 'détente from below', joining activists from East and West in collaborative undertakings that defied the rigid boundaries of the cold war epitomised by the Berlin Wall (Kaldor, Holden and Falk 1989; Keck and Sikkink 1998). What is notable about these developments is that they took shape almost entirely outside the United Nations. At the same time, some NGOs and private citizens were advising government delegations and providing them with valuable information behind the scenes at major law-making conferences sponsored by the United Nations, particularly assisting understaffed and inexperienced Third World governments to be better informed about proposed treaty arrangements affecting their interests. One of the first of these settings that demonstrated the invaluable informal contributions of these NGOs was the decade-long negotiations under UN auspices that produced the Law of the Sea Convention in 1982, which has provided the world with an impressive, if imperfect, public order of the oceans. Another instance, although technically outside the formal purview of the United Nations (with the International Red Cross as the formal sponsor) was

UN scheme), were not to be noticed, much less heeded, in the conduct of the central activities of the UN. The UN was, as clearly intended by its founding governments, a club of, by, and for states, and dominated by the strongest states, suggesting the persistence, if not the resurgence, of geopolitics as the foundation of world order in the decades following the Second World War. No feature of the UN better expressed the blatantly geopolitical character of the organisation than the veto power given to the five permanent members (P-5), which effectively acknowledged the inability of the UN to address threats to global security generated by the

the effort during the 1970s to supplement the Geneva Conventions of 1949, setting forth international humanitarian law by addressing the newly important problems associated with civil wars (Weston, Falk and Charlesworth 1997: 237–60). Without the informational resources provided by NGOs and individuals recruited from civil society, Third World delegations would have been overwhelmed and easily manipulated by the negotiating positions and pressure tactics relied upon by leading countries, especially the United States. To some extent, civil society initiatives in these settings contributed to levelling the playing field, but by no means to an extent that would achieve the *political* (as distinct from *juridical*) equality of sovereign states.

It was only, however, with the onset of global conferences on policy issues, pioneered and prefigured by the Stockholm Conference on the Human Environment in 1971, that the UN became a major arena for transnational civil forces, both as a source of pressure exerted on intergovernmental activities and as an occasion for transnational civil society networking and organising. Unlike the earlier low-profile roles intended to hide the influence of the NGOs in intergovernmental negotiations, here the intention was primarily to exert highly visible influence on the most powerful states and to gain attention for dissident views in the global media assembled to cover the event, although the supportive NGO roles of providing information and analysing policy options continued to be an invaluable equaliser on such occasions. This dynamic reached a climax in the 1990s with a series of high-profile UN conferences that featured strong and vivid participation by civil society actors, and the early articulation by commentators on the international scene of the presence of new political formation identified as 'global civil society' (Pianta 2001; Box 5.1). The very success of this informal penetration of UN processes induced a backlash on the part of several leading governments that sensed a loss of control by states of the policy-forming process, which made the holding of such conferences politically difficult. Representatives of large states described these conferences as 'spectacles' and as 'a waste of money and time', but the real objection was their showcasing of the vitality of civil society actors and networks that so often put governments on the defensive with respect to global policy debates. In effect, civil society actors were creative in their discovery of ways to make effective use of the United Nations to promote their aspirations, but the

statist and geopolitical structuring of influence at the UN, which endures, also displayed its capacity to hit back, to control the purse strings of global diplomacy, and essentially to shut off these informal, yet effective, channels of civil society access with respect to global policy formation on major issues.

The UN Secretary-General: balancing contending forces

The Secretary-General, as political leader and moral authority figure, has struggled to balance the contending forces and aspirations of the organisation. To gain help and support he constituted two prominent panels to study reform prospects, and to deliver reports in 2004. The first of these panels was composed of 'eminent persons', chaired by Fernando Henrique Cardoso, former President of Brazil, and charged with looking into the relations between the United Nations and civil society. It issued its report, *We the Peoples*, on 7 June 2004 (UN 2004a). It covers the subject matter comprehensively, offering 30 proposals for reform. The second initiative was charged with reconsidering the role of the United Nations with respect to peace and security. It was similarly constituted, chaired by Anand Panyarachun, former Prime Minister of Thailand, and submitted its report on 4 December 2004 to the Secretary-General (UN 2004b). The High-Level Panel report is exclusively dedicated to the substantive issues associated with the current global setting, and does not *directly* acknowledge the role or significance of global civil society, but its language and approach do reflect, to some degree, civil society perspectives, including especially its call for reconfiguring security as 'human security' rather than as either 'national security' or 'collective security'. At the same time, both panels were chaired and composed of individuals whose qualifications were based on their statist credentials, having held high positions in governments or intergovernmental institutions; and their recommendations for reform are sensible but not bold or imaginative. The reports also reflect pressures to be geopolitically credible and balanced. For instance, the most interesting and widely noticed discussion in the High-Level Panel on Security is its acknowledgement that anticipatory self-defence may be justifiable in a post-9/11 world, but that the legitimacy of such a claim depends on Security Council authorisation, thereby acknowledging the substantive merits of the Bush doctrine of pre-emptive war while reaffirming the UN procedural role in identifying

Table 5.1: Major UN conferences and summits of the 1990s

	Context/aims	Civil society role/conference outcomes
World Summit for Children, New York, September 1990	This was the first of the big UN conferences that brought together many heads of state and civil society actors. It built on a previous series of conferences on development issues that began in the 1970s.	Since 1990, 12 major UN conferences have addressed issues of global scope that, being beyond the capacities of individual states, needed concerted international effort. The mechanisms and agreements forged at these conferences committed member states to address pressing problems and needs. Non-state actors have played an increasingly significant role in this process, particularly NGOs. The cumulative effect of the conference process was a consensus on the concept of and agenda for development.
Conference on Environment and Development (UNCED), Rio de Janeiro, June 1992 'Earth Summit'	Two decades after the Stockholm Conference on the Environment, UNCED convened the largest ever gathering of heads of state (108 out of 172 government representatives) to discuss any issue to consider the implications of economic development for the planet. Inspired by mounting concern about climate change, pollution, biodiversity loss, and destruction of natural resources, the Earth Summit established a new framework, 'sustainable development'.	The Earth Summit attracted 2,400 representatives of civil society organisations and 17,000 individuals to the parallel NGO forum. News of the summit, transmitted by the 10,000 journalists who attended, created a sense of urgency about the environment. The visibility and strength of the NGO presence and its framing of the environmental issues set a precedent, influencing all subsequent UN conferences. Whether these focused on human rights, population, social development, women or human settlements, they could no longer be considered in isolation from sustainable development. Agenda 21, a global blueprint for sustainable development, became the basis for many national plans; more than 1,800 cities and towns have since created their own local Agenda 21. The UN Commission on Sustainable Development was established to monitor implementation of Rio agreements. A 1997 special session of the UN General Assembly on implementation of Agenda 21 found that, despite some progress, the environment continued to deteriorate. UNCED also led to four international treaties on climate change, biological diversity, desertification and high-seas fishing.
World Conference on Human Rights (WCHR), Vienna, June 1993	Building on the rights to a healthy environment and development that had been established at UNCED, WCHR reaffirmed international commitment to all human rights.	Civil society played a leading role in emphasising the universality and indivisibility of all human rights – both civil and political, and economic, social and cultural. WHCR led to the first Commissioner for Human Rights in 1994, and strengthened monitoring mechanisms. WCHR also instigated the inclusion of human rights as an integral part of UN peacekeeping missions, and made the link between democracy, development and human rights.

	Context/aims	Civil society role/conference outcomes
International Conference on Population and Development, Cairo, September 1994	This conference built a consensus for integrating family planning into a holistic approach to reproductive health services and established that women's education and empowerment was key to population stabilisation and sustainable development.	The Cairo Programme of Action marked the first time that the international community explicitly recognised that reproductive rights are human rights, called for the recognition of unsafe abortion as a major public health concern, and rejected the use of sterilisation and population targets in family planning initiatives. The programme also stressed the importance of empowering women to take charge of their reproductive lives, and laid out a 20-year plan for furthering reproductive and sexual rights worldwide.
World Summit for Social Development (WSSD), Copenhagen, March 1995	WSSD brought together 117 heads of state who committed their governments to eradicating poverty.	This summit agreed to the Copenhagen Declaration and Programme of Action for enhancing social development and ensuring human well-being. Some countries have set target dates for reducing poverty and launched assessments to plan long-term strategies. Civil society actors focused attention on the negative side of economic globalisation, the growing gaps between rich and poor, and increasing insecurity about employment and social services.
Fourth World Conference on Women, Beijing, September 1995 'Beijing Women's Conference'	This conference brought together 189 government representatives and a plethora of civil society actors – in total almost 50,000 people – to address the advancement of women. Gender roles, family structures, reproductive rights, the girl-child and violence against women were some of the areas/ issues considered.	The Beijing Declaration and Platform for Action committed governments to a five-year action plan to enhance the social, economic and political empowerment of women, improve their health, advance their education and promote their marital and sexual rights. New initiatives to implement the action plan were announced by 130 countries. The key message was that issues addressed in the Platform for Action were global and universal; implementation required changes in attitudes, values and practices at all levels – the 'mainstreaming' of a gender perspective. Like UNCED, the Beijing Women's Conference attracted thousands of NGO representatives and individuals to the parallel NGO forum, which influenced the agenda and final documents, and become involved in civil society networks.

Table 5.1 continued

	Context/aims	Civil society role/conference outcomes
Special Session of the General Assembly: Women 2000: Gender Equality, Development and Peace for the 21st Century, New York, June 2000 'Beijing plus 5'/ 'Women 2000'	This event brought together 150 countries and thousands of NGOS, many of them accredited at the Fourth World Conference on Women, in order to review progress on agreements made in Beijing.	The special session of the General Assembly reaffirmed commitment to the Beijing Declaration and Platform for Action. It also emphasised the importance of mainstreaming gender into actions and agreements reached at other UN conferences.
World Summit for Social Development + 5, Geneva, June/July 2000 'Social Summit +5'	A total of 35 heads of state and 4,791 official delegates, alongside 2,045 NGO representatives, attended this summit, which reviewed progress since the Copenhagen Summit of 1995.	This summit approved the Millennium Development Goal of halving extreme poverty by 2015, which would require the active involvement of civil society and those in poverty. Further, the summit stressed that achieving the Copenhagen Declaration would require universal access to high-quality education, health and other basic social services, and equal opportunities for active participation and sharing development benefits.
Millennium Summit, New York, September 2000	147 heads of state gathered to examine the role of the UN in the twenty-first century on issues as diverse as international security, international development, women's rights and the environment.	The Millennium Declaration outlined a blueprint for achieving a more peaceful, prosperous and just world through eight Millennium Development Goals (MDGs) designed to tackle extreme poverty by setting ambitious targets for 2015. The UN called on civil society to support the MDGs; and the declaration emphasised the need for strong partnerships with civil society organisations in order to fulfil the goals. However, civil society groups argued that the lack of appropriate participation was a major reason for the slow diffusion and limited awareness of the MDGs among the public, and slow pace of action. A follow-up summit in New York in September 2005 is intended to review progress since the declaration.

	Context/aims	Civil society role/conference outcomes
World Conference Against Racism and Racial Discrimination, Xenophobia and Related Intolerance, Durban, South Africa, August/September 2001	The conference focused on the following issues: minorities, gender, education, religion, HIV and AIDS, indigenous people, trafficking of women	Controversy marked this conference, including attempts to equate Zionism with racism, the accusation that Israel was conducting ethnic cleansing and the debate about slavery and reparations. The Israeli and US delegations left before agreement was reached. In the end, the Durban Declaration recognised that slavery was a crime against humanity but did not include demand for reparations; it also recognised the 'plight' of Palestinians.
International Conference on Financing for Development, Mexico, March 2002	This conference considered new approaches to domestic and international finance to promote more equitable global development.	This marked a major step up in overseas development assistance, with the US announcing a US$5 billion increase and the EU an US $8 billion increase. Through-out the process, the UN collaborated with a wide range of organisations, including the IMF, the World Bank, the WTO, business associations and corporations. NGO participation was modest.
World Summit on Sustainable Development, Johannesburg, August/September 2002 'Rio +10'	Building on the Earth Summit, the WSSD tackled a broad agenda: social (HIV, gender, health, food, cities); economic (investment, tourism, global public goods); environment (water, climate change, oceans).	The Johannesburg Declaration reaffirmed commitment to Agenda 21 and the Rio Declaration of 1992 but highlighted the challenges posed by poverty, the growing divide between rich and poor and the effects of globalisation. The Civil Society Global Forum, involving a broad range of non-state actors, organised a series of events parallel to the official summit.
Third United Nations Conference on the least developed countries, Brussels, May 2004	This conference, which brought together 193 governments and thousands of civil society actors, was dedicated to the eradication of extreme poverty in the world's least developed countries (LDCs).	Participating governments committed themselves to improving the quality of the lives of the more than 600 million people living in the world's poorest countries via a programme of development assistance, debt cancellation, and private investment. The Brussels Declaration on LDCs stated that a 'transparent, non-discriminatory and rules-based' multilateral trading system was essential for LDCs to reap the benefits of globalisation, and that their accession to the WTO should be encouraged.

appropriate circumstances. Credibility with civil society audiences is less crucial, but not entirely irrelevant to the prospects for exerting influence.

Kofi Annan submitted his own report on UN reform to the General Assembly, titled *In Larger Freedom: Towards Development, Security and Human Rights For All*, on 21 March 2005 (UN 2005). It incorporates the main recommendations of the earlier two reports, giving special attention to the High-Level Panel's proposals relating to Security Council reform and issues associated with the definition of terrorism and the recasting of the UN approach to claims of anticipatory self-defence.

The role of civil society: UN reform or human development?

In the background is the question of whether civil society actors should devote their limited energies and even more limited resources to this debate on UN reform or concentrate most of their efforts on grass-roots contributions to human betterment. This is an old debate that revives the view that civil society undertaking to shape a consensus on UN reform via the report of an independent international commission had led nowhere, and were largely ignored within the United Nations itself (Commission on Global Governance 1995). In contrast, the report by the International Commission on Intervention and State Sovereignty, essentially a civil society initiative although with ties to states, adopted an approach to humanitarian intervention that has now been taken over by the official bodies developing reform initiatives within the United Nations (International Commission on Intervention and State Sovereignty 2001). The issue of UN reform overlaps with and is intimately related to discourses on 'global governance' (examples include Falk 1995; Slaughter 2004; Etzioni 2004; Held 1995). It is notable and appropriate that *Global Civil Society 2004/5* features as its lead chapter a contribution by Kenneth Anderson and David Rieff that counsels international NGOs to give up the pretensions associated with claiming the existence of 'global civil society' and stop trying to play a role in the construction of global governance. In their words:

> ...international NGOs should give up their claims to represent global civil society, give up their dreams of representing the peoples of the world – indeed, devote fewer of their resources to advocacy and more time and care to the actual needs of their

actual constituencies, and re-establish their claims of expertise and competence. (Anderson and Rieff 2005: 36)

Such an admonition can be heard either as a rather sinister message to get out of the way of a resilient geopolitically administered world order, or merely as pragmatic counsel to civil society actors to conserve their energies and resources to achieve maximum effectiveness. (The advice is rendered more controversial, and in my view dubious, by the authors' insistence that if international NGOs and their intellectual spokespersons and allies continue to criticise the United States' role in the post-9/11 world, it would be 'the surest' way to guarantee the 'irrelevance' of civil society perspectives and values' (2005: 37–8). Such a direction of advice would suggest that civil society actors have little or no part to play in shaping the debate on UN reform or, more generally, on the future shape of global governance, but should content themselves with services to humanity performed in the niches of relief work and by mounting local grassroots protests directed at particular projects.)

There is some confusion here with respect to language. Anderson and Rieff are directing their attention to activist NGOs, whereas international commissions drawing their membership from the ranks of prominent individuals, while being part of civil society, are not regarded as posing fundamental challenges to the established order, but rather appear to be appendages that are seeking helpful adjustments.

The special nature of UN reform

There is a final preliminary issue bearing on the nature of 'reform' within the UN context. It should be understood that the basic reformist process has been informal, continuous, and internal to the UN system, filling in gaps by practice and reinterpreting the text of Charter provisions in the light of changing values and norms. This reflects, above all, the difficulty of achieving formal explicit changes due to the cumbersome character of the amendment procedure and a result of the political obstacles blocking the formation of a requisite consensus, especially among the P-5 (Article 108 of the UN Charter requires a two-thirds vote of the General Assembly that is then 'ratified in accordance with their respective constitutional processes by two thirds of the Members of the United Nations, including all the permanent members of the Security

UN peacekeepers in Bosnia Herzegovina ©*Paul Lowe/Panos Pictures*

Council'). The informal or de facto process of reform has many important examples. Already in the 1950s, the Security Council found a way to circumvent the difficulty of confronting the prospect of blockage due to the Soviet boycott (prompted by the failure to accredit the Communist government in Beijing as representing China) during the Korean War. Article 27(3) requires that decisions of the Security Council on substantive issues be supported by nine members, 'including the concurring votes of the permanent members'. A common-sense reading of this text would suggest that absence or abstention prevents a Security Council decision, but the practice established the precedent that the council can reach a valid decision provided only that the permanent members do not cast a negative vote. In the guise of interpretation this is quite a modification of the veto power as expressed in the Charter provision. (For a juridical justification of this interpretation, see McDougal and Gardner 1951.) Another potential way to circumvent a veto was

established by the Uniting for Peace resolution[2], which gave the General Assembly the capacity to recommend action in the peace and security context if the Security Council was gridlocked by the veto. This initiative was also adopted in the setting of the Korean War and based on cold war geopolitics in the 1950s, which gave the West an assured majority in the General Assembly and an associated confidence that the outcome of UN action would always be in its favour.

The Uniting for Peace approach was discreetly abandoned by the West as soon as it became apparent that the United States and the West might invoke the veto and that their majorities in the General Assembly were no longer assured as formerly colonised countries expanded its membership. It was the politically changed circumstances of decolonisation, and the altered composition of the General Assembly, and not the

---

2 *UN General Assembly Resolution 337 (V) of 3 November 1950.*

Box 5.2: Uneasy yet close: human rights NGOs and the UN

The driving force of civil society

The rise of NGOs as a major actor in the UN human rights system is a remarkable story. Behind so many, apparently governmental, human rights initiatives in the UN stands civil society, advocating, informing and raising its voice. NGOs, together with the media, are the conscience of governments; they expose wrongs, educate, mobilise, advocate reform and articulate aspirations of peoples around the world. Especially since the end of the cold war, the character of civil society in the UN has changed, with large numbers of national NGOs from developing countries now participating directly in the UN's work. Yet member states – and the UN bureaucracy that they finance and try to control – have an uneasy relationship with the NGOs that so often challenge their political will and criticise their performance.

The UN Commission on Human Rights – the UN's main intergovernmental body dealing with human rights, which is likely to be transformed into a new Human Rights Council – is often silent and riven by political divisions and compromises. Yet, when it does act on serious violations in a country, it is usually because of NGOs and the media. The hundreds of NGOs that lobby at the commission give its annual six-week meeting in Geneva a sharpness and provide a stark mirror on to the world, which is often the only way to provoke intergovernmental action. Formal 'consultative status' gives NGOs the right to be present and speak at such human rights meetings. But it is through the thousands of informal interactions with government delegations outside the formal conference room that civil society is able to offer its expertise and pressure governments to act.

Over many decades, NGOs have set tomorrow's human rights agenda, bringing women's rights into the mainstream of the human rights discourse, focusing on how to end the recruitment of child soldiers or calling for recognition of the rights of marginalised groups, such as indigenous peoples, disabled people or those who suffer discrimination because of their sexual orientation. NGOs were behind so many of the international human rights standards negotiated in the UN and now used around the world, such as the Convention against Torture or the Declaration on Human Rights Defenders. NGOs active in the UN, however, were slow to advocate economic, social and cultural rights as equal in importance to civil and political rights.

Major new UN institutions, such as the International Criminal Court and the UN High Commissioner for Human Rights, were successfully created because of the mobilising power of NGOs over many decades. The International Commission of Jurists, for example, called for the High Commissioner post as early as 1965, almost 30 years before it was created in 1993.

Over the years, the UN Commission on Human Rights has appointed more than 40 independent experts to investigate abuses in particular countries, or on specific human rights issues from the right to housing to extrajudicial executions. Yet these experts would be paralysed without the information NGOs provide every day on individual cases and patterns of human rights violations around the world – information that enables them to send urgent appeals, to assess patterns around the world and to mount effective missions to countries.

The system of elected expert bodies that examine whether states have implemented their legal obligations under human rights treaties they have ratified did not formally build in any role for civil society. Yet these experts quickly found, in practice, that they needed civil society facts and views as an alternative to the often self-serving information supplied by government departments alone – a role that has now been more formally and openly recognised by these expert treaty bodies.

Most of this human rights advocacy has been focused on bodies that meet in Geneva. New York, where little overtly human rights work is carried out and government delegations are less used to civil society participation, is a much more hostile environment for NGOs. Although, since the mid-1990s, even leaders of large international NGOs have informally addressed members of the Security Council, the General Assembly generally excludes NGOs from its deliberations. In countries around the world, UN agencies on the ground are still often apprehensive about being seen to be too open to civil society, although this is changing. In practice, NGOs are even contracted by UN agencies to implement projects in areas such as refugee assistance, child rights and combating HIV and AIDS.

Why does civil society use the UN?

Civil society groups frame their grievances in the language of international human rights and seek action from UN intergovernmental bodies and expert mechanisms because these are potentially powerful advocacy tools. The common discourse of human rights crosses cultures and opens the door to building global coalitions and alliances. International recognition in the UN of an issue, such as the fact that female genital mutilation is a violation of human rights and is not just a health or cultural issue, can flow back to influence government policies and empower local groups. NGOs have sometimes successfully lobbied for expert missions to be sent to their country or for a human rights field operation to be set up. Victims can sometimes obtain remedies for violations from UN expert mechanisms when domestic complaints procedures fail. In UN gatherings, national NGOs also often find they have interaction with their government representatives that is denied to them back home.

Tensions and opportunities in UN reform

The drive for reform of the UN's institutions has again revealed the underlying tensions between civil society and the UN. Most governments publicly accept that a reformed UN should at least maintain the existing level of NGO access. The High-Level Panel *We the Peoples: Civil Society, the UN and Global Governance* made many recommendations to strengthen the work of civil society in the UN. Yet some governments also believe that NGOs, independent experts and international civil servants in UN agencies are gaining too much influence at the expense of the fundamental intergovernmental character of UN decision making. The UN reform process is opening up old agreements and compromises on NGO participation. It is not yet clear whether this will result in stronger or weaker civil society participation.

Governments – and some in civil society – are also asking why NGOs should be listened to in the UN. Whom do NGOs represent? What legitimacy do unelected, self-proclaimed NGOs have in the process of global governance? To whom are NGOs accountable? Civil society has only just begun to respond to this critique. With the huge increase in the number of NGOs competing for time to speak and even for physical space, governments are seeking to cut down on what they see as the proliferation of NGOs and to channel NGO involvement away from the intergovernmental proceedings towards separate 'consultations' with NGOs. NGOs are seeking to preserve their access, while increasingly acting jointly in coalitions and alliances to limit individual interventions.

Even the definition of NGO is being broadened, with business groups and parliamentarians also now often described as 'civil society actors' in the UN. Civil society also points to the rise in the UN of so-called GONGOs – government-owned-NGOs. Closely allied to, or created and financed by governments, GONGOs discredit the essential non-governmental character of civil society advocacy.

Nicholas Howen, Secretary-General, International Commission of Jurists, Geneva (www.icj.org)

Charter's conception of the roles of the main organs, that closed this escape route from the paralysing clutches of the veto in crises of war and peace.

A second example of de facto reform is the significant development of coercive peacemaking under Chapter VI of the UN Charter during the tenure of Secretary-General Dag Hammarskjöld in the 1960s. It was described at the time as an 'innovation' neither prescribed nor proscribed by the Charter, but useful in dealing with situations other than war making, addressed in Chapter VII, that called for UN peace-keeping. A third example of increasing importance since the end of the cold war is the narrowing of the significance and scope of the prohibition on the UN in Article 2(7) of the Charter to refrain from intervention 'in matters that are essentially within the domestic jurisdiction of any state'. Such a strict conception of Westphalian deference to territorial sovereignty reflected the ethos of 1945, but as civil wars became internationalised and as acute violations of human rights, particularly 'ethnic cleansing' and genocide, became challenges to the organised international community, the UN norm of non-intervention was gradually qualified. This process reached a climax in the period after the Kosovo War in 1999, and produced a doctrine of humanitarian intervention, rationalised as 'a responsibility to protect' (Independent International Commission on Kosovo 2000: 163–8).

A final unconsummated instance of reform by inter-pretation, practice, experience, and reasonableness relates to the High-Level Panel on Security's recommended expansion of the idea of self-defence beyond the image in the Charter language that would appear to rule out anticipatory claims. Article 51 appears to limit claims by the words 'if an armed attacks occurs' and, although this restrictive language has long been eroded by state practice and by the commentary of some international law experts, it has not been directly challenged by the recent panel until now (Arend and Beck 1993). As suggested above, it represents a geopolitical compromise that is unlikely to be accepted by the current United States political leadership or even possibly by the opposition that in the 2004 presidential election affirmed that the United States would not await UN authorisation to pursue by war its security interests. What is most relevant here is that the High-Level Panel recognised the need for adjustment with respect to this core idea in the Charter, offered a practical suggestion for closing the gap

between legal rules and security threats, and explicitly declared in its report that it was not necessary to amend the language of the Charter, even when addressing this fundamental matter of discretion to use international force. Presumably, the reluctance to recommend a formal change expresses both the cumbersomeness of the amendment procedure and also the likelihood that such a change would be controversial with a large number of member states.

> **widely needed and generally accepted reforms are often blocked by the entrenched interests of particular members in retaining outmoded features**

From the foregoing it becomes evident that, while the case for reform is strong, political obstacles often make formal adjustments by way of amendments difficult, if not impossible. Further, the poster child of reform – restructuring the Security Council with respect to membership, size, and availability of the veto – does require a formal amendment, but it is also made problematic by an absence of agreement among members about the specifics of the reform measure. Finally, UN experience demonstrates that significant reform initiatives can proceed by way of practice and interpretation, which has enabled the UN throughout its history to respond with an impressive degree of flexibility to changes in the global settings. So two conclusions emerge: the UN has great difficulties making needed reforms that require formal amend-ments; but the UN has devised effective informal approaches that have successfully enabled many adjustments in the framing of UN action.

A critical analytical approach

It is often implicitly assumed in discussions about both the United Nations and global civil society that their influence is inherently beneficial for the pursuit of widely shared world order goals associated with what I have called elsewhere 'humane global governance' (Falk 1995; 2004). In both instances, such an assumption is misleading. Any political actor, however benign its mandate, can be twisted by pressures from without and subversion from within to pursue policies that corrupt and deform. The United Nations has not always adhered to its lofty goals, as when, for instance, it persisted for 12 years with a programme of sanctions despite evidence of severe harm to the civilian population of Iraq in the aftermath of the 1991 Gulf War. Other instances involve the inexcusable breaches of discipline by UN peacekeeping forces that have involved alleged sexual exploitation of minors and other vulnerable persons. The Secretary-General in his recent report on UN reform says: 'I have enacted a policy of "zero tolerance" towards such offences that applies to all personnel engaged in United Nations operations' (Annan 2005: 31). And then there are a variety of bureaucratic lapses. The recent investigation of the oil-for-food programme revealed a series of actions by UN staff that condoned or was complicit in corruption.

Even if civil society actors are restricted to those that affirm positive world order values, the initiatives taken by a given actor or individual may be corrupt, not reflective of democratic procedures, and regressive in impact. Therefore, a critical posture needs to be adopted by those who purport to discuss the United Nations from the perspective of global civil society.

The interest of civil society in a robust United Nations that is strengthened in response to globalisation and the various issues relating to 'new wars' is taken as a premise in the discussion that follows. In other words, the focus is placed on the UN system as addressing substantive concerns relating to human security as well as accommodating the participation of global civil society within a structure that was made by and for sovereign states.

A reformist perspective

How should the 'citizenry' of global civil society, acknowledging multiple identities, think about the reform of the United Nations? This overall question gives rise to two different concerns. First, how can the United Nations as a generally benevolent element in world order be strengthened to help achieve a more peaceful, fair, sustainable, and just life for the peoples of the planet, considered both as individual subjects and as members of various communities? Second, how can the role and world views of global civil society be made more effective within the United Nations, including the participation of its representatives in the work of the organisation? Responses to these questions are made against the background of the discussion in the prior section.

The structures and norms of the world have altered so much since 1945 that it is tempting to suggest that the United Nations inscribes within its multitude of actors and operations a set of arrangements that no longer reflect the fundamental characteristics of world order, and that it might be best to redesign a world organisation that takes proper account of the emergence of global civil society, of market forces, and of radical shifts in relative power among states and regions. That is, UN reformism is not responsive to the real challenge of adjustment, which is structural renewal, or at least transformation. Such an outlook makes sense from the apolitical perspective of pure reason, but it is not worth seriously entertaining, as starting over is, at this point, completely beyond the horizons of possibility, and any such advocacy by civil society actors would exhibit a spirit of futility. The only practical course is to strengthen the United Nations as it has evolved over the course of its history. Such an effort is difficult enough if ambitiously conceived, and may turn out also to be impossible, as it must overcome the resistance of entrenched interests to reforms that are otherwise widely supported and seem sensible. For instance, enlarging the permanent membership of the Security Council is opposed in some governmental quarters because it will allegedly produce a more unwieldy body that is less able to respond effectively to crises. At the same time, recasting the composition of membership within the scope of the present frame of 15 members seems virtually impossible due to the refusal of Britain and France to give up their individual status and agree to a consolidation of European membership. This would dilute their independent roles as permanent members, but greatly facilitate the restructuring of the Security Council. In effect, widely needed and generally accepted reforms are often blocked by the entrenched vested interests of particular members in retaining outmoded features. The nationalist myopia of a single country can often outweigh the more general interest of all states in enhancing UN effectiveness and legitimacy. The Security Council expansion debacle shows the most dysfunctional features of the UN reform process.

The establishment of the UN in the first place was feasible only because the historical climate that existed immediately after the Second World War strongly supported steps at the global level to prevent the recurrence of strategic warfare in the form of a third world war. This shared resolve reflected the enormous casualties of the war just ended, as well as the shock

The worldwide demonstrations of 2003 against the Iraq war were faciliated by the failure of the UN Security Council to endorse the US-led invasion ©*Marcus Rose/Ingsight*

of the atomic bombs dropped on Japan. It also reflected the capacity of the victorious powers in the war to impose their will on the post-war world. Political space existed, but only for a short time, to institute a new type of global architecture that was intended to build upon and correct the deficiencies of the League of Nations that had emerged after the First World War in a somewhat analogous political climate. The structures embodied in the United Nations, even under these favorable circumstances, were shaped by the persisting primacy of state sovereignty as the constitutive principle of world order. As a result, the United Nations as established fell far short of what would be needed to realise the aspirations announced in the Charter, but even the scaled-back arrangements agreed upon in San Francisco would have been impossible only a year or so later, as the hard lines of tension and distrust associated with the cold war began to define the new geopolitical condition of bipolarity. Had the world leaders not seized the moment in 1945, it is rather doubtful whether the United Nations would have been established in any form, and world order would have been entirely based on regional blocs of states and traditional alliances.

The period following the cold war is, disappointedly, no more favourable to UN reform despite the disappearance of the strategic conflict and ideological bipolarity that had earlier blocked agreements associated with strengthening the United Nations. In some ways, this is surprising, and mainly reflects what might be best described as the imperial tendencies and lack of constructive leadership in the United States, as well as the neoliberal orientations of the main managers of the world economy, who adhered to the so-called Washington consensus, as modified over the years. In effect, these characteristics of the global setting meant that leaders from the North were reluctant to entrust global policy to the United Nations, preferring either unilateral geopolitics managed from Washington, or policy arenas removed from Third World influence, such as the G8 annual economic summits or the yearly meetings of the World Economic Forum at Davos.

These obstacles to needed UN reform are serious, but they should not obscure the actual and potential roles of the United Nations in promoting goals that accord with the dominant viewpoints of global civil society. The existence of a global organisation with nearly universal membership of states creates a framework for dialogue and initiative that exerts a significant impact on the media and on world public opinion. Such universality, sustained now for 60 years, contrasts with the experience of the League of Nations, which leading states, such as the United States, never joined, and from which important countries, such as the Soviet Union, withdrew out of disgust. The UN Charter, together with lawmaking treaties that bind all governments, provides an authoritative framework for judging whether contested action by a state is consistent with international law, and this is of decisive importance for articulating and unifying the global voices of civil society. The mobilisation of opposition to the Iraq war, culminating in the 15 February 2003 worldwide demonstrations, were greatly facilitated by the existence of the UN norms and by the failure of the Security Council to endorse the proposed US-led invasion of Iraq. The UN has provided crucial support for some of the leading projects of global civil society, including decolonisation and self-determination, anti-apartheid, democracy, development, human rights, humanitarian intervention, accountability for international crimes, peacekeeping, environmental protection, and consciousness raising with respect to such issues as demographic pressures, poverty, joblessness, migration, refugees, transnational crime, and social and economic justice.

In approaching the subject matter of UN reform from a global civil society perspective, it is helpful to distinguish horizontal from vertical reforms. Horizontal reforms are associated with adjustments at the intergovernmental level of participation by sovereign states, currently the only members of the organisation. The expansion of the Security Council is a prototypical example of a horizontal reform. It seeks to make the system more legitimate with respect to the relations among sovereign states by enhancing the representativeness of the UN's most important organ, which alone enjoys the authority to render decisions relating to war and peace binding on sovereign states. Such reforms are not, by any means, irrelevant to the concerns and goals of civil society. Any step that makes the UN more effective and legitimate, especially in relation to peace and security, helps realise a central goal of global civil society to achieve a more humane and law-based approach to global governance.

Despite the diversity of perspectives, there is a rather widespread consensus that the participation of states in governance structures should not be downgraded or bypassed, but that it remains crucial for the foreseeable future. A role for global civil society actors is to exert influence to ensure that this participation increasingly reflects widely shared humane values, such as those enshrined in the Charter itself. In this respect, monitoring the Security Council in relation to the Charter framework and world order values, would be itself expressive of a global civil society contribution that is meant to improve the performance of the UN, even while conceding its essentially statist modes of operation. Such concessions are particularly relevant in the setting of the Security Council, where governments are most insistent on statist prerogatives, including high levels of non-transparency. The more informal modes of functioning of some of the specialised agencies, including the World Health Organization (WHO), UNICEF, and the International Labour Organization (ILO), as well as the back-burner character of the subject matter, allow for a more direct and collaborative interface between these actors within the UN system and representatives of global civil society.

At the same time, the most direct and characteristic UN-related projects of civil society are associated with vertical reforms, taking greater account of actors other than states and recognising transnational social forces whose prominence and role exhibit the growing obsolescence of any system of global governance that relies exclusively on a Westphalian conception of world order. The remainder of this chapter is mainly devoted to exploring this vertical approach to UN reform, but it pays some attention to the proposed direction of horizontal reforms touching on the interests of global civil society, especially as affected by the proposed recommendations of the Secretary-General's High-Level Panel on Security. It is also the case that there is often an interplay between global civil society initiatives of a horizontal character and changing perspectives of the United Nations, even in the most recalcitrant context of peace and security. An important illustration of this hybridity arises in relation to the debate on humanitarian intervention that became so significant in the 1990s, especially in light of controversies surrounding the UN responses and non-responses to Somalia, Rwanda, Bosnia, and Kosovo. At the instigation of the Canadian government, a commission of eminent persons was formed under the chairmanship of Gareth Evans and Mohamed Sahnoun, which produced a report under the title *The Responsibility to Protect* that essentially staked out ground that has emerged as a consensus among members of the United Nations (International Commission on Intervention and State Sovereignty 2001). The essential move in the report was to shift the language from that of 'humanitarian intervention', always threatening to the prerogatives of governments, to that of 'a responsibility to protect', on the part of international society, those peoples who are vulnerable to an impending humanitarian catastrophe. By situating this duty to act within the international community, the report also moved on to positive ground rather than challenging so frontally the totemic ideal of territorial sovereignty. Beyond this, an independent commission of private individuals (although with strong public credentials) is definitely an example of a vertical under-taking reshaping the diplomacy, and quite likely the behaviour, of horizontal interactions among the membership of the United Nations.

UN reform from the perspective of global civil society

Aside from participation and influence within the UN system (or what is being identified here as 'vertical reform'), and the relations between the UN and global civil society, there is the overall concern with the future role of the UN: seeking to prevent aggressive war; to promote a more equitable and sustainable world economy; to respond more quickly and effectively to humanitarian and natural disasters; to uphold human rights and the rule of law; and to contribute to the emergence of a humane and democratic structure of global governance engages members of global civil society as world citizens. The foundation for such a discussion is provided by the report of the High-Level Panel convened by the Secretary-General issued under the title *A More Secure World: Our Shared Responsibility* (UN 2004b). The report is comprehensive, and can be discussed only selectively, in relation to its central concern with expanding the understanding of and approach to the core responsibility of the UN to facilitate collective security. The report is written from a statist standpoint, with issues of feasibility in mind, and only tangentially refers to or reflects the influence of global civil society perspectives. Civil society activists concerned with global policy should read this report both for its conceptual contributions and as an expression of the best intergovernmental thinking about the role of the United Nations in the twenty-first

century and of how to depict 'security' as a central preoccupation. The strong endorsement of the findings of the report by Kofi Annan also makes its impact likely to be strong in the discussions of UN reform at the 2005 session of the General Assembly dedicated to the implementation of the MDGs set five years earlier (Annan 2005).

The main premise of *A More Secure World* is that it is no longer viable to limit the security concerns of states to conflicts between sovereign states. It is necessary to consider conflicts *within* states, as well as conditions of infectious disease, extreme poverty, and acute oppression. In the words of the report (UN 2004b:1), 'the indivisibility of security, economic development, and human freedom' must be the basis for UN thinking about effectiveness. In a nod to civil society perspectives, it is acknowledged that a new orientation toward security is implied by the nomenclature of 'human security'. While affirming the role of the UN in addressing the security challenge, the report argues that 'the front-line actors' that 'continue to be individual sovereign States' bear the main burden of responsibility. Further, security rests on 'three pillars': threats to security are interconnected and require attention at national, regional, and global levels; no state can address these threats on its own; and not every state has the capacity to uphold its responsibilities to its own people or to ensure that harm to neighbours will not be done (UN 2004b:1).

In its synopsis, there is little doubt that the report seeks to address the United States as the primary and controversial actor, exhibiting sympathy with its circumstances but warning against its displays of unilateralism, especially with respect to war making. This spirit is well conveyed by the following sentence:

Recommendations that ignore underlying power realities will be doomed to failure or irrelevance, but recommendations that simply reflect raw distributions of power and make no effort to bolster international principles are unlikely to gain the widespread adherence required to shift international behaviour. (UN 2004b: 4)

The report advocates not structural changes in the UN but a more adaptive use of existing institutional mechanisms. While recognising the need to think of self-defence in the light of changing technologies and conflict patterns, it affirms the adequacy of existing

Rwandans remember those who died in the genocide of 1994 – and protest at the failure of the international community to prevent it
©*Paul Lowe/Panos Pictures*

Charter language, which conveys both confidence in the susceptibility of the text to interpretation and the difficulty of prescribing any formal changes that would require calling into play the formal amendment process of the Charter. In essence, the pre-emptive thinking of the United States after 9/11 is affirmed as reasonable in concept but its unilateral enactment is rejected. In relation to the Iraq war, the only application of this Bush doctrine to date, the UN report certainly implies, without expressly saying so, that the United States was wrong to invade Iraq without Security Council authorisation. It is also possible for Washington to read the UN report as saying that the Security Council should not have withheld its authorisation given the demonstration of an Iraqi threat, although in light of the failure to find weapons of mass destruction, such a reading seems strained, to say the least. The report of the High-Level Panel sets forth five criteria that should be relied upon by the Security Council in debates and discussions pertaining to the use of military force:

seriousness of threat, proper purpose, last resort, proportional means, and balance of consequences (UN 2004b: 67). This set of criteria amounts to a revival of a just war approach to the use of force, combining considerations of law, morality, and politics to shape a new perspective on the relation of war to international law and the UN Charter, given post-9/11 realities.

The High-Level Panel also endorses the approach to humanitarian intervention adopted by the International Commission on State Sovereignty and Intervention. This is not surprising considering that the earlier report had been so favorably received in international circles and that the forceful co-chair of the latter was Gareth Evans, who was also a member of the High-Level Panel (International Commission on State Sovereignty and Intervention 2001). In essence, state sovereignty is overridden if a humanitarian catastrophe is unfolding within a state, but the political language of response is shifted from encroachment on the state to the duty of the international community

UN REFORM

Forced to flee: a UN camp provides shelter for 20,000 internally displaced people in the Democratic Republic of Congo
©Sven Torfinn/Panos Pictures

to act. The approach is well-expressed by the High-Level Panel:

> We endorse the emerging norm that there is a
> collective international responsibility to protect,
> exercisable by the Security Council authorizing
> military intervention as a last resort, in the event
> of genocide or other large-scale killing, ethnic
> cleansing or serious violations of international
> humanitarian law which sovereign Governments
> have proved powerless or unwilling to prevent.
> (UN 2004:b66)

There is no mention of the status of a claim (as was made under NATO auspices in relation to Kosovo in 1999) to protect by a state or a group of states in the event of the failure of the Security Council to mandate action. Does such a residual responsibility exist? This issue has been variously resolved in relation to Kosovo, Rwanda and, more recently, the Sudan, but there is, as yet, no consensus on the permissibility under inter-national law of humanitarian intervention undertaken by states or regional actors (Independent International Commission on Kosovo 2000).

Again, the statist constraints on the political imag-ination of the High-Level Panel are apparent. There is no discussion, much less advocacy, of the establish-ment of a UN emergency service that could implement the 'responsibility to protect' norm, and thereby somewhat diminish the problems posed by an absence of a consensus in the Security Council. Furthermore, there is no consideration of whether the UN could become more effective and legitimate if it could put its funding on a basis that was not as tied to geopolitical control. As discussed below, several variations on the initial proposal of a Tobin Tax on transnational currency transactions have been floating around for decades.

Such desirable reforms, which also seem necessary if the goal of UN reform is to make the organisation effective and legitimate in relation to collective security, are not regarded as feasible within the framework of statist geopolitics that continues to set operative limits within the UN system. What should global civil society do about these limits? Respect them or seek to foster a climate of opinion that weakens or circumvents them? These questions deserve widespread debate in civil society circles concerned with establishing global democracy.

---

it is important for global civil society to unite behind the terminology and outlook of 'human security', thereby placing peoples and their concerns at the centre of security discourse

---

The successful movement to establish an International Criminal Court (ICC) is illustrative of a reformist move that came into being, at least formally, outside of these limits on feasibility. William Pace, a leader of the NGO coalition that collaborated with governments in the late 1990s, likes to tell the story that he was advised by many within the UN that the ICC project was impossibly utopian given the firmness of United States opposition. In this instance, the mobilisation of global civil society appeared to create a momentum that overcame geopolitical resistance. Of course, the success may be less than meets the eye if the ICC fails to produce significant indictments and prosecutions in coming years. The first real opportunity for the ICC seems likely to arise out of its anticipated role in dealing with allegations of crimes against humanity in the context of the Darfur genocide in Sudan. There are other important indications that civil society initiatives can obtain results despite geopolitical opposition: the separate requests to the International Court of Justice for Advisory Opinions with respect to the legality of nuclear weapons and of the Israeli security wall; the push for a treaty of prohibition on the use of anti-personnel landmines; and widespread adherence to the Kyoto Protocol restricting greenhouse gas emissions. Such successes should not be overstated. A minority of opposing states can still nullify the 'success' by refusing to comply with or by simply ignoring the institutional or normative claims. The lesson here is that global civil society, acting in collaboration with sympathetic governments, can pursue reformist projects that stretch, if not break free of, the geopolitical limits on political action, and that such action is an indispensable contribution to the global reform process, within and without the

United Nations.

On the central issue of global security, it is important for global civil society forces to unite behind the terminology and outlook of 'human security', thereby placing peoples and their concerns at the centre of security discourse. At this point, within UN circles, especially the Security Council, the notion of security, despite some willingness to acknowledge its wider reach, remains focused on war and violence as related to the security of sovereign states. Even with the greater willingness to discuss the responsibility of the UN to protect vulnerable peoples facing genocidal threats, the political will of the organisation depends on support from major states, and whether this support is forthcoming depends on national interests. The situation is more encouraging in the setting of *natural disasters*, exhibiting more sense of human solidarity, and a willingness of states, regions, NGOs, and international institutions to work together for shared humanitarian goals. The response to the humanitarian catastrophe produced by the Indian Ocean tsunami at the end of 2004 is illustrative of levels of cooperation and rapid response unimaginable in the context of a human rights crisis. It is instructive to compare the responses of the world to genocidal threats in Rwanda, Sudan, and even Bosnia with the response to the tsunami.

Bringing global civil society into the UN: proposals and prospects for vertical reform

There is no doubt that one of the major trends in world politics since 1945 is the complex and contradictory rise of non-state actors as participants in world order. This rise has been celebrated in certain circles as crucial for a positive view of the human future, and bemoaned in others as the onset of global chaos, being prominently described by some influential commentators as an 'age of terrorism'. All along, developing countries' efforts within the UN to exercise their right of development were resisted by the North as being essentially anti-capitalist. The North used its influence within the UN to marginalise certain arenas receptive to Third World aspirations – for instance the UN Conference on Trade and Development (UNCTAD) and the ILO. This resistance also expressed itself through the successful effort by the United States to terminate altogether the UN Center of Information on World Corporations in 1991, apparently a move that was demanded by Washington as the price for supporting the selection of Boutros Boutros Ghali as Secretary-General. In other words, to the extent that civil society activism, reinforcing Third World outlooks at the UN, was seen to conflict with the precepts of a neoliberal world economy, it was regarded as a threat to the prevailing ideology of the 'club' that the leading states in the North wanted the UN to remain. The fierceness of these UN struggles relating to economic ideology subsided after the collapse of socialism, but they could re-emerge at any point, especially if the leftist swing in Latin America continues.

> What is missing from the Cardoso Report are bold proposals that would give global civil society and its representatives an assured and distinct role in future UN activities

Kofi Annan has tried to mediate between these contradictory tendencies. He has consistently, during his tenure as Secretary-General, called for the incorporation of civil society perspectives, as well as global market perspectives, into the operations of the United Nations. Annan has also clearly recognised the magnitude of the challenges posed by non-state transnational terrorism and crime, particularly in the aftermath of the 9/11 attacks. The membership of the United Nations, although somewhat divided on how to respond to these calls for adaptive change, has been able to find spaces for multinational corporations to participate within the UN, in diverse ways: by receiving funds for specific programmes; by establishing advisory bodies drawn from the world of business (as in relation to environmental policy); and by creating a global compact that allows companies to agree voluntarily to pledge adherence to international standards bearing on human rights, labour practices, and environmental protection. By contrast, the informal efforts of global civil society to participate in UN activities have generally been treated by the mainstream media as confrontational, especially with respect to global policy conferences such as the Copenhagen Social Summit in 1995 and the Durban Conference on Racism in 2001. These concerns about the outlook of global civil society were confirmed for conservative statist and economistic forces by the street demonstrations on the occasion of UN gatherings and those of the organised world community, starting

with the opposition to the WTO (technically not part of the UN system) at its December 1999 meetings in Seattle. The visibility of the non-state presence and the articulation of demands that appeared critical of and hostile towards corporate globalisation and United States geopolitical leadership produced an anti-global civil society backlash. This found tangible expression in efforts to eliminate UN arenas of civil society voice and networking, especially the large conferences on major global policy issues.

In the spirit of Annan's fork-in-the-road speech, UN reform needed to explore, among other topics, facilitating a better connection between global civil society and the organisation. As mentioned earlier, in 2003, Annan established a so-called Panel of Eminent Persons on United Nations–Civil Society Relations under the chairmanship of Fernando Henrique Cardoso (Cardoso Panel). The Cardoso Panel report emphasises intangible encouragements to civil society by way of calls on the UN system to consult more with multiple constituencies in addition to governments affected by policy and to establish a spirit of engagement at the level of international institutions and national governments (UN 2004a). Of the 30 proposals set forth in some detail, none is of major consequence, although there is a motif of soft advocacy on behalf of greater global civil society participation as integral to a more effective United Nations in the future. The fourth proposal is indicative of the approach taken – geopolitically sceptical while still promoting a more positive future for civil society activities within the frame of the United Nations. The language of the proposal is revealing: 'The United Nations should *retain* the global conference mechanism but use it *sparingly* to address major emerging policy issues' (emphasis added) in circumstances where public understanding and opinions are important as the basis for 'concerted global action'. Further, '(t)he participation of civil society and other constituencies should be planned in collaboration with their networks' (UN 2004a). Here the word 'planned' acknowledges statist concerns about spontaneous or uncontrolled forms of participation.

There is also a conscious effort to portray the relations between civil society and the private sector in positive terms, based on collaborative action via the embrace of ideas about 'partnerships', the Global Compact, and the establishment of a new Office of Constituency Engagement and Partnerships (Proposal 24) that would include 'a civil society unit' and 'the Global Compact

176

Fifth Assembly of the Peoples' UN, Perugia, Italy °*Foto Belfiore*

Office', as well as an 'Elected Representatives Liaison Unit' (to connect with parliamentary representatives, thereby giving national democracy a global reach), a 'Partnership Development Unit' (incorporating efforts to foster private sector partnerships), and the secretariat of the recently established 'Permanent Forum on Indigenous Issues' (UN 2004a). This is a catch-all bureaucratic consolidation that draws inspiration from fashionable ideas of the 1990s, including 'stakeholder democracy' as a self-conscious way of acknowledging the multiplicity of constituencies affected by private and public policy decisions, and of new modalities of networking as creating cooperative connections between constituencies that might otherwise be devoting their energies to adversarial activities.

What is missing from the Cardoso Report are bold proposals that would give global civil society and its representatives an assured and distinct role in future UN activities, and reflect the less politically constrained views prevalent in those circles of global civil society that think seriously and positively about UN reform. The reliance on consultation and exhortation to engage civil society is not likely to produce relations of trust or to establish significantly more robust channels of influence. The Cardoso Report, despite its consoling rhetoric about the significance of civil society, reads overall like an effort to achieve 'pacification' and 'cosmetic adjustment' and minor bureaucratic accommodations, rather than the scale of 'reform' that seems calibrated to the issues or the demands of reformers. None of the real priorities of civil society with respect to the UN institutional modifications that move towards the consensus goals of global civil society relating to democratisation and effectiveness – namely, participation, accountability, transparency, constitutionalism, autonomy (vis-à-vis geopolitics), and humane governance – are addressed in a positive and direct way, if at all. As well, there is no wider vision of a peaceful, just future based on a broad series of moves in the direction of nuclear disarmament, dialogue among civilisations, and global governance resting on the normative foundations of international law and a non-violent geopolitics.

UN REFORM

Box 5.3: The UN Global Compact

Partly intended as a response to the challenges posed by globalisation, the United Nations Global Compact represents an attempt to move beyond the state-centric nature of the UN policy system. On 26 July 2000, the UN set up the Global Compact scheme to facilitate greater cooperation and exchange between corporate, non-governmental, governmental and UN-based actors in the areas of human rights, corruption, environmental protection and labour standards. Interestingly, whereas the Cardoso Report (UN 2004a) has been criticised for including business interests and parliamentarian actors in the definition of global civil society, the Global Compact makes a positive case for bringing the corporate world, governments and international, regional and national civil society actors together in order to promote good corporate citizenship. The overall aim is to establish a cooperative network, capable of realising the UN Secretary-General's vision of 'a more sustainable and inclusive global economy.' Whether this goal is achievable remains to be seen.

The origins of the Global Compact initiative date back to a speech by Kofi Annan at the World Economic Forum in January 1999, where he urged business leaders, together with various NGOs and governments, to join the scheme by lending their support to its original nine, and now ten, core principles. These principles are derived from various already existing UN documents, primarily the Universal Declaration of Human Rights, the International Labour Organization's Declaration of Fundamental Principles and Rights at Work, the Rio Declaration on Environment and Development, and the United Nations Convention Against Corruption, which together represent the UN's global social agenda (UN URL). To be good corporate citizens, businesses should:

1. support human rights generally
2. ensure they are not complicit in human rights abuses
3. uphold freedom of association
4. eliminate forced and compulsory labour
5. abolish child labour
6. eliminate discriminatory practices in respect of employment and occupation
7. adopt a precautionary approach to environmental challenges
8. undertake initiatives to promote greater environmental responsibility
9. encourage the development and diffusion of environmentally friendly technologies
10. work against all forms of corruption.

At first sight, these principles appear rather vague, but there have been further specifications of their content, including some theoretical issues (such as different types of complicity in human rights abuses) and general strategies for their implementation by the UN. Yet more concrete guidelines, according to which corporate behaviour could be assessed, would be desirable (see below).

Given the variety of influences within the UN on the formulation of the Global Compact, it is unsurprising that, in terms of its structure, the scheme is a network of several UN agencies rather than a clearly demarcated body in its own right. The main coordinating body is the New York-based Global Compact Office, which closely cooperates with the Office of the High Commissioner for Human Rights, the United Nations Environment Programme, the International Labour Organization, the United Nations Development Programme, the United Nations Industrial Development Organisation, and the United Nations Office on Drugs and Crime. To realise the ten principles, all these UN bodies facilitate interaction between corporations, global civil society and governments through various loosely defined mechanisms, including policy dialogues, education, and local structures.

However, neither the Global Compact office nor any other UN body has the power to regulate the conduct of any member of the scheme, as membership and compliance are entirely voluntary. Obviously, the issue of enforcing the ten principles and monitoring the behaviour of participants is a vital one, because, as it stands now, the success of the scheme largely depends on the willingness of corporations to play by the rules. The Global Compact relies on the 'enlightened business interests of corporations'. To retain their membership, corporations have to publish an annual report on their practical commitment to the Global Compact agenda. But some member companies have yet to identify any practical projects designed to realise the ten principles. The US clothing giant GAP is a fitting example: according to the UN Global Compact website, the company has done little more than publish its Social Responsibility Report in 2003. Hence, the question whether companies merely sign up to the Global Compact for public relations reasons looms large. For instance, German pharmaceutical and chemical giant Bayer has been criticised by the NGO Corpwatch for 'whitewashing' its image through participation in the Global Compact (Mimkes 2002). Similarly, US sportswear giant Nike, also a member of the Global Compact, has been accused by an umbrella group of American and Canadian labour unions of preventing its workers from joining trade unions. Because the Global Compact cannot address these allegations, the unions are considering filing a complaint at the ILO (Logan 2004). Indeed, as critics such as Amnesty International (2003) have pointed out, one of the weaknesses of the scheme is that it lacks the mechanism to deal with non-compliance or low compliance.

As for the involvement of global civil society actors, the Global Compact hopes that NGOs, labour organisations and corporations will organise, with support from relevant UN bodies, practical cooperation on certain policy issues. Controversially, the scheme assumes that corporations and various NGOs have similar interests. Consequently, there is the open question of the issues, if any, on which cooperation is possible and fruitful.

Lastly, for the success of the scheme, participation is crucial. As of May 2005, there were 1,999 corporate members of the Global Compact. But an overview of corporate membership according to select countries indicates limited commitment from companies in some of the world's biggest economies:

Number of companies that have signed up to the Global Compact, selected countries

France	UK	Germany	USA	Brazil	Japan	Sri Lanka	China	India	Bangladesh
366	53	36	69	106	32	36	45	93	4

Source: UN (URL)

The only Western country seriously committed to the Global Compact scheme is France, with a stunning 366 participants, leaving far behind fellow G8 members UK, Germany and, especially in view of the size of its economy, the United States. It is all the more worrying that in the economically booming regions of the world, particularly in the case of China and Bangladesh, commitment to the Global Compact is low. However, the UN has recently increased its effort to broaden the appeal of the scheme in China, with a two-day conference in Shanghai scheduled for 30 November – 1 December 2005.

Another problem facing the UN is that many high-profile international organisations have not yet signed up: energy giant Halliburton, Coca-Cola, Microsoft, Puma and Adidas, despite their international dealings, are not part of the Global Compact. The UN thus needs a strategy to expand aggressively the scheme and make it more attractive to companies. If hundreds of thousands of workers, predominantly in the developing world, remain excluded from the minimal protection offered by the ten principles of the Global Compact, then it is difficult to see what difference this initiative could make.

As for its future, in 2004, McKinsey & Company assessed the impact of the Global Compact. Although its report painted a positive picture, McKinsey & Company (2004) pointed out that, in order to achieve its objectives, various reforms would be necessary:

• Communication structures, particularly between the various UN bodies, need to be improved.
• Participation needs to be made more attractive.
• The currently loose network structures need to be formalised.
• The governance structure of the Global Compact needs to be reformed to manage different participants' expectations.
• The aims of the network need to be executed and communicated more consistently than they are presently.

The Global Compact Summit held in New York in 2004 showed that the UN is well aware of these challenges: in his address to delegates, Secretary-General Kofi Annan stressed that, among others things, the governance of the Global Compact needed reforming, although actual proposals have remained rather vague (UN 2004c).

Despite the criticisms outlined above, the Global Compact is a unique experiment that, in the words of the UN, attempts to fuse 'ideas of universal social standards with the power of markets' (UN 2004c). And the UN, with its various bodies, worldwide infrastructure, access to research and expertise, and close relations to state and non-state actors, is in a strong position to carry it out. As Annan has observed, 'If not us, then who?' (UN 2004c).

Alex Leveringhaus, Department of Government, LSE

Three global civil society initiatives

From the perspective of global civil society, the efforts to date by the UN to accommodate the rise of civil society transnationalism or to move towards the realisation of consensus goals are unsatisfactory (Held 2004). In contrast, a variety of bold proposals, some long supported in civic arenas, are favoured by broad sectors of global civil society. The illustrative articulation of some of the more promising proposals is of substantive interest, as well as expressing the spirit of what might be described as reform-from-below and reform-from-without. This chapter sets forth the bare outline of three such proposals. Their concreteness should be interpreted as a disregard of the wider challenge of reconstituting a visionary imaginary for the United Nations that responds to the realities of the early twenty-first century.

A UN parliament or assembly

From the perspective of global democracy, there is general agreement within global civil society that the constitution and modus operandi of the UN do not allow for sufficient participation by representatives of civil society. A popular mode of global civil society participation to overcome this deficiency would be the addition of an organ to the UN that would function as a representative body selected directly or indirectly by global civil society. This line of reformist thinking takes comfort from the existence and development of the European Parliament, which, in the course of several decades, has moved from being a marginalised talking shop to a respected institutional pillar whose democratic character has enhanced the legitimacy of European regionalism (Falk and Strauss 2000).

> a campaign on behalf of some institutional presence for global civil society within the structure of the United Nations is likely to build momentum and generate worldwide excitement

There are many approaches to establishing some sort of global parliamentary presence, including proposals that prefer establishment outside the purview of the UN, for reasons of effectiveness or feasibility. In this chapter, the parliamentary innovation is considered only within the setting of the UN system. The most conservative approach would be to invite national parliaments to designate one or more delegates from their ranks to serve in a UN parliament consisting of such legislative representatives. Presumably, in most cases, these representatives would have been elected by a fair democratic process, and thus would have some connection with popular wishes and the priorities of their national communities. It might be a practical first step to establish a UN assembly on this basis, especially if it included a sunset provision of, say, five years, after which direct elections to the body would be organised in all countries or regions that agreed to take part. More ambitiously, an amendment to the Charter could oblige all members to take part, as well as giving the new body a definite place within the UN system.

The initial point of such an initiative is to establish a distinct and exclusive space for global civil society within the larger confines of the United Nations. If established so as to be a conduit for grassroots priorities in various locales around the world, its challenge to govern-mental and market-oriented thinking would likely be vivid and illuminating. For this reason alone, the proposal is threatening to the statist establishment and nationalist consciousness, and is currently not under serious consideration. The experience in the 1990s with global civil society activism at major UN policy conferences gave leading states an unwelcome taste of global democracy, causing a backlash that can be understood only as anti-democratic, that is, as opposed to conferring status and allowing voice to the representatives of global civil society. This backlash has a paradoxical dimension, given the vigorous engagement of these very same states in the promotion of democracy and democratic values at the national level, and their accompanying rationale about thereby promoting regional and global security communities.

In the lead-up to the millennium, Kofi Annan floated a proposal to arrange a one-off assembly of civil society representatives to be organised by and held at the United Nations. But even this gesture proved to be too much for several influential governments, evidently worried about any further erosion of their traditional roles as *exclusive* representatives of their citizenry. In the end, a stimulating set of civil society sessions was held at the same time as the Special Millennium Session of the General Assembly, but informally and not in the UN buildings.

There are undeniably a variety of obstacles in addition to the opposition of those states that seek to keep the world as statist as possible. It would be difficult, if not

Father and son create a shelter in a UN camp for those forced from their homes in Darfur °*Pep Bonnet/Panos Pictures*

impossible, to arrange the selection of appropriate representatives from countries that do not even possess democratically elected national legislative organs. It would be burdensome to administer any sort of selection process because of the vastness of the task and the unevenness of circumstances on the ground. Further, there are related problems associated with balancing claims to representation based on population against those based on ethnic, civilisational, and religious identity. It would also be a long struggle to provide such an entity responsive to the peoples of the world with a sufficient budget, and likely an even longer one to confer real functions and authority, and achieve a legitimate stature as a vital element of global governance.

Nevertheless, a campaign on behalf of some institutional presence for global civil society within the structure of the United Nations is likely to build momentum and generate worldwide excitement. Such a campaign would also give tangible expression to the advocacy of global democracy. It is hard to imagine an adequately reformed UN without the establishment of ways to ensure that it was committed to the encouragement of global democracy, and that a key part of that commitment was to create a political space reserved for representatives of global civil society. While so affirming, the immediate prospects of UN support are not bright. Astonishingly, the Cardoso Report, with its mission of enhancing relations between the UN and civil society, does not even mention the idea of a global parliament. It is doubtful that this was an oversight; it probably reflects the avoidance of proposals that would likely be dismissed by weighty statesmen as 'utopian' or worse, and could be read as offensive to the tender sensibilities of the geopolitical patrons of the United Nations. A bedevilling feature of this reformist dynamic is the degree to which supervening political pressures keep the most helpful initiatives from even reaching the stage of preliminary discussion.

UN REFORM

181

Table 5.2: **Global civil society (GCS) and UN reform**

	Position on the UN	Position on GCS and UN reform	Examples of GCS actors
Moderate reformers	UN needs to be reformed, but incrementally and modestly.	GCS, including business groups, would be part of UN reform – GCS would coexist with state actors but with subordinate status. GCS can help somewhat at the level of implementation and consultation. The Cardoso Report (UN 2004a) expresses the spirit of the moderate reformers, who also favour achieving a more representative Security Council and adapting prohibition on non-defensive force to the challenges of twenty-first century conflict.	Earthaction Citizens for Global Solutions World Federation of United Nations Associations Professor Jeffrey Sachs
Sceptical reformers	UN needs to be reformed.	Supportive of moderate UN reform in principle, but very worried that the attempts at greater incorporation of GCS into the UN could be co-opted by established economic and political groups (such as business groups and parliamentarians) for their own purposes. It remains unclear, though, what sort of changes to UN–GCS relations sceptical reformers view as constructive.	Third World Network Women's International League for Peace and Freedom World Federalist Movement Amnesty International Civicus/World Alliance for Citizen Participation Asian Civil Society Forum Global Policy Forum
Radical reformers	UN system needs to be fundamentally over-hauled. Currently proposed UN reforms are not far-reaching enough. The UN needs to be fully democra-tised and a wholly new system of democratic global governance needs to be established.	GCS must play a vital part within a fully reformed democratic UN system of global governance. GCS can mediate between international institutions and a global citizenry. However, it remains unclear what role GCS should play until the democratic idea is achieved.	Action for Economic Reform World Campaign for in-depth reform of the system of international institutions Tavola Della Pace

	Position on the UN	Position on GCS and UN reform	Examples of GCS actors
Statists	UN should remain a marginal global actor and the role of dominant states should not be diminished.	No formal role for GCS is needed or desirable.	Move America Forward
Geopolitical realists	Maximum freedom of action for the US within the UN system, minimum intrusion on sovereign rights; UN as talking shop, with the US primarily responsible for global governance.	UN can be effective only if a hegemonic actor guides its essential operations. GCS would encumber this undertaking and should not be allowed to participate.	American Enterprise Institute Heritage Foundation Hoover Institution NGO Watch
No position taken	Preoccupied with substantive work/activism associated with a focused issue area.	No position on UN reform or GCS–UN relations.	ActionAid Oxfam Christian Aid Friends of the Earth

UN Emergency Peace Service

A working group of peace activists and NGO leaders have been developing for some years a proposal for the creation of a UN Emergency Peace Service (UNEPS). The central idea is to have a small, highly trained, professional corps that would be available at short notice and on the longest possible geopolitical leash to prevent and contain humanitarian catastrophes, especially those with genocidal overtones. Undertakings of this sort were done on an ad hoc basis during the 1990s; but without sufficient political will on the part of major states, and thus without an appropriate definition of UN mission and without the provision of adequate capabilities. The UN thus often operated ineffectually in situations of humanitarian emergency, which discredited the system and provided too little, too late for peoples being victimised. The genocide in Rwanda in 1994 remains a paradigmatic instance of UN failure, and the current feeble response to the mass killings and crimes against humanity in the Darfur region of Sudan is a continuing reminder of how ill-equipped the UN is to discharge its 'responsibility to protect', even in response to extreme conditions. It is still relevant to recall the devastating critiques of the UN failures to protect vulnerable peoples in either Bosnia or Rwanda (Rieff 1995; Melvern 2000).

The establishment of UNEPS would provide the UN with standby capabilities to act quickly and within an existing bureaucratic frame, thereby minimising political friction, whenever an imminent threat of genocide or other atrocity-producing situation arose. This capability could be flexibly shaped also to facilitate a usefully quick reaction by the UN to the sort of regional disaster resulting from the South Asian tsunami of December 2004. Of course, it would be naive to believe that the mere existence of UNEPS would ensure effectiveness and legitimacy. Powerful governments would undoubtedly find ways to obstruct UN responses by exerting back-channel pressures and manipulating the purse strings. At the same time, the mere existence of UNEPS would signal a growing commitment by the UN to overcoming humanitarian emergencies in a manner that was far less closely tied to the vagaries of domestic politics. It should be recalled that it took only a small number of US deaths, 18, in 1993, to bring a major peacekeeping operation in Somalia to a sudden halt, contributing as well to a political climate that produced the non-response to Rwanda in 1994 and the woefully inadequate engage-ment with 'ethnic cleansing' in Bosnia.

At times, the role of global civil society is to incubate an idea or initiative until the intergovernmental mood shifts into a supportive mode. This occurred in relation to criminal accountability for political leaders. Governments gave the initial push after the Second World War at the Nuremberg and Tokyo trials, but then backed off. This commitment to accountability was kept alive in the United States and Europe by activists during the cold war who relied on this framework of laws to oppose wars of aggression and improper weaponry and military doctrine and tactics. And then in the aftermath of the cold war, with the break-up of former Yugoslavia and the brutalities of the conflicts in Africa, a new intergovernmental set of initiatives revived the idea of accountability, even leading, against some geopolitical objection, to the formation of an International Criminal Court. In relation to UNEPS, it may also be necessary to push the idea and then wait patiently until a propitious conjuncture of happenings engages political forces throughout the world.

A Tobin Tax

One reformist idea that has been around in a variety of forms is a tax on international transactions. James Tobin, a Nobel laureate in economics, initially proposed a tiny tax on currency trading as a way to build up the financial resources of the UN and to create greater independence for the organisation. Variations have been proposed over the years, including a tax on supersonic flight, an energy tax, and a tax on seabed resources. These are all feasible ways to enhance the financial capabilities of the UN and to provide it with a greater degree of independence and institutional self-confidence.

But as with the global parliament or UNEPS, that is the point! The resistance to the Tobin Tax is not about money, it is about power. The main geopolitical actors are unwilling to allow the UN to become an independent actor that can fulfil the goals of the 'responsibility to protect' ethos in an efficient and a political manner. It is unlikely that independent financing for the UN will occur without a major global civil society movement that would have to be on a scale comparable to that which brought the ICC into being. In most respects, the ICC would seem far more threatening to statist prerogatives than would independent financing for the UN. In this sense, the political will of global civil society must be strengthened if such an indispensable reform is to become a live political project in the years ahead.

Conclusion

Part of the glory of global civil society is its diversity of viewpoints, priorities, activist styles and goals. This chapter has assumed that it is still possible to write on the basis of 'an overlapping consensus' with respect to UN reform, that is, sufficiently shared views on core issues to enable the presentation of ideas and recommendations without detailing lines of divergence. In this sense, while acknowledging the existence of influential anti-UN NGOs in the United States, it excludes their perspectives on reform from discussions of a recommended approach to be adopted by global civil society.

---

there is no substitute for encouraging the moral and political imagination of citizens of global civil society to determine the horizons of possibility for the peoples of the world

---

Further, no effort has been made in this chapter to consider radical alternatives such as abandoning the United Nations as a site of struggle for a better world. The slogan of the World Social Forum, 'another world is possible', does not entail rejecting those features of the existing world order that hold some promise for the present and future. The United Nations, despite limitations and disappointments, remains a source of hope for improving the circumstances of humanity. It deserves the attention of global civil society, both in appreciation of its substantial achievements and to monitor its failures to uphold the UN Charter and the rule of law. The progressive reform of the UN is an integral aspect of any plausible programme for the extension of democracy and the material foundations of human dignity to disadvantaged states and regions, as well as to the world. In a broader sense, a more effective and democratic UN is indispensable to building a world order premised on the 'cosmopolitan democracy' school of thought (Archibugi 2003; Archibugi and Held 1995).

In the end, there is no substitute for encouraging the moral and political imagination of citizens of global civil society to determine the horizons of possibility for the peoples of the world[3]. Many changes that occurred in the 1990s were judged 'impossible' by custodians of the reasonable, and if their counsel had been heeded, Eastern Europe might still be under the dominion of corrupt, authoritarian rule, South Africa could still be a haven for apartheid governance, and the cold war might never have ended.

Given the widely acknowledged transformations of the global setting in the course of recent decades, it certainly seems opportune to give free rein to the imaginative energies of global civil society. And this does not mean an embrace of fantasy but rather an engagement in the struggle to produce the sort of world order that seems most compatible with physical and spiritual survival of the peoples of the earth, in the realisation that we will never know without such a struggle what the true limits of the possible are. Such an orientation towards the life-world should also guide our thinking on this crucial topic of UN reform. In more tangible forms, such an outlook would insist upon serious efforts to achieve nuclear disarmament, the elimination of acute poverty and preventable disease, and the establishment of emergency regimes to avoid climate change, to provide early warning of disasters, and to ensure a viable energy future for the peoples of the world. At the outer horizon of aspiration, voices from global civil society should be exploring and advocating the viability of a non-violent geopolitics that alone has the capacity to revolutionise prospects for a hopeful human future.

---

3 For a seminal account by a leading philosopher of the social imaginary that has informed modernity, which is suggestive of reflections on the future of humanity, see Taylor (2004).

REFERENCES

Amnesty International (2003) 'Amnesty International
    and the United Nations Global Compact'.
    http://web.amnesty.org/pages/ec-gcletter070403-eng
    (consulted 12 April 2005).

Anderson, K. and Rieff, D. (2005) 'Global Civil Society:
    A Sceptical View', in H. Anheier, M. Glasius and M. Kaldor
    (eds), *Global Civil Society 2004/5*. London: Sage.

Annan, K. (2005) '"In Larger Freedom"': Decision Time
    at the UN.' *Foreign Affairs*, 84(3): 63–74.

Archibugi, D. (ed.) (2003) *Debating Cosmopolitics*.
    London: Verso.

Archibugi, D. and Held, D. (eds) (1995) *Cosmopolitan
    Democracy: An Agenda for a New World Order*.
    Cambridge: Polity Press.

Arend, A. C. and Beck, R. J. (1993) *International Law
    and the Use of Force*. London: Routledge.

BBC News (2003) 'Annan Calls for Reform', 23 September.
    http://news.bbc.co.uk/1/hi/world/americas/3133364.stm
    (consulted 14 July 2005).

Commission on Global Governance (1995) *Our Global
    Neighborhood*. Oxford: Oxford University Press.

Etzioni, A. (2004) *From Empire to Community: A New Approach
    to International Relations*. New York: Palgrave Macmillan.

Falk, R. (1995) *On Humane Global Governance: Toward a New
    Global Politics*. Cambridge: Polity Press.

– (2004) *The Declining World Order: America's Imperial
    Geopolitics*. New York: Routledge.

– and Strauss, A. (2000) 'On the Creation of a Global
    Peoples' Assembly: Legitimacy and the Power of Popular
    Sovereignty'. *Stanford Journal of International Law*,
    36(2): 191–219.

Gold, D. (2004) *Tower of Babel: How the UN has fueled Chaos*.
    New York: Crown Forum.

Held, D. (1995) *Democracy and the Global Order*.
    Cambridge: Polity Press.

– (2004) *Global Covenant: The Social Democratic Alternative
    to the Washington Consensus*. Cambridge: Polity Press.

Independent International Commission on Kosovo (2000)
    *Kosovo Report: Conflict, International Responses,
    Lessons Learned*. Oxford: Oxford University Press.

International Commission on Intervention and State
    Sovereignty (2001). *The Responsibility to Protect*.
    Ottawa: International Development Research Centre.

Kaldor, M., Holden, G. and Falk, R. (eds) (1989) *The New
    Détente: Rethinking East-West Relations*. London: Verso.

Keck, M and Sikkink, K (1998) *Activists Beyond Borders:
    Advocacy Networks in International Politics*. Ithaca,
    NY: Cornell University Press.

Logan, M. (2004) 'Nike Complaint Spotlights UN Partnership
    with Business'. *Global Policy Forum*.
    www.globalpolicy.org/reform/business/2004/0429nike.htm
    (consulted 12 April 2005).

McDougal, M. and Gardner, R. (1951) 'The Veto and the
    Charter: An Interpretation for Survival.' *Yale Law Journal*,
    60: 258–92.

McKinsey & Company (2004) *Assessing the Global Compact's
    Impact*. www.unglobalcompact.org/content/NewsDocs/
    Summit/imp_ass.pdf (accessed 12 April 2005).

Melvern, L. (2000) *A People Betrayed: The Role of the West
    in Rwanda*. London: Zed.

Mimkes, P. (2002) 'Bayer and the UN Global Compact: How
    and Why a Major Pharmaceutical and Chemical Company
    "Bluewashes" its Image'. *CorpWatch*.
    www.corpwatch.org/article.php?id=3129
    (consulted 12 April 2005).

Perle, R. (2003) 'Thank God for the Death of the UN: Its Abject
    Failure Gave Us Only Anarchy, We Need Order'. *The Guardian*,
    20 March.

Pianta, M. (2001) 'Parallel Summits of Global Civil Society',
    in H. Anheier, M. Glasius and M. Kaldor (eds), *Global Civil
    Society Yearbook 2001*. Oxford, UK: Oxford University Press.

Rieff, D. (1995) *Slaughterhouse*. New York: Simon & Schuster.

Slaughter, Anne-Marie (2004) *A New World Order*. Princeton,
    NJ: Princeton University Press.

Taylor, C. (2004) *Modern Social Imaginaries*.
    Durham, NC: Duke University Press.

UN (URL) *The Global Compact*.
    www.unglobalcompact.org/Portal/Default.asp?
    (consulted 18 June 2005).

– (2004) The UN System, DPI/2342. New York: UN Department
    of Public Information.

– (2004a) *We the Peoples: Civil Society, the United Nations, and
    Global Governance*. Report of the Panel of Eminent Persons
    on United Nations-Civil Society Relations (Cardoso Report).
    A/58/817. New York: United Nations.

– (2004b) *A More Secure World: Our Shared Responsibility*.
    Report of the Secretary-General's High-Level Panel on
    Threats, Challenges and Change. New York: United Nations.

– (2004c) *The Global Compact Leaders Summit: Final Report*.
    New York: United Nations. www.unglobalcompact.org/content/
    NewsDocs/Summit/summit_rep_fin.pdf
    (consulted 5 April 2005).

– (2005) *In Larger Freedom: Towards Development, Security, and
    Human Rights for All*. Report of the Secretary-General.
    A/59/2005. New York: United Nations.

UNGA (United Nations General Assembly) (2004) *Modalities,
    format and organization of the high-level plenary meeting
    of the sixtieth session of the General Assembly*. A/59/545.
    New York: United Nations.

Weston, B., Falk, R. and Charlesworth, H. (eds) (1997)
    *Supplement to Basic Documents of International Law
    and World Order*. St Paul, MN: West Publishing Co.

PART 3: INFRASTRUCTURE

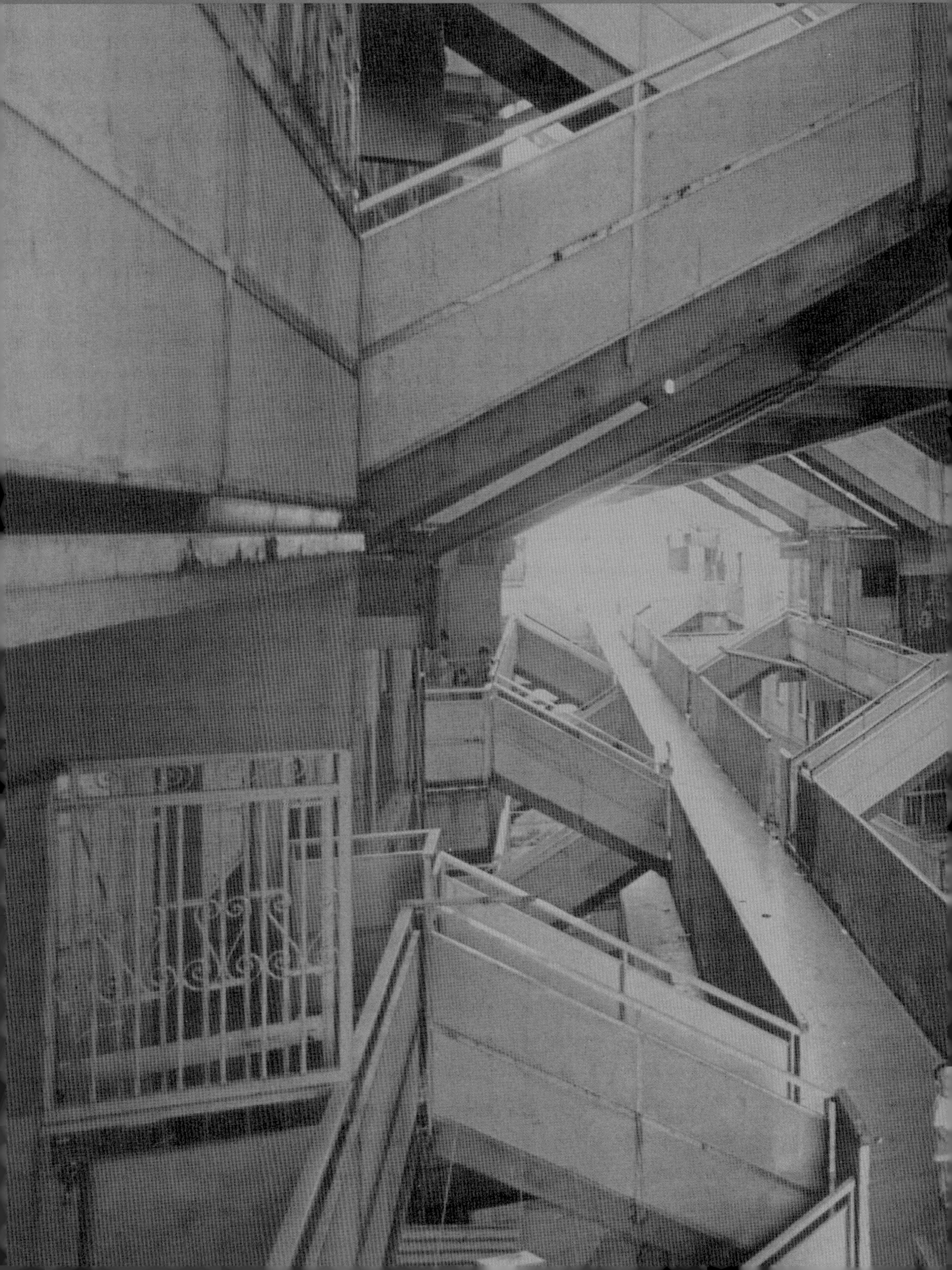

THE ROLE OF SOCIAL FORUMS IN GLOBAL CIVIL SOCIETY: RADICAL BEACON OR STRATEGIC INFRASTRUCTURE?

Marlies Glasius and Jill Timms

Introduction

Local, national, regional, thematic and global social forums have mushroomed in recent years, inspired, either directly or indirectly, by the World Social Forum[1] and its Charter of Principles (WSF 2001). A social forum can be understood as a space that facilitates people coming together, either in person or virtually, to engage with each other on political issues. But it is more than that. As we show below, the real news about the social forums is not what issues are being discussed or what strategies are hammered out, but the ways in which people approach organising and decision making. They are experiments in organisational form. They give rise to uneven attempts to practise politics in horizontal, network-based ways that are meant to be more participatory and democratic than conventional structures. These efforts are subject to sometimes productive and sometimes vicious confrontation, and often fail dismally. But, as we show, the major tensions are all about methods, and 'emancipation' is among the most prominent subjects discussed at the forums. We therefore suggest that what is most ground-breaking in social forums, and what most attracts people to them, is the experimentation with form itself. It becomes part of the substantive message that 'Another World Is Possible', and it creates a new kind of space for global civil society.

Countless articles are available on different aspects of social forums, especially online but increasingly also in academic publications. Most, however, are based on personal experiences, and most focus on the global and regional levels. Of course, we, too, draw on personal experiences, but in addition we have mapped and analysed global, regional, thematic, national and local social forums, undertaken a content analysis of World Social Forum programmes and selected regional, national and local social forum programmes, and pulled together other current research. We aim to provide a helicopter view of social forums, as well as a critical analysis of their functions in global civil society and the tensions inherent in or attendant on this form of organising.

The first section of this chapter examines the political and philosophical origins of social forums and the distinctive principles associated with them. In the next section, we describe what is actually happening: the people and activities involved at the world, regional, national, and local levels. The third section discusses the major issues and themes on which social forums focus. In the fourth section, we aim to draw out the areas of tension and the failures of social forums, including ideological clashes and organisational challenges encountered in putting the social forum principles into practice. In concluding, we examine the implications of the experiences of social forums for global civil society, and look to what their future role could be.

Origins and principles

Origins

Opposition to the World Economic Forum (WEF) was first expressed in a protest meeting and demonstration in Davos in January 1999. Members of Le Monde Diplomatique/ATTAC (originally, the Association for the Taxation of Financial Transactions for the Aid of Citizens) and the Brazilian Landless Movement (MST) were among the participants. A year later, Oded Grajew, a Brazilian social entrepreneur (Grenier 2004: 133–4), and Chico Whitaker, director of the Brazilian Commission for Justice and Peace, met with Bernard Cassen, director of the French ATTAC and Le Monde Diplomatique, to discuss the possibility of a larger alternative forum (Whitaker 2004a; Teivainen 2002).

Their discussion produced three central ideas for the forum. First of all, it should be held in the South, and more concretely in the Brazilian city of Porto Alegre.

The authors wish to thank Fiona Holland, Jeff Juris, and Mary Kaldor for their useful comments and suggestions on previous drafts of this chapter. They also thank all social forum participants and organisers who took the time to talk to them and answer their questions.
1 The websites of social forums are listed separately in the References section.

*Second, the name should be World Social Forum
(WSF), changing only one key word from the
adversary's name. And third, it should be organised
over the same dates as the WEF, partially because
this symbolism was considered attractive for the
media.* (Teivanen 2002: 623)

Soon afterwards, the mayor of Porto Alegre and the
governor of the state, Rio Grande do Sul, both officials
of the Partido dos Trabalhadores (PT, Workers' Party),
agreed to support the forum financially and logistically.
The first WSF, which took place in Porto Alegre,
Brazil, in January 2001, marked the beginning of the
social forum phenomenon. It was the first global civil
society event designed to take place in the South, with
the express purpose of bringing together activists and
global civil society organisations working on diverse
issues, through diverse methods, within a format
described as a social forum.

But the Forum, of course, has other antecedents.
Five interrelated strands can be detected. The first
goes back at least to the 1970s, although it could be
dated back to earlier national anti-colonial struggles.
It is connected to the idea of the New International
Economic Order, which sought to give Third World
governments more say in global affairs and in the
management of their own economies. This strand of
activism is associated with anti-imperialism (taking
the empire to be the West, and more specifically the
United States), state socialism, and national solutions
to economic problems.

The second strand is that of communist and socialist
party activism of all stripes: Leninist, Trotskyist, Stalinist,
Maoist, Guevarist, Sandinista, social democratic, and
so on. To the extent that they have survived the end of
the cold war, parties have been a surprisingly large
presence, and sometimes a source of tension, at the
social forums.

The third strand is that of the 'new social movements',
which are often associated with the student protests
of 1968, particularly the women's movement, the
peace movement and the environmental movement.
While all these concerns have found their way into the
social forums, the most important legacy of the new
social movements for the forums is their preoccupation
with the 'life world' and with practising politics in
a different way. Where older movements sought to
challenge and perhaps capture power, these movements took an interest in ideas about deconstructing

and reconfiguring it (Melucci 1980; Cohen 1985;
Wainwright 2004c). To some extent, these ideas were
also taken up by anti-authoritarian intellectuals in
Eastern Europe and Latin America in the 1980s
(Kaldor 2003).

The fourth strand is that of parallel NGO forums to
the large United Nations conferences of the 1990s
(Pianta 2001; Krut 1997). These meetings, dealing with
the environment, human rights, gender and social
policy and development issues, attracted an increasing
number of professional NGOs, there to lobby governments but also to network with each other. Ideologically,
these NGO forums were not very close to the social
forum phenomenon, but they created the habit among
NGOs and wider civil society activists of going to
broad-based international meetings, a function that
the World Social Forum has, to some, extent taken over.

The fifth, most recent and most significant, strand is
that of the anti-globalisation movement, more
accurately described as the 'global anti-capitalist
movement'. It famously burst on the scene in Seattle
in December 1999, but already had roots in the protests
against the 1992 quincentenary of Columbus's visit to
America, in the Zapatista uprising in 1994 and
subsequent international jungle-meets, in the 50
Years Is Enough Network, in the Reclaim the Streets
campaign, in the MST, in the Ogoni struggle and its
solidarity network, in the campaign against the
Multilateral Agreement on Investment, in the G8
protests in Birmingham in 1998, and in the foundation
of ATTAC. It has been described in many other places
(see Kingsnorth 2003; Desai and Said 2001; Scholte
2002; Van Rooy 2004; Juris 2004).

From the perspective of the social forums, three
characteristics of this disparate anti-capitalist
movement are particularly important: it attracted large
numbers of cyber-savvy young people, particularly in
Europe and Latin America; it had a belief in 'civil
society' quite alien to orthodox Marxist ideologies; and
it sought out targets other than the state, including
multinational corporations and international financial
institutions. In a way, the World Social Forum was an
idea waiting to happen. As early as 1997, for instance,
the South Centre's Third World Forum in Dakar,
published the World Forum for Alternatives Manifesto
(1997), which sought to 'Make the economy serve the
peoples of the world; Break down the wall between
North and South; Rebuild and democratize the state;
Recreate the citizenry; Globalize social struggles; and

Box 6.1: World Social Forum Charter of Principles

The committee of Brazilian organizations that conceived of, and organized, the first World Social Forum, held in Porto Alegre from January 25th to 30th, 2001, after evaluating the results of that Forum and the expectations it raised, consider it necessary and legitimate to draw up a Charter of Principles to guide the continued pursuit of that initiative. While the principles contained in this Charter – to be respected by all those who wish to take part in the process and to organize new editions of the World Social Forum – are a consolidation of the decisions that presided over the holding of the Porto Alegre Forum and ensured its success, they extend the reach of those decisions and define orientations that flow from their logic.

1. The World Social Forum is an open meeting place for reflective thinking, democratic debate of ideas, formulation of proposals, free exchange of experiences and interlinking for effective action, by groups and movements of civil society that are opposed to neoliberalism and to domination of the world by capital and any form of imperialism, and are committed to building a planetary society directed towards fruitful relationships among Humankind and between it and the Earth.

2. The World Social Forum at Porto Alegre was an event localized in time and place. From now on, in the certainty proclaimed at Porto Alegre that 'another world is possible', it becomes a permanent process of seeking and building alternatives, which cannot be reduced to the events supporting it.

3. The World Social Forum is a world process. All the meetings that are held as part of this process have an international dimension.

4. The alternatives proposed at the World Social Forum stand in opposition to a process of globalization commanded by the large multinational corporations and by the governments and international institutions at the service of those corporations interests, with the complicity of national governments. They are designed to ensure that globalization in solidarity will prevail as a new stage in world history. This will respect universal human rights, and those of all citizens – men and women – of all nations and the environment and will rest on democratic international systems and institutions at the service of social justice, equality and the sovereignty of peoples.

5. The World Social Forum brings together and interlinks only organizations and movements of civil society from all the countries in the world, but intends neither to be a body representing world civil society.

6. The meetings of the World Social Forum do not deliberate on behalf of the World Social Forum as a body. No-one, therefore, will be authorized, on behalf of any of the editions of the Forum, to express positions claiming to be those of all its participants. The participants in the Forum shall not be called on to take decisions as a body, whether by vote or acclamation, on declarations or proposals for action that would commit all, or the majority, of them and that propose to be taken as establishing positions of the Forum as a body. It thus does not constitute a locus of power to be disputed by the participants in its meetings, nor does it intend to constitute the only option for interrelation and action by the organizations and movements that participate in it.

7. Nonetheless, organizations or groups of organizations that participate in the Forums meetings must be assured the right, during such meetings, to deliberate on declarations or actions they may decide on, whether singly or in coordination with other participants. The World Social Forum undertakes to circulate such decisions widely by the means at its disposal, without directing, hierarchizing, censuring or restricting them, but as deliberations of the organizations or groups of organizations that made the decisions.

8. The World Social Forum is a plural, diversified, non-confessional, non-governmental and non-party context that, in a decentralized fashion, interrelates organizations and movements engaged in concrete action at levels from the local to the international to build another world.

9. The World Social Forum will always be a forum open to pluralism and to the diversity of activities and ways of engaging of the organizations and movements that decide to participate in it, as well as the diversity of genders, ethnicities, cultures, generations and physical capacities, providing they abide by this Charter of Principles. Neither party representations nor military organizations shall participate in the Forum. Government leaders and members of legislatures who accept the commitments of this Charter may be invited to participate in a personal capacity.

10. The World Social Forum is opposed to all totalitarian and reductionist views of economy, development and history and to the use of violence as a means of social control by the State. It upholds respect for Human Rights, the practices of real democracy, participatory democracy, peaceful relations, in equality and solidarity, among people, ethnicities, genders and peoples, and condemns all forms of domination and all subjection of one person by another.

11. As a forum for debate, the World Social Forum is a movement of ideas that prompts reflection, and the transparent circulation of the results of that reflection, on the mechanisms and instruments of domination by capital, on means and actions to resist and overcome that domination, and on the alternatives proposed to solve the problems of exclusion and social inequality that the process of capitalist globalization with its racist, sexist and environmentally destructive dimensions is creating internationally and within countries.

12. As a framework for the exchange of experiences, the World Social Forum encourages understanding and mutual recognition among its participant organizations and movements, and places special value on the exchange among them, particularly on all that society is building to centre economic activity and political action on meeting the needs of people and respecting nature, in the present and for future generations.

13. As a context for interrelations, the World Social Forum seeks to strengthen and create new national and international links among organizations and movements of society, that – in both public and private life – will increase the capacity for non-violent social resistance to the process of dehumanization the world is undergoing and to the violence used by the State, and reinforce the humanizing measures being taken by the action of these movements and organizations.

14. The World Social Forum is a process that encourages its participant organizations and movements to situate their actions, from the local level to the national level and seeking active participation in international contexts, as issues of planetary citizenship, and to introduce onto the global agenda the change-inducing practices that they are experimenting in building a new world in solidarity.

Approved and adopted in São Paulo, on April 9, 2001, by the organizations that make up the World Social Forum Organizing Committee, approved with modifications by the World Social Forum International Council on June 10, 2001.

Source: WSF (2001)

Build on people's resistance' in order to create a World Forum for Alternatives. The aim of the first World Social Forum was, similarly, to provide an alternative to neoliberal prescriptions, with actual proposals for overcoming economic and social problems. However, in the light of later developments, it is worth quoting Chico Whitaker on the tight and top-down structure that was envisaged for the first Forum:

> ...we have been working against the clock to ensure attendance by participants all over the world, with quotas set for each continent and each type of activity. The programme drawn up provides for two kinds of dynamics: morning panels – 4 running simultaneously on all four days, with four participants each chosen from among leading names in the fight against the One Truth [neo-liberalism]; and in the early afternoon, workshops coordinated by the participants themselves to exchange experiences and for discussions, and in the late afternoon, meetings for networking. Also planned are sessions for testimonies from people involved in different kinds of struggle, and an extensive parallel programme in Porto Alegre city for all those unable to participate directly in the forum, which is open only to people appointed and registered by social organizations. (Whitaker 2004a: 16).

Approximately 1,500 participants were expected, but more than 10,000 showed up (Wallerstein 2004). Although the Forum was not accorded the dramatic media footage that attended other summits of global civil society (for example, the World Trade Organization (WTO) protests in Seattle in 1999; see Pianta 2001), the success of the event as an alternative form inspired immediate plans for the next WSF.

Charter

The World Social Forum Charter of Principles was drawn up by the Brazilian Organising Committee (see Box 6.1 and Figure 6.1) after the runaway success of the first WSF in an attempt to evaluate the results of that Forum and the expectations it raised. It was subsequently approved with modifications by the World Social Forum International Council on 10 June 2001 (see Sen et al 2004 for both versions, the differences between them, and the subsequent confusion).

It is very much a foundational document and is much cited, discussed and debated within the movement. It has inspired the initiation of hundreds of social forums throughout the world, as it provides them with a connection to each other, a shared system of purpose and of method. The section on 'sites of tension', below, discusses extensively how different social forums deal in practice with the precepts of the Charter. Some central points in this document that have become relevant to all social forums inspired by the WSF can be highlighted:

- The Forum is not a neutral space. Articles 1, 4 and 10 in particular set out the broad position of those who engage as being against neoliberal and corporate globalisation and for social justice.
- The Forum is an ongoing initiative. The Forum does not only exist during annual gatherings but rather, as described in Article 2, should be seen as the continuous process of working towards alternatives.
- The Forum is not representative or decision making. The Forum is not representative of global civil society (Article 3) and as a body cannot make decisions (Article 6). The implication is that people and organisations can make their own decisions but not as a collective forum. Voting is avoided and consensus-seeking given preference. However, the WSF annual meeting, and now others, are directly followed by an Assembly of Social Movements. This is a gathering that aims to set out a collective position and to make decisions on collective action. An example of this was the global day of protest against the war in Iraq on 15 February 2003, which had been circulated before but was formally adopted during the Assembly of Social Movements following the third edition of the WSF.
- The Forum undertakes to be a transparent and participatory process. It endeavours to circulate the results of debates as transparently as possible (see Articles 6 and 11). This has resulted in various records of events being openly available to all. These include the ever-growing Library of Alternatives (WSF URLa) and Memorials from each of the WSFs (WSF URLb), which include programmes, reports, statistics, and news articles.
- The Forum aims to be inclusive but non-party political. Diversity in participation is actively encouraged for all except for party or military representatives, and government members may contribute only in a personal capacity (Article 9). As Sen (2004: 72) has pointed out, this clause was much broadened in the amended International

Council version.

- The Forum is non-violent. This has been seen as central and one of the limits on an otherwise very broad canvass of activity that can be associated with forums (Article 13).
- The agenda and activities of the Forum are at the global level. Throughout the Charter and particularly in Articles 1 and 14, the global nature of the problems being faced is stressed and a sense of global citizenship is privileged.

Together, these principles set social forums apart from previous and other civil society activities at the global level (Pianta 2001; Cock 2004).

Spread of the forums

Originally, the WSF International Committee had no intention of developing or linking to any other social forums. However, the large Italian delegation to the first WSF was immediately interested in the forum idea, which could bring together different Italian constituencies and build on the existing 'social centres' in many Italian towns. Hence, against the express wishes of the Brazilian organisers of the WSF, the Italian organisers of the counter-summit to the G8 meeting in Genoa decided to call the event a social forum. Many of the Italian social centres subsequently converted themselves into 'social forums', and Italians have since flocked to both the World and the European Social Forums in large numbers. At the same time, a meeting of social activists in Durban, South Africa, reacting against what they considered the remote and elitist nature of the NGO Forum during the World Conference Against Racism, called itself the Durban Social Forum (see Kaldor, Anheier and Glasius 2003: 23–4).

The second World Social Forum was again held in Porto Alegre, deemed symbolic due to the local government's pioneering work on social inclusion, including experiments of participatory budgeting (Wainwright 2004b). It attracted 68,000 visitors.

The International Committee then agreed to the development of regional social forums, such as the European one, and systems began to be set in place for thematic and regional forums to take place before the next WSF, when they would be invited to report back on their experiences. The committee seems not to have considered local and national forums; and other regional and thematic forums sprang up spontaneously without connection to the master plan.

This means that these social forums are inspired by, but not in any way authorised by or accountable to, the WSF or its committees. So it is important to note that any group can describe itself as a social forum. However, adoption of the name usually means that it has found some form of inspiration in the WSF and its Charter of Principles.

What is happening?

Since 2002, social forums of many types, active at different levels, have flourished. It is difficult to obtain an accurate picture of their exact number and nature because social forums do not register anywhere; what constitutes a forum is interpreted in different ways; there is no complete way of assessing whether a forum adopts the Charter of Principles; and forums become visible only when they take part in a larger activity or have a website.

Our attempt to map the social forums is primarily based on internet research. This has many shortcomings. First of all, it excludes any social forum activism without a web presence. However, this is a very web-based movement, even in the developing world. Still, websites are no guarantee of accurate information, and more often than not they are out of date. Even when we can read the website, find out what types of activities the social forum (SF) in question is (according to the web) involved in and get a sense of the type of language it uses, this gives only a very partial and superficial picture of the forum, no substitute for being there and taking part. Moreover, internet research marginalises any SF activism with a web presence that is not in a west European language we can read (such as Hungarian, Turkish, Arabic, or Persian). Nonetheless, we hope this piece of tracking is of service to researchers and activists, and we aim to continue correcting and updating the underlying database.

Map 6.1: Social forums, by type and year

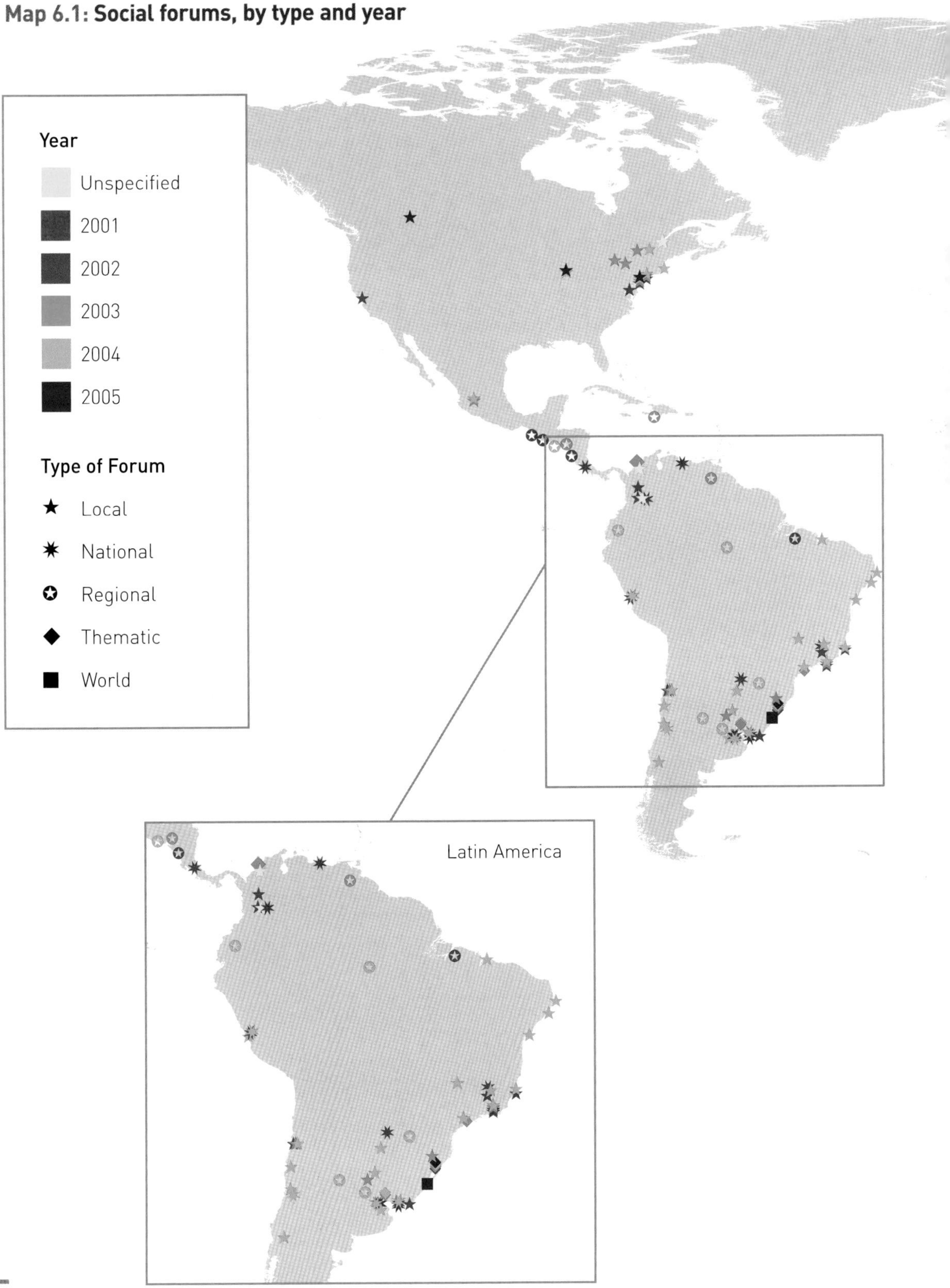

Year
- Unspecified
- 2001
- 2002
- 2003
- 2004
- 2005

Type of Forum
- ★ Local
- ✳ National
- ✪ Regional
- ◆ Thematic
- ■ World

Latin America

Western Europe

Table 6.1: Growth of social forums, 2001–4

	2001	2002	2003	2004
Regional and thematic SFs	3	6	14	12
National SFs	0	11	24	23
Local SFs	2	30	60	74

Note: These numbers exclude local social forums in Italy (c 180) and Greece (c 50). For other caveats see page 195 and Map 6.1.

Map 6.1, which updates the work done by Kaldor, Anheier and Glasius (2003: 20–3), shows where there have been social forums in the sense of major, usually annual, events. But, as discussed below, this is not the only form social forums take. Table 6.1 gives the cumulative number of forums either as annual events or as a more permanent presence. It shows strong growth rates in 2002 and 2003, with stabilisation of regional, thematic and national social forums alongside continued growth of local social forums in 2004. The figures for 2005 are too incomplete for inclusion, but it is clear that new forums continue to be established in all regions of the world with the possible exception of Asia. Our figures should be treated as very conservative because of all the restrictions enumerated above and because local forums in Greece and Italy were not considered – there are too many to keep track of there.

World forums

The WSF is the most institutionalised of the social forums. It has now taken place four times in Porto Alegre, Brazil, and once – the fourth edition – in Mumbai, India. The basic structure for the organising of the fifth WSF in 2005 is presented in Figure 6.1. The International Council is responsible for regular meetings to discuss methodology and resolve the problems faced; the organisation of the Forum should therefore not be seen as a set formalised procedure but one that is continuing to emerge. However, problems with this structure, and also with the transparency of the processes, continue to be experienced. We return to these below.

How significant are the WSFs? Table 6.2 offers a comparison of the main statistics on attendance and activities at each of these annual meetings. The growth in registered participants is noteworthy, and this represents only those who actually paid to register for entry into the formal sessions. Many of the cultural events, marches, and so forth do not need registration to take part. Moreover, the Forum always attracts a substantial number of visitors who have principled objections to registration per se or to the entrance fee, and try to participate without paying.

The WSF is where veteran activists come to debate, network, and strategise, and where a new generation is having its 'Woodstock experience'. But perhaps a better comparison than Woodstock is the Edinburgh Fringe Festival, which also began as counterfoil to a more elite gathering and has now completely overshadowed it, with hundreds of thousands of visitors coming to see thousands of self-organised and uncensored performances. The World Social Forum is like an Edinburgh Festival of politics. The analogy has become even more appropriate under the 'new methodology' adopted in 2005, which saw the much-criticised formally organised plenaries abandoned. As is suggested by the following quotation, every participant's experience of the World Social Forum is different.

The World Social Forum is like a resonant piece of jazz or a picture that looks different from every angle. How we make sense of it and what it means to us depends on our perceptions. (Wainwright 2004a: xvii)

Perhaps even more crucially, it depends on what one decides actually to do at the Forum – what selections one makes from the bewilderingly lengthy programme. It would be possible to attend and never go near any workshops or seminars, focusing on the parties, concerts, films and other cultural events. It would also be possible to spend 12 hours each day locked in serious debate on issues as diverse as the experience of women in Turkish politics, how to mobilise a global boycott against Coca-Cola, or the philosophy of truth. You could spend your days in large meetings, hearing the global social justice gospel handed down by Walden Bello, Vandana Shiva, Samir Amin and Susan George. Or you could seek out the most marginal meetings, discussing 'Revolution in Asia: China 1926' or 'Housing Rights of Plantation Workers in Sri Lanka'. Or, with a modicum of bad luck, you could spend all your time travelling between changed venues and cancelled events.

Figure 6.1: Organising structure of the World Social Forum 2005

The International Council

Responsibilities: Discussion of the future of the WSF, annual events for the discussion of methodology and general political issues.

Delegates
129 organisations

Member organisations

The Secretariat

Base: São Paulo, Brazil

Responsibilities: Forum process coordination

Member organisations: Abong, ATTAC, CBJP, Cives, CUT, Ibase, MST and Social Network for Justice and Human Rights

Comments: These organisations were the original eight involved, joined by the Indian Organising Committee following the WSF in Mumbai.

Observers

Organising committees of:

Africa Social Forum

Americas Social Forum

European Social Forum

Mediterranean Social Forum

Pan-Amazonian Social Forum

Thematic Social Forum: Democracy, Human Rights, War and Drug Traffic

Funders Network on Trade and Globalisation

Brazilian Organising Committee

Base: Porto Alegre

Responsibilities: Translating the methodology and principles of the International Council into the organising and plan for the fifth Social Forum. This includes the events layout, methods for setting the programme, facilitating participation, and providing for the technical and physiological needs of programme organisers and participants, such as arranging free use of technology, voluntary translation, supply via solidarity economy and promoting a sustainable environment, among other aspects.

Members: 23 organisations which are divided into eight working groups:

Culture	*Space*
Translation	*Environment and sustainability*
Communication	*Free software*
Call for action	*Solidarity economy*

Note: Although this is the structure being used for the fifth WSF, it is similar in character to previous ones.

Source: WSF

Table 6.2: Statistics of the World Social Forum, 2001–5

	2001	2002	2003	2004*	2005
Registered participants	4,702	12,274	27,000	74,126	155,000
Estimated total participants	20,000	68,000	100,000	111,000	200,000
Registered organisations	500	5,000	n/a	1,653	6,872
Countries represented	117	131	123	132	135
Registed journalists	1,870	3,356	4,094	3,200	6,823
Volunteers	860	400	650	800	3,100
Interpreters	51	n/a	n/a	180	533
Official languages	n/a	n/a	n/a	13	16
Estimated youth camp participants	2,000	16,000	26,000	5,000	35,000
Total events	458	718	1,372	1,470	2,157

*The method of registration in Mumbai was different from that in Porto Alegre and the youth camp was situated at a distance from the main event. This may account for the reduction in the number of organisations and youths.

Sources: World Social Forum; Intercontinental Youth Camp (URL)

At its best, the Forum has the potential for learning, debating, developing alternative ideas, learning practical skills, promoting campaigns, networking with other activists and organisations, and experiencing different cultures through people, food and events. At its worst, it can be a stale litany of endless harangues against the usual suspects: neoliberal institutions, global corporations, the military–industrial complex, and, of course, George W Bush, without an alternative in sight. The only thing that would not be possible would be to participate in the World Social Forum and avoid politics.

So far, four out of the five World Social Forums have taken place in Porto Alegre. However, in 2006 the World Social Forum will take a different form, being spread out in different countries. With this change of direction, the International Council is taking a large gamble. A tried and trusted recipe, which has continued to attract more and more participants, has been abandoned in favour of experimentation. As is customary in the World Social Forum process, the decision was taken without prior consultation of ordinary participants. Moreover, the choice of sites is controversial: Venezuela has been confirmed at the time of writing, with Morocco and Pakistan also likely venues. Each of these sites risks being hostage to government interference, in the form of restrictions or

propaganda or both, to a much larger extent than was the case in either Porto Alegre or Mumbai. The 2007 WSF is then committed to be in Africa, with the African Social Forums being largely responsible for the organisation (see below and Box 6.2 for further details on this and the importance of location).

Regional forums

At the regional level, the African, European and Pan-Amazonian Social Forums are among the most established, having occurred three or four times each. Their proceedings strongly resemble those of the World Social Forum.

The African Social Forum (ASF) started rather modestly, essentially as an NGO forum, attracting approximately 200 participants to its first two editions in 2002 and 2003. At the second of these forums, a decision was made to convene sub-regional forums, but only the Southern Africa Social Forum (SASF) has actually been held at the time of writing, in Lusaka in 2003. Delegates at the SASF expressed surprise and anger when they were told the that ASF scheduled for January 2004 had been scrapped in favour of a get-together of African delegates to the World Social Forum in Mumbai. 'I have just paid for my own Bus fare to attend this forum and I definitely cannot afford an air

The ESF in London 2004 °*Jill Timms*

ticket to India', said a delegate from Tanzania (Muyoba 2003). The ASF has more generally come under criticism for being a forum for people with 'passports, visas, money, and credit cards' (Tleane 2004), and it has since vowed to raise funds for sponsored participation and to focus more on including peasants, workers and youth. It launched a slightly more ambitious third edition in Lusaka in December 2004, as well as 'mandating' a number of national social forums in Africa (see below).

Apart from the usual focus against neoliberalism, anti-imperialist ideology is a strong mark of the ASF. Thus, in an ASF council meeting in July 2004 in Cairo, a presentation on Darfur by a Sudanese human rights activist was followed by:

a lengthy debate on the possible implication of the African social movement in the resolution of the crisis with a view to avoiding an instrumentalisation of the situation by external forces solely motivated by the predation of the natural resources of this part of the continent. (African Social Forum 2004)

In other words, the meeting would not consider backing a call for intervention. The final declaration signed by a number of participants (which in accordance with the Charter is not a declaration by the Forum itself) lamely calls on 'the Sudanese social movement to mobilize to peacefully regulate the political, social, cultural, ethnic and economic conflict in Darfur' instead.

In the Americas, the Pan-Amazonian Forum, linking Brazil, Bolivia, Colombia, Ecuador, French Guyana, Peru, Surinam and Venezuela, has been going strong since 2002 and was in its fourth edition in January 2005. Organised primarily by the Brazilian trade unions, its focus is against the Free Trade Association of the Americas (FTAA) and the Plan Pueblo Panama. It also appears to have an anti-US and pro-Hugo Chavez orientation, describing the third Pan-Amazonian Forum in Ciudad Guayana, Venezuela, as taking place in 'a country engaged in the struggle against imperialist impositions from the government of the United States' (authors' translation). The Social Forum of the Americas is more of a newcomer; its first edition, after being postponed, was eventually held in Quito, Ecuador, in July 2004. It had a strong emphasis on indigenous issues and, again, against the FTAA. It appears to focus primarily on Latin America, with very little information available in English. The idea of a North American Social Forum has been intermittently discussed on e-lists, and two sessions were devoted to the idea at the 2004 New York Social Forum, but there

Box 6.2: From Porto Alegre to Mumbai and beyond: the World Social Forum goes global

An explosion of energy and inspiration found the ideal venue at the 2004 WSF in India: during the six days, 130,000 participants could choose from eight conferences, eight panels and 1,400 seminars (organised by participants themselves) as well as numerous marches, rallies, songs and dances, all of which added to the diverse flavour of the event.

The process that led to Mumbai began in 2001, early in the history of the WSF, and culminated in a confrontation during a meeting of the International Council in January 2003 in Porte Alegre. On one side were those who argued that Latin America needed the exposure provided by hosting the WSF, and who feared the phenomenon would be threatened if it moved prematurely to other shores. Others argued that the relative lack of participation by Africans and Asians in WSFs to date threatened the legitimacy of an ostensibly global event. In addition, the organisational process was an increasing challenge for the Brazilian left which, from late 2002, was involved directly in the exhilarating process of contributing to the running of the country.

The nature of the conflicts at the global level in the run-up to the 2004 WSF weakened the confidence of the Brazilian activists, and later the European and African partners, in the Indian process. Lack of information, differences in organisational practices, personal misunderstandings, and intermittent interaction and knowledge sharing caused widespread frustration. The concerns of the international partners, which were often shared with the Indian organisers, generated a tense relationship. A critical debate took place on the mailing list of the International Council: in a well-crafted e-mail, the Indian organisers highlighted the complexities of a process involving more than 200 organisations, compared with the eight of the Brazilian Organising Committee, and invited suggestions – but not sterile criticisms from far away. This was a turning point in transnational relations among the actors of the WSF process. A positive consequence of the successful resolution of these intercontinental conflicts was the intensification of proactive strategies in conflict management within the Indian process.

The fourth WSF in Mumbai was the culmination of an innovative organisational process that had been riven with conflict from the beginning, often teetering on the verge of collapse under the weight of apparently irreconcilable differences. Conflicts were inherent in the 2004 WSF and an expression of the exuberant creativity of those involved; sometimes they caused polarisation and confrontation, at other times they generated inventive conflict management strategies with inspirational outcomes – including Mumbai itself. The success of the fourth WSF, despite the conflict inherent in its organisation, indicates that the foundations of a strong counter-hegemonic movement lie beneath the surface of India's labyrinthine political system. Plagued by sectarianism, authoritarianism and a tendency to promote personality over policy, the progressive left in India has been challenged by the experience of organising and participating in the WSF, which represents a new dimension in Indian politics.

The main area of conflict revolved around the identities of actors involved in the organisation of the WSF, and the process of negotiating those identities. For the first time in Indian politics, a wide range of people came together to organise a joint activity: social movements, mass organisations linked to the communist parties, large NGOs and small grassroots organisations, peasants, Dalits, trade unions, women's organisations and indigenous groups. However, the process of collaboration was not easy and not always successful.

Representatives of large NGOs, the crucial link to the international funding of the event, were often resented by grassroots groups and activists, who accused them of lacking political perspicacity and adopting a technocratic approach to social change. For their part, NGOs voiced concerns about corruption, clientelism and nepotism, which they argued was facilitated by actors who camouflaged their true party affiliations behind unions and research centres. Social movements, with a substantial grassroots following, sought to resist the dirigisme and vanguardism of some and the technocratic, apolitical approach of others. Women's organisations launched frequent accusations of paternalism against some of the key figures in the process. Dalits accused organisers of denying them a role in the process and thereby maintaining the unfair tradition of upper-class, high-caste politics. Furthermore, the limited attendance of the Adivasis and peasants at the WSF demonstrated a bourgeois approach to progressive politics on the part of the urban middle class, who traditionally have sought to play down the role of the rural poor in Indian politics. This criticism was voiced throughout the process and gave rise to a parallel forum: Mumbai Resistance.

Finally, a major conflict between the Organising Committee and part of the Muslim community exposed the inability of the WSF process to engage with one of the most significant political issues in Indian society, namely, discrimination against Muslims by the governing Hindu community. In strongly worded letters to the Organising

Committee, Ahmed (not his real name) complained that non-Indian Muslims had a greater chance of participating in the WSF process than Indian Muslims, which he alleged was a consequence of the organisers bowing to the dictates of the Hindu fundamentalist government in Mumbai, without which the WSF would not have been possible.

How were these various conflicts resolved? The concept of the WSF as an 'open space' was used differently by different actors: to silence criticism, to impose authority (in a traditional manner but in a new language), to bring new allies into the process, to explain inevitable failures (such as the non-inclusion of more Indian Muslims into the process, to name just one), to placate controversy and to win arguments. Thus, the concept of open space was expanded to new limits, and, despite criticism, it was accepted as the most appropriate mechanism for reaching agreement in the short term – although it also served merely to postpone confrontation. This conflict management strategy succeeded in maintaining collaboration between a wide range of actors who were often distrustful of each other: it proved to be the strongest hegemonic instrument used by the organisers of the WSF to create a powerful goal-oriented coalition. The notion of open space depoliticised tensions and conflict, forcing all to consider the immediate outcome of the process they were involved in. Confrontations and fractured relationships were put aside for the sake of the organisational success of the event. These tensions may well resurface in the future, further testing this risky strategy. However, three years of uninterrupted collaboration may have provided the necessary tools and trust needed to transform destructive confrontations into creative solutions for the Indian/Asian Social Forum in January 2006.

Mumbai proved that the organisational process of the WSF was able to adapt to a different place and culture. This was not achieved without conflict and confrontation. But these experiences, listed below, generated creative outcomes that have become the common heritage of the global WSF process:

- The number of panels and conferences organised by the WSF limited the Organising Committee's influence over the themes under discussion in major gatherings.
- WSF India brought many Indian activists into the International Council, laying the foundations for a more inclusive process that would later include African activists. This improved the legitimacy of the WSF as a global forum.
- A single location with more spontaneous cultural events made Mumbai a more dynamic and diverse event than the WSFs held at the Catholic University of Porto Alegre.
- Experimentation with an FM-based translation system proposed by Indian activists, coupled with a digital system designed by French activists, was further developed in WSF 2005.
- Key actors in the organisation of Mumbai also participated in the design of the venue and the translation system of the fifth WSF in Porte Alegre, thus initiating a global process.
- Mumbai changed the character of the WSF, encouraging participation by a wide range of individuals and organisations from varied social backgrounds. The Indian mobilisation proved that the division of the social arena into sectors (women's movements, mass organisations, trade unions, NGOs, Dalits, peasants, Adivasis) and regions (Indian states) was successful, though problematic.
- Finance and accounting systems were made more transparent and were openly discussed in meetings of the Organising Committee that were always open to observers.
- An impressive cultural programme aimed to offer different perspectives on political activism instead of merely entertainment.
- The information and communication infrastructure was based entirely on free software, affirming the right to free knowledge in the information age against the oppressive power of monopolies.

Although not exhaustive, this list illustrates the confidence of WSF activists in an increasingly global process that embraces political creativity, growing legitimacy and a strong potential to foster change in the direction envisaged by the WSF Charter of Principles, that is, towards a more fair, equal and just world where human rights are universally respected.

Beyond the success of the Indian organisational process, Mumbai demonstrated the flexibility of the WSF's identity, which enables it to adapt to local social and political contexts without losing its energy. After the fifth WSF in Brazil in 2005, the phenomenon is ready for further global journeys. In 2006, the WSF will take place in a decentralised fashion in South America, Africa and Asia. In 2007, it will take place in a unified form in Africa.

Guiseppe Caruso, School of Oriental and African Studies, University of London

Families are welcome at social forums ©*Jill Timms*

ering after the WSF, was first held in Florence 2002. The ESF has since been held in Paris and in London, and will be held in Athens next in 2006. The organisation of the 2004 ESF in London served to highlight many of the tensions experienced more widely within the forum movement (discussed below and also in Boxes 6.3 and 6.4).

Thematic forums

The thematic forums are possibly the least well-known forums. They usually build on earlier networks relating to the theme in question, but, in addition, they have adopted the 'social forum' title as an indication of their affinity with the forms (exchange of experience and debate) and the politics (global, anti-neoliberal) of the World Social Forum. The Social Forum on Health in Argentina has now convened three times, attracting participants mainly from the Latin-American region. It has two stated aims: to promote and defend a free, equal and high quality public health system, accessible to all; and promotion of the idea of health as a human and citizen's right (authors' translation). In January 2005, the first World Social Forum on Health, apparently unconnected with the Argentine effort, was held in Porto Alegre, preceding the WSF.

The World Education Forum, also in its third edition in 2005, has preceded the WSF in recent years. It now attracts 22,000 participants from 47 countries, mainly teachers, to an astounding 1,200 workshops on didactic topics in the broadest sense.

The World Social Thematic Forum on Democracy, Human Rights, War and Drug Trafficking, focusing especially on the last of these, was held in Cartagena de Indias, Colombia, in June 2003. While intended to discuss these issues as global problems, the forum was situated in Colombia precisely to be at the heart of the problem, not just as a gesture of solidarity but to open up space for debate on issues that are taboo and dangerous to discuss in Colombia itself (authors' translation).

The Social Forum on Climate Change, held in Moscow in June 2003, was not really a thematic social forum like the others but more a matter of brand name adoption: it was the title adopted by the NGO parallel summit to the World Conference on Climate Change, held at the same time and place. There are also smaller thematic forums, particularly in Argentina, where the combination of the social forum idea with a specific focus has found particular resonance.

are no definitive plans at the time of writing.

The Asian Social Forum, which was held in Hyderabad in 2003, has remained a one-off so far. In the subsequent year, the Indians were swamped with organising the WSF in Mumbai, and took some time to regroup (an Indian or Asian SF is planned for January 2006). Moreover, the website of the Asian Social Forum was superseded by the WSF India, so that the institutional memory of the Asian SF, which attracted 11,000 participants, is entirely lost. The Oceania Social Forum, which had also been planned for 2003, was downsized to a more modest New Zealand Social Forum, which appears on current information to have been a one-off. The Mediterranean Social Forum is ambitious, but slow to get off the ground; after a few postponements, it is now due for June 2005. It has a strong input from environmental groups and also emphasises migration and the Middle East peace process.

The European Social Forum (ESF), the largest gath-

Discussion at the Argentina Social Forum, 2002 °Pablo García

National and local forums

The national and local social forums can be seen as one of the most significant developments to have come out of the idea of the WSF. The decision by the Italian delegation at the first WSF to hold the G8 counter-summit in Genoa under the heading of a 'social forum' resulted in a format capable of unifying the Italian left (Cannavo 2001; Sullo 2001a; 2001b). More than 200,000 people, mainly Italians, united in Genoa, and many carried away with them the idea of a social forum. There are now at least 180 local social forums in Italy. Since then, the idea has spread from southern to northern Europe, from Porto Alegre to the rest of Latin America, from South America to North America, to Australia, and most lately also to Africa. The only continent where national and local forums appear to be virtually absent is Asia, despite strong Indian and South Korean participation in the World Social Forum.

While many local social forums simply adopt the format of the WSF, organising a one- to three-day event with workshops, panels, and plenary discussions on a wide number of topics, other organisational forms are also being experimented with. For example, Brisbane (Australia) SF operates its forums on an 'open space' principle. This means that the agenda is determined by participants on the day of the meeting, to promote participation and to provide a space for all voices on all issues (although more recently advance booking of workshops on particular issues has been encouraged). The 2004 Duisburg (Germany) SF has also experimented with this form. Some social forums, including those of Belgium, Berlin and Madrid, have become permanent organisations, whose main activity is to disseminate information about and mobilise for demonstrations and other social forums. Argentina and North Germany SF have evolved into websites that list and support the local social forums there. Castile (Spain) and Orleans (France) SF are primarily websites servicing local associations and social movements. Others, such as Düsseldorf, Paris Centre, or Toronto SF, mount regular campaigns, debates, or conferences.

Some social forums are particularly concerned with organising themselves according to democratic and participatory principles. New York City and Sydney SF have developed particularly elaborate rules to regulate decision making by consensus, as mandated by the WSF Charter. Many social forums come up against a paradox as soon as they want to adopt the principles in the WSF Charter (WSF 2001) for themselves: one of those principles is that 'the participants ... shall not be called on to take decisions as a body, whether by vote or acclamation'. Hence, the act of adoption is itself in breach of the Charter. Many social forums adopt the Charter anyway, while others just refer to it as a source of inspiration.

Many social forums have carefully worded founding documents or, as the German SFs call them, 'self-understandings', which are sometimes written by an individual but often agreed upon in an elaborate consensus-making process. Thus, the Alpes du Sud SF intends to 'reappropriate the city as a space for debate and collective action' (authors' translation); the Berlin SF is explicit about the various allegiances of different members, but at the same time insists that it represents 'nothing, really nothing whatsoever' (authors' translation); the Limburg (Belgium) SF is a permanent forum 'for research and elaboration of alternatives' (authors' translation); and the Chicago SF 'aims toward building a different kind of globalization, one that is rooted in solidarity, equity, and environmental protection and human rights. Of particular importance to this process is the linking of local struggles with global concerns'.

Some countries show a decentralising tendency, with the national forums in Argentina, Belgium and Chile now playing a supporting role for local forums. In Uruguay, the process began in a highly organised manner; in Germany, more organically, with local forums eventually leading to the organisation of a national forum. Some of the most active countries, including Italy and France, have never had a national forum, and Brazil has had only one; but both the former have hosted the ESF and the latter successive WSFs. While in most countries, regions and cities social forums have been almost entirely spontaneous occurrences, in Africa the process has been more top-down. National social forums began to be held after the Organising Committee of the African SF had decided that this would be desirable in order to make grassroots connections. They are mainly organised by donor-sponsored NGOs rather than assorted individuals and groups. Thus, an organisation called Agency for Co-operation and Research in Development

(ACORD) recently celebrated 'a decision by the Horn and East Africa Sub-Regional working group to give ACORD's Uganda Area Programme the mandate to organize the Uganda Social Forum' (ACORD URL).

Social forums also seem to be surprisingly absent in a few countries that are not just considered to have an active civil society but that played a significant role in the global anti-capitalist movement, including Mexico, the Philippines, South Africa and South Korea. It would appear that social forums come into existence not necessarily in the most auspicious circumstances, but rather where there are enough people who feel that such a space or structure would fulfil a need that is currently not being met.

Pre- and post-forum activities

A particular activity worthy of note is the use of communications technology to promote debate and engagement both within and between different social forums. An example is the Tarnais Social Forum in France, which has attempted to make its website function as an interactive virtual social forum with a technology called SPIP. Others include WIKI boards to ensure that the ability to paste ideas and plans is not the prerogative of only a few and that any member of the group can edit and add to the information on the website.

The use of e-mailing groups, discussion boards and websites to upload and download materials has become a central method of promoting participation, consensus building and transparency. Records can be kept of the progress of discussions and outcomes can be viewed by all, such as in the Memorials provided on the website of the WSF (WSF URLb). All resources on the WSF website and many other forum websites are 'copyleft', which means that they are free and can be altered for educational purposes, with the proviso that any amended materials are also freely available.

Another method of developing the continual engagement of the forum is dissemination to local meetings. For example, an educational initiative called Voices from Mumbai aims 'to promote networks, information sharing and events in order to raise public awareness about the World Social Forum (WSF), and encourage local activity related and connected to the WSF and its areas of concern, and other related mobilisation initiatives' (Voices from Mumbai URL). This has involved a mobile exhibition touring public spaces, accompanied by related events to promote knowledge of the WSF and

Ideologies for sale at the forum ©Richard Nagle

debate around critical issues, and the development of educational materials to be disseminated to a wide range of groups and interested individuals. Again, all materials are copyleft and the website itself enables and facilitates continued debate.

Accounts of what actually happens at the World and other social forums, and the experiences of people who have participated, have been documented extensively in the alternative press and on related websites (see Waterman and Timms 2004; *Transform! Europe* 2004; Sen et al 2004; Voices from Mumbai URL; OpenDemocracy URL). Indeed, at the 2005 WSF an extensive project was developed to facilitate and promote the concept of sharing and free press coverage (WSF URLb). This involved a bank of images that could be shared and downloaded; a Forum of Radios with free access to programming for all; a Forum for Television that brought together different organisations to make one-hour programmes on the forum using a free signal; and other information-sharing techniques. The use of new media is not just intended to disseminate information, it is one of several deliberate attempts to foster horizontal and participatory practices through the technology. To what extent they actually succeed is

a subject of academic debate (see Juris 2004 for a sanguine view; Le Grignou and Patou 2004 for more sceptical conclusions).

Counter-forums

The World Social Forum began as a counter-forum to the World Economic Forum. Now social forums are themselves increasingly facing counter-forums. The first edition in 2001 saw a challenge from the right in the form of the World Forum of Liberties, organised two months later by 'various business organisations and right-wing groups of Rio Grande do Sul' critical of the WSF (Teivanen 2002). But most of the challenges have come from anarchist and youth movements to the left of WSF and ESF (see below). Just as Falk (1999) describes the 'anti-capitalist movement' as a new political resistance to the policies of the elite from those below, now we are seeing a resistance from below within the social forums movement against those organising from above.

As described by Jeff Juris (Box 6.3), autonomous spaces are now a standard feature of the largest forums, and they have received a certain level of tacit recognition from the organising committees. 'Allied

Box 6.3: Alternative spaces within and beyond social forums

Since its inception in January 2001, the WSF has been presented by its organisers as heir to the wave of resistance against corporate globalisation that burst on to the public radar screen during the protests against the World Trade Organization in Seattle in 1999. The WSF, designed to generate positive alternatives, was viewed as a broad space of convergence for reflection and debate among all those opposed to neoliberal capitalism. Whereas counter-summit actions had given widespread visibility to the new movement, WSF organisers felt it was time to build a concrete vision for an alternative world. However, many of those who had been most active in organising earlier mass protests, particularly more radical grassroots and direct action-oriented sectors, remained sceptical. They felt the WSF represented an attempt by forces of the traditional left, including leftist political parties, trade unions, and large non-governmental organisations, to establish an hegemony over a new kind of movement that had largely escaped their control.

Many radicals argued that the WSF was inherently reformist in nature, and that anti-capitalists and all those opposed to state-oriented and social democratic approaches should focus on building their own grass-roots networks, such as People's Global Action (PGA) (Grubacic 2003). Others, however, rejected the top-down representative structure of the WSF, which was seen as violating the decentralised, directly democratic modus operandi that had emerged within the broader movement. A well-known anarchist thus characterised the WSF as 'a supranational, nongovernmental body that seeks to shape the global agenda, with no accountability to and far removed from those whose daily lives are affected' (Millstein 2002). According to this view, the hierarchical command logic of the WSF is intrinsically antithetical to the horizontal networking logic that grassroots activists are trying to promote (Juris 2004). At the same time, the social forums themselves are constituted by an ongoing conflict between networking and command logics (Juris 2004; 2005; forthcoming). This partly involves a debate between those who view the forum as an open space (Sen 2004) and others who see it as a 'movement of movements' (Patomäki and Teivanen 2004).

However, many radicals recognised the strategic importance of the forum as a space of popular expression far exceeding the designs of its organisers. As a Brazilian media activist argued after the third edition of the WSF, 'The social forums are attracting a wide range of people, many of whom we really want to bring to our part of the movement' (Ortellado 2003). This position has become widely shared, leading to what many refer to as a strategy of 'contamination'. With respect to the European Social Forum (ESF), Linden Farrer (2002) argues, 'The best way of working with the ESF [is] being constructive in criticism, attempting to change the organization from inside and outside, preventing liberals from tending towards their self-destructive habits of strengthening existing structures of government.' Indeed, since the WSF was established, radical grassroots activists have organised numerous alternative spaces during world and regional social forums. Moreover, the strategy of building autonomous spaces, 'separate, yet connected' to official events embodies an emerging networking logic, involving, in part, decentralised coordination among diverse, autonomous elements (Juris forthcoming).

The Intergalactika Laboratory of Disobedience organised during the Youth Camp at the 2002 WSF became a model for future autonomous spaces, even if not necessarily conceived in these terms. Intergalactika provided an informal, participatory forum of exchange for younger, direct action-oriented activists from Europe and South and North America. The grassroots ambience provided an explicit contrast to the massive lecture halls housing official plenaries. In addition to discussions and workshops around diverse forms of resistance, activists shared their ideas and experiences, while organising confrontational direct actions against the official forum to make its contradictions visible. For example, at one point, a large group of activists from Intergalactika, including a Brazilian anarchist Samba band, denounced the official VIP room by occupying the space through a roving dance party. The VIP room was conspicuously absent the following year.

Following that experience, grassroots activists around Europe developed a proposal for an 'Autonomous space' at the ESF in Florence in November 2002 through a series of debates at PGA, No Border, and other gatherings the previous summer. Radicals continued to disagree about whether to participate in the official forum, but arrived at a compromise solution involving the organisation of a space beyond, but not against, the ESF. As the final proposal put it, 'this space would maintain its autonomy with respect to the "official"...

ESF, but at the same time remain connected... This would mean... having one foot outside and another inside'
(Nadir URL). At the same time, what began as a single project would divide into several alternative initiatives,
including the Eur@action Hub, a space for networking and experimentation with new digital technologies, the
No Work, No Shop space organised by the Italian Desobbedientes, Thematic Squares run by Italian
autonomous workers, and a feminist space called Next Genderation.

After Florence, the practice of creating alternative spaces within and beyond the forum caught on. For
example, the 2003 WSF in Porto Alegre featured several autonomous initiatives, including a new Hub Project,
the second edition of Intergalactika, a gathering of PGA-inspired groups, and a *Z Magazine* forum called Life
After Capitalism. For its part, the second ESF in Paris in November 2003 featured an autonomous media
centre and lab and a direct action space called Space Towards the Globalisation of Disobedient Struggles
and Actions (GLAD).

The fourth edition of the WSF in India represented an important watershed. Moving the practice beyond largely
urban European and Latin American-based autonomous groups, radical worker and peasant movements
organised several alternative spaces in Mumbai, including the Peoples Movements Encounter II, a small PGA
meeting and, perhaps most notably, Mumbai Resistance (MR). MR2004 involved a coalition of roughly 300
political movements and organisations, including Lohiaites, Marxists, Leninists, Maoists, and Sarvodaya workers.
It was conceived at the International Thessaloniki Resistance Camp in June 2003, and took concrete form
when the Coordinating Group of the International League of Peoples' Struggles (ILPS), decided, in July 2003,
to organise a parallel event during the 2004 WSF. Although the Maoist and Gandhian peasant movements that
organised Mumbai Resistance differed from their 'libertarian' counterparts behind previous alternative
initiatives, they were just as vocal in denouncing forum organisers for their timid critique of capitalism, and
even more so in rejecting their funding practices, which relied on large international agencies.

Indeed, the cultural politics surrounding social forums vary with the social, cultural, and political context
within particular locales (see Box 6.2). Grassroots autonomous spaces reached their fullest expression during
the October 2004 ESF in London, where a heated conflict had raged for months between self-styled
'horizontals' and their counterparts from traditional political formations dubbed the 'verticals' (see Box 6.4;
Nunes 2004). In the midst of this battle, a diverse group of grassroots activists – some against the forum,
others promoting reform – decided to organise a series of autonomous spaces, including the anti-authoritarian
forums: Beyond ESF, Radical Theory Forum, Indymedia Center, a direct-action project called the Laboratory
for Insurrectionary Imagination, Mobile Carnival Forum, Solidarity Village, Women's Open Day, and a conference
called Life Despite Capitalism.

Despite differences in vision and position vis-à-vis ESF, these diverse projects, which involved thousands
of participants in an array of projects, actions, and debates, were united in their commitment to a horizontal,
directly democratic process and form. Activists associated with various autonomous spaces also carried out
non-violent direct action, occupying a stage where the Mayor of London was scheduled to speak, to denounce
his heavy-handed tactics during the organising process.

Mass-based movements are always diverse phenomena shot through with internal conflict and differentiation.
Building alternative spaces within and beyond the forums represents an effective strategy for coordinating
across diversity and difference, thus maintaining a certain unity in debate and action without ideological
uniformity or hegemonic control. Indeed, the 2003 edition of the WSF in Porto Alegre incorporated some of
these lessons by moving away from a centralised format towards a more horizontal design involving a series
of thematic terrains, consultation process, and increased emphasis on self-organised workshops. Moreover,
rather than remaining on the margins of the forum, the 2005 Youth Camp, which housed numerous grassroots
projects, including the Caracol Intergalactika, was situated squarely at the centre. In this limited sense, the
contamination strategy may be working, as alternative spaces, within and beyond social forums, help move
them towards greater internal democracy and decentralisation.

Jeff Juris, University of Southern California

Preparing for anti-war protests at the ESF ©*Richard Nagle*

aim of developing sustainable economic and political alternatives to corporate-led globalisation, and privileges diversity, equality and non-violence (see Box 6.1). It is, therefore, unsurprising that democracy, rights, civil society, environment and the public sector have been dominant official themes from the beginning.

War and peace have become issues since 2002, clearly reflecting growing anti-war sentiment surrounding military actions in Afghanistan and Iraq. Media and communications have become important as the WSF has found it necessary to disseminate ideas and report on its activities without relying on the mainstream press, and as the increased use of technology and associated interest in alternative media have been picked up by the organising committee. Culture is another change, becoming a more central part of the WSF.

It is not possible, however, to infer from Table 6.3 how accurately these themes reflect what is actually discussed during each Forum, especially at the level of the workshops that make up by far the majority of events. Accordingly, we have attempted a content analysis of workshop programmes at world, region, national and local social forums over a three-year period. The forums vary enormously in the number of events organised. The WSF has grown from 732 workshops in 2003 to 2,157 in 2005. On top of that, there are over 200 cultural events each year. The continental African SF is no bigger than the very local Puy de Dôme SF, with 14–24 workshops per forum. The national Uruguay SF and the local Skåne SF in Sweden are much more ambitious, with around 100 workshops each time. Table 6.4 identifies major patterns in the focus of the workshops and how these are developing, and suggests variations between the different levels of social forums.

Content analysis of workshops

The central idea of any content analysis is that the words in the text are classified into a much smaller number of content categories (Popping 1999: 12). But we have to sound a note of caution about the methodology: not every workshop listed in the programme will actually have taken place. For those that did occur, we have no idea how many people were involved or how accurately the discussion reflected the title. Indeed, the process of assigning titles to particular categories is a subjective exercise, as each is open to interpretation (Popping 1999: 15). A system

events, fringe events, and autonomous spaces' were, for instance, listed in the official programme for the first time by ESF 2004 in London.

Themes of the forums

In this third section of the chapter, we present our research findings into the major issues being discussed and debated at social forums. One set of information on major themes is readily available for the WSFs and some other forums, as official thematic areas are decided on during the preparatory stages of the Forum. These have been collated in Table 6.3.

The number of official themes increased significantly in 2005, as these were used to determine the physical spaces where events took place. However, the themes for each year are quite predictable given the Forums' opposition to global capitalism, neoliberalism and war. The WSF Charter of Principles clearly expresses the

Table 6.3: Official thematic areas in all World Social Forums

WSF 2001
1. Production of wealth and social reproduction
2. Access to wealth and sustainability
3. Asserting civil society and the public realm
4. Democracy and citizen power

WSF 2002
1. Production of wealth and social reproduction
2. Access to wealth and sustainability
3. Civil society and the public arena
4. Political power and ethics in the new society

WSF 2003
1. Democratic sustainable development
2. Principles and values, human rights, diversity and equality
3. Media, culture and counter-hegemony
4. Political power, civil society and democracy
5. Democratic world order, fight against militarism and promoting peace

WSF 2004[a]
1. Militarism, war and peace
2. Media, information, knowledge and culture
3. Democracy, ecological and economic security
   i. Debt, finance and trade
   ii. Land, water and food sovereignty
   iii. Labour and world of work in production and social reproduction
   iv. Social sectors – food, health, education and social security
4. Exclusions, discrimination, dignity, rights and quality
   i. Nation, State, citizenship, law and justice
   ii. Caste, race and other forms of descent/work-based exclusions
   iii. Religion, culture and identities
   iv. Patriarchy, gender and sexuality

WSF 2005[b]
A. Autonomous thought, reappropriation and socialisation of knowledge and technologies
B. Defending diversity, plurality and identities
C. Arts and creation: weaving and building people's resistance culture
D. Communication – counter-hegemonic practices, rights and alternatives
E. Assuring and defending Earth and people's common goods – as alternative to commodification and transnational control
F. Social struggles and democratic alternatives – against neoliberal domination
G. Peace, demilitarisation and struggle against war, free trade and debt
H. Towards construction of international democratic order and people's integration
I. Sovereign economies for and of people – against neoliberal capitalism
J. Human rights and dignity for a just and egalitarian world
K. Ethics, cosmovisions and spiritualities – resistance and challenges for a new world

a In this year sub-themes were also included.
b These themes determined the physical organisation of the Forum as well, with each theme having a specific location for all the associated events.

Source: World Social Forum

Table 6.4: Content analysis of social forum programmes[a]

World Social Forum[b]	2003		2004		2005[c]	
Democracy and governance	144	5.1%	241	5.7%	452	6.2%
Human rights	47	1.7%	248	5.9%	449	6.2%
International institutions	55	2.0%	86	2.0%	180	2.5%
Indigenous people/race/ethnicity	42	1.5%	110	2.6%	121	1.7%
Violence and non-violence	55	2.0%	76	1.8%	139	1.9%
War and peace	109	3.9%	257	6.1%	359	5.0%
Politics/Law/Governance		**16.1%**		**24.1%**		**23.5%**
Alternative and solidarity economy	111	3.9%	177	4.2%	369	5.1%
Debt	7	0.2%	27	0.6%	40	0.6%
Labour	87	3.1%	190	4.5%	322	4.5%
Marxism/socialism/revolution	74	2.6%	75	1.8%	166	2.3%
Multinational corporations	41	1.5%	84	2.0%	151	2.1%
Poverty and development	144	5.1%	103	2.4%	188	2.6%
Public services	76	2.7%	74	1.8%	108	1.5%
Trade and finance policy	163	5.8%	103	2.4%	198	2.7%
Economy		**25.0%**		**19.7%**		**21.3%**
Agriculture/food/water	170	6.0%	238	5.6%	321	4.4%
Environment	107	3.8%	149	3.5%	292	4.0%
Health	81	2.9%	91	2.2%	204	2.8%
Science and technology	15	0.5%	55	1.3%	160	2.2%
Environment/Science/Health		**13.3%**		**12.6%**		**13.5%**
Activism and networking	73	2.6%	212	5.0%	351	4.9%
Children and youth	81	2.9%	112	2.7%	313	4.3%
Education	155	5.5%	78	1.8%	331	4.6%
Gender	93	3.3%	189	4.5%	298	4.1%
Media and communications	60	2.1%	79	1.9%	162	2.2%
Religion/spirituality/ethics	55	2.0%	108	2.6%	235	3.2%
Social forums	13	0.5%	74	1.8%	106	1.5%
Emancipation		**18.8%**		**20.2%**		**24.8%**
Cultural events	**712**	**25.3%**	**911**	**21.6%**	**1047**	**14.5%**
Other	**44**	**1.6%**	**74**	**1.8%**	**171**[d]	**2.4%**
Total events counted	**938**		**1407**		**2411**	

African Regional Social Forum	2002		2003		2004	
Democracy and governance	6	8.3%		0.0%	3	4.0%
Human rights	3	4.2%		0.0%		0.0%
International institutions	3	4.2%	6	12.5%	7	9.3%
Indigenous people/race/ethnicity		0.0%		0.0%		0.0%
Violence and non-violence		0.0%		0.0%		0.0%
War and peace	6	8.3%	6	12.5%	6	8.0%
Politics/Law/Governance		**25.0%**		**25.0%**		**21.3%**
Alternative and solidarity economy	6	8.3%	3	6.3%	9	12.0%
Debt	6	8.3%	3	6.3%	4	5.3%
Labour		0.0%		0.0%		0.0%
Marxism/socialism/revolution		0.0%		0.0%		0.0%
Multinational corporations		0.0%		0.0%		0.0%
Poverty and development		0.0%	8	16.7%	8	10.7%
Public services[e]	2	2.8%	2	4.2%		0.0%
Trade and finance policy	10	13.9%	5	10.4%	7	9.3%
Economy		**33.3%**		**43.8%**		**37.3%**
Agriculture/food/water		0.0%	6	12.5%	6	8.0%
Environment		0.0%		0.0%		0.0%
Health		0.0%		0.0%		0.0%
Science and technology		0.0%		0.0%		0.0%
Environment/Science/Health		**0.0%**		**12.5%**		**8.0%**
Activism and networking		0.0%		0.0%	5	6.7%
Children and youth		0.0%		0.0%	3	4.0%
Education		0.0%		0.0%	6	8.0%
Gender	9	12.5%		0.0%	3	4.0%
Media and communications		0.0%	3	6.3%	6	8.0%
Religion/spirituality/ethics		0.0%		0.0%		0.0%
Social forums		0.0%	3	6.3%		0.0%
Emancipation		**12.5%**		**12.5%**		**30.7%**
Cultural events	9	12.5%	3	6.3%		**0.0%**
Other[f]	12	16.7%		0.0%	2	2.7%
Total events counted	**24**		**16**		**25**	

Table 6.4 continued

Uruguay National Social Forum	2002[g]		2003[h]		2004[i]	
Democracy and governance	21	5.2%	15	5.3%	19	6.2%
Human rights	18	4.4%	12	4.2%	17	5.6%
International institutions	5	1.2%	3	1.1%	2	0.7%
Indigenous people/race/ethnicity	14	3.5%	10	3.5%	6	2.0%
Violence and non-violence	10	2.5%	1	0.4%	1	0.3%
War and peace		0.0%	4	1.4%		0.0%
Politics/Law/Governance		**16.8%**		**15.8%**		**14.7%**
Alternative and solidarity economy	26	6.4%	18	6.3%	31	10.1%
Debt		0.0%		0.0%	3	1.0%
Labour	22	5.4%	10	3.5%	21	6.9%
Marxism/socialism/revolution	7	1.7%	5	1.8%		0.0%
Multinational corporations		0.0%	3	1.1%	3	1.0%
Poverty and development	12	3.0%	9	3.2%	7	2.3%
Public services	4	1.0%	6	2.1%	8	2.6%
Trade and finance policy	10	2.5%	22	7.7%	3	1.0%
Economy		**20.0%**		**25.6%**		**24.8%**
Agriculture/food/water	18	4.4%	14	4.9%	27	8.8%
Environment	20	4.9%	5	1.8%	10	3.3%
Health	21	5.2%	25	8.8%	16	5.2%
Science and technology	6	1.5%	1	0.4%	0	0.0%
Environment/Science/Health		**16.0%**		**15.8%**		**17.3%**
Activism and networking	15	3.7%	25	8.8%	22	7.2%
Children and youth	22	5.4%	10	3.5%	16	5.2%
Education	15	3.7%	19	6.7%	7	2.3%
Gender	34	8.4%	14	4.9%	16	5.2%
Media and communications	17	4.2%	6	2.1%	16	5.2%
Religion/spirituality/ethics	9	2.2%	18	6.3%	14	4.6%
Social forums	3	0.7%		0.0%		0.0%
Emancipation		**28.4%**		**32.3%**		**29.7%**
Cultural events	39	9.6%	21	7.4%	29	9.5%
Other	37	9.1%	9	3.2%	12	3.9%
Total events counted	135		95		102	

Puy de Dôme Local Social Forum (France)	2002		2003		2004	
Democracy and governance	8	11.1%	2	4.2%		0.0%
Human rights	1	1.4%	4	8.3%		0.0%
International institutions	2	2.8%	1	2.1%	3	7.1%
Indigenous people/race/ethnicity		0.0%		0.0%		0.0%
Violence and non-violence		0.0%		0.0%		0.0%
War and peace	1	1.4%		0.0%		0.0%
Politics/Law/Governance		**16.7%**		**14.6%**		**7.1%**
Alternative and solidarity economy		0.0%		0.0%		0.0%
Debt		0.0%		0.0%		0.0%
Labour		0.0%		0.0%	3	7.1%
Marxism/socialism/revolution		0.0%		0.0%		0.0%
Multinational corporations		0.0%		0.0%		0.0%
Poverty and development		0.0%		0.0%		0.0%
Public services		0.0%	3	6.3%	3	7.1%
Trade and finance policy		0.0%		0.0%	3	7.1%
Economy		**0.0%**		**6.3%**		**21.4%**
Agriculture/food[j]/water	2	2.8%	5	10.4%	7	16.7%
Environment	1	1.4%	3	6.3%		0.0%
Health		0.0%		0.0%		0.0%
Science and technology		0.0%		0.0%	1	2.4%
Environment/Science/Health		**4.2%**		**16.7%**		**19.0%**
Activism and networking	3	4.2%		0.0%	3	7.1%
Children and youth	4	5.6%	2	4.2%		0.0%
Education		0.0%		0.0%		0.0%
Gender	2	2.8%		0.0%		0.0%
Media and communications		0.0%		0.0%		0.0%
Religion/spirituality/ethics		0.0%		0.0%		0.0%
Social forums	3	4.2%		0.0%		0.0%
Emancipation		**16.7%**		**4.2%**		**7.1%**
Cultural events	45	**62.5%**	28	**58.3%**	19	**45.2%**
Other		**0.0%**		**0.0%**		**0.0%**
Total events counted	**24**		**16**		**14**	

Table 6.4 continued

Skåne Local Social Forum (Sweden)	2002		2004	
Democracy and governance	8	2.8%	23	5.2%
Human rights	14	4.9%	21	4.7%
International institutions	7	2.5%	16	3.6%
Indigenous people/race/ethnicity	5	1.8%	16	3.6%
Violence and non-violence		0.0%		0.0%
War and peace	11	3.9%	24	5.4%
Politics/Law/Governance		**15.8%**		**22.5%**
Alternative and solidarity economy	7	2.5%	5	1.1%
Debt	3	1.1%	2	0.5%
Labour	4	1.4%	11	2.5%
Marxism/socialism/revolution[k]	12	4.2%	24	5.4%
Multinational corporations	1	0.4%		0.0%
Poverty and development	4	1.4%	15	3.4%
Public services	3	1.1%	9	2.0%
Trade and finance policy	27	9.5%	4	0.9%
Economy		**21.4%**		**15.8%**
Agriculture/food/water		0.0%	5	1.1%
Environment	12	4.2%	16	3.6%
Health	7	2.5%	11	2.5%
Science and technology		0.0%	3	0.7%
Environment/Science/Health		**6.7%**		**7.9%**
Activism and networking	14	4.9%	30	6.8%
Children and youth	2	0.7%	6	1.4%
Education	1	0.4%	3	0.7%
Gender	4	1.4%	9	2.0%
Media and communications	17	6.0%	12	2.7%
Religion/spirituality/ethics	9	3.2%	9	2.0%
Social forums	6	2.1%	8	1.8%
Emancipation		**18.6%**		**17.3%**
Cultural events[l]	101	35.4%	148	33.3%
Other	6	2.1%	14	3.2%
Total events counted	95		148	

a Each workshop on the social forum programmes was given a value of three. Since the three points were assigned to an appropriate category or categories, the figures represent these values, not numbers of workshops. But the total number of workshops counted for each year is noted in the table. For a full explanation of methodology and caveats, see the main text.
b Our analysis of WSF programmes has focused on the workshops, as it is inequitable to compare large plenaries with the much more prevalent workshop format. All workshops that appeared in the official programme have been included, as well as cultural events, but plenaries, public meetings, testimonies, conferences, opening and closing events, and events at related social forums (including the youth camp) have been excluded.
c In this year, events were organised in spaces or terrains, one for each of the thematic areas. Within these there was more repetition of events than in previous years, but each time a workshop was run it has been counted.
d 'Other' might have increased because the programme was more self-organised, and more mistakes, mistranslations and untitled events were included, such as listings described just as 'workshop'. It was also found that the number of book launches included as 'other' was increased this year.
e Based on this particular programme, kinds of public services are not distinguished for 2002 and 2003.
f The high 'other' in 2002 is caused by a mysterious workshop on 'responding to social demands', which ran four times.
g Minus pre-meetings, including simultaneous Montevideo SF, film, video, and demonstration.
h Minus plenaries, including market, photo exhibition, and demonstration, with music and dance counted as one workshop.
i Minus plenaries, including market, and demonstrations with music and dance sites counted as one workshop each.
j Communal eating of local food, a popular activity at this forum, has been counted as 1 x food and 2 x culture.
k Uncritical celebrations of solidarity with Cuba, Venezuela and North Korea have been counted in this category.
l Repeat theatre and musical performances have been counted only once.

Confessional box from Earthly Sins at ESF 2004 ©*Jill Timms*

of scoring was used whereby each workshop was given a value of three. These three points were then assigned to the categories that most closely reflected the workshop title.

A growing number of workshops rising to nearly a quarter of the total at the WSF in 2004 and 2005 were focused on issues of politics/law/governance. Particularly important aspects were democracy and human rights; war and peace was another significant topic. In the African forum this is only the third largest topic area, and dropping, with international institutions and war being the main points of interest. In the Uruguay and Puy de Dôme forums there is a decreasing interest, but it remains one of the most significant areas.

Predictably, the economy has been a significant theme, with a quarter of all workshops being about an aspect of the economy at the WSF in 2003. This proportion has hovered at around 20 per cent. It is still the largest area of interest for the African and Puy de Dôme forums. The categories of multinational companies and alternative and solidarity economy have been the topics of increasing numbers of workshops, suggesting that people are increasingly moving on from critiques of neo-liberalism (captured mainly in the trade and finance category) to interest in economic alternatives, as well as concrete campaigns. Workshops on work and labour have slightly increased at the WSF and also in all the other forums except the African. This could be due to increasing involvement of trade unions (see Waterman and Timms 2004).

Interest in environmental issues has been steady but low at the 2003–5 WSFs, at 3–4 per cent of workshops. There has been a slight decrease in interest at the other forums, but if we widen the category to include issues of agriculture, health and science, this is a significant area to be considered. In particular, workshops on agriculture at the WSF seem to have decreased in number, but there has been an increase in those focusing on the issue of water.

The most significant theme identified for workshops in the 2005 WSF, now discussed at a quarter of all events, is what we have called emancipation. Within this category, activism and networking is the most important topic. The percentage would be even higher if we had not classified social forums as a separate topic. This suggests that, in the actual workshops, self-reflection and sharing of experience and skills on the methods of doing politics have become the main item on the agenda. In the African SF, too, emancipation has eclipsed politics as the second largest category after the economy, whereas in Uruguay, it has consistently been the largest category. In the local forums, it is significant but overshadowed by the related category of culture.

The prominence of this category, which includes workshops about culture but more frequently cultural events featuring song, dance, theatre or film, has been as astonishing as the focus on emancipation. Culture was easily the biggest category at both local forums, with between 45 per cent and 62 per cent at Puy de Dôme and a third or more at Skåne, suggesting that these social forums can be defined as pre-dominantly cultural events. At the WSF, cultural events have risen in absolute numbers, but fallen in percentage points against the ever-rising number of workshops. Our numbers do not, however, include impromptu or unofficial events. The focus on culture again suggests a preoccupation with the manner of engaging in politics instead of with substance only. It demonstrates that sit-and-talk is not the only model of activist engagement, and many others are explored.

Diversity of form and focus

One certain conclusion that can be drawn from our data and other research is that social forums are very diverse in both their form and the issues discussed within them. We have identified some common themes and patterns, but it is also important to recognise that no list of categories can do justice to the vast range of topics involved. In the 2005 WSF programme, we found intriguing ones such as 'Firefly expedition', 'Unlearning' and 'Project K' (all categorised as 'other').

Other regional, national and local social forums are equally bewildering in their variety. Like their global counterpart, they are products of negotiations between different local (and sometimes international) con-stituents. Despite their smaller size, their character and purpose are still very much in the eye of the beholder, as emerges from two very different descriptions of the 2004 Zimbabwe Social Forum (ZSF). A participant in the Youth Camp enthused:

When it happened minds came together. Struggles converged like many rivulets forming a powerful river

…The Freedom Youth Camp was a space where hundreds of young radicals had fiery discussions on sexism, grassroots democracy, non-violent direct action, alternative youth culture and a web of other subversive realities. In the camp the Students' Solidarity Trust hosted a heated discussion on 'Student Victimisation' which saw youths erupting into toyi toyi war dances before sitting down, sweaty, and looking at the history of Zim university students in struggles against Rhodesian colonialism, followed by IMF-imposed structural adjustment programmes and now a brutal bourgeois black regime… A grassroots movement was born. The fattened spider should be wriggling in fear. (Monro 2004)

An observer from a Danish donor organisation, which part-funded the forum, described the same forum as follows:

…the program was promising a range of interesting sessions from morning till late. Four huge tents provided the possibility of housing four different sessions at the same time, and despite the lively debates and the seemingly never-ending flow of questions from the audience the discussions were generally marked by timeliness and discipline, which made the program run smoothly and satisfactory … In essence, the ZSF was a platform for sensitising and educating the general populace on the causes of the present challenges to development at local, national and global level. Secondly, and even more important, the ZSF endeavoured to come up with coping strategies and find a way forward. (MS 2004)

Nonetheless, some meaningful comments can be made about the major themes that national and local social forums have developed and the ways in which these are shaped by their local environment. In Latin America, economic issues like the FTAA, on the one hand and solidarity economy (discussed further in Box 6.6), on the other, continue to be hot items on the agenda, as are indigenous issues and the legacy of the dictatorships. In Spain, many city social forums emerged as counter-forums to official European Union meetings during the Spanish presidency in 2002, and the EU was therefore their main topic. Many have since withered. In France, social forums are much more rural than elsewhere, with regional forums rotat-ing between small towns. There is much emphasis on

Box 6.4: Exception or rule? The case of the London European Social Forum 2004

The third European Social Forum (ESF) took place in London, 14–17 October 2004, attracting over 20,000 delegates from across the continent for three days of discussion, networking, strategising and, at times, intense political dispute.

Many observers dubbed this third ESF 'the London exception', expressing concerns that its practices had failed to live up to social forum principles. The label also implies that the difficulties of the London ESF were the product of local circumstances: a fragmented and sectarian left and relatively weak social movements. There is some truth in this, as a lack of civil society involvement resulted in an organising process that was particularly focused around the Greater London Authority's (GLA) City Hall, where agendas were set and the vast majority of preparatory meetings were held. This led French and Italian delegations – the main power brokers in the ESF's internal disputes – to the verge of withdrawing their support altogether. But the difficulties in London were also part of the bigger problem of how the forum relates to state institutions, and the lines of this debate were not drawn in London.

Virtually all major social forums (with the exception of the 2004 WSF in Mumbai) have relied on state funding, despite their formal status as civil society initiatives. In Porto Alegre, this works, with occasional friction, because the city government's participatory ethos means that it has learned to recognise the benefits of the forum's relative autonomy. But the same was not true in London, where the unwritten rule that local authorities should restrict themselves to logistical support was broken. The Mayor's Office, most of whose senior staff are affiliates to a tightly-knit (post-)Trotskyite grouping called Socialist Action, has a heavily centralised approach to London governance; it extended this same managerialism to the ESF, with practical tasks outsourced or dealt with bureaucratically. The lines of accountability within the ESF office (a vital aspect of the forum's informal decision making structure) led to the GLA, which also hosted private weekly coordinating meetings of its own in parallel with the 'official' ESF process. Other tasks, such as the website and 'event management', were outsourced – albeit to ethical companies. But the lack of accountability inherent in these contractual arrangements meant that the forum was not able to operate as a space of practical experimentation, prefiguring the 'other world' that it promises to bring about. Underlying these decisions was a tendency – by no means unique to the third ESF, although seen in exacerbated form there – to treat the ESF as an event rather than a process, subordinating the ongoing dynamic of pan-European social movement networking to the perceived need for administrative 'efficiency'.

Paradoxically, the lack of a significant left party in the UK contributed to this situation. The background involvement of political parties is another unwritten rule of forum organising, despite the Charter of Principles proclaiming the social forum to be a 'non-party context'. In principle, the London ESF offered a rare opportunity to break this mould. In practice, it proved that the forums currently rely upon such parties to mediate the relationship with local government, as well as allowing them a space within which to articulate their political demands and organise collective activities. In the case of London, the GLA took on this role by proxy. Political parties were still present, however, with Socialist Action (Labour Party centrists) forging an unlikely alliance with the Socialist Workers Party (SWP) and some members of the Communist Party of Britain. These same groups sought to involve the British trade unions in the forum, with mixed success: several held seminars, and both the public sector union Unison and the Transport and General Workers' Union offered financial and logistical support. However, this did not translate into significant involvement by branch-level trade unionists, and there are few signs that British trade unions will remain involved in the forum process after London.

This is just one symptom of the forum's failure, thus far, to fully 'Europeanise' itself. Although a lower turnout meant that the proportion of international delegates at the London forum increased, it remained way below 50 per cent. The organising process still has a long way to travel to overcome its methodological nationalism, too. In 2004, as in previous years, the ESF continued to assign national quotas to the selection of its plenary speakers – a process well suited to political party involvement (and, in the case of London 2004, manipulation).

With crisis comes renewal, however. Discontent with the 'official' London ESF process resulted in the spread of a number of 'autonomous spaces', a label that fuses a statement of formal organisational independence with a political conception of 'autonomy', drawing on post-Marxist and anarchist traditions. These spaces did not necessarily share a common ideological position, but all shared a concern with the third ESF's 'vertical' organising processes. This culminated in a stage invasion at a Saturday night plenary where London Mayor Ken Livingstone was scheduled to speak (he did not turn up), with activists from the autonomous spaces unfurling a banner that read 'ESF – another world is for sale'. But this wasn't simply an inside–outside conflict, as dissidents from the ESF Organising Committee also joined the protest. The boundary between the 'official' and autonomous spaces was porous in another sense, too, as the constant flow of participants between them meant that the latter were not simply fringe events but became integral to the experience of the London ESF as a whole. This new dynamic could even be seen as a model for re-conceptualising the social forum 'as a constellation of related self-organised convergence spaces without a centre' (Nunes 2004). Rather than viewing the forum as a singular open space, we might then begin to understand it as a complex pattern of interlocking networked spaces – an organisational logic that, to some extent, mirrors the mass direct actions against multilateral institutions in places like Prague, Quebec, and Genoa.

In the aftermath of the London ESF, reflective meetings of the ESF Preparatory Assembly in Paris, Brussels and Athens drew something approximating to this conclusion – though in watered-down form. The next ESF, to be held in Athens in spring 2006, will be structured around thematic terrains (as was the WSF 2005), and the process has already started with a European-wide consultation, which is more closely in keeping with the forum's participatory principles. There will, no doubt, be efforts to marginalise the results of this process or read them selectively, but it nevertheless signals that another forum might yet be possible.

Oscar Reyes, University of East London

local food and culture, and agriculture. The Cyprus, Israel and Pakistan Social Forums (none of which is well-represented on the internet) have a predictable focus on peace and reconciliation.

Many German city forums are almost entirely devoted to fighting the German government's austerity measures, with the global connection just a footnote. In the Middle East, by contrast, social forum activity does not always seem well-embedded, and can almost seem like a form of escapism from local problems: the Istanbul SF focuses on attending European meetings, the Morocco SF has much more text in French and English on its website than in Arabic, and the Iran SF appears to be a diasporic aspiration rather than a real forum based in Iran.

But most forums either combine local and globally focused activities or apply global analysis to local issues. Thus the Cardiff SF campaigns against the yuppific-ation of the Grangetown neighbourhood, but also organises to protest at the G8 meeting in Scotland in July 2005. In Santa Fe, Argentina, a thematic-local social forum was held titled 'Neoliberal Policies and Natural Disasters: The Santa Fe Flood'. The Mapuche SF in Chile dealt with the effect of the Asia-Pacific Economic Cooperation (APEC) on indigenous people in general and the Mapuche in particular.

Two main findings emerge from our investigation of the themes of social forums. The first is their diversity and their ability to adapt and evolve in response to local concerns and current issues. What is unclear, as yet, is whether the social forums are serving to lead on these issues or are merely following the interests driven by established civil society organisations. The second is a strong and growing interest in the processes and structures of political organising.

Sites of tension

The spread and popularity of the social forums suggest that the principles underlying them do offer a potential new structure for the activities of global civil society, or at least a significant section of it. The WSF Charter of Principles is a unique document to which social forums can continually turn for guidance. The challenge facing social forums is not only to develop alternatives to existing policies to promote social justice but also to find new workable processes and methods of organising to develop these alternatives. However, as set out in the first section of this chapter, the origins of the social forum movement are multifaceted and

complex. Therefore, social forums have not started in a politically neutral environment, and the space they occupy has already been claimed by long-established civil society organisations with long-established beliefs, organising structures and processes. These different traditions can make seemingly mundane organisational issues deeply divisive.

Horizontals versus verticals

One of the most central ideological clashes played out in social forums can be conceptualised as the problem of the 'horizontals' versus the 'verticals'. The terms were coined by self-invented horizontals (from the idea of the 'horizontality' of the anti-capitalist movement) during the fraught preparations for ESF 2004. 'Verticals' refers to members of organisations that have established hierarchical structures and are used to working with organisations of a similar kind and using traditional forms of decision making and planning, such as majority voting and electing representatives to committees, and whose activists think in this way and prefer this method of working. 'Horizontals' refers to members of civil society organisations with 'flat' and flexible structures, or indeed people with no specific organisational affiliation, who work to develop alternative methods of decision making through consensus building or allowing multiple outcomes.

Verticals are typically from trade unions, political parties and larger non-governmental organisations. Horizontals are typically found among small solidarity groups and anarchist outfits, disillusioned former party activists, and frequently also students and academics. It needs to be noted, however, that these 'horizontals' and 'verticals' are ideal types, and in reality the division between them can be understood only through a knowledge of particular contexts.

Some of the bitterest divisions between those inter-ested in debating innovative, more democratic ways to organise and so on, and those who wanted to 'get on with it', usually on the basis of existing methods such as representation, majority voting and bargaining, were evident at the ESF in London in 2004 (see Box 6.4). But the tension runs through many forums, and is often dealt with more productively than in that instance.

Organisations can move towards new methods (see Waterman and Timms 2004 on the attempts made by some trade unions and other labour organisations), and it may not be impossible for horizontals to work with verticals. As suggested above, the increasing emphasis on self-organisation and accommodation of autonomous spaces points at an evolution in this direction within the larger forums.

Nonetheless, decision making in relation to the actual organising of the larger forums will continue to be marked by conflict, as old-fashioned, formally democratic vertical structures are rejected but no recipes have yet been developed for horizontal and consensus decision making involving thousands of people. The smaller forums may occasionally experience what Ricardo Blaug (1999: 136) calls 'an outbreak of democracy':

The primary characteristic must be that of noise. All accounts note that speech becomes animated, and debate heated. This sudden increase in discussion follows upon the discovery of a common preoccupation. Now, people are keen to be heard, they listen to others with interest, and concern is expressed to elicit all views. Exclusionary tactics are directly challenged, as are attempts to distort the needs and interests of others. Whatever the common interest under discussion, all salient facts are actively explored, and the group, now pooling its cognitive resources, confronts the matter at hand in its full complexity.

However, as Blaug notes, such outbreaks do not usually last. So the jury is still out on whether the commitment to new participatory forms is sustainable. It is likely that the social forum phenomenon will continue to oscillate between more traditional forms of organising and the 'tyranny of structurelessness' (Freeman 1972). A conflict-ridden process of continuous challenges to either tendency may in fact be the best way forward for social forums.

Deliberation versus struggle

A related but different area of tension is between the 'deliberation' and the 'struggle' functions that social forums seek to combine. The Charter of Principles brings together two very different strands of thought about the function of (global) civil society (see Box 6.1). The first is the idea of a deliberative space, articulated by Kant and elaborated by Habermas. This kind of thinking is reflected in Article 1 of the Charter, decreeing that the WSF should provide a space for communication that is 'open', 'democratic' and 'free'. The second idea is derived from Gramsci and sees

civil society as being engaged in a counter-hegemonic struggle. This is reflected in the second part of Article 1, which defines what the groups coming together in the Forum have to be against: here is the idea – quite against Marx – that groups and movements of civil society can be fighting 'domination of the world by capital and any form of imperialism'. Article 11 is a similar mix of Habermasian debate and reflection, and Gramscian struggle to 'resist and overcome domination', while the final Article 14 again reflects Kantian cosmopolitanism. While the WSF's broad aim of opposing neoliberalism and corporate domination could be seen as neo-Gramscian, some of its unique features, such as its prohibition on party representation, on voting and on taking positions as an organisation, owe more to the deliberation than to the struggle tradition (see also Glasius 2005).

But the two traditions are necessarily at odds with each other. While deliberation values plurality and diversity and debate for its own sake, effective action against the domination of capital requires a certain level of unity. Conversely, a debate that is a priori against something can never an entirely open debate. The Zapatista movement, an important intellectual forerunner of the social forums, sought to resolve this dilemma with its formula of 'One big no and many yesses' (Kingsnorth 2003; Klein 2001). Patomäki and Teivanen (2004) have described this tension as one between being a space and being a movement, and Teivanen (2003) elsewhere calls it 'arena or actor'. This is the main subject of the debate between Whitaker, Sousa Santos and Cassen elsewhere in this Yearbook.

The same dilemma rears its head in national and local social forums. Some lean much more towards one direction than the other. The manifesto of the Madrid Social Forum, for instance, while much more anti-militarist than anti-capitalist, is clearly in struggle or movement mode. It declares that its aims are 'the defence of peace, solidarity, human rights and democratic liberties', and that in order to do so, it must form an 'action unit' launching a 'great offensive' with a 'single vocation' and, in a peculiar piece of double-speak, be a 'space of tolerance and necessary consensus' of the left in Madrid (Madrid Social Forum 2003, authors' translation). A mark of social forums with a struggle conception is that they often fail to take seriously the WSF Charter's prohibition on adopting political positions. Thus, the Senegal SF has adopted a petition against the privatisation of the national lottery (*Indymedia* 2005); the Kenya SF has addressed itself to a WTO meeting (Kenya Social Forum 2005); and the Hamburg South SF has adopted a declaration of solidarity with the striking workers at a local Opel car factory (Hamburg South Social Forum 2004).

An increasing number of recent local and national social forums, by contrast, emphasise open space, plurality and debate. Thus, the Ivry (France) SF identifies itself as a 'simple meeting space for those organizations and individuals who share the objections and aspirations of the "altermondialiste" movement. One comes to be mutually informed, to debate, to deepen knowledge on questions of common interest and to propose initiatives. These are then carried out by whoever is interested' (authors' translation). The Melbourne SF is 'an annual open space event, and a network, for facilitating debate, self-expression and imagination in addressing global issues. In particular for seeking out, articulating and helping to establish more sustainable and just versions of globalisation'. The Netherlands SF, finally, is 'an open meeting place for the exchange of ideas, the creation and the strengthening of networks and a breeding ground for action' (authors' translation). Social forums that emphasise the 'open space' or 'debate' function often refer to the 2003 article by Chico Whitaker (2004b), 'The WSF as an Open Space', which has been translated into many languages.

At the World Social Forum, this particular tension had been muted because of the large size of the forum and through the device of having a separate 'assembly of social movements' that could adopt positions. In 2005, however, it came to a head when a group of 19 launched what it called 'the Porto Alegre Consensus' as 'a synthesis of what the WSF is proposing globally'. The group included WSF co-founder Bernard Cassen, two Nobel Prize winners, and other anti-globalisation stars such as Aminata Traoré (the only woman in the group), Samir Amin, and Walden Bello. However, Chico Whitaker, another founder of the WSF, said that it should be seen as only one of 'dozens, maybe hundreds of other proposals' (Anthony and Silva 2005); and Candido Grzybowski, another member of the Brazilian Organising Committee, felt that, while he had nothing against the contents of the manifesto, 'it goes against the very spirit of the Forum. Here, all proposals are equally important and not only that of a group of intellectuals, even when they are very significant

persons' (Anthony and Silva 2005).

The 150,000 or so other participants in the fifth WSF took relatively little notice of the manifesto, and it seems not to have become the latter-day heir to the Communist Manifesto that the authors may have hoped it would be. Indeed, it takes some effort to find the manifesto on the internet (an English version can be found at OD Today 2005).

The deliberation versus struggle, or space versus movement, controversy seems at the moment to be veering towards deliberation and space. Nonetheless, one should not be too sentimental about the openness of social forum spaces. First of all, there remains a logical contradiction in the idea of an open space against something. Second, as we discuss in the next sections, the social forums do not altogether succeed in providing a horizontal gathering place for the world's marginalised people.

Leadership

Both the tendency towards horizontality and the celebration of diversity in social forums are legacies of the movements of 1968. But, even more than these movements, the anti-capitalist movement and its associated social forum manifestation reject the idea of leadership. This has two unfortunate side effects.

First, the organisers behind the large regional and world forums remain shadowy figures. Potential participants may discover, for instance, that the next WSF will be decentralised or that the next ESF is to be in Greece, but the vast majority of them would be hard put to name any of the members of the Organising Committee or the International Council. Thus, there are no faces associated with the decision making process and it is difficult even to discover to whom suggestions or grievances should be addressed, let alone how to become part of the process. In the local social forums, this is much less of a problem, as organising meetings are usually 'open to all', although more ethnographic research would be required to discover how such bodies function in practice.

Second, no new leaders appear to have emerged from the social forum phenomenon. Rare candidates for leadership roles, such as Naomi Klein or Arundhati Roy, emphatically reject any mantle of leadership. Yet the social forums are not, in practice, the leader-free zones that some would like them to be. Instead, veteran leaders of older social movements and even politicians have stepped into the vacuum. This would include the drafters of the Porto Alegre Consensus, whose age probably averages 60 or 70. Long-time darlings of the left, like José Bové, John Pilger and even 87-year-old Ahmed Ben Bella, are staples of the regional and national forums. And when the World Social Forum officially abolished the plenaries with star speakers, the biggest draw became Venezuelan President Hugo Chavez, drawing a crowd of 20,000.

In view of this development, the question can be asked whether the suspicion of leadership has gone too far, and whether the anti-capitalist movement should have emphasised better, more participatory leadership rather than celebrating leaderlessness. Under the present dispensation, it is hard to decide which is worse: grassroots activists turned off by the likes of Walden Bello, Noam Chomsky or Hugo Chavez, or grassroots activists actually turned on by them!

Inclusion and exclusion

One of the distinguishing features of the WSF Charter is its celebration of diversity. However, while another world may be possible, the forums are still of this world, and they struggle to avoid reproducing existing inequalities within the forums. In the official plenaries, for instance, world and regional forums typically allocate speakers based on percentages of representation by gender and national or regional identity. Paradoxically, this process of apportioning reproduces exactly the kind of nationality-based interest politics that the social forums are meant to break through. The self-organised sessions, meanwhile, are heavily dominated by the host nationality and by the regions where social forum organising is most developed: Latin America, especially Brazil, and Southern Europe. Moreover, as Smith (2005) notes for the ESF, 'the larger, better-organized and better resourced interests are most likely to be heard and to dictate the agenda'.

Statements about the importance of including women or the disabled do not necessarily translate into crèche facilities or accommodation of special needs, such as disabled access or sign language. Worse, social forums turn out not necessarily to be a safe space for women. A shocking 90 incidents of violence against women at the Youth Camp were reported at the 2005 WSF, including sexual harassment and even rape, prompting the formation of a 'Lilac Brigade' designed to help women suffering from abuse (Obando, 2005).

Moreover, little effort is made to attract to social forums participants who do not have access to or do not use the internet. Perhaps one of the most persistent criticisms of social forums, particularly in Africa but elsewhere too, is that they are in fact elitist forms of 'champagne activism', open only to those who can afford the time and money to fly around the world discussing global problems.

Due to the specific format of social forums, there is also a continuing tension between making progress in the development of strategies and alternatives, and outreach, as new participants continually need to be 'socialised' into the process and the background to the forum process explained. Youth have been given much attention, but at the same time they have often been kept somewhat remote through the organisation of separate Youth Camps. The 2005 WSF improved on this by putting the youth camp at the centre of the site.

In the Americas there has been repeated tension over inclusiveness towards indigenous peoples. At the Northwest Social Forum in the US, an ambitious three-day event was cancelled at short notice after the withdrawal of the indigenous and youth committees, which had felt increasingly marginalised in the decision making and concluded that the agreed values of grassroots initiative, independent priority setting, and shared and equal leadership had been breached (Northwest Social Forum 2004a; 2004b). At the WSF, too, the marginalisation of indigenous people has been the subject of controversy (Nunes, Dowling and Juris 2005)

One area in which the major social forums have been particularly proactive in accommodating diversity is that of language. This has been almost entirely due to Babels, a volunteer organisation set up in September 2002 to meet the needs of the European Social Forum in Florence. It now has 13 national coordination centres to provide translation at world, regional and national social forums, and remains entirely a voluntary effort. (The importance of Babels is discussed in Box 6.5.) Nonetheless, language remains a problem at the regional and world forums. At the 2005 WSF, due to reduced funding from the local authorities, translators were in very short supply, and British, Chinese and Indian participants were seen walking disconsolately from tent to tent in search of some sessions where English was spoken.

Box 6.5: Babels and the politics of language within the social forums

It is the need for social forum activists and organisers to communicate across myriad language communities that explains the role of Babels, the international network of volunteer interpreters and translators allied to the social forum movement. Babels was born in the run-up to the first ESF in Florence in 2002 out of a mixture of political principle and financial necessity. Many activists had disapproved of the hiring of professional interpreters and corporate equipment for the WSFs in 2001 and 2002 – the huge expense and use of the market went against the spirit of solidarity economy and alternatives to neoliberalism that Porto Alegre was supposed to symbolise. Communication activists linked to ATTAC France proposed that all interpreters for Florence be volunteers; and although the Italian organisers stuck to the traditional market route, an eleventh-hour emergency call for volunteers was made when the costs became too high, and 350 volunteer Babels interpreters and translators eventually helped the first ESF take place.

The Babels experiment in Florence just about worked but was completely chaotic: coordinators had few resources to work with and were even forced to squat in a medieval tower to get their own office space. The experience prompted a greater consideration of language issues for the second ESF in 2003 in Paris. Babels was given a relatively large pot of money (£200,000) with which to coordinate and innovate. Boosted by its participation in the counter-G8 conferences in Evian and Annemasse, and the emergence of new coordinations across Europe, Babels assembled over 1,000 volunteers for Paris from a pool four times that number. Since then, the network has grown rapidly and participated in an increasing range of forums and events. In 2004 alone, Babels took part in the Mumbai WSF, the first Social Forum of the Americas in Quito, Ecuador, and the third ESF in London. The last of these welcomed 500 Babelitos from 22 countries, who in turn enabled some 20,000 participants from more than 60 countries to express themselves in 25 different languages over three days. The number of volunteer interpreters and translators registered in the Babels database is now over 9,000, representing more than 60 languages.

Increasingly indispensable to social forums, Babels is becoming a political actor in its own right. Like the social forums, it has a charter of principles. Its main precondition for involvement in any civil society event or process is the 100 per cent volunteer rule: interpreters and translators can receive travel and subsistence expenses but no income for working. Babels must also be involved in the political process from the beginning and treated as an organiser of a social forum like any other, not a 'free' service provider. Perhaps most difficult of all is Babels' commitment to defend and promote 'the right of everybody to express themselves in the language of their choice' (Babels URL). In practice, these preconditions are nearly always abused by social forum organisers, and the biggest problem remains the presence of a 'language hierarchy' within any forum.

What is most striking about Babels is its determination to develop language and communication systems that are alternative to the free market. In its efforts to respect language diversity, Babels is developing innovatory new language tools through activities such as the Lexicon Project (Babels URL). This is an ongoing effort by volunteers from a wide range of countries and backgrounds (teachers, students, professionals, activists) to create a comprehensive glossary of words and phrases to help interpreters and translators best reflect different meanings according to different national, cultural and politico-historical contexts. Babels is consciously creating a process of 'contamination' in which the excellent language skills of the politically sympathetic trained interpreter or translator interact with the deeper political knowledge of the language-fluent activist to improve constantly the communications medium within the social forums.

Lexicons are being formed in conjunction with the Situational Preparation Project, more commonly known as Sitprep, which records WSF and ESF plenaries and seminars in a wide range of languages on to DVD to allow any volunteer – experienced or inexperienced – to prepare more realistically for simultaneous translation in the social forum. Significantly for Babels, the moves to create a systematic 'memory' of each social forum will allow the quality of interpretation to be assessed and new online 'distance practice' materials for inexperienced volunteers created.

More problematic is the widespread commitment within Babels to 'horizontality' – Babelitos supposedly eschew leaders and hierarchies and instead seek to work collectively as equals in a network organisation based upon creative thinking and consensus. In reality, horizontality remains more an ideal than a working practice. In many ways, Babels has been a victim of its own success. When Babels was just a handful of coordinators, decision making was relatively straightforward, but the mushrooming of new coordinations across Europe and increasingly the global South, and the huge growth in the number of registered volunteers on the database without a concomitant political process to both renew the shared principles underpinning the network and create a coherent framework of decision making, have created a classic 'tyranny of structureless-ness'. The result is that, far from being a horizontal network across borders, Babels has evolved into something of an unsatisfactory hybrid comprising a massive pool of volunteer labour, a set of national coordinations that are often in conflict with each other, and a hidden hierarchy with a strong French centre. Opening up and levelling down Babels' democratic process is not helped by the top-down and centralised way in which forums such as the ESF have been traditionally organised.

Babels has recently become a controversial actor within the social forums. During the ESF in London, the marginalisation of language needs and the undemocratic organising process dominated by the Greater London Authority led Babels to issue a number of critical public statements and nearly to pull out on several occasions. The fact that Babels stepped back from the brink each time was partly due to the difficulties of reaching consensus among people from different backgrounds and perspectives. Moreover, the UK coordinators of Babels who agreed to participate in the 2005 ESF did so with their political eyes wide open. The reality is that the social forums, and especially the ESF, are not politically 'pure' spaces where everyone works together in mutual respect and harmony. They are instead political battlegrounds where self-interested factions fight for leadership and control and are met with resistance from those opposed to vanguardism. Babels thus currently accepts that the innovations and alternatives being generated by projects like itself come not only from the annual process of organising the ESF and WSF, but also from struggle against those within them.

Stuart Hodkinson, Associate Editor of Red Pepper *magazine*

At the political level there is a real issue about the amount of effort devoted to bringing new people, young or otherwise, to the forums, and engaging with new constituencies and challenging and politicising them. At the 2004 ESF, for instance, engagement with the Islamic world was a major item on the agenda, but a 'large majority of participants were white' (Smith 2005). Indeed, the vast majority of Londoners of all colours were probably unaware that the ESF was taking place in their city. Similar comments have been made about the Asian SF in Hyderabad. Many city social forums similarly consist of very small groups of 'usual suspects'. Only a few, such as for instance the Boston SF and various German SFs, have had a strong media policy.

Political parties and government relations

It is clearly set out in the WSF Charter of Principles that political parties should not be a part of social forums, but people can of course belong to a party and also contribute to a forum in a personal capacity. In practice, the attitude of political parties has almost entirely determined the character of many social forums. In Brazil, the World Social Forums could not have been organised without the enthusiastic financial, logistical and symbolic support of the Brazilian Workers' Party (PT), which has a history of cordial relations with civil society 'fellow travellers' (Wainwright 2003: 44). In Italy, too, there is a history of long-standing if fraught relations between the Communist Party, civil society activists and left intellectuals. Both of the Communist Party's descendants, the reformist Democratici di Sinistra and the hard-line Rifondazione Comunista, have backed the social forum movement enthusiastically. The former controlled both the region of Tuscany and the city council of Florence in 2002, and subsidised the European Social Forum there. However, it would appear that in both Brazil and Italy the parties recognised that attempts to dominate the forum agenda or to use it for overt party-political propaganda would lead to a more conflictual and less successful forum, and ultimately reflect badly on the parties themselves. Nonetheless, the authors have witnessed some fairly open party propaganda from the PT at the WSF.

In India and in the UK, party attitudes have been rather different. As Jai Sen describes, the preparations for the WSF in India

...came to be strongly dominated by formations within the organised Left. Some argued that this was the case only because these formations were willing to make available their networks and cadres to the Forum and do the dog work required in organising such a process and event. Many outside the Left however, felt that the Forum was highly exclusive and unwelcoming and/or not addressing key issues, and kept away from it. (Sen 2004)

The experience of preparing for the European Social Forum in London was, as Massimo De Angelis (2004) has pointed out, very similar, with the Trotskyite Socialist Workers' Party and a more shadowy group called Socialist Action connected to Ken Livingstone, dominating the proceedings (see Box 6.4). Like their Brazilian and Italian counterparts, these parties see the forum as an opportunity but, unlike them, they look upon it as straightforward power politics and grab as much of it as they can at the expense of diversity and deliberative politics. Whereas in Mumbai the parties' influence was counterbalanced by strong social movements and well-funded NGOs, in London they prevailed in all organisational struggles. What both types of parties have in common, however, and what non-party activists need to acknowledge, is cadres of committed volunteers, which almost no other social forum-related organisation can command (ATTAC and Babels may be exceptions).

Similar tensions are sometimes played out in local social forums. In Gironde, France, the first forum in 2003 (significantly opened on 1 May) was firmly in the hands of left-wing political parties, which formed the majority of the secretariat. In what seems partly a horizontal–vertical conflict, protests against this 'guiding hand' led to the establishment of an alternative website, which declared itself 'within the Charter' and the official organisers 'outside the Charter'. Since then, the parties have lost the elections and withdrawn from the organisation, leading to a smaller but more associational forum (authors' translation).

To what extent a social forum succeeds in being a new, more open and more diverse form of politics appears then to depend not so much on whether political parties have a presence, which seems almost inevitable, but rather on whether the parties themselves have changed and recognised that a different relationship with civil society is necessary.

'Knitting' a web with plastic bags to highlight waste at the ESF ©*Richard Nagle*

Violence

In addition to avoiding party politics, the WSF Charter of Principles specifies that the Forum should involve only those who do not engage in violence. Article 13 clearly states that the Forum aims to increase the capacity of 'non-violent social resistance' (see Box 6.1). As this Charter forms a basis for the development of social forums at all levels, or is expected to do so, it could be argued that the growth of social forums has put a formerly direct action-oriented anti-capitalist movement on a trajectory of strict non-violence. But this raises two problems.

First, it is difficult to prevent members of groups that use violence from participating, especially when they do so in a personal capacity. The nature of social forums provides many opportunities for members of these groups to participate in or link themselves with forums without disclosing their violent associations. Small groups of protesters do attend with the intention of using violence, although this has not been an obvious problem at the majority of forums.

Second, the mainstream media image of the anti-capitalist movement, which is intertwined with the development of the social forums, has often focused on incidents of violence or conflict with authorities. Two striking examples are the 'battle of Seattle' in 1999 and the 2001 'social forum' in Genoa. The focus on violence in media reporting on Seattle has since been criticised as inaccurate (FAIR 2001). In Genoa, again, much of the mainstream media characterised participants as violent and aggressive (Andretta and Mosca 2004), although it has since become clear that the police brutality was much more severe (Burbach 2001; BBC News 2001). Thus, the movement is associated with violence while at the same time non-violent events go largely unreported.

These tensions are currently being explored within social forums in two ways. The first is to make violence and non-violence an explicit theme for discussion and debate within the forums (representing 2–2.5 per cent of the topics at the WSF). The second is to try to counter a potentially negative public image of social forums in the mainstream press with increasing support for fairer coverage of the forums by the alternative media. Integrating the mainstream press into forum facilities is also being used as a way to ensure that the non-violent nature of the forums can be reported accurately.

Table 6.5: **Financial sponsors of the World Social Forum**

WSF 2003	WSF 2004	WSF 2005
Sponsors of the WSF process	**Sponsors of the WSF process**	**Sponsors of the WSF process and the WSF in Porto Alegre**
BR Petrobras	BR Petrobras	Banco do Brasil
Ford Foundation	Caixa do Brasil	Brasil Governo Federal
Fundação Banco do Brasil	Correios	BR Petrobras
Governo do Rio de Grande do Sol	Ford Foundation	Caixa do Brasil
Prefeitura do Municipio de Porto Alegre	Fundação Banco do Brasil	Correios
		Christian Aid
Sponsors of the WSF in Porto Alegre	**Sponsors of the WSF in Mumbai**	CAFOD
ActionAid	ActionAid	Comité Catholique Contre la Faim et pour le Développement (CCFD)
CAFOD	Alternatives, Canada	Electobras
Comité Catholique Contre la Faim et pour le Développement (CCFD)	ATTAC Norway	Evangelischer Entwicklungsdienst (EED)
Evangelischer Entwicklungsdienst (EED)	Comité Catholique Contre la Faim et pour le Développement (CCFD)	Ford Foundation
Heinrich Boll Foundation	Christian Aid	Fundação Banco do Brasil
Inter Church Organisation for Development Cooperation (ICCO)	Development and Peace	Furnas
Misereor International	Evangelischer Entwicklungsdienst (EED)	Governo do Rio de Grande do Sol
Oxfam International	Funders Network on Trade and Globalisation (FNTG)	Inter Church Organisation for Development Cooperation (ICCO)
Oxfam Belgium	Heinrich Boll Foundation	Infraero, Brazilian Airports
Oxfam Great Britain	Humanist Institute for Co-operation with Developing Countries (HIVOS)	Misereor International
Oxfam Hong Kong	Inter Church Organisation for Development Cooperation (ICCO)	Oxfam Netherlands
Oxfam Netherlands	Members of India General Council for their solidarity contribution	Prefeitura do Municipio de Porto Alegre
Oxfam Spain	Oxfam International	Rockefeller Brothers Fund
	Solidago Foundation	
	Solidarités, Norway	
	Swedish International Development Cooperation Agency (SIDA)	
	Swiss Agency for Development and Cooperation	
	Tides Foundation	
	World Council of Churches	

Notes: Information is not available on the amount of sponsorship offered by any of the organisations or on the funding of WSF 2001 and 2002. The information for 2005 does not distinguish between those who sponsored the process and those who sponsored the forum event.

Source: World Social Forum

Funding and resources

Who actually pays for social forums to take place? The issue of funding is not a simple one, at the world, national or local level. The cost of achieving a continuous forum or of staging major events can be great, especially when they aim to allow space, facilities and access for all. This is much more than a practical matter as sources of, and decisions about, funding have been political issues since the first WSF, and the controversy has increased with the number and size of forums. The actors involved and the size and nature of contributions differ greatly depending on the type and level of the social forum. However, tensions regarding the power of funders and the nature of their associations arise at all levels.

Table 6.5 shows the organisations that have contributed to the WSFs of 2003, 2004 and 2005. In 2003 and 2004, a distinction was made between those sponsors who supported the WSF process and those who contributed to the forum event. Sponsoring organisations include government institutions, business corporations, philanthropic foundations, and a range of NGOs, including charities and religious institutions.

It is from these sources of funding that important political tensions arise. The WSF Charter of Principles, particularly Articles 1 and 4, expresses opposition to corporate-led globalisation and neoliberal economic policies (see Box 6.1). Therefore, accepting funding from corporations and related foundations can appear to be in breach of the Charter. Accepting government funding has also been criticised as opposed to the spirit of the Charter, as Article 8 describes the Forum as non-governmental and Article 9 prevents government representatives from taking part, except in a personal capacity.

Criticism of the funding policy has led WSF organisers to make information about funding available on the official website. However, no information is given on the size or conditions of each organisation's contribution. During 2003 and 2004, corporate, foundation and government funding was mainly donated to the process of the WSF while NGO contributions were donated to the actual event so as to get around the charge that the WSF events were sponsored by the very multinationals to which the Charter expresses opposition (BBC News 2004).

A close examination of the sponsors of the 2003 and 2004 events soon discloses links between these NGOs and business corporations. Indeed, a great number of the civil society organisations that contributed sponsorship are in turn funded by corporate philanthropy and state bodies. An example of this is the Funders Network on Trade and Globalization, which is made up of many different organisations, each with its own funding (FNTG URL), whose deepening relationship with the Organising Committee of the WSF is documented by Caruso (nd). In addition, the funding of many WSF participants, both individuals and organisations, can be traced back at least in part to promoters of capitalist globalisation. This can include the funding of participants' travel to the forum to take part and to organise workshops and events (*Aspects of India's Economy* 2003).

State funding is equally problematic: the 2004 ESF in London was severely criticised for accepting a £400,000 donation from Ken Livingstone, the Mayor of London, and the Greater London Authority (see Box 6.4).

Funding is problematic not only because it may conflict with the Charter of Principles but also because of the power of the funders and the potential for their policies and aims to influence the social forums through the conditions that come with their donations.

Beyond major funding, there are politics involved in all financing decisions: the acceptance of donations, the pricing of event tickets, the setting of budgets and decisions on how money should be spent. They relate not only to the sources of funding but also to tensions between those who think austere, volunteerist initiatives are best, and those who believe money should be spent to raise the profile of forums. Although tensions surrounding funding are increasingly important and problematic as needs increase, they are spurring debate and sometimes provoke creative alternatives, in the best traditions of the forum ideal. As described in Box 6.6, some forums are much better than others at drawing required goods and services from 'solidarity economy', that is, from organisations that privilege equitable or environmental principles over the capitalist pursuit of profit.

Box 6.6: The social forum is not for sale?

'Our world is not for sale' has become one of the core slogans of anti-capitalist movements. It can be clearly seen and heard at many social forums, expressing opposition towards unlimited exploitation of the planet's resources for profit. Indeed, an important focus of debate at forums has been a critique of privatisation policies and unrestricted commercialism, and the development of ideas for alternative economic systems, such as popular or solidarity economy. Arruda (2003) defines solidarity economy as 'all production, distribution and consumption activities that contribute to the democratization of the economy based on citizens commitments both at a local and global level'. Solidarity economy is concerned with bringing about social change through the ways that people buy goods and services, how they save their money, and how they exchange and produce, including initiatives such as ethical investment, fair trade, community agriculture and other forms of collective ownership. The increasing importance of this theme to WSF programmes can be seen in the content analysis in Table 6.4; Article 4 of the WSF Charter of Principles (see Box 6.1) specifically calls for alternatives to a globalisation dominated by large multinationals.

But do the forums live up to these principles or are they becoming commercial events? Are organisers and participants ethical consumers who promote solidarity economy? Or is the format of the social forum 'for sale'? As discussed in this chapter, sourcing funding for forums from multinational corporations and state bodies is contentious, risking as it does contravening the WSF Charter of Principles. Here we focus on the commercialism at forums themselves. The extent of commercialisation varies among the various types and levels of forums but, because each is expected to adhere to the spirit of the Charter, comments can be made on the common barriers to achieving this.

Every forum consumes goods and services – otherwise it could not take place. Participants need transport to reach the venue, and food and accommodation during the event. Organisers must arrange stalls, security and translation services. Therefore, unsurprisingly, some commercialism surrounds each forum, especially the larger annual ones. Mushinge and Mulilo (2005) complain that the 'World social forum is a money spinner', with local hoteliers, airlines and taxi companies forming syndicates to inflate prices to exploit participants. However, this is true of all large events, especially those that attract people from abroad who may not be familiar with local prices. To counter this, forum organisers, particularly at the world and regional levels, attempt to provide for as many needs as possible.

Two examples from recent forums illustrate how decision making guided by the Charter of Principles not only enables adherence to the notion of ethical consumption but encourages the development of solidarity economy. Babels is the unique voluntary network of translators, described in more detail in Box 6.5, which evolved from the need for cost-only translation services in order to promote inclusion and sharing of abilities. The second example is from the WSF in January 2005. Partly due to the efforts of a working group on solidarity economy, and partly because of government support over a number of years, a significant proportion of the goods and services required for the operation of the WSF were produced by more than 1,500 workers in 35 solidarity economy initiatives. For example, cotton bags for registered forum participants were made using environmentally friendly techniques from recycled materials by 500 workers in a not-for-profit cooperative (World Social Forum). By contrast, the 2004 ESF forum in London was criticised for using mainly commercial services and suppliers, including, for example, outsourcing security to a Scottish company, which transported staff by coach from Glasgow (Tempest 2004).

Beyond the services consumed by forum organisers, there is also potential for commercialism within the forum generated by the needs of participants. The World Social Forums at Mumbai in 2004 and Porto Alegre in 2005 were palpably different from previous events, due to the privileging of solidarity economy initiatives for participants' needs. This was most visible in the area of food, with cooperatives offering organic and local dishes, and recycling rubbish. In Mumbai these stalls often also provided information on social action and campaigns in the region where the food was sourced. This approach to resources has been particularly prominent at some local social forums, for example in France, where issues of agricultural reform are high on the agenda. Indeed, the 2003 ESF in Paris was praised for the way organic 'slow food' was promoted, supporting solidarity economy and also environmentally friendly food production techniques. By contrast, the 2004 ESF in London was criticised for failing to follow this example, and for the lack of support for solidarity economy initiatives at the main event. Refreshments were available mainly from in-house caterers at the hired venue, Alexandra Palace, and from commercial 'burger-vans', which paid for the opportunity to sell their wares to participants. Moreover, most of the food available was unsuitable for the significant proportions of vegans and vegetarians at the ESF (Tempest 2004).

Many social forums do involve some element of commercialisation beyond the provision of essentials, such as food, water and accommodation. Most, especially larger, forums often create space for stalls that sell goods as well as promote causes and provide information. Again, the extent of commercialism varies. Positive examples include a stall in Mumbai run by women from a refuge selling pottery to help fund their charity and also to offer information about their campaign for women's protection. On the other hand, there are plenty of examples of commercial stalls, selling a vast range of mass-produced, fashionable items. Heath and Potter (2005) claim that the commercialisation of symbols, such as alternative Coca-Cola logos, Che Guevara images and anti-war slogans on T-shirts, posters and badges, actually demonstrates how the 'counter-culture' has become consumer culture. The proliferation of these stalls has led to the complaint that they make the event nothing more than a conference, with people buying the symbols of causes with which they want to be associated, but not necessarily learning about them or indeed supporting them in any practical way. Another example of this is the presence of universities at the official ESF in London; one stall promoted degree courses in drama, reminiscent of a careers fair rather than a forum of political alternatives.

So is the social forum for sale? This is a danger when the provision of services and consumables is not planned according to the Charter's principles. Where this happens, the forum can become more of a sales floor with a discussion area where the themes of debate are not mirrored by the choices available to participants. Yet, when the principles of solidarity economy are supported, they lead not only to increasingly innovative forms of exchange, production and service provision, but also to a lasting network and infrastructure for maintaining such provision beyond the annual forum.

Jill Timms, LSE

Raising the issue of agriculture at the third WSF in Brazil, 2003 ©Jill Timms

Conclusions

It is often asked what the World Social Forum and its many varied siblings have actually accomplished. No concrete or obvious examples of political triumphs can be cited. However, that is no proof of a lack of achievement. If the forum is conceived of as a space rather than a movement, then, by its nature, success can be attributed not to it but only to the various groups and movements within it. Despite the new 'mural of proposals' of the WSF, many of its activities remain rather subterraneous. In the smaller forums, connections are sometimes more evident. There is clearly a close connection, for instance, between the German social forums and protests about welfare reform.

The influence of the social forums might also be gauged from the evolution of the forum they originally set out to challenge. In 2005, poverty, debt, climate change and equitable globalisation were the main issues addressed by the World Economic Forum (WEF), which set itself the task of implementing concrete measures, including 'the adoption of technology to reduce the emission of greenhouse gases, the creation of a fund to accelerate financial aid to the poorest nations and the removal of trade barriers that deprive developing countries of the dividends of global economic growth' (WEF 2005a). This does not quite sound like the language of the WSF, but it has crept much closer to it. Jacques Chirac, the French President, actually proposed a tax on international financial transactions to the 2005 WEF (WEF 2005b). Indeed, the mood of the meeting was such that Sir Digby Jones, head of the Confederation of British Industry, complained:

> The pendulum is swinging too far in favour of the NGOs. The World Economic Forum is caving in to them. Davos has been hijacked by those who want business to apologise for itself ...We have heard how we are greedy and how we pollute, and how we have got to help Africa. But a celebration of business? No. (Elliott 2005)

Again, there is no hard evidence that this shift in priorities can be attributed to the social forums but, as World Bank and IMF officials visit the WSF incognito (as we have been confidentially advised), there is good reason to believe that it plays a role in the permeation of ideas from the anti-capitalist movement into mainstream global politics.

On the basis of our content analysis, there is much less reason to believe that, as some radicals fear (see Box 6.3), the WSF has been is similarly contaminated by WEF ideas. In 2005, we found only two very small workshops (organised by Civicus and the Danish Confederation of Trade Unions respectively) that suggested explicitly in their workshop titles that civil society might even consider (critical) collaboration with international financial institutions. But it remains to be seen what effect increased interest from funding foundations, corporations, and government might have on actual content.

Even if it remains problematic to attribute specific results to specific forums, it is clear that the forums disseminate ideas and ways of looking at particular problems. A clear example is the method of participatory budgeting pioneered by the Porto Alegre city council, forms of which are now practised by dozens of city councils in Latin America, Europe, and New Zealand. Another theme that has emerged very strongly from the forums – indeed, the mural of proposals teems with it – is the right to water. It connects to earlier campaigns against dams as well as the privatisation of public services, while using the language of human rights. A more recent theme that we will probably hear more of is 'the right to the city'. These are clear examples of the 'discursive infrastructure' created by the coming together and interaction of different types of groups in the social forums; another is the emergence of a 'climate justice movement (Newell, this volume). A more self-conscious effort in this direction is that of the 'intermovement dialogues' initiated by a number of feminist groups in Mumbai in 2004 and continued in Porto Alegre to explore commonalities and conflicts between themselves and anti-racist, labour and sexual rights movements (Feminist Dialogues 2005).

It has emerged very clearly from our research that social forums continue to flourish. The World Social Forum has ever higher numbers of participants and events, and the number of local social forums continues to rise. In a few places like Spain and Colombia, they seem to be largely a spent force, but in Scandinavia and France they are still going strong and in Africa and Germany they are just beginning. However, as we have shown, the social forum movement is only very partially the diverse, dynamic and innovative factory of alternatives it is sometimes portrayed to be. In terms of both its organisation and the rhetoric of its staple speakers, it is and always has been substantially influenced by an Old Left that is hierarchical in its institutions and backward-looking in its solutions to global problems.

Because social forums are still such a young phenomenon, it is impossible to tell at this point whether they will still be a feature of the global civil society landscape in five, ten or twenty years' time, and indeed what shape that feature might have. Part of the attraction will be strategic. The World Social Forum, much more than the regional, national and local ones, has already developed into a 'must-go' for global civil society activists of different ideological persuasions, simply because of the serendipity of finding so many of one's contacts in the same place at the same time. For the local and national forums, this is much less of a raison d'être, but there the purpose of breaching differences and avoiding parallel universes could be more prominent. In this sense, social forums fit within an older tradition of movements such as the anti-colonial movement, the peace movement and in certain countries the communist movement, of encouraging a 'big tent' where different groups can peddle their causes under a single broad ideology. Manifestations of the big tent idea will undoubtedly remain a feature of global civil society, but it is more doubtful whether the unique features of social forums, including self-organisation, consensus-seeking rather than voting, and the avoidance of collective adoption of positions, will survive.

This may depend on whether the social forums remain true to their roots in the anti-capitalist movement or emancipate themselves from this heritage. If social forums remain closely linked to the anti-capitalist movement, their fortunes will follow those of the movement itself. On present evidence it may be partly co-opted and partly marginalised, as is the story of many social movements.

But one of the most exciting things that has come out of the anti-capitalist movement, and has found further expression in the social forums, is the obsession with transforming the organisational process itself. We have shown that social forums have the potential to emancipate forms of organising from residual vanguardism in the movement that spawned them. When they succeed, they simultaneously expand and reconfigure the infrastructure of global civil society.'

REFERENCES

ACORD (URL) 'ACORD Participates in African Social Forum.' www.acord.org.uk/asf.htm (consulted 18 April 2005).

Andretta, M. and Mosca, L. (2004) 'Understanding the Genoa Protest', in R. Taylor (ed) *Creating a Better World: Interpreting Global Civil Society*. Bloomsfield, CT: Kumarian Press.

Anthony, D. and Silva, J. (2005) 'World Social Forum: The Consensus of Porto Alegre?', *Terra Viva*, 30 January. www.ipsnews.net/new_nota.asp?idnews=27250 (consulted 19 April 2005).

Arruda, M (2003) 'What is a Solidarity Economy?' Paper presented at WSF 2003. www.tni.org/archives/arruda/solecon.htm (consulted 10 March 2005).

ASF (African Social Forum) (2004) 'Summary of Proceedings and Decisions of the African Social Forum Council'. Cairo, 27–30 July. www.forumsocialafricain.org/english/caire.htm (consulted 18 April 2005).

Aspects of India's Economy (2003) 'Economics and Politics of the WSF, Appendix II: , Funds for the World Social Forum', *Aspects of India's Economy*, No 35 (September). www.rupe-india.org/35/app2.html (consulted 10 April 2005).

Babels (URL) www.babels.org (consulted 10 April 2005).

BBC News (2001) 'Genoa Violence Claims Police Scalps', 2 August. http://news.bbc.co.uk/1/hi/world/europe/1471107.stm (consulted 30 March 2005).

– (2004) 'Q&A: World Social Forum'. http://news.bbc.co.uk/2/hi/south_asia/3383737.stm (consulted 5 March 2005).

Blaug, Ricardo (1999) *Democracy Real and Ideal*: Discourse Ethics and Radical Politics. Albany: State University of New York Press.

Burbach, R. (2001) 'The Blood of Genoa', *Spotlight*, 1 August. www.redress.btinternet.co.uk/genoa.htm (consulted 10 April 2005).

Cannavo, S. (2001) 'Porto Alegre, Un Altra Strada per l'Umanita', *Carta*, 5 February.

Caruso, G. (n.d.) 'Funders and Funders' Networks in Global Civil Society: The Case of the Funders' Network on Trade and Globalization and the World Social Forum' (unpublished manuscript).

Cock, J. (2004) 'The World Social Forum and New Forms of Social Activism,' in R. Taylor (ed.), *Creating a Better World: Interpreting Global Civil Society*. Bloomsfield, CT: Kumarian Press.

Cohen, J. (1985) 'Strategy or Identity', *Social Research*, 52: 663–716.

De Angelis, M. (2004) '"There Are Many Alternatives!" versus "There is No Alternative!" A World Social Forum Book and the WSF Process', *The Commoner*, No 9 (Spring/Summer). www.commoner.org.uk/tinavstama.htm (consulted 15 March 2005).

Desai, M. and Said, Y. (2001) 'The New Anti-Capitalist Movement: Money and Global Civil Society', in H. Anheier, M. Glasius and M. Kaldor (eds), *Global Civil Society 2001*. Oxford: Oxford University Press.

Elliott, Larry (2005) 'CBI Chief Claims Davos Hijacked by NGOs', *Guardian*, 31 January.

FAIR (2001) 'WTO coverage: Prattle in Seattle'. www.fair.org/activism/wto-prattle.html (consulted 20 April 2005).

Falk, R. (1999) *Predatory Globalization: A Critique*. Cambridge: Polity Press.

Farrer, L. (2002) 'World Forum Movement: Abandon or Contaminate?' www.nadir.org/nadir/initiativ/agp/free/wsf/worldforum.htm (consulted 9 April 2005).

Feminist Dialogues (2005) 'Dialogue Between Movements to Discuss the Politics of Differences', 24 January. http://feministdialogue.isiswomen.org/modules.php?op=mod load&name=News&file=article&sid=9&mode=thread&order =0&thold=0 (consulted 19 April 2005).

FNTG (URL) Funders Network on Trade and Globalization. www.fntg.org/index.php (consulted 12 May 2005).

Foro Social de Madrid (2003) 'Manifiesto del Foro Social de Madrid', 17 December. www.nodo50.org/estudiantesdeizquierdas/article.php3?id_ar ticle=29 (consulted 9 April 2005).

Freeman, Jo (1972) 'The Tyranny of Structurelessness', *Berkeley Journal of Sociology*, 17: 151–65.

Glasius, M. (2005) 'Deliberation or Struggle? Civil Society Traditions Behind the Social Forums', *Ephemera*, 5(2). www.ephemeraweb.org (consulted 24 May 2005).

Grenier, P (2004) 'The New Pioneers: The People Behind Global Civil Society', in H. Anheier, M. Glasius and M. Kaldor (eds.), *Global Civil Society 2004/5*. London: Sage.

Grubacic, A. (2003) 'Life After Social Forums: New Radicalism and the Questions of Attitude Towards Social Forums'. www.nadir.org/nadir/initiativ/agp/free/wsf/life-after-sf.htm (consulted 9 April 2005).

Hamburg South Social Forum (2004) 'Solidaritätserklärung des Sozialforums Hamburger Süden mit den Aktionen der Opel-Beschäftigten' [Declaration of Solidarity of the Hamburg South Social Forum with the Actions of the Opel Employees], 17 October. www.sozialforum-hh.de/inhalt/harburg/detail.php?nr=703 &kategorie=harburg (consulted 19 April 2005).

Heath, J. and Potter, A. (2005) *The Rebel Sell: How the Counterculture Became the Consumer Culture*. Albany, OR: Capstone Publishing.

Indymedia (2005) 'Senegalese NGOs Fight Lottery Privatisation', 19 March. http://newswire.indymedia.org/pt/newswire/2004/03/801064. shtml (consulted 19 April 2005).

Intercontinental Youth Camp (URL) http://english.acampamentofsm.org (consulted 1 April 2005).

Juris, J. (2004) 'Networked Social Movements: Global Movements for Global Justice', in Manuel Castells (ed.), *The Network Society: A Cross-Cultural Perspective*. London: Edward Elgar.

– (2005) 'The New Digital Media and Activist Networking within Anti-Corporate Globalization Movements', in E. Klinenberg (ed.), *Cultural Production in a Digital Age* (Special edition of The Annals of the American Academy of Political and Social Science). New York: Sage.

– (forthcoming) 'Social Forums and their Margins: Networking Logics and the Cultural Politics of Autonomous Space', in S. Bohm, S. Sullivan and O. Reyes (eds), *www.ephemeraweb.org*

Kaldor, M. (2003) Global Civil Society: An Answer to War. Cambridge: Polity.

Kaldor, M., Anheier, H. and Glasius, M. (2003) 'Global Civil Society in an Era of Regressive Globalisation', in M. Kaldor, H. Anheier and M. Glasius (eds), Global Civil Society 2003. Oxford: Oxford University Press.

Kenya Social Forum (2005) 'Don't Trade Away Our Farmers and Our Workers Livelihoods!'. Statement from Kenyan Civil Society in Relation to the WTO Mini Ministerial in Kenya 2nd–4th March 2005. www.ogiek.org/news/news-post-05-03-4.htm (consulted 19 April 2005).

Kingsnorth, P. (2003) One No, Many Yeses: A Journey to the Heart of the Global Resistance Movement. London: Free Press.

Klein, N. (2001) 'The Unknown Icon', Guardian, 3 March.

Krut, Riva (1997) Globalization and Civil Society: NGO Influence in International Decision-Making. Geneva: United Nations Research Institute for Social Development.

Le Grignou, B. and Patou, C. (2004) 'ATTAC(k)ing Expertise: Does the Internet Really Democratize Knowledge', in Win van de Donk et al. (eds), Cyberprotest: New Media, Citizens and Social Movements. London: Routledge.

Melucci, A. (1980) 'The New Social Movements: A Theoretical Approach', Social Science Information, 19(2): 199–226.

Millstein, C (2002) 'Another World is Possible... But What Kind, and Shaped by Whom?', Anarchist Opinion. www.infoshop.org/rants/cindy_awip.html (consulted 9 April 2005).

Monro, S. (2004) 'Zimbabwe Social Forum: the Future Beckons', Workers' Liberty, 23 November. www.workersliberty.org/node/view/3407 (consulted 19 April 2005).

MS (Mellemfolkeligt Samvirke) (2004) 'MS-Zimbabwe Supports a Successful Social Forum'. zimbabwe.ms.dk/articles/zimsocforum.htm (consulted 19 April 2005).

Mushinge, G. and Mulilo, D. (2005) 'World Social Forum is a Money Spinner'. V International Ciranda of Independent Information. www.ciranda.net/cgi-bin/twiki/view/English/WebHome?inc1=Artigos&inc2=NewsItem20050131214036DeborahMoreira&CGISESSID=b52f07b1db251c152db3f2ebe655f28e, (consulted 2 March 2005).

Muyoba, N. (2003) 'SASF calls on the Africa Social Forum to be held in Africa', SASF News, No 3 (November). http://earth.prohosting.com/sasf2003 (consulted 19 May 2005).

Nadir (URL) www.nadir.org (consulted 9 April 2005).

Northwest Social Forum (2004a) 'Indigenous Programming Committee Statement on the Northwest Social Forum', 23 September. www.nwsocialforum.org/?q=news/ipcstatement (consulted 19 April 2005).

– (2004b) 'Voice, Mind, Music: Youth Planning Committee Statement', 28 September. www.nwsocialforum.org/?q=news/ypcstatement (consulted 19 April 2005).

Nunes, R. (2004) 'Territory and Deterritory: Inside and Outside the ESF 2004, New Movement Subjectivities'. www.euromovements.info/newsletter/nunes.htm?sid=04/10/29/1410226 (consulted 12 May 2005).

Nunes, R., Dowling, E. and Juris, J. (2005) 'The Fertility of the Borders: the Caracol Intergalactika at the WSF 2005'. Red Pepper, March.

Obando, Ana Elena (2005). 'Sexism in the World Social Forum: Is Another World Possible?'. Women's Human Rights Net, February. http://www.whrnet.org/docs/issue-sexism_wsf.html

OD Today (2005) 'Porto Alegre Manifesto in English', 11 February. http://opendemocracy.typepad.com/wsf/2005/02/previous_posts_.html (consulted 19 April 2005).

OpenDemocracy (URL) DIY World. www.opendemocracy.net/debates/issue-3-91.jsp (consulted 15 April 2005).

Ortellado, P. (2003) 'Whose Movement?' www.nadir.org/nadir/initiativ/agp/free/wsf/whosement.htm (consulted 9 April 2005).

Patomäki, H. and Teivanen, T. (2004) 'The World Social Forum: An Open Space or a Movement of Movements?', Theory, Culture & Society, 21(6): 145–54.

Pianta, M (2001) 'Parallel Summits of Global Civil Society', in H. Anheier, M. Glasius, and M. Kaldor (eds), Global Civil Society 2001. Oxford: Oxford University Press.

Scholte, J. (ed.) (2002) Civil Society and Global Finance. London: Routledge.

Sen, J. (2004). 'The Long March to Another World: Reflections of a Member of the WSF India Committee in 2002 on the First Year of the World Social Forum Process in India', in J. Sen et al (eds), World Social Forum: Challenging Empires. New Delhi: The Viveka Foundation.

Sen, J., Anand, A., Escobar, A. and Waterman, P. (eds) (2004) World Social Forum: Challenging Empires. New Delhi: The Viveka Foundation.

Smith, J. (2005) 'Observations from the European Social Forum, London 2004: A Cooperative Research Initiative', 12 January. www.kent.ac.uk/sspssr/demos (consulted

Sullo, Pierluigi (2001a) 'Allegri Saluti, Cartoline dal Nuovo Mondo', Il Manifesto, 31 January.

– (2001b) 'Note Allegre Dopo Il Forum', Il Manifesto, 4 February.

Teivanen, T. (2002) 'The World Social Forum and Global Democratisation: Learning from Porto Alegre', Third World Quarterly, 23(4): 621–32.

– (2003) 'World Social Forum: What Should It Be When it Grows Up?', DIY World, openDemocracy, 10 July. http://opendemocracy.net/debates/article-6-91-1342.jsp (consulted 19 May 2005).

Tempest, M. (2004) 'ESF Closes with Mass Protest', Guardian, 18 October.

Tleane, C. (2004) 'Forum to Confront Critical Questions', African Flame, No 1, 10 December.

Transform! Europe (2004) 'World Social Forum: A Debate on the Challenges for its future', Newsletter 1, March. www.transform.it/newsletter/newsletter01.pdf (consulted 19 April 2005).

Van Rooy, Alison (2004) The Global Legitimacy Game: Civil Society, Globalisation and Protest. Basingstoke: Palgrave Macmillan.

Voices from Mumbai (URL) www.voicesfrommumbai.webhop.org (consulted 5 March 2005).

Wainwright, H. (2003) *Reclaim the State: Experiments in Popular Democracy*. London: Verso.

– (2004a) 'The Forum as Jazz', in J. Sen et al (eds), *World Social Forum: Challenging Empires*. New Delhi: The Viveka Foundation.

– (2004b) 'Civil Society, Democracy and Power: Global Connections', in H. Anheier, M. Glasius, and M. Kaldor (eds), *Global Civil Society 2004/5*. London: Sage.

– (2004c) 'Western Europe: Democratic Civil Society versus Neoliberalism', in M. Glasius, D. Lewis and M. Seckinelgin (eds), *Exploring Civil Society: Political and Cultural Contexts*. London: Routledge.

Wallerstein, Immanuel (2004) 'The Rising Strength of the World Social Forum', *Transform! Europe*, Newsletter 1, March. www.transform.it/newsletter/newsletter01.pdf (consulted 19 April 2005).

Waterman, P. and Timms, J. (2004) 'Trade Union Internationalism and a Global Civil Society in the Making', in H. Anheier, M. Glasius and M. Kaldor (eds), *Global Civil Society 2004/5*. London: Sage Publications.

WEF (World Economic Forum) (2005a) 'Annual Meeting Sets Action Priorities for 2005'. www.weforum.org/site/homepublic.nsf/Content/Annual+Meeting+2005#21, (consulted 19 April 2005).

– (2005b) 'Chirac Proposes Voluntary Tax to Fight Poverty'. www.weforum.org/site/homepublic.nsf/Content/Annual+Meeting+2005#21, (consulted 19 April 2005).

Whitaker, Francisco (Chico) (2004a) 'World Social Forum: Origins and Aims'. *Transform! Europe*, Newsletter 1, March (first published January 2004). www.transform.it/newsletter/newsletter01.pdf (consulted 19 April 2005).

– (2004b) 'The WSF as Open Space', in J. Sen et al. (eds), *World Social Forum: Challenging Empires*. New Delhi: The Viveka Foundation. www.choike.org/documentos/wsf_s302_whitaker.pdf (consulted 1 April 2005).

World Forum for Alternatives Manifesto (1997) *South Letter*, No 28. www.southcentre.org/southletter/sl28/SL28%20HTMLtrans-04.htm (consulted 19 April 2005).

WSF (World Social Forum) (2001) *World Social Forum Charter of Principles*, 10 June. www.nycsocialforum.org/about_wsf/wsf_charter.html (consulted 10 February 2005).

– (URLa) Alternative Media. www.forumsocialmundial.org.br/dinamic.php?pagina=fsmMidiaEN (consulted 10 April 2005).

– (URLb) Memorials. www.forumsocialmundial.org.br/main.php?id_menu=14&cd_language=2 (consulted 5 April 2005).

Social forum websites (consulted 25 April 2005)

African Social Forum 2002. www.enda.sn/objectifs.htm

African Social Forum 2003. www.enda.sn/Forum%20social/english

African Social Forum 2004. www.forumsocialafricain.org/english/index.htm

Alpes du Sud Social Forum. www.fsas.ras.eu.org

Argentina Social Forum. www.forosocialargentino.org

Belgium Social Forum. www.wsf.be

Berlin Social Forum. www.sozialforum-berlin.de

Boston Social Forum. www.bostonsocialforum.org/news.php

Brisbane Social Forum. www.brisbanesocialforum.org

Cardiff Social Forum. www.cardiffsocialforum.org.uk

Castile Social Forum. www.forocastellano.org

Chicago Social Forum. www.chicagosocialforum.org

Chile Social Forum. www.forosocialchileno.cl

Düsseldorf Social Forum. http://duesseldorfersozialforum.de

Duisburg Social Forum. www.sozialforum-duisburg.de

European Social Forum. www.fse-esf.org

Gironde Social Forum. www.fsl33.net

Gironde Social Forum (alternative website). http://fsl33.apinc.org

Iran Social Forum. www.iransocialforum.org

Istanbul Social Forum. www.geocities.com/sosyalforum

Ivry Social Forum. www.fsivry.free.fr

Kenya Social Forum. www.socialforum.or.ke/about.htm

Limburg Social Forum. www.lsf.be/index2.php

Madrid Social Forum (new URL). www.forosocialmadrid.org

Mapuche Social Forum. www.forosocialchileno.cl/forosgrande.htm

Mediterranean Social Forum 2005. www.fsmed.info

Melbourne Social Forum. www.melbournesocialforum.org

Morocco Social Forum. www.forumsocialmaroc.org

Netherlands Social Forum. www.sociaalforum.nl

New York City Social Forum. www.nycsocialforum.org

New Zealand Social Forum 2003. www.socialforum.org.nz

North Germany Social Forum. www.ndsf.org

Northwest Social Forum (US). www.nwsocialforum.org

Orleans Social Forum. www.associations45.ras.eu.org

Pan Amazonian Social Forum. www.ivforumpan.com.br

Paris Centre Social Forum. www.fsl-paris-centre.net

Santa Fe Social Forum. www.fsmsantafe.lunix.com.ar

Social Forum in Germany. www.sozialforum2005.de

Social Forum of the Americas (2004). www.forosocialamericas.org

Social Forum on Climate Change. www.environmentaldefense.org/article.cfm?contentid=3066

Social Forum on Health in Argentina. www.cicop.org.ar/forosalud

Southern African Social Forum (2003). earth.prohosting.com/sasf2003

Sydney Social Forum. www.sydneysocialforum.org

World Social Thematic Forum Democracy, Human Rights, War and Drug Trafficking. www.fsmt.org.co/presentation.htm

Toronto Social Forum. www.torontosocialforum.ca

Uruguay Social Forum. www.forosocialuruguay.org.uy

World Education Forum. www.portoalegre.rs.gov.br/fme

World Social Forum. www.forumsocialmundial.org.br

World Social Forum India. www.wsfindia.org/index.php.

World Social Forum on Health. www.transhumanism.org/index.php/WTA/index

CHAPTER 7

GLOBAL CONNECTEDNESS:
THE STRUCTURE OF TRANSNATIONAL NGO NETWORKS

Hagai Katz and Helmut Anheier

Introduction

Globalisation involves the movement of objects (such as goods, services, finance and other resources), meaning (for example, language, symbols, knowledge and identities) and people across regional and intercontinental space. It is a process that turns what has been local and national into transnational and increasingly global flows – be it in the field of trade, information technologies, or epidemics such as HIV/AIDS and SARS (Kaul 2003). Among the consequences of globalisation are the increasing scope and scale of existing supranational structures and patterns, and the emergence of new ones. International nongovernmental organisations (INGOs), transnational corporations (TNCs), states, international governmental organisations (IGOs), and, of course, individuals participate in a great variety of international forums, conventions, meetings, organisations, and coalitions. In other words, they are creating transnational networks of many kinds.

It is useful to view these transnational networks as some kind of 'global infrastructure' generated by, and allowing for, the flow of resources, information, knowledge, influence, legitimacy, and so on. For example, TNCs form networks of finance-product-service-consumption chains around transnational markets, involving organisations (firms, regulatory agencies) and individuals as employees and consumers. Similarly, the international system of law and politics, based on bilateral and multilateral contracts, generates a network of international relations, just as links among diaspora communities or political activists form transnational networks between individuals. Last but not least, INGOs form networks based on information exchange, project collaboration, participation in meetings and forums, or joint membership in advocacy coalitions.

Network metaphors are indeed very common in the globalisation literature. Terms like 'inter-connectedness' or 'woven world' (Yergin and Stanislav 1998) seek to express how transnational actors connect formerly disparate entities and issues. John Keane (2001: 23–4) describes global civil society as an 'interconnected and multilayered social space' comprised of 'cross border networks (and) chains of interaction' linking the local to the global. James Rosenau (1995) describes global governance as a framework of horizontal relations between states and between non-state actors. David Held's notion of global governance (2004) suggests a complicated web of interrelated global issue networks, some that are issue-specific and others more general, together forming a large web of governments, NGOs, IGOs, TNCs and other interested parties. The inter-organisational structure around the International Criminal Court (ICC) is an example of one such global issue network (for a brief analysis of the ICC see the methods chapter in this volume), where INGOs, IGOs and governments came together and developed a new global governance institution.

> network structures bound the possibilities of action; they prevent some actions but encourage and facilitate others

Ulrich Beck (1999) proposes to examine the scale, density, and stability of such regional–global networks, the social spaces they create and the cultural images they carry. In his view, the continued expansion and contraction along local–global axes creates patterns of varying density and centrality in these global networks. Manuel Castells (1996) takes this imagery further to argue that networks increasingly form meta-networks at the transnational level and create a system of 'decentralized concentration', where a multiplicity of interconnected tasks takes place in different sites. Since the 1970s, Castells points out, enabling technologies such as IT and the internet have brought about the ascendancy of a 'network society', whose processes occur in a new type of space which he labels the 'space of flows'. This space, comprising a myriad of exchanges, has come to dominate the 'space of places' of territorially defined units of states, regions and neighbourhoods thanks to its greater flexibility and compatibility with the new logic of network society. Nodes and hubs in this space of flows construct the social organisation of this network society. For Castells, this new space is at the core of the globalisation process; and, for understanding global civil society within the larger process of a shift from 'place' to 'flows,' networks are the central concept.

Yet what precisely are the characteristic network structures of global civil society, as measured through INGO networks? Presumably, such a network would involve activists as well as representatives of civil society organisations of many kinds. It would also include inter-organisational relationships like coalitions among INGOs as well as funding flows between philanthropic institutions and recipient groups. These connections form structures and patterns, which involve numerous types of actors – individuals such as citizens, activists and scientists, organisations, governments, corporations, as well as others. But why is it important to know about such network structures, and how would this improve our understanding of global civil society? These are the major questions that we address in the present chapter.

INGO networks are obviously limited in terms of the kind of relationship they include; most notably, they leave out networks among individuals as well as between individuals and organisations. They also do not cover other more organised relations that are important in global civil society, such as social movements, social forums, and the like. Yet at a minimum they allow us to ask important questions about the potential of INGO networks for global action and mobilisation processes within the broader conext of the structural patterns of economic and political globalisation.

At one level, network structures bound the possibilities of action; they prevent some actions but encourage and facilitate others. As Cox (1993: 36) puts it, the structural constraints define 'the limits of the possible'. At the same time, however, action defines and modifies structure; actors can create new links, altering the structure, and as a result also the repertoire of actions available to them (Diani 2003a; 2003c; Cox 1993). In this sense, networks are structures created through agency, and analysing such networks provides us with the opportunity to capture the dualistic nature of action and structure. Specifically, looking at the network structures of global civil society will help us better understand their spatial patterns in terms of centre-periphery and inclusion

and exclusion, and whether they and the spaces they create promote or hinder collective action at the global level, and to what end.

This brings us to the issue of global governance. Global civil society is often presented as the remedy for some of the problems of global governance (Kaldor 2003; Kaldor, Anheier and Glasius 2003; Held 2004). As Riva Krut (1997) maintains, global civil society has two major roles in global governance – as part of the system of checks and balances, promoting the transparency and accountability of global governance institutions, and as representatives of the weak and marginalised, a window for popular participation in global governance. Some of the authors of recent accounts of global civil society's role in global governance argue that NGOs are still marginal in many of the circles of power in the global governance system (Held 2004), and are mostly treated as 'second priority' players (Scholte 2004). Can global civil society, as measured here in terms of INGO relations, compensate for weaknesses of the global governance system?

While a fuller set of answers is developed in the course of this chapter (and specifically in Katz 2005), it is useful to summarise our key insights at the outset. Our analysis finds the structural pattern generated by INGO networks relatively coherent and little fragmented, which is conducive to alleviating the political-jurisdictional gap in global governance. In other words, global civil society as measured by INGO networks can be a holistic and coherent 'actor' in the global governance system, one that can address many of the critical issues synergistically. By contrast, however, it is unlikely that this very same pattern could contribute to increased representativeness or inclusion in the global governance system, let alone heighten substantially the participation of currently marginalised constituencies. As we shall see, the network structure is very sparse and reveals a pronounced centre-periphery structure, and it is simply too concentrated in the North. As a result, its capacity to make authentic voices of Southern communities heard in the corridors of global power remains limited. In the concluding section of this chapter we address the implications of these findings.

The authors would like to thank Professor Jan De Leew from the Department of Statistics, UCLA, for his help with the correspondence analysis.

Figure 7.1: Climate Action Network's global network structure

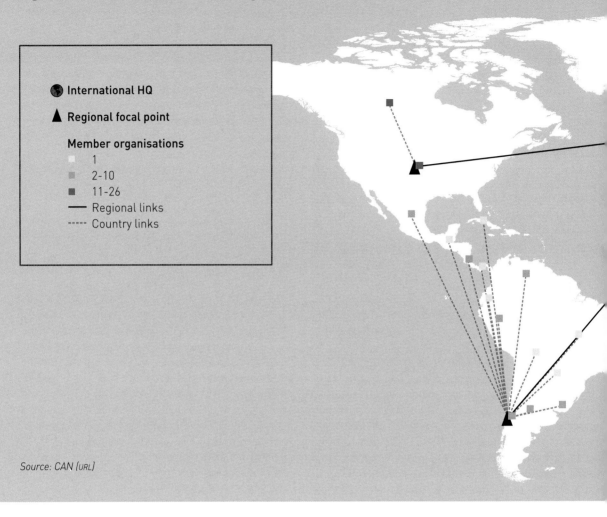

Source: CAN (URL)

Global civil society networks

Global civil society is a very relational, networked phenomenon (Anheier and Katz 2004). Indeed, as we have already illustrated, the globalisation and civil society literature is rich in network metaphors. Yet network metaphors of global civil society more often than not remain abstract, with little empirical research using network concepts, and still fewer studies implementing network analysis methods. As Peter Waterman (2000: 144) humorously puts it, 'network babble therefore needs, today, to be replaced by network analysis'. Many writers decry the lack of evidence-based network studies of global civil society. Townsend (1999) points out that, despite frequent reference to the 'network' character of global civil

society as a structured space, analytical portraits or global maps showing the implied connectedness and resulting patterns are still missing. As a first step, some authors suggest that civil society be studied by focusing on the relationships between different INGOs (Florini and Simmons 2000; Deacon 1997). Yet to date no such studies have explored such networks systematically at a global level.

What is a network?

A network is a set of links or ties connecting nodes. The nodes are typically people or organisations, and the links involve many different types of relations and flows: contracts, joint projects, including funding, joint board members, information exchange, and even affect

relations. Networks are a way of measuring the patterns and structures of social life, including, as we do here, organisational and inter-organisational links. In global civil society specific organisations and networks can be highly complex structures, as is evident in the organisational design of the global Climate Action Network shown in Figure 7.1. The global Climate Action Network, 'a worldwide network of over 340 Non- Governmental Organisations (NGOs) working to promote government and individual action to limit human-induced climate change to ecologically sustainable levels' (CAN URL) is one INGO network with a highly complex design that includes multiple headquarters and a decentralised federated structure. Yet, however complex, it is only one fragment of the full network of global civil society.

Of course, the complete structure of the global civil society network adds to this one complex network thousands of other networks and individual organisations, intra- and inter-organisational networks, some even more complex than the global Climate Action Network, and involves more nodes and links than can be displayed in a graph. Therefore, much of what network analysis does is to examine complex personal or inter-organisational networks to reveal the underlying patterns that might lend themselves more easily to some forms of understanding (Anheier and Katz 2004).

This chapter focuses exclusively on inter-organisational networks among INGOs. Although such networks are a major part of the global civil society infrastructure, they leave out two important aspects: network ties among individuals such as civil society leaders; and inter-organisational connections generated by person-to-person contacts across institutions. In particular, interlocking network structures are critical for information flows, mobilisation of resources and the overall degree of inclusion or exclusion of given fields.

In this box, I briefly illustrate these aspects, using the example of international scientific communities as a case in point. Scientists and academics generally form interpersonal ties based on collegiality, information exchange or joint projects and publications. They also establish affiliations with institutions, for example, as members of advisory committees or funding bodies, or acting as external examiners. By doing so, they generate two networks: an interpersonal one linking scientists, and an institutional one linking scientists to organisations. Although networks among civil society activists differ from those among academics in many respects, they have in common that they are communities of meaning and knowledge, so that examining one could help us to understand the other.

Who joins international scientific communities? And how are the scientists who work on international scientific assessments connected? Since the late 1980s, scholars have studied such international communities, exploring 'networks of knowledge-based experts' or what have come to be called 'epistemic communities' (Haas 1992: 2; see also Haas 1989; 1990; Lidskog and Sundqvist 2002). Scholars have used this notion to describe the relationship between scientific communities and international policies such as the Mediterranean Plan of Action (Haas 1989; 1990), the International Food Aid Regime (Hopkins 1992), and the international management of whaling (Peterson 1992), focusing mainly on how epistemic communities address the uncertainties surrounding specific social problems.

The Millennium Ecosystem Assessment (MA) is a case in point. Launched in 2001 by the Secretary General of the United Nations as 'an international work program designed to meet the needs of decision makers and the public for scientific information concerning the consequences of ecosystem change for human well-being and options for responding to those changes' (MA URL), the MA aims to involve the top scientists from around the world in the evaluation of the state of the science of biodiversity and ecosystem loss. Through its four working groups (sub-global, conditions, scenarios, and responses), members of the MA, its Board, and other participants have nominated over 3,000 scientists to participate in the assessment[a], more than 500 of whom have contributed to drafting the group's First Assessment Review, which is scheduled to be published in late 2005.

Although the organisers of this scientific assessment set out to bring together a group of scientists who were diverse in terms of geography and disciplines, and working on issues related to its focus, it is probable that the MA's formation, which involved a multi-stage nominations process, involved a relatively homophilous group of scholars. 'Homophily' is the tendency of individuals to associate with those similar to them, and 'implies that distance in terms of social characteristics translates into network distance...' (McPherson, Smith-Lovin and Cook 2001: 416; see also McPherson and Smith-Lovin 1987; Ruef, Aldrich and Carter 2003). Consequently, the scientists conscripted into this network of biodiversity specialists had central social characteristics in common.

Using data collected through participant observation and a survey of the MA's members, I examined whether the nominations process limited the representation of scholars who were not already involved in other international communities. Such constraints could imply limitations on, for example, particular disciplines and scientific perspectives and on representatives from less developed regions of the world. Preliminary data analyses suggest that that recruitment into the MA frequently occurred through homophilous network ties. In other words, most participants in this scientific assessment had already worked together through other international organisations at least once – which also suggests a certain path dependency and reproduction of network ties[b]. Table 7.1 presents descriptive statistics of the connections among members of the MA. These findings are particularly interesting when one examines the most common ties among the MA's participants, all of which provided backing for the MA itself[c].

Table 7.1: Organisational ties among participants in the Millennium Ecosystem Assessment

Observations (N)	368		
Minimum	1	Mean	2.68
Maximum	17	Standard deviation	2.45

In many cases, participants in the MA had multiple common ties through international organisations. Figure 7.2 presents a map of the inter-organisational network created by the connections among these scholars. The density of this network supports the supposition that there was considerable homophily within the MA. In many cases, participants had collaborated on other United Nations-sponsored projects prior to their association through the MA.

Figure 7.2: Millennium Ecosystem Assessment: inter-organisational ties through individual participants

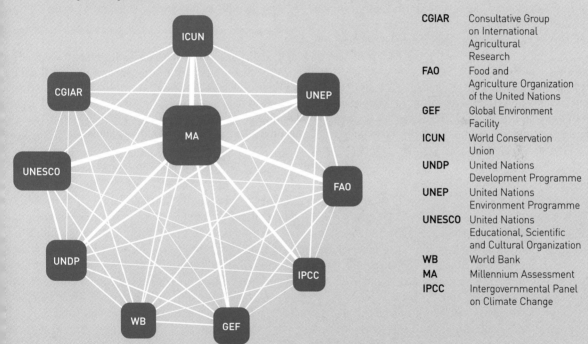

CGIAR	Consultative Group on International Agricultural Research
FAO	Food and Agriculture Organization of the United Nations
GEF	Global Environment Facility
ICUN	World Conservation Union
UNDP	United Nations Development Programme
UNEP	United Nations Environment Programme
UNESCO	United Nations Educational, Scientific and Cultural Organization
WB	World Bank
MA	Millennium Assessment
IPCC	Intergovernmental Panel on Climate Change

This finding has significant implications for global civil society networks and for the tensions between network diversity and efficiency. Because individuals involved tend to nominate others who are similar to them and with whom they have interacted in the past, interpersonal transnational networks are likely to generate homophilous structures and appear exclusive rather than inclusive. By implication, more diverse networks would require more exhaustive reviews of potential members, and the recruitment process would have to extend beyond the common connections among those already participating in the international community. This extension, however, adds to the costs of organising and maintaining the network.

a This process began with multiple nominations from the director and board of the MA. Although some people involved in the MA were self-nominated, their self-nominations had to be approved by a chair of one of the working groups.
b The international organisations listed in the survey include those that provided funding and support for the MA as well as the other major international environmental assessments.
c The most common organisations, besides the MA itself, are the Food and Agriculture Organization of the UN (FAO), United Nations Development Programme (UNDP), the United Nations Environment Programme (UNEP), and the World Conservation Union (IUCN).

Dana R. Fisher, Department of Sociology, Columbia University

Networks matter

Why study the networks of global civil society? The answer is simple: because network structure has an impact on outcomes for the individuals and organisations involved as well as for the network as a whole. The social movement literature is very instructive in illustrating this point: activist networks are affected by the overall configuration of the network structures they are part of, and how these structures influence the potential for collective action (Diani 2003a; McAdam 2003). Most social movement scholars agree that network structure is crucial to the development of movement formation; since actors are usually drawn to a movement by people they know (Gould 2003; see also Chapter 8, this volume). Established associational networks play a central role in facilitating contention. If a mobilising structure is absent, incipient movements lack the capacity to act, even if the opportunity to do so arises (McAdam 2003: 290–1).

Both Mario Diani (2003a; 2003b) and Beth Caniglia (2002) highlight the importance of centrality and brokerage in the network on the network's influence on policy-making. Diani suggests that centrality (a node is considered central when it is connected to more nodes) correlates with leadership and public visibility and has an influence on agenda-setting. In the network he studied (a network of environmental organisations in Milan), more central organisations were generally perceived (by outsiders as well as insiders) as representative of the entire network and the issues it promoted. Brokerage (when a node helps to connect otherwise disconnected nodes), on the other hand, contributed mostly to the integration of the network, and was mostly done behind the scenes. Brokerage was not associated with visibility, as centrality was found to be, but it was found to facilitate communication lines between different subgroups of the movement and to connect divergent organisations. Moreover, Caniglia concludes that brokerage and centrality roles in NGO networks correlate with greater connectedness to international governmental organisations (IGOs). In other words, NGOs central in the NGO network assume brokerage roles in relation to international organisations more generally.

Compositional diversity of the network has also been identified as a factor in successful movements or coalitions. Sanjeev Khagram (2002) points out that a diverse composition, mixing local and global actors grassroots and elite organisations, differing ideolo-gies, and different strategies (for example, passive resistance, lobbying, confrontation), is what made the coalitions around the Narmada Valley dams in India so successful in their attempt to change the World Bank's politics of development. The Narmada campaigns were successful in part due to the broadbased, interlaced set of issues and organisations that featured in the campaign, including environmental concerns, anti-capitalism, human rights, and development, among others.

> network structure has an impact on outcomes for the individuals and organisations involved as well as for the network as a whole

Looking at a different movement, Elizabeth Donnelly (2002) shows that, as the global scope of the debt reduction network grew, so did its impact. This increase was made possible by greater compatibility between the scope and breadth of anti-debt network and the multilateral nature of world trade and debt. Compositional diversity of networks implies a mix of different issues and interests for achieving greater impact. In this context, Diani (2003c) notes that network diversity is multiplicative, as it opens channels of communication to varied populations of organisations. In turn, issue diversity is also linked to strategic diversity, flexibility, and adjustment to change. By implication, the challenge of movements is to balance too much diversity, which can lead to lack of coherence, and too little diversity around single issues that opponents can more easily isolate or otherwise neutralise.

Global network patterns and functions

What emerges from this brief review of transnational social movements and networks is the close link between inter-organisational relations and trans-national connectedness. Yet what overall patterns of connectedness can we hypothesise? What role or functions would such an emerging 'organisational infrastructure' of global civil society perform? And critically: what is the relation between structure and function? In approaching these questions, it is useful to seek theoretical guidance from the civil society literature first.

Antonio Gramsci and his followers see in a dense

Table 7.2: Sample network matrix

	To Organisation A	Organisation B	Organisation C	...
From **Organisation A**	–	1	1	...
Organisation B	0	–	0	...
Organisation C	1	0	–	...
...	...	...	...	–

network of connectedness and in a solid organisational infrastructure a precondition for the development of civil society into a counter-hegemonic bloc – a bloc that can challenge existing power structures[1]. We suggest that what holds for national systems could also apply to the global level: such a bloc would serve the function of offering a viable alternative in the systems of global governance to global neo-liberalism (Cox 1993; 1996; 2002; Gill 1993; Gramsci 1971) or other dominant ideologies and institutions that are seen as problematic or unjust. Such a bloc would incorporate a wide range of parties that take issue with prevailing policies and patterns of economic and political globalisation – and do so across regions, classes, constituencies, and so forth. This bloc, as an all-inclusive network, would help guarantee more equal and fuller representation of interests in the global governance system, and thereby also reaffirm the legitimacy that is the consequence of such fuller representation.

Specifically, in the case of INGOs several characteristics would indicate the presence of a bloc. First, INGO networks would have to show global reach or, in Held and McGrew's term (2002), 'extensity'. Second, this global reach must show some spread in numbers and centrality; that is, it should allow for multiple centres of influence and a brokerage role to emerge. Third, it must show compositional diversity and incorporate different issues, coalitions and interests. If these characteristics are present, INGO networks can help reaffirm full and significant participation of more peoples and communities in the processes of global governance, setting the priorities of global governance institutions, and keeping an eye on governments and TNCs.

Another aspect of the reach of the global civil society network is the enhancement of the local-global nexus.

Local presence has the important potential of generating local grassroots activism and empowering such local activism with the support of an international backing. According to Margaret Keck and Kathryn Sikkink (1998), a local-global mix allows for the so-called boomerang effect, whereby the organisations of local protestors against national governments forge links with INGOs in other countries, which, in turn, mobilise their own governments and other constituencies to exert pressure on their behalf from outside. Hence, participation in such global civil society networks potentially allows access to power – it allows local INGOs to reach, if by proxy, the centres of decision making in Brussels, New York and London. It provides them with indirect access to large influential INGOs, governments and IGOs.

Castells (1997) argues that avoiding localism is important to thwart the attempts of global capitalist elites to co-opt and weaken resistance, since to be able to have impact on the circles of power of the network society, which are placeless, resistance identities need to become placeless as well. Expanding local campaigns into global networks (as Zapatistas did) elevates them from operating in the space of places to operating in the space of flows, thus giving them greater visibility where it really counts.

But what if transnational NGO connectedness is very uneven across regions and fields, and what if the organisational infrastructure does not reflect Gramscian

---

1 Obviously, Gramsci didn't advocate network density, if only because the concept wasn't in existence in his time. However, Gramsci advocated the development of a counter-hegemonic historic bloc which, he argued, to be of value should include all of the subaltern groups and interests, including workers and other groups. When read with a network mindset, this translates into a dense network in the sense that many of the ties that can possibly exist between those subaltern groups are actually in existence.

Figure 7.3: **Network densities: INGOs and other global networks**

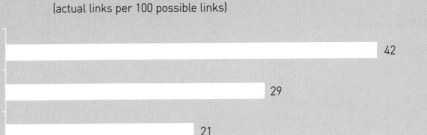

Network density
(actual links per 100 possible links)

International students flows (countries)	42
World trade flows (countries)	29
Embassy links (countries)	21
INGO links (countries)	14
Refugees flows (countries)	11

0   5   10   15   20   25   30   35   40   45

blocs, boomerang patterns or local-global relations? What if emerging network patterns are more reflective of existing power structures than counter-hegemonic tendencies? What do structural patterns say about the potential of global civil society in relation to global governance problems?

Data and methods

We analyse the relations among INGOs as an initial step toward improving our understanding of the network structure of global civil society. Of course, we are well aware that INGOs are not the only element of global civil society, and that concentrating on organisations leaves out the important aspect of transnational interpersonal connections. Nonetheless, INGOs are a prominent part of the infrastructure of global civil society, and are among its most visible or tangible actors (Anheier and Katz 2003; Boli and Thomas 1997; Castells 1997; Cox 1993; Falk 2003). Since ties among formal organisations by definition tend to be less ephemeral than individual ties, the study of such ties provides a glimpse into aspects of the longer-term structures of global civil society.

Yet inter-organisational relations are only one part

of the total set of links connecting INGOs. Individuals, too, connect INGOs in many ways, including but not limited to overlapping memberships, friendships, participation in meetings and conferences, and even marriage. However permanent or transient they may be, such personal ties between organisations through the individuals that intertwine them can be of substantial importance, revealing informal layers of politics and influence. An example of one such study is presented in Box 7.1, in which Dana Fisher looks at how and why links between individuals create a network of inter-organisational connections. In Chapter 8 in this volume, Castells and his colleagues discuss another facet of the role of informal and interpersonal links and communications in developing and mobilising civil society. They show how interpersonal networks facilitate organisation and mobilisation, between organisations, between organisations and activists, or among previously unorganised masses, especially when such networks are reinforced by advanced technologies such as mobile telephony and text messaging. In some cases, they show, chaotic interpersonal networks are more effective in mobilising for action than more organised ones.

Table 7.3: Organisations and links by regions and World Bank income groups

World Bank income groups	Organisations (%)	Links sent (%)	Links received (%)
High income	81	81	80
Middle income	11	11	11
Low income	6	6	6

Regions	Organisations (%)	Links sent (%)	Links received (%)
East Asia & Pacific	8	8	8
Europe & Central Asia	54	56	54
EU-15	47	48	47
Latin America & Caribbean	5	5	5
Middle East & North Africa	2	2	2
North America	23	20	22
South Asia	2	2	2
Sub-Saharan Africa	5	5	5
Grand total	**10,001**	**9,863**	**29,863**

While no picture of global civil society can be complete without these two elements (inter-organisational and interpersonal), individual-level data is rare and the cost of collecting it prohibitive. Of course, even for INGOs themselves the data situation is far from ideal. At the very least, to find initial answers to the above questions we need data on a substantial share of the thousands of INGOs operating in and across different fields and parts of the world. Fortunately, the Brussels-based Union of International Associations (UIA) collects information on approximately 45,000 international organisations and associations on an ongoing basis, including INGOs and other types of international organisations, associations, conferences, treaties and more[2]. The descriptions of organisations in UIA's database are based on information received from a variety of sources but primarily from INGOs themselves, through an annual survey questionnaire administered by UIA.

Developing the network dataset

Our access to UIA's database was limited to a subset of organisations that were selected in an iterative process with the use of UIA's subject classification[3]. We selected organisations deemed relevant to global governance according to the stated subjects they address or the fields in which they operate. While arguably every inter-organisational tie is a potential channel of information, thereby adding to the density of global civil society networks, some links are unlikely to be instrumental, or play a role in, global governance processes. In other words, we excluded organisations that are primarily self-interested and narrow in scope, such the International Association of Stamp Collectors and similar clubs. We also excluded organisations that at least at face value appeared only remotely relevant to global governance issues, such as the Association for Computational Linguistics, and organisations that are of an extremely expressive nature and imply no action orientation whatsoever, such as Crystal Consciousness[4].

---

2 For more details on the UIA, its publications and work, see UIA (URL).

3 UIA classifies all organisations in the database into 1,283 subject categories, allowing for multiple classifications. In other words, each organisation can be associated with more than one subject category (UIA URL).

4 All names of organisations mentioned in this paragraph are real, and are extracted from UIA's online databases (UIA URL).

The selection process started by identifying UIA subject groups that correspond to thematic issues in panels at the 2004 World Social Forum that were set up by the organising committee of the forum, which consisted of 67 Indian organisations including trade unions, women's groups, farmers' networks, as well as 27 social movements and NGOs (for the committee's roles and responsibilities, see WSF 2004a). The World Social Forum is considered to be the central and most comprehensive global civil society event in recent years. It is the most global civil society event, both in its attendance and in the approach to the issues discussed in it. As well, it serves as a convergence point for nodes of existing networks and as a launching pad for new ones (Cock 2004). The World Social Forum is therefore here assumed to reflect the central issues concerning global civil society actors today.

---

the matrix of country interconnections through INGO links is considerably denser, but still not as dense and well-connected as other global networks, notably those that pertain to the global economy and to inter-state relations

---

The panels covered the following issues: Globalisation, Global Governance and the Nation State; The World Trade Organization; Militarism, War and Peace; Political Parties and Social Movements; Media, Culture and Knowledge; Wars against Women, Women against Wars; Globalisation Economic and Social Security; Globalisation and its Alternatives; Discrimination and Oppression: Racism and Casteism; Work and the World of Labour; The Struggle against Neoliberalism and War and the Significance of WSF Religious, Ethnic and Linguistic Exclusion and Oppression; Food Sovereignty and Natural Resources (WSF 2004b). These issues were associated with corresponding UIA subject groups: Peace and Justice, Societal Problems, Community, Conditions of Trade, and Freedom and Liberation. Not all of the issues had exactly corresponding subject groups in the UIA classification, but those that did not were covered by the more general subject groups such as Community or Peace and Justice.

We then looked at the list of organisations in the UIA's database included in each of these five UIA subject groups, and listed other subject groups with which they were associated, and the number of times those subject groups appeared. Subject groups with which at least 10 per cent of the organisations in the core groups were associated were singled out and listed in a second list of subject groups. Thereafter we looked into the organisations associated with the second list of subject groups, and likewise identified additional subject groups with which organisations listed in them were associated. This process was repeated five times, resulting in a list of 356 subject groups. Only subject groups that were counted at least twice were selected (the median number of times subject groups surfaced in the process was two). In the end, this step-wise procedure yielded 181 subject groups (14 per cent of UIA's 1,283 groups). In our final network data-set we included the organisations listed in these groups, as well as those in other groups that were linked to them. The final set of INGOs totaled 10,001 organisations (48.5 per cent of the total number of international NGOs in UIA's database[5]). In network analysis terms, they comprise a square matrix of 10,001 entries, with $N*(N-1)$ or just over 100 million possible links.

Based on this selection, UIA staff extracted from their database a directed, binary matrix of links in which the existence of a link between one organisation and another is coded as '1' and the absence of a link is coded '0'. In Table 7.2, for example, organisation A argues it has a link with organisation B, as indicated by the '1' in the cell from organisation A to organisation B; but this link is not reciprocal as organisation B reports no link with organisation A, as indicated by the '0' in the cell from organisation B to organisation A.

The matrix was created through a purposive sample of egocentric networks: nodes were included if they had links from organisations in the sample subject groups. So if organisation A was included in one of the selected subject groups, it would be included in the sample. If organisation A states that it has a link to organisation B, organisation B is also included in the sample even if it is not in the selected subject groups.

In its database UIA collects information on different types of links between INGOs[6]. These include the following:

- links through founding or establishment – organisation A took part in the founding of organisation B;
- structural link: for example, sister organisation or subsidiary organisation;
- link through shared or mutual assignment of key

Table 7.4: Organisations and links by country, top 20 countries

Rank	Organisations	%	Rank	Links sent	%	Rank	Links received	%
1	USA	19.6	1	USA	17.4	1	USA	19.0
2	UK	10.0	2	UK	10.5	2	UK	9.7
3	Belgium	9.3	3	Belgium	10.1	3	Belgium	9.5
4	France	7.8	4	France	8.0	4	France	7.8
5	Germany	4.8	5	Switzerland	5.8	5	Germany	4.8
6	Switzerland	4.2	6	Germany	4.6	6	Switzerland	4.3
7	Netherlands	3.9	7	Netherlands	4.0	7	Netherlands	4.0
8	Canada	3.0	8	Italy	3.1	8	Italy	3.1
9	Italy	3.0	9	Canada	2.9	9	Canada	3.0
10	Spain	1.6	10	Austria	1.6	10	Spain	1.8
11	Sweden	1.5	11	Australia	1.5	11	Austria	1.6
12	Australia	1.5	12	Sweden	1.5	12	Denmark	1.6
13	Austria	1.5	13	Denmark	1.4	13	Sweden	1.5
14	Japan	1.4	14	Spain	1.3	14	Japan	1.5
15	Denmark	1.4	15	Japan	1.2	15	Australia	1.5
16	India	1.2	16	India	1.2	16	India	1.3
17	Norway	0.9	17	Norway	1.0	17	Kenya	0.9
18	Kenya	0.9	18	Venezuela	0.9	18	Norway	0.9
19	Finland	0.8	19	Philippines	0.8	19	Finland	0.8
20	Philippines	0.8	20	Kenya	0.7	20	Philippines	0.8

staff, as when two organisations have the same CEO, or when organisation A nominates board members in organisation B;

- financial links, such as when organisation A donates money to organisation B, or when two or more organisations run shared fund-raising campaigns;
- activity links – joint activities or activities aimed at the cited organisation, as when organisation A collects information for organisation B;
- publication links: joint publications or publications about another organisation, as when organisation A publishes regular reports on the conduct of organisation B;
- membership links, such as those between a federation of organisations and its members; and
- other forms of relation with another NGO that were not classified.

However, since UIA did not make available to us such detailed data, we make no distinction between different types of links, and all the types of links mentioned above are treated in our analysis in the same way. Hence, the '1' from organisation A to organisation B in the example above would mean that any of the above types of links exists between these two organisations. Recall that

---

5 According to UIA criteria, this covers organisations of types A to G, excluding bodies coded 'governmental'.
6 It should be note that the UIA database probably does not cover all the NGOs involved in international activities, particularly those working in regions where, and around issues on which, data is hard to obtain. Also, since the database is generated mostly from self-reporting, bias can be expected in the data it contains. Nonetheless, it is still the most comprehensive and expansive database on such organisations, and has been used in many previous works (including previous editions of the Global Civil Society Yearbook) as well as by other authors such as Boli and Thomas (1997).

Box 7.2: Civil Society and communication information policy – mapping the WSIS Global Civil Society Network

Communication and information policy (CIP) is often overlooked by analysts of transnational civil society. The use of the internet as a tool of civil society actors has been widely noted, but usually the causes involve other policy domains, such as trade, human rights or environmentalism. Yet the issues surrounding the governance of the internet itself are of critical importance in their own right.

As a policy domain CIP involves such issues as telecommunications infrastructure regulation and development, privacy and freedom of expression, free software, intellectual property protection and the public domain, mass media regulation, technical standards and internet governance.

The World Summit on the Information Society (WSIS) has generated significant activity in global civil society. WSIS provided an opportunity for civil society actors in all CIP-related issue networks to converge on a common forum. Can this activity be characterised as a global social movement, comparable to environmentalism, or is it just a collection of issue networks? Who is involved and how wide and deep is the network?

To answer those questions, researchers at Syracuse University's Convergence Center performed a social network analysis of 50 individuals involved in transnational civil society action around CIP issues. Each respondent generated an average of ten names of people to whom they were connected in interactions regarding CIP. This produced a network structure of 345 unique individuals. The results showed that WSIS has indeed brought together a broad range of CIP-issue networks, but there are still some barriers to integration of different regions and issue areas.

Figure 7.4 shows the entire interpersonal network. Note the lingering significance of geography and the importance of intermediaries in connecting NGOs to the WSIS process. In the overall network map, considered clockwise, North Americans (represented by the semi-circles) cluster around 8–10 am, Latin Americans (diamonds) cluster around noon–1 pm. Africans (circles) tend to be found at 4–5 pm, Europeans (squares) tend to be distributed around the centre.

Figure 7.4: Transnational CIP interpersonal network

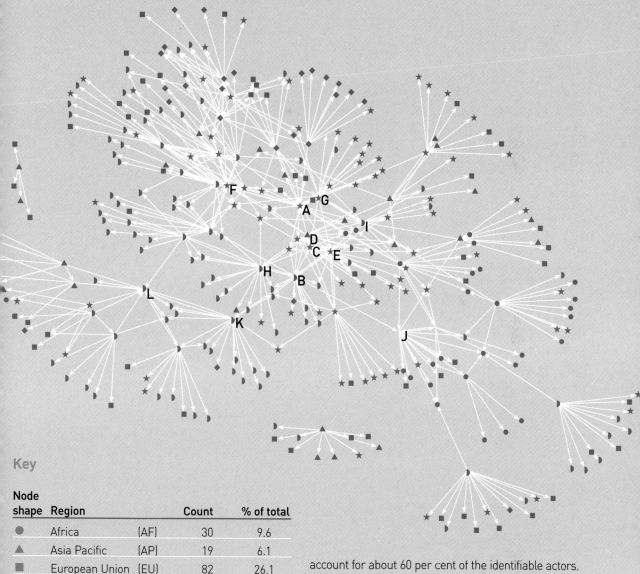

Key

Node shape

Node shape	Region		Count	% of total
●	Africa	(AF)	30	9.6
▲	Asia Pacific	(AP)	19	6.1
■	European Union	(EU)	82	26.1
◆	Latin America	(LA)	26	8.3
◗	North America	(NA)	103	32.8
★	Unidentified		54	17.2

Although geographically diverse, the WSIS civil society network is Europe-centred. If one uses 'degree' or 'closeness' as the measure of centrality (see Table 7.5), five of the top seven most central actors are in Europe. Although there are more North Americans, the Europeans are less regionally clustered. North Americans and Europeans combined account for about 60 per cent of the identifiable actors. A striking feature of the diagram is the minimal involvement of Asians (triangles) in the global civil society network: only 6 per cent of the identifiable actors are from Asia. There are only two Asians with significant centrality, and both are in Japan. India and China are notable by their relative absence. Most Latin Americans are connected to the WSIS civil society process via the Communication Rights in the Information Society (CRIS) campaign. Africans are connected through individuals associated with the Association for Progressive Communications (APC), the WSIS Civil Society Bureau, and development agencies.

Table 7.5: Ten most central actors by closeness

Ind.	Region	Issue	Measure of centrality Degree	Closeness	Betweenness
A	EU	Multiple	8.307	35.129	31.354
B	NA	Privacy; internet governance	5.431	34.701	30.692
C	EU	Internet governance	4.792	32.741	8.997
D	AP	Internet governance	4.792	32.706	9.311
E	EU	Privacy	5.751	31.841	8.208
F	EU	Communication rights	5.751	31.841	16.080
G	EU	UN process	6.070	30.716	10.289
H	NA	Internet governance	5.431	30.477	8.257
I	NA	UN process	4.153	29.753	7.554
J	AF	ICT dev; internet governance	5.431	29.473	22.947

Note: Disconnected nodes removed for analysis.

Table 7.5 reveals a concentration of centrality on individual A. By any mathematical measure (degree, closeness, and betweenness) this individual is the hub of the WSIS-CS network. This individual's organisation is involved in a variety of CIP issues, from gender to ICT development to the internet. Following in rank are six individuals who focus on internet governance, privacy, and communication rights, and two who are concerned with civil society participation in UN processes. Among other things, this data shows the degree to which the growing prominence of internet governance has brought into the centre of the WSIS network individuals who are strongly associated with that issue and active in the civil society institutions of the Internet Corporation for Assigned Names and Numbers (ICANN).

Betweenness measures the degree to which a given individual connects other members of the network who are otherwise disconnected. Nodes with high levels of betweenness (individuals A, B, J, K and L) can act as gatekeepers of information flow or as liaisons between different parts of the network. In this case the same individual, A, has the highest rank, but there is a significantly different ordering below. North American activists in WSIS (including individuals K and L in Figure 7.4 whose betweenness scores exceed 17) tend to have higher betweenness scores because North American civil society advocacy groups are less integrated in the WSIS process than European groups. Likewise, African civil society tends to be connected to WSIS through a small number of intermediaries (such as individual J).

Source: Convergence Center (URL)   Milton Mueller, Brenden Kuerbis and Christiane Pagé, Syracuse University

our data contains only formal inter-organisational links; and links between organisations by way of individuals active in them are not covered. Also, in order to preserve their anonymity, UIA did not include the actual names of INGOs. However, a separate file listed information on activities and headquarter country.

We used a variety of network analytic techniques, including centrality, density and clustering measures as well as blockmodel, correspondence and cluster analysis[7]. In addition, we used other readily available data-sets as part of our overall analysis to provide some basis for comparing our results with other global patterns. These included refugee flows across borders, international student exchanges, ambassadorial and consular links, and trade flows[8].

The structure of the global INGO network

What is the scale and pattern of the global INGO network? How dense are the links in this network and how does the INGO network density compare to that of other global networks? We will present our key empirical results, and then explore their implications.

A sparse network

Analysis reveals that network density (calculated as the ratio of the number of existing links to that of all possible links in the network) is very thin: only 0.03 per cent. In other words, for every 10,000 possible links between INGOs in our sample, only three links exist in the data reported. Densities improve when we look at how INGO links connect countries. As Figure 7.3 shows, the matrix of country interconnections through INGO links is considerably denser, but still not as dense and well-connected as other global networks, notably those that pertain to the global economy and to inter-state relations.

If global civil society is to become a counterweight to economic globalisation in the Gramscian sense of a historic bloc and, possibly, to have a reforming and humanising impact on global injustices, our results indicate that it still has a long way to go before its network density approaches that of international trade and transnational corporations. Across the 222 countries and regions included, the trade network is omnipresent. By contrast, the INGO network analysed here covers only 168 countries and far fewer links between them. This means that economic globalisation extends farther and deeper than INGOs do.

As Figure 7.3 shows, most other networks analysed here are denser than the INGO network. The only network less dense is that of refugee flows (UNHCR 2004: Table 8). This comes as no surprise, especially since only few countries serve as hosts for this type of flow, and refugee flows are rarely reciprocal. Other networks are considerably denser: countries are 50 per cent more connected by placing embassies in each other (Maher et al. 2001), 100 per cent more connected by trade flows (UN URL), and 300 per cent more connected by international students' flows (UNESCO 2004) than they are by INGOs.

A pronounced core-periphery structure

A well-known trait of global civil society is its uneven global distribution (Anheier and Stares 2002; Anheier and Katz 2003; Kaldor, Anheier, and Glasius 2003), with concentrations in some parts of the world and a virtual absence in others. The picture that emerges with INGOs is no different. INGOs in our network – that is, organisations that deal with issues related to core global governance issues – come predominantly from the developed world: 81 per cent of the organisations in the network are from high-income economies, 54 per cent from Europe and Central Asia (but almost all of those are from European Union member states) and 23 per cent from North America (Table 7.3). The distribution of network links, both sent and received, is basically the same.

A glimpse at the distribution of organisations in the network by countries in Table 7.4 shows that the US alone accounts for 20 per cent of all organisations in the network. The 15 countries that were EU members in 2003 account for 47 per cent. In other words, while the US is the central country of INGO networks, the EU is its central region. Together, the EU and the US represent 66 per cent of all organisations, 65 per cent of all links sent, and 66 per cent of all links received.

Similar Western European bias was found in the work done by Milton Mueller et al. on global civil society networks dealing with communication information policy (see Box 7.2). Since they analyse individual networks, the similar findings suggest that comparable

---

7   For a comprehensive review see Wasserman and Faust (1994); for an application to global civil society networks see Anheier and Katz (2004).

8   Sources for this network data include, respectively: UNHCR (2004); UNESCO (2004); Maher et al. (2001); UN (2005).

patterns can be found in the organisational level and the individual level of global civil society networks. It is worth noting, however, that the structure Mueller et al. find may reflect the issue their network deals with, namely, IT and communications, which is strongly affected by the global digital divide. It is not surprising, then, to find there such a Eurocentric bias. Networks dealing with other issues might not be as centred in the developed North, as was shown in numerous cases (see for example the Latin American bias in the networks of international farmers' associations, Edelman 2003).

By contrast, among the top 20 countries represented in the network, only three are developing nations: India, Kenya, and the Philippines. All three rank 16th or lower, in terms of their share both in the total number of organisations and in the total number of links. In the count of outgoing links, Venezuela makes an appearance in the 18th place. Hence, it appears that developed countries are home to the majority of the network's nodes as well as the bulk of the links. Yet it also turns out that the description offered by some (for example, Lindenberg and Bryant 2001), whereby the shape of the global INGO network resembles a star, with Northern INGOs being the hub of the star and Southern INGOs the spokes, fails to receive much empirical support in our analysis. If such an unequal relationship actually held, we would expect the share of Southern INGOs in the number of links to be smaller than their share in the number of organisations. Our findings show, however, that the share of Southern INGOs in the number of network nodes closely reflects their share in the number of network links. One can deduce that organisations in the global South, once they emerge, create just as many links on average as their Northern counterparts. But they create more links with Northern INGOs, particularly in a few selected nations, than with other Southern INGOs.

Preliminary analyses of INGO networks in a smaller sample taken from the UIA database, and of INGOs participating in events during the 2004 World Social Forum (Anheier and Katz 2004), show in each case a clear core-periphery structure whereby Northern INGOs form the core and INGOs from the global South are located at the periphery. Our current data, too, reveal such a sharp distinction between a core and a periphery at the country level. A core-periphery analysis on the country matrix (generated from the INGO matrix as input) places three countries at the core of INGO network structure – the US, the UK, and

Belgium. All other countries are placed at the periphery. This finding clearly reflects the impact of political centres of power (US and EU) and the legacy of colonial and post-colonial history (London).

As Table 7.6 shows, the core countries play a major role in the network. Links between INGOs in the three core countries account for 15 per cent of the links in the entire network, and links from periphery organisations to the core and vice versa account for 47 per cent of the total. In all, almost two in every three links between NGOs in our network involve an organisation in Belgium, the UK or the US. Finally, links among NGOs in peripheral countries account for 38 per cent of the total connectivity in the network, divided between 165 countries. Moreover, under a tenth of those, or 3 per cent of all links, are between two developing or in-transition countries. The rest (35 per cent of total links) involve at least one developed country. In other words, the structure of the network reveals a coherent and well-connected centre located entirely in the developed North, and a dispersed and less well-connected periphery which includes the entire global South.

When we examine the spatial distribution of network centrality (using degree centrality scores, which measure centrality by number of connected nodes), this core-periphery structure becomes very clear. As Figure 7.5 shows, the network density is far higher in Western Europe and the north-eastern seaboard of North America than anywhere else. Yet, several secondary network hubs seem to be emerging in the developing world: Nairobi, Johannesburg and Lagos in Africa; New Delhi in Asia; Buenos Aires, São Paolo and Caracas in Latin America; Cairo, Amman and Jerusalem in the Middle East. Yet from this map we also see that vast areas of the world, among them highly vulnerable and fragile regions, are not included in the INGO network structure.

A mostly cohesive structure

The core-periphery analysis tells us how egalitarian the INGO network is in terms of the distribution of links. In our case it actually tells us that the network is unevenly divided between North and South, and between the capitals of global governance and finance and the rest of the world. But, while the core-periphery analysis tells us that the network has a clear hierarchical structure, it does not tell us whether the network is fragmented or cohesive. A network can be hierarchical but still be cohesive in that it is not

Table 7.6: Core-periphery links

	Share of total links (%)
Links involving core countries	62
Within-core links	15
Core-periphery links	47
Within-periphery links	38
All links	100 (= 29,863)

broken into loosely connected sub-networks. Such cohesiveness is important if we want INGOs to serve as an infrastructure for a global, rather than a loosely associated collection of regional, interest-bound, or sectarian, civil societies. As mentioned above, networks' diversity can have a considerable impact on their effectiveness.

The key question here is this: what is the degree of fragmentation of the global INGO network? To answer it, we need to analyse the network for clustering. Is the network completely unified in one more or less inclusive structure, or is it broken up into mutually exclusive groups? Or is the structure somewhere in between these two extremes, as suggested by Richard Falk's observations (2003) that global civil society is still divided into partly complementary and partly overlapping, movements? Curiously, all three possibilities seem to be valid at the same time, at least to some extent. To find this out, we performed correspondence analysis[9] on the INGO matrix. Correspondence analysis looks at the patterns of connections in the networks, and draws the nodes in a multidimensional space based on how similar their connections are. Two organisations that have an identical set of links will be charted next to each other. As Figure 7.6 shows, the analysis produced six clusters (few organisations were not included in any of those clusters). The first of the clusters is extremely large, and it accounts for over nine-tenths of the entire network in term of nodes as well as of links (Table 7.7). It includes all but 11 of the major hubs of the network (164 organisations in our network which have at least 25 links with other organisations). This group of well-connected organisations is also extremely interconnected, creating a very dense web of links between them. By contrast, the major cluster and the minor clusters are to a great

extent disconnected from each other. Given the fact that over 90 per cent of the network is contained in one cluster, this finding is not so alarming. It means that, overall, the network is considerably unified and that fragmentation in the network is limited, but at the same time it shows that global civil society has a marginal tendency to form disparate, cohesive and exclusive blocs, a fact whose scope and impact should be followed closely in the future.

A look at the composition of the clusters by subjects as well as by countries reveals no particular patterns; that is, none of the clusters is issue-specific or region-specific. All clusters have a similar mix of organisations from all regions and income groups dealing with all manner of issues. This reflects a network that is substantially cohesive in terms of who is connected with whom, while at the same time being extremely diverse.

We now explore the implications of our findings. We test them against conventional expectations about INGOs within the broader context of global governance.

Implications

Analysing the network among 10,001 INGOs and 29,863 links revealed three major results. First, the network, as measured by the UIA annual survey, is very sparse, which indicates that the inter-organisational infrastructure of global civil society is less developed than other globalisation processes. Second, a pronounced centre-periphery structure reproduces rather than compensates for North-South splits in

9 Developed by Michael Greenacre and Jörg Blasius (1994), correspondence analysis is used in network analysis to extract cohesive groups (groups that have more links between their members, and fewer links with members from other groups) from a larger matrix, by locating groups of nodes with similar tie patterns (for a succinct summary, see Clausen 1998).

Figure 7.5: Spatial distribution of network centrality

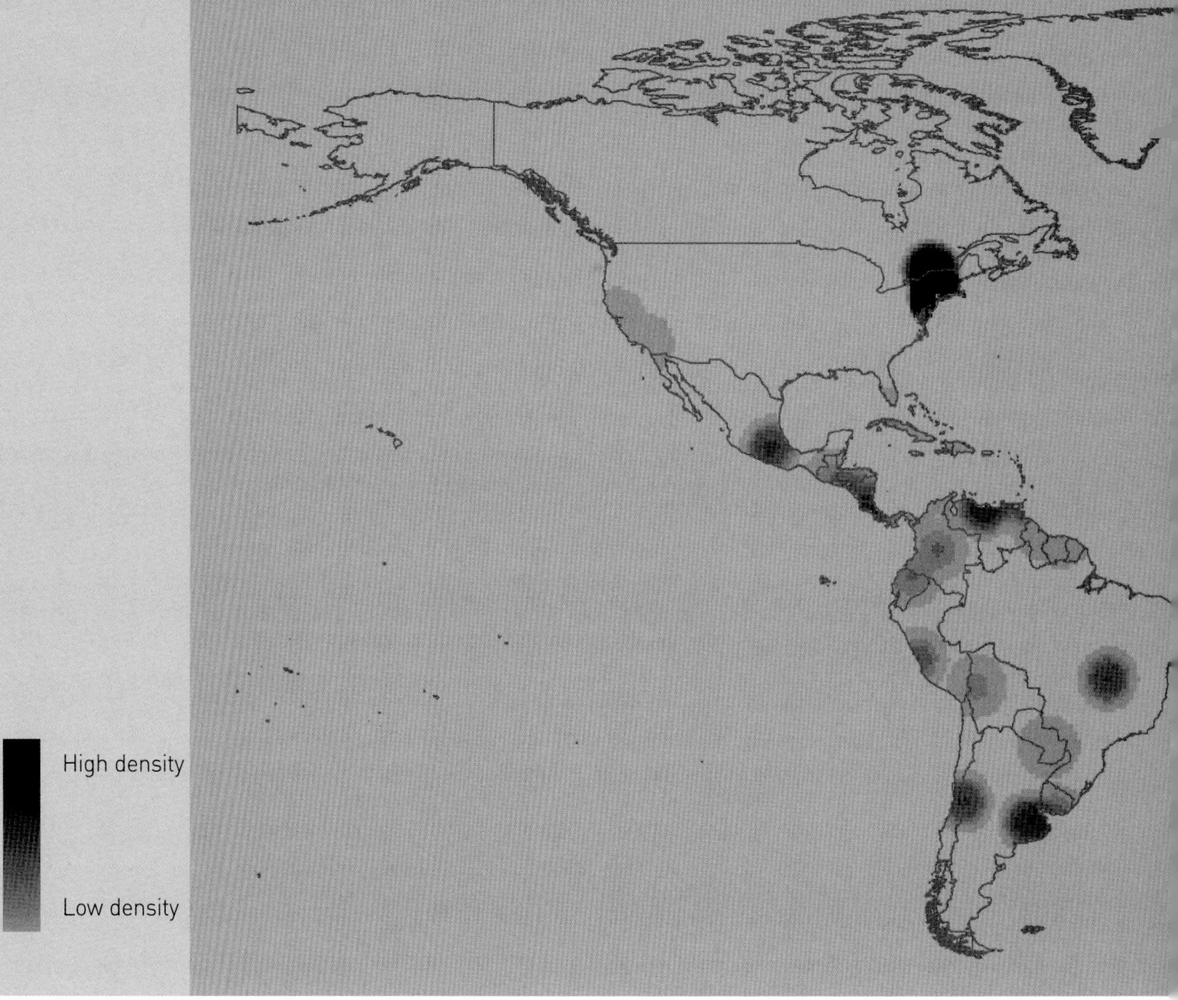

High density

Low density

other dimensions of globalisation, notably trade flows. Third, correspondence analysis points to a cohesive network with some marginal, almost negligible, tendencies towards fragmentation.

INGOs are frequently portrayed as a potential counterweight to the ills of globalisation (Clark 2003; Lindenberg and Bryant 2001; Kaldor, Anheier, and Glasius 2003). Keeping markets and governments at bay, they are seen as organisations dedicated to international understanding, introducing greater participation, giving voice to under-represented groups and encouraging greater global equity. As quintessential institutions of global civil society, it is argued, INGOs are the human face of globalisation, and at the forefront of a struggle for better global governance.

Clearly, these statements are based on a mix of implicit assumptions and reflect normative expectations. In particular they assume some form of combined or collective action among INGOs, however loosely coordinated or structured, toward humanising globalisation or some related goal; they also assume a generally positive INGO contribution to the creation of an effective counterweight vis-à-vis global market players and hegemonic states.

But how real are these expectations? While the analysis presented here is only preliminary, and based on partial and incomplete information, our results nonetheless lead us to be cautious about the structural impact of INGOs. Our findings reveal a very sparse network, unevenly dispersed around the globe,

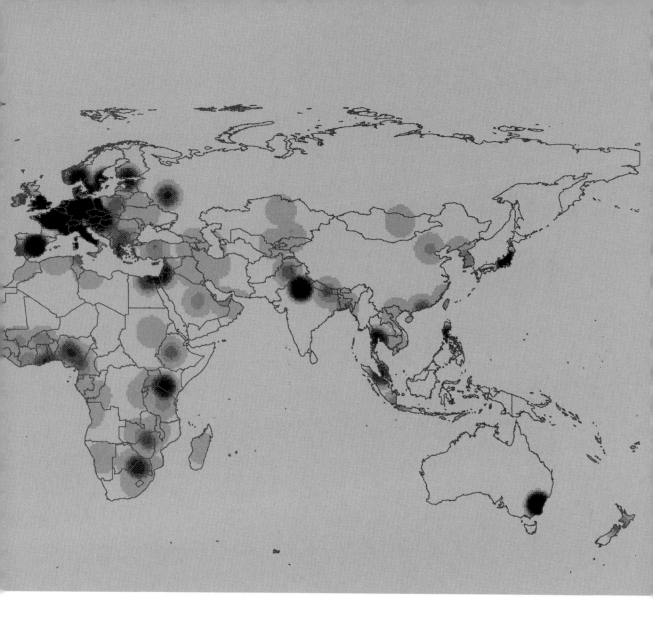

with Europe and North America accounting for largest share of the nodes and links of the network. While some minor Southern foci exist, the global INGO network is still predominantly a Northern and Western phenomenon. Furthermore, it is highly concentrated where the global centres of power – political and economic – are located: in New York, Washington, London and Brussels.

As we have seen, the network of INGOs, comprising the infrastructure of global civil society, is only slightly fragmented, but when fragmentation occurs it creates relatively isolated pockets. These pockets are not distinguishable in terms of issue or regional focus, and so it is more likely from the knowledge we posses at the moment that they are competing rather than

complementary. What does this mean for global civil society and global governance?

The end of the cold war and the processes of globalisation have engendered change and ambiguity in the locus of power in the world system. David Held (2004: 89–93) describes two main gaps that have evolved in the global governance system as a result of these changes: jurisdictional and incentive. The jurisdictional gap has to do with the incongruence between current policy-making units, which are for the most part local, and the global scope and character of present social problems. The incentive gap relates to the unwillingness of institutions, in particular international organisations like the UN, the IMF or the World Bank, to undertake policy innovation

Figure 7.6: **Clusters of connectivity in the global civil society network**

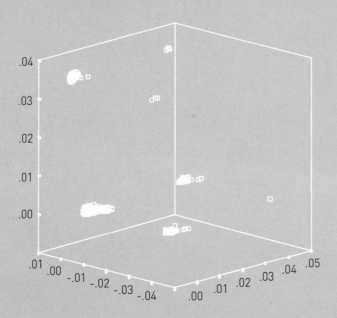

and reform. The result is not only an incoherent system but also an institutional vacuum: we lack institutions that address many of the issues at hand. The current system is crippled by a lack of clear distribution of labour, overlapping jurisdictions, and procedural ambiguity. This melange of political and legal structures, John Keane (2001) argues, is present in many policy areas, involving nation states and regional and local governments, inter-governmental agencies and programmes, inter-governmental structures, INGOs and TNCs. The system of global governance also includes global accords, treaties, and conventions; policy summits and meetings; and more forms of public deliberation and conflict resolution.

Held (2004: 90, 94) adds that the lack of ownership of global problems causes some problems to be claimed by several institutions, often in an uncoordinated and even conflicting fashion, while other problems or issues are tossed between institutions like hot potatoes, eventually falling between the cracks in the global governance system. In addition, in the absence of any significant supranational entity to regulate global governance processes, particularly in light of the deepening weakness of the UN system (Krut 1997; Ollila 2003), global governance actors lack any motivation to act and often prefer to free ride.

Equity and representation are also prominent problems in the systems of global governance. Global governance is distorted in the sense that it promotes the interests of the most powerful states and global social actors (IGOs, TNCs) and impedes the achievement of global social justice and human security (Rosenau 2002; Held 2004). It is a product of global power inequalities, and reproduces those very inequalities. TNCs, largely unchecked by most governments, enjoy increasing power, while they remain accountable primarily to their shareholders, who are typically in the industrial North. This situation increases other deficits in the global governance system, that is, the lack of equity and representation characteristic of global governance institutions, most specifically around issues of welfare, human security and poverty reduction, issues which have no strong actor to promote them.

The result of this uneven 'playing field' is an increasing

Table 7.7: Organisations and links by cluster

Cluster	Organisations (%)	Links sent (%)	Links received (%)	Ratio sent/received
1	93.20%	93.60%	91.14%	1.03
2	1.37%	1.23%	1.74%	0.71
3	0.94%	0.91%	1.28%	0.71
4	1.02%	1.28%	1.37%	0.93
5	1.36%	1.01%	1.81%	0.56
6	2.02%	1.86%	2.60%	0.71

gap between the level of development of rules promoting free markets and those promoting social justice (Held 2004: 92; Held and McGrew 2002: 1–21). Under-representation of global constituencies, especially among poor nations and indigenous people, is exacerbated by the unequal decision making structures of some prominent IGOs, particularly those dealing with economic regulation such as the WTO and the IMF, and the complete absence of many countries from bodies such as G8. Held (2004: 15) points out that the key mechanism for popular participation in political processes in democratic systems, namely, electoral and campaigning politics, is not relevant to global governance institutions, since they have no direct link to a politically bounded population.

Moreover, the limited access to and supervision of global governance institutions that most governments enjoy is usually in the hands of state bureaucrats who have no direct ties to voters (Scholte 2004). Many governance institutions lack mechanisms to introduce popular inputs in their deliberations, and in many cases the introduction of INGOs is no more than a token gesture (Held 2004). Consequently, there is growing incongruence between those affected by public goods (and 'bads') and those involved in deciding on and providing them. In addition, systems of global governance lack the checks and balances that are essential for democratic regimes.

Can global civil society, and especially its most prominent actors – INGOs – cure these ills of the global governance system? Our results suggest an answer to this question along the lines of 'potentially and to some extent yes, but currently no'. Our findings can be divided into 'good news' and 'bad news'. Let's start with the good news. Our analysis finds the global civil society network notably cohesive, as indicated by its low level of fragmentation. Such cohesion means that there is only one INGO network in which almost all INGOs are reachable, and only a few are relatively disconnected in smaller sub-groups. The import of this is that potentially all INGOs in this network can be brought to the discussion table, directly or indirectly, and that all voices, regions, issues and constituencies are represented in this network. This characteristic of the INGO network is conducive to alleviating the jurisdictional gap – global civil society can be a holistic and coherent actor in the global governance system, one that can address many critical issues synergistically. This compositional diversity, as shown in the cases of the Narmada dam and the debt reduction networks discussed above, also enhances the effectiveness of the network.

This characteristic of global civil society is also conducive to the development of a global movement of sorts, perhaps a version of Antonio Gramsci's counter-hegemonic historic bloc. For Gramsci, an opposition movement to hegemonic institutions can develop into a true counter-hegemonic historic bloc only if all the subaltern groups are represented in it. The existing data show that, at least at the level of the organisational networks of global civil society, the INGO network is all-inclusive, and practically all the actors in our analysis are included in the main network cluster. Any exclusions from the main cluster are not systematic, that is, our findings show that no single region or constituency is excluded from the global structure. The very low degree of fragmentation we found in this giant network is one precondition of the emergence of a global bloc. Other preconditions exist, of course, and, as we discuss below, a few of them are still to be met.

This optimistic finding is by no means enough to secure either a change to the global governance system or the development of a global counter-hegemonic movement. The bad news that emerges from our study is that the global INGO network is greatly underdeveloped, especially in the developing world. The overall sparseness of the global INGO network and it limited global reach relative to other global networks, particularly those of international relations and global trade, restricts its capacity to become a serious and viable force in the global governance system. First, it is less omnipresent, and lacks a local footing in all the places where it is relevant. While international organisations such as Greenpeace or Human Rights Watch address problems related to their organisational mandate anywhere in the world, even if local NGOs are not linked to the global network we have analysed here, the additional benefit of local-global collaboration and the potential advantage of the 'boomerang effect' (Keck and Sikkink 1998) will be missing from such action.

Another concern is the underdevelopment of the INGO presence and structure in the South. Indeed, our findings show that even though INGOs from the global South are symmetrically and proportionally involved in the global INGO network, there are simply not enough of them, and those few are locked into a peripheral position. As it appears now, it is not very likely that global civil society in its current structure can contribute to increasing the representativeness of the global governance system, or increase substantially the participation of currently marginalised con-stituencies in global governance processes. It is too concentrated in the North, its density in the South is dismal, and as a result its capacity to legitimately make the authentic voices of Southern communities heard in the corridors of global power is very limited.

Presumably, were the number of INGOs in the South to increase, and at a faster rate than the centre, and were present patterns of inclusion to continue and strengthen, particularly an intentional thickening of the links between Northern and Southern NGOs, such a future global INGO network would be more likely to accrue the global reach needed for it to become a significant element of the infrastructure of global civil society. It could even become an effective element of global governance, and achieve better representation and improved legitimacy based on greater inclusion and participation. Only then, we suggest, could the global INGO network serve as the vehicle for the emergence of a historic bloc and potentially act as a countervailing force in the globalisation process.

Anheier, Helmut K. and Katz, Hagai (2003) 'Mapping Global Civil Society', in M. Kaldor, H. Anheir and M. Glasius (eds.), *Global Civil Society 2003*. Oxford: Oxford University Press.

– (2004) 'Network Approaches to Global Civil Society', in H. Anheier, M. Glasius and M. Kaldor (eds.), *Global Civil Society 2004/5*. London: Sage.

– and Stares, Sally (2002)'Introducing the Global Civil Society Index', in M. Glasius, M. Kaldor and H. Anheier (eds.), *Global Civil Society 2002*. Oxford: Oxford University Press.

Beck, Ulrich (1999) *What is Globalisation?* Cambridge: Polity Press.

Boli, John and George M Thomas (1997). 'World Culture in the World Polity: A Century of International Non-Governmental Organisation', *Annual Sociological Review*, 62: 171–90.

CAN [Climate Action Network] (URL) www.climatenetwork.org (consulted April 27, 2005).

Caniglia, Beth (2002). 'Elite Alliances and Transnational Environmental Movement Organisations', in J. Smith and H. Johnston (eds.), *Globalisation and Resistance: Tranasnational Dimensions* Of Social Movements. Lanham, MD: Rowman and Littlefield.

Castells, Manuel (1996) *The Rise of the Network Society*. Oxford: Blackwell.

– (1997) *The Power of Identity*. Malden, MA: Blackwell.

Clark, John (2003) *Worlds Apart: Civil Society and the Battle for Ethical Globalisation*. Bloomfield, CT: Kumarian Press.

Clausen, Sten-Erik (1998) *Applied Correspondence Analysis: An Introduction*. Thousand Oaks, CA: Sage.

Cock, Jacklyn (2004) 'The World Social Forum and New Forms of Social Activism', in R. Taylor (ed.), *Creating a Better World: Interpreting Global Civil Society*. Bloomfield, CT: Kumarian Press.

Convergence Center (URL) http://dcc.syr.edu/overview.htm (consulted 10 June 2005).

Cox, Robert W. (1993) .'Gramsci, Hegemony and International Relations', in S. Gill (ed.), *Gramsci, Historical Materialism and International Relations*. Cambridge and New York: Cambridge University Press.

– (1996) *Approaches to World Order*. Cambridge: Cambridge University Press.

– (2002) *The Political Economy of a Plural World: Globalisation and Civilization*. New York: Routledge.

Deacon, Bob (1997) *Global Social Policy: International Organisations and the Future of Welfare*. London: Sage.

Diani, Mario (2003a) 'Introduction', in M. Diani and D. McAdam (eds.), *Social Movements and Networks: Relational Approaches to Collective Action*. Oxford and New York: Oxford University Press.

– (2003b) 'Leaders or Brokers: Positions and Influence in Social Movement Networks', in M. Diani and D. McAdam (eds.), *Social Movements and Networks: Relational Approaches to Collective Action*. Oxford and New York: Oxford University Press.

– (2003c) .Networks and Social Movements: A Research Programme', in M. Diani and D. McAdam (eds.), *Social Movements and Networks: Relational Approaches to Collective Action*. Oxford and New York: Oxford University Press.

Donnelly, Elizabeth A. (2002) 'Proclaiming Jubilee: The Debt and Structural Adjustment Network', in S. Khagram, J. V. Riker and K. Sikkink (eds.), *Restructuring World Politics: Transnational Social Movements, Networks, and Norms*. Minneapolis: University of Minnesota Press.

Edelman, Mark (2003) 'International Peasant and Farmers Movements and Networks', in M. Kaldor, H. Anheier and M. Glasius (eds.), *Global Civil Society 2003*. Oxford: Oxford University Press.

Falk, Richard (2003) 'On the Political Relevance of Global Civil Society', in J. H. Dunning (ed.), *Making Globalisation Good: The Moral Challenges of Global Capitalism*. Oxford and New York: Oxford University Press.

Florini, Ann and Simmons, P. J. (2000) 'What the World Needs Now?', in A. Florini (ed.), *The Third Force: The Rise of Transnational Civil Society*. Tokyo and Washington DC: Japan Center for International Exchange and Carnegie Endowment for International Peace.

Gill, Stephen (1993) 'Gramsci and Global Politics: Towards a Post-Hegemonic Research Agenda', in S. Gill (ed.), *Gramsci, Historical Materialism and International Relations*. Cambridge and New York: Cambridge University Press.

Gould, Roger V. (2003). 'Why Do Networks Matter? Rationalist and Structuralist Interpretations', in M. Diani and D. McAdam (eds.), *Social Movements and Networks: Relational Approaches to Collective Action*. Oxford and New York: Oxford University Press.

Gramsci, Antonio (1971) *Selections from the Prison Notebooks of Antonio Gramsci*. (ed. Q. Hoare and G. Nowell-Smith). London: Lawrence and Wishart.

Greenacre, Michael and Blasius, Jörg (eds.) (1994) *Correspondence Analysis in the Social Sciences: Recent Developments and Applications*. London: Academic Press.

Haas, Peter M. (1992) 'Epistemic Communities and International Policy Coordination– Introduction', *International Organization*, 46: 1–35.

– (1989) 'Do Regimes Matter? Epistemic Communities and Mediterranean Pollution Control', *International Organization*, 43: 377–403.

– (1990) *Saving the Mediterranean: The Politics of Environmental Cooperation*. New York: Columbia University Press.

Held, David (2004) *Global Covenant: The Social Democratic Alternative to the Washington Consensus*. Cambridge: Polity.

– and McGrew, Anthony G. (2002) *Governing Globalisation: Power, Authority, and Global Governance*. Cambridge and Malden, MA: Polity.

Hopkins, R. F. (1992) 'Reform in the International Food Aid Regime: The Role of Consensual Knowledge', *International Organization*, 46: 225–64.

Kaldor, Mary (2003) *Global Civil Society: An Answer to War*. Cambridge: Polity Press.

–, Anheier, Helmut and Glasius, Marlies (2003) 'Global Civil Society in an Era of Regressive Globalisation', in M. Kaldor, H. Anheier and M. Glasius (eds.), *Global Civil Society 2003*. Oxford: Oxford University Press.

Katz, Hagai (2005). 'Global Civil Society and Global Governance: Co-opted or Counter-hegemonic? Analysing International NGO Networks in the Context of Gramscian Theory' (Ph.D. dissertation). Los Angeles: School of Public Affairs, UCLA.

Kaul, I., Conceicao P., Le Goulvern K., Mendoza R. (eds) (2003) *Providing global public goods: managing globalisation*. New York: Oxford University Press.

Keane, John (2001) 'Global Civil Society?', in H. Anheier, M. Glasius and M. Kaldor (eds), *Global Civil Society 2001*. Oxford: Oxford University Press.

Keck, Margaret and Sikkink, Kathryn (1998) *Activists Beyond Borders: Advocacy Networks in International Politics*. Ithaca, NY: Cornell University Press.

Khagram, Sanjeev (2002) 'Restructuring the global Politics of Development: The Case of India's Narmada Valley Dams', in S. Khagram, J. V. Riker and K. Sikkink (eds.), *Restructuring World Politics: Transnational Social Movements, Networks, and Norms*. Minneapolis: University of Minnesota Press.

Krut, Riva (1997) *Globalisation and Civil Society: NGO Influence in International Decision-Making*, UNRISD Discussion Paper No. 83. New York: The United Nations Research Institute for Social Development (UNRISD).

Lidskog, R. and Sundqvist, G. (2002) 'The Role of Science in Environmental Regimes: The Case of LRTAP', *European Journal of International Relations*, 8: 77–101.

Lindenberg, Marc and Bryant, Coralie (2001) *Going Global: Transforming Relief and Development NGOs*. Bloomfield, CT: Kumarian Press.

MA (Millennium Ecosystem Assessment) (URL) 'About the Millennium Ecosystem Assessment'. www.millenniumassessment.org/en/about.overview.aspx? (consulted 21 January 2003).

McAdam, Doug (2003) 'Beyond Structural Analysis: Toward a More Dynamic View of Social Movements', in M. Diani and D. McAdam (eds.), *Social Movements and Networks: Relational Approaches to Collective Action*. Oxford: New York: Oxford University Press.

McPherson, M. and Smith-Lovin, L. (1987) 'Homophily in Voluntary Organizations: Status Distance and the Composition of Face-to-Face Groups', *American Sociological Review*, 52: 370–9.

– and Cook, J. M (2001) 'Birds of a Feather: Homophily in Social Networks', *Annual Review of Sociology*, 27: 415–44.

Maher, Joanne et al. (eds.) (2001) *Europa World Year Book 2001, Vols I and II*. London: Europa Publications.

Ollila, Eeva (2003) *Global Health-Related Public-Private Partnerships and the United Nations*, Policy Brief. Helsinki and Sheffield: Globalism and Social Policy Programme (GASPP).

Peterson, M. J. (1992) 'Whalers, Cetologists, Environmentalists, and the International Management of Whaling', *International Organization*, 46: 147–86.

Rosenau, James N. (1995) 'Governance and Democracy in a Globalising World', in D. Archibugi, D. Held and M. Kohler (eds.), *Re-imagining Political Community: Studies in Cosmopolitan Democracy*. Cambridge: Polity Press.

– (2002) 'Governance in a New Global Order', in D. Held and A. G. McGrew (eds.), Governing Globalisation : *Power, Authority, and Global Governance*. Cambridge and Malden, MA: Polity Press.

Ruef, M., Aldrich, H. and Carter, N. (2003) 'The Structure of Founding Teams: Homophily, Strong Ties, and Isolation among US Entrepreneur', *American Sociological Review*, 68: 195–222.

Scholte, Jan Aart (2004) 'Civil Society and Democratically Accountable Global Governance', *Government and Opposition*, 39(2): 211–33.

Townsend, J. G (1999) 'Are Non-governmental Organisations Working in Development a Transnational Community?', *Journal of International Development*, 11: 613–23.

UIA (Union of International Associations) (URL) www.uia.org (consulted April 27, 2005).

UN (United Nations) (URL) UN *Commodity Trade Statistics Database (UN Comtrade)*. New York: Statistics Division, UN. http://unstats.un.org/unsd/comtrade (consulted February 6, 2005).

UNESCO (2004) *Global and Internationally Comparable Statistics on Education, Science, Technology, Culture and Communication*. Paris: Institute for Statistics, UNESCO. www.uis.unesco.org (consulted 6 February 2005).

UNHCR (2004) *2003 Global Refugee Trends*. Geneva: Population Data Unit/PGDS, Division of Operational Support, UNHCR.

Wasserman, Stanley and Faust, Katherine (1994) *Social Network Analysis: Methods and Applications* (Structural Analysis in the Social Sciences, 8). Cambridge and New York: Cambridge University Press.

Waterman, Peter (2000) 'Social Movements, Local Places and Globalised Places: Implications for Globalisation from Below', in B. K. Gills (ed.), *Globalisation and the Politics of Resistance*. London: McMillan.

WSF (World Social Forum) (2004a) 'Organisation Structure'. www.wsfindia.org/orgstructure.php (consulted April 22, 2005).

– (2004b) 'Programme: WSF Organised'. www.forumsocialmundial.org.br/dinamic.asp?pagina=programa_coindia_ing (consulted April 22, 2005).

Yergin, D. A. and Stanislav, J. (1998) *The Commanding Heights: The Battle between Government and the Marketplace that is Remaking the Modern World*. New York: Simon and Schuster.

CHAPTER 8

ELECTRONIC COMMUNICATION AND SOCIO-POLITICAL MOBILISATION: A NEW FORM OF CIVIL SOCIETY

Manuel Castells, Mireia Fernandez-Ardevol, Jack Linchuan Qiu and Araba Sey

Introduction: civil society and communication technology

The structuring of civil society evolves with its institutional, cultural, and technological context. The more this context maximises the chances of autonomy vis-à-vis the state, the more civil society empowers itself. Interactive electronic communication, and particularly wireless communication, provides a powerful platform for political autonomy on the basis of independent channels of autonomous communication, from person to person, and from group to group. The communication networks that mobile telephony makes possible can be formed and re-formed instantly, and messages are received from a known source, enhancing their credibility. The network logic of the communication process makes it a high-volume communication channel, but with a considerable degree of personalisation and interactivity. In this sense, the wide availability of individually controlled wireless communication effectively bypasses the mass media as a source of information, and creates a new public space.

Without prejudging on the desirability of political autonomy (because, naturally, it can be used to support very different kinds of political values and interests), we have observed a growing tendency by people in different contexts to use wireless communication to voice their discontent with the powers that be, and to organise protests by inducing 'flash mobilisations' that have sometimes made a considerable impact on formal politics and government decisions. To document this tendency, and to explore its implications, we analyse in this chapter four cases of political mobilisation in which wireless communication played a significant role. These are the ousting of President Estrada from the Philippines in 2001, the election of Korean President Moo-Hyun in 2002, the electoral defeat of the Spanish Partido Popular in 2004, and the organisation of a series of protests during the United States Republican Party's national convention in 2004. In the final section of our chapter, we consider two cases in which wireless communication did not result in socio-political mobilisation,

and emphasise the importance of political frameworks and institutions in shaping the uses of technology. Thus we briefly discuss the factors underlying the political apathy of mobile phone subscribers in Japan and especially in China during the SARS epidemic of 2003. In our view, any attempt to understand civil society, both global and local, in the twenty-first century will have to pay attention to the interplay between institutions, technology and values in the process and outcomes of social organisation and social mobilisation.

The Philippines: People Power II

In January 2001, thousands of cell phone touting Filipinos took part in massive demonstrations now dubbed 'People Power II' (following the original People Power movement that overthrew Ferdinand and Imelda Marcos in 1986). This four-day event has become legendary as the first occasion in human history when the mobile phone played an instrumental role in removing the head of the government of a nation-state (Bagalawis 2001; Salterio 2001: 25).

On 30 June 1998, Joseph Estrada, a well-known actor and populist candidate, was sworn in as the 13th President of the Philippines. From the beginning of his presidency, Estrada was subjected to allegations of corruption, including mishandling of public funds, accepting bribery, and using illegal income to buy houses for his mistresses. The most serious charge that led to his expulsion from office came in October 2000, when he was accused of receiving US$80 million from a gambling pay-off scheme and several more million from tobacco tax kickbacks. On 12 October, Vice-President Gloria Macapagal Arroyo, a Harvard-trained economist and the daughter of former President Diosdado Macapagal, resigned from the cabinet and later become the leader of what would soon become People Power II (*Pamantalaang Mindanaw* 2000).

On 18 October 2000, opposition groups filed an impeachment motion against Estrada in the House of Representatives. Protests started to emerge in Manila. In less than a month, dozens of senior officials and lawmakers from Estrada's ruling party withdrew their support, including both the Senate president and the House speaker. On 7 December, the Senate impeachment trial formally began. Multiple investigations took place, revealing more and more evidence against Estrada.

> **News coverage of the demonstrations invariably highlights the role of new communication technologies, especially short message service (SMS) and the internet, in facilitating the protests**

Soon, a violent disaster disrupted the political life of the entire country. On 30 December 2000, five bombs exploded in Manila, killing 22 people and injuring more than 120 (*Philippine Daily Inquirer* 2001). The explosions were synchronised to hit the city's crowded public spaces, including the airport, a light-rail train, a bus, a gas station, and a park near the US embassy (*The Australian* 2001). A police investigation incriminated Jemaah Islamiyah, a Muslim rebel group that was later linked to Al-Qaeda (Associated Press 2003), although many suspected at the time that the explosions were linked to Estrada's impeachment trial.

On 16 January 2001, the Senate in a critical session voted by 11 votes to 10 not to open an envelope that was believed to contain records of Estrada's secret transactions. Within hours, enraged Manila residents – many of them following instructions received on their cell phones – gathered in the historic Shrine at Epifnio de los Santos Avenue, also known as Edsa, the site of the People Power revolt of 1986, to protest against perceived injustice and demand the immediate removal of Estrada from the presidency.

The massive demonstrations of People Power II lasted for four days, 16–20 January. The group of senator-judges serving at the impeachment trial resigned on 17 January and the case was suspended indefinitely. With increasing pressure from protesters led by Gloria Arroyo and other former officials, the defence secretary and finance secretary resigned on 19 January to join the opposition. By then, the Estrada cabinet had basically collapsed, with most of its key posts abandoned; most importantly, the military had sided with demonstrators. On 20 January, Estrada was escorted out of the Malacanang Palace by the armed forces chief of staff and vice chief of staff. By the end of

the day, the Supreme Court had declared the presidency vacant, Gloria Arroyo had been sworn in, and People Power II concluded on a triumphant note.

News coverage of the demonstrations invariably highlights the role of new communication technologies, especially short message service (SMS) and the internet, in facilitating the protests. In one account, anti-Estrada information began to accumulate in online forums as soon as he took office in 1998, amounting to some 200 websites and about 100 e-mail discussion groups by the time People Power II started (Pabico nd). A famous online forum is E-Lagda.com, which collected 91,000 e-signatures to support the impeachment through both the internet and SMS (Bagalawis 2001). Besides imparting pure information, many internet and text messages poked fun at Estrada, his (allegedly) corrupt life, and his poor English.

While this kind of semi-serious communication continued for more than two years, allowing for the expression of widespread discontent, it was text messaging that made possible the swift gathering of tens of thousands of people immediately after the crucial Senate vote of 16 January. According to a member of the Generation Txt who joined the demonstrations, she was on a date in the evening when the news broke (Uy-Tioco 2003: 1–2). She first received a message from her best friend: 'I THNK UD BETR GO HME NW (I think you'd better go home now)'. But by the time she got home, already quite late in the evening, she received numerous messages from others such as: 'NOISE BARRAGE AT 11PM', 'GO 2 EDSA, WEAR BLACK 2 MOURN D DEATH F DEMOCRACY.' She then quickly followed the instructions:

> *I barely had time to kick off my high heels and slip on my sneakers when my mom, brother, and I jumped into the car and joined the cars in our neighborhood in honking horns in protest. And then to Edsa we went. At midnight, there were a couple of hundred people. Families clad in pajamas, teenagers in party clothes, men and women in suits fresh from happy hour, college students clutching books obviously coming from a study group, nuns and priests.*

The authors wish to acknowledge the support of the Annenberg Foundation and of the Annenberg School for Communication in the preparation of this chapter.

ELECTRONIC COMMUNICATION

©Marc Schlossman/Panos Pictures

During the week of People Power II, Smart Communications Inc transmitted 70 million text messages, and Globe Telecom, the other main SMS operator, handled 45 million messages each day as opposed to its normal daily average of 24.7 million (Bagalawis 2001). The demonstrators were using text messages so actively that they seriously strained the networks covering Edsa. According to Smart's public affairs officer, 'The sudden increase in the volume of messages being handled at that time was so tremendous that sometimes the signals were not coming through, especially in the Edsa area.' High-level representatives from Globe admitted similar difficulty, saying that mobile cell sites had to be transferred from the Senate and rural Bicol to ease equipment load, alleviate congestion, and provide back-up contingency (Bagalawis 2001).

Most English-language Filipino media regard the overthrow of Estrada as a positive development in the country's democratic life. Comparing People Power II with the People Power movement of 1986, they argue that there was less violence and military involvement (Andrade-Jimenez 2001); that the demonstration was more centred on information and IT. '[T]he wired and

wireless media became effective messengers of information – be it jokes, rumors, petitions, angry e-mails or factoids – that made People Power II much wider in scope and broader in reach than its predecessor' (Bagalawis 2001). Moreover, the speed of IT-based mobilisation was much faster. Whereas Marcos managed to continue his rule for almost two decades despite serious allegations of corruption and human rights violations, Estrada was ousted after only two-and-a-half years, less than half the six-year presidential term (Andrade-Jimenez 2001; Pabico nd).

For these reasons, Helen Andrade-Jimenez claimed that 'People Power II showed the power of the internet and mobile communications technology – not to mention broadcast media – not only to shape public opinion but also to mobilize civil society when push came to a shove' (Andrade-Jimenez 2001). According to these accounts, the victory of People Power II was the victory of new technologies, especially the mobile phone and the internet. These media accounts, however, need to be treated with caution. After all, '[n]early all the accounts of People Power II available to us come from middle-class writers or by way of a middle-class controlled media with strong nationalist sentiments' (Rafael 2003: 401). Written in the immediate aftermath of the protests, most accounts are excessively celebratory, glossing over many issues important to our understanding of the role of the mobile phone in this political movement.

First, characterising People Power II as non-violent and information centred is to oversimplify it. The military was never a non-factor in the process. It was only after the armed forces sided with the protestors that Estrada retreated and was 'escorted' out of his presidential palace by military commanders. Moreover, the deadly synchronised explosions that killed 22 Manila residents and injured more than 120 took place only 17 days before People Power II. Given the sensitive timing in the middle of the impeachment trial, such a violent incident clearly threatened everyone – especially senator-judges – with an all-out civil war on top of the ongoing clashes with the Muslim rebels accused of perpetrating the 30 December bombing. Such a civil war was quite possible because, despite the corruption charges, Estrada had overwhelming support in the countryside and among the poor, as shown in his landslide victory in the 1998 election. In fact, in a seldom-told story, on 25 April 2001, three months after People Power II, Estrada was formally arrested on charges of graft and corruption, soon after which 'a crowd of perhaps one hundred thousand formed at Edsa and demanded Estrada's release and reinstatement' (Rafael 2003: 422):

Unlike those who had gathered there during People Power II, the crowd in what came to be billed as the 'Poor People Power' was trucked in by Estrada's political operatives from the slums and nearby provinces and provided with money, food, and, on at least certain occasions, alcohol. In place of cell phones, many reportedly were armed with slingshots, homemade guns, knives, and steel pipes. English-language news reports described this crowd as unruly and uncivilized and castigated protestors for strewing garbage on the Edsa Shrine, harassing reporters, and publicly urinating near the giant statue of the Virgin Mary of Edsa. (Rafael 2003: 422)

Besides showing the potential for large-scale violence during the impeachment trial, Poor People Power calls into question the proclaimed importance of new media because, although most poor demonstrators did not have cell phones (let alone internet access), this particular crowd was also able to gather in virtually no time[1]. They had to be 'trucked in' since, unlike the middle-class protestors, they had no other means of transportation (see the quotation on page 267 from Uy-Tioco for the usage of private cars in People Power II). Meanwhile, as Rafael (2003: 422–3) points out, the negative descriptions of the Poor People Power in part reflected the class positioning of Filipino English-language newspapers:

Other accounts qualified these depictions by pointing out that many in the crowd [of Poor People Power] were not merely hired thugs or demented loyalists [of Estrada] but poor people who had legitimate complaints. They had been largely ignored by the elite politicians, the Catholic Church hierarchy, the middle-class-dominated left-wing groups, and the NGOs. Even though Estrada manipulated them, the protestors saw their ex-president as a patron who had given them hope by way of occasional handouts and who addressed them in their vernacular. ...Generation Txt spoke of democratization, accountability, and civil society; the 'tsingelas crowd,' so called because of the cheap rubber slippers many protestors wore, was fixated on its 'idol,' Estrada.

Poor People Power was finally dispersed by the military after five days (Rafael 2003: 425). This incident, seldom incorporated in the narrative of People Power II, shows the oversimplifying nature of the 'People Power' label with respect to the deep-seated class problems in the Philippines that offer more fundamental explanations for the social unrest described above and beyond the over-celebrated power of the new media in and of themselves. Almost 40 per cent of Filipinos live on a daily income of one US dollar (Bociurkiw 2001). Of the country's total population of 80 million (National Statistical Coordination Board URL), only about 13.8 per cent had access to mobile phones in 2001. The scope of the cell phone's political influence was therefore still quite limited. Although some members of the lower classes also took part in People Power II, they were, like the 'tsingelas crowd', presumed to be 'voiceless' in the 'telecommunicative fantasies' about the cell phone (Rafael 2003: 400).

---

1 *It is unclear, however, to what extent the organisers of Poor People Power, the 'political operatives' of Estrada, were relying on mobile phones at the time.*

©Ami Vitale/Panos Pictures

The contradiction of class interests was most acutely presented in a book – titled *Power Grab* (Arillo 2003), whose summary was prominently featured on Estrada's official website[2]. It maintains that:

[Estrada] lost his job when white-collar mobsters and plunderers, backed by seditious communists, do-gooder prelates, traditional politicians, and misguided police and military generals, banded together and toppled his regime, first, by using massive disinformation and black propaganda carefully crafted to provide half-true, misleading, or wholly false information to deceive and anger the public.

Quite apart fom the highly partisan language, this pro-Estrada writer obviously agrees that communication technologies played a pivotal role, though not to inform and mobilise in a positive sense but to disseminate 'disinformation', 'to deceive and anger the public', and to 'misguide' police and generals. The question that emerges is: given that Estrada was the sitting president, why he did not prevent the 'disinformation'

and vicious mobilisation against himself? Did he think the new technology was invincible since 'one could imagine each user becoming his or her own broadcasting station: a node in a wider network of communication that the state could not possibly monitor, much less control'? (Rafael 2003: 403). More likely, as Rafael continues, the new technologies, especially the cell phone, were powerful because there was a need for 'the power to overcome the crowded conditions and congested surroundings brought about by state's inability to order everyday life' (2003: 403). In other words, the existence of a relatively weak state was a condition for the key role of the mobile phone and the internet in this case. The outcome might have been very different had there been stronger state control. Although there were some indications that Estrada was attempting to acquire the technology to monitor cell phone use, '[i]t is doubtful, however, that cell phone surveillance technology was available to the Estrada administration' (Rafael 2003:

2 www.erap.com (consulted 3 June 2004).

403)[3]. Besides problems in technologies, this probably reflected Estrada's life first as a successful film star (making him overconfident about the image that film, TV, and radio had created of him), then as a long-time, small-town politician (making him unprepared for the power of the new communications media in Manila) (Pabico nd).

It should also be pointed out that other social forces were playing critical roles, especially the Catholic Church and the radio and other media under its influence. A Catholic nun was among the first openly to accuse Estrada's family of mishandling public funds (Uy-Tioco 2003: 9). Cardinal Sin, the head of the Roman Catholic Church in the Philippines, had been among the most prominent anti-Estrada leaders since the beginning of the impeachment in October 2000 (BBC News 2000; Gaspar 2001). Moreover, while many were suspicious of the credibility of SMS messages because so many of them consisted of ungrounded rumours, religious organisations were deliberately involved to add legitimacy to anti-Estrada text messages. As one activist reveals in a listserv post:

> I was certain [texting] would not be taken seriously unless it was backed up by some kind of authority figure to give it some sort of legitimacy. A priest who was with us suggested that Radio Veritas [the church-owned broadcasting station] should get involved in disseminating the particulars ... We [then] formulated a test message ... and sent it out that night and I turned off my phone ... By the time I turned it on in the morning, the message had come back to me three times ... I am now a firm believer in the power of the text! (quoted in Rafael 2003: 408)

As mentioned earlier, mobile phones also worked closely with hundreds of anti-Estrada websites and listservs during the movement. In addition to famous online forums such as E-Lagda.com, blogging sites were also involved, such as 'The Secret Diary of Erap Estrada (erap.blogspot.com)' (Andrade-Jimenez 2001). It is thus erroneous to give all the credit to texting, since mobile phones had to function in this particular media environment, which reflected the middle-class-dominated power structure at the time. It is within this larger framework that we should acknowledge that the mobile phone – as a medium that is portable, personal, and prepared to receive and

deliver messages anytime, anywhere – can perform a mobilisation function much more efficiently than other communication channels at the tipping point of an emerging political movement.

On the other hand, as a tool of political communication, texting has a serious limitation: it allows short messages to be copied and distributed quickly and widely, but it permits very little editing or elaboration based on the original message. It is suited for simple coordinating messages, such as specifying the time and location of a gathering and what to wear (black clothes, in this case). However, it is highly insufficient for civic deliberation. With SMS, the messages were 'mechanically augmented but semantically unaltered ... producing a "technological revolution" that sets the question of social revolution aside' (Rafael 2003: 409–10). 'Texting is thus "revolutionary" in a reformist sense' (Rafael 2003: 410). If a real revolution were to take place that fundamentally altered a social structure, it would most likely involve other media, including not only the internet, which has been accompanying the cell phone in most political mobilisations, but also traditional mass media and interpersonal communication.

Finally, there was a global dimension to People Power II. New media technologies, especially the internet, enabled the global Filipino diaspora to participate more easily (Andrade-Jimenez 2001). Since overseas Filipinos are more sympathetic toward middle-class appeals, they added significantly to the oppositional force. Moreover, Estrada has been an outspoken nationalist for most of his political life. He was named the Most Outstanding Mayor and Foremost Nationalist in 1972 (Alfredson and Vigilar 2001). In 1991, he was the first senator to propose the termination of the US military bases in the Philippines. He therefore had little support from global capital or the US government, which would rather watch him being replaced by Gloria Arroyo, who was more Westernised and represented middle-class interests.

To sum up, during People Power II, the mobile phone, and especially text messaging, did play a major role in message dissemination, political mobilisation, and the coordination of campaign logistics. Because it allows instant communication at any time, anywhere,

---

3 In 2000 and 2001, even if there were mobile phone surveillance systems, they must have been still too primitive to be used during large-scale political movements such as People Power II.

©Mark Henley/Panos Pictures

Wireless communication and the 'people who love Roh' in South Korea

On 19 December 2002, South Korea elected its new president, Roh Moo-Hyun, a major part of whose victory has been widely attributed to 'Nosamo', an online supporter group known by this Korean acronym of 'people who love Roh'. The success of Roh and of Nosamo is now 'a textbook example for the power of IT' (Hachigian and Wu 2003: 68), which systematically utilised a combination of the internet and mobile phone-based communication While the internet-based campaign had lasted for years, providing the core political networks, it was the mobile phones that mobilised large numbers of young voters on the election day and finally reversed the voting result (Fulford 2003; S-D Kim nd; Rhee 2003).

Nosamo is not a random phenomenon. It is rather a strategic coalition of liberal pro-reform political forces and new communication technologies that came together in response to pressing issues such as economic growth and the problem of regionalism. Based on the nation's high internet and mobile phone penetration rates, it also draws on the pro-democracy student demonstrations of the 1980s (Fairclough 2004; J-M Kim 2001: 49). This is a very sensible strategy given that the traditional media, especially newspapers, are predominantly conservative (S-D Kim nd). These 'old' media had little appeal to young people in their twenties and thirties; yet this age group is a baby-boom generation that makes up slightly more than half the total number of voters (J-M Kim 2001).

Roh Moo-Hyun, a self-educated labour lawyer, assumed the presidency at the rather young age of 56. He differed from most other politicians in having a more radical reformist agenda that, on the one hand, favoured a fundamental overhaul of the *chaebols*, the family-dominated conglomerates that 'have long funded the country's political machinery' (Fairclough 2004), and, on the other hand, attempted to transcend the boundaries of regionalism, a deep-rooted structural problem in Korean politics (Rhee 2003: 95). In addition to these particular political stances, Roh was also known for his highly idealistic personality[4] because, despite repeatedly failing to win elections (as mayor of Pusan and then as a member of the national assembly), he refused to compromise or switch parties as many

---

4 For this, some analysts would even characterise him as 'unrealistic, foolhardy' (Rhee 2003: 95).

it is most suited to assembling large-scale demonstrations immediately after emergent political events such as the senators' decision on the impeachment trial on 16 January 2001, or events during the Korean presidential election of 2002. However, the social influence of the mobile phone was limited by the digital divide. It is often a tool serving the interests of the middle class, traditional stakeholders (such as the Catholic Church), and global capital. It does not always have high credibility or sufficient capacity to spur two-way civic deliberation. For these reasons, mobile phones and texting have to work closely with other media, such as the internet and radio as shown in this case, in order to lead to actual political consequences at the national level.

other opposition figures did. This iconoclastic image won him 'an almost cult-like following among young Koreans' (Demick 2003).

Roh's age, policy, and personality assured him of great popularity among young voters, 'just as President Bill Clinton appealed to many American baby boomers' (Fairclough 2004). At the core of his support is the generation of the so-called '386ers', those who were in their thirties during the presidential election, who grew up in the 1980s with Korea's pro-democracy movement, and were born in the 1960s at the dawn of South Korea's industrialisation era (Fairclough 2004). Unlike the older generations, the 386ers are 'more skeptical of the US in part because Washington backed the same military rulers they fought against as college students' (Fairclough 2004). In addition, there were also large numbers of younger supporters in their twenties, such as Hwang Myong-Pil, a stock trader who quit his well-paid job to become a full-time volunteer at Nosamo (Demick 2003). Together, the twenty- and thirty-somethings were Korea's baby-boom generation, accounting for slightly more than half the voter population (J-M Kim 2001; Rhee 2003). Most of these young activists regarded themselves as having inherited the revolutionary spirit of the student demonstrations of more than a decade ago. At large political gatherings, they would chant songs dating back to the pro-democracy movement of the 1980s, such as 'Morning Dew' (Korea Times 2002).

To reach this critical cohort of voters, Roh experimented with online campaigns back in 1995, when he was running for election as mayor of Pusan. It 'fits in with his political philosophy of openness and direct communication with the people'[5]. Many of his closest aides in the presidential election were former student activists (Fairclough 2004). This was a highly innovative approach, not only because it used new technology but also because it appealed to the younger generation in a more substantial way than the predominantly conservative traditional media that formed part of the Korean political machine. Consequently, young people had been feeling cynical and disenfranchised in the political process:

Nearly a third of the nation's twenty-somethings didn't bother to vote in the 1997 presidential election. Less than 40 per cent of the 8 million people in their twenties voted in parliamentary elections in April last year [2000], far below the 57 per cent national

average. (J-M Kim 2001: 49)

It was at this historic moment of low voting turnout among young people, when Roh Moo-Hyun lost his second race in the parliamentary election, that Nosamo (www.nosamo.org) came into being. On 6 June 2000, Nosamo was formed by around 100 founding members who convened in Taejon (Korea Times 2002). While Roh's campaign team had been actively utilising the new media, Nosamo was a voluntary organisation self-funded by membership fees and only informally affiliated with Roh (Rhee 2003: 95). Within five months, its membership had mushroomed: from around 100 to nearly 5,000 in November 2001 (J-M Kim 2001: 50), and then to 70–80,000 by the end of 2002, amounting to a most formidable political force[6].

During the presidential election of 2002, Nosamo members raised more than US$7 million over the internet (Demick 2003). They used electronic bulletins, online polls, and text messages to formulate collective decisions and coordinate campaign activities. 'All the decisions about their activities are made through an electronic voting system and the final decision making online committee has its monthly meeting in chat rooms' (J-M Kim 2001: 50). Among a variety of logistical tasks, one was to ensure that people wore yellow outfits when attending political rallies – yellow being the colour symbolising Roh's campaign (Korea Times 2002).

At times, members of Nosamo could act quite aggressively. For instance, a professor made a comment perceived to be critical of Roh supporters on a television talk show. He was subjected to hundreds of angry e-mails and was widely lambasted in the Nosamo forum (Demick 2003). Because of this and similar activities, Nosamo was criticised for behaving like 'Internet Red Guards' with 'violent words in cyberspace and an appeal to populism' (Demick 2003). About a month before the presidential election, South Korea's election commission barred the group from raising money for the candidate (Demick 2003), and the organisation's website was forced to close until the election day (Korea Times 2002).

5 Min-Kyung Bae, head of the Cyber Culture Research Association in Seoul, quoted in Demick (2003).
6 Estimates of the number of Nosamo members vary from 70,000 (Korea Times 2002) to 80,000 (Demick 2003).

Meanwhile, the rather unconventional approaches of Roh Moo-Hyun continued to work to his disadvantage. Mainstream media, most of which belonged to the conservative camp, kept casting him in a negative light (Rhee 2003; S-D Kim nd). A few months before the election, Roh was so far down in the opinion polls that members of his own Millennium Democratic Party (MDP) tried to force him out of the race (Demick 2003). On the eve of election, Roh's key campaign partner, the multi-millionaire Chung Mong-Joon, suddenly withdrew his support, dealing a heavy blow to the entire campaign at the last minute (*Korea Times* 2002).

...it would be an exaggeration to attribute to the mobile phone some kind of magical, innate political power as the sole or even the most important media device

---

As the day of the election dawned on 19 December 2002, Nosamo members were struck by a deep sense of crisis. With their main website having been closed for the month preceding election eve, young activists started the day by posting online messages such as 'Let's go vote!' (Rhee 2003: 96)[7]. By 11 am exit polls showed that Roh was losing by a margin of 1 to 2 per cent (Fulford 2003; Rhee 2003: 96). At midday, '[h]is supporters hit the chat rooms to drum up support. Within minutes more than 800,000 e-mails were sent to mobile phones to urge supporters to go out and vote. Traditionally apathetic young voters surged to the polls, and by 2 pm, Roh took the lead and went on to win the election' (Fulford 2003).

Several elements contributed to this historic event, when mobile phones for the first time played a significant part in determining the outcome of a presidential election. First, a large-scale grassroots political network was already centred on Nosamo, whose members not only had frequent online exchanges but also met offline. Second, Roh Moo-Hyun's centre-left policies and iconoclastic image energised young liberals, many of whom were highly motivated and ready to act promptly at a time of crisis. Third, Chung Mong-Joon's sudden withdrawal of support on election eve and the temporary trailing of Roh created an urgent need to rally public support. And the mobile phone – the quintessential grassroots communication gadget that is always on, 'anywhere,

anytime,' – turned out to be the best medium for these rallying calls. Given the strength of youth networks (Yoon 2003a; 2003b) and the demographic fact that people in their twenties and thirties made up slightly more than half the total number of voters (J-M Kim 2001: 49), young people mobilised through mobile messages became a decisive voting bloc. At the end of the day, 'sixty percent of voters in their 20s and 30s cast ballots for Roh' (Rhee 2003: 95).

After President Roh took office, Nosamo decided to remain active following an internal poll in January 2003 (*Korea Herald* 2003). Nosamo members continued to 'solicit suggestions for appointees to Cabinet positions and engage in debates over topics ranging from North Korea's nuclear programme, to whether it would be more appropriate for Roh to take up golf or jogging as president' (Demick 2003). In fact, like any long-term civic group, they played a relatively independent watchdog role in observing, and sometimes criticising, Roh's presidential decisions. Back in 2001, a founding member of Nosamo was quoted as saying that 'We're using the Net to support him. But we want to say "no" when he makes any decision which we think is wrong' (J-M Kim 2001: 50). On 24 March 2003, Nosamo adopted a statement opposing the US-led war in Iraq and the decision of South Korea to dispatch engineering and medical troops there (*Korea Times* 2003). Yet the Roh administration proceeded with the plan, causing some Nosamo members to withdraw from the group; one of them said:

I withdrew from Nosamo because President Roh Moo-Hyun has shown us drastically different aspects since becoming president. I do not love Roh Moo-Hyun anymore. I hate the sight of the president supporting the barbaric war of the United States killing innocent civilians of Iraq. (Korea Times 2003)

In spring 2004, Nosamo again played a major role in staging support for Roh during an impeachment investigation against him on charges of violating Korean laws barring partisan remarks within a period of 17 days preceding parliamentary elections (Len 2004). During this election, the liberal Uri Party, which had Roh's support, used mobile phones for campaigning

---

7   It is, however, difficult to find other actual mobilisation short messages in primary and secondary sources, unlike news accounts on the People Power II movement in the Philippines.

Improvised memorial at Atocha Station, Madrid ©*Matia Costa/Panos Pictures*

purposes. Along with the usual policy statements, candidate profiles, and scheduled appearances, Nosamo's website also encouraged supporters to copy 'Get out and vote' messages and send them out by mobile phone to ten friends who were then, in turn, asked to forward the message to ten of their friends (Salmon 2004).

The socio-political uses of the mobile phone are still increasing as Korean society further transforms and the technology further diffuses and becomes more mature. Again, the role of the mobile has to be understood as closely related to other media, especially the online bulletin board system (BBS). These new media function most importantly as a catalyst for the mobilisation of existing youth networks, giving rise to groups, such as Nosamo, that are, in one sense, new political forces whose historical origins, however, can be traced back at least two decades. That said, it would be an exaggeration to attribute to the mobile phone some kind of magical, innate political power as the sole or even the most important media device. Yet it would be equally erroneous to ignore the unique capacity of the mobile phone – as a gadget of 'perpetual contact' – to promote the swift mobilisation of certain marginalised social groups at critical political moments such as the Korean presidential election of 2002.

Terrorism, political manipulation, autonomous communication, social mobilisation, and political change: Spain, March 2004[8]

On 11 March 2004, a Madrid-based, mainly Moroccan, radical Islamic group associated with Al-Qaeda conducted in Madrid the largest terrorist attack in Europe, bombing three suburban trains, killing 199 people and wounding over 1,000. The bombing was conducted by remote-control-activated cell phones. Indeed, it was the discovery of a cell phone calling card in an unexploded bag that led to the identification of the phone and the arrest of the culprits. Al-Qaeda took responsibility for the bombing later that evening. The attack took place in a very particular political context, four days before the Spanish parliamentary elections, which were dominated by the debate on the participation of Spain in the Iraq war, a policy opposed by the vast majority of Spanish citizens. Yet the conservative party, Partido Popular (PP), was considered the likely

---

8 The reconstruction of the events in Spain is based on the researchers' direct observations and on reports in the Spanish press. As of January 2005, there were few bibliographic references on the subject, but we wish to refer to the following: Cué (2004), Juan (2004), Partal and Otamendi (2004), Rodríguez (2004), Spanish Parliament (2004), de Ugarte (2004), VVAA (2004).

winner of the election, based on its record in economic policy and its stand on Basque terrorism. However, in the last weeks before the election the young, charismatic Socialist leader Jose Luis Rodriguez Zapatero waged an impressive electoral campaign, so that on 10 March 2004, opinion polls rendered the result of the election too close to call one way or the other.

In this political context, as soon as the Madrid terror attack occurred, and before any evidence surfaced, the PP government stated with total conviction that ETA, the Basque terrorist group, was behind the bombing. As the hours went by, it became increasingly likely that Al-Qaeda was the culprit. Yet the Minister of the Interior and the government's spokesman continued to insist that ETA was responsible, until the evening of 13 March. The government calculated that holding the Basque terrorists responsible would favour the PP in the elections, while acknowledging that Islamic terrorists were probably responsible would indicate to Spaniards the high price they were paying for their government's policy in Iraq, thus potentially inciting them to vote against the government. In the minds of millions of Spaniards (67 per cent of them) the government was manipulating information about the attack, seeking political advantage. This widespread feeling was an important factor in the unexpected political defeat of the PP on 14 March, leading to the election of a Socialist government and to the immediate withdrawal of Spanish troops from Iraq.

A parliamentary commission investigating the events of 11–14 March produced evidence that, without necessarily lying, at the very least the PP government had delayed the publication of some critical information, and stated as facts propositions that were still under scrutiny. There was clearly an inclination to favour the hypothesis of Basque terrorism and not to give priority to following the Islamic trail, in spite of the early leads of the police in this direction. But, regardless of the extent of manipulation that actually took place, what counts is that thousands of citizens were convinced, on 12 and 13 March, that such manipulation was happening, and that they decided to diffuse their views to the entire population through wireless communication and the internet. The main television networks, under the direct or indirect control of the government, were supporting the Basque terrorist hypothesis, as did most of the radio networks (though not the largest one) and most of the print media, after the Prime Minister personally called the editors of the main newspapers and gave them his word that the attack was carried out by ETA.

Thus, oppositional views on the actual source of terror had to find alternative channels of communication to be heard. The use of these alternative communication channels led to mobilisations against the PP on Saturday 13 March, a 'day of reflection' when, under Spanish law, political demonstrations and public statements are forbidden. Yet the actions of thousands of protestors, most of them youths, made an impact on public opinion, and particularly on the two million new voters – young people who usually have a higher abstention rate or vote for minority parties rather than for Socialists or Conservatives. In this election, there were 2.5 million more voters than in the 2000 parliamentary election, and about 1 million voters switched to the Socialists, seeking to punish the government both for its policy on Iraq and for its perceived manipulation of information. The Socialist Party won a clear majority in an election that saw a 77 per cent turnout. This discussion, on the basis of published reports, explores the process through which alternative communications channels were created and used efficiently.

...on Saturday morning, a number of activists, mostly individuals without any current political affiliations, and independently of the mainstream parties, started to circulate text messages

---

The process of alternative communication started with the outpouring of emotion that surrounded the street demonstrations on Friday 12 March, called by the government with the support of all political forces. This is important: it was in the physical gathering that people first started to react and to oppose the official version of the facts, independently of political parties that remained silent for the occasion. While the demonstration was called against terrorism and in support of the constitution (an oblique reference to Basque separatism), many of the participants were displaying banners opposing the war in Iraq. The demonstration was intended to mark the end of political statements, leading to the day of reflection on Saturday and to the election on Sunday. Yet on Saturday morning a number of activists, mostly individuals without any current political affiliations, and independently of the mainstream parties, started to circulate text messages to the addresses programmed in their cell phones. In the messages they denounced the manipulation of information and called for a demonstration at 6 pm in front of the headquarters of the PP in Madrid and then in other Spanish cities. This was in fact outlawed, and naturally did not receive any support, explicit or implicit, from any party, although some of the participants in these gatherings were members of left-wing parties, particularly of the United Left (a small party in parliament that includes the remnants of the Communist Party in Spain). But most of the activists were participants in the anti-war movement, and most of the people gathering in front of the PP headquarters were simply those reached by the network of SMSs. The earliest and most famous of these messages, all fitting within the 160 characters frame of the SMS format, was the following:

Aznar off the hook? ¿They call it day of reflection and Urdaci works? Today, 13M, 18h. PP headquarters, Genova street, 13. No parties. Silent for truth. Forward it! ('Pasalo!').

The reference to Urdaci must be explained: he was the notorious anchorman of Spanish national television, well known for his manipulation of political news (in fact, sentenced for such by the court). In the meantime, Spanish national television continued to defend the story of Basque terrorism, and, in the evening before the election, changed its regular programming to broadcast a documentary film on the assassination of a Socialist politician by Basque terrorists.

On Saturday, SMS traffic increased by 40 per cent over a regular Saturday, reaching a higher volume than on a regular Monday, an all-time record for these messages. The critical point is that, while most messages were very similar, the sender for each receiver was someone known, someone who had the receiver's address in his or her cell phone's address book. Thus, the network of diffusion was at the same time increasing at an exponential rate but without losing the proximity of the source, according to the well-known 'small world' phenomenon[9].

The internet started to become an alternative channel of communication earlier, on 11 March particularly, but also on the 12th. On the one hand, people used the internet to look for other sources of information, particularly from abroad. But there were also a number of initiatives, including some by journalists acting on their own, to set up a website with information and debates from various sources.

Interestingly enough, the PP started an SMS network with a different message: 'ETA are the authors of the massacre. Pasalo!' But it diffused mainly through party channels, did not reach a critical mass of known person to known person, and, more importantly, was not credible for the thousands of people who were already doubting the government's word.

The context provided by the mainstream media was also meaningful. Major television networks were very soon ignored as unreliable sources of information. Through their hesitancy newspapers made themselves unreliable, although *La Vanguardia* in Barcelona, printed in its front page on Saturday an article supporting the claim that Al-Qaeda was responsible for the attack. On the other hand, SER, the major private radio network, on the initiative of its journalists, immediately looked for evidence elsewhere than on the Basque trail. Sometimes it did so too eagerly, as it diffused some inaccurate information; yet most of its reports proved to be accurate. As a result, many people treated their radios (including their portable radios) as their source of information, and then interacted with SMS and cell phone calls. People used voice communication for direct discussion with close friends, and SMS for diffusing personally crafted messages or for forwarding received messages that they agreed with.

Thus, the context of communication was provided by the physical gathering in the streets, at the beginning of the formation of public opinion, and as a result of the process of political communication: the congregation in front of the PP buildings was the proof of the usefulness of the message. Then the street action attracted the attention of some radio and television networks (regional television and CNN-Spain) and ultimately, on Saturday at 20.20, forced the Minister of the Interior to appear on national television acknowledging Al Qaeda's possible role. Yet later on, the leading candidate of the PP also appeared on national television denouncing the demonstrators, unwittingly fuelling the crisis of trust that they had induced. An error of political communication thus amplified the effect of the demonstrations.

---

9 *The small world phenomenon (also known as the small world effect) is the hypothesis that everyone in the world can be reached through a short chain of social acquaintances. The concept gave rise to the famous phrase 'six degrees of separation' after a small world experiment by psychologist Stanley Milgram (1967), which found that two random US citizens were connected by an average of six acquaintances.*

Protesters demonstrate against the Republican convention
in New York ©Teun Voeten/Panos Pictures

The Mobilisation around the Republican National Convention in New York

The US Republican Party held its 2004 National Convention (RNC) from 30 August to 2 September amid heightened expectations of disturbances caused by anti-Bush activists. The run-up to the New York convention was characterised by reports and rumours of planned and potentially spontaneous protests and of how the police and security agencies were preparing to deal with these incidents (Carpenter 2004; Gibbs 2004; Shachtman 2004; Terdiman 2004). Comparisons were made to the battle of Seattle in 1999, when over 40,000 protesters descended on the city from all over the world to protest against the policies of the World Trade Organization (WTO), leading to scenes of violence and contributing to the breakdown of the WTO talks. What was particularly interesting about these reports was that the central role of wireless communication was taken for granted, not just in the protests but in all aspects of the convention. In the event, several (mostly non-violent) protests were indeed coordinated primarily via wireless communication and the internet, leading to over 17,000 arrests. The convention itself was hardly affected by the protests apart from a few minor disruptions. In fact, President Bush experienced a bounce of two percentage points in the polls (among likely voters) after the convention (*The Economist* 2004; Jones 2004). These events occurred too recently for any judgements to be made about their immediate or long-term impact. Preliminary examination, however, indicates that this was a case where the use of wireless communication technologies served to enhance efficiency but not to effect change.

News reports indicate that protests began as early as 27 August with the largest, a march organised by an anti-Iraq group, United for Peace and Justice, on 29 August. Although the police did not give an estimate of numbers, organisers of the march said there were about 500,000 people, the largest ever convention protest (Hauser 2004). Protesters marched past Madison Square Garden, the site of the convention, chanting anti-Bush slogans, led by prominent person-alities such as Jesse Jackson and film-maker Michael Moore. Other protests followed throughout the four days of the convention, all helped by the use of cell phones and text messaging.

Wireless communication, especially text messages, featured prominently as a means of coordinating the

The internet was important as a source of information and a forum of debate in the days preceding the demonstrations. But the critical events were the demonstrations of Saturday 13 March – typical flash mob phenomena prompted by a massive network of SMSs that increased the effect of communication exponentially through interpersonal channels. They happened first in Madrid, but diffused to Barcelona and ultimately to all Spanish cities because, naturally, address books in cell phones include friends and acquaintances in other cities.

This experience in Spain, coming three years after the flash mob mobilisation that forced the resignation of Estrada in the Philippines, will remain a turning point in the history of political communication. Armed with their cell phones, and connected to the internet, individuals and grassroots activists are able to set up powerful, broad, personalised, instant networks of com-munication. Whatever the merits of this phenomenon (as it is subject, of course, to the diffusion of harmful, misleading information), this form of autonomous communication rings a warning bell about the control of information by governments and mainstream media.

Box 8.1: Sample of Republican National Convention reports from TxtMob

15:32:02:   About 100 people at war resisters vigil – ground zero, need more

16:15:19:   Half of WRL march is being detained by orange netting on Fulton btwn Church and Broadway

17:06:57:   Bryant Park near Public Library – lots of police gathering and waiting

18:03:30:   police pushing people off library steps/also police vans headed south on 5th ave from 20th st

18:11:15:   large #'s of cops headed west towards public library, scooters

19:26:17:   Pepper spray used at Herald Square (33rd and 6th). About 1000 people there, traffic almost blocked

19:51:45:   union Square – medics and marching band targeted. Medic also snatched at Herald Square

19:53:20:   Union Sq. at 16th st. things arrests getting violent, people completely penned in.

20:01:20:   Video cameras needed at Irving and E16th, near Union Square.

20:44:02:   26th and Park, spontaneous march being chased on foot by police. Arrests.

23:27:45:   Busses full arrestees are lined up on the West Side HW btwn 15 &18 St waiting to enter pier 57

23:42:46:   Lots of arrestees tonight! Show them your support! Meet folks as there released @ 100 Center St. 9am-1am

Source: Rubin (2004)

activities of protesters and sending out alerts about ongoing activities, such as spontaneous gatherings or police arrests, at least from the perspective of news coverage of the protests. For example, text messages were used to call a spontaneous rally on 1 September at the pier where arrested protesters were being held by the police (Simon 2004). Other people used text messages to decide which protests they would attend, or to avoid 'hot spots' where police brutality was taking place. Especially prominent were warning messages about where police were located and whether they were arresting protesters (see Box 8.1).

The pre-conference hype about protest activities was to some extent accurate, but also exaggerated the potential for wireless communication to cause any major upsets at the conference. For the most part, the protests were widespread but not revolutionary. This happened for a number of reasons. First, the use of wireless communication as a protest tool had been so widely anticipated that it was incorporated into the strategies of the security forces. For one thing, security detail used wireless monitoring techniques

themselves, such as head-mounted miniature video cameras that transmitted footage from the security personnel's location to a mobile command centre (Reardon 2004). Security personnel also allegedly infiltrated protesters' planning meetings and monitored text messaging and other communication services used by activists (Gibbs 2004; Gibson 2004). For example, during the convention protesters using indymedia's website to transmit messages soon realised that the 'police were on to them'. Thereafter, 'calls for "direct action" stayed posted only for a couple of minutes and used code words for location' (Becker and Port 2004).

Second, and linked to the above point, unlike some radical protests that were generated spontaneously, such as those discussed in our other three case studies, a high level of central management was associated with wireless use in the RNC context. Most of the protests and protest strategies were carefully planned, some as much as a year in advance (Archibold 2003). In addition, protest groups had to obtain a permit to demonstrate, of which eventually

29 were granted (Archibold 2004). The locations and routes of protests were mapped out in detail (Slackman 2004), and each protest was closely monitored by the police. Generally, those who tried to implement protests without a permit ended up being arrested for unlawful assembly, and their numbers were never large enough to change the tone of the protest environment. Although thousands of demonstrators gathered at Central Park after the 29 August march, in defiance of a court decision not to allow protests in that area, there is no indication that this gathering had any effect on the progress of the convention.

> ...the single-mindedness associated with other protests that have effected immediate change was absent from these demonstrations

Another example of central management was the use of specially tailored text messaging systems such as Ruckus, TxtMob (probably the most popular service used at the RNC), which was specifically designed by the Institute for Applied Autonomy for use by activists to broadcast messages during the Democratic and Republican conventions, or MoPort, which allowed individuals to 'mobblog' by sending pictures of the protests from their mobile devices to be downloaded onto the internet. The objective of MoPort was 'to join the disparate streams into a collective reporting effort' (Dayal 2004). It is possible that there was a need for such centrally organised services because of the lack of a common standard to allow people to send text messages to people on different phone networks. While these types of services effectively brought together communities of like-minded people for the purpose of activism, they lacked the character of direct person-to-person texting based on interpersonal relationships, because users have to sign up to send or receive messages through the service provider's server. Incidentally, for a period during the convention, users of TxtMob had problems receiving messages, for which the service provider gave no explanation, leading to conspiracy theories that some cell phone companies (T-Mobile and Sprint) had deliberately blocked messages. The current explanation is that this may have been the work of a spam filter that tagged messages going out from the same server to more than 100 people as spam (Di Justo 2004;

Lebkowsky 2004). The blackout effectively shut down a flash mob organised by A31 Action coalition, partly because potential participants did not know where the starting point was, although it is not clear why other forms of communication, such as mobile phone calls, could not have served as effective substitutes. This illustrates the limitations of communications technology, especially centralised systems.

The energy of protests was also affected by the fact that they involved several groups with different agendas, from anti-war to animal rights to abortion rights. Admittedly, the convergence of all these groups in one place against a central political institution would be a formidable force. At the same time, the single-mindedness associated with other protests that have effected immediate change was absent from these demonstrations. This can also be linked to the apparent absence of measurable goals. With the election too far away for them to galvanise action to vote against President Bush, and no chance of overturning the Republican Party's nomination of Bush as its candidate for 2004, protesters marched with such goals as:

to regain the integrity of our country... to regain our moral authority... to extend the ban on assault weapons... for more police on our streets... for more port security... for a plan to get out of Iraq (Jackson 2004) or

we want to take charge and reach the right people and influence them to go on and spread the message that this is a corrupt government. (protester quoted by CNN 2004)

It seems, then, that so far the use of wireless communication has not had any significant effect on political events in the United States, at least on the surface. Yet social undercurrents may develop and change people's minds and influence their political behaviour. Indeed, in so far as the protesters' objective was peacefully to make their voice heard during a central political event while avoiding clashes with the police, one can say that the protests were successful. However, we do not have evidence to claim that they had any direct impact on the political process itself.

Texting in Shanghai, China ©*Qilai Shen/Panos Pictures*

Mobile communication without social mobilisation: Japan and China

There are other cases where wireless communication was not used for social mobilisation, such as in Japan, or where initial political developments were crushed by the state, such as in China. While our discussion of these two additional cases is less detailed, due to the lack of studies of them, they do demonstrate that, in line with our earlier claim, the particular usage of wireless technologies is shaped by the social context and political structures of a given society.

In Japan, despite the very high penetration of mobile phone and mobile internet services, so far we have not identified any instances of grassroots socio-political mobilisation that utilised wireless communication, despite several months of literature search among academic and journalistic sources. The Japanese authorities did make some effort to use mobile technologies as a broadcasting system of some sort: for example, the 'Lion Heart' e-newsletter from the office of Prime Minister Junichiro Koizumi, which had 1.7 million subscribers through personal computers and mobile phones by March 2004 (PR

Newswire 2004; Reuters 2001). At the local level, city governments, such as that of Sagamihara in Kanagawa Prefecture in the southern part of Tokyo, also launched an m-government experiment in April 2004 that allowed users to report damage or defects they found in streets and public signs by sending pictures from their camera phones (Suzuki 2004). These are, however, state initiatives that operate top-down rather than examples of socio-political mobilisation that starts within the networks of ordinary mobile-equipped citizens and their organisations, as in the other cases we have discussed. The lack of grassroots political usage among Japanese mobile subscribers is an interesting issue and remains to be explored. At this initial stage, however, we suspect it has to do with the ultra-consumerist tendency of Japan's mobile culture and the relative inactivity of alternative political forces outside the mainstream in general, which is a result of the wider social and cultural framework of Japanese politics that goes way beyond the mobile culture per se.

China is a more extreme case, given its authoritarian political system, which is fundamentally at odds with spontaneous grassroots mobilisation. Hence, despite fast growth in the mobile phone market, the new technologies have so far seldom been put to socio-political uses. And, as in Japan, those few instances have been state-sponsored experiments. For example, during the National People's Congress in March 2002, Xinhua News Agency teamed up with China Mobile to offer the public a chance to text message their concerns and proposals to the country's lawmakers (Zhao forthcoming). Yet there was little indication of the trial's level of success, particularly due to the very limited content capacity of SMS. It may be unrealistic for text messages to convey anything more than a quick request or a short complaint, not to mention any deliberation in the full sense.

Meanwhile, the Chinese authorities have been seeking to limit the use of new communication technologies, including wireless technologies, by political dissidents. The Telecom Ordinance of 2000 outlawed the transmission of harmful information via any telecom facilities (Fries 2000: 43–4)[10]. Later widely known for its influence on the establishment of China's internet censorship regime, this measure was initially designed, in large part, to counter the subversive potential of pagers at the time of its initial promulgation in the mid-1990s. Meanwhile, it provided the legal basis for further, more specific, controls over the mobile phone and SMS.

Although the Chinese authorities are stepping up their regulatory efforts, some elements of Chinese society have nonetheless started to use pagers and cell phones for alternative or even oppositional political organisation. Despite the lack of systematic examination, it is likely that three social groups may have used wireless technologies to further their political ends. First is the Falungong group that Beijing denounces as an 'evil cult'. Second, there have been constant demonstrations by laid-off urbanites or pensioners, such as the massive protests of workers in the petroleum and machinery industries in north-east China in 2002 (Associated Press 2002). Third, in the countryside there have also been protests against the misconduct and corruption of local officials (Duffy and Zhao 2004). Some members of these movements, especially the organisers, may have used wireless technologies (especially the low-end applications such as prepaid phone cards and Little Smart) for small-scale coordination. However, this technical adoption is yet to have any significant impact upon the existing power balance, because, so far, all these perceived challenges to the state have been kept under control at the national level, despite sporadic outbursts in certain localities.

On the basis of her observations, Yuezhi Zhao (forthcoming: 18–19) concluded that, whereas there are some small-scale ICT-facilitated urban movements in China, it is unlikely that they will be connected with the country's 800 million peasants. Moreover, due to the privileged positions of the information-haves, those who have access to the new technologies are 'not necessarily the ones most ready to act upon this critical information' (forthcoming: 20).

Finally, the SARS outbreak of 2003 serves as another indication of the very limited nature of the socio-political uses of mobile phones in general and SMS messages in particular. At the very beginning, no news media or internet outlets reported the epidemic. But victims and their friends and families, especially those who worked in local hospitals of Guangdong, started to text message people they know about this strange, deadly disease. The SMS alerts spread quickly among urban residents in Guangdong and then outside the province to reach the rest of the country. But at this time, public hygiene and propaganda authorities in Beijing decided to expel this 'rumour' by launching a mass media campaign claiming that the infections were no more than a variant of pneumonia, that it was already under control, and that the public panic partially induced by text messages was groundless. This official campaign via traditional media effectively undermined earlier information disseminated via mobile phones, because SMS was perceived to be a medium of lower credibility and there was no other source of information. As a result, most people, including experienced foreign analysts living in south China, chose to believe the official version[11] – to witness a few weeks later the horror of SARS in full swing. Given that the power of the mobile phone was so inadequate for the sustenance of a non-state information system, even about a life-and-death issue of such immediate concern, it would be much more difficult for the new technologies to be applied to other autonomous socio-political uses with any significant consequences, at least in the short run.

---

10 See also the Ordinance at www.isc.org.cn/20020417/ca38931.htm (consulted 29 June 2004).
11 Personal communications with members of the China IT Group.

Conclusion: civil society in the new technological context: the building of autonomy though communication networks

The above cases illustrate the diverse outcomes that the use of communication technologies can mediate. In three of the cases (the Philippines, Korea and Spain) the outcome was substantial in so far as it affected the choice of a government. The fourth process we examined (in the United States) had a limited impact on US politics, and hardly affected the results of the November 2004 presidential election. In the Philippines, wireless communication was employed to oust a sitting president before his term of office ended; in South Korea, the same technologies were used to change the fortunes of a presidential contender who was trailing in the polls. In Spain, text messaging not only was used to galvanise people to vote a government out of power but was also used extensively to supplant, supplement and debunk government propaganda and mainstream media. In the United States, text messaging and other wireless technologies were employed (by protesters and police) as efficient tools to coordinate and monitor protest activities during a political convention. Finally, in Japan and China, socio-political usage of mobile phones is minimal, despite the rapid diffusion of communications technology in these two countries.

A critical difference between the United States and the other three examples is that in the Philippines, Korea and Spain, a combination of factors converged to stimulate spontaneous uprisings, whereas in the United States, the process was more centrally managed, thus removing, to some extent, the element of interpersonal communication based on friendship networks. Significantly, there were no surprises in the US case; everyone had anticipated how wireless communication would likely be used. Conversely, in the other cases, events were less charted and less predictable, and there were no effective countermeasures.

As we have already noted in the various case studies, in order not to be deterministic about the impact of new communications technologies, we should recognise that other communication processes and media, both wired and unwired, were also important in these processes. We certainly know that revolutionary political mobilisations have occurred in countries where wireless communication is lacking. When wireless communication has had some political impetus, some or all of these other processes have been in play,

including a precipitating event strong enough to arouse anger or other emotions, activist instigators, support from respected institutions such as the Church, and supplementary information from mainstream media and/or internet sources. In addition, people involved feel that they really can bring about change and tend to have a focused goal, which can sometimes be directly implemented through the voting process.

We have also noted that communication is a double-edged sword. Speed of information flow through interpersonal networks that has the ability to move people to act can as easily be used to spread rumours or inaccurate information as to spread hidden truths. Also, in so far as there is some differentiation in the diffusion and usage patterns of wireless communication technologies among countries, as well as on the basis of age, gender and socio-economic status, the process of political mobilisation using this means could be limited to certain privileged groups.

Still, based on these case studies, it cannot be denied that access to and use of wireless communications technology adds a beneficial tool to the arsenal of those who seek to influence politics and the political process outside formal channels. Arguably, other media such as wired phones, radio or TV could perform the same rallying function as wireless methods, but not in as timely a manner, not with the ability to reach people wherever they are, and not free of the production constraints associated with traditional media. Wireless communications methods and applications such as cell phones and text messaging, then, do not replace, but add to, and even change, the media ecology, expanding the information networks available to individuals to include the interpersonal level. The shape of civil society, both local and global, is being transformed by new forms of communication that increase people's autonomy to retrieve their own sources of information and to develop their own communication channels. Throughout history, information has always been power, and communication the foundation of counter-power. Therefore, the technology of information and communication is a fundamental dimension of civil society in our time.

Alfredson, Kirsty and Vigilar, Rufi (2001) 'The Rise and Fall of Joseph Estrada', *CNN.com World*, 2 May. http://edition.cnn.com/2001/WORLD/asiapcf/southeast/04/22/estrada.profile/ (consulted 12 June 2004).

Andrade-Jimenez, Helen S. (2001) 'Technology Changing Political Dynamics,' *it matters*, 29 January. http://itmatters.com.ph/news/news_01292001a.html (consulted 3 June 2004).

Archibold, R. C. (2003) 'Protest Groups Planning for Republican Convention', *New York Times*, 10 August: 29.

– (2004) 'Days of Protests, Vigils and Street Theater (Thongs, Too)', *New York Times*, 26 August: B 7.

Arillo, Cecilio T. (2002) *Power Grab*. Manila: Charles Morgan Printing & Equipment, Inc.

Associated Press (2002) 'Laid off Chinese Protest en Masse', 18 March.

– (2003) 'Terror Attacks Believed Linked to Al-Qaida', 20 November.

The Australian (2001) 'Manila on Alert after Blasts', I January.

Bagalawis, Jennifer E. (2001) 'How IT Helped Topple a President', *Computer World*, 30 January. http://wireless.itworld.com/4273/CW_1-31-01_it/pfindex.html (consulted 3 June 2004).

BBC News (2000) 'Cardinal Sin tells Estrada to Quit', 11 October. http://news.bbc.co.uk/1/hi/world/asia-pacific/967115.stm (consulted 14 June 2004).

Becker, M. and Port, B. (2004) 'At GOP Convention, a Technological Battle', *New York Daily News*, 3 September. http://pqasb.pqarchiver.com/nydailynews/687890221.html?did=687890221&fmt=abs&fmts=ft&date=sep+3%2c+2004&author=maki+becker+and+bob+port+daily+news+staff+writers&desc=protesters+click+with+new+media+to+mobilize (consulted 8 September 2004).

Bociurkiw, Michael (2001) 'Revolution by Cell Phone', *Forbes*, 10 September: 28.

Carpenter, S. (2004) 'Pirate Radio to Moor at Republican Convention', *Los Angeles Times*, 27 August: E1.

Chang, S.-J. (2003). 'The Internet Economy of Korea', in B. Kogut (ed.), T*he Global Internet Economy*. Cambridge, MA: The MIT Press, pp. 262–89.

CNN (2004) 'GOP Convention Protest Covers Miles of New York', 30 August. http://usgovinfo.about.com/gi/dynamic/offsite.htm?site=http://www.cnn.com/2004/ALLPOLITICS/08/29/gop.main/index.html (consulted 11 September 2004).

Cué, C. E. (2004) *¡Pásalo! Los cuatro días de marzo que cambiaron el país*. Barcelona: Ediciones Península.

Dayal, G. (2004) 'Yury and his Magicbike', *Village Voice*, 29 August. www.villagevoice.com/issues/0435/dayal.php (consulted 31 August 2004).

Demick, B. (2003) 'Netizens Crusade Buoys New South Korean Leader', *Los Angeles Times*, 10 February: A3.

de Ugarte, D. (2004) *11M. Redes para ganar una Guerra*. Barcelona: Ed. Icaria.

Di Justo, P. (2004) 'Protests Powered by Cellphone', *New York Times*, 9 September. http://tech2.nytimes.com/mem/technology/techreview.html?res=9404E2DE1730F93AA3575AC0A9629C8B63 (consulted 8 September 2004).

Duffy, R. and Zhao, Y. (2004) 'Short-circuited: Communication and Working Class Struggle in China', paper presented at the China's Media Today and Tomorrow Symposium, 14 May, University of Westminster.

The Economist (2004) 'How Big was the Bounce?', 9 September. www.economist.com/world/na/displayStory.cfm?story_id=3177113 (consulted 13 September 2004).

Fairclough, G. (2004) 'Generation Why? The 386ers of Korea Question Old Rules', *Wall Street Journal*, 14 April: A1.

Fries, Manuel (2000) *China and Cyberspace: The Development of the Chinese National Information Infrastructure*. Bochum: Bochum University Press.

Fulford, B. (2003). 'Korea's Weird Wired World', Forbes, 21 July: 92.

Gaspar, Karl (2001). 'Once Again, an Outpouring in the Streets Brings Change to the Philippines', *Sojourners Magazine*, March–April: 15.

Gibbs, C. (2004) 'SMS to Aid Protesters at GOP Convention', *RCR Wireless News*, 30 August.

Gibson, G. (2004) 'The Republican Convention is Expected to Draw Hundreds of Thousands of Protesters Eager to Air their Discontent with The Bush Administration', *Baltimore Sun*, 22 August: 1F.

Hachigian, N. and Wu, L. (2003) *The Information Revolution in Asia*. Santa Monica, CA: RAND Corporation.

Hauser, C. (2004). 'Marchers Denounce Bush as They Pass G.O.P. Convention Hall', *New York Times*, 20 August. www.nytimes.com/2004/08/29/politics/campaign/29CND-PORT.html?ex=1114488000&en=f3897bb7d72df891&ei=5070 (consulted 23 April 2005).

Jackson, J. (2004) Speech made at the United for Peace and Justice protest during the 2004 Republican National Convention, 29 August. www.democracynow.org/article.pl?sid=04/08/30/1453250 (consulted 23 April 2005).

Jones, J. (2004) 'Bush Gets Small Convention Bounce, Leads Kerry by Seven', Gallup Poll, 6 September. ww.gallup.com/poll/content/login.aspx?ci=12922 (consulted 13 September 2004).

Juan, M. (2004) *11/M. La trama completa*, Barcelona: Ediciones de la Tempestad.

Kim, J.-M. (2001) 'Caught in a Political Net', *Far Eastern Economic Review*, 1 November: 49–50.

Kim, S.-D. (n.d.) 'President of Cyberspace', *Netpolitique*. www.netpolitique.net/php/articles/kimsd_art.php3 (consulted 21 May 2004).

Korea Herald (2003) 'Roh's Support Group Decides Not to Disband', 20 January.

Korea Times (2003) 'Nosamo Opposes Assistance to Iraq War', 24 March.

– (2002) 'History for "Nosamo", Makers of Presidents'. 19 December.

Lebkowsky J. (2004). 'More on SMS-bocking During the RNC', *Smartmobs*, 4 September. www.smartmobs.com/archive/2004/09/04/more_on_smsblo.html (consulted 13 September 2004).

Len, S. (2004) 'President's Impeachment Stirs Angry Protests in South Korea', *New York Times*, 13 March: A2.

Milgram, S. (1967) 'The Small World Problem', *Psychology Today*, 1(1): 60–7.

National Statistical Coordination Board (URL) 'Per Capita GNP'. www.nscb.gov.ph/sna/2002/4q-2002/2002per4.asp (consulted 12 June 2004).

Pabico (n.d.) 'Hypertext Revolution,' *I Magazine*. www.pldt.com/hypertext.htm (consulted 5 June 2004).

Pacheco, I. (2004) *11-M. La respuesta*. Madrid: Asociación Cultural Amigos del Arte Popular.

Pamantalaang Mindanaw (2000) 'President for Impeachment, Anyone?' 16 October. www.mindanaw.com/2000/10/16gloria.html (consulted 10 June 2004).

Partal, V. and Otamendi, M. (2004) *11-M. El periodismo en crisi*. Barcelona: Edicions Ara LLibres.

Philippine Daily Inquirer (2001) 'Estrada Suspends Talks with MLF', 7 January: 2.

PR Newswire (2004) 'Prime Minister Koizumi's E-mail Magazine Now in English', 10 March. www.prnewswire.co.uk/cgi/news/release?id=118889 (consulted 21 April 2004).

Rafael, Vicente (2003). 'The Cell Phone and the Crowd: Messianic Politics in the Contemporary Philippines', *Popular Culture*, 15(3): 399–425.

Reardon, M. (2004) 'Wireless Gets Workout at RNC', *CNET News.com*. http://news.com.com/Wireless+tech+gets+workout+at+RNC/2100-1033_3-5330792.html (consulted 31 August 2004).

Reuters (2001) 'Japan PM's Million-Human E-Mail', *Wired News*, 14 June. www.wired.com/news/politics/0,1283,44528,00.html (consulted 20 April 2004).

Rhee, I.-Y. (2003) 'The Korean Election Shows a Shift in Media Power', *Nieman Reports*, 57 (1): 95–6.

Rodríguez, P. (2004) *11-M Mentira de Estado: Los tres días que acabaron con Aznar*. Barcelona: Ediciones B.

Rubin, J. (2004) 'Ruckus RNC 2004 Text Alerts: updates and information on demonstration activities during the Republican National Convention 2004 in New York City'. www.joshrubin.com/coolhunting/archives/2004/09/rnc_text_alerts.html (consulted 24 April 2005).

Salmon, A. (2004). 'Parties Rallying Behind Internet in Race for Votes', *Washington Times*, 11 April.

Salterio, Leah (2001). 'Text Power in Edsa 2001', *Philippine Daily Inquirer*, 22 January: 25.

Shachtman, N. (2004). 'Political Protesters Hear Call with Text Messaging', *Chicago Tribune*, 28 August. www.chicagotribune.com/technology/chi-0408280053aug28,1,6383205.story?coll=chi-technology-hed&ctrack=1&cset=true (consulted 23 April 2005).

Slackman, M. (2004) 'If a Protest Is Planned to a T, Is It a Protest?', *New York Times*, 22 August. http://query.nytimes.com/gst/abstract.html?res=F00D12FE3C5A0C718EDDA10894DC404482&incamp=archive:search (consulted 23 April 2005).

Simon, E. (2004) 'Protesters Using Text Messages to Plan', *Associated Press*, 1 September. http://pqasb.pqarchiver.com/ap/689698741.html?did=689698741&FMT=ABS&FMTS=FT&date=Sep+1%2C+2004&author=ELLEN+SIMON&desc=Protesters+get+%27txt+msgs%27+to+join+marches%2C+avoid+violence (consulted 9 September 2004).

Spanish Parliament (2004) *Comisión de Investigación sobre el 11 de Marzo de 2004*. Madrid: Cortes Generales, Diario de Sesiones del Congreso de los Diputados, n. 2–12 July. www.congreso.es/pdf/comision_investigacion/04/julio_04.htm (consulted September 2004).

Suzuki, Atsushi (2004) 'Case study 45: Sagamihara, Kanagawa Prefecture' (in Japanese). Nikkei BP Government Technology, 21 June.

Terdiman, D. (2004) 'Text Messages for Critical Mass', *Wired News*, 12 August. www.wired.com/news/politics/0,1283,64536,00.html?tw=wn_tophead_3 (consulted 31 August 2004).

Uy-Tioco, Cecilia A. S. (2003) 'The Cell Phone and Edsa 2: The Role of Communication Technology in Ousting a President', paper presented to the 4th Critical Themes In Media Studies Conference, New School University, New York, 11 October.

Yoon, K.-W. (2003a) 'Youth sociality and globalization: An ethnographic study of young Koreans' mobile phone use', Ph.D. dissertation, Birmingham, UK: University of Buckingham.

– (2003b). 'Retraditionalizing the Mobile: Young people's Sociality and Mobile Phone Use in Seoul, South Korea', *European Journal of Cultural Studie*s, 6(3): 327–43.

VV.AA. (2004) *¡Pásalo! Relatos y Análisis sobre el 11-M y los días que le siguieron*. Madrid: Traficantes de Sueños. www.nodo50.org/ts/editorial/librospdf/pasalo.pdf www.traficantes.net (consulted 22 April 2005).

Zhao, Y. (forthcoming) 'Marketization and the Social Biases of the Chinese "Information Revolution"', in G. Murdoch and J. Wasko (eds), *Media in the Age of Marketisation*. Cresskill, NJ: Hampton Press.

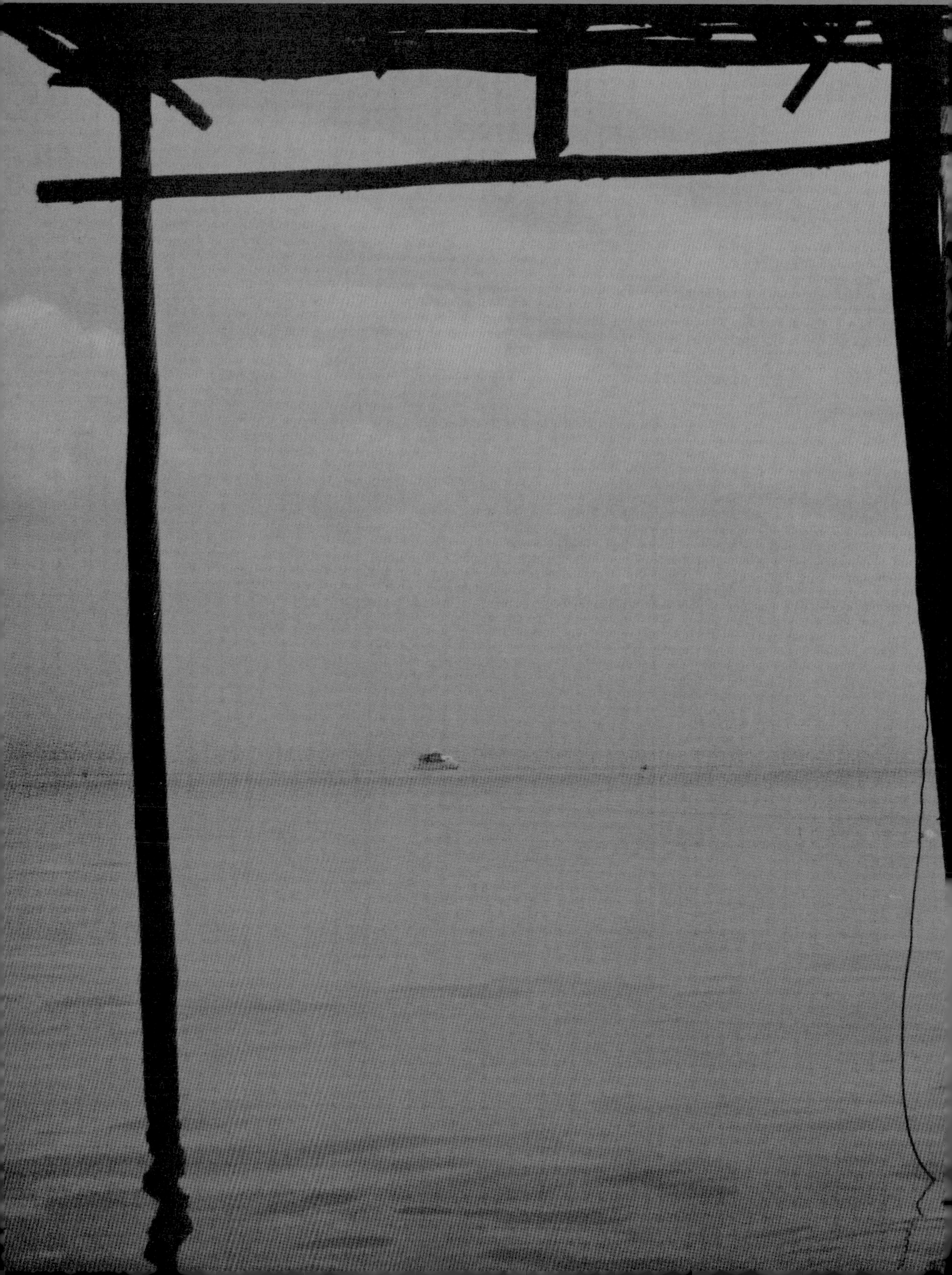

LEARNING FROM HISTORY?
COMPARATIVE HISTORICAL METHODS
AND RESEARCHING GLOBAL CIVIL SOCIETY
Helmut Anheier and Hagai Katz

Why comparative and historical analysis?

Each Global Civil Society Yearbook explores a different approach to measuring and analysing global civil society. We addressed the measurement of global civil society in 2001, introduced the Global Civil Society Index in 2002, examined geographical information systems for analysing the spatial patterns of global civil society in 2003, and in 2004/5 looked at network analysis. This 2005/6 Yearbook reviews comparative historical methods. We are interested in finding out how useful the various approaches and tools of comparative historical analysis are for understanding global civil society as a historical process.

'Historical process' has both a general and particular meaning. For one, global civil society itself is part of a wider historical globalisation process that seems to follow some kind of trajectory in terms of structure, function, impact and growth. As such, it exists in the context of other globalisation processes, and is shaped by a variety of factors that change over time in strength and direction. For example, economic globalisation or migration movements can expand, contract and even reverse themselves. Such broader developments are part of what historians call the 'long duree' after the seminal work of Ferdinand Braudel on medieval Europe.

Besides this more general understanding of historical process are more specific concerns about particular events and developments and their genesis and outcomes that are part of, or effect, global civil society. Examples of the former include anti-globalisation movements, the worldwide protest against the Iraq war in February 2003, the World Social Forums; examples of the latter are events like September 11, 2001, the Darfur crises, and the Balkan wars of the 1990s. Clearly, to help us understand the changing contours and roles of global civil society, we need to analyse these events, their origins, developments and impact – and we need a set analytic approaches that assist us in this task. How did the World Social Forums come about and what factors or conditions are related

to their success or failure? Why did the events following the December 2004 tsunami happen the way they did? How did the global mobilisation process against the Iraq war unfold? What are the patterns of complex historical developments leading to events such as the Darfur crisis, and what more general theoretical lessons can we learn from finding answers to these questions? This is where comparative historical methods become relevant.

Comparative historical methods are located between the social sciences, in particular sociology and political science on the one hand and history and the humanities on the other. They both seek to strike a compromise between the ideographic model of historical studies (that is, the principle of comprehensiveness or explaining particular events as fully as possible) and the nomothetic social science model (that is, the principle of parsimony or explaining classes of events with the least number of factors). An example of the first model would be an account of all the factors and developments leading to the events of 1989 in Central and Eastern Europe; an example of the latter would be a statistical analysis of causal variables predicting regime change. In the case of global civil society, the ideographic model would focus on particular events or developments such as the 2004 World Social Forum, whereas the social science approach would try to examine the phenomenon of social forums more generally.

Each approach has its advantages and disadvantages. For one, the ideographic approach of history raises the question of generalisability and predictive power beyond the particular event or events under consideration, whereas the social science approach can be criticised for its superficiality and insensitivity to nuances and subtle differences. For much of the last few decades, the social science model, typically in the form of statistical analysis and based on the notion of causality and inference, has been dominant. Yet persistent methodological problems have since the 1980s rekindled interest in historical analysis under the name of comparative historical methods (Tilly 1984; Chase-Dunn 1989; Ragin 1987; 2000; Kiser and Hechter 1991; Bollen, Entwisle and Alderson 1993; Sartori 1994; Abbott 1995).

These newer approaches have in common that they are based on mathematical-logical reasoning rather than statistical assumptions, and that they are case-sensitive rather than variable-driven. In other words, in contrast to more standard historical analysis, comparative historical methods go beyond both the descriptive narrative and the particularity of single events or phenomena and seek more general insights. The two kinds of approach we introduce in much of the remainder of this chapter try to attempt just that. But first we should briefly review the critical issues behind the development of comparative historical models. These are the small N problem, Galton's problem, and the black box problem.

Small N problem. This problem refers to the limited number of cases available for exploring topics such as revolutions, regime changes, or social movements with conventional statistical methods. There are simply not that many French Revolutions, tsunamis or civil rights movements 'out there' for social scientists to study using multivariate analysis based on normal distributions. As a consequence, it is difficult to derive probabilistic answers. Moreover, a lack of statistical degrees of freedom may lead to unstable results, creating uneasy tensions between the nomothetic explanations of the social science mode and the descriptive accuracy of ideography. Yet how can we derive broader lessons from single or few cases? This is the realm of the comparative method.

Galton's problem. This problem is named after the Victorian polymath Sir Francis Galton (1822–1911), who questioned the independence of many cultural, social and technological developments within par-ticular groups of related societies, and suggested that exchanges, borrowing and copying among cultures and societies led to complex patterns of diffusion. Examples would be democratisation or economic development, where developments in one country are influenced by prior developments in others and vice versa. In methodological terms, this means 'contam-inations' of units of analysis (such as country, society) and predictive variables (that is, factors). Galton's problem undermines statistical models that are based on the independence of units of analysis, and

brings into question the very notion of isolated and identifiable developments. Clearly, this fundamental methodological problem is particularly relevant in the field of globalisation research. Both the comparative methods and event sequence models are a response to this basic problem.

Black box problem. This problem refers to the nomothetic notion of causality that tends to neglect the actual causal process and, while concentrating on the 'why', leaves the 'how' of causality unspecified. This is typically the case with models based on input-output approaches to causality: observable inputs as the cause are tested in relation to observable outputs as the effects, while the actual causal process remains unobserved: the 'black box'. The methodological danger here is a neglect of time-sensitive and conditional factors. Too easily variables are assigned agency and become reified as actors in simplified cause-effect relations. For example, price changes (the effect) are explained by pointing to supply and demand fluctuations (the causes), yet behind such 'market forces' are complex processes of observations, interpretations, actions and reactions by individual people and the organisations and interests they represent. From a methodological perspective, we need to look inside the black box, which is what event structure analysis and sequencing models try to do (more on this below).

Global civil society involves shifting units of analysis among processes that span the local, regional, national, international and transnational. This makes events, rather than fixed geographical entities more central to the analysis of global civil society, be they demonstrations, forums, movement, or positions. This, in turn, implies that we focus on the sequentiality and causality of events, on the importance of event patterns, and on the causal combinations among factors involved in terms of necessary and sufficient conditions. The evolution of events, the development of organisations, networks and movements, political positions and coali-tions over time, rather than the diachronic statistical analysis of conventional social science: these form the locus and focus of comparative historical research.

In profound ways, comparative historical methods are attempts to go beyond the limitations of what Beck (2003), Shaw (2003) and others have labelled 'method-ological nationalism', the tendency of the social sciences to remain in the statistical and conceptual categories of the nation state. As we have pointed out repeatedly in these methodological essays, this tendency has become a persistent handicap: it equates nation, culture and polity, and ultimately discourages thinking beyond nineteenth and twentieth century categories. As an approach, it seems increasingly at odds with the realities of a globalising world. Indeed, Galton's problem looms large, as does the small-N problem. Consequently, we are urged to focus on the causal complexity of process and events other than attributes of nation states.

The comparative method

From among the growing repertoire of comparative historical methods that have been developed in recent decades, we select two broad classes that have proved useful for generating insights into complex transnational phenomena and that have gained wider acceptance in the social science research community. The first is called the qualitative comparative method, and analyses the causal relations between factors and outcomes as well as among the factors themselves. The second analyses event sequences and event structures. We introduce each in turn.

Many of the recent developments of comparative historical methods, and indeed their renaissance among a growing number of social scientists, go back to a highly influential book by Charles Ragin (1987; see also Ragin and Sonnett 2004). He makes a case for the comparative approach by pointing to two challenges: first, the small-N problem limits the use of multivariate statistical methods analysts can use in explaining outcomes; and second, the interpretation of factors and outcomes involves a level of causal complexity that goes beyond the capacity of conventional statistical models.

Causal complexity refers both to the 'causal chemistry' involved and to the outcome as such. For example, the fall of the Berlin Wall in 1989 was just one event in a wider set of events, and by itself and in combination with other events and factors caused various other outcomes. Conversely, the event we describe as the fall of the Berlin Wall contained many smaller events and actions within itself that through a sequence of causal interactions and combination made it possible. We could make similar cases for culminating events that triggered regime changes but also those that failed to do so (for example, Tiananmen Square in 1989). A main objective of comparative analysis is to look closer at the causal combinations among factors that lead to specified events and outcomes.

The challenge lies in the potentially large number of factors involved or that can be identified as significant in producing an event such as the fall of the Berlin Wall: citizen mobilisation, disenchantment with the ruling Socialist Unity Party, the role of the churches and roundtables, the reluctance of then President of the Soviet Union Mikhail Gorbachev to call in the Soviet army to quell unrest, the cautious role of the West, the prior events in Hungary, and so on. We could easily list many more such factors on empirical and theoretical grounds. While political and sociological theory helps identify the most significant ones, the problem of causal complexity increases when we add a second, third or fourth, and so on, case of regime changing events, such as Romania in 1989, the Soviet Union in 1991 or Serbia in 2001. While each case involves unique factors, other factors may be present across the various cases. Even if we limited ourselves to three causal factors accounting for regime-changes events, we would have 2^n or 8 combinations to examine. With five factors, the number of combinations rises to 2^5 or 32, and with ten to over 1,000.

How can we deal with such combinatorial complexity when comparing relatively small numbers of cases that involve multiple causal factors? The comparative method developed by Ragin (1987) and further developed since then (Ragin 2000; Ragin and Sonnett 2004) proposes a Boolean approach to this problem. The comparative method and the accompanying software program QCA and QCA2 now include a range of approaches and tools[1]. As these go well beyond the confines of this chapter, we offer a basic introduction to illustrate the usefulness of the comparative analysis for issues of interest to global civil society research.

The basic analytic thinking behind QCA is Boolean and combinatorial. It begins by assuming that factors and outcomes can have two states or conditions: present or absent, coded 1 and 0 respectively. In the examples below, we denote presence with capital letters and absence in lower case. Thus,

$$A + B = C$$

---

1 The website Small-N Compass (URL) hosted by the Catholic University of Leuven includes many useful links to the comparative methods and also offers QCA and QCA2 as free downloads inclusive of manuals and methodological guidance.

Table M1: Truth table for success and failure of social forums

Factor A Leadership	Factor B Coordination	Factor C Resources	Outcome S Success	Number of cases observed
1	0	1	1	4
0	1	0	1	2
1	1	0	1	3
1	1	1	1	6
1	0	0	0	6
0	0	1	0	2
0	1	1	0	2
0	0	0	0	5

means that the presence of either factor A or B causes the outcome C, whereas as

AB = C

implies that the combined presence of A and B produces outcome C. The first 'either-or' case is called a Boolean addition, and the combined case a Boolean multiplication. Boolean analysis is combinatorial in nature, and the absence of a factor and outcome has the same logical status as their presence. The following expression

AB + Cde = F

states that the presence of F is brought about either by the joint presence of A and B as factors or by the presence of C combined with the joint absence of D and E. If we were to find a second case with the following combination for producing F

AB + CDE = F

we would conclude that either the absence or presence of both D and E is immaterial to the presence of F, and, consequently, could simplify the expression to

AB + C = F.

With the basic tools of Boolean algebra to hand, we would examine available cases where the outcome F is either present or absent, and look for causal factors (A ... E), and then begin a stepwise process of analysis by reducing the inherent complexity among the causal factors involved in producing the outcome or event F. We illustrate this stepwise analysis using a hypothetical though theory-grounded example from the sociology of social movements: the successful or unsuccessful outcome of a social forum.

Of course, for the purposes of this exercise we assume that we have a definition of what constitutes success and failure of the social forum, and we also assume the same for the measurement of the three factors that we associate with forum success: the presence of local leadership (A); the degree of coordination with related causes, organisations and networks (B); and the availability of financial and human resources for organising and holding the forum (C). In other words, we hypothesise that

ABC = S

and examine actual cases to see whether the three factors were present, in what combinations, and leading to what outcome. Recall that three factors yield eight logical combinations, so that each of the 30 cases examined would be assigned to one of the rows of what is called a truth table. Table M1 present the truth table, where 1 means presence and 0 absence of factors and outcome.

Table M2: Implication chart for forum success

Reduced terms (rows)/ unreduced terms (columns)	ABC	AbC	Abc	ABc
AC	X	X	X	
AB	X		X	
Bc				X

With the truth table completed, we can now state the unreduced Boolean expression for predicting successful social forums:

S = AbC + aBc + ABc + ABC.

In other words, based on our observations of 30 cases, social forums are successful if we find

- the presence of local leadership and resources combined with the absence of coordination
- the presence of coordination combined with the absence of leadership and resources
- the presence of leadership combined with the absence of coordination and resources, or
- the combined presence of all three factors.

Note that we can state the unreduced Boolean expression for failed social forums as

s = Abc + abC + aBC + abc.

However, does combinatorial logic mean that we are adding complexity upon complexity? No, as the unreduced expression is simply input for the first analytic step in applying the comparative method. We are now looking for a way to simplify the expression, and do so through Boolean minimisation, which states that, if two Boolean expressions differ in only one causal condition yet produce the same outcome, then the causal condition that distinguishes the two can be considered irrelevant and can be removed. This is what we did in the first example above when simplifying

AB + Cde = F and AB + CDE = F to AB + C = F.

Applied to the unreduced Boolean expression for outcome S, the minimisation of

ABC and AbC to AC
ABC and ABc to AB
ABc and aBc to Bc

yields the following reduced Boolean expression

S = AC + AB + Bc

which states that forums are successful if leadership and resources are present, or leadership and coordination, or coordination with the absence of resources. With the reduced expression at hand we can now consider Boolean implications – a process by which the use of implication charts can further simplify the reduced Boolean expression for forum success.

A Boolean expression is said to imply another if the second is a subset of the first. For example, the product AB implies ABC and Abc, as shown above, and Bc implies Abc and aBc. Applied to the relationship between the reduced and the unreduced form predicting movement success, implication means that there are more implicants than are needed. In other words, the equation S = AC + AB + Bc may include redundant terms or combinations among factors.

To identify redundant or surplus terms in the reduced expression, we refer to the implication chart in Table M2. As we can see, the combination AC is implicated in ABC, AbC and Abc, and thereby covers also two of the terms AB implicates. This makes AB a subset of AC, and therefore redundant. As a result, we have two prime implicants, AC and Bc, as the 'combinatorial essence of the causal chemistry' producing successful social forums, or

S = AC + Bc

This states that forums are successful if leadership and coordination are present, or with the presence of coordination and the absence of resources. What then, can we say about the conditions for failure? What causal combinations are associated with a lack of success? Rather than repeating the minimisation and implication process for failure, we apply what is referred to as De Morgan's Law to the conditions for success, and turn presence into absence, absence into presence, multiplication into addition, and addition into multiplication. This transforms $S = AC + Bc$ into

$$s = (a + c)(b + C) = ab + aC + cb.$$

Put differently, forums fail if lack of leadership coincides with a lack of coordination or the presence of resources, or if both resources and coordination are absent.

Applying the comparative method is both a rigorous logical exercise and an interpretative analysis where the researcher goes back and forth between formal and substantive levels of discourse. Indeed, as Ragin (1987) suggests, the comparative method can be used for examining theoretical arguments and hypotheses, and explores overlap and contradictions. Let's briefly illustrate the potential of the comparative method in this respect as well by evaluating two theoretical arguments about the occurrence of peasant revolts.

The first theory suggests that peasant revolts happen under commercialization pressures (B) or when the absence of peasant traditionalism (a) combined with the presence of a peasant middle class (C) and landed elite that live on the land (lack of absentee landlords – d):

$$T1 = B + aCd.$$

The second theory states that revolts happen if peasant traditionalism combines with commercialisation or the presence of a middle class with absentee landlords:

$$T2 = AB + CD.$$

Boolean algebra allows us to map areas of agreement and disagreement between both theoretical arguments. We use the intersection of T1 and T2 to yield a subset of causal combinations that are included in both theories

$$T1 * T2 = (B + aCd)(AB + CD) = AB + BCD.$$

This shows that a subset of the causal conditions included in T1 is confirmed: all expressions include commercialisation pressures (B), giving more weight to this factor. Yet it is also possible to model causal combinations that were found to produce peasant revolts according to T2 but that were not hypothesised by T1. This is the intersection of t1 and T2. Applying de Morgan's law to T1 produces

$$t1 = Ab + bc + bD$$

and multiplied by T2 gives

$$t1 * T2 = (Ab + bc + bD)(AB + CD)$$
$$= AbCD + bCD = bCD.$$

The term bCD pinpoints a major shortcoming of existing theories, which fail to predict peasant revolts under social conditions that consist of a lack of commercialisation, with the presence of both middle class peasants and absentee landlords. By the same approach, we can model causal combinations included in T1 but not T2.

More generally, we can use the evaluation of theoretical arguments also as an approach to hypothesis testing. If T1 is the hypothesis, and T2 what we found empirically studying cases of peasant revolts, T1 * T2 would yield those causal combinations hypothesised and found; t1 * T2 those found but not hypothesised; and T1 * t2 those factors hypothesised but not found.

In conclusion, the comparative method is an evolving field. In recent years, the introduction of fuzzy set approaches has lifted one of the limitations of the Boolean truth table, which required that causal conditions are simple present/absence dichotomies falling into crisp categories. Many phenomena and causal relations, however, are a matter of degree and cannot be forced into two exclusive states or conditions. For example, while some membership organisations are democratic, others are not, but many will be more or less democratic. Ragin (2000; 2004) has introduced an approach to applying fuzzy set mathematics to the comparative method, which we intend to review and introduce in a future edition of the Global Civil Society Yearbook.

Analysing event sequences

Event sequences and event structure methods take a different approach to comparative historical analysis. They focus on analysing developments through time rather than the causal combinations among factors. Conventional quantitative methods in the social sciences predominantly deal with the attributes of actors and the correlations between them, but focus less on their actions and their causes. While the attribute-correlation approach has yielded much valuable knowledge, it is not as applicable to various areas of social research such as organisational evolution, individual career patterns, or sequences of events. More generally, standard statistical approaches are limited when events and actions and their causal interpretation are analysed in a temporal context (Abbott 1995).

Approaches to event sequence analysis reflect a shift in social science from the analysis of entities and their variable attributes to the analysis of events in context

---

Events and actions are highly contextual. They can be fully understood only in the full sequence in which they occur. Only then can we gain insight into the 'cause' of these actions and events (or, more precisely, their narrative construction; Griffin 1993). When analysing a sequence of events, we try to identify a causal logic which is grounded in time and which allows us to better understand how and why the event unfolded they way it did and with what implications. Such an analysis allows us to figure out how past events enable and constrain future events, and to understand the 'path dependency' that is characteristic of social and political history (Aminzade 1992).

Approaches to event sequence analysis reflect a shift in social science from the analysis of entities and their variable attributes to the analysis of events in context. Event series can be examined in part, step by step, or as whole series of single or combined sequences. Step by step analysis leads to the use of time series methodologies such as event history analysis (Yamaguchi 1991). The analysis of whole sequences leads to two methodologies that have become more salient in addressing event sequence research questions: optimal matching, most notably

represented in the work of Andrew Abbott (Abbott and Tsay 2000), and event structure analysis, developed by David Heise (Heise 1991).

Optimal matching

Originally developed for the analysis of DNA sequences, optimal matching (OM) is primarily a technique for searching general patterns based on sequence similarity (Abbott and Tsay 2000). It requires a set of event sequences and coding scheme. An example of event sequences would be the careers of a sample of NGO leaders, coded so as to distinguish education and training, managerial and non-managerial positions, employment in government and in the corporate sector, and so forth. The actual applications of OM vary greatly, from analysis of rhetoric sequences in speeches and written documents to people's daily activities and the development of welfare regimes (see Abbott and Tsay, 2000, for a review of OM applications).

Once event data have been converted into sequences with the use of standard codes, the sequences are processed with an algorithm that calculates the distance between all sequences in the data-set. The distance between event sequences is calculated based on the number of replacements (**in**serts or **del**etes called 'indels') required to make them identical. Not all indels are of equal importance, and a 'cost matrix' specifies the relative weight of each replacement. The result of the algorithm is a matrix of distance scores of sequences from each other. The matrix can then be analysed with scaling techniques (such as cluster analysis or multidimensional scaling) or network analysis techniques (finding cohesive groups). The result is a categorisation of the data-set of sequences into a number of typical sequence patterns. It is a method to find regularities in complex events data, and can be used for reducing complex data into general patterns and to classify sequences of events empirically.

Event structure analysis

Optimal matching is more appropriate for studies that require analysis and comparison of large numbers of event sequences, while event structure analysis (ESA) is more appropriate for studies with a small set of cases. This makes ESA more compatible with the current state of data on global civil society events, which frequently report on single in-depth cases rather than large and consistent databases[2]. While OM uses lists of events and event characteristics as a starting point for analysis, ESA adopts a very different approach.

> **ESA more compatible with the current state of data on global civil society events, which frequently report on single in-depth cases rather than large and consistent databases**

ESA is used to extract the structure of events and their causal and temporal relationships from a narrative. It is an interpretive method driven by the analyst's understanding of the underlying issues and the historical context of the events. Notably, the narrative itself comes from a narrator with some sort of bias or agenda, however implicit or explicit, conscious or unconscious, in construing events in a certain order and sequence. This subjective interpretation of real events is reinterpreted by the researcher. Thus, a narrative is but one account of reality among others, and analysts can use different narrations of the same sequences to obtain a more complete account of the actual events and their unfolding.

The causal logic of sequences often remains implicit, and it is hard to discern from a narrative whether the linkage between events is causal or merely descriptive (Griffin 1993). Temporal sequence doesn't necessarily imply some causal relations between events. A future event cannot cause a past event, but at the same time the fact that one event happened first doesn't necessarily mean that it caused all subsequent events. Thus, analysts attempt to 'unpack' the narrative (Abrams 1982) and reconstitute it by building causal interpretations of historical events. This involves examining whether a preceding event is causally linked to a subsequent event, and also asking whether the event could have happened in different (historically plausible, within the relevant historical context)

circumstances; that is, counterfactual reasoning (Weber 1949 [1905]).

ESA is a computer-aided analysis in which a narrative and the events extracted from it are analysed by means of an interrogative process. The programme requires repeated re-examination and reinterpretation of the data within a strict logical framework. Ethno2[3], the program developed by Heise (1991), is especially appropriate for this type of historical interrogation (Griffin 1993). It combines interpretive power and methodological rigour with a consideration of context and contingency with a rule-bound logical analysis that is conducive to replication and generalisation (Stevenson, Zinzow, and Sridharan 2003)[4].

Ethno2 requires the researcher to comb the narrative and pull out the events that comprise it. The list of events (plus optionally the text that defines each event in the narrative) is then entered as raw data into Ethno2's interface, and a brief description of each event is added. Once the events are entered, the linking process can begin. The programme doesn't determine the logical structure of the sequence but rather elicits it from the expert through a series of questions on the relations between events. Following the temporal order of events, the programme asks the analyst whether event B requires event A (or whether event A is a prerequisite for event B). It continues the interrogation until all events are linked to other events, and the last event in the sequence is reached. As the programme progresses with the interrogation, it draws a chart of the causal structure of the event sequence.

Upon completion of the linking sequence, the analyst turns to test that logical structure and check whether the logical structure matches the sequence of events as it unfolded. To create the event structure,

---

2 ESA is technically and computationally much easier to use than OM and therefore more approachable for persons with less developed computer and quantitative skills. ESA and OM can be combined, and ESA can be used to generate sequences for comparison with the use of OM methods.

3 The programme is freely available for online or offline use at www.indiana.edu/~socpsy/ESA/. The website also includes useful tutorials and program manual files.

4 The application of ESA to the analysis of social change and the role non-profit organisations play in planned social change is offered by Stevenson, Zinzow, and Sridharan (2003). Others used it to study organisational life histories. Looking at events leading to the demise of non-profit organisations and testing various theories explaining the demise of organisations, Hager and Galaskiewicz (2002) identified precipitating events as well as patterned events that ultimately resulted in closure.

the programme follows several basic logical constraints and rules on the behaviour of events: (a) it assumes that an event cannot occur until all of its prerequisites have occurred; (b) it assumes that an event depletes its prerequisites, that is, uses up the conditions which the prerequisites created; and (c) it assumes an event isn't repeated until the conditions it created are used up by some other event.

In the process of testing the event structure, the programme tests each event and link in the structure (in temporal order) to see whether it conforms to the rules. If an event in the structure violates these logical requirements, the programme calls this to the scholar's attention and asks him to consider how the error can be fixed. It allows the analyst to introduce structural changes into the chart, which better reflect the real-life behaviour of actors and events. It allows the analyst to remove illogical links, to determine that certain events can be a prerequisite for more than one event, and to add events that were missed and can explain inconsistencies. The end result is a diagram that validates the temporal and causal structure of the event sequence. In addition, the analyst can enter information on each event, such as the actors involved, the actions they engaged, and the product of their actions. Consequently, we can analyse the associations between actors, actions, strategies, products and so forth, which emerge from the sequence.

As Griffin (1993: 1128) commented, ESA requires '...probes into events and their historical and structural contexts, separation of causal significance from temporal sequence, the interweaving of the general and the particular, and confrontation with the silences imposed by the paucity of hard evidence'. This is precisely what we think is needed for the analysis of global civil society events. Therefore, we illustrate the application of ESA on one important event in which global civil society actors played an key role – the establishment of the International Criminal Court.

Event structure analysis of the emergence of the International Criminal Court

The narrative we use here to illustrate the utility of ESA for the study of global civil society is the first two chapters in a book by one of the Global Civil Society Yearbook's editors, Marlies Glasius: *The International Criminal Court: A Global Civil Society Achievement* (2005). The chapters tell the history of the establishment of the International Criminal Court (ICC) from the early days of international humanitarian law in the late nineteenth century to current developments and actions, such as the US campaign against the ICC. For the purpose of this chapter we limited the sequence of events; our analysis starts with the war crime tribunals in Yugoslavia and Rwanda and ends with the acceptance of the ICC statute in Rome on 17 July 1998.

Table M3: Events included in the event structure analysis of the International Criminal Court

	Code	Event
1	Pre HR	Preexisting human rights regime
2	Yugo	Ethnic cleansing, Yugoslavia
3	T Yugo	Ad hoc tribunal, Yugoslavia
4	Rwnd	Genocide, Rwanda
5	T Rwnd	Tribunal, Rwanda
6	Preced	Successful precedent (Yugoslavia and Rwanda tribunals)
7	ILC Drft	International Law Commission (ILC) issues draft
8	Gov Sup	ILC draft receives support from some governments
9	Gov Res	ILC draft receives resistance from some governments
10	UN Asmb	UN assembly discusses ILC draft

11	NGO-UN	5–6 NGOs in UN general assembly session
12	Scom Est	UN establishes Ad hoc states committee
13	Cicc Est	NGOs establish the Coalition for the International Criminal Court (CICC)
14	Pcom Est	ILC establishes preparatory Committee (Prepcom)
15	Pcom-NGO	NGO delegations at Prepcom
16	LMG Est	Like-minded group of states (LMG) emerges
17	LMG-NGO	LMG connects with NGOs
18	Pcom Wg	Prepcom decides to operate in working groups
19	LMG Pos	LMG issues cornerstone positions
20	LMG Coh	LMG is not polarised North-South
21	CICC 800	CICC reaches 800 members (by time of Rome conference)
22	LMG 61	LMG reaches 61 members (by time of Rome conference)
23	NGO Dbt	Global specialist debate – meetings worldwide: NGOs, government officials and individuals participate
24	CICC Acred	CICC assigned NGO accreditation for Rome
25	Rome	Rome conference
26	No P Frm	No parallel forum to Rome conference
27	NGO 236	236 NGOs have formal representation in Rome
28	Disem	NGOs disseminate data from proceedings
29	NGO lc	NGOs lobby conference participants
30	NGO lh	NGO lobby home government
31	C-C Crd	Conference-to-capital coordination
32	Rome Coh	Rome conference is not polarised North-South
33	LMG Lead	LMG representatives hold conference leadership
34	NGO-Gov	NGO collaborate with LMG delegates
35	CICC-LMG	Informal fora between LMG-CICC
36	Strt Act	Street action during Rome conference is marginal
37	Res Def	Resistance of various nations to ICC in Rome conference defused
38	Sc Obj	Security council members raise objections in Rome
39	Sc Dfct	European security council members 'defect' to LMG
40	Res Frg	Animosities prevent development of 'unlike-minded' group
41	R Disc	Rome conference issues first discussion paper
42	R Prop	Rome conference issues statute part II proposal
43	R Pack	Rome conference issues 'take it or leave it' package
44	Amend	Resisting governments (India, US) suggest amendments
45	V Amend	Rome conference vote 'no action on' amendments
46	ICC Statute	ICC statute adopted

We went through the narrative and extracted the 46 events listed in Table M3. Deciding what constitutes an event is in itself an interpretive task. Most events are easy to identify; others are more difficult. We followed Griffin (1993) who, in his analysis of a 1930 lynching in Mississippi, defines non-actions (for example, a sheriff refraining from action to prevent lynching) as events, and treats general facts and developments as events as well (for example, racist organisations operating in the region at the time). In our analysis 'No P Frm', which stands for the lack of a parallel forum to the Rome conference, is a significant non-action at a time when few important international meetings were unaccompanied by a parallel forum (Pianta 2001) and had important consequences. 'Pre HR' is a general development, standing for the overall pre-existing human rights international regime and summarising 100 years of humanitarian and human rights law.

With events entered, Ethno2 interrogates to find the causal links between the events in the sequence. We can illustrate the process and the thinking behind this interrogation only through a selection of sections. When considering the links for the event of the establishment of the Coalition for the International Criminal Court (CICC Est) the programme started with the following sequence of questions, trying to link the current event with preceding ones, from the most recent in the sequence and proceeding backwards.

The programme started by asking:

- Does *NGOs establish the Coalition for the International Criminal Court (CICC)* require *UN establishes Ad hoc states committee* or a similar event?

To answer this question we returned to the narrative: '...it was the disappointment with this general assembly decision [to establish the states' committee] that led civil society activists to set up the Coalition for the International Criminal Court' (Glasius 2005). Hence, we answered 'yes' to this question. Ethno2 drew a line between these two nodes in the chart. Then the programme asked us the next question, following the sequence:

- Does *NGOs establish the Coalition for the International Criminal Court (CICC)* require *5-6 NGOs in UN General Assembly session* or a similar event?

Again, reading the narrative, we find that '...a phone-call between two of these observers... resulted in an invitation to a number of groups to discuss the formation of an NGO coalition' (Glasius 2005). Thus it is clear that the establishment of the coalition is a consequence of those few organisations' presence in the UN assembly. Accordingly, we answered 'yes' to the question and another line was added to the growing chart[5].

Thus, in the series of queries the programme helped us ascertain that the establishment of the CICC was the result of the UN General Assembly's decision to establish a states' committee, due to the disagreement about the ILC's ICC statute draft. This was a rather short sequence of questions, as we were at the beginning of our list of events. Later on certain events required as many as 31 queries to establish their causal linkage in the overall structure of the sequence. In all, 348 elicitations were made, resulting in an unverified first draft of the event structure chart.

> **Deciding what constitutes an event is in itself an interpretive task. Most events are easy to identify; others are more difficult**

The next step was to test the draft chart. In the process of testing Ethno asked us a few dozen more questions, trying to validate the chart based on Ethno2's inherent logical constraints, mentioned above. The programme starts validating the chart from the first event to the last (in temporal order), and whenever it finds an incongruence between the chart and its logical constraints it asks the researcher how to proceed. For example, when it reached the Pcom Est event it encountered a problem. The programme expects each event to be a requisite of only one other event, unless otherwise instructed. In this case it found that the event Scom Est was already 'used up' by the event CICC Est. To ameliorate this incongruence it gave us three options: (a) to disconnect the link between CICC

---

5 Since the events UN Asmb, Gov Sup, Gov Res and ILC Drft were already declared requisites to Scom Est, the programme assumed they are also requisites (once and twice removed) for CICC Est and did not query us about the links between these events and CICC Est.

Figure M1: Realisation of the ICC statute: event structure

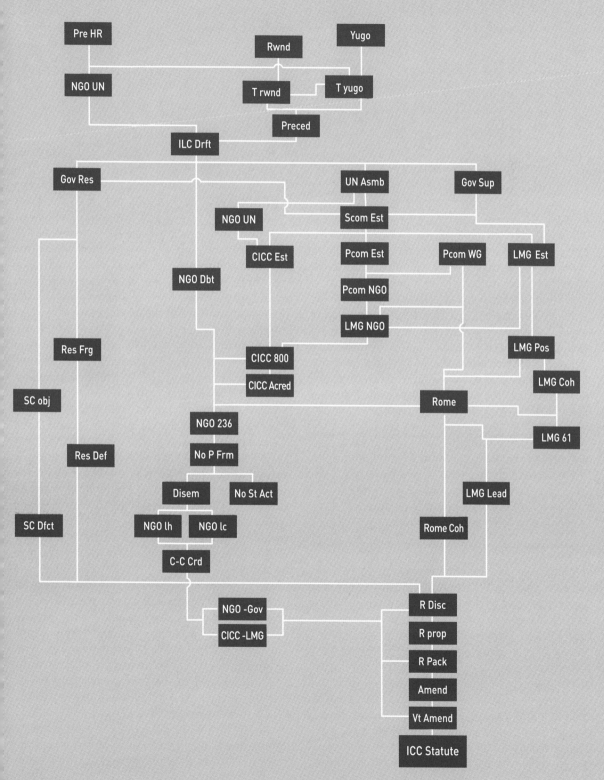

Table M4: Associations of GCS (CICC; NGOs)

Action associations	Count	Person associations	Count
Collaborate	6	GCS	26
Establish	2	ILC	2
Inform	2	LMG	6
Issue statement	2	Rome	6
Lobby	6	Governments	10
Observe	1	PrepCom	2
Participate	8	UN Assembly	1

Est and Scom Est, which we didn't consider; (b) to consider the possibility that an unrecorded event explains the occurrence of Pcom Est, which we also rejected; and (c) to define the events so that Scom Est is not used up by CICC Est, thus actually relaxing the logical constraints of the programme and determining that Scom Est can have multiple consequences, a decision that is not unreasonable in the complex world of international politics. A few dozen such elicitations later, all logical inconsistencies were settled, and the result was the chart shown in Figure M1.

> The figure turns the implicit connections between events in the narrative into a structure of causes and effects, and as a result makes it possible to point out different aspects of the history of the ICC

What do we learn from the figure? The figure is not a simple replication of Glasius's account. Rather, it is best understood as a interpretive 'unpacking' of the original, based on a combination of our reading of the text and our knowledge of its context and related issues. What it adds is something very different from the narrative: a causal analysis of the narrative. It turns the implicit connections between events in the narrative into a structure of causes and effects, and as a result makes it possible to point out different aspects of the history of the ICC – critical events, causal interrelations between events, and potential 'breaking points' in the process. Figure M1 tells us how actions

and events are causally interwoven and reveals the structure of the specific history we are studying. Importantly, from the event structure we can see which actions are key to the entire sequence.

Indeed, four distinct though intertwined parallel tracks lead to the approval of the ICC statute in Rome. Those streams, from the left, include government resistance to the ICC, NGO advocacy on behalf of the ICC, the formal actions by the UN and its committees, and government support for the ICC. The CICC seems to play an important role in both connecting NGO activities to the governments in favour of the ICC and in empowering NGOs in Rome due to its sheer size (CICC 800) and clout (CICC Acrd). Also, the figure shows that the combination of conference and home lobbying, and the resulting conference-to-capital coordination (C-C Crd), allowed NGOs in general and the CICC in particular, to gain access to government delegations in Rome, and consequently allowed their views to be heard and considered in the developing of the statute.

The structure demonstrates the importance of agency and contingency in the development of action – the ICC statute was never destined to be, rather it was a contingent outcome of a number of unfolding sequences that caused it. The entire process was triggered by the atrocities performed in the Balkans and in Africa, and by the international response to them that set up a legal and political precedent for the ICC. The emergence of the CICC was contingent on the presence of NGOs in the UN. The role that these events – the Balkan and Rwanda atrocities and the presence of NGOs in the UN General Assembly – play in the sequence is very telling in terms of what events open a 'window of opportunity' for change in international regimes, as well as what actions global civil society actors need to engage in to be able to take advantage of such windows of opportunity.

ESA proves to be a valuable methodology, permitting scholars of global civil society to investigate the causal relationships between actions and their consequences and to determine the likely outcome of combinations of actions and events in the wider context of other players in the global governance arena

---

Using event features, the analyst can use Ethno2 to analyse the associations between actors, actions, instruments, and other aspects of the events in the sequence. We limited the analysis to actions and persons for all events in which NGOs and the CICC were participants, introducing GCS (global civil society) as a generalised actor (not shown in Figure M1), which is associated with both global civil society actors in the chart – NGOs, CICC. In Table M4, we can see with whom global civil society as a generalised actor interacted, and how frequently. These results can be compared across global civil society campaigns and be used as predictors of successful ones.

ESA proves to be a valuable methodology, permitting scholars of global civil society to investigate the causal relationships between actions and their consequences and to determine the likely outcome of combinations of actions and events in the wider context of other players in the global governance arena. It is demanding in terms of time and complexity, but is very permissive in terms of the data it requires. All ESA requires is a detailed narrative and a knowledgeable person to interpret it.

Conclusion

The purpose of this chapter is to explore comparative historical research methods for examining aspects of global civil society. Of course, given the exploratory nature of the work presented here, we have been able to do little but scratch the surface of what are undoubtedly complex methodological and analytical problems. Nonetheless, we hope that our attempts to use different units of analysis to emphasise causal combinations and sequences of events have at least pointed the way for future work in this area. We are encouraged by the ease at which comparative historical methods lend themselves to units of analysis other than the nation state, their sensitivity to small-N scenarios, and their capacity to take account of Galton's problem and the causal relationships behind events and outcomes.

Next steps would include a closer look at our Chronology section to see how we could both improve event coverage and the analysis of what is reported. Potentially useful topics not yet explored include the examination of theoretical arguments around global civil society, transnational social movements, and the relationship between civil and uncivil society (crime, terrorists, supremacists, and fundamentalists; and the movements, networks, and organisations they create and operate), and their relationship to other globalisation drivers. Of course, there may be other areas that are worth exploring. Nonetheless, we hope to have shown the potential of the comparative historical approaches to overcome the legacy of methodological nationalism.

Abbott, A. (1995) 'Sequence Analysis: New Methods for Old Ideas', *Annual Review of Sociology*, 21: 93–113.

– and Tsay, A. (2000) 'Sequence Analysis and Optimal Matching Methods in Sociology: Review and Prospect', *Sociological Methods & Research*, 29: 3–33.

Abrams, P. (1982) *Historical Sociology*. Shepton Mallet: Open Books.

Aminzade, R. (1992) 'Historical Sociology and Time', *Sociological Methods & Research*, 20: 456–80.

Beck, U. (2003) 'The Analysis of Global Inequality: From National to Cosmopolitan Perspective', in M. Kaldor, H. Anheier and M. Glasius (eds.), *Global Civil Society 2003*. Oxford: Oxford University Press.

Bollen, K., Entwisle, B. and Alderson, A. (1993) 'Macrocomparative Research Methods', *Annual Review of Sociology*, 19: 321–51.

Chase-Dunn, C. (1989) *Global Formations: Structure of the World Economy*. Oxford: Blackwell.

Glasius, M. (2005) *The International Criminal Court: A Global Civil Society Achievement*. Oxford: Routledge.

Griffin, L. (1993). 'Narrative, Event-Structure Analysis, and Causal Interpretation in Historical Sociology', *American Journal of sociology*, 98: 1094–133.

Hager, M. and Galaskiewicz, J. (2002) 'Studying Closure Among Nonprofit Organizations Using Event Structure Analysis and Network Methods'. Paper delivered at Fourth Annual Health Care Organizations Conference, Berkeley, CA, 6–7 June.

Heise, D. (1991) 'Event Structure Analysis: A qualitative Model of Quantitative Research', in N. Fielding and R. M. Lee (eds.), *Using Computers in Qualitative Research*. London and Newbury Park: Sage.

Kiser, E. and Hechter, M. (1991) 'The Role of General Theory in Comparative Historical Sociology', *American Journal of Sociology*, 97: 1–30.

Pianta, M. (2001) 'Parallel Summits of Global Civil Society', in H. Anheier, M. Glasius and M. Kaldor (eds.), *Global Civil Society 2001*. Oxford: Oxford University Press.

Ragin, C. (1987) *The Comparative Method*. Berkeley: University of California Press.

– (2000) *Fuzzy-Set Social Science*. Chicago: University of Chicago Press.

– (2004) 'From Fuzzy Sets to Crisp Truth Tables'. Working paper. Arizona: Department of Sociology, University of Arizona. www.compasss.org/Raginfztt_April05.pdf (consulted 29 June 2005).

– and Sonnett, J. (2004) 'Between Complexity and Parsimony: Limited Diversity, Counterfactual Cases and Comparative Analysis', in S. Kropp and M. Minkenberg (eds.), *Vergleichen in der Politikwissenschaft*. Wiesbaden: VS Verlag fuer Sozialwissenschaften.

Sartori, G. (1994) 'Compare Why and How: Comparing, Miscomparing and the Comparative Method', in M. Dogan and A. Kazancigil (eds.), *Comparing Nations: Concepts, Strategies, Substance*. Oxford: Blackwell.

Shaw, M. (2004) 'The Global Transformation of the Social Sciences', in M. Kaldor, H. Anheier and M. Glasius (eds.), *Global Civil Society 2003*. Oxford: Oxford University Press.

Small-N Compass (URL) http://smalln.spri.ucl.ac.be (consulted 24 June 2005).

Stevenson, W., Zinzow, H. and Sridharan, S. (2003) 'Using Event Structure Analysis to Understand Planned Social Change', *International Journal of Qualitative Methods*, 2 (2), Article 5. www.ualberta.ca/~iiqm/backissues/2_2/html/stevensonetal.htm (consulted 29 June 2005).

Tilly, C. (1984) *Big Structures, Large Processes, Huge Comparisons*. New York: Russell Sage.

Weber, M. (1949 [1905]) *Max Weber on the Methodology of the Social Sciences* (trans. and ed. E. Shils and H. Finch). Glencoe, IL: Free Press.

Yamaguchi, K. (1991). *Event History Analysis: Applied Social Research Methods Series* V. 28. Newbury Park, CA: Sage Publications.

Note on Data

Relation to data programme Global Civil Society 2005/6

We have updated the information presented in the 2004/5 edition of the Yearbook wherever possible. Those indicators repeated from the 2004/5 data programme represent more recent or updated figures. In order to facilitate comparisons, country data are grouped by income and region, using World Bank classifications.

We have added new indicators where we judge them to be valuable, sometimes representing a departure from those presented last year. Such indicators are found in our records on governance and accountability, environment, and political rights and civil liberties. In these records we present survey data asking for opinions regarding international development and UN reform, data on paper production and on freedom of religion and press freedom. This year we include eight new records: INGO networks, NGOs and global governance, NGO-government relations, attitudes towards NGOs, tsunami relief, international philanthropy, attitudes towards the United States and attitudes towards corporate responsibility. Thus we introduce the following data sources to the Yearbook:

- Food and Agricultural Organisation of the United Nations (http://faostat.fao.org/)
- Council of Europe (www.coe.int)
- Professor Peter Willetts (www.staff.city.ac.uk/p.willetts)
- OECD Development Assistance Committee (www.oecd.org/dac)
- UN Global Compact (www.unglobalcompact.org)
- EuropeAid (www.europa.eu.int/comm/europeaid/index_en.htm)
- US Aid for International Development (www.usaid.gov)
- Eurbarometer of the European Commission (www.europa.eu.int/comm/public_opinion/)
- Globescan (formally Environics) (www.globescan.com)
- National Memorial Institute for the Prevention of Terrorism (www.tkb.org)
- ReliefWeb (www.reliefweb.int)
- United Nations Office for the Coordination of Humanitarian Affairs (http://ochaonline.un.org/)
- International Federation of Red Cross and Red Crescent Societies (www.ifrc.org)
- Foundation Center (www.fdncenter.org)
- Worldwide Initiatives for Grant-Maker Support (www.wingsweb.org)
- Program on International Policy Attitudes (www.pipa.org)

We continue using graphical formats for presentation of the data. Network diagrams are given for the records on world trade, students abroad, and international philanthropy. Each network diagram is created using a different method that best suits the data at hand. Key details of these methods are given in the headers for these records and in the relevant entries in the Glossary.

For some elements of last year's data programme we have been unable to obtain updated or equivalent data. Thus, we have decided not to reproduce the data on NGOs in countries and cities, country participation in NGOs, links between international organisations, INGO networks, meetings of IGOs and INGOs, NGOs by purpose, and employment, volunteering and revenue of NGOs. Two records from previous years have been reintroduced where data availability made this possible: students abroad, and human rights violations.

All data from previous Yearbooks remain available on our website at: **www.lse.ac.uk/Depts/global/researchgcspub.htm**

Sources and explanatory notes

Brief references to sources are found at the end of each record. All major terms used in the records are briefly defined in the Glossary. As will become clear, comparative information is not available for some countries and variables. A blank entry indicates that the data are not available, not comparable, or otherwise of insufficient quality to warrant reporting. To improve readability of the data and to facilitate interpretation, each record is preceded by a brief description of the information presented that points to some of the key findings.

Time periods

Dependent on data availability, data are reported for 1994 and 2004 or the closest years possible.

Countries

Countries in these tables are generally independent states with currently more than 100,000 inhabitants according to the most recent population estimates. Short or conventional country names are used. It is not the intention of the editors to take a position with regard to the political or diplomatic implications of geographical names or continental groupings used.

China, Hong Kong, Macao, Taiwan, and Tibet

Hong Kong became a Special Administrative Region (SAR) of China in 1997 after formal transfer from the UK. Macao became a SAR of China in 1999 after formal transfer from Portugal. Data for China before these dates do not include Hong Kong and Macao; thereafter they do unless otherwise stated. Tibet was annexed by the People's Republic of China in 1949. Data for Tibet are included in those for China and Tibet. Taiwan became the home of Chinese nationalists fleeing Communist rule on the mainland and claims separate status from the People's Republic of China. Data for Taiwan, which is not recognised by the United Nations as an independent country, is not included in most of the tables. Entries for Taiwan are presented in Records 20, 21 and 22.

Czechoslovakia
Czechoslovakia ceased to exist (in UN terms) on 31 December 1992. Its successor states, the Czech Republic and the Slovak Republic, became UN members in 1993. Figures predating 1993 are given for the Czech Republic and Slovakia separately where possible, or otherwise not at all.

Ethiopia and Eritrea
Eritrea became independent from Ethiopia in 1993. Data for Ethiopia until 1993 include Eritrea, later data do not.

Germany
The Federal Republic of Germany and the German Democratic Republic were unified in 1990. Data for 1990 and 1991 include both unless otherwise indicated.

Indonesia and East Timor
The Indonesian occupation of East Timor ended in late 1999. After a transitional period under the authority of the United Nations, East Timor became independent on 20 May 2002. Data for 1999 and after are presented separately for Indonesia and East Timor wherever possible. All data for Indonesia also include Irian Jaya (West Papua), the status of which has been in dispute since the 1960s.

Israel and the Occupied Territories
Data for Israel generally include both the occupied territories and territories administered by the Palestinian Authority. Records 8, 11, 12, 15, 16, 21 and 22 contain separate entries for territories named as 'Palestinian Authority' or 'West Bank & Gaza'.

Morocco and the Western Sahara
The Western Sahara (formerly Spanish Sahara) was annexed by Morocco in the 1970s. Unless otherwise stated, data are amalgamated for 'Morocco and the Western Sahara'.

Yugoslavia and Serbia & Montenegro
The Socialist Federal Republic of Yugoslavia dissolved in 1991 into Bosnia and Herzegovina, the Republic of Croatia, the Republic of Slovenia, the former Yugoslav Republic of Macedonia, and the Federal Republic of Yugoslavia. In February 2003 the Federal Republic of Yugoslavia was renamed Serbia and Montenegro, reflecting the implementation of constitutional change

to a looser federation of its two republics. For ease of presentation, the name 'Serbia and Montenegro' is used throughout these records, where the 'Federal Republic of Yugoslavia' would have applied pre-2003. Wherever possible, including for 1990, data are given separately for Serbia & Montenegro and the other constituent states of the former Yugoslavia.

USSR
The Union of Soviet Socialist Republics (USSR) dissolved in 1991 into Armenia, Azerbaijan, Belarus, Georgia, Kazakhstan, Kyrgyzstan, Republic of Moldova, Russian Federation, Tajikistan, Turkmenistan, Ukraine, and Uzbekistan. 1990 and 1991 data for the Russian Federation refer only to the Russian Federation, except where they are indicated to relate to the USSR.

Aggregations
Where possible we present data for groups of countries (by region and economy) as well as for individual countries. These groups are generally classified according to World Bank definitions. The aggregations are weighted differently depending on the data presented. To give an example, in Record 1 we present figures for trade as a percentage of GDP. The aggregate figure for South Asia is calculated as the sum of trade for Afghanistan, Bangladesh, Bhutan, India, Maldives, Nepal, Pakistan and Sri Lanka, divided by the sum of GDP for those countries, and multiplied by 100 to generate a percentage, ie

Trade as % GDP for South Asia =

$$\frac{\text{Afghan trade} + \text{Bangladeshi trade} + }{\text{Afghan GDP} + \text{Bangladeshi GDP} + ...} \times 100$$

Most aggregate figures given are calculated in this way. Similarly, the aggregations given in the first two tables of Record 19 and in Record 24 are weighted by population.

By contrast, in Records 17, 20 and 21 the data in the main tables represent counts or sums (eg number of NGOs, or amount of US$ contributions to a cause) rather than ratios (as in the case of 'trade as % GDP'), so the aggregate figures are simple sums. For example, in Record 17 the aggregate figure for South Asia's participation in the WTO's 1999 Seattle conference is simply the sum of the numbers of NGOs involved from the countries in that region. Each country's contribution to the regional or world figure is given equal weight under this method of aggregation.

Record 1: Global economy

The first table contains data on the globalisation of domestic economies. It shows total trade, foreign direct investment (FDI), and receipts of official development aid, presented as a percentage of GDP. It also includes information on changes over time between 1993 and 2003, with the use of the latest figures available. We try to show the extent to which national economies are parts of an emerging global economy, and where economic growth or contraction has been most pronounced in this respect since the mid-1990s. The table shows significant increases in trade and direct investments between 1993 and 2003 for most countries, and decreases in official development aid for many countries, contrasted with increases in aid in middle- and low-income economies in Europe and Central Asia.

Country	Trade			Official development aid*			Foreign direct investment					
	Total trade in % GDP 1993	Total trade in % GDP 2003	% change 1993-2003	Aid (% of GNI) 1993	Aid (% of GNI) 2003	% change 1993-2003	Inward FDI stock in % GDP 1993	Inward FDI stock in % GDP 2003	% change 1993-2003	Outward FDI stock in % GDP 1993	Outward FDI stock in % GDP 2003	% change 1993-2003
East Asia & Pacific												
Low income economies												
Cambodia	49.2	133.3	171	12.4	12.5	1	5.1	49.1	858	5.7	6.1	6
Indonesia	50.5	56.9	13	1.3	0.9	-31	27.9	27.6	-1	0.1	1.3	2,387
Korea, Dem. Rep.							6.1	9.1	49			
Laos	52.6	50.8	-4	15.2	14.3	-6	4.3	30.3	605		14.9	
Mongolia	190.4	147.9	-22	20.3	19.7	-3	2.6	36.2	1,271			
Myanmar	4.0						3.7	7.5	102			
Papua New Guinea	89.6			6.6	8.1	22	37.0	66.5	80	5.8	19.2	228
Solomon Islands	151.7	64.8	-57	22.1	24.4	10	43.0	49.9	16			
Vietnam	66.2	127.3	92	2.0	4.5	126	15.4	48.5	214			
Middle income economies												
China**	35.7	66.1	85	0.7	0.1	-87	10.6	35.6	236	2.0	2.6	34
Fiji	111.8			3.9	2.6	-33	30.5	36.3	19	3.3		
Malaysia	157.9	207.6	31	0.1	0.1	-23	30.8	57.1	86	7.5	28.8	284
Micronesia				29.8	44.0	48						
Philippines	71.2	99.0	39	2.7	0.9	-68	8.1	14.3	77	1.0	1.2	27
Samoa				31.1	12.5	-60	13.4	16.9	26			
Thailand	80.2	124.6	55	0.5	-0.7	-246	11.3	25.8	129	0.8	2.3	199
Tonga	67.4			22.2	17.1	-23	3.4	16.3	385			
Vanuatu	104.2			19.4	11.6	-40	95.8	172.5	80			
High income economies												
Australia	37.7	41.9	11				26.0	33.3	28	12.5	22.4	78
Brunei							1.0	160.6	15,308	1.3	3.7	193

Country	Trade			Official development aid*			Foreign direct investment					
	Total trade in % GDP 1993	Total trade in % GDP 2003	% change 1993-2003	Aid (% of GNI) 1993	Aid (% of GNI) 2003	% change 1993-2003	Inward FDI stock in % GDP 1993	Inward FDI stock in % GDP 2003	% change 1993-2003	Outward FDI stock in % GDP 1993	Outward FDI stock in % GDP 2003	% change 1993-2003
Japan	16.0	22.0	38				0.4	2.1	438	5.9	7.8	31
Korea, Rep.	53.2	73.8	39	0.0	-0.1	565	2.1	9.0	320	1.6	6.5	316
New Caledonia	43.4			12.9			3.2	4.0	24			
New Zealand	58.6	63.1	8				33.7	50.6	50	9.6	11.7	21
Europe & Central Asia												
Low income economies												
Armenia	108.0	81.7	-24	10.0	8.5	-14	1.7	30.3	1,715		2.0	
Azerbaijan	133.4	109.6	-18	2.1	4.4	112	1.8	121.0	6,463		17.6	
Georgia	118.6	78.2	-34	4.4	5.5	24	0.8	26.3	3,168			
Kyrgyzstan	74.7	80.3	7	5.5	10.7	93	1.0	26.2	2,504		2.3	
Moldova	94.7	141.3	49	1.2	5.1	319	3.2	40.3	1,160	1.6	1.2	-27
Tajikistan		139.3		1.6	9.9	523	2.6	14.4	445			
Ukraine	52.1	101.2	94	0.5	0.7	29	1.5	14.7	893	0.2	0.3	37
Uzbekistan	64.3	66.3	3	0.5	2.0	312	1.0	10.4	903			
Middle income economies												
Albania	77.7	61.3	-21	24.4	5.4	-78	6.4	18.0	183	2.2	1.5	-33
Belarus	151.0	136.8	-9	1.1	0.2	-84	0.4	10.8	2,861		0.0	
Bosnia & Herzegovina		84.4		36.3	7.4	-80		17.2		0.1	0.6	634
Bulgaria	84.0	116.2	38	1.1	2.1	98	2.3	25.4	1,002	1.0	0.7	-29
Croatia	106.0	103.9	-2	0.0	0.4		2.3	40.1	1,673	6.3	8.1	28
Czech Republic	110.1	127.8	16	0.3	0.3	6	9.0	45.4	402	0.5	1.9	298
Estonia	136.4	158.0	16	1.1	1.0	-10	16.5	79.0	380	3.9	12.4	217
Hungary	61.0	133.0	118	0.4	0.3	-29	14.3	51.8	262	0.6	4.7	716
Kazakhstan	84.6	94.5	12	0.1	1.0	1,119	10.8	63.8	488		1.1	
Latvia	129.5	104.0	-20	0.7	1.0	46	10.2	32.3	217	16.6	1.0	-94
Lithuania	172.9	113.8	-34	0.8	2.1	151	5.1	27.7	439		0.7	
Macedonia	101.4	88.6	-13	0.1	5.0	3,684	0.7	22.4	3,055		0.0	
Poland	44.9	47.3	5	1.3	0.6	-55	2.9	25.2	762	0.2	0.9	303
Romania	51.0	71.6	40	0.6	1.1	67	0.8	22.3	2,633	0.4	0.4	-5
Russian Federation	68.7	52.6	-23	0.6	0.3	-47	1.5	12.1	709	1.4	12.0	745
Serbia & Montenegro		67.5			6.4		1.6	17.1	941			

Country	Trade			Official development aid*			Foreign direct investment					
	Total trade in % GDP 1993	Total trade in % GDP 2003	% change 1993-2003	Aid (% of GNI) 1993	Aid (% of GNI) 2003	% change 1993-2003	Inward FDI stock in % GDP 1993	Inward FDI stock in % GDP 2003	% change 1993-2003	Outward FDI stock in % GDP 1993	Outward FDI stock in % GDP 2003	% change 1993-2003
Slovakia	117.7	157.6	34	0.4	0.5	30	3.0	31.5	953	0.8	1.7	110
Slovenia	116.4	119.3	2	0.1	0.2	321	7.5	15.6	108	2.2	6.5	194
Turkey	33.0	58.6	78	0.2	0.1	-68	7.5	7.5	0	0.7	2.3	225
Turkmenistan	98.8			1.0	0.4	-56	1.4	8.8	536			
High income economies												
Austria	71.5	102.1	43				6.1	23.7	288	4.4	23.3	435
Belgium & Luxembourg***	128.3	165.8	29				41.1	108.4	164	27.3	101.9	273
Cyprus	95.4			0.5			17.2	44.2	157	2.8	12.3	342
Denmark	64.0	80.4	26				10.5	36.0	242	11.4	36.4	220
Finland	59.5	67.0	13				4.9	28.7	488	10.6	42.5	300
France	40.0	50.4	26				10.6	24.7	133	12.4	36.6	194
Germany	45.4	67.7	49				6.6	22.7	242	9.1	25.9	184
Greece	42.4	47.8	13				9.5	9.9	3	3.2	5.8	84
Iceland	63.7	73.9	16				2.0	8.3	324	1.9	13.1	586
Ireland	121.4	*168.7*	*39*				75.0	125.8	68	23.8	21.8	-8
Italy	41.3	50.2	22				5.3	11.8	124	8.2	16.3	98
Netherlands	99.5	*120.1*	*21*				23.0	65.5	185	37.1	74.9	102
Norway	69.6	69.1	-1				11.6	20.3	75	10.8	18.3	70
Portugal	60.3	67.9	13				19.0	36.3	91	2.5	26.2	926
Spain	37.4	57.7	54				16.1	27.5	71	4.8	24.7	414
Sweden	60.1	80.8	34				6.6	47.6	619	22.9	62.9	174
Switzerland	66.0	*81.0*	*23*				16.4	49.3	202	38.7	110.4	185
United Kingdom	52.0	53.2	2				18.6	37.4	101	25.5	62.8	146
Latin America & Caribbean												
Low income economies												
Haiti	31.7	*50.1*	*58*	7.2	6.9	-4	10.2	9.3	-9		0.2	
Nicaragua	68.3	75.5	11	24.1	21.0	-13	7.8	47.6	510		0.5	
Middle income economies												
Argentina	16.2	39.1	141	0.1	0.1	-8	7.8	27.1	246	3.4	16.4	381
Barbados	109.3	*107.5*	*-2*	0.3	0.8	210	12.2	17.4	42	1.7	1.6	-5
Belize	112.1	120.8	8	5.7	1.3	-77	25.6	50.7	98	4.9	6.0	24

Country	Trade			Official development aid*			Foreign direct investment					
	Total trade in % GDP 1993	Total trade in % GDP 2003	% change 1993–2003	Aid (% of GNI) 1993	Aid (% of GNI) 2003	% change 1993–2003	Inward FDI stock in % GDP 1993	Inward FDI stock in % GDP 2003	% change 1993–2003	Outward FDI stock in % GDP 1993	Outward FDI stock in % GDP 2003	% change 1993–2003
Bolivia	47.5	48.8	3	10.2	12.3	20	22.9	87.0	281	0.2	0.5	102
Brazil	19.6	30.0	53	0.0	0.1	33	8.0	26.7	232	9.7	11.3	16
Chile	57.4	68.3	19	0.4	0.1	-73	24.7	65.5	165	1.6	19.3	1,142
Colombia	35.2	43.9	25	0.2	1.1	574	7.1	24.7	249	1.0	4.6	368
Costa Rica	78.0	95.4	22	1.1	0.2	-85	21.8	39.5	82	0.6	1.0	73
Cuba							0.1	0.3	89			
Dominican Republic	67.8	106.3	57	0.0	0.5	-3,312	8.6	35.7	317	0.1	0.4	413
Ecuador	51.8	52.6	2	1.7	0.7	-59	17.2	41.0	138		1.0	
El Salvador	53.5	70.0	31	5.8	1.3	-78	3.7	17.4	375	0.8	1.0	27
Grenada	117.1	104.5	-11	3.3	3.0	-9	60.2	152.5	153			
Guatemala	43.8	44.2	1	1.9	1.0	-46	18.1	17.6	-3		0.2	
Guyana	254.6	199.0	-22	28.6	12.4	-57	58.0	114.5	98	0.4		
Honduras	74.2	90.2	22	9.9	5.7	-42	15.3	30.2	98			
Jamaica	104.3	99.9	-4	2.2	0.0	-98	27.2	66.4	144	4.0	12.8	221
Mexico	34.4	58.5	70	0.1	0.0	-84	10.1	27.0	168	0.4	2.2	409
Panama	189.7	116.7	-38	1.0	0.3	-75	36.1	76.4	112	64.1	82.4	28
Paraguay	84.8	79.0	-7	1.9	0.8	-55	9.7	15.1	55	1.9	2.6	31
Peru	28.8	35.3	23	1.7	0.9	-49	4.7	21.0	345	0.3	1.3	328
St. Lucia	141.3	125.0	-11	5.6	2.3	-59	90.6	129.3	43	0.2		
St. Vincent & the Grenadines	117.9	112.3	-5	6.0	1.8	-70	42.4	154.2	264			
Suriname	42.7	66.2	55	20.1	0.9	-95						
Trinidad & Tobago	83.1	90.9	9	0.0	0.0	-151	61.6	93.7	52	0.5	7.9	1,517
Uruguay	38.7	48.8	26	0.8	0.2	-80	7.5	13.9	86	1.2	2.4	97
Venezuela	54.1	45.6	-16	0.1	0.1	40	8.6	44.5	416	5.8	10.3	79
High income economies												
Bahamas				0.0	0.1	162	21.4	44.8	109	44.7	30.5	-32
Middle East & North Africa												
Low income economies												
Yemen	92.3	67.1	-27	7.0	2.4	-65	10.5	12.9	23	0.0	0.1	105
Middle income economies												
Algeria	44.9	63.3	41	0.5	0.4	-23	2.9	9.7	238	0.5	0.7	48

Country	Trade			Official development aid*			Foreign direct investment					
	Total trade in % GDP 1993	Total trade in % GDP 2003	% change 1993–2003	Aid (% of GNI) 1993	Aid (% of GNI) 2003	% change 1993–2003	Inward FDI stock in % GDP 1993	Inward FDI stock in % GDP 2003	% change 1993–2003	Outward FDI stock in % GDP 1993	Outward FDI stock in % GDP 2003	% change 1993–2003
Djibouti					12.1		2.5	8.3	230			
Egypt	58.4	45.3	-22	5.1	1.1	-79	24.8	27.5	11	0.5	0.9	93
Iran	46.8	48.2	3	0.2	0.1	-58	2.1	2.0	-3	0.0	4.7	28,684
Jordan	131.7	114.6	-13	5.9	12.6	115	10.8	28.3	163	0.7		
Lebanon	80.5	52.4	-35	1.8	1.3	-29	1.1	10.8	910	1.3	2.8	107
Libya	59.8	84.4	41							0.5	7.5	1,279
Malta	200.4	176.8	-12	1.1	0.2	-81	26.5	53.6	102	1.0	5.8	467
Morocco	58.1	68.7	18	2.8	1.2	-56	8.0	26.0	224	2.1	2.0	-8
Oman	91.0	92.3	1	0.4	0.2	-53	16.8	13.0	-23	0.0	0.1	105
Saudi Arabia	68.2	71.0	4	0.0	0.0	-53	20.2	12.3	-39	1.1	1.1	-7
Syria	68.8	73.2	6	1.9	0.8	-60	3.1	7.8	149			
Tunisia	88.4	90.3	2	1.6	1.3	-22	59.7	65.8	10	0.2	0.2	13
High income economies												
Bahrain	164.6	146.1	-11	1.9	1.0	-50	33.9	74.0	118	16.6	31.9	93
Israel & Occupied Territories****	81.0	73.3	-9	0.0	9.4		75.0	26.1	-65	3.8	10.4	172
Kuwait	92.1	87.9	-5	0.0	0.0	175	0.4	1.6	329	22.3	4.7	-79
Qatar				0.0			3.1	15.3	387		2.0	
United Arab Emirates	124.5			0.0			3.7	5.4	45	0.3	6.2	1,796
North America												
High income economies												
Canada	61.1	78.7	29				19.3	32.3	67	16.7	36.1	116
United States	20.8	23.4	12				7.1	14.3	102	8.6	19.1	122
South Asia												
Low income economies												
Afghanistan		145.6					0.3	0.5	68			
Bangladesh	23.1	34.2	48	4.0	2.5	-37	1.0	4.8	376	0.0	0.1	444
Bhutan	75.4	64.6	-14	30.4	13.2	-57	0.9	0.6	-34			
India	20.0	30.5	52	0.5	0.2	-71	0.9	5.2	484	0.0	0.9	3,698
Nepal	47.2	45.4	-4	9.9	8.0	-20	0.7	2.5	275			
Pakistan	38.7	40.8	5	1.9	1.3	-31	4.6	10.1	122	0.6	0.8	39

Country	Trade			Official development aid*			Foreign direct investment					
	Total trade in % GDP 1993	Total trade in % GDP 2003	% change 1993–2003	Aid (% of GNI) 1993	Aid (% of GNI) 2003	% change 1993–2003	Inward FDI stock in % GDP 1993	Inward FDI stock in % GDP 2003	% change 1993–2003	Outward FDI stock in % GDP 1993	Outward FDI stock in % GDP 2003	% change 1993–2003
Middle income economies												
Maldives		151.3		10.4	2.6	-75	14.0	21.4	53			
Sri Lanka	77.1	78.1	1	6.5	3.7	-43	10.2	16.6	63	0.2	0.6	187
Sub-Saharan Africa												
Low income economies												
Angola	109.1	138.1	27	9.0	4.6	-48	43.1	133.5	209			
Benin	41.9	40.8	-3	13.9	8.5	-39	17.0	19.0	12	0.1	1.9	2,138
Burkina Faso	33.1	31.9	-4	20.0	10.8	-46	1.5	4.3	175	0.2	0.7	272
Burundi	39.8	24.7	-38	23.4	39.0	67	3.3	8.1	147		0.3	
Cameroon	33.1	50.9	54	4.9	7.5	54	8.7	13.5	55	1.8	2.0	11
Central African Republic	36.3	55.0	51	13.5	4.2	-69	5.8	9.5	65	2.6	3.5	33
Chad	42.6	73.2	72	15.5	10.6	-32	18.6	116.0	524	5.7	3.2	-43
Comoros	54.7	37.0	-32	17.5	7.6	-57	6.9	8.2	18	0.6	0.6	-7
Congo, Dem. Rep.	20.4	*40.9*	*100*	1.8	99.9	5,468	5.3	17.2	225			
Congo, Rep.	94.4	130.7	38	7.5	2.6	-65	33.4	63.4	90			
Côte d'Ivoire	55.3	80.5	45	7.9	1.9	-75	11.1	27.7	149	3.8	4.6	23
Equatorial Guinea	39.7			35.2			58.6	130.3	122		0.1	
Eritrea	102.1	112.8	10	12.1	34.2	181		28.1				
Ethiopia	28.3	53.7	89	17.7	22.8	29	2.5	17.0	577		8.3	
Gambia	133.0	85.9	-35	23.5	16.2	-31	47.6	101.5	113	7.8	16.6	114
Ghana	56.7	92.5	63	10.7	12.2	14	8.1	23.6	191		7.1	
Guinea	46.6	46.6	0	13.0	6.6	-49	4.0	8.4	108		0.4	
Guinea-Bissau	41.6	73.4	77	42.6	63.6	49	8.2	16.0	95			
Kenya	84.1	54.2	-36	19.9	3.4	-83	12.6	7.4	-41	1.8	0.9	-53
Lesotho	142.3	136.6	-4	11.8	5.7	-52	13.9	39.9	188			
Madagascar	39.9	53.1	33	11.2	10.0	-11	4.7	8.7	87	0.1	0.1	60
Malawi	48.4	68.1	41	24.5	29.8	22	8.5	19.7	131		1.3	
Mali	47.1	57.2	22	13.5	12.7	-6	1.0	17.8	1,705	0.9	4.2	372
Mauritania	103.5	109.4	6	37.2	20.9	-44	8.8	51.0	481	0.3	0.3	-14
Mozambique	61.6	62.1	1	65.0	25.1	-61	6.0	43.9	633			
Niger	33.7	41.2	22	21.7	16.7	-23	14.8	16.7	13	4.5	5.1	13

Country	Trade			Official development aid*			Foreign direct investment					
	Total trade in % GDP 1993	Total trade in % GDP 2003	% change 1993–2003	Aid (% of GNI) 1993	Aid (% of GNI) 2003	% change 1993–2003	Inward FDI stock in % GDP 1993	Inward FDI stock in % GDP 2003	% change 1993–2003	Outward FDI stock in % GDP 1993	Outward FDI stock in % GDP 2003	% change 1993–2003
Nigeria	97.3	90.9	-7	1.5	0.6	-58	34.7	49.1	42	11.6	9.6	-17
Rwanda	25.7	36.2	41	18.2	20.0	10	11.8	17.3	46		0.4	
São Tomé & Principe	111.0	120.6	9	110.7	75.0	-32		48.2				
Senegal	50.3	68.9	37	9.5	7.0	-26	5.0	15.3	206	1.5	2.5	63
Sierra Leone	43.3	71.9	66	30.3	39.0	29		3.3				
Somalia								0.3				
Sudan		28.4		6.5	3.8	-41	0.6	26.1	4,261			
Tanzania	65.7	45.6	-31	23.2	16.3	-30	3.6	25.8	616			
Togo	56.5	81.2	44	8.0	2.6	-67	20.4	30.7	50	3.1	6.3	103
Uganda	28.2	38.7	37	19.2	15.6	-19	1.9	32.7	1,586	1.6	3.7	133
Zambia	74.0	48.5	-34	28.9	13.4	-54	34.9	54.4	56			
Zimbabwe	63.2	45.8	-27	7.9			2.8	46.2	1,550	1.7	10.3	512
Middle income economies												
Botswana	86.2	78.4	-9	2.9	0.4	-86	26.9	15.2	-44	12.6	18.3	45
Cape Verde	62.6	100.2	60	32.7	18.3	-44	2.7	25.5	857	1.0	1.0	-5
Gabon	83.3	103.4	24	2.6	-0.2	-108	21.6	0.4	-98	3.8	5.2	36
Mauritius	122.2	117.0	-4	0.8	-0.3	-137	6.7	14.6	120	2.7	3.3	21
Namibia	108.6	86.1	-21	5.3	3.2	-40	52.4	25.6	-51	2.8	0.7	-76
South Africa	39.3	54.6	39	0.2	0.4	85	8.2	19.0	132	13.8	15.1	10
Swaziland	177.4	177.2	0	5.2	1.4	-72	45.0	40.4	-10	5.1	3.2	-37

Region	Trade			Official development aid*			Foreign direct investment					
	Total trade in % GDP 1993	Total trade in % GDP 2003	% change 1993–2003	Aid (% of GNI) 1993	Aid (% of GNI) 2003	% change 1993–2003	Inward FDI stock in % GDP 1993	Inward FDI stock in % GDP 2003	% change 1993–2003	Outward FDI stock in % GDP 1993	Outward FDI stock in % GDP 2003	% change 1993–2003
Low income	34.3	44.8	31	4.1	3.0	-26	10.5	25.8	145	1.5	2.1	46
Middle income	46.9	62.5	33	0.7	0.4	-39	10.3	23.1	124	5.5	7.9	43
Low & middle income	45.1	60.0	33	1.4	1.1	-22						
East Asia & Pacific	49.3	80.8	64	1.1	0.4	-67						
Europe & Central Asia	63.9	69.8	9	1.0	0.8	-23						
Latin America & Caribbean	31.9	45.8	44	0.4	0.4	-6						
Middle East & North Africa	62.6	61.6	-2	1.3	1.0	-20						
South Asia	24.2	33.5	38	1.4	0.8	-42						
Sub-Saharan Africa	56.2	64.5	15	6.3	6.0	-6						
High income	36.9	*45.0*	*22*	0.0	0.0	-62	25.7	49.4	92	5.7	27.8	384
World	38.4	*47.6*	*24*	0.3	0.2	-17	9.5	22.9	141	9.2	22.9	148

Where data for a particular year are not available, figures are taken from the year before or after as an estimate. These figures, and estimates based on them, are presented in italics.

* Official development aid includes both official development assistance and official aid.

** Data for Hong Kong, Macao and Taiwan are not included in this table.

*** FDI data are not supplied for Belgium and Luxembourg individually: figures for Trade and Aid for Belgium and Luxembourg together are estimates calculated by UCLA (these are averages, weighted by population).

**** Separate data for Israel and the Occupied Territories (The Palestinian Authority) were not available for 1993. For reasons of comparability data are presented in one figure (these are averages, weighted by population).

Sources: World Development Indicators 2005, WDI Online, World Bank,
http://devdata.worldbank.org/dataonline; UNCTAD Foreign Direct Investment database,
http://stats.unctad.org/restricted/eng/ReportFolders/Rfview/Explorerp.asp

Record 2: **Global trade**

This record shows the unevenness of economic globalisation as measured by trade flows. The network graph offers a simplified and consolidated view of trade flows among major world regions for 2003. The graph should be interpreted by reference to the thickness of the lines between regions (indicating volumes of trade), the position of the regions (spatial centrality reflecting a central position in the trading system), and the size of the regions (reflecting total trade flows into and out of each region). There is a clear distinction between core, semi-periphery and periphery in the world trade system. Thus, the US, European Union (EU) and East Asia occupy the most central positions within this network, with the greatest amounts of trade flowing between the EU and the US. Japan, Europe and Central Asia, the Middle East and North Africa, and South Asia are at the semi-periphery, and Sub-Saharan Africa and Latin America are at the outer periphery.

The accompanying table illustrates a general trend of increased overall centralisation in the network of world trade between 2000 and 2003 (calculated on the basis of the gap between the most centralised and least centralised nodes in the network). This means that trade is becoming more concentrated in the rich regions. A growing share of world trade is channelled between the US, the EU, and East Asia and the Pacific. South Asian countries are becoming more central while Japan's centrality has declined due to its continuing economic crisis (centrality in the global trade network is determined not only by a particular region's share of total world trade but also the 'strength' of the regions it trades with).

Direction of flow (export region → import region)*	Amount of trade in % world trade** 2003
East Asia & Pacific → Europe & Central Asia	0.3
East Asia & Pacific → European Union	1.6
East Asia & Pacific → Japan	1.5
East Asia & Pacific → Latin America & Caribbean	0.2
East Asia & Pacific → Middle East & North Africa	0.2
East Asia & Pacific → South Asia	0.2
East Asia & Pacific → Sub-Saharan Africa	0.4
East Asia & Pacific → United States	2.1
Within East Asia & Pacific	1.1
Europe & Central Asia → East Asia & Pacific	0.2
Europe & Central Asia → European Union	3.1
Europe & Central Asia → Middle East & North Africa	0.2
Europe & Central Asia → South Asia	0.1
Europe & Central Asia → United States	0.2
Within Europe & Central Asia	1.7
European Union → East Asia & Pacific	1.0
European Union → Europe & Central Asia	3.5
European Union → Japan	0.6
European Union → Latin America & Caribbean	0.7
European Union → Middle East & North Africa	1.0
European Union → South Asia	0.3
European Union → Sub-Saharan Africa	0.6

Direction of flow (export region → import region)*	Amount of trade in % world trade** 2003
European Union → United States	3.5
Within European Union	24.5
Japan → East Asia & Pacific	1.4
Japan → Europe & Central Asia	0.1
Japan → European Union	1.0
Japan → Latin America & Caribbean	0.2
Japan → Middle East & North Africa	0.1
Japan → South Asia	0.1
Japan → Sub-Saharan Africa	0.1
Japan → United States	1.6
Latin America & Caribbean → East Asia & Pacific	0.2
Latin America & Caribbean → Europe & Central Asia	0.1
Latin America & Caribbean → European Union	0.6
Latin America & Caribbean → Japan	0.1
Latin America & Caribbean → Middle East & North Africa	0.1
Latin America & Caribbean → United States	3.0
Within Latin America & Caribbean	0.8
Middle East & North Africa → East Asia & Pacific	0.3
Middle East & North Africa → Europe & Central Asia	0.1
Middle East & North Africa → European Union	0.9
Middle East & North Africa → Japan	0.3
Middle East & North Africa → South Asia	0.1
Middle East & North Africa → Sub-Saharan Africa	0.1
Middle East & North Africa → United States	0.4
Within Middle East & North Africa	0.1
South Asia → East Asia & Pacific	0.1
South Asia → European Union	0.3
South Asia → Middle East & North Africa	0.1
South Asia → United States	0.2
Within South Asia	0.1
Sub-Saharan Africa → East Asia & Pacific	0.1
Sub-Saharan Africa → European Union	0.5
Sub-Saharan Africa → Japan	0.1
Sub-Saharan Africa → South Asia	0.1
Sub-Saharan Africa → United States	0.3
Within Sub-Saharan Africa	0.2

Direction of flow (export region → import region)*	Amount of trade in % world trade** 2003
United States → East Asia & Pacific	0.8
United States → Europe & Central Asia	0.1
United States → European Union	2.1
United States → Japan	0.7
United States → Latin America & Caribbean	2.0
United States → Middle East & North Africa	0.1
United States → South Asia	0.1
United States → Sub-Saharan Africa	0.1

* European Union Countries: Austria, Belgium, Denmark, Finland, France, Germany, Greece, Ireland, Italy, Luxembourg, The Netherlands, Portugal, Spain, Sweden, United Kingdom. All other regions represented in the diagram comprise the countries listed in Record 1.

** Only flows amounting to at least 0.1% of total world trade are included in this table. Flows not associated with a region are also excluded from the table. Figures do not therefore sum to 100%.

Source: World Bank, World Development Indicators 2005: Table 6.2. Direction and growth of merchandise trade; Direction of trade 2003; http://www.worldbank.org/data/wdi2005/wditext/Section6.htm.

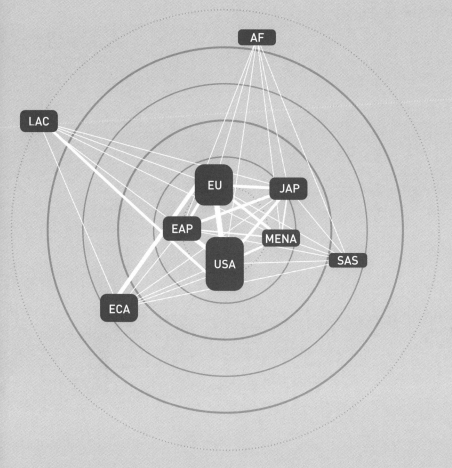

EAP   East Asia & Pacific

ECA   Europe & Central Asia

EU   European Union

JAP   Japan

LAC   Latin America
       & Caribbean

MENA   Middle East
       & North Africa

SAS   South Asia

USA   United States

Changes in trade network centrality, 2000-2003

Node	Region	Network centrality		Change in centrality (% change) 2000-2003
		2000	2003	
LAC	Latin America & Caribbean	9.5	7.4	-22
AF	Sub-Saharan Africa	7.7	9.2	19
JAP	Japan	13.0	10.1	-22
ECA	Europe & Central Asia	9.5	10.3	8
MENA	Middle East & North Africa	12.0	11.8	-1
SAS	South Asia	9.5	12.1	27
EAP	East Asia & Pacific	13.0	13.0	1
EU	European Union	13.0	13.0	1
USA	United States	13.0	13.0	1
Network centralisation		2.1	2.2	5

Record 3: Transnationality of top 100 transnational corporations (TNCs)

This record suggests the importance of TNCs, and the globalised economy they create, as a major reference point for the development of global civil society – from the growing numbers and influence of highly mobile groups of managers and professionals working for TNCs to activists protesting against certain corporate practices and cultures. The names and global headquarter countries for the 100 largest non-financial corporations are listed, alongside figures on their sizes and foreign shares of assets, sales, and employment for 2001. TNCs are listed in order of degree of transnationality, with the most transnational companies at the top, where higher index numbers (and lower rank numbers) indicate an overall greater extent of transnationality. The table shows that the majority of large TNCs are located in North America and Western Europe, with a few in South-East Asia and only one in Latin America. All the newcomers to this list are from developed nations, with only one being neither European nor American.

Ranking by TNI*				US $ billions and number of employees, 2002									
				Assets			Sales			Employment			
2002	2001	Corporation & industry	Country	Foreign	Total	% Foreign	Foreign	Total	% Foreign	Foreign	Total	% Foreign	TNI* (%)
1	1	NTL Inc *Telecommunications*	United States	12.9	13.0	98.6	3.3	3.3	100.0	14,922	15,130	98.6	99.1
2	2	Thomson Corporation *Media*	Canada	18.1	18.5	97.8	7.7	7.9	97.7	41,300	42,000	98.3	97.9
3	4	Holcim AG *Construction materials*	Switzerland	17.5	18.4	95.3	7.9	8.4	93.9	49,765	51,115	97.4	95.5
4	–	CRH Plc *Lumber & other building materials dealers*	Ireland	10.6	11.1	95.8	9.5	10.2	93.4	47,335	49,889	94.9	94.7
5	3	ABB *Machinery & equipment*	Switzerland	28.2	29.5	95.3	17.1	18.3	93.7	131,321	139,051	94.4	94.5
6	5	Roche Group *Pharmaceuticals*	Switzerland	40.2	46.2	87.0	18.8	19.2	98.2	61,090	69,659	87.7	91.0
7	–	Interbrew SA *Beverages*	Belgium	10.7	11.7	91.3	6.0	6.6	90.7	31,682	35,044	90.4	90.8
8	–	Publicis Groupe SA *Business services*	France	11.0	11.5	95.8	2.4	2.8	87.0	31,871	35,681	89.3	90.7
9	11	News Corporation *Media*	Australia	40.3	45.2	89.2	16.0	17.4	92.0	31,220	35,000	89.2	90.1
10	7	Philips Electronics *Electrical & electronic equipment*	Netherlands	27.9	33.8	82.4	28.7	30.1	95.3	140,827	170,087	82.8	86.8
11	13	Vodafone Group Plc *Telecommunications*	United Kingdom	207.6	232.9	89.2	33.6	42.3	79.5	56,667	66,667	85.0	84.5
12	12	Nortel Networks *Machinery & equipment*	Canada	13.4	16.0	83.9	9.9	10.6	93.6	26,820	36,960	72.6	83.4
13	14	Astrazeneca Plc *Pharmaceuticals*	United Kingdom	14.8	21.6	68.6	17.0	17.8	95.1	46,800	57,500	81.4	81.7
14	15	British Petroleum Company Plc – *Petroleum*	United Kingdom	126.1	159.1	79.3	146.0	180.2	81.0	97,400	116,300	83.7	81.3
15	19	Reed Elseviero *Publishing & printing*	United Kingdom/ Netherlands	11.7	14.0	83.5	5.7	7.5	76.1	27,300	36,100	75.6	78.4
16	–	Alcan Inc. *Metal & metal products*	Canada	11.7	17.5	66.6	11.5	12.5	92.0	38,000	50,000	76.0	78.2

Ranking by TNI* 2002	2001	Corporation & industry	Country	Assets Foreign	Assets Total	Assets % Foreign	Sales Foreign	Sales Total	Sales % Foreign	Employment Foreign	Employment Total	Employment % Foreign	TNI* [%]
				US $ billions and number of employees, 2002									
17	18	Suez *Electricity, gas & water*	France	38.7	44.8	86.5	34.2	43.6	78.4	138,200	198,750	69.5	78.1
18	16	Danone Groupe SA *Food & beverages*	France	11.3	16.2	69.7	9.5	12.8	74.0	79,945	92,209	86.7	76.8
19	33	Royal Ahold NV *Retail*	Netherlands	20.6	25.9	79.4	46.3	59.3	78.2	236,698	341,909	69.2	75.6
20	21	Total Fina Elf *Petroleum*	France	79.0	89.5	88.4	77.5	97.0	79.9	68,554	121,469	56.4	74.9
21	26	BHP Billiton Group *Mining & quarrying*	Australia	13.8	20.6	66.8	15.7	17.5	89.9	23,259	34,801	66.8	74.5
22	10	Diageo Plc *Beverages*	United Kingdom	18.5	26.7	69.3	12.6	15.0	84.4	26,999	38,955	69.3	74.3
23	22	Volvo Group *Motor vehicles*	Sweden	17.4	27.4	63.7	18.0	19.2	93.5	45,740	71,160	64.3	73.8
24	41	Lvmh Moët-Hennessy Louis Vuitton SA *Luxury goods*	France	16.4	22.5	73.1	10.0	12.0	83.0	33,996	53,812	63.2	73.1
25	32	Coca-Cola Company *Beverages*	United States	17.4	24.5	70.9	13.1	19.4	67.6	45,100	56,000	80.5	73.0
26	23	Nokia *Machinery & equipment*	Finland	14.5	24.5	59.4	28.1	28.4	98.8	30,099	52,714	57.1	71.8
27	38	Hutchison Whampoa Ltd. *Diversified*	Hong Kong, China	48.0	63.3	75.9	8.1	14.2	56.8	124,942	154,813	80.7	71.1
28	25	Anglo American *Mining & quarrying*	United Kingdom	22.5	33.6	66.9	12.8	20.5	62.6	147,000	177,000	83.1	70.8
29	44	Honda Motor Co Ltd. *Motor vehicles*	Japan	43.6	63.8	68.5	49.2	65.4	75.2	42,885	63,310	67.7	70.5
30	24	AES Corporation *Electricity, gas & water*	United States	22.8	33.8	67.5	6.5	8.6	75.8	24,284	36,000	67.5	70.2
31	27	Compagnie De Saint-Gobain SA *Construction materials*	France	22.4	31.6	70.8	19.7	28.6	68.8	122,373	172,357	71.0	70.2
32	–	Novartis *Pharmaceuticals*	Switzerland	25.9	45.6	56.8	20.6	20.9	98.5	40,282	72,877	55.3	70.2
33	30	Cemex S.A. *Construction materials*	Mexico	12.2	16.0	76.0	4.4	7.0	62.1	17,568	26,752	65.7	67.9
34	29	GlaxoSmithKline Plc *Pharmaceuticals*	United Kingdom	20.0	35.8	55.8	29.3	31.9	91.9	58,471	104,499	56.0	67.9
35	17	Stora Enso OY *Paper*	Finland	13.1	19.1	68.7	8.2	12.1	67.5	29,177	43,853	66.5	67.6
36	34	British American Tobacco Group *Tobacco*	United Kingdom	15.6	26.1	59.7	25.0	37.1	67.5	60,107	85,819	70.0	65.7
37	40	Aventis SA *Pharmaceuticals*	France	23.8	32.6	72.9	14.8	19.5	75.7	37,802	78,099	48.4	65.7
38	36	Vivendi Universal *Media*	France	49.7	72.7	68.3	30.0	55.0	54.6	45,772	61,815	74.0	65.7

2002	2001	Corporation & industry	Country	Assets Foreign	Assets Total	Assets % Foreign	Sales Foreign	Sales Total	Sales % Foreign	Employment Foreign	Employment Total	Employment % Foreign	TNI* (%)
				US $ billions and number of employees, 2002									
39	39	ExxonMobil Corporation *Petroleum*	United States	60.8	94.9	64.0	141.3	200.9	70.3	56,000	92,000	60.9	65.1
40	35	Unilever *Diversified*	United Kingdom/ Netherlands	27.9	46.8	59.8	27.6	46.1	59.9	193,000	258,000	74.8	64.8
41	43	Bertelsmann *Media*	Germany	14.1	23.3	60.7	11.9	17.3	68.9	48,920	80,632	60.7	63.4
42	45	Carrefour SA *Retail*	France	28.6	40.8	70.1	31.8	65.0	48.9	271,031	386,762	70.1	63.0
43	48	Royal Dutch/Shell Group *Petroleum*	United Kingdom/ Netherlands	94.4	145.4	64.9	114.3	179.4	63.7	65,000	111,000	58.6	62.4
44	–	Siemens AG *Electrical & electronic equipment*	Germany	47.5	76.5	62.1	50.7	77.2	65.7	251,340	426,000	59.0	62.3
45	37	Singtel Ltd. *Telecommunications*	Singapore	15.8	19.1	82.7	3.2	5.8	56.0	9,877	21,716	45.5	61.4
46	20	Nestlé SA *Food & beverages*	Switzerland	36.1	63.0	57.4	34.9	57.5	60.6	150,232	254,199	59.1	59.0
47	42	Alcatel *Machinery & equipment*	France	12.7	27.1	46.8	10.0	15.7	63.7	50,559	75,940	66.6	59.0
48	57	ChevronTexaco Corp. *Petroleum*	United States	48.5	77.4	62.7	55.1	98.7	55.8	37,038	66,038	56.1	58.2
49	49	McDonald's Corporation *Restaurant*	United States	13.8	24.0	57.4	9.0	15.4	58.1	237,269	413,000	57.5	57.7
50	53	Sony Corporation *Electrical & electronic equipment*	Japan	29.8	69.5	42.9	42.9	61.3	69.9	94,000	161,100	58.3	57.1
51	51	Volkswagen Group *Motor vehicles*	Germany	57.1	114.2	50.0	59.7	82.2	72.5	157,887	324,892	48.6	57.1
52	59	Pinault-Printemps Redoute SA *Retail*	France	19.2	31.5	61.1	13.9	25.9	53.8	53,871	108,423	49.7	54.9
53	54	BASF AG *Chemicals*	Germany	22.7	36.8	61.7	17.9	30.5	58.7	39,078	89,398	43.7	54.7
54	60	BMW AG *Motor vehicles*	Germany	37.6	58.2	64.6	30.2	40.0	75.5	20,120	96,263	20.9	53.7
55	73	Procter & Gamble *Diversified*	United States	20.3	43.7	46.4	21.5	43.4	49.6	61,200	98,000	62.4	52.8
56	67	Scottish Power *Electric utilities*	United Kingdom	13.0	19.9	65.2	4.0	7.6	52.8	6,268	15,490	40.5	52.8
57	66	Dow Chemical Company *Chemicals*	United States	17.4	39.6	43.9	16.4	27.6	59.2	24,725	49,959	49.5	50.9
58	65	IBM *Electrical & electronic equipment*	United States	35.0	96.5	36.2	48.4	81.2	59.6	178,602	315,889	56.5	50.8
59	52	Telefonica SA *Telecommunications*	Spain	35.7	71.3	50.1	11.3	26.9	42.0	88,401	152,845	57.8	50.0
60	75	Eni Group *Petroleum*	Italy	37.0	69.0	53.6	22.8	45.3	50.3	36,973	80,655	45.8	49.9

Ranking by TNI* 2002	2001	Corporation & industry	Country	Assets Foreign	Assets Total	Assets % Foreign	Sales Foreign	Sales Total	Sales % Foreign	Employment Foreign	Employment Total	Employment % Foreign	TNI* (%)
61	–	France Telecom *Telecommunications*	France	73.5	111.7	65.7	18.2	44.1	41.2	102,016	243,573	41.9	49.6
62	63	Fiat Spa *Motor vehicles*	Italy	46.2	97.0	47.6	24.6	52.6	46.7	98,703	186,492	52.9	49.1
63	85	Ford Motor Company *Motor vehicles*	United States	165.0	295.2	55.9	54.5	163.4	33.3	188,453	350,321	53.8	47.7
64	68	Pfizer Inc *Pharmaceuticals*	United States	21.2	46.4	45.6	11.6	32.4	35.9	72,000	120,000	60.0	47.2
65	74	Matsushita Electric Industrial Co., Ltd. *Electrical & electronic equipment*	Japan	17.9	65.0	27.6	32.4	60.7	53.3	166,873	288,324	57.9	46.3
66	61	Hewlett-Packard *Electrical & electronic equipment*	United States	28.2	70.7	39.9	33.3	56.6	58.8	56,326	141,000	39.9	46.2
67	–	Metro AG *Retail*	Germany	11.8	24.0	49.2	22.5	48.7	46.3	84,825	196,462	43.2	46.2
68	69	Repsol YPF SA *Petroleum*	Spain	23.1	39.9	57.9	11.3	34.5	32.7	14,072	30,110	46.7	45.8
69	47	Toyota Motor Corporation *Motor vehicles*	Japan	79.4	167.3	47.5	72.8	127.1	57.3	85,057	264,096	32.2	45.7
70	62	Motorola Inc *Machinery & equipment*	United States	10.4	31.2	33.5	18.2	37.6	48.3	53,350	97,000	55.0	45.6
71	58	Bayer AG *Pharmaceuticals/chemicals*	Germany	18.0	43.7	41.1	14.9	28.0	53.3	52,000	122,600	42.4	45.6
72	71	Thyssenkrupp AG *Metal & metal products*	Germany	12.8	30.6	41.8	15.5	33.7	45.9	88,404	191,254	46.2	44.6
73	79	Alcoa *Metal & metal products*	United States	11.1	29.8	37.3	7.4	20.3	36.4	73,500	127,000	57.9	43.9
74	81	RWE Group *Electricity, gas & water*	Germany	50.7	105.1	48.2	17.6	44.1	40.0	55,563	131,765	42.2	43.4
75	80	Abbott Laboratories *Pharmaceuticals*	United States	11.1	24.3	45.6	6.7	17.7	37.8	33,000	71,819	45.9	43.1
76	28	National Grid Transco *Energy*	United Kingdom	16.5	35.6	46.5	6.2	13.5	45.8	9,975	27,308	36.5	42.9
77	78	Du Pont (E.I.) De Nemours – *Chemicals*	United States	13.0	34.6	37.7	12.6	24.0	52.4	29,755	79,000	37.7	42.6
78	–	Canadian National Railway Company *Transportation*	Canada	12.1	21.7	55.4	2.4	6.1	39.0	6,879	22,114	31.1	41.9
79	–	Endesa *Electricity, gas & water*	Spain	22.5	50.5	44.5	5.5	16.3	33.9	12,334	26,354	46.8	41.7
80	83	General Electric *Electrical & electronic equipment*	United States	229.0	575.2	39.8	45.4	131.7	34.5	150,000	315,000	47.6	40.6
81	94	Mitsui & Co Ltd *Wholesale trade*	Japan	21.0	54.3	38.7	47.0	108.5	43.3	14,611	37,734	38.7	40.2

Ranking by TNI*				US $ billions and number of employees, 2002									
				Assets			Sales			Employment			
2002	2001	Corporation & industry	Country	Foreign	Total	% Foreign	Foreign	Total	% Foreign	Foreign	Total	% Foreign	TNI* (%)
82	86	E.On *Electricity, gas & water*	Germany	52.3	118.5	44.1	13.1	35.1	37.4	42,063	107,856	39.0	40.2
83	76	Renault SA *Motor vehicles*	France	17.4	55.8	31.3	21.2	34.4	61.7	35,351	132,351	26.7	39.9
84	–	Samsung Electronics Co., Ltd. *Electrical & electronic equipment*	Republic of Korea	11.4	52.0	21.9	28.3	47.7	59.4	28,300	82,400	34.3	38.5
85	96	Deutsche Post World Net *Transport & storage*	Germany	22.8	170.5	13.4	21.8	37.1	58.8	108,609	327,676	33.1	35.1
86	84	Johnson & Johnson *Pharmaceuticals*	United States	12.8	40.6	31.6	13.8	36.3	38.1	34,218	108,300	31.6	33.8
87	–	ConocoPhillips *Petroleum*	United States	32.1	76.8	41.8	10.1	56.7	17.8	23,934	57,300	41.8	33.8
88	90	Philip Morris Companies Inc *Diversified*	United States	21.5	87.5	24.6	35.7	80.4	44.4	40,795	166,000	24.6	31.2
89	91	Electricité de France *Electricity, gas & water*	France	47.4	151.8	31.2	12.6	45.7	27.4	50,437	171,995	29.3	29.3
90	87	General Motors *Motor vehicles*	United States	107.9	370.8	29.1	48.1	186.8	25.7	101,000	350,000	28.9	27.9
91	92	Merck & Co *Pharmaceuticals*	United States	11.4	47.6	23.9	8.3	51.8	16.0	28,600	77,300	37.0	25.7
92	98	Hitachi Ltd *Electrical & electronic equipment*	Japan	20.2	84.5	23.9	15.6	67.2	23.2	83,478	339,572	24.6	23.9
93	97	DaimlerChrysler AG *Motor vehicles*	Germany/ United States	35.8	196.4	18.2	46.1	141.5	32.6	72,560	365,571	19.8	23.6
94	95	Wal-Mart Stores *Retail*	United States	30.7	94.7	32.4	40.8	244.5	16.7	300,000	1,400,000	21.4	23.5
95	88	Mitsubishi Corporation *Wholesale trade*	Japan	17.3	67.2	25.7	15.6	109.3	14.3	12,182	47,370	25.7	21.9
96	–	AOL Time Warner Inc *Media*	United States	23.5	115.5	20.3	8.3	41.0	20.3	18,555	91,250	20.3	20.3
97	–	Telecom Italia *Telecommunications*	Italy	17.3	84.9	20.3	6.7	33.0	20.3	21,653	106,620	20.3	20.3
98	–	Duke Energy Corporation *Electricity, gas & water*	United States	12.2	49.1	24.9	2.2	15.7	13.9	4,400	22,000	20.0	19.6
99	82	Deutsche Telekom AG *Telecommunications*	Germany	19.2	120.6	15.9	0.3	24.4	1.3	78,146	255,969	30.5	15.9
100	100	Verizon Communications *Telecommunications*	United States	14.2	167.5	8.5	3.3	67.6	4.8	19,513	229,497	8.5	7.3

*TNI = Transnationality Index (average of the ratios of foreign to total assets, sales and employment).

List includes non-financial TNCs only.

Definitions of 'foreign' are not straightforward for some TNCs; see notes accompanying this information in World Investment Report for more details.

Source: UNCTAD, World Investment Report 2004: The Shift towards Services, Annex table A.I.3. The world's top 100 non-financial TNCs, ranked by foreign assets, 2002, pp. 276-278, http://www.unctad.org/en/docs/wir2004annexes_en.pdf

Record 4: **Students abroad**

Students are major transmitters of knowledge and ideas, and interlocutors among cultures. The growing practice of studying abroad may therefore be one catalyst for the emergence and spread of global civil society. The data show that high-income economies in North America and Europe are the main destinations of international students. Middle-income European and Central Asian countries and middle-income East Asian countries are the largest sources of international students. The diagram reflects the structure of the global network created by international student flows. It is an optimised network diagram (spring optimisation – see Glossary) in which pairs of nodes (regions) with greater numbers of students moving between them are placed further apart. It shows again a core periphery structure, where student flow is concentrated in the core and relatively little student flow is found in the periphery. Here the core consists mostly of high- and middle-income economies, particularly the developed nations in North America, Europe and East Asia/Pacific, while low-income economies are in the periphery.

Direction of flow (region of origin → host region)	Number of students, 2001-2002*
East Asia & Pacific, Low income → East Asia & Pacific, Middle income	1,989
East Asia & Pacific, Low income → East Asia & Pacific, High income	4,224
East Asia & Pacific, Low income → Europe & Central Asia, Low income	24
East Asia & Pacific, Low income → Europe & Central Asia, Middle income	1,004
East Asia & Pacific, Low income → Europe & Central Asia, High income	5,231
East Asia & Pacific, Low income → Latin America & Caribbean, Middle income	2,152
East Asia & Pacific, Low income → Middle East & North Africa, Middle income	362
East Asia & Pacific, Low income → North America, High income	16,149
East Asia & Pacific, Middle income → East Asia & Pacific, Middle income	1,921
East Asia & Pacific, Middle income → East Asia & Pacific, High income	53,782
East Asia & Pacific, Middle income → Europe & Central Asia, Low income	67
East Asia & Pacific, Middle income → Europe & Central Asia, Middle income	963
East Asia & Pacific, Middle income → Europe & Central Asia, High income	16,213
East Asia & Pacific, Middle income → Latin America & Caribbean, Middle income	1,956
East Asia & Pacific, Middle income → Middle East & North Africa, Middle income	66
East Asia & Pacific, Middle income → Middle East & North Africa, High income	2
East Asia & Pacific, Middle income → North America, High income	86,060
East Asia & Pacific, High income → East Asia & Pacific, Middle income	967
East Asia & Pacific, High income → East Asia & Pacific, High income	21,911
East Asia & Pacific, High income → Europe & Central Asia, Low income	1
East Asia & Pacific, High income → Europe & Central Asia, Middle income	227
East Asia & Pacific, High income → Europe & Central Asia, High income	16,508
East Asia & Pacific, High income → Latin America & Caribbean, Middle income	470
East Asia & Pacific, High income → Middle East & North Africa, Middle income	11
East Asia & Pacific, High income → Middle East & North Africa, High income	2
East Asia & Pacific, High income → North America, High income	112,984
Europe & Central Asia, Low income → East Asia & Pacific, Middle income	30
Europe & Central Asia, Low income → East Asia & Pacific, High income	147

Direction of flow (region of origin → host region)	Number of students, 2001-2002*
Europe & Central Asia, Low income → Europe & Central Asia, Low income	8,821
Europe & Central Asia, Low income → Europe & Central Asia, Middle income	13,616
Europe & Central Asia, Low income → Europe & Central Asia, High income	3,349
Europe & Central Asia, Low income → Latin America & Caribbean, Middle income	27,241
Europe & Central Asia, Low income → Middle East & North Africa, Middle income	177
Europe & Central Asia, Low income → North America, High income	1,645
Europe & Central Asia, Middle income → East Asia & Pacific, Middle income	212
Europe & Central Asia, Middle income → East Asia & Pacific, High income	1,202
Europe & Central Asia, Middle income → Europe & Central Asia, Low income	9,901
Europe & Central Asia, Middle income → Europe & Central Asia, Middle income	63,950
Europe & Central Asia, Middle income → Europe & Central Asia, High income	93,109
Europe & Central Asia, Middle income → Latin America & Caribbean, Middle income	127,903
Europe & Central Asia, Middle income → Middle East & North Africa, Middle income	120
Europe & Central Asia, Middle income → Middle East & North Africa, High income	9
Europe & Central Asia, Middle income → North America, High income	41,254
Europe & Central Asia, High income → East Asia & Pacific, Middle income	162
Europe & Central Asia, High income → East Asia & Pacific, High income	2,292
Europe & Central Asia, High income → Europe & Central Asia, Low income	41
Europe & Central Asia, High income → Europe & Central Asia, Middle income	5,574
Europe & Central Asia, High income → Europe & Central Asia, High income	82,500
Europe & Central Asia, High income → Latin America & Caribbean, Middle income	11,261
Europe & Central Asia, High income → Middle East & North Africa, Middle income	55
Europe & Central Asia, High income → Middle East & North Africa, High income	7
Europe & Central Asia, High income → North America, High income	53,160
Latin America & Caribbean, Low income → East Asia & Pacific, High income	4
Latin America & Caribbean, Low income → Europe & Central Asia, Middle income	3
Latin America & Caribbean, Low income → Europe & Central Asia, High income	155
Latin America & Caribbean, Low income → Latin America & Caribbean, Middle income	1,624
Latin America & Caribbean, Low income → North America, High income	1,856
Latin America & Caribbean, Middle income → East Asia & Pacific, Middle income	12
Latin America & Caribbean, Middle income → East Asia & Pacific, High income	1,192
Latin America & Caribbean, Middle income → Europe & Central Asia, Middle income	248
Latin America & Caribbean, Middle income → Europe & Central Asia, High income	17,726
Latin America & Caribbean, Middle income → Latin America & Caribbean, Middle income	10,294
Latin America & Caribbean, Middle income → Middle East & North Africa, Middle income	9
Latin America & Caribbean, Middle income → North America, High income	62,767
Latin America & Caribbean, High income → East Asia & Pacific, High income	3
Latin America & Caribbean, High income → Europe & Central Asia, Middle income	3

Direction of flow (region of origin → host region)	Number of students, 2001-2002*
Latin America & Caribbean, High income → Europe & Central Asia, High income	10
Latin America & Caribbean, High income → Latin America & Caribbean, Middle income	736
Latin America & Caribbean, High income → North America, High income	1,840
Middle East & North Africa, Low income → East Asia & Pacific, High income	6
Middle East & North Africa, Low income → Europe & Central Asia, Low income	13
Middle East & North Africa, Low income → Europe & Central Asia, Middle income	128
Middle East & North Africa, Low income → Europe & Central Asia, High income	150
Middle East & North Africa, Low income → Latin America & Caribbean, Middle income	283
Middle East & North Africa, Low income → Middle East & North Africa, Middle income	706
Middle East & North Africa, Low income → Middle East & North Africa, High income	69
Middle East & North Africa, Low income → North America, High income	436
Middle East & North Africa, Middle income → East Asia & Pacific, Middle income	857
Middle East & North Africa, Middle income → East Asia & Pacific, High income	754
Middle East & North Africa, Middle income → Europe & Central Asia, Low income	1,225
Middle East & North Africa, Middle income → Europe & Central Asia, Middle income	3,540
Middle East & North Africa, Middle income → Europe & Central Asia, High income	24,047
Middle East & North Africa, Middle income → Latin America & Caribbean, Middle income	7,594
Middle East & North Africa, Middle income → Middle East & North Africa, Middle income	1,613
Middle East & North Africa, Middle income → Middle East & North Africa, High income	1,176
Middle East & North Africa, Middle income → North America, High income	19,599
Middle East & North Africa, High income → East Asia & Pacific, Middle income	7
Middle East & North Africa, High income → East Asia & Pacific, High income	76
Middle East & North Africa, High income → Europe & Central Asia, Low income	106
Middle East & North Africa, High income → Europe & Central Asia, Middle income	1,222
Middle East & North Africa, High income → Europe & Central Asia, High income	1,085
Middle East & North Africa, High income → Latin America & Caribbean, Middle income	2,640
Middle East & North Africa, High income → Middle East & North Africa, Middle income	543
Middle East & North Africa, High income → Middle East & North Africa, High income	143
Middle East & North Africa, High income → North America, High income	11,580
North America, High income → East Asia & Pacific, Middle income	607
North America, High income → East Asia & Pacific, High income	2,265
North America, High income → Europe & Central Asia, Low income	1
North America, High income → Europe & Central Asia, Middle income	1,040
North America, High income → Europe & Central Asia, High income	5,721
North America, High income → Latin America & Caribbean, Middle income	3,656
North America, High income → Middle East & North Africa, Middle income	41
North America, High income → Middle East & North Africa, High income	5
North America, High income → North America, High income	26,514
South Asia, Low income → East Asia & Pacific, Middle income	927

Direction of flow (region of origin → host region)	Number of students, 2001-2002*
South Asia, Low income → East Asia & Pacific, High income	1,967
South Asia, Low income → Europe & Central Asia, Low income	540
South Asia, Low income → Europe & Central Asia, Middle income	800
South Asia, Low income → Europe & Central Asia, High income	4,452
South Asia, Low income → Latin America & Caribbean, Middle income	1,635
South Asia, Low income → Middle East & North Africa, Middle income	1,917
South Asia, Low income → Middle East & North Africa, High income	31
South Asia, Low income → North America, High income	82,604
South Asia, Middle income → East Asia & Pacific, Middle income	23
South Asia, Middle income → East Asia & Pacific, High income	481
South Asia, Middle income → Europe & Central Asia, Low income	54
South Asia, Middle income → Europe & Central Asia, Middle income	88
South Asia, Middle income → Europe & Central Asia, High income	229
South Asia, Middle income → Latin America & Caribbean, Middle income	235
South Asia, Middle income → Middle East & North Africa, Middle income	694
South Asia, Middle income → North America, High income	2,085
Sub-Saharan Africa, Low income → East Asia & Pacific, Middle income	299
Sub-Saharan Africa, Low income → East Asia & Pacific, High income	497
Sub-Saharan Africa, Low income → Europe & Central Asia, Low income	96
Sub-Saharan Africa, Low income → Europe & Central Asia, Middle income	898
Sub-Saharan Africa, Low income → Europe & Central Asia, High income	11,222
Sub-Saharan Africa, Low income → Latin America & Caribbean, Middle income	2,714
Sub-Saharan Africa, Low income → Middle East & North Africa, Middle income	429
Sub-Saharan Africa, Low income → Middle East & North Africa, High income	86
Sub-Saharan Africa, Low income → North America, High income	28,639
Sub-Saharan Africa, Low income → Sub-Saharan Africa, Low income	1,010
Sub-Saharan Africa, Middle income → East Asia & Pacific, Middle income	10
Sub-Saharan Africa, Middle income → East Asia & Pacific, High income	92
Sub-Saharan Africa, Middle income → Europe & Central Asia, Middle income	64
Sub-Saharan Africa, Middle income → Europe & Central Asia, High income	429
Sub-Saharan Africa, Middle income → Latin America & Caribbean, Middle income	626
Sub-Saharan Africa, Middle income → Middle East & North Africa, Middle income	7
Sub-Saharan Africa, Middle income → Middle East & North Africa, High income	27
Sub-Saharan Africa, Middle income → North America, High income	3,833

* Only students flows associated with specific countries are included

Source: UNESCO Institute for Statistics

Global students flows, 2003

The relative importance of nations in the network is indicated by the number of links an organisation sends or receives, which is also expressed as a percentage of the total links

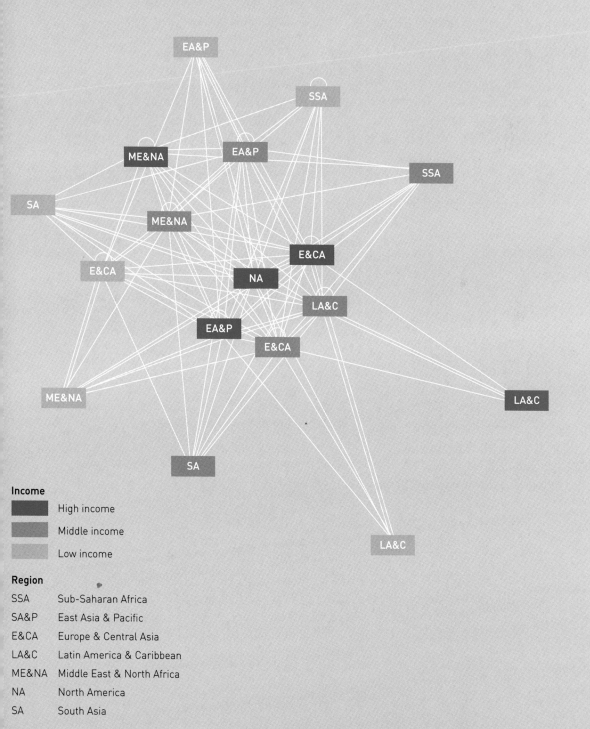

Income

■ High income

■ Middle income

■ Low income

Region

SSA   Sub-Saharan Africa
SA&P   East Asia & Pacific
E&CA   Europe & Central Asia
LA&C   Latin America & Caribbean
ME&NA   Middle East & North Africa
NA   North America
SA   South Asia

Record 5: Trafficking in persons

One of the major vehicles and consequences of globalisation is the flow of people across national boundaries. One such flow, albeit a negative aspect of globalisation, is trafficking of people. Trafficking is defined as 'the recruitment, harbouring, transportation, provision, or obtaining of a person for labour or services, through the use of force, fraud or coercion for the purpose of subjection to involuntary servitude, peonage, debt bondage, or slavery'. While no accurate quantitative data exists (the US government estimates up to 900,000 people are trafficked annually worldwide), the US State Department does issue a report that provides a qualitative assessment of the forms and scope of trafficking by country. In the table below, a country is designated 'yes' if the report lists it as an origin of trafficking, or as a transit country for trafficked people, or as a destination for trafficking. The report also identifies countries where internal trafficking exists. The table reveals that low- and middle-income economies, especially in Africa, Latin America and Eastern Europe, are the main sources of trafficking, and often are also destinations of trafficking, while high-income economies are usually destinations of trafficking.

Country	International trafficking			Internal trafficking
	Source	Transit	Destination	
East Asia & Pacific				
Low income economies				
Cambodia	yes	yes	yes	
Indonesia	yes	yes	yes	yes
Korea, Dem. Rep.	yes			yes
Laos	yes	yes	yes	
Myanmar	yes		yes	yes
Vietnam	yes	yes		yes
Middle income economies				
China	yes	yes	yes	yes
Malaysia	yes	yes	yes	
Philippines	yes	yes	yes	yes
Thailand	yes	yes	yes	yes
High income economies				
Australia			yes	
Korea, Rep.	yes	yes	yes	
Japan			yes	
New Zealand			yes	yes
Singapore			yes	
Europe & Central Asia				
Low income economies				
Armenia	yes	yes		
Azerbaijan	yes	yes		yes
Georgia	yes	yes	yes	
Kyrgyzstan	yes	yes		yes
Moldova	yes	yes		

Country	International trafficking			Internal trafficking
	Source	Transit	Destination	
Tajikistan	yes			
Ukraine	yes	yes		
Uzbekistan	yes	yes		yes
Middle income economies				
Albania	yes	yes		
Belarus	yes			
Bosnia & Herzegovina	yes	yes	yes	yes
Bulgaria	yes	yes	yes	
Croatia		yes	yes	
Czech Republic	yes	yes	yes	yes
Estonia	yes			yes
Hungary	yes	yes	yes	
Kazakhstan	yes	yes	yes	yes
Latvia	yes			yes
Lithuania	yes	yes		
Macedonia	yes	yes	yes	yes
Poland	yes	yes	yes	yes
Romania	yes	yes		
Russian Federation	yes	yes	yes	yes
Serbia & Montenegro	yes	yes	yes	yes
Slovakia	yes	yes		
Slovenia	yes	yes	yes	
Turkey		yes	yes	
High income economies				
Austria		yes	yes	
Belgium		yes	yes	
Cyprus			yes	
Denmark		yes	yes	
Finland	yes	yes		
France		yes	yes	
Germany		yes	yes	
Greece		yes	yes	
Italy		yes	yes	
Netherlands		yes	yes	yes
Norway			yes	
Portugal		yes	yes	

Country	International trafficking			Internal trafficking
	Source	Transit	Destination	
Spain		yes	yes	
Sweden		yes	yes	
Switzerland		yes	yes	
United Kingdom		yes	yes	
Latin America & Caribbean				
Low income economies				
Nicaragua	yes	yes		yes
Middle income economies				
Argentina	yes		yes	yes
Belize		yes	yes	yes
Bolivia	yes	yes		
Brazil	yes		yes	yes
Chile	yes		yes	yes
Colombia	yes	yes		yes
Costa Rica		yes	yes	yes
Cuba				yes
Dominican Republic	yes	yes	yes	
Ecuador	yes	yes	yes	yes
El Salvador	yes	yes	yes	yes
Guatemala	yes	yes	yes	yes
Guyana	yes	yes	yes	yes
Honduras	yes	yes		yes
Jamaica		yes		yes
Mexico	yes	yes	yes	yes
Panama	yes	yes	yes	yes
Paraguay	yes		yes	yes
Peru	yes	yes		yes
Suriname		yes	yes	
Venezuela	yes	yes	yes	yes
Middle East & North Africa				
Middle income economies				
Egypt		yes		
Iran	yes	yes	yes	yes
Lebanon			yes	
Morocco	yes	yes	yes	yes
Saudi Arabia			yes	

Country	International trafficking			Internal trafficking
	Source	Transit	Destination	
High income economies				
Bahrain			yes	
Israel			yes	
Kuwait			yes	yes
Qatar			yes	
United Arab Emirates			yes	
North America				
High income economies				
Canada		yes	yes	yes
South Asia				
Low income economies				
Afghanistan	yes	yes		yes
Bangladesh	yes	yes		yes
India	yes	yes	yes	yes
Nepal	yes			yes
Pakistan	yes	yes	yes	yes
Middle income economies				
Sri Lanka	yes			yes
Sub-Saharan Africa				
Low income economies				
Angola	yes			yes
Benin	yes	yes	yes	yes
Burkina Faso	yes	yes	yes	yes
Burundi	yes	yes		yes
Cameroon	yes	yes	yes	yes
Congo, Dem. Rep.	yes			yes
Côte d'Ivoire	yes	yes	yes	yes
Equatorial Guinea		yes	yes	
Ethiopia	yes			yes
Gambia	yes	yes	yes	yes
Ghana	yes	yes	yes	yes
Guinea	yes	yes	yes	yes
Kenya	yes	yes	yes	yes
Madagascar				yes
Malawi	yes		yes	yes
Mali	yes	yes	yes	

Country	International trafficking			Internal trafficking
	Source	Transit	Destination	
Mauritania	yes		yes	
Mozambique	yes			
Niger	yes	yes		yes
Nigeria	yes	yes	yes	yes
Rwanda	yes			yes
Senegal	yes	yes	yes	
Sierra Leone	yes	yes	yes	yes
Sudan	yes		yes	yes
Tanzania	yes		yes	yes
Togo	yes		yes	
Uganda				yes
Zambia	yes	yes		
Zimbabwe	yes	yes		yes
Middle income economies				
Gabon			yes	
Mauritius	yes		yes	yes
South Africa	yes	yes	yes	yes

Lack of data for a country does not necessarily mean that it does not have a trafficking problem: rather it may be that credible information regarding trafficking is not available. Hence, missing data should be treated with caution. Countries excluded from this list may or may not have a trafficking problem, but credible information regarding trafficking is not provided by the US Secretary of State.

Source: US Department of State, (June 2004). Victims of Trafficking and Violence Protection Act of 2000: Trafficking in Persons Report, 2004. Office of the Under Secretary for Global Affairs, Office to Monitor and Combat Trafficking in Persons, Publication 11150, www.state.gov/g/tip/rls/tiprpt/2004

Record 6: Air travel and international tourism

Air travel facilitates global activism and creates economic as well as social ties. International tourism is certainly a measure of globalisation; it can be a point of contact between people from different regions and cultures. The table contains data on air transport and international tourism for 1993 and 2003, including the percentage change during this time period.

The table shows general growth throughout the world in international travel, with exceptional growth in outbound tourism in low- and middle-income countries in Asia and Europe. The overall number of air transport passengers has increased dramatically when compared with the global rates in low-income countries in South and East Asia. Tourism, both inbound and outbound, has increased, especially in Africa, although the total volume is still relatively small.

| | Air transport | | | | | International tourism | | | | | | | | | |
| | Passengers carried | | | | | Inbound tourists | | | | | Outbound tourists | | | | |
Country	Total (1000s) 1993	Per capita 1993	Total (1000s) 2003	Per capita 2003	% change in total 1993-2003	Total (1000s) 1993	Per capita 1993	Total (1000s) 2003	Per capita 2003	% change in total 1993-2003	Total (1000s) 1993	Per capita 1993	Total (1000s) 2003	Per capita 2003	% change in total 1993-2003
East Asia & Pacific															
Low income economies															
Cambodia			116	0.01		118	0.01	701	0.05	494	44	*0.00*			
Indonesia	12,009	0.06	12,221	0.05	2	3,403	0.02	4,467	0.02	31	1,146	0.01			
Korea, Dem. Rep.	242	0.01	75	0.00	-69	*117*	*0.01*								
Laos	119	0.03	219	0.04	85	36	0.01	196	0.03	444					
Mongolia	630	0.27	295	0.11	-53	131	0.06	201	0.07	53					
Myanmar	319	0.01	1,117	0.03	251	48	0.00	206	0.00	329					
Papua New Guinea	866	0.21	691	0.13	-20	34	0.01	56	0.01	65	52	0.01	92	*0.02*	77
Solomon Islands	75	0.20	68	0.13	-9	12	0.03								
Vietnam	1,200	0.02	4,553	0.06	279	670	0.01								
Middle income economies															
China	31,313	0.03	86,041	0.07	175	18,982	0.02	32,970	0.03	74	3,740	0.00	20,222	0.02	441
Fiji	424	0.56	972	1.12	129	287	0.38	431	0.50	50	64	0.08	104	0.12	63
Malaysia	13,101	0.70	15,214	0.66	16	6,504	0.35	10,577	0.46	63	17,008	0.91			
Philippines	6,526	0.10	6,467	0.08	-1	1,372	0.02	1,907	0.02	39	1,316	0.02	1,803	0.02	37
Samoa			198	1.11		47	0.26	92	0.52	96					
Thailand	10,197	0.18	16,623	0.26	63	5,761	0.10	10,082	0.16	75	1,540	0.03	2,152	0.03	40
Tonga	35	0.38	61	0.56	72	26	0.28	*37*	*0.34*	42					
Vanuatu	67	0.40	83	0.42	25	44	0.27	50	0.25	14	9	0.05	13	0.07	44
High income economies															
Australia	26,929	1.52	41,386	2.10	54	2,996	0.17	4,354	0.22	45	2,267	0.13	3,388	0.17	49

| Country | Air tranport | | | | | International tourism | | | | | | | | | |
| | Passengers carried | | | | | Inbound tourists | | | | | Outbound tourists | | | | |
	Total (1000s) 1993	Per capita 1993	Total (1000s) 2003	Per capita 2003	% change in total 1993-2003	Total (1000s) 1993	Per capita 1993	Total (1000s) 2003	Per capita 2003	% change in total 1993-2003	Total (1000s) 1993	Per capita 1993	Total (1000s) 2003	Per capita 2003	% change in total 1993-2003
Brunei	604	2.15	955	2.67	58	489	1.74				300	1.07			
Korea, Rep.	21,426	0.48	33,334	0.69	56	3,331	0.08	4,754	0.10	43	2,420	0.05	7,086	0.15	193
Japan	80,064	0.64	103,606	0.81	29	3,410	0.03	5,212	0.04	53	11,934	0.10	13,296	0.10	11
New Zealand	6,291	1.81	12,259	3.10	95	1,157	0.33	2,104	0.53	82	800	0.23	1,374	0.35	72
Singapore	9,271	2.79	14,737	3.45	59	5,804	1.74	5,705	1.33	-2	2,156	0.65	4,221	0.99	96
Europe & Central Asia															
Low income economies															
Armenia			367	0.12		9	0.00	206	0.07	2,189			169	0.06	
Azerbaijan	1,383	0.18	684	0.09	-51	70	0.01	834	0.11	1,091	47	0.01	1,141	0.15	2,328
Georgia	170	0.03	124	0.03	-27			298	0.06				317	0.07	
Kyrgyzstan	464	0.10	206	0.04	-56			140	0.03		42	0.01	45	0.01	7
Moldova	312	0.07	179	0.04	-43	56	0.01	21	0.00	-63	33	0.01	67	0.02	103
Tajikistan	783	0.14	413	0.06	-47										
Ukraine	1,278	0.02	1,477	0.03	16	3,610	0.07	6,326	0.13	75	4,901	0.09	9,270	0.19	89
Uzbekistan	2,217	0.10	1,466	0.06	-34	92	0.00	231	0.01	151			400	0.02	
Middle income economies															
Albania	9	0.00	159	0.05	1,646	45	0.01				3	0.00			
Belarus	805	0.08	234	0.02	-71	184	0.02				488	0.05			
Bosnia & Herzegovina			73	0.02				165	0.04						
Bulgaria	916	0.11	75	0.01	-92	3,182	0.38	4,048	0.53	27	2,142	0.25	3,403	0.45	59
Croatia	432	0.10	1,267	0.28	193	1,521	0.34	7,409	1.65	387					
Czech Republic	1,025	0.10	3,392	0.33	231	11,500	1.11	5,076	0.50	-56	30,980	3.00	36,074	3.52	16
Estonia	128	0.09	395	0.29	210	470	0.32	1,462	1.08	211	46	0.03	2,075	1.54	4,411
Hungary	1,217	0.12	2,369	0.24	95	2,788	0.27	2,948	0.29	6	12,115	1.17	14,283	1.42	18
Kazakhstan	706	0.04	1,010	0.07	43			2,410	0.16				2,374	0.16	
Latvia	111	0.04	340	0.15	205	622	0.24	971	0.42	56	2,269	0.88	2,286	0.98	1
Lithuania	150	0.04	329	0.09	120	780	0.21	1,491	0.41	91	2,353	0.64	3,502	0.97	49
Macedonia	188	0.10	201	0.10	7	208	0.11	158	0.08	-24					
Poland	1,270	0.03	3,252	0.08	156	16,930	0.44	13,720	0.36	-19	31,395	0.82	38,730	1.00	23
Romania	979	0.04	1,251	0.06	28	2,911	0.13	3,204	0.14	10	10,757	0.47	5,757	0.26	-46
Russian Federation	36,124	0.24	22,723	0.16	-37	5,896	0.04	7,943	0.05	35	9,181	0.06	20,343	0.14	122

Country	Air tranport Passengers carried					International tourism Inbound tourists					International tourism Outbound tourists				
	Total (1000s) 1993	Per capita 1993	Total (1000s) 2003	Per capita 2003	% change in total 1993-2003	Total (1000s) 1993	Per capita 1993	Total (1000s) 2003	Per capita 2003	% change in total 1993-2003	Total (1000s) 1993	Per capita 1993	Total (1000s) 2003	Per capita 2003	% change in total 1993-2003
Serbia & Montenegro			1,298	0.12		275	0.03	481	0.04	75					
Slovakia	18	0.00	208	0.04	1,039	653	0.12	1,387	0.26	112	159	0.03	408	0.08	157
Slovenia	291	0.15	758	0.38	160	624	0.31	1,373	0.68	120			2,114	1.05	
Turkey	6,077	0.10	10,701	0.16	76	5,904	0.10	13,341	0.20	126	3,311	0.06	5,928	0.09	79
Turkmenistan	748	0.19	1,412	0.30	89	50	0.01				18	0.00			
High income economies															
Austria	3,297	0.41	6,903	0.85	109	18,257	2.29	19,078	2.34	4	2,792	0.35	5,060	0.62	81
Belgium	3,651	0.36	2,904	0.28	-20	5,120	0.51	6,690	0.65	31			7,268	0.70	
Cyprus	1,011	1.41	1,883	2.44	86	1,841	2.56	2,303	2.98	25	266	0.37	629	0.82	136
Denmark	5,078	0.98	5,886	1.09	16	2,068	0.40	2,016	0.37	-3			5,564	1.03	
Finland	3,948	0.78	6,184	1.19	57	1,679	0.33	2,601	0.50	55	4,110	0.81	5,585	1.07	36
France	35,626	0.62	47,259	0.79	33	60,565	1.05	75,048	1.25	24	16,401	0.28	17,426	0.29	6
Germany	29,363	0.36	72,693	0.88	148	14,348	0.18	18,399	0.22	28			74,600	0.91	
Greece	5,478	0.53	7,519	0.71	37	9,413	0.91	*14,180*	*1.33*	*51*	1,861	0.18			
Iceland	801	3.07	1,134	3.90	42	157	0.60	771	2.65	391	141	0.54			
Ireland	4,650	1.30	28,864	7.36	521	3,888	1.09	6,774	1.73	74	2,056	0.57	*4,634*	*1.18*	*125*
Italy	21,901	0.38	34,953	0.60	60	26,379	0.46	39,604	0.68	50			26,817	0.46	
Luxembourg	471	1.18	854	1.87	81	791	1.99	867	1.90	10					
Netherlands	11,775	0.77	23,455	1.45	99	5,757	0.38	9,181	0.57	59	12,110	0.79	*16,760*	*1.03*	*38*
Norway	10,384	2.41	12,779	2.81	23	2,556	0.59	3,146	0.69	23	493	0.11			
Portugal	4,379	0.44	7,590	0.72	73	8,434	0.85	11,707	1.12	39	*227*	*0.02*			
Spain	22,279	0.56	42,507	1.06	91	37,268	0.94	52,478	1.30	41	*3,527*	*0.09*	4,094	0.10	*16*
Sweden	9,719	1.11	11,586	1.29	19	1,692	0.19	7,627	0.85	351	12,044	1.37	12,579	1.40	4
Switzerland	9,152	1.30	10,589	1.43	16	12,400	1.76	6,530	0.88	-47	9,620	1.36	*11,427*	1.54	19
United Kingdom	50,188	0.86	76,377	1.27	52	19,863	0.34	24,785	0.41	25	36,720	0.63	61,453	1.02	67
Latin America & Caribbean															
Low income economies															
Haiti						77	0.01								
Nicaragua	34	0.01				198	0.05	526	0.10	166	226	0.05	562	0.11 \	149
Middle income economies															
Argentina	5,105	0.15	6,030	0.16	18	1,918	0.06	3,374	0.09	76	3,757	0.11	3,346	0.09	-11

Country	Air transport Passengers carried					International tourism Inbound tourists					Outbound tourists				
	Total (1000s) 1993	Per capita 1993	Total (1000s) 2003	Per capita 2003	% change in total 1993-2003	Total (1000s) 1993	Per capita 1993	Total (1000s) 2003	Per capita 2003	% change in total 1993-2003	Total (1000s) 1993	Per capita 1993	Total (1000s) 2003	Per capita 2003	% change in total 1993-2003
Barbados						396	1.49	531	1.92	34					
Belize						117	0.57	221	0.83	89					
Bolivia	1,117	0.16	1,768	0.21	58	244	0.03	352	0.04	44	243	0.03	672	0.08	177
Brazil	16,536	0.10	32,372	0.18	96	1,572	0.01	3,783	0.02	141	1,400	0.01	1,861	0.01	33
Chile	2,360	0.17	5,247	0.33	122	1,412	0.10	1,614	0.10	14	842	0.06	2,100	0.13	149
Colombia	6,930	0.20	9,143	0.22	32	1,047	0.03	541	0.01	-48	911	0.03	1,241	0.03	36
Costa Rica	690	0.21	781	0.20	13	684	0.21	1,113	0.29	63	260	0.08	364	0.09	40
Cuba	624	0.06	611	0.05	-2	544	0.05	1,656	0.15	204	64	0.01	111	0.01	73
Dominican Republic	328	0.04				1,609	0.22	3,282	0.38	104	152	0.02	321	0.04	111
Ecuador	2,122	0.19	1,123	0.09	-47	471	0.04	761	0.06	62	235	0.02	613	0.05	161
El Salvador	1,243	0.23	2,966	0.46	139	267	0.05	857	0.13	221	330	0.06	940	0.15	185
Guatemala	240	0.02				562	0.05	880	0.06	57	329	0.03	658	0.05	100
Guyana	115	0.15				107	0.14	101	0.13	-6					
Honduras	602	0.12				261	0.05	610	0.09	134	172	0.03	277	0.04	61
Jamaica	1,038	0.41	1,838	0.68	77	1,105	0.44	1,350	0.50	22					
Mexico	16,485	0.18	20,688	0.20	25	16,440	0.18	18,665	0.18	14	10,185	0.11	11,044	0.11	8
Panama	321	0.13	1,264	0.43	294	300	0.12	566	0.19	89	172	0.07	227	0.08	32
Paraguay	338	0.07	313	0.05	-7	404	0.09	268	0.04	-34	334	0.07	141	0.02	-58
Peru	1,362	0.06	2,233	0.08	64	272	0.01	931	0.03	242	466	0.02	889	0.03	91
St. Lucia						194	1.35	277	1.71	43					
Suriname	96	0.24	258	0.59	169	39	0.10								
Trinidad & Tobago	1,389	1.18	1,084	0.98	-22	249	0.21	384	0.35	54	198	0.17			
Uruguay	503	0.16	464	0.14	-8	1,735	0.55	1,420	0.42	-18			495	0.15	
Venezuela	6,814	0.33	3,824	0.16	-44	396	0.02	337	0.01	-15	477	0.02	832	0.03	74
High income economies															
Bahamas	862	3.21	1,601	5.38	86	1,489	5.55	1,510	5.08	1					
Middle East & North Africa															
Low income economies															
Yemen	848	0.06	844	0.04	0	70	0.01								
Middle income economies															
Algeria	3,255	0.12	3,293	0.10	1	1,128	0.04	1,166	0.04	3	2,838	0.11	1,254	0.04	-56

Country	Air tranport — Passengers carried					International tourism — Inbound tourists					International tourism — Outbound tourists				
	Total (1000s) 1993	Per capita 1993	Total (1000s) 2003	Per capita 2003	% change in total 1993–2003	Total (1000s) 1993	Per capita 1993	Total (1000s) 2003	Per capita 2003	% change in total 1993–2003	Total (1000s) 1993	Per capita 1993	Total (1000s) 2003	Per capita 2003	% change in total 1993–2003
Djibouti						25	0.06								
Egypt	2,881	0.05	4,172	0.06	45	2,291	0.04	5,746	0.08	151	2,679	0.04	3,644	0.05	36
Iran	5,352	0.09	9,554	0.14	79	304	0.01	*1,585*	*0.02*	*421*	738	0.01	*2,921*	*0.04*	*296*
Iraq	*32*	*0.00*				123	0.01				199	0.01			
Jordan	1,186	0.30	1,353	0.25	14	766	0.19	1,573	0.29	105	1,128	0.28	1,533	0.28	36
Lebanon	677	0.21	935	0.25	38	311	0.10	1,016	0.27	227					
Libya	853	0.19	627	0.11	-27	63	0.01	142	0.03	125	183	0.04			
Malta	797	2.15	1,309	3.31	64	1,063	2.87	1,127	2.85	6	136	0.37			
Morocco	2,140	0.08	2,565	0.08	20	4,027	0.15	4,552	0.14	13	1,376	0.05	1,694	0.05	23
Oman	1,180	0.59	2,777	0.99	135	256	0.13	*817*	*0.29*	*219*			*2,060*	*0.73*	
Saudi Arabia	11,864	0.66	13,822	0.55	16	2,869	0.16	7,332	0.29	156			4,104	0.16	
Syria	485	0.04	908	0.05	87	703	0.05	2,788	0.16	297	1,521	0.11	3,932	0.22	159
Tunisia	1,351	0.16	1,720	0.17	27	3,656	0.42	5,114	0.52	40	1,838	0.21	2,274	0.23	24
High income economies															
Bahrain	1,080	1.99	1,851	2.77	71	1,761	3.24	2,955	4.43	68					
Israel	2,569	0.51	3,672	0.60	43	1,656	0.33	1,063	0.17	-36	1,409	0.28	3,299	0.54	134
Kuwait	1,554	1.05	2,198	1.01	41	73	0.05								
Qatar	1,080	1.94	3,184	3.90	195	160	0.29								
United Arab Emirates	2,936	1.40	11,384	4.58	288	1,088	0.52	5,871	2.36	440					
North America															
High income economies															
Canada	17,517	0.61	35,884	1.11	105	15,105	0.52	17,534	0.54	16	20,561	0.71	17,739	0.55	-14
United States	469,926	1.81	588,997	2.03	25	45,779	0.18	40,356	0.14	-12	44,411	0.17	54,206	0.19	22
South Asia															
Low income economies															
Afghanistan	197	0.01													
Bangladesh	1,083	0.01	1,579	0.01	46	127	0.00	*207*	*0.00*	*63*	760	0.01			
Bhutan	9	0.01	36	0.02	318	3	0.00	6	0.00	100					
India	9,442	0.01	19,456	0.02	106	1,765	0.00	*2,384*	*0.00*	*35*	2,733	0.00	*4,205*	*0.00*	*54*
Nepal	633	0.03	625	0.02	-1	294	0.01	338	0.01	15	64	0.00	258	0.01	303
Pakistan	5,647	0.05	4,477	0.03	-21	379	0.00	479	0.00	26					

| | Air tranport | | | | | International tourism | | | | | | | | | |
| | Passengers carried | | | | | Inbound tourists | | | | | Outbound tourists | | | | |
Country	Total (1000s) 1993	Per capita 1993	Total (1000s) 2003	Per capita 2003	% change in total 1993-2003	Total (1000s) 1993	Per capita 1993	Total (1000s) 2003	Per capita 2003	% change in total 1993-2003	Total (1000s) 1993	Per capita 1993	Total (1000s) 2003	Per capita 2003	% change in total 1993-2003
Middle income economies															
Maldives	9	0.04	60	0.18	540	241	1.00	564	1.71	134	28	0.12	44	0.13	57
Sri Lanka	994	0.06	1,958	0.10	97	392	0.02	501	0.03	28	416	0.02	561	0.03	35
Sub-Saharan Africa															
Low income economies															
Angola	334	0.04	198	0.02	-41	21	0.00	107	0.01	410	4	*0.00*			
Benin	68	0.01				140	0.03	*72*	*0.01*	-49	418	0.08			
Burkina Faso	129	0.01	55	0.00	-58	111	0.01	163	0.01	47					
Burundi	9	0.00				75	0.01				34	0.01			
Cameroon	275	0.02	315	0.02	15	81	0.01	*226*	*0.01*	179					
Central African Republic	68	0.02				21	0.01								
Chad	85	0.01				21	0.00	21	0.00	0					
Comoros	26	0.06				24	0.05	*19*	*0.03*	-21					
Congo, Dem. Rep.	84	0.00				22	0.00	35	0.00	59					
Congo, Rep.	231	0.10	52	0.02	-77	36	0.01								
Côte d'Ivoire	186	0.01				159	0.01				4	*0.00*			
Equatorial Guinea	14	0.04													
Eritrea						176	0.05	80	0.02	-55					
Ethiopia	752	0.01	1,147	0.02	53	93	0.00	*156*	*0.00*	68	101	0.00			
Gambia						76	0.07	*79*	*0.05*	4					
Ghana	152	0.01	241	0.01	58	257	0.02	*483*	*0.02*	88					
Guinea	24	0.00						44	0.00						
Guinea-Bissau	21	0.02													
Kenya	770	0.03	1,678	0.05	118	826	0.03	927	0.03	12	*162*	*0.01*			
Lesotho	21	0.01				130	0.07	*124*	*0.07*	-5	*254*	*0.14*			
Liberia	*32*	*0.02*													
Madagascar	419	0.03	404	0.02	-4	55	0.00	139	0.01	153	32	0.00			
Malawi	132	0.01	109	0.01	-18	153	0.02	421	0.04	175					
Mali	68	0.01				30	0.00	70	0.01	133					
Mauritania	215	0.10	116	0.04	-46										
Mozambique	206	0.02	281	0.01	36			*943*	*0.05*						

Country	Air transport — Passengers carried					International tourism — Inbound tourists					International tourism — Outbound tourists				
	Total (1000s) 1993	Per capita 1993	Total (1000s) 2003	Per capita 2003	% change in total 1993–2003	Total (1000s) 1993	Per capita 1993	Total (1000s) 2003	Per capita 2003	% change in total 1993–2003	Total (1000s) 1993	Per capita 1993	Total (1000s) 2003	Per capita 2003	% change in total 1993–2003
Niger	68	0.01				12	0.00	58	0.01	383	16	0.00			
Nigeria	608	0.01	520	0.00	-14	192	0.00	887	0.01	362					
Rwanda	9	0.00													
São Tomé & Principe	22	0.17	36	0.20	60	3	0.02								
Senegal	140	0.02	130	0.01	-7	168	0.02	354	0.03	111					
Sierra Leone	18	0.00	14	0.00	-22	91	0.02	37	0.01	-59			13	0.00	
Somalia															
Sudan	408	0.01	421	0.01	3	37	0.00	52	0.00	41	185	0.01			
Tanzania	189	0.01	150	0.00	-21	223	0.01	552	0.02	148	120	0.00			
Togo	68	0.02				24	0.01	61	0.01	154					
Uganda	78	0.00	40	0.00	-49	116	0.01	305	0.01	163			387	0.02	
Zambia	219	0.03	51	0.00	-77	157	0.02	578	0.05	268					
Zimbabwe	595	0.05	201	0.02	-66	951	0.09				418	0.04			
Middle income economies															
Botswana	123	0.09	183	0.11	49	607	0.44	975	0.60	61	327	0.24			
Cape Verde	100	0.27	253	0.61	153	27	0.07	126	0.31	367					
Gabon	302	0.30	386	0.29	28	125	0.12	222	0.17	78			236	0.18	
Mauritius	582	0.53	1,035	0.86	78	375	0.34	702	0.58	87	105	0.09	161	0.13	53
Namibia	179	0.11	266	0.13	49	255	0.16	695	0.35	173					
South Africa	5,582	0.14	9,481	0.21	70	3,358	0.08	6,505	0.15	94	1,516	0.04	3,794	0.09	150
Swaziland	58	0.06				272	0.27	256	0.22	-6					

Region	Air tranport					International tourism									
	Passengers carried					Inbound tourists					Outbound tourists				
	Total (1000s) 1993	Per capita 1993	Total (1000s) 2003	Per capita 2003	% change in total 1993-2003	Total (1000s) 1993	Per capita 1993	Total (1000s) 2003	Per capita 2003	% change in total 1993-2003	Total (1000s) 1993	Per capita 1993	Total (1000s) 2003	Per capita 2003	% change in total 1993-2003
Low income	31,826	0.01	42,573	0.02	34	12,723	0.01	*16,746*	*0.01*	*32*					
Middle income	234,048	0.09	340,444	0.12	45	147,042	0.06	222,163	0.08	51	177,035	0.07	*283,702*	*0.10*	*60*
Low & middle income:															
East Asia & Pacific	77,191	0.05	145,041	0.08	88	38,573	0.02	64,926	0.03	68					
Europe & Central Asia	57,331	0.12	55,604	0.12	-3	61,804	0.13	75,701	0.16	22	130,068	0.28	156,807	0.33	21
Latin America & Caribbean	67,346	0.15	93,435	0.17	39	32,511	0.07	45,316	0.08	39	21,424	0.05	27,381	0.05	
Middle East & North Africa	32,071	0.12	42,570	0.13	33	16,726	0.06	32,268	0.10	93	16,630	0.06	19,072	0.06	
South Asia	18,014	0.02	28,192	0.02	57	3,263	0.00	*4,333*	*0.00*	*33*	4,567	0.00	6,994	*0.00*	*53*
Sub-Saharan Africa	13,923	0.03	18,174	0.03	31	10,455	0.02	*19,438*	*0.03*	*86*					
High income	876,390	1.00	1,296,821	1.39	48	340,009	0.39	432,522	0.46	27	242,036	0.28	387,248	0.42	60
World	1,142,265	0.21	1,679,838	0.27	47	508,424	0.09	681,723	0.11	34	450,949	0.08	802,249	0.13	78

Data on inbound and outbound tourists refer to numbers of arrivals and departures, not numbers of people.

Where data for a particular year are not available, figures are taken from the year before or after as an estimate. These figures, and estimates based on them, are presented in italics.

Per capita estimates (aggregate and individual country level) are calculated using total midyear country population figures from the US Bureau of the Census International Data Base.

Sources: World Bank, World Development Indicators 2005 (WDI-Online), http://devdata.worldbank.org/dataonline/; US Census Bureau, Population Division, International Programs Center, International Data Base (IDB), http://www.census.gov/ipc/www/idbsprd.html

Record 7: Media and communication

Communications and news are major facilitators of globalisation, as well as of dissent from it. This record offers an indication of people's exposure to media as well as their local and transnational communication with each other. The data show ownership of television sets and cable TV subscribers, telephone communication infrastructure, volume of cellular and international telephone communication and ownership of personal computers and internet access, all for the latest available year and with a time comparison where feasible.

The table shows that exposure to media and communication technologies has grown throughout the globe, particularly in South and East Asia. People in the developing world are also much better connected, thanks partly to the rapid expansion of cellular communications. Conversely, international communication has declined in low- and middle-income Asian and African nations. Data on computer and internet use reveal the 'digital divide' between developed nations and the rest of the world, but also vast variations in internet access between developing countries in different regions.

Country	Television sets per 1000 people			Cable television subscribers per 1000 people			Main telephone lines per 1000 people			Cellular mobile telephone subscribers per 1000 people			International telecom, outgoing traffic (minutes per subscriber)			Personal Computers per 1000 people 2003	Internet users per 1000 people 2003
	1992	2002	% change 1992-2002	1997	2002	% change 1997-2002	1992	2002	% change 1992-2002	1993	2003	% change 1993-2003	1993	2003	% change 1993-2003		
East Asia & Pacific																	
Low income economies																	
Cambodia	7.9	7.6	-4				0.4	2.6	491	0.5	35.2	6,996	1,257.4	146.7	-88	2.3	2.5
Indonesia	76.1	153.0	101	0.1	0.3	470	10.0	39.4	296	0.3	87.4	30,511	82.8	37.3	-55	11.9	37.6
Korea, Dem. Rep.	18.7	162.0	768		0.0		23.1	41.0	77	0.0	0.0		6.1				
Laos	6.5	51.9	698		0.0		1.9	12.3	542	0.1	19.8	26,068	119.9	104.1	-13	3.5	3.3
Mongolia	32.5	79.2	144	11.3	18.5	64	30.7	56.2	83	0.0	129.8		12.3	33.1	170	77.3	58.1
Myanmar	4.0	7.6	90				2.7	6.8	151	0.0	1.2	8,282	22.2	26.0	17	5.6	0.5
Papua New Guinea	2.5	23.1	823	4.2			9.5	11.7	23	0.0	2.7		549.2			58.7	13.7
Solomon Islands	5.9	10.5	77				15.8	13.1	-17	0.0	3.1		330.8			40.5	5.2
Vietnam	43.2	197.4	357				3.7	54.1	1,377	0.1	33.7	58,808	76.9	17.1	-78	9.8	43.0
Middle income economies																	
China	190.1	350.3	84	40.0	75.0	88	14.5	209.0	1,343	0.5	214.8	40,174	51.9	3.8	-93	27.6	63.2
Fiji	26.8	117.5	338				71.8	123.5	72	0.0	133.1		245.4			50.9	66.6
Malaysia	149.3	209.6	40	5.2	0.0		125.5	181.6	45	17.7	442.0	2,397	107.1			166.9	344.1
Philippines	78.4	182.4	133	6.9	37.0	436	13.2	41.2	213	1.6	269.5	17,098	155.6	51.6	-67	27.7	44.0
Samoa	98.2	148.2	51	2.8	1.8	-35	43.1	72.9	69	0.0	57.6		535.2	559.2	4	6.7	22.2
Thailand	157.0	300.4	91	8.2	12.9	58	39.3	104.9	167	7.3	394.2	5,266	73.7	51.7	-30	39.8	110.5
Tonga	10.4	70.6	580	0.0			61.2	112.9	84	0.0	33.8		251.2			20.2	29.2
Vanuatu	9.7	13.0	34				25.7	31.5	22	0.0	37.6		611.7			14.8	36.1
High income economies																	
Australia	564.8	722.1	28	35.0	76.3	118	483.7	542.3	12	39.1	719.5	1,741	85.5			601.8	566.7

Country	Television sets per 1000 people			Cable television subscribers per 1000 people			Main telephone lines per 1000 people			Cellular mobile telephone subscribers per 1000 people			International telecom, outgoing traffic (minutes per subscriber)			Personal Computers per 1000 people 2003	Internet users per 1000 people 2003
	1992	2002	% change 1992-2002	1997	2002	% change 1997-2002	1992	2002	% change 1992-2002	1993	2003	% change 1993-2003	1993	2003	% change 1993-2003		
Brunei	242.7	628.7	159		70.2		202.0	255.7	27	30.4			424.3			76.7	102.3
Korea, Rep.	209.4	458.2	119	148.0	282.2	91	378.5	538.3	42	10.7	700.9	6,450	21.3	44.8	110	558.0	609.7
Japan	635.1	784.7	24	114.8	183.1	59	471.5	471.9	0	17.1	679.0	3,875	24.0	37.1	55	382.2	482.7
New Zealand	492.4	573.7	17	1.3	7.1	430	451.1	448.5	-1	40.7	648.3	1,492	144.4	312.6	116	413.8	526.3
Singapore	324.9	302.6	-7	27.4	84.5	208	375.7	450.3	20	54.0	852.5	1,479	399.0	1,019.6	156	622.0	508.8
Europe & Central Asia																	
Low income economies																	
Armenia	209.5	228.8	9	0.4	1.2	196	156.4	148.3	-5	0.0	30.1		91.7	65.8	-28	15.8	36.8
Azerbaijan	205.5	331.7	61	0.1	0.6	626	84.2	114.3	36	0.0	128.1		42.5	44.9	6		36.9
Georgia	220.2	357.3	62	2.5	12.4	389	104.9	133.0	27	0.0	106.8					35.2	23.9
Kyrgyzstan	22.3	48.6	118		3.1		82.0	76.1	-7	0.0	26.6		3.4	66.1	1,821	14.4	38.4
Moldova	289.7	296.1	2	16.1	13.3	-17	120.4	219.3	82	0.0	132.0		138.2	79.0	-43	21.3	79.8
Tajikistan	197.1	356.7	81	0.0	0.1		47.0	37.5	-20	0.0	7.3		1.0	46.7	4,550		0.6
Ukraine	329.8			15.7	38.6	146	149.9	216.1	44	0.0	135.9	10,905,584	4.9	36.3	647	19.8	18.8
Uzbekistan	182.6	280.3	54		3.7		70.6	67.0	-5	0.0	12.5	54,639	17.3	36.2	109		19.2
Middle income economies																	
Albania	91.8	318.2	246	0.0	2.3		13.7	83.0	508	0.0	358.0		648.2	281.8	-57	11.7	9.8
Belarus	270.6	361.8	34		77.2		177.1	311.1	76	0.0	113.2	357,921	82.9	87.3	5		141.0
Bosnia & Herzegovina	90.1				19.4		143.9	244.8	70	0.0	274.0		0.8				26.2
Bulgaria	269.3			24.1	93.5	289	284.6	380.5	34	0.1	466.4	394,917	31.8	30.8	-3	51.9	205.8
Croatia	232.8				8.1		220.2	417.2	89	2.4	583.7	23,827	113.3	197.7	74	173.8	231.8
Czech Republic	348.8	538.0	54	67.9	94.4	39	190.9	360.3	89	1.4	964.6	70,858	94.6	95.1	1	177.4	308.0
Estonia	375.6	501.8	34	15.1	107.0	609	230.6	341.2	48	4.8	777.4	16,222	117.7	190.2	62	440.4	444.1
Hungary	420.8	474.9	13	146.5	170.1	16	145.3	348.6	140	4.4	768.8	17,239	142.4	43.7	-69	108.4	232.2
Kazakhstan	222.6	338.0	52		6.6		116.6	130.4	12	0.0	64.3		2.8	63.2	2,129		15.7
Latvia	419.7	850.2	103	48.5	132.2	172	266.4	285.4	7	1.5	525.8	35,965	51.1	75.9	49	188.0	403.6
Lithuania	339.5	486.6	43	47.0	75.1	60	230.5	239.2	4	0.3	629.7	188,718	63.8	42.6	-33	109.7	201.9
Macedonia	179.9						166.3	271.3	63	0.0	177.0		85.1	115.5	36		48.5
Poland	273.7	228.8	-16	72.1	91.4	27	114.8	318.7	178	0.4	450.9	110,393	61.8	147.0	138	142.0	232.5
Romania	199.0	697.4	250	114.3	152.2	33	114.4	199.4	74	0.0	324.2	922,345	24.0	38.6	61	96.6	184.0
Russian Federation	370.8			78.0	43.6	-44	158.5	242.2	53	0.1	249.3	369,232	37.5	34.3	-8	88.7	40.9

Country	Television sets per 1000 people			Cable television subscribers per 1000 people			Main telephone lines per 1000 people			Cellular mobile telephone subscribers per 1000 people			International telecom, outgoing traffic (minutes per subscriber)			Personal Computers per 1000 people 2003	Internet users per 1000 people 2003
	1992	2002	% change 1992-2002	1997	2002	% change 1997-2002	1992	2002	% change 1992-2002	1993	2003	% change 1993-2003	1993	2003	% change 1993-2003		
Serbia & Montenegro	172.6						182.0	242.7	33	0.0	337.8		94.5	120.8	28	27.1	78.7
Slovakia	282.5	409.0	45				167.3	240.8	44	0.6	684.2	116,723	34.2	134.5	293	236.2	255.9
Slovenia	293.1	365.7	25	126.0	160.3	27	265.2	406.8	53	3.3	870.9	26,571	117.6	105.6	-10	325.5	400.6
Turkey	256.8	423.1	65	8.2	14.2	73	183.8	267.5	46	1.4	394.4	27,769	24.9	49.7	99	43.1	84.9
Turkmenistan	198.5	182.0	-8				61.5	77.1	25	0.0	1.7		44.3	64.4	45		1.7
High income economies																	
Austria	473.2	637.3	35	111.5	132.0	18	448.0	480.7	7	27.6	878.8	3,080	214.4	371.0	73	374.1	462.0
Belgium	452.4	540.8	20	361.6	374.7	4	437.4	489.2	12	6.7	792.8	11,655	222.8	352.1	58	318.1	385.6
Cyprus	338.8	386.3	14	0.0	0.0		509.0	571.9	12	25.0	744.0	2,873	301.6	810.5	169	269.9	337.1
Denmark	536.4	859.0	60	239.0	236.7	-1	589.6	669.3	14	68.9	883.2	1,182	146.6	225.1	54	576.8	541.0
Finland	499.5	670.3	34	170.0	199.7	17	544.1	492.0	-10	96.3	909.6	844	86.1	172.2	100	441.7	533.8
France	568.3	631.9	11	40.3	57.5	43	537.7	566.0	5	10.0	695.9	6,891	78.5	138.6	77	347.1	365.6
Germany	479.2	660.6	38	210.8	249.9	19	454.9	657.3	45	21.8	785.2	3,499	121.7	167.4	38	484.7	472.5
Greece	203.5	519.1	155	0.0	0.0		457.0	453.9	-1	4.6	902.3	19,411	71.3	173.1	143	81.7	150.0
Iceland	423.4			4.4	122.8	2,692	542.0	659.9	22	65.7	965.6	1,369	167.7			451.4	674.7
Ireland	310.2	694.5	124	159.8	143.0	-11	328.1	491.3	50	17.1	879.6	5,033	269.9	441.1	63	420.8	316.7
Italy	428.2			0.8	1.4	71	423.6	484.0	14	21.2	1,017.6	4,709	66.9			230.7	336.7
Luxembourg	555.4	598.0	8	97.4	334.4	243	539.7	797.5	48	12.8	1,193.8	9,250	901.5	1,202.5	33	620.2	376.5
Netherlands	487.5	648.3	33	378.0	401.4	6	499.7	614.3	23	14.1	767.6	5,329	162.2			466.6	521.9
Norway	423.4	884.2	109	159.6	184.5	16	539.8	713.5	32	85.9	908.9	958	161.1	164.8	2	528.3	345.7
Portugal	354.3	413.4	17	38.5	122.1	218	329.6	411.1	25	10.2	898.5	8,674	71.4	124.4	74	134.4	193.5
Spain	402.5	564.0	40	11.8	19.9	70	364.7	433.8	19	6.6	909.1	13,713	59.4	183.3	209	196.0	239.1
Sweden	467.1	965.2	107	218.1	246.0	13	675.8	735.7	9	88.6	980.5	1,007	128.6			621.3	573.1
Switzerland	401.5	552.1	38	352.3	376.2	7	612.0	744.2	22	37.0	843.4	2,181	368.6			708.7	398.5
United Kingdom	432.7	950.5	120	40.2	57.2	42	469.7	590.6	26	39.0	840.7	2,057	118.2	257.9	118	405.7	423.1
Latin America & Caribbean																	
Low income economies																	
Haiti	4.7	60.1	1,168		7.2		6.5	16.8	158	0.0	38.4		422.1				18.0
Nicaragua	65.6	122.6	87	7.8			16.2	37.4	130	0.1	85.1	107,994	311.3	108.5	-65	28.8	17.3
Middle income economies																	
Argentina	267.0	325.8	22	160.6	162.9	1	119.6	218.8	83	3.4	177.6	5,182	31.9	53.3	67	82.0	112.0
Barbados	278.0	328.0	18	0.0	0.0		317.4	496.8	57	6.0	519.1	8,551	310.3			104.1	370.8

DATA PROGRAMME

Country	Television sets per 1000 people			Cable television subscribers per 1000 people			Main telephone lines per 1000 people			Cellular mobile telephone subscribers per 1000 people			International telecom, outgoing traffic (minutes per subscriber)			Personal Computers per 1000 people 2003	Internet users per 1000 people 2003
	1992	2002	% change 1992-2002	1997	2002	% change 1997-2002	1992	2002	% change 1992-2002	1993	2003	% change 1993-2003	1993	2003	% change 1993-2003		
Belize	154.2	182.5	18				143.3	112.7	-21	2.0	204.6	10,116	192.4	380.2	98	127.0	108.9
Bolivia	120.7			4.7	7.4	57	32.8	72.3	120	0.4	152.1	40,312	62.8	67.8	8	22.8	32.4
Brazil	214.2	369.4	72	12.9	13.4	4	74.6	222.9	199	1.2	263.6	21,849	13.3	20.8	56	74.8	82.2
Chile	221.6	522.8	136	43.7	57.4	31	110.4	221.0	100	6.2	511.4	8,166	47.2	78.9	67	119.3	272.0
Colombia	115.4	302.9	163	9.6			84.6	179.3	112	0.0	141.3		32.7	43.6	33	49.3	52.5
Costa Rica	225.0			13.8			116.1	250.5	116	1.4	111.0	7,575	104.4	124.7	19	218.1	287.5
Cuba	176.5	251.0	42				31.9			0.0	1.6	3,364	26.1			23.9	8.7
Dominican Republic	87.0			16.0			69.6	115.4	66	1.4	271.4	19,852	109.6	244.9	123		102.4
Ecuador	102.4	236.8	131	11.7	33.8	188	54.5	122.4	125	0.0	189.2		56.2			32.4	46.0
El Salvador	142.6	232.8	63	34.2			32.2	115.5	259	0.3	176.5	58,183	326.0			33.1	82.9
Guatemala	54.6	145.5	167	28.5			24.2	70.5	191	0.3	131.5	41,898	121.2	172.5	42	14.4	33.3
Guyana	39.4	97.7	148				50.5	91.5	81	1.3	99.3	7,795	375.8	234.3	-38	27.3	142.2
Honduras	74.7	119.4	60	8.1	21.6	167	21.0	48.1	130	0.0	48.7		317.5			14.6	39.7
Jamaica	137.4	373.6	172	99.0			86.0	169.7	97	6.3	534.8	8,416	240.1	310.2	29	53.7	228.5
Mexico	182.0	282.0	55	14.5	24.3	68	83.6	157.7	89	4.2	291.1	6,775	97.0	133.6	38	83.0	120.0
Panama	168.8	191.1	13				103.0	122.0	18	0.0	267.6		157.6			38.3	61.6
Paraguay	59.7			9.8	21.3	117	30.6	46.1	51	0.7	298.5	40,881	108.7	103.9	-4	34.6	20.2
Peru	98.0	172.5	76	10.4	16.6	60	29.7	67.1	126	1.6	106.1	6,516	57.9	82.0	41	43.0	103.9
St. Lucia	203.5	296.0	45				175.7	319.5	82	3.7	89.5	2,293	510.6	305.2	-40	150.0	82.4
Suriname	134.5	261.4	94	8.5	6.2	-26	114.1	151.7	33	2.6	320.3	12,202	153.1	428.9	180	45.5	43.7
Trinidad & Tobago	333.3	345.4	4				158.3	249.8	58	1.4	278.1	20,037	218.8			79.5	106.0
Uruguay	463.2			104.7			168.4	279.6	66	1.6	192.6	12,107	71.7			110.1	119.0
Venezuela	161.4	186.1	15	17.4	36.3	109	99.6	110.6	11	8.7	273.0	3,026	63.9			60.9	60.3
High income economies																	
Bahamas	231.2	247.6	7	162.6			284.5	415.3	46	9.0	366.7	3,990	580.2	570.7	-2		264.9
Middle East & North Africa																	
Low income economies																	
Yemen	272.2	307.8	13				12.1	27.8	130	0.4	34.7	8,862	124.1	81.0	-35	7.4	5.1
Middle income economies																	
Algeria	76.1	113.5	49	0.0	0.0		39.7	69.3	74	0.2	45.6	25,531	73.3			8.3	16.0
Djibouti	46.3	77.6	68	15.3			13.2	15.2	15	0.0	34.4		654.3	598.9	-8	21.7	9.7
Egypt	137.3	228.8	67		0.0		39.6	127.3	221	0.1	84.5	69,204	35.7	35.1	-2	29.1	43.7

Country	Television sets per 1000 people			Cable television subscribers per 1000 people			Main telephone lines per 1000 people			Cellular mobile telephone subscribers per 1000 people			International telecom, outgoing traffic (minutes per subscriber)			Personal Computers per 1000 people 2003	Internet users per 1000 people 2003
	1992	2002	% change 1992-2002	1997	2002	% change 1997-2002	1992	2002	% change 1992-2002	1993	2003	% change 1993-2003	1993	2003	% change 1993-2003		
Iran	68.8	172.9	151	0.0			62.6	219.7	251	0.0	50.9		43.4	22.6	-48	90.5	72.4
Iraq	73.7						35.3	27.8	-21	0.0	3.2		17.6			8.3	1.0
Jordan	137.9	177.1	28	0.2			72.7	113.6	56	0.4	241.9	66,216	172.4	380.3	121	44.7	81.1
Lebanon	351.9	356.7	1	1.4	29.9	1,986	151.6	198.8	31	0.0	227.0		35.2			100.0	142.9
Libya	99.5			0.0			47.6	135.6	185	0.0	23.0		160.7			23.4	28.9
Malta	355.5	566.3	59	158.1	240.2	52	429.9	520.7	21	14.5	725.0	4,912	142.0	210.6	48	255.1	303.0
Morocco	147.1	166.7	13	0.0			31.7	40.5	28	0.3	243.4	94,260	151.2			19.9	33.2
Oman	627.2	553.3	-12	0.0	0.0		73.2	83.9	15	2.8	229.3	8,139	305.4	728.6	139	37.4	70.9
Saudi Arabia	251.6	265.5	6		0.3		93.1	155.4	67	0.9	321.1	34,921	281.7	577.6	105	136.7	66.6
Syria	65.6	182.4	178		0.0		42.3	123.2	191	0.0	65.2		64.6			28.5	34.8
Tunisia	153.1	206.8	35				48.7	117.7	142	0.0	192.1	73,198	164.7			40.5	63.7
High income economies																	
Bahrain	422.4	427.8	1	5.5	11.8	116	233.0	267.6	15	21.3	638.4	2,900	619.2	1,251.7	102	159.2	216.1
Israel	268.5	330.4	23	174.1	184.0	6	363.1	458.2	26	12.0	960.7	7,935	89.6	385.1	330	242.6	301.4
Kuwait	343.5	417.6	22				200.7	198.2	-1	36.0	578.1	1,504	326.3	503.2	54	161.0	228.2
Qatar	407.5	426.2	5	49.9	115.5	131	210.7	261.2	24	8.2	533.1	6,408	528.4	1,575.6	198	163.8	199.3
United Arab Emirates	183.8	251.6	37				263.4	281.1	7	33.6	735.7	2,089	648.9	1,732.0	167	119.9	274.8
North America																	
High income economies																	
Canada	642.5	690.6	7	273.3	252.9	-7	599.0	629.0	5	47.8	416.8	773	141.6	0.4	-100	487.0	483.9
United States	772.8	937.5	21	243.1	255.0	5	573.8	621.3	8	62.0	543.0	775	76.9	216.6	182	659.8	555.8
South Asia	35.2	84.4	140	16.4	37.3	128	8.4	38.9	362	0.0	22.5	122,324	60.4	35.1	-42		
Low income economies																	
Afghanistan	9.8	14.2	45		0.0		1.7	1.8	9	0.0	10.0		16.5				1.0
Bangladesh	10.4	59.0	465		27.0		2.1	5.5	160	0.0	10.1	235,321	60.4			7.8	1.8
Bhutan		26.7		0.0	16.2		7.0	34.3	393	0.0	10.9		181.7			13.6	20.4
India	39.6	82.8	109	18.8	38.9	107	8.9	46.3	418	0.0	24.7		35.9	15.9	-56	7.2	17.5
Nepal	2.4	8.5	257	0.2			3.7	15.7	319	0.0	2.1		158.4	101.6	-36	3.7	3.4
Pakistan	33.5	150.2	348	0.1	26.7	43,189	12.4	26.6	114	0.1	17.5	13,368	36.4	35.1	-4	4.2	10.3
Middle income economies																	
Maldives	44.8	131.0	192	0.0			43.0	102.0	137	0.0	149.1		198.5	244.9	23	71.2	53.4
Sri Lanka	50.4	117.4	133	0.0	0.3		9.3	49.0	428	0.4	72.7	19,795	123.1			17.0	13.0

Country	Television sets per 1000 people			Cable television subscribers per 1000 people			Main telephone lines per 1000 people			Cellular mobile telephone subscribers per 1000 people			International telecom, outgoing traffic (minutes per subscriber)			Personal Computers per 1000 people 2003	Internet users per 1000 people 2003
	1992	2002	% change 1992-2002	1997	2002	% change 1997-2002	1992	2002	% change 1992-2002	1993	2003	% change 1993-2003	1993	2003	% change 1993-2003		
Sub-Saharan Africa																	
Low income economies																	
Angola	6.3	52.5	738				5.2	6.7	29	0.1	9.3	8,614	269.2	403.5	50	1.9	2.9
Benin	11.2	11.5	3				4.0	9.5	136	0.0	33.6		216.1			3.7	10.0
Burkina Faso	5.6	79.4	1,328	0.0	0.0		2.3	5.3	134	0.0	18.5		266.0	307.0	15	2.1	3.9
Burundi	1.1	31.5	2,885		0.0		2.7	3.4	26	0.1	9.0	14,715	108.7	126.8	17	1.8	2.0
Cameroon	26.3	74.6	184				4.6	7.0	53	0.0	66.2		428.1			5.7	3.8
Central African Republic	4.6	5.8	27				2.1	2.3	6	0.0	9.7		306.4	466.1	52	2.0	1.4
Chad	1.4	1.9	40	0.0			0.7	1.5	104	0.0	8.0		368.5			1.7	1.9
Comoros	3.1	3.7	18				7.0	16.6	136	0.0	2.5		296.3	373.0	26	5.8	6.3
Congo, Dem. Rep.	1.4	1.9	38				0.9	0.2	-78		18.9						1.0
Congo, Rep.	6.3	12.9	103				7.8	2.0	-75	0.0	94.3		260.4			4.3	4.3
Côte d'Ivoire	60.0	61.2	2	0.0	0.0		6.8	14.3	109	0.0	77.0		243.2	273.6	12	9.3	14.4
Equatorial Guinea	48.6			0.0			3.4	17.7	415	0.0	76.4		377.3			6.9	3.6
Eritrea	5.9	50.3	753		0.0		3.9	9.2	133	0.0	0.0		54.0	126.7	135	2.9	7.2
Ethiopia	3.0	5.7	90	0.0			2.6	6.3	145	0.0	1.4		82.4	36.3	-56	2.2	1.1
Gambia	0.5	15.0	2,881				15.9	28.0	76	0.4	72.9	16,261	240.9	352.0	46	14.3	18.8
Ghana	40.4	52.6	30		0.3		3.0	13.5	355	0.1	35.6	33,546	186.3	212.6	14	3.8	7.8
Guinea	7.1	47.1	561	0.0	0.0		1.8	3.4	90	0.0	14.4	223,282	380.3			5.5	5.2
Guinea-Bissau		35.9					6.5	8.2	27	0.0	1.0		172.9				14.8
Kenya	17.6	26.0	48		0.5		8.9	10.4	16	0.0	50.2	103,910	96.3			6.5	12.7
Lesotho	6.2	34.6	457				7.6	13.2	74	0.0	42.5		1,235.9	64.3	-95		13.8
Liberia	18.5						1.7			0.0			508.9				
Madagascar	21.8	25.5	17				2.8	3.6	28	0.0	17.4		124.3	111.2	-11	4.9	4.3
Malawi		3.9			0.0		3.6	8.1	123	0.0	12.9		233.8			1.5	3.4
Mali	10.5	32.9	214	0.0			1.6	5.3	238	0.0	23.0		408.3			1.4	2.4
Mauritania	23.7	43.6	84				3.5	13.9	293	0.0	127.5		570.4	392.9	-31	10.8	4.4
Mozambique	3.0	13.7	354				3.8	4.6	21	0.0	22.8		199.1	274.1	38	4.5	2.8
Niger	11.0	9.8	-11				1.2	1.9	55	0.0	2.0		288.4			0.6	1.3
Nigeria	38.0	102.6	170		0.5		3.4	6.9	104	0.1	25.5	28,430	128.9	123.8	-4	7.0	6.1
Rwanda	0.8						1.9	2.8	47	0.0	16.0		358.2				3.1
São Tomé & Principe		92.7					19.6	45.9	134	0.0	31.7		175.0	194.9	11		98.7

Country	Television sets per 1000 people			Cable television subscribers per 1000 people			Main telephone lines per 1000 people			Cellular mobile telephone subscribers per 1000 people			International telecom, outgoing traffic (minutes per subscriber)			Personal Computers per 1000 people 2003	Internet users per 1000 people 2003
	1992	2002	% change 1992-2002	1997	2002	% change 1997-2002	1992	2002	% change 1992-2002	1993	2003	% change 1993-2003	1993	2003	% change 1993-2003		
Senegal	46.5	77.5	67		0.1		8.1	22.1	173	0.0	55.6		246.4			21.2	21.7
Sierra Leone	10.6	13.2	24	0.0			3.4	4.8	44	0.0	13.4		107.0				1.6
Somalia	12.7	14.4	14				1.7	9.8	487	0.0	3.4						
Sudan	79.4	386.4	386	0.0	0.0		2.6	27.0	954	0.0	19.5		153.2			6.1	9.0
Tanzania	5.8	44.6	673		0.2		3.2	4.2	33	0.0	25.2		57.9	72.9	26	5.7	7.1
Togo	6.6	123.1	1,753				4.5	12.1	172	0.0	44.0		546.5	349.4	-36	32.0	42.0
Uganda	17.4	17.9	3		0.3		1.2	2.4	105	0.0	30.3		130.0			4.0	4.9
Zambia	36.5	51.0	40		1.2		9.2	7.9	-14	0.0	21.5		147.2	177.9	21	8.5	6.1
Zimbabwe	26.9	55.6	107				12.2	25.6	110	0.0	32.2		312.3			52.7	43.0
Middle income economies																	
Botswana	19.1	44.0	130				31.2	74.9	140	0.0	297.1		687.3	424.7	-38	40.7	34.9
Cape Verde	2.8	100.7	3,530				41.2	156.3	279	0.0	116.3		164.4	121.6	-26	77.7	43.6
Gabon	48.4	307.9	536	1.8	11.5	557	29.4	28.7	-2	1.2	224.4	18,879	477.6	854.2	79	22.4	26.2
Mauritius	185.1	299.1	62				98.0	285.2	191	3.7	267.0	7,116	167.4	124.7	-26	148.7	122.9
Namibia	27.6	269.1	873		16.0		44.9	66.2	47	0.0	116.3		623.6	499.1	-20	99.3	33.8
South Africa	105.4	177.2	68		0.0		95.1	106.6	12	1.1	363.6	34,266	71.0	117.1	65	72.6	68.2
Swaziland	24.7	33.9	37				19.2	44.3	130	0.0	84.3		1,018.3	656.8	-36	28.7	25.9

Region	Television sets per 1000 people			Cable television subscribers per 1000 people			Main telephone lines per 1000 people			Cellular mobile telephone subscribers per 1000 people			International telecom, outgoing traffic (minutes per subscriber)			Personal Computers per 1000 people 2003	Internet users per 1000 people 2003
	1992	2002	% change 1992-2002	1997	2002	% change 1997-2002	1992	2002	% change 1992-2002	1993	2003	% change 1993-2003	1993	2003	% change 1993-2003		
Low income	35.3	83.6	137		27.2		8.3	32.2	290	0.0	23.5	93,572	172.9	108.5	-37	6.9	16.2
Middle income	187.3	279.6	49	37.4	57.3	53	53.0	177.5	235	1.1	225.0	20,927	84.0	93.0	11	42.9	115.9
Low & middle income	124.9	189.9	52	29.8	40.2	35	34.5	112.0	225	0.6	136.8	21,161	117.7	103.9	-12	28.4	75.1
East Asia & Pacific	155.8	317.3	104	36.3	70.1	93	15.4	161.4	950	0.9	195.4	20,677	79.9	42.4	-47	26.3	68.2
Europe & Central Asia	295.4			55.4	47.5	-14	149.1	228.0	53	0.4	300.5	70,545	56.4	66.0	17	73.4	161.0
Latin America & Caribbean	178.3	289.3	62	26.3	33.5	27	75.7	169.8	124	2.2	246.3	10,855	97.0	106.2	10	67.4	106.1
Middle East & North Africa	129.6	200.5	55				48.7	135.4	178	0.2	102.1	53,360	124.1	131.6	6	38.2	48.3
South Asia	35.2	84.4	140	16.4	37.3	128	8.4	38.9	362	0.0	22.5	122,324	60.4	35.1	-42	6.8	10.5
Sub-Saharan Africa	28.5	68.8	141				10.3	10.7	3	0.1	51.2	44,022	242.1	208.2	-14	11.9	19.7
High income	559.8	734.9	31	155.3	190.9	23	492.5	559.9	14	34.5	707.7	1,949	121.7	214.1	76	466.5	376.8
World	197.4	275.4	40	56.6	65.5	16	110.1	183.0	66	6.3	222.7	3,447	119.0	123.2	4	101.3	149.9

Empty cells indicate that data were unavailable. In such instances, where possible, figures are taken from the year before or after as an estimate. These figures, and estimates based on them, are presented in italics.

Sources: World Bank, World Development Indicators 2005 (WDI-Online); International Telecommunications Union (ITU), ICT – Free statistics homepage, www.itu.int/ITU-D/ict/statistics

Record 8: Governance and accountability

The first section of this record presents findings from the third wave of the 2020 Fund's Global Stakeholder Panel, in which international leaders from all sectors were asked to prioritize different aspects of global civil society involvement in UN reforms. Respondents favoured reforming multilateral agencies, such as the World Trade Organization and the World Bank, and including more representatives from poor communities in international discussions. Including representatives of business in global governance was unpopular in all parts of the world, except North America.

The second part of the record shows a Voice and Accountability Index developed by The World Bank Institute researchers, in their project Governance Matters. The Voice and Accountability Index measures the extent to which citizens of a country participate in the selection of government and the level of independence of the media. The index comprises various indicators from 25 different sources, which measure different aspects of the political process, civil liberties and political rights. Index values are ranked on a 1–100 scale (see www.worldbank.org/wbi/governance/pdf/govmatters3_wber.pdf for more information on index methodology).

High-income countries in Europe and North America and in parts of Latin America score highest in the index. The table shows the change in a country's rank between 1996 and 2003. Over half of the countries in the table exhibited decreases in voice and accountability; and, with a few exceptions (including Israel, Kuwait, United Arab Emirates and Singapore), all of the nations with a five-point decrease or more in their rank are low- to middle-income economies.

Thinking about actions to facilitate greater international development, please assess the impact that each of the following could have. "Development" here means efforts to meet the basic needs of people (economic, environmental, health, nutrition, social services, governance, infrastructure) and to improve the standard of living in society.

% respondents	Region								Per-Capita Income		
	Sub-Saharan Africa	Asia	Middle East & North Africa	Latin America & the Carribean	North America	Western Europe	Eastern Europe & Central Asia	Pacific	Low income economies	Middle income economies	High income economies
Establish greater accountability and transparency of international institutions involved in development											
% responding 'positive' or 'very positive' impact	87	90	73	92	76	75	65	70	87	85	75
% respondents listing this as one of the three most urgent actions that need to be implemented first to foster greater international development	24	34	22	22	21	21	28	28	24	28	22
Establish greater accountability and transparency of multinational companies providing foreign direct investment (FDI)											
% responding 'positive' or 'very positive' impact	80	83	64	88	75	74	61	70	80	82	74
% respondents listing this as one of the three most urgent actions that need to be implemented first to foster greater international development	14	17	44	16	17	18	8	11	16	15	17

Please assess the influence that you think each of the following has had to date in facilitating development in developing countries.

% respondents

% responding 'positive influence' or 'very positive influence'											
UN and its agencies (UNDP, UNEP, etc.)	47	55	27	46	58	65	61	65	50	51	62
International Monetary Fund (IMF)	8	15	18	6	10	12	16	4	11	9	11
The World Bank	15	23	45	18	17	18	39	15	20	21	18
Respondent's national government	25	30	45	14	29	35	16	35	23	20	33
Nongovernmental organisations (NGOs)	66	59	100	63	73	73	81	80	60	74	74
Faith based Organisations	49	24	27	28	32	31	29	35	36	31	31
Trade unions	45	20	36	22	31	30	26	37	31	25	31
Social movements	49	55	91	66	66	58	52	61	52	67	61
Trade agreements between governments	13	20	45	24	19	20	32	11	19	26	19
Governments of developing countries	9	18	9	10	5	5	19	11	13	13	5
Governments of developed countries	22	30	36	11	11	11	35	11	25	19	11
The European Union	33	42	27	39	31	36	68	30	37	47	33
The United States	20	17	27	6	12	7	23	7	19	12	9
Transnational corporations (TNCs)	10	18	18	7	10	10	10	4	16	9	9

The United Nations is currently exploring possible reforms to its management and operation. Please rate each of the following on the priority you think it should have in UN reform.

% respondents	Region								Per-Capita Income			
	Sub-Saharan Africa	Asia	Middle East & North Africa	Latin America & the Carribean	North America	Western Europe	Eastern Europe & Central Asia	Pacific	Low income economies	Middle income economies	High income economies	% considering this one of top 3 priorities
% stating reform 'should be a priority' or 'should be a major priority'												
Creating ad-hoc expert groups to recommend specific policies and implementation strategies to the UN	54	61	82	49	56	53	74	52	48	67	54	9
Increasing the capacity of and opportunities for developing countries to fully participate in UN processes	91	82	91	82	66	70	61	78	85	80	69	19
Expanding the formal roles of accredited NGOs within the UN's processes and operations	85	68	91	72	57	53	68	61	75	76	55	9
Expanding the formal roles of accredited trade union organisations within the UN's processes and operations	58	56	45	46	31	34	39	37	56	46	33	1
Expanding the formal roles of accredited international business organisations within the UN's processes and operations	42	46	27	42	19	27	42	28	44	38	24	1
Formalising partnerships with international business organisations, NGOs and trade unions as key instruments for implementing UN mandates	74	70	55	65	47	53	52	67	69	61	53	14
Acknowledging the role of broad-based coalitions of NGOs and like-minded states to campaign outside UN structures for objectives that are consistent with UN goals (e.g. Land Mines Treaty)	80	73	91	79	70	64	71	63	75	79	67	8
Establishing a new global tax on international transactions to fund the United Nations directly, rather than the current reliance on support from member governments	64	59	55	67	56	57	52	70	63	64	57	25

Source: 2020 Fund (2005), What Global Leaders Want? Report of the Third Survey of the 2020 Global Stakeholder Panel; http://www.2020fund.org/gsp_results.htm

Voice and accountability

Country	Voice & accountability ranking		Rank change 1996-2004
	1996	2004	
East Asia & Pacific			
Low income economies			
Cambodia	27.7	24.8	-3
East Timor		52.9	
Indonesia	16.2	35.9	20
Korea, Dem. Rep.	0.5	0.5	0
Laos	17.8	6.8	-11
Mongolia	62.8	59.7	-3
Myanmar	1.6	0.0	-2
Papua New Guinea	57.6	45.6	-12
Solomon Islands	80.1	49.5	-31
Vietnam	11.5	7.3	-4
Middle income economies			
China*	12.0	7.3	-5
Fiji	49.7	51.0	1
Malaysia	51.8	37.4	-14
Micronesia	85.9	80.1	-6
Philippines	58.6	47.6	-11
Samoa	70.7	68.4	-2
Thailand	52.9	52.4	-1
Tonga	52.4	38.3	-14
Vanuatu	63.9	67.5	4
High income economies			
Australia	99.0	95.6	-3
Austria	91.6	91.3	0
Brunei	22.5	17.5	-5
Japan	81.2	78.2	-3
Korea, Rep.	68.1	68.9	1
New Zealand	96.3	97.1	1
Singapore	63.4	43.2	-20
Europe & Central Asia			
Low income economies			
Azerbaijan	18.8	23.3	5
Georgia	33.5	39.3	6

Country	Voice & accountability ranking		Rank change 1996-2004
	1996	2004	
Kyrgyzstan	34.6	20.4	-14
Moldova	44.5	34.5	-10
Tajikistan	6.8	16.5	10
Uzbekistan	7.9	3.4	-5
Middle income economies			
Albania	41.4	48.1	7
Armenia	31.4	29.6	-2
Belarus	20.4	7.3	-13
Bosnia & Herzegovina	15.2	42.2	27
Bulgaria	58.1	65.0	7
Croatia	34.0	60.2	26
Czech Republic	79.6	81.1	2
Estonia	71.2	85.0	14
Hungary	79.1	87.4	8
Kazakhstan	20.9	13.6	-7
Latvia	64.9	76.2	11
Lithuania	69.6	77.2	8
Macedonia	50.8	46.1	-5
Poland	76.4	85.0	9
Romania	54.5	56.8	2
Russian Federation	39.8	25.7	-14
Slovakia	62.3	83.5	21
Turkey	38.2	41.7	4
Turkmenistan	2.1	1.5	-1
Ukraine	39.3	31.1	-8
High income economies			
Belgium	93.2	93.7	1
Cyprus	78.0	79.1	1
Denmark	99.5	100.0	1
Finland	98.4	98.5	0
France	94.8	90.8	-4
Germany	95.8	94.7	-1
Greece	75.4	73.3	-2
Iceland	92.7	96.6	4
Ireland	93.7	92.7	-1
Italy	82.2	82.0	0

Country	Voice & accountability ranking		Rank change 1996-2004
	1996	2004	
Luxembourg	94.2	95.6	1
Malta	82.7	91.7	9
Netherlands	96.9	97.6	1
Norway	100.0	99.5	-1
Portugal	90.1	93.2	3
Slovenia	75.9	84.5	9
Spain	84.8	87.9	3
Sweden	97.4	99.0	2
Switzerland	97.9	97.6	0
United Kingdom	91.1	94.2	3
Latin America & Caribbean			
Low income economies			
Haiti	36.1	8.7	-27
Nicaragua	43.5	48.5	5
Middle income economies			
Argentina	66.5	62.1	-4
Belize	81.7	73.3	-8
Bolivia	56.5	47.1	-9
Brazil	59.7	55.8	-4
Chile	74.9	83.0	8
Colombia	50.3	34.5	-16
Costa Rica	90.6	84.0	-7
Cuba	8.4	1.9	-7
Dominican Republic	53.4	53.9	1
Ecuador	55.5	40.8	-15
El Salvador	44.0	53.4	9
Guatemala	28.8	36.4	8
Guyana	73.8	66.0	-8
Honduras	40.3	46.1	6
Jamaica	66.0	63.6	-2
Mexico	42.9	56.8	14
Panama	61.8	63.6	2
Paraguay	38.7	40.3	2
Peru	27.2	44.7	18
St. Lucia	83.8	77.2	-7
St. Vincent & the Grenadines	84.3	76.2	-8

Country	Voice & accountability ranking		Rank change 1996-2004
	1996	2004	
Suriname	51.3	65.5	14
Trinidad & Tobago	70.2	62.1	-8
Uruguay	71.7	79.1	7
Venezuela	55.0	35.4	-20
High income economies			
Bahamas	83.2	86.4	3
Barbados	86.4	87.9	2
Middle East & North Africa			
Low income economies			
Yemen	23.6	22.8	-1
Middle income economies			
Algeria	15.7	23.8	8
Djibouti	25.7	25.2	-1
Egypt	26.7	20.9	-6
Iran	18.3	10.7	-8
Iraq	1.0	4.4	3
Jordan	48.7	29.1	-20
Lebanon	36.6	25.7	-11
Libya	5.2	2.9	-2
Morocco	29.3	32.5	3
Oman	30.4	24.3	-6
Palestinian Authority	3.1	12.1	9
Saudi Arabia	14.7	5.8	-9
Syria	10.5	3.9	-7
Tunisia	33.0	17.5	-16
High income economies			
Bahrain	23.0	27.7	5
Israel*	80.6	60.2	-20
Kuwait	46.1	34.0	-12
Qatar	24.6	26.7	2
United Arab Emirates	28.3	21.8	-7
North America			
High income economies			
Canada	92.1	94.7	3
United States	95.3	89.3	-6

Country	Voice & accountability ranking		Rank change 1996-2004
	1996	2004	
South Asia			
Low income economies			
Afghanistan	3.7	11.2	8
Bangladesh	41.9	28.6	-13
Bhutan	9.4	14.6	5
India	60.7	53.9	-7
Nepal	57.1	22.3	-35
Pakistan	22.0	11.7	-10
Middle income economies			
Maldives	21.5	19.9	-2
Sri Lanka	45.0	41.3	-4
Sub-Saharan Africa			
Low income economies			
Angola	6.3	21.4	15
Benin	69.1	55.3	-14
Burkina Faso	35.6	36.9	1
Burundi	13.1	16.0	3
Cameroon	19.9	14.6	-5
Central African Republic	47.1	14.1	-33
Chad	26.2	18.9	-7
Comoros	49.2	42.2	-7
Congo, Rep.	14.1	26.7	13
Congo, Dem. Rep.	13.6	5.3	-8
Côte d'Ivoire	46.6	9.7	-37
Equatorial Guinea	4.7	4.4	0
Eritrea	17.3	1.0	-16
Ethiopia	30.9	17.5	-13
Gambia	11.0	32.0	21
Ghana	40.8	57.8	17
Guinea	16.8	16.5	0
Guinea-Bissau	31.9	31.1	-1
Kenya	35.1	39.3	4
Lesotho	53.9	54.9	1
Liberia	7.3	12.6	5
Madagascar	60.2	49.0	-11
Malawi	37.2	33.0	-4

Country	Voice & accountability ranking		Rank change 1996-2004
	1996	2004	
Mali	61.3	56.3	-5
Mauritania	24.1	15.5	-9
Mozambique	45.5	43.2	-2
Niger	37.7	44.2	7
Nigeria	4.2	30.1	26
Rwanda	5.8	18.9	13
São Tomé & Principe	72.8	64.6	-8
Senegal	47.6	51.5	4
Sierra Leone	9.9	33.5	24
Somalia	0.0	6.3	6
Sudan	2.6	2.4	0
Tanzania	25.1	38.3	13
Togo	19.4	13.1	-6
Uganda	29.8	30.6	1
Zambia	48.2	37.4	-11
Zimbabwe	42.4	9.2	-33
Middle income economies			
Botswana	68.6	68.9	0
Cape Verde	74.3	71.4	-3
Gabon	32.5	28.2	-4
Mauritius	72.3	74.8	3
Namibia	64.4	61.2	-3
South Africa	67.5	72.3	5
Swaziland	12.6	10.2	-2

* China excludes Hong Kong and Macao.

Source: World Bank Institute: Governance Indicators: 1996-2004; http://worldbank.org/wbi/governance/govdata/index.html

Global civil society is both dependent on the international rule of law and one of the main actors pushing for the adoption and enforcement of international law. The table indicates which countries have ratified the major human rights, humanitarian, disarmament, and environmental treaties, and in which years, according to the most recent data available. It shows how many countries have ratified each particular treaty, and how many of the listed treaties each country has ratified. The number of listed treaties ratified by each country since 2000 is also shown. In terms of the number of treaties ratified, it seems that low- and middle-income countries in Europe and Central Asia, Latin America and Africa are catching up with high-income economies. The highest numbers of recent ratifications are of humanitarian and environmental law treaties.

Key

ICESCR	International Covenant on Economic, Social and Cultural Rights (As of 09 June 2004)
ICCPR	International Convenant on Civil and Political Rights (As of 09 June 2004)
ICCPR-OP1	Optional Protocol to the International Convenant on Civil and Political Rights (As of 09 June 2004)
ICCPR-OP2	Second Optional Protocol to the International Convenant on Civil and Political Rights (As of 09 June 2004)
CERD	International Convention on the Elimination of all forms of Racial Discrimination (As of 09 June 2004)
CEDAW	Convention on the Elimination of All Forms of Discrimination Against Women (As of 09 June 2004)
CAT	Convention against Torture and Other Cruel, Inhuman or Degrading Treatment or Punishment (As of 09 June 2004)
Gen	Convention on the Prevention and Punishment of the Crime of the Genocide (As of 09 October 2001)
ILO 87	Freedom of Association and Protection of the Right to Organise Convention (Accessed 18 May 2005)
CSR	Convention relating to the Status of Refugees (Accessed 18 May 2005)
ICC	Rome Statute on the International Criminal Court (As of 12 May 2005)
CWC	Chemical Weapons Convention (As of 21 May 2005)
BWC	Biological Weapons Convention (Accessed 18 May 2005)
LMC	Convention on the Prohibition of the Use, Stockpiling, Production and Transfer of Anti-Personnel Mines and on their Destruction (Accessed 18 May 2005)
Geneva	Geneva Conventions (As of 29 March 2005)
Prot 1	First Additional Protocol to the Geneva Conventions (As of 29 March 2005)
Prot 2	Second Additional Protocol to the Geneva Conventions (As of 29 March 2005)
BC	Basel Convention on the Control of Transboundary Movements of Hazardous Wastes and Their Disposal (As of 8 April 2005)
CBD	Convention on Biological Diversity (Accessed 18 May 2005)
UNFCCC	United Nations Framework Convention on Climate Change (As of 24 May 2004)
KP	Kyoto Protocol to United Nations Framework Convention on Climate Change (As of 29 April 2005)
VCPOL	Vienna Convention for the Protection of Ozone Layer (As of 29 March 2005)

Country	Human Rights											Humanitarian Law						Environmental Law						
	ICESCR	ICCPR	ICCPR-OP1	ICCPR-OP2	CERD	CEDAW	CAT	Gen	ILO 87	CSR	ICC	CWC	BWC	LMC	Geneva	Prot 1	Prot2	BC	CBD	UNFCCC	KP	VCPOL	Total	Ratified since 2000
East Asia & Pacific																								
Low income economies																								
Cambodia	92	92			83	92	92	50	99	92	02		83	99	58	98	98	01	95	95	02	01	**19**	**4**
Indonesia & East Timor					99	84	98		98			98	92		58			93	94	94		92	**11**	**0**
Korea, Dem. Rep.	81	81				01		89					87		57	88			94	94		95	**10**	**1**
Laos	00				74	81		50				97	73		56	80	80		96	95	03	98	**13**	**2**
Mongolia	74	74	91		69	81	02	67	69		02	95	72		58	95	95	97	93	93	99	96	**19**	**2**
Myanmar						97		56	55						92				94	94	03	93	**8**	**1**
Papua New Guinea					82	95		82	00	86		94	80		76			95	93	93	02	92	**13**	**2**
Solomon Islands	82				82	02				95			81	99	81	88	88		95	94	03	93	**13**	**2**
Vietnam	82	82			82	82		81				98	80		57	81		95	94	94	02	94	**14**	**1**
Middle income economies																								
China & Tibet	01				81	80	88	83		82		97	84		56	83	83	91	93	93		89	**15**	**1**
Fiji					73	95		73	02	72	99	93	73	98	71				93	93	98	89	**14**	**1**
Malaysia						95		94				00	91	99	62			93	94	94	02	89	**11**	**2**
Philippines	74	86	89		67	81	86	50	53	81		96	73	00	52		86	93	93	94	03	91	**19**	**2**
Samoa						92				88	02	02		98	84	84	84	02	94	94	00	92	**13**	**4**
Thailand	99	96				85						03	75	98	54			97	04	94	02	89	**12**	**3**
Tonga					72			72					76		78	03	03	98	98			98	**9**	**2**
Vanuatu						95						03	90		82	85	85		93	93	01	94	**10**	**2**
High income economies																								
Australia	75	80	91	90	75	83	89	49	73	54	02	94	77	99	58	91	91	92	93	92		87	**21**	**1**
Brunei												97	91		91	91	91	02				90	**7**	**1**
Korea, Rep.	90	90	90		78	84	95	50		92	02	97	87		66	82	82	94	94	93	02	92	**19**	**2**
Japan	79	79			95	85	99		65	81		95	82	98	53	04	04	93	93	93		88	**17**	**2**
New Zealand	78	78	89	90	72	85	89	78		60	00	96	72	99	59	88	88	94	93	93	02	87	**21**	**2**
Singapore						95		95				97	75		73			96	95	97		89	**9**	**0**
Europe & Central Asia																								
Low income economies																								
Armenia	93	93	93		93	93	93	93		93		94	94		93	93	93	99	93	94	03	99	**18**	**1**
Azerbaijan	92	92	01	99	96	95	96	96	92	93		00			93			01	00	95	00	96	**17**	**5**
Georgia	94	94	94	99	99	94	94	93	99	99	03	95	96		93	93	93	99	94	94	99	96	**21**	**1**
Kyrgyzstan	94	94	95		97	97	97	97	92	96					92	92	92	96	96	00	03	00	**17**	**3**

Country	Human Rights											Humanitarian Law						Environmental Law					Total	Ratified since 2000
	ICESCR	ICCPR	ICCPR-OP1	ICCPR-OP2	CERD	CEDAW	CAT	Gen	ILO 87	CSR	ICC	CWC	BWC	LMC	Geneva	Prot 1	Prot2	BC	CBD	UNFCCC	KP	VCPOL		
Moldova	93	93			93	94	95	93	96	02		96		00	93	93	93	98	95	95	03	96	18	3
Tajikistan	99	99	99		95	93	95		93	93	00	95		99	93	93	93		97	98		96	17	1
Ukraine	73	73	91		69	81	87	54	56			98	75		54	90	90	99	95	97	04	86	18	1
Uzbekistan	95	95	95		95	95	95	99				96	96		93	93	93	96	95	93	99	93	17	0
Middle income economies																								
Albania	91	91			94	94	94	55	57	92	03	94	92	00	57	93	93	99	94	94		99	19	2
Belarus	73	73	92		69	81	87	54	56	01		96	75	03	54	89	89	99	93	00		86	19	3
Bosnia & Herzegovina	92	93	95	01	93	93	93	92	93	93	02	97	94	98	92	92	92	01	02	00		92	21	5
Bulgaria	70	70	92	99	66	82	86	50	59	93	02	94	72	98	54	89	89	96	96	95	02	90	22	2
Croatia	91	92	95	95	92	92	92	92	91	92	01	95	93	98	92	92	92	94	96	96		91	21	1
Czech Republic	93	93	93		93	93	93	93	93	93		96	93	93	93	93	93	93	93	93	01	93	20	1
Estonia	91	91	91		91	91	91	91	94	97	02	99	93		93	93	93	92	94	94	02	96	20	2
Hungary	74	74	88	94	67	80	87	52	57	89	01	96	72	98	54	89	89	90	94	94	02	88	22	2
Kazakhstan	03				98	98	98	98	00	99		00			92	92	92	03	94	95		98	15	4
Latvia	92	92	94		92	92	92	92	92	97	02	96	97		91	91	91	92	95	95	02	95	20	2
Lithuania	91	91	91	02	98	94	96	96	94	97	03	98	98	03	96	00	00	99	96	95	03	95	22	6
Macedonia	94	94	94	95	94	94	94	94	91	94	02	97	96	94	93	93	93	97	97	98		94	21	1
Poland	77	77	91		68	80	89	50	57	91	01	95	73		54	91	91	92	96	99	02	90	20	2
Romania	74	74	93	91	70	82	90	50	57	91	02	95	79	00	54	90	90	91	94	94	01	93	22	3
Russian Federation	73	73	91		69	81	87	54	56	93		97	75		54	89	89	95	95	94	04	86	19	1
Slovakia	93	93	93	99	93	93	93	93	93	93	02	95	93	99	93	93	93	93	94	94	02	93	22	2
Slovenia	92	92	93	94	92	92	93	92	92	92	01	97	92	98	92	92	92	93	96	95	02	92	22	2
Turkey	03	03			02	85	88	50	93	62		97	74	03	54			94	97	04		91	16	5
Turkmenistan	97	97	97	00	94	97	99		97	98		94	96	98	92	92	92	96	96	95	00	93	20	2
Yugoslavia	01	01	01	01	01	82	01	01	00	01		00			01	01	01	00	02	97		92	18	15
High income economies																								
Austria	78	78	87	93	72	82	87	58	50	54	00	95	73	98	53	82	82	93	94	94	02	87	22	2
Belgium	83	83	94	98	75	85	99	51	51	53	00	97	79	98	52	86	86	93	96	96	02	88	22	2
Cyprus	69	69	92	99	67	85	91	82	66	63	02	98	73	03	62	79	96	92	96	97	99	92	22	2
Denmark	72	72	72	94	71	83	87	51	51	52	01	95	73	98	51	82	82	94	93	93	02	88	22	2
Finland	75	75	75	91	70	86	89	59	50	68	00	95	74		55	80	80	91	94	94	02	86	21	2
France	80	80	84		71	83	86	50	51	54	00	95	84	98	51	01	84	91	94	94		87	20	2
Germany	73	73	93	92	69	85	90	54	57	53	00	94	72	98	54	91	91	95	93	93	02	88	22	2

Country	Human Rights										Humanitarian Law							Environmental Law					Total	Ratified since 2000
	ICESCR	ICCPR	ICCPR-OP1	ICCPR-OP2	CERD	CEDAW	CAT	Gen	ILO 87	CSR	ICC	CWC	BWC	LMC	Geneva	Prot 1	Prot2	BC	CBD	UNFCCC	KP	VCPOL		
Greece	85	97	97	97	70	83	88	54	62	60	02	94	75	03	56	89	93	94	94	94	02	88	22	3
Iceland	79	79	79	91	67	85	96	49	50	55	00	97	73	99	65	87	87	95	94	93	02	89	22	2
Ireland	89	89	89	93	00	85	02	76	55	56	02	96	72	97	62	99	99	94	96	94	02	88	22	4
Italy	78	78	78	95	76	85	89	52	58	54	99	95	75	99	51	86	86	94	94	94	02	88	22	1
Luxembourg	83	83	83	92	78	89	87	81	58	53	00	97	76	99	53	89	89	94	94	94	02	88	22	2
Netherlands	78	78	78	91	71	91	88	66	50	56	01	95	81	99	54	87	87	93	94	93	02	88	22	2
Norway	72	72	72	91	70	81	86	49	49	53	00	94	73	98	51	81	81	90	93	93	02	86	22	2
Portugal	78	78	83	90	82	80	89	99	77	60	02	96	75	99	61	92	92	94	93	93		88	21	1
Spain	77	77	85	91	68	84	87	68	77	78	00	94	79	99	52	89	89	94	93	93	02	88	22	2
Sweden	71	71	71	90	71	80	86	52	49	54	01	93	76	98	53	79	79	91	93	93	02	86	22	2
Switzerland	92	92		94	94	97	86	00	75	55	01	95	76	98	50	82	82	90	94	93	03	87	21	3
United Kingdom	76	76		99	69	86	88	70	49	54	01	96	75	98	57	98	98	94	94	93	02	87	21	2
Latin America & Caribbean																								
Low income economies																								
Haiti		91			72	81		50	79	84					57				96	96		00	10	1
Nicaragua	80	80	80		78	81		52	67	80		99	75	98	53	99	99	97	95	95	99	93	19	0
Middle income economies																								
Argentina	86	86	86		68	85	86	56	60	61	01	95	79	99	56	86	86	91	94	93	01	90	21	2
Barbados	73	73	73		72	80		80	67		02		73	99	68	90	90	95	93	94	00	92	18	2
Belize		96			01	90	86	98	83	90	00	03	86	98	84	84	84	97	93	94	03	97	19	4
Bolivia	82	82	82		70	90	99		65	82	02	98	75	98	76	83	83	96	94	94	99	94	20	1
Brazil	92	92			68	84	89	52		60	02	96	73	99	57	92	92	92	94	94	02	90	19	2
Chile	72	72	92		71	89	88	53	99	72		96	80	01	50	91	91	92	94	94	02	90	20	2
Colombia	69	69	69	97	81	82	87	59	76	61	02	00	83	00	61	93	95	96	94	95	01	90	22	4
Costa Rica	68	68	68	98	67	86	93	50	60	78	01	96	93	99	69	83	83	95	94	94	02	91	22	2
Cuba					72	80	95	53	52			97	76		54	82	99	94	94	94	02	92	15	1
Dominican Republic	78	78	78		83	82		56	78		05		73	00	58	94	94	00	96	98	02	93	18	4
Ecuador	69	69	69	93	66	81	88	49	67	55	02	95	75	99	54	79	79	93	93	94	00	90	22	2
El Salvador	79	79	95		79	81	96	50		83		95	91	99	53	78	78	91	94	95	98	92	19	0
Guatemala	88	92	00		83	82	90	50	52	83			73	99	52	87	87	95	95	95	99	87	19	1
Guyana	77	77	93		77	80	88		67		04	97		03	68	88	88	01	94	94	03	93	18	4
Honduras	81	97			02	83	96	52	56	92	02		79	98	65	95	95	95	95	95	00	93	19	3
Jamaica	75	75			71	84		68	62	64		00	75	98	64	86	86	03	95	94	99	93	18	2

Country	Human Rights											Humanitarian Law						Environmental Law					Total	Ratified since 2000
	ICESCR	ICCPR	ICCPR-OP1	ICCPR-OP2	CERD	CEDAW	CAT	Gen	ILO 87	CSR	ICC	CWC	BWC	LMC	Geneva	Prot 1	Prot2	BC	CBD	UNFCCC	KP	VCPOL		
Mexico	81	81	02		75	81	86	52	61	00		94	74	98	52	83		91	93	93	00	87	19	3
Panama	77	77	77	93	67	81	87	50	58	78	02	98	74	98	56	95	95	91	95	95	99	89	22	1
Paraguay	92	92	95		03	87	90	01	62	70	01	96	76	98	61	90	90	95	94	94	99	92	21	3
Peru	78	78	80		71	82	88	60	60	64	01	95	85	98	56	89	89	93	93	93	02	89	21	2
St. Lucia					90	82			80			97	86	99	81	82	82	93	93	93		93	13	0
St. Vincent & the Grenadines	81	81	81		81	81	01	81	01	93		02	99	01	81	83	83	96	96	96	04	96	20	5
Suriname	76	76	76		84	93			76	78		97	93		76	85	85	96	97			97	15	0
Trinidad & Tobago	78	78			73	90			63	00	99	97		98	63	01	01	94	96	94	99	89	17	3
Uruguay	70	70	70	93	68	81	86	67	54	70	02	94	81	01	69	85	85	91	93	94	01	89	22	3
Venezuela	78	78	78	93	67	83	91	60	82		00	97	78	99	56	98	98	98	94	94		88	20	1
High income economies																								
Bahamas					75	93		75	01	93			86	98	75	80	80	92	93	94	99	93	15	1
Middle East & North Africa																								
Low income economies																								
Yemen	87	87			72	84	91	87	76	80		00	79	98	70	90	90	96	96	96		96	18	1
Middle income economies																								
Algeria	89	89	89		72	96	89	63	62	63		95	01	01	62	89	89	98	95	93		92	19	2
Djibouti	02	02	02	02		98	02		78	77	02			98	78	91	91	02	94	95	02	99	18	8
Egypt	82	82			67	81	86	52	57	81					52	92	92	93	94	94		88	15	0
Iran	75	75			68			56		76		97	73		57			93	96	96		90	12	0
Iraq	71	71			70	86		59					91		56								7	0
Jordan	75	75			74	92	91	50			02	97	75	98	51	79	79	89	93	93	03	89	18	2
Lebanon	72	72			71	97	00	53					75		51	97	97	94	94	94		93	14	1
Libya	70	70	89		68	89	89	89	00			04	82		56	78	78	01	01	99		90	17	4
Malta	90	90	90	94	71	91	90		65	71	02	97	75	01	68	89	89	00	00	94	01	88	21	5
Morocco & Western Sahara	79	79			70	93	93	58		56		95	02		56			95	95	95	02	95	15	2
Oman												95	92		74	84	84	95	95	95		99	9	0
Saudi Arabia					97	00	97	50				96	72		63	87		90		94		93	11	1
Syria	69	69			69			55	60						53	83		92	96	96		89	11	0
Tunisia	69	69			67	85	88	56	57	57		97	73	99	57	79	79	95	93	93	03	89	19	2
High income economies																								
Bahrain					90	02	98	90				97	88		71	86	86	92	96	94		90	13	1
Israel & Occupied Territiories	91	91			79	91	91	50	57	54					51			94	95	96	04	92	14	1

Country	Human Rights											Humanitarian Law						Environmental Law					Total	Ratified since 2000
	ICESCR	ICCPR	ICCPR-OP1	ICCPR-OP2	CERD	CEDAW	CAT	Gen	ILO 87	CSR	ICC	CWC	BWC	LMC	Geneva	Prot 1	Prot2	BC	CBD	UNFCCC	KP	VCPOL		
Kuwait	96	96			68	94	96	95	61			97	72		67	85	85	93	02	94		92	16	1
Qatar					76		00					97	75	98	75	88		95	96	96		96	11	1
United Arab Emirates					74							00			72	83	83	92	00	95		89	9	2
North America																								
High income economies																								
Canada	76	76	76		70	81	87	52	72	69	00	95	72	97	65	90	90	92	92	92	02	86	21	2
United States		92			94		94	88				97	75		55					92		86	9	0
South Asia																								
Low income economies																								
Afghanistan	83	83			83	03	87	56	57		03		75	02	56				02	02			13	5
Bangladesh	98	00			79	84	98	98	72			97	85	00	72	80	80	93	94	94	01	90	18	3
Bhutan					81								78		91			02	95	95	02		7	2
India	79	79			68	93		59				96	74		50			92	94	93	02	91	13	1
Nepal	91	91	91	98	71	91	91	69				97			64			96	93	94		94	14	0
Pakistan					66	96		57	51			97	74		51			94	94	94		92	11	0
Middle income economies																								
Maldives					84	93		84				94	93	00	91	91	91	92	92	92	98	88	14	1
Sri Lanka	80	80	97		82	81	94	50	95			94	86		59			92	94	93	02	89	16	1
Sub-Saharan Africa																								
Low income economies																								
Angola	92	92	92			86			01	81				02	84	84			98	00		00	12	4
Benin	92	92	92			92	92		60	62	02	98	75	98	61	86	86	97	94	94		93	18	1
Burkina Faso	99	99	99		74	87	99	65	60	80	04	97	91	98	61	87	87	99	93	93		89	20	1
Burundi	90	90			77	92	93	97	93	63	04	98			71	93	93	97	97	97	01	97	18	2
Cameroon	84	84	84		71	94	86		60	61		96		02	63	84	84	01	94	94	02	89	18	3
Central African Republic	81	81	81		71	91			60	62	01			02	66	84	84		95	95		93	15	2
Chad	95	95	95		77	95	95		60	81				99	70	97	97		94	94		89	15	0
Comoros						94			78					02	85	85	85	94	94	94		94	10	1
Congo, Rep.	83	83	83		88	82			60	62	04		78	01	67	83	83	96				94	15	2
Congo, Dem. Rep.	76	76	76		76	86	96	62	01	65	02		75	02	61	82	02	94	94	95		94	19	4
Côte d'Ivoire	92	92	97		73	95	95	95	60	61		95		00	61	89	89	94	94	94		93	18	1
Equatorial Guinea	87	87	87		02	84	02		01	86		97	89	98	86	86	86	03	94	00	00	88	20	6
Eritrea	01	02			01	95	00					00	01		00				96	95			10	7

Country	ICESCR	ICCPR	ICCPR-OP1	ICCPR-OP2	CERD	CEDAW	CAT	Gen	ILO 87	CSR	ICC	CWC	BWC	LMC	Geneva	Prot 1	Prot2	BC	CBD	UNFCCC	KP	VCPOL	Total	Ratified since 2000
	Human Rights											Humanitarian Law						Environmental Law						
Ethiopia	93	93			76	81	94	49	63	69		96	75		69	94	94	00	94	94		94	17	1
Gambia	78	79	88		78	93		78	00	66	02	98	91	02	66	89	89	97	94	94	01	90	20	4
Ghana	00	00	00		66	86	00	58	65	63	99	97	75	00	58	78	78	03	94	95	03	89	21	7
Guinea	78	78	93		77	82	89	00	59	65	03	97		98	84	84	84	95	93	93	00	92	20	3
Guinea-Bissau	92	00				85				76			76	01	74	86	86		95	95		02	12	3
Kenya	72	72			01	84	97			66	05	97	76	01	66	99	99	00	94	94		88	17	4
Lesotho	92	92	00		71	95	01	74	66	81	00	94	77	98	68	94	94	00	95	95	00	94	21	5
Liberia					76	84		50	62	64	04			99	54	88	88		00	02	02	96	14	4
Madagascar	71	71	71		69	89			60	67				04	63	92	92	99	96	99	03	96	16	2
Malawi	93	93	96		96	87	96		99	87	02	98		98	68	91	91	94	94	94	01	91	19	2
Mali	74	74	01		74	85	99	74	60	73	00	97	02	98	65	89	89	00	95	94	02	94	21	5
Mozambique		93		93	83	97	99	83	96	83		00		98	83	83	02	97	95	95		94	17	2
Niger	86	86	86		67	99	98		61	61	02	97	72	99	64	79	79	98	95	95	04	92	20	2
Nigeria	93	93			67	85	01		60	67	01	99	73	01	61	88	88	91	94	94		88	18	3
Rwanda	75	75			75	81		75	88	80		04	75	00	64	84	84		96	98		01	16	3
São Tomé & Principe						03			92	78		03	79	03	76	96	96		99	99		01	12	4
Senegal	78	78	78		72	85	86	83	60	63	99	98	75	98	63	85	85	92	94	94	01	93	21	1
Sierra Leone	96	96	96		67	88	01		61	81	00	04	76	04	65	86	86		94	95		01	18	5
Somalia	90	90	90		75		90			78					62							01	8	1
Sudan	86	76			77					74		99		03	57				95	93		93	10	1
Tanzania	76	76			72	85		84	00	64	02	98		00	62	83	83	93	96	96	02	93	18	4
Togo	84	84	88		72	83	87	84	60	62		97	76	00	62	84	84		95	95		91	18	1
Uganda	87	95	95		80	85	86	95		76	02	01	92	99	64	91	91	99	93	93	02	88	20	3
Zambia	84	84	84		72	85	98		96	69	02	01		01	66	95	95	94	93	93		90	18	3
Zimbabwe	91	91			91	91		91	03	81		97	90	98	83	92	92		94	92		92	16	1
Middle income economies																								
Botswana		00			74	96	00		97	69	00	98	92	00	68	79	79	98	95	94	03	91	18	5
Cape Verde	93	93	00	00	79	80	92		99			03	77	01	84	95	95	99	95	95		01	18	5
Gabon	83	83			80	83	00	83	60	64	00	00		00	65	80	80		97	98		94	17	4
Mauritius	73	73	73		72	84	92		05		02	93	72	97	70	82	82	92	92	92	01	92	19	3
Namibia	94	94	94	94	82	92	94	94	95	95	02	95		98	91	94	94	95	97	95	03	93	21	2
South Africa		99	02	02	98	95	98	98	96	96	00	95	75	98	52	95	95	94	95	97	02	90	21	4
Swaziland					69				78	00		96	91	98	73	95	95		94	96		92	12	1

Country	Human Rights										Humanitarian Law							Environmental Law					Total	Ratified since 2000
	ICESCR	ICCPR	ICCPR-OP1	ICCPR-OP2	CERD	CEDAW	CAT	Gen	ILO 87	CSR	ICC	CWC	BWC	LMC	Geneva	Prot 1	Prot2	BC	CBD	UNFCCC	KP	VCPOL		
Total States in table	143	145	101	46	158	163	127	129	136	131	90	144	138	123	174	149	143	145	169	170	107	170	3,001	
Total States Parties*	146	148	102	47	166	171	132	132	143	139	95	154	165	131	190	161	156	156	187	188	108	185	3,202	
Ratified since 2000 (States in table)	8	8	10	7	9	6	14	4	15	6	85	23	3	43	2	6	7	21	10	8	92	10		397

* Total States Parties refers to the total number of ratifications for each treaty, including from those countries with populations of less than 100,000 that are not included in this table.

Sources: Office of the UN High Commissioner for Human Rights, www.unhchr.ch/pdf/report.pdf, www.unhchr.ch/html/menu3/b/treaty2ref.htm, www.unhchr.ch/html/menu3/b/treaty1gen.htm; United Nations, www.un.org/law/icc/statute/status.htm; International Criminal Court, www.iccnow.org/countryinfo/worldsigsandratifications.html; International Labour Organization, www.ilo.org/ilolex/cgi-lex/ratifce.pl?C087, Organisation for the Prohibition of Chemical Weapons, www.opcw.org/html/db/members_frameset.html; Federation of American Scientists, www.fas.org/nuke/control/bwc/text/bwcsig.htm; Secretariat, Basel Convention on the Control of Transboundary Movements of Hazardous Wastes and Their Disposal, www.basel.int/ratif/ratif.html; Secretariat, United Nations Framework Convention on Climate Change, unfccc.int/resource/conv/ratlist.pdf, unfccc.int/resource/kpstats.pdf, unfccc.int/files/essential_background/kyoto_protocol/application/pdf/kpstats,pdf; United Nations Environment Programme, www.unep.org/ozone/Treaties_and_Ratification/2C_ratificationTable.asp; International Committee of the Red Cross, www.icrc.org/eng/party_gc, www.icrc.org/eng/party_cmines; Convention on Biological Diversity, www.biodiv.org/world/parties.asp www.fas.org/nuke/control/bwc/text/bwcsig.htm

Record 10: Human rights violations

Global civil society is instrumental in exposing human rights violations. At the same time, human rights violations form one of the main threats to the survival of local civil societies. While Record 9 shows the extent to which states have committed themselves to abide by international law, this table shows the extent to which they actually respect international human rights law. The table displays information on human rights abuses by country, covering extrajudicial executions and disappearances, arbitrary detentions, torture, freedom of expression, and the situation of minorities, using the latest information available from two sources: Amnesty International (report of 2005) and the US State Department (reports of 2004). The inclusion of data from Human Rights Watch is no longer possible because the organisation has stopped producing annual country reports.

This year, Amnesty International and the US State Department report human rights violations (including reports of discrimination against minorities in developed nations) in more countries than in the 2003 Yearbook, when we last reported human right violations.

Country	Disappearances & extrajudicial executions		Arbitrary detentions		Torture		Discrimination against minorities		Restricted freedom of expression & association	
	AI	SD	AI	SD	AI	SD	AI	SD	AI	SD
East Asia & Pacific										
Low income economies										
Cambodia		yes		yes	yes	yes		yes	yes	yes
Indonesia	yes	yes	yes	yes	yes	yes		yes	yes	yes
Korea, Dem. Rep.	yes	yes	yes	yes	yes	yes		yes	yes	yes
Laos		yes		yes	yes	yes	yes	yes	yes	yes
Mongolia				yes		yes			yes	
Myanmar		yes		yes		yes	yes	yes	yes	yes
Papua New Guinea		yes								
Solomon Islands										
Vietnam		yes		yes		yes	yes	yes	yes	yes
Middle income economies										
China & Tibet		yes	yes	yes	yes	yes	yes		yes	yes
Fiji							yes	yes		yes
Malaysia			yes	yes		yes		yes	yes	yes
Philippines	yes	yes	yes	yes	yes	yes		yes		
Samoa										
Thailand	yes	yes		yes		yes	yes	yes		yes
Tonga										yes
Vanuatu										
High income economies										
Australia							yes	yes		
Brunei			yes	yes	yes					yes
Korea, Rep.				yes			yes	yes		yes
Japan						yes		yes		
New Zealand										

Country	Disappearances & extrajudicial executions		Arbitrary detentions		Torture		Discrimination against minorities		Restricted freedom of expression & association	
	AI	SD	AI	SD	AI	SD	AI	SD	AI	SD
Singapore			yes	yes					yes	yes
Europe & Central Asia										
Low income economies										
Armenia				yes				yes	yes	yes
Azerbaijan				yes		yes		yes	yes	yes
Georgia				yes	yes	yes	yes	yes	yes	yes
Kyrgyzstan		yes		yes			yes	yes		yes
Moldova		yes	yes	yes	yes	yes		yes		yes
Tajikistan				yes	yes	yes			yes	yes
Ukraine		yes		yes	yes	yes		yes	yes	yes
Uzbekistan		yes	yes	yes	yes	yes				yes
Middle income economies										
Albania		yes		yes	yes	yes		yes		yes
Belarus		yes		yes		yes		yes	yes	yes
Bosnia & Herzegovina								yes		yes
Bulgaria			yes	yes	yes		yes	yes		yes
Croatia							yes	yes		yes
Czech Republic							yes	yes		
Estonia										
Hungary							yes	yes		
Kazakhstan				yes		yes	yes	yes	yes	yes
Latvia						yes				
Lithuania						yes		yes		
Macedonia				yes		yes	yes	yes		
Malta			yes							
Poland							yes	yes	yes	yes
Romania		yes		yes	yes	yes	yes	yes		yes
Russian Federation	yes	yes		yes	yes	yes	yes	yes	yes	yes
Serbia & Montenegro	yes			yes	yes	yes	yes	yes		yes
Slovakia							yes	yes		yes
Slovenia								yes		
Turkey	yes	yes		yes	yes	yes		yes	yes	yes
Turkmenistan			yes	yes		yes	yes	yes	yes	yes
High income economies										
Austria										
Belgium							yes	yes		

Country	Disappearances & extrajudicial executions		Arbitrary detentions		Torture		Discrimination against minorities		Restricted freedom of expression & association	
	AI	SD	AI	SD	AI	SD	AI	SD	AI	SD
Cyprus						yes	yes			
Denmark										
Finland							yes			
France							yes	yes		
Germany								yes		yes
Greece				yes		yes	yes	yes		yes
Iceland								yes		
Ireland							yes	yes		
Italy							yes			
Luxembourg										
Netherlands										
Norway										
Portugal										
Spain					yes	yes	yes	yes		
Sweden							yes			
Switzerland				yes			yes			
United Kingdom										
Latin America & Caribbean										
Low income economies										
Haiti	yes	yes	yes	yes	yes	yes			yes	yes
Nicaragua		yes		yes		yes		yes		
Middle income economies										
Argentina				yes	yes	yes				
Barbados										
Belize		yes		yes						
Bolivia				yes	yes			yes		yes
Brazil	yes	yes		yes	yes	yes	yes	yes	yes	
Chile				yes			yes	yes		
Colombia	yes	yes	yes	yes	yes	yes		yes	yes	yes
Costa Rica										
Cuba				yes					yes	yes
Dominican Republic	yes	yes		yes	yes	yes		yes	yes	yes
Ecuador		yes		yes		yes	yes	yes	yes	yes
El Salvador				yes				yes		
Guatemala		yes		yes		yes		yes	yes	yes
Guyana	yes	yes			yes			yes		

Country	Disappearances & extrajudicial executions		Arbitrary detentions		Torture		Discrimination against minorities		Restricted freedom of expression & association	
	AI	SD	AI	SD	AI	SD	AI	SD	AI	SD
Honduras		yes		yes		yes	yes	yes	yes	yes
Jamaica	yes	yes		yes	yes		yes	yes		
Mexico		yes	yes	yes	yes	yes	yes	yes	yes	yes
Panama								yes		yes
Paraguay		yes		yes	yes	yes	yes	yes		yes
Peru					yes	yes		yes	yes	
St. Lucia										
Suriname								yes		
Trinidad & Tobago					yes					
Uruguay					yes			yes		
Venezuela	yes	yes	yes	yes	yes	yes		yes	yes	yes
High income economies										
Bahamas		yes		yes				yes		
Middle East & North Africa										
Low income economies										
Yemen	yes		yes	yes	yes	yes		yes	yes	yes
Middle income economies										
Algeria	yes	yes		yes	yes	yes		yes	yes	yes
Djibouti		yes		yes				yes		yes
Egypt		yes	yes	yes	yes	yes		yes	yes	yes
Iran		yes	yes	yes	yes	yes	yes	yes	yes	yes
Iraq	yes	yes	yes	yes	yes	yes				
Jordan				yes	yes	yes		yes		yes
Lebanon		yes	yes	yes	yes	yes	yes	yes	yes	yes
Libya		yes	yes	yes	yes	yes		yes	yes	yes
Morocco & Western Sahara				yes	yes	yes			yes	yes
Oman				yes						yes
Saudi Arabia	yes		yes	yes	yes			yes	yes	yes
Syria		yes		yes	yes	yes	yes	yes	yes	yes
Tunisia				yes	yes	yes			yes	yes
High income economies										
Bahrain								yes	yes	yes
Israel & Occupied Territories	yes		yes		yes	yes	yes	yes		
Kuwait					yes	yes		yes	yes	yes
Qatar								yes		yes
United Arab Emirates	yes		yes					yes	yes	yes

Country	Disappearances & extrajudicial executions		Arbitrary detentions		Torture		Discrimination against minorities		Restricted freedom of expression & association	
	AI	SD	AI	SD	AI	SD	AI	SD	AI	SD
North America										
High income economies										
Canada							yes			
United States	yes		yes		yes					
South Asia										
Low income economies										
Afghanistan	yes	yes	yes	yes	yes	yes		yes		yes
Bangladesh	yes	yes	yes	yes		yes	yes	yes	yes	yes
Bhutan							yes	yes	yes	yes
India		yes	yes	yes	yes	yes	yes	yes		
Nepal	yes	yes	yes	yes	yes	yes	yes	yes	yes	yes
Pakistan	yes	yes	yes	yes		yes	yes	yes	yes	yes
Middle income economies										
Maldives			yes	yes						yes
Sri Lanka	yes			yes	yes	yes	yes	yes		
Sub-Saharan Africa										
Low income economies										
Angola		yes		yes		yes		yes		yes
Benin				yes						yes
Burkina Faso		yes		yes		yes		yes		yes
Burundi	yes	yes	yes	yes	yes	yes		yes	yes	yes
Cameroon		yes		yes	yes	yes		yes	yes	yes
Central African Republic		yes		yes		yes		yes	yes	yes
Chad		yes		yes		yes		yes	yes	yes
Comoros								yes		yes
Congo, Dem Rep.	yes	yes	yes	yes	yes	yes		yes		yes
Congo, Rep.	yes			yes				yes	yes	yes
Côte d'Ivoire	yes	yes		yes				yes		yes
Equatorial Guinea	yes	yes	yes	yes	yes	yes		yes		yes
Eritrea		yes	yes	yes	yes	yes		yes	yes	yes
Ethiopia	yes	yes	yes	yes	yes	yes	yes	yes	yes	yes
Gambia				yes		yes				yes
Ghana		yes		yes				yes		yes
Guinea		yes	yes	yes		yes		yes		yes
Guinea-Bissau		yes		yes				yes		
Kenya		yes		yes	yes	yes		yes		yes

Country	Disappearances & extrajudicial executions		Arbitrary detentions		Torture		Discrimination against minorities		Restricted freedom of expression & association	
	AI	SD	AI	SD	AI	SD	AI	SD	AI	SD
Lesotho						yes				
Liberia				yes				yes		yes
Madagascar				yes				yes		yes
Malawi				yes	yes					yes
Mali				yes				yes		
Mauritania				yes	yes	yes		yes		yes
Mozambique		yes		yes		yes				yes
Niger		yes		yes				yes	yes	
Nigeria		yes		yes		yes		yes	yes	yes
Rwanda		yes		yes		yes		yes	yes	yes
São Tomé & Principe										
Senegal				yes					yes	
Sierra Leone				yes				yes		yes
Somalia		yes	yes	yes	yes	yes	yes	yes	yes	yes
Sudan	yes	yes	yes	yes	yes	yes	yes	yes	yes	yes
Tanzania		yes		yes		yes	yes	yes	yes	yes
Togo		yes	yes	yes	yes	yes		yes	yes	yes
Uganda		yes		yes	yes	yes	yes	yes	yes	yes
Zambia		yes	yes	yes	yes	yes		yes	yes	yes
Zimbabwe		yes	yes	yes	yes	yes		yes	yes	yes
Middle income economies										
Botswana								yes		yes
Cape Verde										
Gabon				yes		yes		yes		yes
Mauritius										
Namibia				yes				yes		
South Africa					yes	yes		yes		
Swaziland		yes		yes	yes	yes		yes		yes

'Yes' denotes a violation. Absence of data indicates that either no violations have been recorded or that no data are available.

Sources: Amnesty International Report 2005, http://web.amnesty.org/report2005/index-eng; U.S. State Department 2004 Country Reports on Human Rights Practices http://www.state.gov/g/drl/rls/hrrpt/2004/index.htm.

This record illustrates another element of the spread of the international rule of law, namely, the realisation of social and economic rights, or social justice. This record contains indicators of poverty, inequality, and social exclusion. Growing inequality appears to be one of the characteristics of globalisation. It can be seen as inhibiting the emergence of global civil society, but it is also one of global civil society's major causes. Figures are given for 1990 and 2002 unless otherwise indicated. The Human Development Index (HDI) is the first indicator listed. It is a composite index of three separate indicators measuring respectively GDP per capita, educational attainment, and life expectancy at birth. Higher numbers suggest higher levels of development. As further measures of social justice, the table also includes the extent of income inequality revealed by the Gini coefficient, with higher numbers indicating greater inequality; the net primary school enrolment ratio (the number of students enrolled in a level of education who are of official school age for that level, as a percentage of the population of official school age for that level); and the ratio of girls to boys in primary education, to indicate gender inequality.

The data show that health, education and equality outcomes in Sub-Saharan Africa are extremely low, affected to a great extent by the HIV and AIDS pandemic, and are worse than the figures we reported last year.

Country	Human Development Index (HDI)			GDP per capita, PPP in current international $			Infant mortality rate (% live births)			Life expectancy at birth (years)			Net primary school enrolment ratio (%)			Ratio of girls to boys in primary education (%)			Income inequality (Gini index)* see note below
	value 1990	value 2002	% change 1990–2002	1992	2002	% change 1992–2002	1990	2002	% change 1990–2002	1992	2002	% change 1992–2002	1990–1991	2001–2002	% change 1990–2002	1990–1991	2001–2002	% change 1990–2002	
East Asia & Pacific																			
Low income economies																			
Cambodia	0.501	0.568	13	1,133	2,060	82	9.5	9.6	1	52	57	11		86			93		40
East Timor		0.436						8.9			49								
Indonesia	0.623	0.692	11	2,410	3,230	34	6.0	3.3	-45	63	67	6	98	92	-6	95	99	4	34
Laos	0.404	0.534	32	952	1,720	81	10.6	8.7	-18	51	54	7		83		77	92	19	37
Mongolia	0.657	0.668	2	1,634	1,710	5	7.3	5.8	-21	64	64	0		87		100	103	3	44
Myanmar		0.551			1,027		10.0	7.7	-23	55	57	3		82		94	100	6	
Papua New Guinea	0.479	0.542	13	2,040	2,270	11	8.3	7.0	-16	56	57	3		77		80	89	11	51
Solomon Islands		0.624		2,010	1,590	-21	3.0	2.0	-33	65	69	6				80			
Vietnam	0.605	0.691	14	1,121	2,300	105	4.0	3.0	-25	66	69	5		94			94		36
Middle income economies																			
China & Tibet**	0.625	0.745	19	1,680	4,580	173	3.8	3.1	-18	69	71	3	97	93	-4	86	101	17	45
Fiji	0.723	0.758	5	3,858	5,440	41	3.5	1.7	-51	67	70	4	101	100	-1		100		
Malaysia	0.722	0.793	10	5,464	9,120	67	1.6	0.8	-49	71	73	2		95		95	100	5	49
Philippines	0.716	0.753	5	3,128	4,170	33	3.7	2.9	-22	67	70	5	98	93	-5	95	102	7	46
Samoa	0.666	0.769	15	3,546	5,600	58	2.7	2.0	-26	68	70	3		95		98	99	1	
Thailand	0.713	0.768	8	4,451	7,010	58	3.7	2.4	-35	70	69	-1		86		94	97	3	43
Tonga		0.787		4,464	6,850	53	3	1.6	-36	70	68	-2		105		92	100	9	
Vanuatu		0.57		2,729	2,890	6	4.6	3.4	-25	65	69	5		93		89	102	15	

Country	Human Development Index (HDI)			GDP per capita, PPP in current international $			Infant mortality rate (% live births)			Life expectancy at birth (years)			Net primary school enrolment ratio (%)			Ratio of girls to boys in primary education (%)			Income inequality (Gini index)* see note below
	value 1990	value 2002	% change 1990-2002	1992	2002	% change 1992-2002	1990	2002	% change 1990-2002	1992	2002	% change 1992-2002	1990-1991	2001-2002	% change 1990-2002	1990-1991	2001-2002	% change 1990-2002	
High income economies																			
Australia	0.888	0.946	7	18,264	28,260	55	0.8	0.6	-25	78	79	2	99	96	-3	95	101	6	35
Brunei		0.867			19,210		0.9	0.6	-36	75	76	2	91		0				
Korea, Rep.	0.815	0.888	9	9,052	16,950	87	1.2	0.5	-59	71	75	6	104	101	-3	94	100	6	32
Japan	0.909	0.938	3	20,788	26,940	30	0.5	0.3	-35	79	82	3	100	101	1	95	100	5	25
New Zealand	0.875	0.926	6	14,249	21,740	53	0.8	0.6	-28	76	78	3	101	98	-3	94	99	5	36
Singapore	0.818	0.902	10	13,492	24,040	78	0.7	0.3	-55	75	78	4				90			43
Europe & Central Asia																			
Low income economies																			
Armenia	0.759	0.754	-1	1,736	3,120	80	1.9	3.0	61	72	72	1		85			99		38
Azerbaijan		0.746		2,313	3,210	39	2.3	7.4	222	70	72	4		80		94	98	4	37
Georgia		0.739		1,905	2,260	19	1.6	2.4	51	73	74	1		91		96	100	4	37
Kyrgyzstan		0.701		1,630	1,620	-1	3.0	5.2	73	68	68	0		90		99	96	-3	29
Moldova	0.759	0.681	-10	1,937	1,470	-24	3.9	2.7	-31	68	69	1		78		97	99	2	36
Tajikistan	0.740	0.671	-9	1,258	980	-22	4.1	5.3	30	68	69	1		105		96	95	-1	35
Ukraine	0.795	0.777	-2	6,229	4,870	-22	1.3	1.6	24	69	70	1		82		96	100	4	29
Uzbekistan	0.731	0.709	-3	1,343	1,670	24	3.5	5.2	50		70					96			27
Middle income economies																			
Albania	0.702	0.781	11	1,893	4,830	155	2.8	2.6	-8	71	74	3		97		93	100	8	28
Belarus	0.809	0.79	-2	4,098	5,520	35	1.2	1.7	43	70	70	0		94			98		30
Bosnia & Herzegovina		0.781			5,970		1.5	1.5	-2	72	74	2							26
Bulgaria	0.786	0.796	1	5,092	7,130	40	1.5	1.4	-5	71	71	-1	86	93	8	93	98	5	32
Croatia	0.797	0.83	4	6,215	10,240	65	1.1	0.7	-35	71	74	4	79	88	11	94	98	4	29
Czech Republic	0.835	0.868	4	10,061	15,780	57	1.1	0.4	-64	72	75	4		88		96	100	4	25
Estonia		0.853		6,085	12,260	101	1.2	1.0	-19	69	72	4		98		94	98	4	37
Hungary	0.804	0.848	5	8,190	13,400	64	1.5	0.8	-46	69	72	4	91	91	0	95	99	4	24
Kazakhstan		0.766		4,214	5,870	39	2.6	6.1	132	68	66	-2		90			99		31
Latvia	0.804	0.823	2	4,756	9,210	94	1.4	1.7	24	68	71	4	83	91	10	96	99	3	32
Lithuania	0.816	0.842	3	7,316	10,320	41	1.0	0.8	-22	70	73	3		97		90	99	10	32
Macedonia		0.793		5,852	6,470	11	3.2	2.2	-30	72	74	2	94	93	-1	93	100	8	28
Poland	0.792	0.85	7	5,828	10,560	81	1.9	0.8	-59	71	74	4	97	98	1	95	100	5	32

Country	Human Development Index (HDI)			GDP per capita, PPP in current international $			Infant mortality rate (% live births)			Life expectancy at birth (years)			Net primary school enrolment ratio (%)			Ratio of girls to boys in primary education (%)			Income inequality (Gini index)* see note below
	value 1990	value 2002	% change 1990–2002	1992	2002	% change 1992–2002	1990	2002	% change 1990–2002	1992	2002	% change 1992–2002	1990–1991	2001–2002	% change 1990–2002	1990–1991	2001–2002	% change 1990–2002	
Romania	0.777	0.778	0	4,631	6,560	42	2.7	1.9	-29	70	71	1	77	93	21	96	99	3	30
Russian Federation	0.824	0.795	-4	7,266	8,230	13	1.7	1.8	3	67	67	0				97			46
Slovakia	0.820	0.842	3	7,634	12,840	68	1.2	0.8	-33	72	74	3		87			102		26
Slovenia	0.845	0.895	6	10,414	18,540	78	0.8	0.4	-52	73	76	4		93			99		28
Turkey	0.686	0.751	9	4,686	6,390	36	5.8	3.6	-38	67	70	6	89	88	-1	89	93	4	40
Turkmenistan		0.752		4,205	4,300	2	4.5	7.6	68	66	67	2							41
High income economies																			
Austria	0.890	0.934	5	20,453	29,220	43	0.8	0.5	-36	76	79	3	90	91	1	95	101	6	30
Belgium	0.896	0.942	5	19,762	27,570	40	0.8	0.5	-37	76	79	3	97	101	4	97	100	3	25
Cyprus	0.845	0.883	4	11,447	18,360	60	1.1	0.5	-55	77	78	2	87	95	9	93	101	9	
Denmark	0.891	0.932	5	21,253	30,940	46	0.8	0.4	-47	75	77	2	98	99	1	96	100	4	25
Finland	0.896	0.935	4	17,312	26,190	51	0.6	0.4	-29	75	78	3	99	100	1	95	100	5	27
France	0.897	0.932	4	19,401	26,920	39	0.7	0.4	-45	77	79	2	101	100	-1	94	100	6	33
Germany	0.885	0.925	5	20,204	27,100	34	0.7	0.4	-43	76	78	3	84	83	-1		102		28
Greece	0.859	0.902	5	12,213	18,720	53	1.0	0.5	-48	77	78	1	94	95	1	94	100	6	35
Iceland	0.913	0.941	3	19,821	29,750	50	0.6	0.3	-49	78	80	2		101			100		
Ireland	0.870	0.936	8	13,861	36,360	162	0.8	0.6	-27	76	77	1	91	94	3	95	101	6	36
Italy	0.879	0.92	5	19,289	26,430	37	0.8	0.4	-51	77	79	2		100		95	100	5	36
Luxembourg	0.884	0.933	6	29,174	61,190	110	0.7	0.5	-32	76	78	3		96		103	100	-3	31
Netherlands	0.902	0.942	4	19,485	29,100	49	0.7	0.5	-30	77	78	1	95	100	5	99	99	0	33
Norway	0.901	0.956	6	23,914	36,600	53	0.7	0.4	-42	77	79	2	100	101	1	95	100	5	26
Portugal	0.819	0.897	10	12,125	18,280	51	1.1	0.5	-54	74	76	3	102			91			39
Spain	0.876	0.922	5	14,180	21,460	51	0.8	0.4	-47	77	79	2	103	104	1	94	99	5	33
Sweden	0.894	0.946	6	17,951	26,050	45	0.6	0.3	-50	78	80	3	100	102	2	95	100	5	25
Switzerland	0.905	0.936	3	24,223	30,010	24	0.7	0.5	-26	78	79	2	84	99	18	96	99	3	33
United Kingdom	0.878	0.936	7	17,134	26,150	53	0.8	0.5	-37	76	78	2	97	101	4	96	100	4	36
Latin America & Caribbean																			
Low income economies																			
Haiti	0.447	0.463	4	1,860	1,610	-13	10.2	7.9	-23	53	49	-8	22			93			
Nicaragua	0.592	0.667	13	3,261	2,470	-24	5.1	3.2	-37	66	69	5	72	82	14	104	101	-3	55
Middle income economies																			
Argentina	0.808	0.853	6	9,227	10,880	18	2.5	1.6	-37	72	74	3		108			100		52

Country	Human Development Index (HDI)			GDP per capita, PPP in current international $			Infant mortality rate (% live births)			Life expectancy at birth (years)			Net primary school enrolment ratio (%)			Ratio of girls to boys in primary education (%)			Income inequality (Gini index)* see note below
	value 1990	value 2002	% change 1990-2002	1992	2002	% change 1992-2002	1990	2002	% change 1990-2002	1992	2002	% change 1992-2002	1990-1991	2001-2002	% change 1990-2002	1990-1991	2001-2002	% change 1990-2002	
Barbados		0.888		10,574	15,290	45	1.2	1.2	3	75	77	2	78	103	32		100		
Belize	0.750	0.737	-2	4,312	6,080	41	3.5	3.4	-2	73	72	-2	98	96	-2	94	100	6	
Bolivia	0.597	0.681	14	1,839	2,460	34	8.0	5.6	-30	59	64	7	91	94	3	90	100	11	45
Brazil	0.713	0.775	9	5,418	7,770	43	4.8	3.0	-37	66	68	3	86	97	13		102		59
Chile	0.782	0.839	7	5,817	9,820	69	1.6	1.0	-38	74	76	2	88	89	1	95	99	4	57
Colombia	0.724	0.773	7	5,228	6,370	22	3.0	1.9	-38	69	72	5		87		111	99	-11	58
Costa Rica	0.787	0.834	6	5,797	8,840	52	1.5	0.9	-39	77	78	2	86	91	6	94	102	9	47
Cuba		0.809			5,259		1.1	0.7	-35	75	77	2	92	96	4	93	99	6	
Dominican Republic	0.677	0.738	9	3,710	6,640	79	5.0	3.2	-36	67	67	0		97			96		47
Ecuador	0.705	0.735	4	2,962	3,580	21	4.5	2.5	-45	69	71	3		102			101		44
El Salvador	0.644	0.72	12	3,341	4,890	46	4.6	3.3	-28	67	71	5	75	89	19		100		53
Guatemala	0.579	0.649	12	3,062	4,080	33	5.6	3.6	-36	63	66	5		85			95		48
Guyana	0.680	0.719	6	3,102	4,260	37	5.9	5.4	-8	65	63	-2	93	98	5	97	97	0	43
Honduras	0.615	0.672	9	2,195	2,600	18	5.0	3.2	-36	65	69	5	89	87	-2	99	102	3	55
Jamaica	0.720	0.764	6	3,322	3,980	20	2.5	1.7	-33	74	76	2	96	95	-1	99	100	1	38
Mexico	0.761	0.802	5	6,728	8,970	33	3.6	2.4	-34	71	73	3	100	101	1	94	101	7	55
Panama	0.747	0.791	6	4,500	6,170	37	2.6	1.9	-27	73	75	2	91	99	9	92	100	9	56
Paraguay	0.717	0.751	5	4,153	4,610	11	3.1	2.6	-17	68	71	3	93	92	-1	93	101	9	57
Peru	0.704	0.752	7	3,281	5,010	53	5.4	3.0	-44	67	70	4		100			100		50
St. Lucia		0.777		4,678	5,300	13	1.9	1.7	-11	72	72	1		103		95	98	3	43
Suriname		0.78			6,590		3.4	3.1	-9	69	71	3		97		96	101	5	
Trinidad & Tobago	0.781	0.801	3	5,973	9,430	58	1.8	1.7	-4	72	71	0	91	94	3	97	100	3	40
Uruguay	0.801	0.833	4	6,703	7,830	17	2.1	1.4	-34	73	75	3	91	90	-1	95	101	6	45
Venezuela	0.757	0.778	3	5,573	5,380	-3	2.5	1.9	-23	72	74	3	88	92	5	99	101	2	49
High income economies															0				
Bahamas	0.822	0.815	-1	13,648	17,280	27	2.8	1.3	-54	69	67	-3	96	86	-10		103		
Middle East & North Africa																			
Low income economies																			
Yemen	0.399	0.482	21	563	870	55	11.0	7.9	-28	53	60	14		67			66		33
Middle income economies																			
Algeria	0.639	0.704	10	4,571	5,760	26	4.6	3.9	-15	68	70	2	93	95	2	81	97	20	35
Djibouti		0.454			1,990		12	10.0	-17	48	46	-5	32	34	6	71	77	8	

Country	Human Development Index (HDI)			GDP per capita, PPP in current international $			Infant mortality rate (% live births)			Life expectancy at birth (years)			Net primary school enrolment ratio (%)			Ratio of girls to boys in primary education (%)			Income inequality (Gini index)* see note below
	value 1990	value 2002	% change 1990-2002	1992	2002	% change 1992-2002	1990	2002	% change 1990-2002	1992	2002	% change 1992-2002	1990-1991	2001-2002	% change 1990-2002	1990-1991	2001-2002	% change 1990-2002	
Egypt	0.574	0.653	14	2,505	3,810	52	6.8	3.5	-48	64	69	7		90		80	96	20	34
Iran	0.645	0.732	13	4,524	6,690	48	5.4	3.5	-35	66	70	7		87		86	98	14	43
Iraq							4.0			59			79			80			
Jordan	0.677	0.75	11	3,468	4,220	22	3.0	2.7	-10	70	71	2	66	91	38	94	101	7	36
Lebanon	0.680	0.758	11	3,052	4,360	43	3.6	2.8	-23	69	74	7		90			99		
Libya		0.794			7,570		3.3	1.6	-51	69	73	5	97			91			
Malta	0.826	0.875	6	10,374	17,640	70	0.9	0.5	-45	76	78	3	99	98	-1	92	101	10	
Morocco & Western Sahara	0.540	0.62	15	2,864	3,810	33	6.6	3.9	-41	64	69	6	58	88	52	66	93	41	40
Oman		0.77		10,207	13,340	31	2.2	1.1	-50	70	72	4	70	75	7	89	101	13	
Palestinian Authority		0.726						2.3		72				95	0		101		
Saudi Arabia	0.706	0.768	9	11,244	12,650	13	3.2	2.3	-28	70	72	3	59	59	0	84	92	10	
Syria	0.634	0.71	12	2,622	3,620	38	3.9	2.3	-41	67	72	6	98	98	0	87	95	9	
Tunisia	0.646	0.745	15	4,278	6,760	58	3.7	2.1	-44	71	73	3	94	97	3	85	99	16	40
High income economies																			
Bahrain		0.843		11,824	17,170	45	2.3	1.3	-43	72	74	3	99	91	-8	95	101	6	
Israel	0.855	0.908	6	14,124	19,530	38	1.0	0.6	-39	76	79	3		100		98	100	2	36
Kuwait		0.838			16,240		1.4	0.9	-34	75	77	2	45	85	89	92	99	8	
Qatar		0.833			19,844		2.1	1.1	-48	73	72	-1	87	94	8	91	98	8	
United Arab Emirates		0.824		20,423	22,420	10	2.0	0.8	-60	74	75	1	94	81	-14	93	97	4	
North America																			
High income economies																			
Canada	0.926	0.943	2	19,447	29,480	52	0.7	0.5	-26	77	79	3	97	100	3	93	100	8	33
United States	0.914	0.939	3	24,865	35,750	44	0.9	0.7	-26	76	77	2	96	93	-3	94	101	7	41
South Asia																			
Low income economies																			
Afghanistan							17			42						52			
Bangladesh	0.416	0.509	22	1,059	1,700	61	9.1	5.1	-44	56	61	9	64	87	36	81	102	26	32
Bhutan		0.536			1,969			7.4		58	63	9							
India	0.511	0.595	16	1,506	2,670	77	8.0	6.7	-16	60	64	6		83		71	83	17	33
Nepal	0.416	0.504	21	941	1,370	46	10.1	6.6	-35	55	60	9		70		56	88	57	37

Country	Human Development Index (HDI)			GDP per capita, PPP in current international $			Infant mortality rate (% live births)			Life expectancy at birth (years)			Net primary school enrolment ratio (%)			Ratio of girls to boys in primary education (%)			Income inequality (Gini index)* see note below
	value 1990	value 2002	% change 1990-2002	1992	2002	% change 1992-2002	1990	2002	% change 1990-2002	1992	2002	% change 1992-2002	1990-1991	2001-2002	% change 1990-2002	1990-1991	2001-2002	% change 1990-2002	
Pakistan	0.442	0.497	12	1,499	1,940	29	11.0	8.3	-25	60	61	2				48			33
Middle income economies																			
Maldives	0.676	0.752	11		4,798		6.0	5.8	-3	63	67	7		96			101		
Sri Lanka	0.697	0.74	6	2,178	3,570	64	1.9	1.7	-8	71	73	2		105		93	100	8	34
Sub-Saharan Africa																			
Low income economies																			
Angola		0.381		2,376	2,130	-10	13.0	15.4	18	46	40	-14		30		92	86	-7	
Benin	0.358	0.421	18	726	1,070	47	10.4	9.3	-11	53	51	-4	49	71	45	50	69	38	
Burkina Faso	0.290	0.302	4	779	1,100	41	11.1	10.7	-3	45	46	2	27	35	30	62	71	15	48
Burundi	0.344	0.339	-1	765	630	-18	11.9	11.4	-4	42	41	-2	52	53	2	84	82	-2	33
Cameroon	0.513	0.501	-2	1,588	2,000	26	8.1	9.5	17	55	47	-15				85			45
Central African Republic	0.372	0.361	-3	958	1,170	22	10.2	11.5	13	48	40	-16	53			65			61
Chad	0.322	0.379	18	877	1,020	16	11.8	11.7	-1	47	45	-4		58		45	67	49	
Comoros	0.502	0.53	6	1,604	1,690	5	8.4	5.9	-30	57	61	5		55		71	84	18	
Congo, Dem. Rep.		0.365		981	650	-34	8.4	12.9	54	52	41	-20	54	35	-35	74	95	28	
Congo, Rep.	0.510	0.494	-3	786	980	25	8.2	8.1	-1	51	48	-5				90			
Côte d'Ivoire	0.415	0.399	-4	1,429	1,520	6	9.5	10.2	7	49	41	-16	47	63	34	71	74	4	45
Equatorial Guinea	0.553	0.703	27	1,135	30,130	2,555	12.1	10.1	-17	48	49	2		85			85		
Eritrea		0.439		582	890	53	8.1	4.7	-42	50	53	6		43		95	86	-9	
Ethiopia	0.297	0.359	21	424	780	84	13.1	11.4	-13	45	46	1		46		66	79	20	30
Gambia		0.452		1,434	1,690	18	10.9	9.1	-16	51	54	6	51	73	43	68	92	35	38
Ghana	0.506	0.568	12	1,465	2,130	45	6.6	5.7	-14	58	58	0		60		82	96	17	30
Guinea		0.425		1,493	2,100	41	12.1	10.9	-10	44	49	10		61		46	78	70	40
Guinea-Bissau	0.304	0.35	15	793	710	-10	14.5	13.0	-10	43	45	5		45			71		47
Kenya	0.533	0.488	-8	932	1,020	9	6.2	7.8	26	57	45	-20		70		95	102	7	45
Lesotho	0.574	0.493	-14	1,305	2,420	85	10.2	6.4	-37	58	36	-38	73	84	15	121	108	-11	63
Liberia							16.8			39									
Madagascar	0.434	0.469	8	742	740	0	10.3	8.4	-18	53	53	1		69		97	101	4	48
Malawi	0.362	0.388	7	437	580	33	12.8	11.4	-11	44	38	-14	50	81	62	82	100	22	50
Mali	0.312	0.326	4	609	930	53	13.6	12.2	-10	44	49	10	21	38	81	59	72	22	51
Mauritania	0.390	0.465	19	1,308	2,220	70	11.2	12.0	7	49	52	6		67		73	96	32	39

Country	Human Development Index (HDI)			GDP per capita, PPP in current international $			Infant mortality rate (% live births)			Life expectancy at birth (years)			Net primary school enrolment ratio (%)			Ratio of girls to boys in primary education (%)			Income inequality (Gini index)* see note below
	value 1990	value 2002	% change 1990–2002	1992	2002	% change 1992–2002	1990	2002	% change 1990–2002	1992	2002	% change 1992–2002	1990–1991	2001–2002	% change 1990–2002	1990–1991	2001–2002	% change 1990–2002	
Mozambique	0.310	0.354	14	528	1,050	99	15.0	12.5	-17	43	39	-11	47	60	28	76	88	16	40
Niger	0.256	0.292	14	686	800	17	15.0	15.6	4	43	46	8	25	34	36	57	68	19	51
Nigeria	0.425	0.466	10	772	860	11	8.6	11.0	27	50	52	4				76			51
Rwanda	0.346	0.431	25	1,012	1,270	25	13.2	9.6	-27	35	39	12	66	84	27	99	103	4	29
São Tomé & Principe		0.645			1,317		6.1	7.5	23	63	70	11		98			94		
Senegal	0.380	0.437	15	1,165	1,580	36	7.4	7.9	7	50	53	5	48	58	21	72	89	24	41
Sierra Leone		0.273		727	520	-28	19.0	16.5	-13	34	34	0				70			0
Somalia							15.2			39									
Sudan	0.419	0.505	21	1,176	1,820	55	9.8	6.4	-34	53	56	5		46		75	83	11	
Tanzania	0.422	0.407	-4	439	580	32	11.5	10.4	-9	49	44	-12	51	54	6	98	100	2	38
Togo	0.465	0.495	6	1,315	1,480	13	8.1	7.9	-2	50	50	0	75	95	27	65	84	29	
Uganda	0.388			780			10.4	8.2	-21	46						80			
Zambia	0.468	0.389	-17	781	840	8	10.7	10.8	1	49	33	-33		66			99		53
Zimbabwe	0.597	0.491	-18	2,162	2,400	11	5.2	7.6	47	56	34	-39		83		99	101	2	57
Middle income economies																			
Botswana	0.653	0.589	-10	4,860	8,170	68	5.5	8.0	47	54	41	-23	93	81	-13	107	104	-3	63
Cape Verde	0.626	0.717	15	2,884	5,000	73	6.4	2.9	-55	66	70	6		101			99		
Gabon		0.648		5,271	6,590	25	7.2	6.0	-16	52	57	8		78			99		
Mauritius	0.723	0.785	9	6,084	10,810	78	2.0	1.7	-17	70	72	3	95	93	-2	98	100	2	
Namibia		0.607		5,055	6,210	23	6.4	5.5	-14	59	45	-23	89	78	-12	108	106	-2	71
South Africa	0.714	0.666	-7	7,943	10,070	27	5.5	5.2	-5	63	49	-22	103	90	-13	98	101	3	59
Swaziland	0.615	0.519	-16	3,539	4,550	29	7.9	10.6	35	58	36	-38	88	77	-13	99	101	2	61

Region	Human Development Index (HDI)	GDP per capita, PPP in current international $			Infant mortality rate (% live births)	Life expectancy at birth (years)		
	value 2002	value 1992	value 12002	% change 1992-2002	value 2002	value 1992	value 2002	% change 1992-2002
Low income	0.557	1,260	2,149	71	12.6	57	59	4
Middle income	0.756	3,530	5,908	67	8.5	68	70	3
Low & middle income:								
East Asia & Pacific	0.740	1,890	4,768	152	8.4	68	70	3
Europe & Central Asia	0.796	5,630	7,192	28	3.4	68	70	1
Latin America & Caribbean	0.777	5,420	7,223	33	8.6	69	71	3
Middle East & North Africa	0.651	4,190	5,069	21	12.8	65	66	2
South Asia	0.584	1,450	2,658	83	12.9	59	63	6
Sub-Saharan Africa	0.465	1,420	1,790	26	13.9	50	46	-7
High income	0.933	19,900	28,741	44	2.2	76	78	3
World	0.729	5,460	7,804	43	9.6	66	67	2

* Survey year for Gini index varies by country. 0 represents perfect equality, 100 represents perfect inequality.

** Data for China & Tibet excludes Hong Kong and Macao.

Sources: Human Development Report 2004, Cultural Liberty in Today's Diverse World, New York: Oxford University Press; http://hdr.undp.org/reports/global/2004/; World Development Indicators 2005 (WDI Online), http://devdata.worldbank.org/dataonline/

Record 12: Corruption

This record examines the state of the rule of law through the prism of corruption. Corruption not only hinders economic development; it inhibits the formation of trust and social capital. Therefore it is likely to be an obstacle to the growth of civil society generally, as well as a focus of civil society activism, both locally and globally. The table presents four types of indicators of corruption. The first three are the Corruption Perceptions Index by Transparency International, the Bribing and Corruption Index, and the Transparency of Government index, the latter two by the Institute for Management Development. For these indicators scores range between 10, indicating high transparency and the absence of bribery and corruption and zero, indicating lack of transparency and high levels of perceived corruption and bribery. The fourth indicator, Control of Corruption Index, which was developed by the World Bank Institute researchers in their project Governance Matters, measures perceptions of corruption, conventionally defined as the exercise of public power for private gain. A higher score in this index represents better control of corruption (a detailed explanation of the index appears in www.worldbank.org/wbi/governance/pdf/govmatters3_wber.pdf). High-income countries tend to score better on all corruption indices in the table. More than half of the countries in the table show a decrease in their control of corruption scores, which is more often true for developing countries, but is apparent also among high-income countries.

Country	Corruption Perceptions Index		Bribing and corruption		Transparency of government		Control of Corruption Index		
	2000	2004	2000	2005	2000	2005	1998	2004	% change 1998-2004
East Asia & Pacific									
Low income economies									
Cambodia							2.7	13.3	393
Indonesia	1.7	2.0	1.3	1.1	5.0	2.7	6.6	17.7	168
Korea, Dem. Rep.							33.9	2.0	-94
Laos							24.6	6.9	-72
Mongolia		3.0					54.6	39.9	-27
Myanmar		1.7					2.2	1.0	-55
Papua New Guinea		2.6					24.0	17.7	-26
Vietnam	2.5	2.6					28.4	27.1	-5
Middle income economies									
China & Tibet*	3.1	3.4	2.2	1.5	6.3	4.4	57.9	39.9	-31
Malaysia	4.8	5.0	3.2	3.4	6.4	5.2	80.9	64.5	-20
Micronesia							48.6	47.8	-2
Philippines	2.8	2.6	1.6	1.0	3.3	2.9	45.9	36.5	-20
Samoa							48.6	59.1	22
Thailand	3.2	3.6	2.0	2.7	4.3	4.7	61.2	49.3	-19
Tonga							48.6	31.5	-35
High income economies									
Australia	8.3	8.8	8.2	8.3	6.9	6.9	93.4	94.1	1
Brunei							66.7	63.1	-5

Country	Corruption Perceptions Index		Bribing and corruption		Transparency of government		Control of Corruption Index		
	2000	2004	2000	2005	2000	2005	1998	2004	% change 1998-2004
Fiji							70.5	54.2	-23
Japan	6.4	6.9	5.3	5.6	3.7	3.7	86.9	86.2	-1
Korea, Rep.	4.0	4.5	2.6		3.7		69.9	62.1	-11
New Zealand	9.4	9.6	8.8	8.5	6.6	6.8	97.8	98.0	0
Singapore	9.1	9.3	8.7	8.2	8.4	7.0	97.3	99.5	2
Europe & Central Asia									
Low income economies									
Armenia	2.5	3.1					23.0	37.4	63
Azerbaijan	1.5	1.9					5.5	10.8	96
Cyprus		5.4					87.4	79.3	-9
Georgia		2.0					27.3	16.3	-40
Kyrgyzstan		2.2					26.2	15.3	-42
Malta		6.8					78.7	87.7	11
Moldova	2.6	2.3					38.3	21.2	-45
Tajikistan		2.0					3.8	8.9	134
Ukraine	1.5	2.2					12.0	18.7	56
Uzbekistan	2.4	2.3					7.7	5.9	-23
Middle income economies									
Albania		2.5					9.8	29.1	197
Belarus	4.1	3.3					29.5	16.3	-45
Bosnia & Herzegovina		3.1					45.4	36.9	-19
Bulgaria	3.5	4.1					39.9	56.2	41
Croatia	3.7	3.5					46.4	60.1	30
Czech Republic	4.3	4.2	1.8	2.7	3.2	2.6	73.2	66.0	-10
Estonia	5.7	6.0		5.7		5.8	76.5	80.3	5
Hungary	5.2	4.8	3.3	3.1	5.2	4.1	79.8	74.4	-7
Kazakhstan	3.0	2.2					13.1	9.9	-24
Latvia	3.4	4.0					61.7	63.1	2
Lithuania	4.1	4.6					67.8	69.0	2
Macedonia		2.7					48.1	38.4	-20
Poland	4.1	3.5	2.9	1.1	3.4	2.2	77.0	61.6	-20
Romania	2.9	2.9		1.0		4.2	44.3	49.3	11
Russian Federation	2.1	2.8	1.9	0.6	2.5	2.7	26.8	29.1	9
Serbia & Montenegro	1.3	2.7					8.2	42.4	417

Country	Corruption Perceptions Index		Bribing and corruption		Transparency of government		Control of Corruption Index		
	2000	2004	2000	2005	2000	2005	1998	2004	% change 1998-2004
Slovakia	3.5	4.0		2.3		5.6	62.8	70.0	11
Slovenia	5.5	6.0	3.7	3.1	3.1	3.7	82.5	83.3	1
Turkey	3.8	3.2	2.6	3.4	6.0	5.0	65.6	50.7	-23
Turkmenistan		2.0					3.3	3.4	3
High income economies									
Austria	7.7	8.4	6.7	7.3	5.3	6.0	91.8	95.6	4
Belgium	6.1	7.5	5.0	6.2	5.9	4.1	86.3	90.1	4
Denmark	9.8	9.5	9.2	9.1	5.5	7.4	99.5	98.0	-2
Finland	10.0	9.7	9.5	9.4	7.6	7.8	98.9	100.0	1
France	6.7	7.1	5.0	6.1	5.8	4.4	90.7	88.7	-2
Germany	7.6	8.2	5.4	6.5	4.5	4.3	94.0	93.1	-1
Greece	4.9	4.3	2.4	2.6	5.5	4.3	83.1	72.9	-12
Iceland	9.1	9.5	8.5	9.3	6.8	6.1	95.1	99.0	4
Ireland	7.2	7.5	6.5	5.7	7.5	5.9	92.3	91.1	-1
Italy	4.6	4.8	2.8	2.9	3.8	3.3	84.7	74.9	-12
Luxembourg	8.6	8.4	7.2	6.4	6.9	5.8	92.9	96.6	4
Netherlands	8.9	8.7	7.8	7.0	7.3	5.9	96.2	95.1	-1
Norway	9.1	8.9	8.3	6.9	5.3	6.3	95.6	96.1	1
Portugal	6.4	6.3	4.3	4.1	5.4	3.6	89.1	86.7	-3
Spain	7.0	7.1	5.3	5.4	6.9	4.1	89.6	89.7	0
Sweden	9.4	9.2	8.4	7.7	4.2	4.9	98.4	97.5	-1
Switzerland	8.6	9.1	7.5	7.7	6.1	6.6	100.0	97.0	-3
United Kingdom	8.7	8.6	7.6	6.8	5.8	3.8	94.5	94.6	0
Latin America & Caribbean									
Low income economies									
Antigua & Barbuda								81.3	
Barbados		7.3						79.8	
Haiti		1.5					13.7	1.0	-93
Nicaragua		2.7					25.7	46.3	80
Middle income economies									
Argentina	3.5	2.5	1.5	0.8	5.2	1.6	59.6	42.9	-28
Belize		3.8					48.6	54.7	13
Bolivia	2.7	2.2					42.1	25.1	-40
Brazil	3.9	3.9	2.6	2.7	5.3	4.0	68.9	53.2	-23

Country	Corruption Perceptions Index		Bribing and corruption		Transparency of government		Control of Corruption Index		
	2000	2004	2000	2005	2000	2005	1998	2004	% change 1998-2004
Chile	7.4	7.4	6.3	6.1	5.6	6.6	85.8	88.7	3
Colombia	3.2	3.8	1.6	2.4	5.0	5.4	30.6	52.2	71
Costa Rica	5.4	4.9					80.3	77.3	-4
Cuba		3.7					53.6	33.0	-38
Dominican Republic		2.9					37.7	41.4	10
Ecuador	2.6	2.4					19.1	26.6	39
El Salvador	4.1	4.2					47.5	43.8	-8
Grenada							63.4	71.9	13
Guatemala		2.2					23.5	27.1	15
Guyana							55.2	44.8	-19
Honduras		2.3					21.9	30.0	37
Jamaica		3.3					55.7	38.4	-31
Mexico	3.3	3.6	2.1	1.8	5.5	4.8	41.0	48.8	19
Panama		3.7					54.1	55.2	2
Paraguay		1.9					9.3	12.8	38
Peru	4.4	3.5					58.5	44.8	-23
St. Kitts & Nevis							63.4	67.5	6
St. Lucia							63.4	64.5	2
St. Vincent & The Grenadines							63.4	67.5	6
Suriname		4.3					66.7	69.0	3
Trinidad & Tobago		4.2					69.4	58.1	-16
Uruguay		6.2					74.9	71.4	-5
Venezuela	2.7	2.3	1.4	0.7	2.4	0.7	21.3	14.3	-33
High income economies									
Bahamas							78.7	88.2	12
Middle East & North Africa									
Low income economies									
Yemen		2.4					32.8	22.7	-31
Middle income economies									
Algeria		2.7					25.1	41.9	67
Djibouti							15.8	14.3	-9
Egypt	3.1	3.2					56.3	51.2	-9
Iran		2.9					27.9	35.0	25
Iraq		2.1					1.6	2.5	56

Country	Corruption Perceptions Index		Bribing and corruption		Transparency of government		Control of Corruption Index		
	2000	2004	2000	2005	2000	2005	1998	2004	% change 1998-2004
Jordan	4.6	5.3		4.7		4.9	71.6	68.5	-4
Lebanon		2.7					47.0	39.9	-15
Libya		2.5					10.9	16.3	50
Morocco	4.7	3.2					62.3	56.7	-9
Oman		6.1					83.6	77.3	-8
Palestinian Authority		2.5						34.5	
Saudi Arabia		3.4					72.7	61.1	-16
Syria		3.4					31.7	27.1	-15
Tunisia	5.2	5.0					68.3	64.5	-6
High income economies									
Bahrain		5.8					73.8	76.8	4
Israel	6.6	6.4	6.0	4.9	5.5	5.3	88.0	78.8	-10
Kuwait		4.6					85.2	76.4	-10
Qatar		5.2					82.0	72.4	-12
United Arab Emirates		6.1					81.4	86.7	7
North America									
High income economies									
Canada	9.2	8.5	8.3	7.0	6.9	5.7	96.7	93.6	-3
United States	7.8	7.5	6.8	6.4	6.2	5.6	91.3	92.6	1
South Asia									
Low income economies									
Afghanistan								3.9	
Bangladesh		1.5					43.7	10.3	-76
Bhutan							75.4	75.4	0
India	2.8	2.8	1.5	1.7	5.0	4.3	60.1	47.3	-21
Nepal		2.8					30.1	33.5	11
Pakistan		2.1					20.2	20.2	0
Middle income economies									
Maldives							34.4	60.6	76
Sri Lanka		3.5					57.4	52.2	-9
Sub-Saharan Africa									
Low income economies									
Angola	1.7	2.0					4.9	8.4	71
Benin		3.2					19.7	46.3	135

Country	Corruption Perceptions Index		Bribing and corruption		Transparency of government		Control of Corruption Index		
	2000	2004	2000	2005	2000	2005	1998	2004	% change 1998-2004
Burkina Faso	3						38.8	44.8	15
Burundi							15.8	6.4	-59
Cameroon	2.0	2.1					4.4	25.1	470
Central African Republic							34.4	3.0	-91
Chad		1.7					14.2	7.4	-48
Comoros							15.8	7.4	-53
Congo, Dem. Rep.		2.0						4.4	
Congo, Rep.		2.3					7.1	11.3	59
Côte d'Ivoire	2.7	2.0					44.8	11.8	-74
Equatorial Guinea							15.8	0.0	-100
Eritrea		2.6					75.4	32.5	-57
Ethiopia	3.2	2.3					56.8	22.2	-61
Gambia		2.8					40.4	33.5	-17
Ghana	3.5	3.6					43.2	51.7	20
Guinea							14.8	24.1	63
Guinea-Bissau							32.2	30.0	-7
Kenya	2.1	2.1					10.4	18.7	80
Lesotho							66.1	55.7	-16
Liberia							0.5	21.2	4,140
Madagascar		3.1					15.3	53.2	248
Malawi	4.1	2.8					39.3	23.6	-40
Mali		3.2					31.1	38.4	23
Mauritania							48.6	58.1	20
Mozambique	2.2	2.8					18.6	24.6	32
Niger		2.2					12.6	20.2	60
Nigeria	1.2	1.6					6.0	8.9	48
Rwanda							34.4	44.3	29
São Tomé & Principe							15.8	32.0	103
Senegal	3.5	3.0					41.5	43.3	4
Sierra Leone		2.3					22.4	19.7	-12
Somalia							0.5	0.5	0
Sudan		2.2					20.8	4.9	-76
Tanzania	2.5	2.8					8.7	36.0	314
Togo							42.6	15.3	-64

Uganda	2.3	2.6					29.0	30.0	3
Zambia	3.4	2.6					33.3	27.1	-19
Zimbabwe	3.0	2.3					60.7	11.8	-81
Middle income economies									
Botswana	6.0	6.0					78.1	80.8	3
Cape Verde							48.6	66.5	37
Gabon		3.3					11.5	35.5	209
Mauritius	4.7	4.1					71.0	67.0	-6
Namibia	5.4	4.1					72.1	62.6	-13
South Africa	5.0	4.6	2.7	2.9	6.0	6.2	74.3	70.9	-5
Swaziland							59.0	13.8	-77

*China & Tibet excludes Hong Kong and Macao

Sources: Transparency International, 2000 Corruption Perceptions Index, www.transparency.org/cpi/2000/cpi2000.html; Transparency International, 2004 Corruption Perceptions Index, http://www.globalcorruptionreport.org/download.html; International Institute for Management Development (2000), The World Competitiveness Yearbook 1999, Institute for Management Development, Lausanne, Switzerland; International Institute for Management Development (2004), Tables 2.3.13 'Transparency' and 2.3.16 'Bribing and Corruption', The World Competitiveness Yearbook 2004, Institute for Management Development, Lausanne, Switzerland; World Bank Institute, Governance Indicators 1996–2004, http://www.worldbank.org/wbi/governance/data.html

Record 13: Refugee populations and flows

This record shows two dimensions of the refugee problem: if a country 'generates' many refugees or internally displaced persons (IDPs), it can be assumed that there is little respect for the international rule of law in that country. On the other hand, countries that host many refugees can be considered as extending international hospitality and bearing the associated financial burden. The table presents data on refugee populations, both in total counts and per 1,000 inhabitants, for 1993 and 2003. In addition, the table provides information on inflows and outflows of refugees during 2003, as well as estimates of IDPs. Negative inflow for a country indicates that there are fewer refugees in that country at the end of the year than at the beginning, while negative outflow indicates that the number of refugees originating from that country decreased over the year.

The table shows that the numbers of refugees across the world decreased in the last decade. Yet refugees are numerous in volatile areas such as Central Asia, Central Africa and the Middle East. Some Western European countries appear as major recipients of refugees, refugees representing more than one per cent of their populations.

| | Refugee populations* | | | | | | IDP populations | | | Refugee flows** | |
| | Total (1000s) | | | per 1000 inhabitants | | | Total (1000s) | | | 2003 (1000s) | |
Country of asylum	1993	2003	% change	1993	2003	% change	2002	2003	% change	Inflow	Outflow
East Asia & Pacific											
Low income economies											
Cambodia	0.0	0.1	100	0.0	0.0	100				-0.1	-2.1
East Timor		0.0			0.0					0.0	-28.0
Indonesia***	2.4	0.2	-930	0.0	0.0	-1,120				-28.4	3.2
Papua New Guinea	7.7	0.0		1.9	0.0						0.0
Vietnam	5.1	15.4	67	0.1	0.2	62				-0.6	-10.5
Middle income economies											
China***	287.4	299.4	4	0.2	0.2	-4				2.1	0.3
Malaysia	0.2	0.4	55	0.0	0.0	44				-50.2	0.1
Philippines	2.5	0.1	-2,215	0.0	0.0	-2,755				0.0	-45.2
Thailand	119.2	119.1	0	2.1	1.9	-12				6.4	-0.1
Tibet											-0.4
High income economies											
Australia	50.6	56.0	10	2.9	2.8	-1				-3.4	0.0
Korea, Rep.	*0.1*	0.0	*-300*	0.0	0.0	-334				0.0	0.0
Japan	6.5	2.3	-187	0.1	0.0	-193				-0.4	0.0
New Zealand	3.9	5.8	33	1.1	1.5	24				0.1	0.0
Singapore	0.0	0.0	100	0.0	0.0	100				0.0	0.0
Europe & Central Asia											
Low income economies											
Armenia	334.0	239.3	-40	103.4	79.7	-30				-8.3	-0.1
Azerbaijan	228.8	0.3	-70,084	30.5	0.0	-73,207	577.2	575.6	0	-0.1	-7.0

| Country of asylum | Refugee populations* | | | | | | IDP populations | | | Refugee flows** | |
| | Total (1000s) | | | per 1000 inhabitants | | | Total (1000s) | | | 2003 (1000s) | |
	1993	2003	% change	1993	2003	% change	2002	2003	% change	Inflow	Outflow
Georgia		3.9			0.8		261.6	260.2	-1	-0.3	-4.5
Kyrgyzstan	21.2	5.6	-279	4.7	1.1	-324				-2.1	0.2
Moldova		0.1			0.0		1.0			-0.1	1.0
Tajikistan	0.3	3.3	91	0.1	0.5	89				-0.1	-4.3
Ukraine	5.2	2.9	-81	0.1	0.1	-67				-0.1	8.9
Uzbekistan	8.0	44.7	82	0.4	1.7	79				-0.3	0.5
Middle income economies											
Albania	3.0	0.0	-11,438	0.9	0.0	-12,041				0.0	-0.4
Belarus	1.8	0.6	-182	0.2	0.1	-181				0.0	1.5
Bosnia & Herzegovina		22.5			5.6		367.5	327.2	-11	-5.5	-108.1
Bulgaria	0.5	4.1	88	0.1	0.5	89				0.4	-0.3
Croatia	287.0	4.4	-6,442	64.0	1.0	-6,459	17.1	12.6	-27	-4.0	-44.6
Czech Republic	0.2	1.5	87	0.0	0.1	87				0.2	-0.3
Hungary	3.0	7.0	57	0.3	0.7	58				0.9	-0.1
Kazakhstan	5.0	15.8	68	0.3	1.0	71				-4.8	0.2
Latvia		0.0			0.0					0.0	0.1
Lithuania		0.4			0.1					0.0	0.2
Macedonia	31.5	0.2	-16,221	16.4	0.1	-17,222	9.4			-2.6	-2.1
Poland	0.8	1.8	56	0.0	0.0	56				0.2	-1.5
Romania	1.2	2.0	40	0.1	0.1	41				0.2	-0.5
Russian Federation		9.9			0.1		371.2	368.2	-1	-5.1	
Serbia & Montenegro	479.1	291.4	-64	45.4	26.9	-68	261.8	256.9	-2	-63.0	-26.7
Slovenia	45.0	2.1	-2,075	22.5	1.0	-2,088				-0.1	-0.2
Turkey	23.3	2.5	-836	0.4	0.0	-976				-0.8	-8.1
Turkmenistan	15.4	13.5	-14	3.9	2.8	-38				-0.2	0.0
High income economies											
Austria	57.7	16.1	-258	7.2	2.0	-266				2.0	0.0
Belgium	24.9	12.6	-98	2.5	1.2	-103				0.0	0.0
Cyprus	0.1	0.3	71	0.1	0.5	69				0.2	0.0
Denmark	44.6	69.9	36	8.6	13.0	34				-3.7	0.0
Finland	8.5	10.8	22	1.7	2.1	19				-1.6	0.0
France	166.3	130.8	-27	2.9	2.2	-33				-1.3	0.0
Germany	1,418.0	960.4	-48	17.5	11.7	-50				-19.6	-0.2
Greece	7.9	2.8	-185	0.8	0.3	-192				0.0	0.0

| Country of asylum | Refugee populations* | | | | | | IDP populations | | | Refugee flows** | |
| | Total (1000s) | | | per 1000 inhabitants | | | Total (1000s) | | | 2003 (1000s) | |
	1993	2003	% change	1993	2003	% change	2002	2003	% change	Inflow	Outflow
Iceland	0.2	0.2	16	0.8	0.8	7				0.0	0.0
Ireland	0.1	6.0	98	0.0	1.5	98				0.6	0.0
Italy	50.3	12.4	-306	0.9	0.2	-313				2.2	0.0
Luxembourg	0.2	1.2	83	0.5	2.6	81				0.0	
Netherlands	43.5	140.9	69	2.8	8.7	67				-7.5	0.0
Norway	38.4	46.1	17	8.9	10.1	12				-4.3	0.0
Portugal	0.6	0.4	-44	0.1	0.0	-51				0.0	0.0
Spain	5.0	5.9	15	0.1	0.1	14				-0.9	0.0
Sweden	162.4	112.2	-45	18.5	12.5	-48				-30.0	0.0
Switzerland	56.6	50.1	-13	8.0	6.8	-18				-4.0	0.0
United Kingdom	57.6	276.5	79	1.0	4.6	78				15.8	0.0
Latin America & Caribbean											
Low income economies											
Nicaragua	5.6	0.3	-1,767	1.4	0.1	-2,268				0.0	-0.1
Middle income economies											
Argentina	11.6	2.6	-339	0.3	0.1	-394				0.2	0.0
Belize	8.9	0.9	-934	43.2	3.2	-1,238				-0.2	0.0
Bolivia	0.7	0.5	-33	0.1	0.1	-62				0.2	0.0
Brazil	6.2	3.2	-94	0.0	0.0	-123				0.0	-0.1
Chile	0.2	0.5	57	0.0	0.0	51				0.1	-0.2
Colombia	0.3	0.2	-61	0.0	0.0	-93	950.0	1,244.1	31	0.0	7.4
Costa Rica	24.8	13.5	-84	7.6	3.5	-120				1.1	0.0
Cuba	3.6	0.8	-331	0.3	0.1	-350				-0.2	-1.9
Ecuador	0.2	6.4	97	0.0	0.5	96				3.1	-0.1
El Salvador	0.2	0.2	19	0.0	0.0	2				0.2	-1.0
Guatemala	4.7	0.7	-557	0.4	0.1	-770				0.0	-7.3
Honduras	0.1	0.0	-335	0.0	0.0	-463				0.0	-0.1
Mexico	52.5	6.1	-764	0.6	0.1	-899				-6.9	0.0
Panama	1.0	1.4	31	0.4	0.5	19				-0.1	0.0
Peru	0.7	0.7	3	0.0	0.0	-16				0.0	-0.8
Suriname	0.1	0.0		0.2	0.0						0.0
Uruguay	0.1	0.1	-10	0.0	0.0	-17				0.0	0.0
Venezuela	2.2	0.1	-3,693	0.1	0.0	-4,417				0.0	0.1

Country of asylum	Refugee populations*						IDP populations			Refugee flows**	
	Total (1000s)			per 1000 inhabitants			Total (1000s)			2003 (1000s)	
	1993	2003	% change	1993	2003	% change	2002	2003	% change	Inflow	Outflow
Middle East & North Africa											
Low income economies											
Yemen	54.5	61.9	12	3.9	3.2	-23				-20.9	0.0
Western Sahara											-0.2
Middle income economies											
Algeria	219.1	169.0	-30	8.1	5.3	-53				-0.2	-0.4
Djibouti	34.1	27.0	-26	86.7	59.1	-47				5.3	0.1
Egypt	6.7	88.7	92	0.1	1.2	91				8.3	-0.7
Iran	2,495.0	984.9	-153	41.1	14.7	-180				-321.7	-5.5
Iraq	109.1	134.2	19	5.9	5.4	-9				0.0	-53.7
Jordan	0.5	1.2	58	0.1	0.2	43				0.0	-0.1
Lebanon	1.2	2.5	52	0.4	0.7	45				-0.3	-1.4
Libya	1.2	11.9	90	0.3	2.2	88				0.2	0.1
Morocco***	0.3	2.1	86	0.0	0.1	83				0.0	0.0
Saudi Arabia	24.0	240.8	90	1.3	9.6	86				-4.4	0.0
Syria	38.7	3.7	-951	2.8	0.2	-1,262				0.8	1.4
Tunisia	0.1	0.1	-1	0.0	0.0	-15				0.0	0.0
High income economies											
Israel		4.2			0.7					0.0	0.1
Kuwait	30.0	1.5	-1,876	20.2	0.7	-2,808				0.0	-0.1
United Arab Emirates	0.4	0.2	-150	0.2	0.1	-197				0.0	0.0
North America											
High income economies											
Canada	183.2	133.1	-38	6.3	4.1	-53				3.1	0.0
United States	623.1	452.5	-38	2.4	1.6	-54				-32.6	0.0
South Asia											
Low income economies											
Afghanistan	32.1	0.0	-458,471	1.7	0.0	-675,351	665.2	184.3	-72	0.0	-374.2
Bangladesh	199.0	19.8	-905	1.7	0.1	-1,106				-2.2	-0.2
India	262.8	164.8	-60	0.3	0.2	-88				-4.1	-0.6
Nepal	85.3	123.7	31	4.1	4.7	12				-8.6	0.3
Pakistan	1,479.3	1,124.3	-32	12.1	7.2	-68				-103.1	1.2
Middle income economies											
Sri Lanka	0.0	0.0	100	0.0	0.0	100	447.1	386.1	-14	0.0	-11.0

Country of asylum	Refugee populations*						IDP populations			Refugee flows**	
	Total (1000s)			per 1000 inhabitants			Total (1000s)			2003 (1000s)	
	1993	2003	% change	1993	2003	% change	2002	2003	% change	Inflow	Outflow
Sub-Saharan Africa											
Low income economies											
Angola	10.9	13.4	19	1.3	1.2	-1	188.7		-100	0.0	-105.9
Benin	156.2	5.0	-3,003	30.4	0.7	-4,151				0.0	0.1
Burkina Faso	6.6	0.5	-1,316	0.7	0.0	-1,773				0.0	-0.1
Burundi	271.9	41.0	-564	48.6	6.7	-624	100.0	2.0	-98	0.4	-43.1
Cameroon	44.0	58.6	25	3.5	3.7	6				0.3	1.0
Central African Republic	44.1	44.8	1	14.4	12.1	-19				-6.0	10.0
Chad	0.1	146.4	100	0.0	15.8	100				111.8	4.9
Congo, Dem. Rep.	572.1	234.0	-144	13.7	4.1	-231	9.0			-98.9	28.5
Congo, Rep.	13.6	91.4	85	5.6	30.9	82				-17.8	0.8
Côte d'Ivoire	251.6	76.0	-231	19.1	4.6	-318	100.0	38.0	-62	31.2	9.9
Eritrea	0.0	3.9	100	0.0	0.9	100				0.3	-194.2
Ethiopia	272.6	130.3	-109	5.1	1.9	-173				-2.7	1.4
Gambia	2.2	7.5	71	2.0	5.0	59				-4.7	-0.1
Ghana	150.1	43.9	-242	8.9	2.1	-317				10.4	0.2
Guinea	577.2	184.3	-213	80.2	20.4	-293				2.2	0.5
Guinea-Bissau	20.7	7.6	-174	19.1	5.5	-244				-0.1	0.0
Kenya	301.6	237.5	-27	11.7	7.4	-58				3.8	0.1
Lesotho	0.1	0.0		0.1	0.0						0.0
Liberia	150.2	34.0	-342	72.8	10.2	-610	304.1	531.6	75	-36.8	77.7
Madagascar	*0.1*	0.0		0.0	0.0						0.0
Malawi	713.6	3.2	-22,186	71.4	0.3	-25,874				1.0	0.0
Mali	15.2	10.0	-52	1.7	0.9	-102				0.9	-0.1
Mauritania	51.5	0.5	-10,742	23.4	0.2	-14,220				0.1	0.4
Mozambique	0.2	0.3	36	0.0	0.0	12				0.1	0.0
Niger	16.7	0.3	-4,991	2.0	0.0	-6,678				0.0	-0.1
Nigeria	4.8	9.2	48	0.1	0.1	33				1.8	-0.2
Rwanda	277.0	36.6	-657	37.1	4.6	-716				5.7	0.1
São Tomé & Principe		0.0			0.0						0.0
Senegal	73.0	20.7	-252	9.1	2.0	-363				0.0	-3.7
Sierra Leone	16.3	61.2	73	3.9	10.7	64				-2.3	-76.9
Somalia	0.4	0.4	-9	0.1	0.0	-44				0.2	-30.1
Sudan	745.2	138.2	-439	25.7	3.6	-610				-190.0	98.0

| Country of asylum | Refugee populations* | | | | | | IDP populations | | | Refugee flows** | |
| | Total (1000s) | | | per 1000 inhabitants | | | Total (1000s) | | | 2003 (1000s) | |
	1993	2003	% change	1993	2003	% change	2002	2003	% change	Inflow	Outflow
Tanzania	564.5	649.8	13	20.5	18.4	-12				-39.6	0.1
Togo	3.3	12.4	73	0.8	2.3	63				0.1	0.1
Uganda	286.5	230.9	-24	15.2	9.0	-68				13.6	-5.2
Zambia	141.1	226.7	38	16.4	21.0	22				-20.1	0.0
Zimbabwe	100.5	12.7	-690	9.1	1.0	-803				3.3	3.1
Middle income economies											
Botswana	0.5	2.8	82	0.4	1.7	79				0.0	0.0
Gabon	0.6	14.0	96	0.6	10.6	94				0.5	0.0
Namibia	0.6	19.8	97	0.4	9.9	96				-2.6	0.0
South Africa	250.0	26.6	-841	6.2	0.6	-930				3.2	0.0
Swaziland	48.9	0.7	-7,028	49.3	0.6	-8,244				0.0	0.0

Region	Refugee populations* Total (1000s)			Refugee populations* per 1000 inhabitants			IDP populations Total (1000s)			Refugee flows** 2003 (1000s)	
	1993	2003	% change	1993	2003	% change	2002	2003	% change	Inflow	Outflow
Low income	8,039.9	4,344.3	-85	4.2	1.9	-125	2,206.8	1,591.7	-28	-411.1	-639.2
Middle income	4,522.8	2,818.9	-60	1.7	0.9	-78	2,424.1	2,595.0	7	-439.1	-311.4
Low & middle income:											
East Asia & Pacific	407.4	449.1	9	0.2	0.2	-1	0.0	0.0		-70.7	-82.7
Europe & Central Asia	1,277.1	678.2	-88	2.7	1.4	-90	1,866.8	1,800.7	-4	-95.4	-196.2
Latin America & Caribbean	109.0	38.3	-184	0.2	0.1	-231	950.0	1,244.1	31	-2.6	-4.1
Middle East & North Africa	2,726.5	1,728.1	-58	10.7	5.5	-92	0.0	0.0		-333.0	-60.3
South Asia	1,552.4	1,432.6	-8	1.3	1.0	-30	1,112.2	570.4	-49	-118.1	-384.6
Sub-Saharan Africa	6,490.2	2,836.9	-129	11.8	4.0	-192	701.8	571.6	-19	-230.4	-222.7
High income	3,171.1	2,517.1	-26	3.5	2.6	-35	0.0	0.0		-56.0	-0.3
World	15,733.7	9,680.3	-63	2.9	1.5	-86	4,630.9	4,186.8	-10	-906.2	-950.9

* The figures for refugee populations are as of end of year.

** Figures for inflow and outflow of refugees were obtained by netting the populations of refugees reported in the beginning of 2003 and at the end of 2003 for the country of asylum in the case of inflow and for the country of origin in the case of outflow. Inflows and outflows based on primae facie arrivals and and individually recognised refugees. IDPs refer to internally displaced persons of concern to/assisted by UNHCR at end of 2003.

*** China: 1993 figures include Tibet; Indonesia: 1993 figures include East Timor; Morocco: 1993 figures include Western Sahara

Empty cells indicate that the value is below 100, zero or not available.

When data for a specific year were not available, data for an adjacent year were substituted. These data and estimates based on them are presented in italics.

Per capita calculations were made by us, using population data from US Census Bureau International Database, www.census.gov/ipc/www/idbsprd.html

Sources: World Development Indicators 2005 (WDI-Online); UNHCR Statstics Online, www.unhcr.ch/cgi-bin/texis/vtx/goto?page=statistics; US Census Bureau International Database, www.census.gov/ipc/www/idbsprd.html

Record 14: **Peacekeeping**

A country's preparedness to contribute part of its armed forces to peacekeeping duties in foreign conflicts can be seen as a commitment to the international rule of law. This record reports the ratio of peacekeeping forces to total military personnel, comparing numbers of military personnel (for 2003, the latest available data) with the total number of forces per country committed to peacekeeping (as of March 2005).

The total number of peacekeeping forces has increased by a third between 2004 and 2005, South Asia and Sub-Saharan African nations being the source of the largest numbers of peacekeepers.

Country	Total military personnel 2003	Peacekeeping forces as of March 2005*	Peacekeeping forces per thousand military personnel
East Asia & Pacific			
Low income economies			
Cambodia	125,000		
Indonesia & East Timor	302,000	201	0.7
Korea, Dem. Rep.	1,082,000		
Laos	29,100		
Mongolia	8,600	5	0.6
Myanmar	488,000		
Papua New Guinea	3,100		
Vietnam	484,000		
Middle income economies			
China & Tibet	2,250,000	850	0.4
Fiji	3,500	137	39.1
Malaysia	104,000	78	0.8
Philippines	106,000	321	3.0
Thailand	314,200	6	0.0
High income economies			
Australia	53,600	110	2.1
Brunei	7,000		
Korea, Rep.	686,000	41	0.1
Japan	239,900	30	0.1
New Zealand	8,600	18	2.1
Singapore	72,500		
Europe & Central Asia			
Low income economies			
Armenia	44,600		
Azerbaijan	66,500		
Georgia	17,500		
Kyrgyzstan	10,900	7	0.6
Moldova	6,900	8	1.2
Tajikistan	6,000		
Ukraine	295,500	531	1.8

Country	Total military personnel 2003	Peacekeeping forces as of March 2005*	Peacekeeping forces per thousand military personnel
Uzbekistan	52,000		
Middle income economies			
Albania	22,000	3	0.1
Belarus	72,900		
Bosnia & Herzegovina		14	
Bulgaria	51,000	10	0.2
Croatia	20,800	31	1.5
Czech Republic	57,000	16	0.3
Estonia	5,500	2	0.4
Hungary	33,400	98	2.9
Kazakhstan	65,800		
Latvia	4,900		
Lithuania	12,700	0	0.0
Macedonia	12,800		
Poland	163,000	597	3.7
Romania	97,200	44	0.5
Russian Federation	960,600	215	0.2
Serbia & Montenegro	74,200	16	0.2
Slovakia	22,000	301	13.7
Slovenia	6,500	2	0.3
Turkey	514,800	5	0.0
Turkmenistan	29,000		
High income economies			
Austria	34,600	390	11.3
Belgium	40,800	18	0.4
Cyprus	10,000		
Denmark	22,800	38	1.7
Finland	27,000	37	1.4
France	259,000	437	1.7
Germany	284,500	27	0.1
Greece	177,600	9	0.1
Ireland	10,400	465	44.7
Italy	200,000	128	0.6
Luxembourg	900		
Netherlands	53,100	18	0.3
Norway	26,600	20	0.8
Portugal	44,900	19	0.4
Spain	150,700	210	1.4

Country	Total military personnel 2003	Peacekeeping forces as of March 2005*	Peacekeeping forces per thousand military personnel
Sweden	27,600	260	9.4
Switzerland	27,500	19	0.7
United Kingdom	212,600	300	1.4
Latin America & Caribbean			
Low income economies			
Nicaragua	14,000		
Middle income economies			
Argentina	71,400	1,002	14.0
Belize	1,100		
Bolivia	31,500	249	7.9
Brazil	287,600	1,361	4.7
Chile	77,300	544	7.0
Colombia	200,000		
Cuba	46,000		
Dominican Republic	24,500	4	0.2
Ecuador	59,500	73	1.2
El Salvador	15,500	11	0.7
Guatemala	31,400	186	5.9
Guyana	1,600		
Honduras	12,000	12	1.0
Jamaica	2,800	0	0.0
Mexico	192,800		
Paraguay	18,600	47	2.5
Peru	100,000	226	2.3
Suriname	1,800		
Trinidad & Tobago	2,700		
Uruguay	24,000	2,589	107.9
Venezuela	82,300		
Middle East & North Africa			
Low income economies			
Yemen	66,700	10	0.1
Middle income economies			
Algeria	127,500	21	0.2
Djibouti	9,800	0	0.0
Egypt	450,000	71	0.2
Iran	540,000	3	0.0
Iraq	389,000		
Jordan	100,500	2,062	20.5

Country	Total military personnel 2003	Peacekeeping forces as of March 2005*	Peacekeeping forces per thousand military personnel
Lebanon	72,100	0	0.0
Libya	76,000		
Malta	2,100		
Morocco & Western Sahara		1,705	
Oman	41,700		
Saudi Arabia	199,500		
Syria	319,000		
Tunisia	35,000	515	14.7
High income economies			
Bahrain	11,200		
Kuwait	15,500		
Qatar	12,400		
United Arab Emirates	50,500		
North America			
High income economies			
Canada	52,300	218	4.2
United States	1,427,000	31	0.0
South Asia			
Low income economies			
Afghanistan	60,000		
Bangladesh	125,500	7,866	62.7
Bhutan			
India	1,325,000	5,706	4.3
Nepal	63,000	2,914	46.3
Pakistan	620,000	9,420	15.2
Middle income economies			
Sri Lanka	152,300	755	5.0
Sub-Saharan Africa			
Low income economies			
Angola	120,000		
Benin	4,600	347	75.4
Burkina Faso	10,800	27	2.5
Burundi	50,500		
Cameroon	23,100	5	0.2
Central African Republic	2,600		
Chad	30,300	11	0.4
Congo, Rep.	10,000	6	0.6
Côte d'Ivoire	17,000	0	0.0

Country	Total military personnel 2003	Peacekeeping forces as of March 2005*	Peacekeeping forces per thousand military personnel
Equatorial Guinea	1,300		
Eritrea	202,000		
Ethiopia	162,400	3,421	21.1
Gambia	800	26	32.5
Ghana	7,000	3,211	458.7
Guinea	9,700	15	1.5
Guinea-Bissau	9,200		
Kenya	24,100	1,427	59.2
Lesotho	2,000		
Liberia	15,000		
Madagascar	13,500	0	0.0
Malawi	5,300	30	5.7
Mali	7,400	59	8.0
Mozambique	8,200	193	23.5
Niger	5,300	398	75.1
Nigeria	78,500	2,809	35.8
Rwanda	51,000		
Senegal	13,600	1,422	104.6
Sierra Leone	13,000	0	0.0
Sudan	104,500		
Tanzania	27,000	16	0.6
Togo	8,500	319	37.5
Uganda	60,000	2	0.0
Zambia	18,100	53	2.9
Zimbabwe	29,000	0	0.0
Middle income economies			
Botswana	9,000		
Cape Verde	1,200		
Gabon	4,700	6	1.3
Namibia	9,000	872	96.9
South Africa	55,700	2,316	41.6
World	**20,358,400**	**60,684**	**3.0**

* Peacekeeping forces here comprise military observers and troops

Country of mission	Region	Name of mission
East Timor	East Asia & Pacific	UNTAET
Cyprus	Europe & Central Asia	UNFICIP
Georgia	Europe & Central Asia	UNIMIG
Kosovo	Europe & Central Asia	UNMIK
Haiti	Latin America & Caribbean	MINUSTAH
Golan Heights	Middle East & North Africa	UNDOF
Lebanon	Middle East & North Africa	UNIFIL
Middle East	Middle East & North Africa	UNTSO
Western Sahara	Middle East & North Africa	MINURSO
India/Pakistan	South Asia	UNMOGIP
Burundi	Sub-Saharan Africa	ONUB
Côte d'Ivoire	Sub-Saharan Africa	UNOCI
Congo, Dem. Rep.	Sub-Saharan Africa	MONUC
Ethipia/Eritrea	Sub-Saharan Africa	UNMEE
Liberia	Sub-Saharan Africa	UNMIL
Sierra Leone	Sub-Saharan Africa	UNAMSIL
Sudan	Sub-Saharan Africa	UNMIS

Sources: United Nations, Department of Peacekeeping Operations, www.un.org/Depts/dpko/dpko/contributors/index.htm; International Institute for Strategic Studies, London: The Military Balance 2004/5. Oxford: Oxford University Press, Table 38 International comparisons of defense expenditure and military manpower, 2001-2003.

Record 15: Environment

This record gives an indication of the extent to which countries protect or harm the global environment, with the use of the latest data available. It is now generally agreed that carbon dioxide emission is a major contributor to the problem of global warming: a large volume of emissions can therefore be considered as an infringement of the environmental element of the international rule of law. It is difficult to evaluate emissions indicators at the country level, since per capita figures may favour populous countries, while per unit of income measures may favour high-income countries (we use purchasing power parity, PPP, which represents the relative value of currencies based on what those currencies will buy in their nation of origin). We therefore present both in the table, for comparison purposes.

The proportion of recycled paper in a country's total paper production is an indicator of the commitment to natural resource conservation. The data show the ratio of new to recovered paper production: figures higher than one indicate recovered paper exceeds new paper production, and figures lower than one reflect the opposite.

The number of environmental conservation treaties ratified or signed is an indicator of a country's commitment to international norms of environmental conservation. The entries in the table indicate the number of environmental conservation treaties signed by each country out of a list of 220 treaties generally pertaining to environmental conservation from the list maintained by the Environmental Treaties and Resource Indicators (ENTRI) project (see table note for a list of treaty categories considered for this table; for a detailed list of treaties included see www.sedac.ciesin.columbia.edu/entri/treatySearch.jsp, updated as of July 2003).

Country	Carbon dioxide emissions — metric tons per capita 1990	2000	% change 1990-2000	kg per PPP $ of GDP 1990	2000	% change 1990-2000	Paper production: ratio of recovered paper to new paper 1993	2003	% change 1993-2003	Number of ratified or signed environmental conservation treaties* Party	Signatory	% party or signatory	% party or signatory since 1995
East Asia & Pacific													
Low income economies													
Cambodia	0.047	0.042	-11		0.024					17	2	8.6	15.8
Indonesia	0.927	1.307	41	0.409	0.429	5	0.1	0.2	27	19	5	10.9	8.3
Korea, Dem. Rep.	12.259	8.481	-31							10	3	5.9	0.0
Laos	0.056	0.078	40	0.054	0.051	-6				11	0	5.0	9.1
Mongolia	4.739	3.126	-34	1.831	1.944	6				13	0	5.9	0.0
Myanmar	0.102	0.192	88				0.0	1.0		13	0	5.9	7.7
Papua New Guinea	0.610	0.473	-23	0.317	0.198	-38				25	3	12.7	7.1
Solomon Islands	0.505	0.394	-22	0.232	0.209	-10				27	2	13.2	3.4
Vietnam	0.339	0.732	116	0.280	0.363	30	1.1	0.4	-68	15	0	6.8	6.7
Middle income economies													
China	2.116	2.210	4	1.325	0.578	-56	0.4	0.4	17	28	1	13.2	6.9
Fiji	1.103	0.894	-19	0.249	0.176	-29				23	3	11.8	11.5
Malaysia	3.037	6.206	104	0.551	0.693	26	0.2	0.7	336	22	1	10.5	8.7
Philippines	0.726	1.012	39	0.187	0.254	36	0.1	0.3	196	20	5	11.4	12.0

Country	Carbon dioxide emissions						Paper production: ratio of recovered paper to new paper		% change	Number of ratified or signed environmental conservation treaties*			
	metric tons per capita		% change	kg per PPP $ of GDP		% change							
	1990	2000	1990-2000	1990	2000	1990-2000	1993	2003	1993-2003	Party	Signatory	% party or signatory	% party or signatory since 1995
Samoa	0.779	0.809	4	0.150	0.159	6				17	2	8.6	15.8
Thailand	1.722	3.271	90	0.385	0.515	34	0.3	0.2	-4	21	3	10.9	12.5
Tonga	0.802	1.207	51	0.167	0.192	15				12	2	6.4	7.1
Vanuatu	0.448	0.409	-9	0.184	0.132	-28				8	8	7.3	12.5
High income economies													
Australia	15.588	17.973	15	0.739	0.686	-7	0.5	0.5	5	52	3	25.0	5.5
Brunei	22.641	*14.150*	*-38*							7	2	4.1	11.1
Korea, Rep.	5.626	9.084	61	0.611	0.598	-2	0.5	0.7	40	30	1	14.1	6.5
Japan	8.667	9.336	8	0.373	0.359	-4	0.5	0.5	-9	41	3	20.0	9.1
New Zealand	6.834	8.312	22	0.414	0.415	0	0.1	0.3	105	43	6	22.3	4.1
Singapore	13.757	14.695	7	0.943	0.625	-34	3.1	3.2	1	6	1	3.2	0.0
Europe & Central Asia													
Low income economies													
Armenia		1.128			0.466					11	1	5.5	8.3
Azerbaijan		3.608			1.403		0.0	0.0		4	1	2.3	0.0
Georgia		1.173			0.624					14	3	7.7	11.8
Kyrgyzstan		0.944			0.605					6	0	2.7	0.0
Moldova		1.536			1.190		0.0	0.0		11	4	6.8	20.0
Tajikistan		0.641			0.799					8	0	3.6	0.0
Ukraine		6.925			1.685		0.7	0.5	-23	25	7	14.5	18.8
Uzbekistan		4.812			3.175					10	0	4.5	20.0
Middle income economies													
Albania	2.218	0.918	-59	0.705	0.249	-65	0.0	0.0		20	5	11.4	28.0
Belarus		5.912			1.231		0.0	0.0		13	5	8.2	5.6
Bosnia & Herzegovina		4.840			0.922					14	2	7.3	18.8
Bulgaria	8.642	5.253	-39	1.190	0.843	-29	0.9	0.5	-49	42	7	22.3	10.2
Croatia		4.470			0.492		0.5	0.0	-100	27	4	14.1	12.9
Czech Republic		11.561			0.828		0.3	0.4	40	34	5	17.7	28.2
Estonia		11.684			1.140		0.2	0.3	34	21	2	10.5	4.3
Hungary	5.644	5.403	-4	0.505	0.425	-16	0.9	0.7	-21	37	5	19.1	9.5
Kazakhstan		8.053			1.753		0.0	0.0		8	1	4.1	11.1
Latvia		2.526			0.332		2.0	1.3	-34	22	3	11.4	12.0

Country	Carbon dioxide emissions						Paper production: ratio of recovered paper to new paper		% change	Number of ratified or signed environmental conservation treaties*			
	metric tons per capita		% change	kg per PPP $ of GDP		% change							
	1990	2000	1990-2000	1990	2000	1990-2000	1993	2003	1993-2003	Party	Signatory	% party or signatory	% party or signatory since 1995
Lithuania		3.386			0.388		0.8	1.1	47	17	4	9.5	23.8
Macedonia		5.521			0.841		0.0	0.1		17	0	7.7	11.8
Poland	9.119	7.797	-14	1.233	0.785	-36	0.1	0.4	148	53	10	28.6	7.9
Romania	6.682	3.844	-42	1.015	0.673	-34	0.6	0.5	-9	39	9	21.8	14.6
Russian Federation		9.859			1.361		0.3	0.3	9	64	4	30.9	1.5
Serbia & Montenegro		*3.716*					0.1	0.0	-100	26	2	12.7	3.6
Slovakia		6.567			0.574		0.3	0.3	13	33	3	16.4	5.6
Slovenia		7.343			0.442		0.2	0.1	-8	33	10	19.5	18.6
Turkey	2.561	3.286	28	0.486	0.526	8	0.5	0.6	19	27	8	15.9	5.7
Turkmenistan		7.450			2.031					8	0	3.6	37.5
High income economies													
Austria	7.445	7.595	2	0.328	0.271	-17	0.1	0.3	292	47	15	28.2	9.7
Belgium**	10.087	9.973	-1	0.451	0.376	-16	0.6	1.1	77	74	15	40.5	6.7
Cyprus	6.826	8.485	24	0.549	0.496	-10	0.0	0.0		26	5	14.1	12.9
Denmark	9.871	8.353	-15	0.404	0.285	-29	1.4	0.9	-36	86	9	43.2	6.3
Finland	10.609	10.330	-3	0.483	0.411	-15	0.0	0.1	15	65	8	33.2	8.2
France	6.301	6.154	-2	0.285	0.243	-15	0.4	0.6	64	93	29	55.5	10.7
Germany	*11.126*	9.555	-14	*0.483*	0.366	-24	0.7	0.6	-2	91	20	50.5	10.8
Greece	7.108	8.208	15	0.508	0.491	-3	0.2	0.2	-16	48	15	28.6	12.7
Iceland	7.931	7.680	-3	0.323	0.267	-17	0.0	0.0		33	13	20.9	10.9
Ireland	8.497	11.076	30	0.556	0.369	-34	0.0	4.7		44	17	27.7	8.2
Italy	7.032	7.422	6	0.322	0.298	-8	0.5	0.6	12	74	16	40.9	7.8
Luxembourg	25.919	19.366	-25	0.824	0.344	-58				43	18	27.7	11.5
Netherlands	10.031	8.723	-13	0.456	0.320	-30	0.7	0.7	0	89	9	44.5	6.1
Norway	7.472	11.114	49	0.284	0.316	12	0.1	0.2	129	80	6	39.1	8.1
Portugal	4.277	5.848	37	0.317	0.337	6	0.3	0.2	-24	63	13	34.5	9.2
Spain	5.454	6.986	28	0.343	0.350	2	0.5	0.7	29	81	8	40.5	7.9
Sweden	5.671	5.293	-7	0.269	0.216	-20	0.1	0.1	25	83	6	40.5	6.7
Switzerland	6.360	5.440	-14	0.221	0.191	-14	0.6	0.6	10	52	19	32.3	14.1
United Kingdom	9.891	9.644	-2	0.486	0.391	-20	0.6	0.8	35	88	14	46.4	4.9

Country	Carbon dioxide emissions						Paper production: ratio of recovered paper to new paper		% change	Number of ratified or signed environmental conservation treaties*			
	metric tons per capita		% change	kg per PPP $ of GDP		% change	ratio of recovered paper to new paper		% change				
	1990	2000	1990–2000	1990	2000	1990–2000	1993	2003	1993–2003	Party	Signatory	% party or signatory	% party or signatory since 1995
Latin America & Caribbean													
Low income economies													
Haiti	0.154	0.179	16	0.062	0.102	65				13	2	6.8	6.7
Nicaragua	0.680	0.737	8	0.230	0.230	0				13	7	9.1	10.0
Middle income economies													
Argentina	3.398	3.855	13	0.383	0.315	-18	0.4	0.7	84	30	8	17.3	7.9
Barbados	4.164	4.405	6	0.314	0.287	-8				14	2	7.3	6.3
Belize	1.648	3.124	90	0.398	0.532	34				15	4	8.6	15.8
Bolivia	0.824	1.330	61	0.389	0.556	43				18	8	11.8	11.5
Brazil	1.369	1.808	32	0.212	0.245	16	0.2	0.4	53	36	2	17.3	10.5
Chile	2.697	3.912	45	0.464	0.425	-8	0.3	0.1	-52	32	4	16.4	2.8
Colombia	1.600	1.381	-14	0.270	0.226	-16	0.5	0.5	-6	19	8	12.3	7.4
Costa Rica	0.957	1.423	49	0.148	0.160	8	0.6	0.6	-5	20	5	11.4	8.0
Cuba	3.016	2.763	-8				1.0	2.4	137	18	6	10.9	0.0
Dominican Republic	1.337	3.009	125	0.328	0.489	49	0.7	0.1	-84	14	4	8.2	5.6
Ecuador	1.614	2.049	27	0.461	0.612	33	0.0	0.7		21	4	11.4	8.0
El Salvador	0.512	1.073	110	0.141	0.228	62	0.3	0.1	-69	14	3	7.7	5.9
Guatemala	0.581	0.868	49	0.168	0.220	31	0.9	0.6	-32	19	4	10.5	4.3
Guyana	1.549	2.105	36	0.445	0.521	17				14	3	7.7	11.8
Honduras	0.532	0.742	39	0.212	0.297	40	0.0	0.5		13	4	7.7	17.6
Jamaica	3.330	4.178	25	0.862	1.145	33	3.3	0.0	-100	17	5	10.0	9.1
Mexico	3.669	4.328	18	0.487	0.485	0	0.4	0.2	-40	25	4	13.2	6.9
Panama	1.305	2.220	70	0.288	0.355	23	0.4	0.0	-100	23	8	14.1	3.2
Paraguay	0.545	0.695	27	0.116	0.151	30	0.0	2.3		19	2	9.5	14.3
Peru	1.004	1.139	13	0.259	0.241	-7	0.6	1.1	92	27	3	13.6	6.7
St. Lucia	1.202	*2.098*	74	0.237	*0.370*	56				12	3	6.8	13.3
Suriname	4.501	4.983	11							15	3	8.2	5.6
Trinidad & Tobago	13.929	20.452	47	2.002	2.285	14	0.0	0.0		19	4	10.5	4.3
Uruguay	1.259	1.628	29	0.175	0.184	5	0.5	0.2	-65	24	8	14.5	9.4
Venezuela	5.760	6.489	13	0.994	1.152	16	0.4	0.3	-40	27	1	12.7	14.3
High income economies													
Bahamas	7.620	5.886	-23	0.449	0.351	-22				11	2	5.9	7.7

Country	Carbon dioxide emissions						Paper production: ratio of recovered paper to new paper		% change	Number of ratified or signed environmental conservation treaties*			
	metric tons per capita		% change	kg per PPP $ of GDP		% change				Party	Signatory	% party or signatory	% party or signatory since 1995
	1990	2000	1990-2000	1990	2000	1990-2000	1993	2003	1993-2003				
Middle East & North Africa													
Low income economies													
Western Sahara										1	0	0.5	0.0
Yemen	*0.698*	0.482	*-31*	*1.188*	0.584	*-51*				13	0	5.9	7.7
Middle income economies													
Algeria	3.215	2.943	-8	0.589	0.543	-8	0.0	0.8	1,715	21	3	10.9	8.3
Djibouti	0.718	0.578	-20		0.300					8	3	5.0	9.1
Egypt	1.438	2.223	55	0.492	0.629	28	0.6	0.8	30	27	4	14.1	12.9
Iran	3.904	4.874	25	0.849	0.874	3	0.3	1.7	465	9	13	10.0	0.0
Iraq	2.725	3.287	2							16	2	3.6	0.0
Jordan	3.213	3.182	-1	0.833	0.814	-2	0.4	0.1	-71	17	1	8.2	22.2
Lebanon	2.501	3.503	40	1.149	0.834	-27				13	4	7.7	0.0
Libya	8.773	10.908	24							12	4	7.3	6.3
Malta	4.611	7.215	56	0.430	0.404	-6	0.0	0.0		16	7	10.5	17.4
Morocco	0.977	1.273	30	0.290	0.367	26	0.3	0.2	-23	24	12	16.4	11.1
Oman	7.092	8.205	16	0.610	0.657	8				10	0	4.5	0.0
Palestinian Authority										2	0	0.9	0.0
Saudi Arabia	11.257	18.064	60	0.953	1.439	51				12	0	5.5	0.0
Syria	2.958	3.347	13	1.116	1.005	-10				11	3	6.4	7.1
Tunisia	1.626	1.923	18	0.358	0.308	-14	0.1	0.1	-15	26	7	15.0	12.1
High income economies													
Bahrain	23.274	29.104	25	1.627	1.834	13				8	0	3.6	0.0
Israel	7.431	10.033	35	0.469	0.487	4	0.5	0.4	-23	19	3	10.0	9.1
Kuwait	19.863	21.867	10	*1.329*	1.389	*5*				7	2	4.1	0.0
Qatar	28.151	69.560	147							6	1	3.2	14.3
United Arab Emirates	34.339	18.144	-47	1.337						6	2	3.6	0.0
North America													
High income economies													
Canada	15.431	14.165	-8	0.660	0.508	-23	0.1	0.1	-39	47	11	26.4	5.2
United States	19.293	19.848	3	0.677	0.582	-14	0.4	0.5	27	60	11	32.3	2.8

Country	Carbon dioxide emissions						Paper production: ratio of recovered paper to new paper		% change	Number of ratified or signed environmental conservation treaties*			
	metric tons per capita		% change	kg per PPP $ of GDP		% change							
	1990	2000	1990–2000	1990	2000	1990–2000	1993	2003	1993–2003	Party	Signatory	% party or signatory	% party or signatory since 1995
South Asia													
Low income economies													
Afghanistan	0.148	0.034	-77							8	6	6.4	0.0
Bangladesh	0.140	0.223	60	0.119	0.144	21				16	4	9.1	10.0
Bhutan	0.214	0.492	130							3	1	1.8	0.0
India	0.795	1.054	33	0.467	0.436	-7	0.2	0.2	1	32	1	15.0	3.0
Nepal	0.035	0.148	326	0.034	0.112	231				13	4	7.7	0.0
Pakistan	0.629	0.759	21	0.403	0.394	-2	0.1	0.6	316	23	8	14.1	3.2
Middle income economies													
Maldives	0.722	1.819	152							6	3	4.1	22.2
Sri Lanka	0.237	0.551	133	0.100	0.160	59	0.7	0.5	-22	20	5	11.4	4.0
Sub-Saharan Africa													
Low income economies													
Angola	0.498	0.517	4	0.205	0.265	29				7	3	4.5	10.0
Benin	0.120	0.260	118	0.146	0.268	83				18	5	10.5	8.7
Burkina Faso	0.112	0.091	-18	0.129	0.090	-30				22	5	12.3	7.4
Burundi	0.036	0.036	0	0.040	0.059	47				7	5	5.5	8.3
Cameroon	0.128	0.433	238	0.062	0.231	273				18	8	11.8	7.7
Central African Republic	0.067	0.073	9	0.054	0.063	17				8	4	5.5	0.0
Chad	0.025	0.016	-35	0.027	0.019	-29				14	4	8.2	5.6
Comoros	0.153	0.144	-5	0.079	0.089	13				8	2	4.5	0.0
Congo, Rep.	0.816	0.525	-36	0.840	0.547	-35				13	8	9.5	0.0
Congo, Dem. Rep.	0.110	0.056	-49	0.068	0.080	18				12	7	8.6	5.3
Côte d'Ivoire	1.006	0.662	-34	0.551	0.418	-24				24	7	14.1	12.9
Equatorial Guinea	0.333	0.448	34	0.257	0.030	-88				14	3	7.7	0.0
Eritrea		0.148			0.199					5	0	2.3	0.0
Ethiopia	0.058	0.087	50	0.093	0.130	39	0.3	0.2	-27	10	7	7.7	11.8
Gambia	0.205	0.207	1	0.113	0.121	7				11	5	7.3	12.5
Ghana	0.231	0.301	30	0.141	0.153	9				19	8	12.3	7.4
Guinea	0.176	0.174	-1	0.099	0.089	-10				24	3	12.3	3.7
Guinea-Bissau	0.753	0.193	-74	0.829	0.243	-71				10	4	6.4	14.3
Kenya	0.249	0.311	25	0.219	0.310	42	0.1	0.5	222	22	4	11.8	3.8

Country	Carbon dioxide emissions						Paper production: ratio of recovered paper to new paper		% change	Number of ratified or signed environmental conservation treaties*			
	metric tons per capita		% change	kg per PPP $ of GDP		% change							
	1990	2000	1990–2000	1990	2000	1990–2000	1993	2003	1993–2003	Party	Signatory	% party or signatory	% party or signatory since 1995
Lesotho										10	6	7.3	6.3
Liberia	0.192	0.128	-34							11	11	10.0	0.0
Madagascar	0.081	0.146	80	0.086	0.178	107	0.8	0.7	-14	16	7	10.5	4.3
Malawi	0.070	0.074	5	0.136	0.124	-9				17	4	9.5	4.8
Mali	0.050	0.051	3	0.073	0.065	-11				21	2	10.5	8.7
Mauritania	1.298	1.161	-11	0.948	0.702	-26				13	9	10.0	9.1
Mozambique	0.070	0.067	-5	0.111	0.076	-31	5.0	0.0	-100	11	3	6.4	7.1
Niger	0.137	0.110	-20	0.154	0.148	-4				23	3	11.8	7.7
Nigeria	0.922	0.285	-69	1.037	0.324	-69	1.6	0.4	-74	25	2	12.3	0.0
Rwanda	0.076	0.074	-3	0.063	0.067	6				8	4	5.5	8.3
São Tomé & Principe	0.573	0.594	4							8	3	5.0	9.1
Senegal	0.396	0.438	11	0.283	0.296	5				31	2	15.0	9.1
Sierra Leone	0.083	0.112	35	0.083	0.244	195				16	5	9.5	4.8
Somalia	0.003									6	4	4.5	0.0
Sudan	0.139	0.166	20	0.121	0.095	-22	2.0	2.0		16	6	10.0	9.1
Tanzania	0.089	0.128	43	0.169	0.247	47				15	5	9.1	10.0
Togo	0.200	0.394	97	0.119	0.249	109				21	4	11.4	8.0
Uganda	0.047	0.066	39	0.054	0.052	-3				20	6	11.8	7.7
Zambia	0.314	0.185	-41	0.327	0.238	-27				16	4	9.1	5.0
Zimbabwe	1.625	1.170	-28	0.597	0.454	-24	0.4	0.9	146	15	3	8.2	5.6
Middle income economies													
Botswana	1.700	2.299	35	0.297	0.306	3				12	5	7.7	5.9
Cape Verde	0.247	0.320	30	0.075	0.068	-8				11	5	7.3	6.3
Gabon	7.004	2.781	-60	1.141	0.454	-60				16	8	10.9	12.5
Mauritius	1.088	2.439	124	0.167	0.253	52				23	3	11.8	3.8
Namibia		0.961			0.158					14	2	7.3	12.5
South Africa	8.270	7.438	-10	0.823	0.788	-4	0.3	0.4	15	38	3	18.6	9.8
Swaziland	0.552	0.365	-34	0.131	0.083	-36				9	7	7.3	6.3

Region	Carbon dioxide emissions					
	metric tons per capita		% change	kg per PPP $ of GDP		% change
	1990	2000	1990-2000	1990	2000	1990-2000
Low income	0.799	0.808	1	0.417	0.401	-0.04
Middle income	3.574	3.236	-9	0.876	0.629	-0.28
Low & middle income	2.446	2.194	-10	0.785	0.581	-0.26
East Asia & Pacific	1.909	2.076	9	0.981	0.541	-0.45
Europe & Central Asia	10.221	6.704	-34	1.359	1.055	-0.22
Latin America & Caribbean	2.217	2.663	20	0.343	0.369	0.08
Middle East & North Africa	3.300	4.180	27	0.699	0.833	0.19
South Asia	0.684	0.901	32	0.429	0.404	-0.06
Sub-Saharan Africa	0.929	0.734	-21	0.545	0.434	-0.20
High income	11.754	12.354	5	0.533	0.452	-0.15
World	3.908	3.802	-3	0.633	0.507	-0.20

* includes 220 treaties in the following categories: animal species protection – management; environmental conservation (general); fishing – management – use of harvestable fish; forest conservation – management – exploitation; hunting – management – use of harvestable species; marine resources conservation – management; natural resources and nature conservation; plant species protection – management; renewable energy sources and energy conservation; soil conservation – management; water resources conservation – management.

** paper production data includes Luxemburg (in 2003 reported paper production in Luxemburg amount to 0).

NB/erratum to Yearbook 2004/05: last year's carbon dioxide data were reported using different measurement units – Metric tons CO2 per terajoule energy and Metric Tons CO2/million ppp.

Sources: World Development Indicators 2005, WDI Online; Food and Agriculture Organization of the United Nations, Forestry Data, FAOSTAT data, 2005, http://faostat.fao.org/; Environmental Treaties and Resource Indicators (ENTRI) project of The Center for International Earth Science Information Network (CIESIN), Earth Institute, Columbia University, sedac.ciesin.columbia.edu/entri/index.jsp

This record displays the extent to which INGOs in different countries are involved in the network of global civil society organisations. The scores in this table were calculated from a network of links between INGOs that make up almost half the entire universe of A–G organisations in the database of the Union of International Associations (UIA) (for more details on the network sample and data, see Chapter 7 of this Yearbook).

The scores illustrate different aspects of network centrality: the share of each country in the total number of organisations participating in the network indicates the inclusiveness of the network. The relative importance of nations in the network is indicated by the number of links an organisation sends or receives, which is also expressed as a percentage of the total sent/received links, respectively. The column 'Dyads connected' represents the number of pairs of organisations that are connected through the organisations in each country, thus measuring the contribution of each country's INGOs to the integration of the global INGO network.

The data reflect the extreme concentration of the network in the developed world (and particularly in four hubs of global civil society – the US, UK, Belgium and France), and the underdevelopment of global civil society in most of the developing world.

| Country | Organisations in network | Inter-organisational links | | | | Dyads connected* |
| | | Outgoing | | Incoming | | |
	%	Number	%	Number	%	Number
East Asia & Pacific						
Low income economies						
Cambodia	0.05	1	0.00	14	0.05	0
East Timor	0.01	0	0.00	6	0.02	0
Indonesia	0.18	52	0.19	54	0.20	46
Korea, Dem. Rep.	0.01	1	0.00	3	0.01	0
Mongolia	0.02	1	0.00	7	0.03	0
Vietnam	0.01	0	0.00	3	0.01	0
Middle income economies						
China & Tibet**	0.13	24	0.34	38	0.49	15
Fiji	0.15	30	0.11	49	0.18	4
Malaysia	0.47	132	0.49	142	0.52	80
Philippines	0.80	224	0.83	225	0.83	83
Samoa	0.02	5	0.02	5	0.02	0
Thailand	0.76	196	0.72	221	0.82	84
Tonga	0.02	3	0.01	12	0.04	0
Vanuatu	0.01	1	0.00	3	0.01	0
High income economies						
Australia	1.53	442	1.63	433	1.60	451
Korea, Rep.	0.22	38	0.14	59	0.22	12
Japan	1.47	358	1.32	436	1.61	269
New Zealand	0.26	74	0.27	77	0.28	26
Singapore	0.32	81	0.30	69	0.25	18

Country	Organisations in network	Inter-organisational links				Dyads connected*
		Outgoing		Incoming		
	%	Number	%	Number	%	Number
Europe & Central Asia						
Low income economies						
Armenia	0.01	0	0.00	4	0.01	0
Azerbaijan	0.01	2	0.01	4	0.01	0
Georgia	0.04	3	0.01	9	0.03	0
Kyrgyzstan	0.02	4	0.01	9	0.03	0
Moldova	0.01	11	0.04	4	0.01	0
Ukraine	0.07	10	0.04	23	0.08	0
Uzbekistan	0.02	0	0.00	4	0.01	0
Middle income economies						
Bosnia & Herzegovina	0.02	0	0.00	7	0.03	0
Bulgaria	0.14	98	0.36	43	0.16	11
Croatia	0.08	6	0.02	24	0.09	0
Czech Republic	0.21	61	0.22	68	0.25	6
Estonia	0.05	14	0.05	13	0.05	0
Hungary	0.32	85	0.31	88	0.32	131
Kazakhstan	0.03	8	0.03	9	0.03	2
Latvia	0.02	5	0.02	5	0.02	0
Lithuania	0.05	24	0.09	16	0.06	2
Macedonia	0.04	7	0.03	11	0.04	0
Poland	0.27	69	0.25	68	0.25	18
Romania	0.10	16	0.06	38	0.14	3
Russian Federation	0.46	136	0.50	134	0.49	71
Serbia & Montenegro	0.05	7	0.03	10	0.04	0
Slovakia	0.08	12	0.04	28	0.10	2
Slovenia	0.09	18	0.07	28	0.10	2
Turkey	0.17	44	0.16	54	0.20	8
High income economies						
Austria	1.49	464	1.71	454	1.68	414
Belgium	9.54	2,689	9.91	2,518	9.29	2,829
Cyprus	0.07	49	0.18	14	0.05	5
Denmark	1.42	417	1.54	457	1.69	554
Finland	0.83	162	0.60	239	0.88	101
France	8.01	2,215	8.16	2,160	7.97	1,851
Germany	4.90	1,302	4.80	1,360	5.02	1,462

Country	Organisations in network %	Inter-organisational links Outgoing Number	Outgoing %	Incoming Number	Incoming %	Dyads connected* Number
Greece	0.51	129	0.48	155	0.57	32
Iceland	0.12	35	0.13	36	0.13	6
Ireland	0.37	95	0.35	97	0.36	29
Italy	3.04	902	3.32	877	3.24	751
Luxembourg	0.26	64	0.24	61	0.23	10
Netherlands	4.01	1,146	4.22	1,154	4.26	1,058
Norway	0.94	296	1.09	263	0.97	238
Portugal	0.35	129	0.48	98	0.36	70
Spain	1.67	380	1.40	539	1.99	393
Sweden	1.56	440	1.62	439	1.62	340
Switzerland	4.26	1,636	6.03	1,200	4.43	1,304
United Kingdom	10.17	2,831	10.44	2,575	9.50	2,362
Latin America & Caribbean						
Low income economies						
Nicaragua	0.09	25	0.09	26	0.10	5
Middle income economies						
Argentina	0.66	200	0.74	179	0.66	112
Barbados	0.11	45	0.17	36	0.13	10
Bolivia	0.07	40	0.15	27	0.10	4
Brazil	0.45	97	0.36	146	0.54	35
Chile	0.40	139	0.51	114	0.42	63
Colombia	0.16	55	0.20	49	0.18	9
Costa Rica	0.48	146	0.54	113	0.42	54
Cuba	0.12	42	0.15	30	0.11	1
Dominican Republic	0.03	5	0.02	7	0.03	0
Ecuador	0.19	64	0.24	37	0.14	5
El Salvador	0.05	3	0.01	14	0.05	0
Guatemala	0.12	23	0.08	44	0.16	2
Guyana	0.04	12	0.04	19	0.07	2
Honduras	0.10	40	0.15	34	0.13	7
Jamaica	0.10	25	0.09	38	0.14	4
Mexico	0.51	108	0.40	163	0.60	59
Panama	0.13	13	0.05	39	0.14	1
Paraguay	0.03	5	0.02	9	0.03	0
Peru	0.26	77	0.28	70	0.26	5

| Country | Organisations in network | Inter-organisational links | | | | Dyads connected* |
| | | Outgoing | | Incoming | | |
	%	Number	%	Number	%	Number
St. Lucia	0.02	0	0.00	9	0.03	0
St. Vincent & the Grenadines	0.03	7	0.03	4	0.01	0
Suriname	0.02	2	0.01	4	0.01	0
Trinidad & Tobago	0.28	83	0.31	76	0.28	194
Uruguay	0.24	56	0.21	73	0.27	3
Venezuela	0.31	262	0.97	99	0.37	135
High income economies						
Bahamas	0.02	1	0.00	10	0.04	0
Middle East & North Africa						
Middle income economies						
Algeria	0.07	6	0.02	14	0.05	1
Egypt	0.37	138	0.51	102	0.38	59
Iran	0.04	4	0.01	10	0.04	0
Iraq	0.05	23	0.08	16	0.06	6
Jordan	0.09	3	0.01	32	0.12	0
Lebanon	0.10	22	0.08	27	0.10	0
Libya	0.03	14	0.05	10	0.04	1
Malta	0.13	37	0.14	34	0.13	3
Morocco	0.05	12	0.04	18	0.07	0
Oman	0.01	0	0.00	1	0.00	0
Palestinian Authority	0.02	2	0.01	4	0.01	0
Saudi Arabia	0.09	54	0.20	23	0.08	6
Syria	0.05	17	0.06	9	0.03	0
Tunisia	0.17	80	0.29	62	0.23	21
High income economies						
Israel	0.68	195	0.72	213	0.79	41
Kuwait	0.04	11	0.04	18	0.07	1
United Arab Emirates	0.05	41	0.15	21	0.08	6
North America						
High income economies						
Canada	3.09	830	3.06	864	3.19	778
United States	19.98	4,198	15.47	4,670	17.23	4,831
South Asia						
Low income economies						
Bangladesh	0.15	34	0.13	41	0.15	28

| Country | Organisations in network % | Inter-organisational links | | | | Dyads connected* |
| | | Outgoing | | Incoming | | |
	%	Number	%	Number	%	Number
India	1.19	344	1.27	393	1.45	376
Nepal	0.18	62	0.23	55	0.20	15
Pakistan	0.19	80	0.29	62	0.23	6
Middle income economies						
Sri Lanka	0.16	67	0.25	50	0.18	11
Sub-Saharan Africa						
Low income economies						
Angola	0.01	0	0.00	2	0.01	0
Benin	0.11	17	0.06	36	0.13	1
Burkina Faso	0.18	44	0.16	51	0.19	5
Burundi	0.01	1	0.00	3	0.01	0
Cameroon	0.15	36	0.13	46	0.17	9
Congo, Rep.	0.02	5	0.02	4	0.01	0
Congo, Dem. Rep.	0.03	1	0.00	5	0.02	0
Côte d'Ivoire	0.16	44	0.16	52	0.19	10
Ethiopia	0.16	85	0.31	49	0.18	61
Gambia	0.04	10	0.04	18	0.07	0
Ghana	0.23	90	0.33	72	0.27	21
Guinea	0.01	3	0.01	4	0.01	0
Kenya	0.88	206	0.76	279	1.03	197
Lesotho	0.02	0	0.00	2	0.01	0
Madagascar	0.01	2	0.01	2	0.01	0
Malawi	0.01	3	0.01	4	0.01	0
Mali	0.06	51	0.19	14	0.05	2
Mauritania	0.01	3	0.01	3	0.01	0
Mozambique	0.04	12	0.04	12	0.04	0
Nigeria	0.33	145	0.53	89	0.33	57
Rwanda	0.03	6	0.02	7	0.03	0
Senegal	0.47	115	0.42	147	0.54	52
Sierra Leone	0.01	0	0.00	4	0.01	0
Sudan	0.04	11	0.04	9	0.03	0
Tanzania	0.15	37	0.14	46	0.17	4
Togo	0.18	73	0.27	57	0.21	51
Uganda	0.15	35	0.13	38	0.14	3
Zambia	0.09	26	0.10	26	0.10	5

| Country | Organisations in network | Inter-organisational links | | | | Dyads connected* |
| | | Outgoing | | Incoming | | |
	%	Number	%	Number	%	Number
Zimbabwe	0.22	92	0.34	63	0.23	24
Middle income economies						
Botswana	0.10	70	0.26	24	0.09	10
Gabon	0.04	6	0.02	9	0.03	0
Mauritius	0.08	2	0.01	29	0.11	0
Namibia	0.04	7	0.03	12	0.04	0
South Africa	0.56	136	0.50	161	0.59	42
Swaziland	0.01	1	0.00	2	0.01	0

* The measure used is *network betweenness centrality*: a measure of the number of times an organisation is part of the shortest path between a pair (dyad) of other organisations.

** China & Tibet includes Hong Kong and Macao

Source: © Union of International Associations

Record 17: **NGOs and global governance**

NGOs have become frequent and often important participants in global governance systems and processes; this record shows how and where they are involved. The first part displays numbers of NGOs participating in the World Trade Organization's ministerial conferences as well as the numbers of INGOs holding participatory status with the Council of Europe. Countries where the World Bank engaged civil society organisations in consultation efforts 2001–04 are also listed, distinguishing between consultation in country assistance strategy and involvement in poverty reduction strategy. The former refers to the World Bank's comprehensive development strategy for any country planning to borrow from World Bank agencies. The latter refers to the process intended to encourage governments to develop their own comprehensive plans to promote economic growth and reduce poverty through wide stakeholder consultation and donor coordination.

The second part of this record details the scope of NGO involvement in the UN, through holding consultative status and through participation in the UN's Global Compact. The first table lists INGOs holding consultative status with the Economic and Social Council (ECOSOC) of the UN, which engages in international cooperation on standards-making and problem-solving in economic and social issues. General Category organisations are those defined as 'concerned with most of the activities of the ECOSOC and its subsidiary bodies'. Usually this includes large established INGOs with a broad geographical reach. Special Category is granted to NGOs 'which have a special competence in, and are concerned specifically with, only a few of the fields of activity covered by the ECOSOC', which are usually smaller and younger. Roster organisations are those that 'can make occasional and useful contributions to the work of ECOSOC', and tend to have a rather narrow and/or technical focus.

The Global Compact is a UN initiative to bring companies together with UN agencies, labour and civil society in order to support universal environmental and social principles, and to catalyse action in support of UN goals, through policy dialogues, learning, country/regional networks, and projects (see Box 5.3 in this Yearbook).

The tables shows a bifurcation in the modes of participation of civil society actors in global governance processes. One mode is consultative status or participation in global governance processes, which is increasing but is the prerogative mostly of NGOs from developed nations. Organisations from developing nations participate in global governance process at the local level, usually by invitation from agencies such as the World Bank.

Country	NGO participation in WTO ministerial conferences		Council of Europe	World Bank, civil society consultation efforts								Total 2001-4
	Seattle, 1999	Doha, 2001	INGOs with participatory status, 2005	Consultation in Country Assistance Strategy				Involvement in Poverty Reduction Strategy				
	number	number	number	2001	2002	2003	2004	2001	2002	2003	2004	
East Asia & Pacific												
Low income economies												
Cambodia						yes		yes		yes		3
Indonesia	2					yes						1
Mongolia							yes	yes		yes		3
Vietnam					yes		yes		yes		yes	4
Middle income economies												
China*						yes						1
Fiji	1	1										
Malaysia	3	6										
Philippines	6	15			yes							1
Thailand	1	10			yes							1
High income economies												
Australia	8	15	1									
Japan	13	42										
Korea, Rep.		6										
New Zealand	1	3										
Europe & Central Asia												
Low income economies												
Armenia										yes		1
Azerbaijan						yes		yes		yes		3
Georgia	2	1								yes		1
Kyrgyzstan				yes		yes		yes		yes	yes	5
Moldova			1								yes	1
Tajikistan									yes			1
Ukraine										yes		1
Uzbekistan					yes							1
Middle income economies												
Albania						yes			yes	yes	yes	4
Belarus					yes							1
Bosnia & Herzegovina				yes					yes		yes	3
Bulgaria					yes							1
Croatia				yes								1

Country	NGO participation in WTO ministerial conferences		Council of Europe	World Bank, civil society consultation efforts								
	Seattle, 1999	Doha, 2001	INGOs with participatory status, 2005	Consultation in Country Assistance Strategy				Involvement in Poverty Reduction Strategy				Total 2001-4
	number	number	number	2001	2002	2003	2004	2001	2002	2003	2004	
Czech Republic		2	1									
Hungary		5			yes							1
Latvia					yes							1
Macedonia		1				yes						1
Poland		1			yes							1
Romania			1									
Russian Federation		1	6		yes							1
Serbia & Montenegro									yes		yes	2
Slovakia							yes					1
Slovenia			1									
Turkey						yes						1
High income economies												
Austria		7	13									
Belgium	37	64	85									
Denmark	3	6	7									
Finland	1	3	3									
France	35	54	90									
Germany	9	29	22									
Greece		1	3									
Iceland	1	1										
Ireland		3	1									
Italy	2	11	16									
Netherlands	12	18	19									
Norway	6	21										
Spain	10	14	2									
Sweden	4	6	3									
Switzerland	16	39	37									
United Kingdom	19	45	42									
Latin America & Caribbean												
Low income economies												
Dominica										yes		1
Nicaragua		2				yes		yes	yes		yes	4

Country	NGO participation in WTO ministerial conferences		Council of Europe	World Bank, civil society consultation efforts								
	Seattle, 1999	Doha, 2001	INGOs with participatory status, 2005	Consultation in Country Assistance Strategy				Involvement in Poverty Reduction Strategy				Total 2001-4
	number	number	number	2001	2002	2003	2004	2001	2002	2003	2004	
Middle income economies												
Argentina	3	1					yes					1
Barbados		1										
Bolivia	1	5					yes					1
Brazil	3	18			yes							1
Chile	1	4	1		yes							1
Colombia		6				yes						1
Costa Rica	1	1					yes					1
Ecuador	4	2				yes						1
El Salvador	1	2		yes								1
Guatemala		3			yes							1
Guyana					yes				yes			2
Honduras		1				yes		yes			yes	3
Mexico	2	33			yes		yes					2
Paraguay	1	1				yes						1
Peru	2	4			yes							1
Trinidad & Tobago	1	1										
Uruguay	3	1	1									
Venezuela	1	1										
Middle East & North Africa												
Low income economies												
Yemen									yes			1
Middle income economies												
Algeria						yes						1
Djibouti								yes			yes	2
Egypt	1	3										
Iran		1										
Jordan		2				yes						1
Lebanon		1										
Tunisia		3					yes					1
North America												
High income economies												
Canada	46	84	2									

	NGO participation in WTO ministerial conferences		Council of Europe	World Bank, civil society consultation efforts									
	Seattle, 1999	Doha, 2001	INGOs with participatory status, 2005	Consultation in Country Assistance Strategy				Involvement in Poverty Reduction Strategy				Total 2001-4
Country	number	number	number	2001	2002	2003	2004	2001	2002	2003	2004	
United States	187	236	5									
South Asia												
Low income economies												
Afghanistan					yes							1
Bangladesh	1	2								yes		1
India	6	34					yes					1
Nepal		4			yes	yes				yes		3
Pakistan		9			yes				yes		yes	3
Middle income economies												
Sri Lanka					yes					yes		2
Sub-Saharan Africa												
Low income economies												
Benin	1	1			yes					yes		2
Burkina Faso		1			yes		yes	yes			yes	4
Burundi										yes		1
Cameroon		3			yes					yes		2
Chad					yes					yes		2
Congo, Dem. Rep.									yes			1
Côte d'Ivoire		2		yes					yes			2
Ethiopia					yes				yes		yes	3
Gambia					yes				yes			2
Ghana	2	4				yes				yes	yes	3
Guinea		1			yes				yes			2
Kenya	5	11									yes	1
Liberia						yes						1
Madagascar		2			yes					yes		2
Malawi		1			yes				yes	yes		3
Mali		2			yes					yes	yes	3
Mauritania				yes					yes	yes		3
Mozambique		1			yes	yes			yes	yes		4
Niger				yes	yes				yes	yes		4
Nigeria		1										
Rwanda					yes				yes			2

Country	NGO participation in WTO ministerial conferences		Council of Europe	World Bank, civil society consultation efforts								
	Seattle, 1999	Doha, 2001	INGOs with participatory status, 2005	Consultation in Country Assistance Strategy				Involvement in Poverty Reduction Strategy				Total 2001-4
	number	number	number	2001	2002	2003	2004	2001	2002	2003	2004	
Senegal	1	1				yes			yes			2
Sierra Leone					yes			yes		yes		3
Somalia						yes						1
Tanzania		1						yes		yes	yes	3
Togo	1	1										
Uganda		10							yes	yes		2
Zambia		3									yes	1
Zimbabwe	4	3										
Middle income economies												
Botswana	1											
Cape Verde									yes			1
Mauritius	1				yes							1
Namibia	1											
South Africa	2	8										

Region	NGO participation in WTO ministerial conferences		Council of Europe	World Bank, civil society consultation efforts								
	Seattle, 1999	Doha, 2001	INGOs with participatory status, 2005	Consultation in Country Assistance Strategy				Involvement in Poverty Reduction Strategy				Total 2001-4
	number	number	number	2001	2002	2003	2004	2001	2002	2003	2004	
Low income	25	101	1	2	10	19	5	10	16	23	14	99
Middle income	41	140	16	3	16	10	6	2	5	2	5	49
Low & middle income:												
East Asia & Pacific	13	32	0	0	3	3	2	2	1	2	1	14
Europe & Central Asia	2	6	15	3	8	4	1	2	4	6	5	33
Latin America & Caribbean	24	87	2	1	6	5	4	2	2	1	2	23
Middle East & North Africa	1	10	0	0	0	2	1	1	1	0	1	6
South Asia	7	49	0	0	3	2	1	1	0	3	1	11
Sub-Saharan Africa	19	57	0	2	6	14	2	4	13	13	9	63
High income	410	708	351	0	0	0	0	0	0	0	0	0
World	476	949	368	5	26	29	11	12	21	25	19	148

* Data for Hong Kong, Macao and Taiwan are not included in this table.

Sources: WTO, http://www.wto.org/english/forums_e/ngo_e/ngo_e.htm; Council of Europe, http://www.coe.int/T/E/NGO/public/Participatory_status/; World Bank, (forthcoming). World Bank-Civil Society, Review of Fiscal Years 2002 – 2004 Engagement, Annex I: Civil Society Consultation Efforts in Country Assistance Strategies (CASs); Annex II – Society Civil Society Involvement Efforts in Poverty Reduction Strategy Papers (PRSPs).

Consultative status of NGOs

Year	Number of NGOs				Year	Number of NGOs			
	General	Special	Roster	Total		General	Special	Roster	Total
1945	0	0	0	0	1976	24	196	466	686
1946	4	0	0	4	1977	26	204	501	731
1947	7	32	2	41	1978	27	203	534	764
1948	9	56	4	69	1979	30	206	357	593
1949	9	77	4	90	1980	30	205	373	608
1950	9	78	110	197	1981	31	215	400	646
1951	9	92	116	217	1982	31	215	400	646
1952	9	100	113	222	1983	31	239	422	692
1953	9	106	124	239	1984	32	236	444	712
1954	9	109	151	269	1985	34	269	457	760
1955	10	110	162	282	1986	34	267	461	762
1956	10	110	172	292	1987	35	299	493	827
1957	10	112	177	299	1988	35	299	493	827
1958	10	112	180	302	1989	36	331	526	893
1959	10	117	200	327	1990	36	331	526	893
1960	10	119	205	334	1991	41	354	533	928
1961	10	120	201	331	1992	41	354	533	928
1962	10	124	198	332	1993	41	373	555	969
1963	10	122	206	338	1994	42	376	551	969
1964	10	131	214	355	1995	69	436	563	1,068
1965	10	131	220	361	1996	80	500	646	1,226
1966	12	135	221	368	1997	88	602	666	1,356
1967	12	143	222	377	1998	103	745	669	1,517
1968	12	143	222	377	1999	111	918	672	1,701
1969	16	116	245	377	2000	120	1003	872	1,995
1970	16	137	266	419	2001	121	1083	885	2,089
1971	16	157	296	469	2002	131	1197	908	2,236
1972	17	168	334	519	2003	131	1317	931	2,379
1973	19	181	381	581	2004	134	1479	922	2,535
1974	20	192	403	615	2005	134	1548	913	2,595
1975	24	194	433	651					

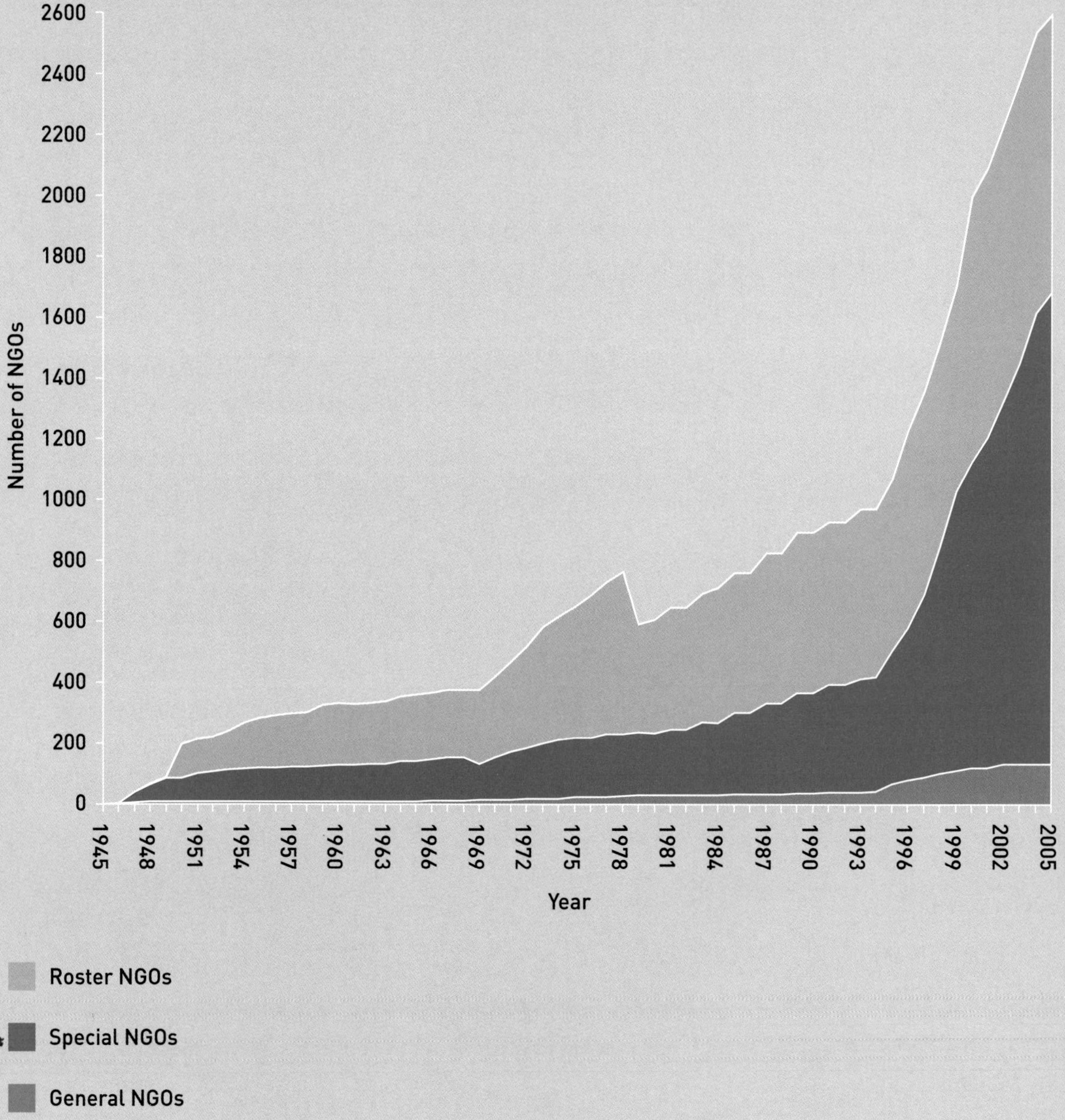
2600
2400
2200
2000
1800
1600
1400
1200
1000
800
600
400
200
0
Number of NGOs
1945
1948
1951
1954
1957
1960
1963
1966
1969
1972
1975
1978
1981
1984
1987
1990
1993
1996
1999
2002
2005
Year
Roster NGOs
Special NGOs
General NGOs

Stakeholders participating in the UN's Global Compact, September 2004

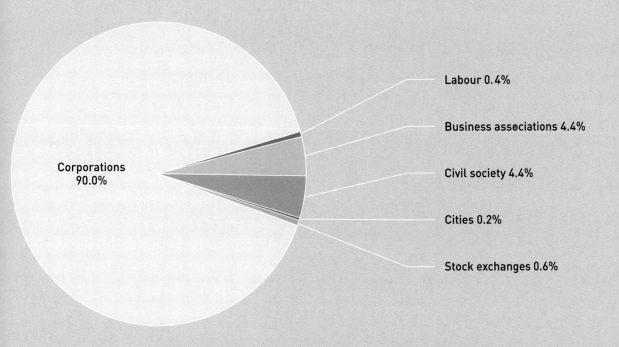

Corporations 90.0%

Labour 0.4%

Business associations 4.4%

Civil society 4.4%

Cities 0.2%

Stock exchanges 0.6%

Type	Number
Corporations	1,999
Labour	9
Business associations	97
Civil society	97
Cities	5
Stock exchanges	13
Academia	n/a*

*The Global Compact included participants from academic institutions, but data for these were not available for this record.

Sources: © Peter Willetts (2002), The Conscience of the World. Washington: The Brookings Institution, http://www.staff.city.ac.uk/p.willetts/NGOS/NGO-GRPH.HTM; UN DESA-NGO section, NGOs in consultative status with ECOSOC, http://www.un.org/esa/coordination/ngo/pdf/INF_List.pdf; UN Global Compact, http://www.unglobalcompact.org

Record 18: **NGO-government relations**

NGOs have complicated relationships with governments, which can entail variously cooperation, dependence, competition, evaluation, and other forms of interaction. The three tables in this record demonstrate two different aspects of government-NGO relations – financial support from governments to NGOs, and evaluation of NGOs by government for the purpose of strategically planning aid policies.

The first table displays financial support given by OECD member states to NGOs in their own countries and to international NGOs, as well as the percentage change in such assistance, which shows a substantial increase in support in most OECD countries, particularly support for international NGOs.

The second table summarises NGO co-financing and decentralised cooperation funds disbursed by the EuropeAid cooperation office, the European Commission organ developed to implement the European Commission's external aid instruments. NGO co-financing and decentralised cooperation funding complements the main funding instruments for development cooperation, such as the European Development Fund (EDF). This type of funding covers activities undertaken by European NGOs in developing countries, to raise public awareness of development issues in European countries and to strengthen civil society in the South. The figures demonstrate the magnitude of sums disbursed, but also the gaps between what is requested and what is actually made available. Actual commitments represent less than one-fifth of requested sums.

The third table lists the scores of the Central and Eastern Europe and Eurasia NGO Sustainability Index, which is issued by the evaluation staff of USAID. This evaluation is used by USAID and other agencies as a management tool to shape funding policies, inform programme design and monitor and measure progress. The index is composed of seven dimensions and a composite index score, which are presented in the table. The table also shows percentage changes in the composite index between 2000 and 2003, which reflect a predominantly negative trend in the sustainability of civil society in the region.

OECD Development Assistance: gross disbursements to NGOs

Donor	Support to national NGOs			Support to international NGOs		
	US $ (million) 1993	US $ (million) 2003	% change 1993-2003	US $ (million) 1993	US $ (million) 2003	% change 1993-2003
Countries						
Australia	17.29	0.89	-95	1.19	0.29	-76
Austria	4.64	0.14	-97	0.55	1.11	102
Belgium	1.69	7.34	334	0.03	5.05	16,733
Canada	128.01	0.66	-99	16.29	12.89	-21
Denmark	6.31	12.36	96			
Finland	4.73	6.00	27	2.17	1.81	-17
France	21.01	28.17	34		5.85	
Germany	195.23			5.32	1.22	-77
Ireland	1.96	74.10	3,681	1.16	29.61	2,453
Italy		34.14		5.34	5.65	6
Japan	131.91	187.68	42	9.84	142.44	1,348
Korea, Rep.		6.66			0.35	
Luxembourg	0.40	26.06	6,415			
Netherlands	208.05	659.53	217		37.20	
New Zealand	1.06	11.07	944	0.16	1.53	856
Norway				7.73	17.13	122
Portugal	0.06	0.65	983		0.23	
Spain		6.90		1.32	1.94	47
Sweden		105.03			1.73	
Switzerland	103.20	46.73	-55	37.23	51.23	38
United Kingdom	48.23	268.34	456	13.62	60.19	342
Multilateral	148.08				1.52	
Aggregations						
G7, total	524.39	518.99	-1	50.41	228.24	353
EU members	492.31	1,228.76	150	29.51	151.59	414
Development Co-operation Directorate (DAC) countries	873.78	1,475.79	69	101.95	377.10	270
Non-DAC bilateral donors		6.66			0.35	
All donors	1,021.86	1,482.45	45	101.95	378.97	272

Source: OECD Development Assistance Committee, http://www1.oecd.org/scripts/cde/viewbase.asp?dbname=cde_dac

EuropeAid – NGO co-financing and decentralised cooperation, 2003

Country	Actions of development				Actions to raise European public awareness of development issues				Actions of strengthening the civil society of the South				Total			
	Requests		Commitments		Requests		Commitments		Requests		Commitments		Requests		Commitments	
	Number	Total Euro	Number	Total Euro	Number	Total Euro	Number	Total Euro	Number	Total Euro	Number	Total Euro	Number	Total Euro	Number	Total Euro
Austria	27	14,056,490	7	3,588,014	5	1,921,527	1	700,903	1	999,540	1	999,540	33	16,977,557	9	5,288,457
Belgium	35	17,997,721	8	3,819,892	7	3,495,490	2	1,109,688	8	4,977,844	3	2,179,510	50	26,471,055	13	7,109,090
Denmark	21	14,144,400	2	1,500,000	6	2,196,996	0	0	0	0	0	0	27	16,341,396	2	1,500,000
Finland	2	1,500,000	0	0	3	1,962,684	0	0	0	0	0	0	5	3,462,684	0	0
France	138	82,372,645	32	19,233,870	20	7,279,122	3	2,091,530	17	10,597,146	5	3,304,586	175	100,248,913	40	24,629,986
Germany	105	61,940,900	20	12,818,991	55	25,251,648	6	2,430,753	9	6,276,034	0	0	169	93,468,582	26	15,249,744
Greece	6	3,446,895	1	415,313	3	1,258,529	0	0	2	1,127,639	0	0	11	5,833,063	1	415,313
Ireland	5	2,584,853	1	750,000	3	900,127	2	579,689	1	852,739	0	0	9	4,337,719	3	1,329,689
Italy	217	134,388,541	19	10,493,041	55	23,098,263	9	4,808,964	26	17,610,875	2	1,887,319	298	175,097,679	30	17,189,324
Luxembourg	1	185,477	1	185,477					1	785,808	1	785,808	2	971,285	2	971,285
Netherlands	48	35,147,305	5	4,815,251	17	6,205,046	4	1,592,874	0	0	0	0	65	41,352,351	9	6,408,125
Portugal	25	15,650,652	6	3,794,024	10	4,598,140	2	864,018	3	1,907,195	1	791,627	38	22,155,987	9	5,449,669
Spain	114	55,302,000	12	5,163,839	24	7,051,574	2	532,273	10	7,601,294	2	1,990,336	148	69,954,868	16	7,686,448
Sweden	3	1,694,705	0	0	2	457,586	1	197,221	3	1,021,388	0	0	8	3,173,679	1	197,221
UK	193	119,464,654	40	24,250,090	44	28,357,467	12	5,780,554	10	7,528,844	1	999,437	247	155,350,965	53	31,030,081
Consortium	76	79,749,874	21	22,149,452									76	79,749,874	21	22,149,452
Total	1,016	639,627,112	175	112,977,254	249	112,112,672	43	19,987,564	91	61,286,346	16	12,938,163	1,356	813,026,130	234	145,902,981

Source: EuropeAid – NGO co-financing and decentralised Cco-operation, 2003, http://europa.eu.int/comm/europeaid/projects/ong_cd/index_en.htm

USAID – Central and Eastern Europe and Eurasia NGO Sustainability Index

Country	Sub-indices scores, 2003							Overall index scores, 1997-2003							
	Legal environment	Organisational capacity	Financial viability	Advocacy	Service provision	Infrastructure	Public image	1997	1998	1999	2000	2001	2002	2003	% change 2000-2003
Albania	3.5	4.2	4.6	3.6	4.0	4.4	4.5	4.4	4.2	4.8	4.6	4.6	4.3	4.1	-11
Armenia	3.8	3.6	5.5	3.8	4.0	4.0	3.9		5.5	5.1	5.0	4.4	4.2	4.1	-18
Azerbaijan	5.0	4.8	5.8	4.8	4.8	4.7	5.3		6.3	5.6	5.0	5.0	5.2	5.0	0
Belarus	6.8	4.8	6.2	5.7	5.1	4.8	5.6				5.7	5.5	5.3	5.6	-2
Bosnia	3.5	3.8	5.4	3.6	4.4	4.5	3.8		5.6	5.3	4.9	4.5	4.2	4.1	-16
Bulgaria	2.0	4.4	3.7	2.5	2.9	2.5	3.4	4.0	3.6	4.0	3.7	3.6	3.1	3.1	-16
Croatia	2.8	3.8	4.4	3.0	3.4	3.6	3.4	4.6	4.4	4.6	4.3	3.8	3.7	3.5	-19
Czech Republic	3.0	2.9	1.9	2.0	2.2	3.0	2.1				2.4	2.3	2.5	2.4	0
Estonia	1.8	2.6	2.6	2.0	2.5	2.0	2.2				2.4	2.1	2.2	2.2	-8
Georgia	3.7	4.0	4.6	4.0	4.4	3.8	4.4		3.6	3.8	4.1	4.0	4.2	4.1	0
Hungary	1.3	2.9	3.3	3.3	2.3	2.4	3.2	2.3	1.6	2.1	2.3	2.6	2.6	2.7	17
Kazakhstan	4.0	3.8	4.7	3.6	3.9	3.6	3.9	4.6	4.2	4.8	4.7	4.3	4.1	3.9	-17
Kosovo	3.2	4.3	5.6	3.8	4.8	3.5	3.9			4.4	4.6	4.6	4.3	4.2	-9
Kyrgyzstan	3.9	4.3	5.0	3.8	3.8	3.8	4.1	4.6	3.8	4.2	4.3	4.3	4.0	4.1	-5
Latvia	2.6	2.9	3.3	2.0	2.5	2.8	2.8	3.6	4.2		2.8	2.9	2.8	2.7	-4
Lithuania	1.6	2.6	3.0	1.6	3.4	2.2	3.3	4.0	3.0	2.9	3.1	2.9	2.7	2.5	-19
Macedonia	2.9	3.7	4.5	3.3	4.0	3.3	3.9	4.4	4.4	4.6	4.6	4.1	4.0	3.7	-20
Moldova	3.7	4.2	5.3	4.1	4.5	3.8	4.2				4.6	4.2	4.2	4.3	-7
Montenegro	3.4	4.8	5.4	4.3	4.2	4.6	4.7			4.6	4.6	4.7	4.6	4.5	-2
Poland	2.0	2.2	2.8	1.9	2.0	1.9	2.2	1.8	2.0	2.1	2.1	2.1	2.2	2.1	0
Romania	4.0	3.8	4.3	3.8	3.1	3.6	4.0	3.6	3.8	4.0	4.1	4.0	3.7	3.8	-7
Russian Federation	4.3	4.3	4.9	4.5	4.1	4.0	4.6	3.4	3.4	4.1	4.3	4.2	4.0	4.4	2
Serbia	4.5	3.8	5.4	3.2	4.1	3.3	3.9	4.8	5.4	5.4	4.6	4.1	4.1	4.0	-13
Slovakia	2.5	2.0	3.2	1.6	2.2	1.9	2.0	2.8	2.8	2.2	1.9	1.9	2.1	2.2	16
Slovenia	3.7	3.5	3.3	3.0	3.0	3.8	3.6							3.4	
Tajikistan	4.3	4.6	5.7	4.5	4.3	4.1	4.4		6.6	6.1	5.4	5.1	4.6	4.6	-15
Turkmenistan	6.7	5.3	6.0	6.1	4.8	5.0	5.9			6.6	6.0	5.8	5.6	5.7	-5
Ukraine	4.0	3.9	4.8	3.4	3.3	3.5	4.4	4.0	4.2	4.1	4.4	4.3	4.0	3.9	-11
Uzbekistan	4.2	4.4	5.5	5.1	4.6	4.5	4.3		4.9	5.3	5.1	4.6	4.7	4.7	-8

Source: USAID (2004), The 2003 Sustainability Index for Central and Eastern Europe and Eurasia, Statistical annexes, http://www.usaid.gov/locations/europe_eurasia/dem_gov/ngoindex/2003/

DATA PROGRAMME

Record 19: Attitudes towards NGOs

The public image of NGOs is extremely diverse. They enjoy considerable public support, which is demonstrated through donations as well as positive attitudes towards them and their work, but they are also subject to much criticism. The tables in this record illustrate some elements of public attitudes towards NGOs.

The first table summarises public attitudes, comparing the levels of trust enjoyed by various civil society groups in Europe. The second table shows which types of civil society actors people trust the most to control the effects of globalisation. Respondents could select more than one organisation, so the percentages do not add up to 100. The data show that, although mostly the level of generalised trust in NGOs is high and rising, respondents were sceptical about NGOs' ability to control globalisation.

The third table displays the respondents' support for global civil society involvement in global governance reforms and sustainable development. The Global Stakeholders Panel is an annual survey of leaders from

Trust in other institutions

I would like to ask you a question about how much trust you have in certain institutions. For each of the following institutions, please tell me if you tend to trust it or tend not to trust it?

% responding 'tend to trust'	Religious institutions			Trade unions			Charitable or voluntary organisations		
	Autumn 2003	Spring 2004	% change 2003-2004	Autumn 2003	Spring 2004	% change 2003-2004	Autumn 2003	Spring 2004	% change 2003-2004
Country									
Belgium	39	33	-15	44	43	-2	58	64	10
Denmark	72	74	3	53	51	-4	57	63	11
Germany	39	37	-5	27	28	4	51	51	0
Greece	60	61	2	44	50	14	63	64	2
Spain	37	58	57	33	53	61	62	26	-58
France	34	52	53	36	53	47	62	24	-61
Ireland	33	38	15	43	48	12	63	64	2
Italy	55	55	0	31	35	13	57	61	7
Luxembourg	36	37	3	44	47	7	58	62	7
Netherlands	38	37	-3	50	54	8	64	60	-6
Austria	44	43	-2	43	38	-12	56	57	2
Portugal	64	63	-2	41	40	-2	61	68	11
Finland	69	71	3	57	53	-7	51	56	10
Sweden	19	21	11	42	49	17	45	46	2
United Kingdom	37	37	0	35	34	-3	68	65	-4
EU15*	42	41	-2	35	36	3	59	61	3

NGOs, governments, and businesses across the world on issues of globalisation and governance. Respondents were asked if a 'global social movement alliance of NGOs and individual citizens' was an effective way to accelerate sustainable development, and to prioritise different forms of NGO involvement in UN reform. The figures demonstrate strong support for the involvement of global civil society in global governance reforms and sustainable development.

A very different expression of attitudes towards NGO is highlighted in the fourth table. It counts acts of terrorism directed towards NGOs between 1991 and 2005. These incidents can be used as an indicator of animosity towards NGOs, although it should be borne in mind that different regions experience varying levels of terrorist activity in general. The data reveal a considerable increase in such incidents, mainly due to terror attacks on NGOs in Afghanistan and Iraq.

Trusting people to control the effects of globalisation

From the following list, who do you trust most to get the effects of globalisation under control?

Respondents selecting as most trustworthy	Green/ environmental/ ecological groups	Trade unions	Consumer rights associations	Anti- or alter- globalisation movements	Non- governmental organisations (NGOs)	Citizens themselves
Country						
Belgium	10	11	25	10	14	28
Denmark	22	9	18	7	10	26
Germany	12	8	26	14	6	23
Greece	21	12	26	20	13	28
Spain	13	7	15	14	15	16
France	20	11	34	22	21	31
Ireland	19	9	22	10	7	16
Italy	17	7	41	13	21	23
Luxembourg	14	11	15	8	11	22
Netherlands	10	10	20	10	4	24
Austria	17	12	19	11	9	21
Portugal	7	6	14	5	5	15
Finland	13	7	15	11	12	30
Sweden	22	8	18	10	5	26
United Kingdom	18	9	16	7	12	21
EU15*	16	9	26	13	13	23

* Figure for EU15 represents an average with countries weighted according their populations (using population estimates from EUROSTAT or national statistical offices).

Source: European Commission, 2004. Eurobarometer 60: Public opinion in the european union, Autumn 2003, Eurobarometer 61: Public opinion in the european union, Fall 2004, http://europa.eu.int/comm/public_opinion/standard_en.htm

Global Stakeholders Panel – Role of global civil society in global governance reforms

	Sub-Saharan Africa	South & East Asia	Middle East & North Africa	Latin America & Caribbean	North America	Western Europe	Eastern Europe & Central Asia	Pacific
Accelerating sustainable development **% responding 'effective' or 'highly effective'**								
Effectiveness of a global social movement alliance of NGOs and individual citizens	72	72	73	72	63	51	48	61
UN reform priorities **% responding 'priority' or 'high priority'**								
Creating a civil society forum (involving NGOs, trade unions and business firms) parallel to the UN General Assembly	91	72	73	79	60	60	74	72
Greater role for NGOs to act as a 'moral compass' for the UN	81	70	73	59	52	46	58	50
Providing greater space for NGOs to voice their views on global issues	90	85	73	83	71	66	81	74
Greater role for NGOs as advisors on UN policy and programmes	83	77	82	75	67	63	77	72
Greater role for NGOs in implementation of UN programmes	81	65	64	80	61	60	81	67
Providing feedback to NGOs on their recommendations to the UN	88	80	64	75	64	57	68	70
Improving NGO capacity to participate in UN policymaking	87	72	73	84	58	55	68	76
Balancing the influence of Northern and Southern NGOs in the UN	88	82	82	84	62	65	58	72
Improving Southern NGOs' capacity to participate in UN policymaking	85	77	73	88	61	68	55	72
Providing a greater NGO role in improving developing country governments' capacity to participate in UN policymaking	83	77	82	79	53	56	58	61
Providing a greater NGO role in representing special interest groups in the UN	79	72	73	76	50	56	55	59
Requiring member governments to better involve NGOs when developing positions on UN matters	81	77	73	75	60	58	52	67

	Low income economies	Middle income economies	High income economies
Accelerating sustainable development			
% responding 'effective' or 'highly effective'			
Effectiveness of a global social movement alliance of NGOs and individual citizens	68	70	57
UN reform priorities			
% responding 'priority' or 'high priority'			
Creating a civil society forum (involving NGOs, trade unions and business firms) parallel to the UN general assembly	79	82	61
Greater role for NGOs to act as a "moral compass" for the UN	71	65	49
Providing greater space for NGOs to voice their views on global issues	84	87	68
Greater role for NGOs as advisors on UN policy and programmes	78	83	64
Greater role for NGOs in implementation of UN programmes	75	80	60
Providing feedback to NGOs on their recommendations to the UN	83	73	61
Improving NGO capacity to participate in UN policymaking	82	79	57
Balancing the influence of Northern and Southern NGOs in the UN	84	79	64
Improving Southern NGOs' capacity to participate in UN policymaking	82	78	65
Providing a greater NGO role in improving developing country governments' capacity to participate in UN policymaking	79	78	55
Providing a greater NGO role in representing special interest groups in the UN	74	75	53
Requiring member governments to better involve NGOs when developing positions on UN matters	76	76	59

Source: 2020 Fund (2005), What Global Leaders Want? Report of the Third Survey of the 2020 Global Stakeholder Panel; http://www.2020fund.org/gsp_results.htm

Terrorist incidents targeting NGOs

Country	1991	1992	1993	1994	1995	1996	1997	1998	1999	2000	2001	2002	2003	2004	2005	1991-1995	1996-2000	2001-2005	% change 1991-5 to 2001-5
East Asia & Pacific																			
Cambodia			2	1		2										3	2		
Indonesia							1			2		1		1			3	2	
Japan													4					4	
Philippines	1											1				1		1	0
Europe & Central Asia																			
Albania							1										1		
Bosnia & Herzegovina				1	1			1								2	1		
France								1									1		
Russian Federation					1	4	3					4	1	1		1	7	6	500
Serbia & Montenegro								1									1		
Switzerland								1									1		
Tajikistan							2	1			1						3	1	
Turkey								1	1		1						2	1	
Latin America & Caribbean																			
Colombia							1	3	4	4	1	1	1	1			12	4	
Guatemala					1											1			
Peru	3						1									3	1		
Middle East & North Africa																			
Iraq		4	1	1	1	1		1				5	9	3		7	2	17	143
Lebanon	1															1			
Yemen			1													1			
South Asia																			
Afghanistan	1	1	1				1					2	26	14		3	1	42	1,300
India												1	1					2	
Nepal														3				3	
Pakistan	7											1	2	1		7		4	-43
Sri Lanka	1															1			
Sub-Saharan Africa																			
Angola					1				1	2						1	3		
Burundi					5	3			1							5	4		

Country	1991	1992	1993	1994	1995	1996	1997	1998	1999	2000	2001	2002	2003	2004	2005	1991-1995	1996-2000	2001-2005	% change 1991-5 to 2001-5
Chad					1											1			
Congo, Dem. Rep.			1			1					1					1	1	1	0
Congo, Rep.							1										1		
Eritrea													1					1	
Ethiopia		1				1		1		1			1			2	2	1	-50
Kenya				1												1			
Liberia		1				2										1	2		
Niger							1										1		
Rwanda							3										3		
Sierra Leone		2	1	1	1					1						5	1		
Somalia	1	1	3	4	3	4	1	1					1	1		12	6	2	-83
Sudan		1			2	1				1						3	2		
Togo													1					1	
Uganda			1				3		1							1	4		
Total	15	11	10	11	17	23	15	13	11	6	4	11	44	31	3	64	68	93	45

An empty cell either indicates no incidents or lack of information.

Source: National Memorial Institute for the Prevention of Terrorism (MIPT), Terrorism Knowledge Base, http://www.tkb.org/Home.jsp

Record 20: **Tsunami relief**

The global response to the tsunami of 26 December 2004 in South Asia can serve as a case study of the systems of relief, highlighting how and from where disaster relief is channelled. This record shows the sources and channels of aid flows of two of the largest actors in the disaster relief arena – the UN Office for the Coordination of Humanitarian Affairs (OCHA) and the International Federation of Red Cross and Red Crescent Societies (IFRCRC).

The first table shows the sources and channels of aid commitments and pledges through OCHA's Indian Ocean Earthquake-Tsunami Flash Appeal. On 6 January 2005, in response to the tsunami in the Indian Ocean, a flash appeal for humanitarian and reconstruction contributions was issued by a group of UN agencies and NGOs to plan and implement a strategic, efficient and coordinated response to assist some five million people affected. The appeal, coordinated by OCHA and UNICEF, originally declared the need for US$353 million in order to provide emergency assistance and to support recovery efforts in the agriculture, education, health care, food, shelter, and water and sanitation sectors. Although it does not include all the funds channelled through OCHA for tsunami aid, the appeal is particularly interesting because it involves collaboration between the UN and NGOs, and it reflects the response of nations and international organisations to humanitarian emergencies and the global infrastructure that emerges to address such emergencies. As of 27 May 2005, more than US$1 billion had been committed, and US$91 million had been pledged. The table reflects the sums of commitments/contributions and uncommitted pledges of donors, and the agencies through which these funds were channelled, as compiled by OCHA on the basis of information provided by donors and NGOs. The data in this table were used to make map I.1 on p 6–7 of the Introduction to this Yearbook.

The second table complements the first by combining relief donated by governments, private donors and local Red Cross/Crescent branches, which were channelled through the IFRCRC. It shows the scope and distribution of these contributions across the globe, and also the centrality of the IFRCRC in the international humanitarian aid regime.

Indian Ocean Earthquake – Tsunami Flash Appeal 2005: commitments/contributions and pledges

Donors	Commitments/ contributions (US$)	Uncommitted pledges (US$)
Countries		
East Asia & Pacific		
Low income economies		
East Timor	50,000	
Middle income economies		
China	18,400,000	1,600,000
High income economies		
Australia	17,442,073	781,250
Brunei		3,658,537
Japan	228,900,000	
Korea, Rep.	2,000,000	3,000,000
New Zealand	14,192,163	1,000,000
Taiwan	250,000	
Europe & Central Asia		
Low income economies		
Azerbaijan	1,000,000	
Georgia		55,866
Middle income economies		
Czech Republic	548,252	
Hungary	108,365	
Kazakhstan	10,000	
Lithuania	133,414	
Poland	300,000	
Romania	151,680	
Russian Federation		22,000,000
Serbia & Montenegro	392,157	
Slovakia	676,080	
Turkey	248,254	
High income economies		
Belgium	5,776,884	
Denmark	15,476,621	
Finland	11,706,236	1,678,000
France	17,159,926	
Germany	69,706,927	
Greece	12,370,874	
Iceland	321,136	159,058

Donors	Commitments/ contributions (US$)	Uncommitted pledges (US$)
Ireland	7,575,861	
Italy	15,813,017	1,356,852
Luxembourg	4,025,681	
Netherlands	30,305,553	
Norway	69,782,699	
Portugal	2,848,707	
Slovenia	135,686	
Spain	88,067	
Sweden	21,607,054	4,266,126
Switzerland	4,816,720	
United Kingdom	60,154,179	12,231,132
Latin America & Caribbean		
Middle income economies		
Guyana	50,000	
Jamaica	244,021	
Mexico	1,100,000	3,800,000
Trinidad & Tobago	1,933,176	
Middle East & North Africa		
Middle income economies		
Algeria	2,000,000	
Saudi Arabia	500,000	
High income economies		
Israel	100,000	
Qatar	3,000,000	
United Arab Emirates	50,000	10,000
North America		
High income economies		
Canada	41,718,097	431,000
United States	59,370,366	
Sub-Saharan Africa		
Low income economies		
Equatorial Guinea	198,826	
Madagascar	80,000	
Mali	199,700	
Mauritania	100,336	
Niger		250,000

Donors	Commitments/ contributions (US$)	Uncommitted pledges (US$)
Nigeria	970,855	
Senegal	198,560	
Non-state Donors		
Intergovernmental organisations		
European Commission EuropeAid Co-operation Office	18,995,929	
European Commission Humanitarian Aid Office	47,622,103	32,069,842
International Labour Organisation (ILO)	636,000	
UN Foundation	3,000	
UN Centre for Human Settlements (UN-HABITAT)	260,000	
United Nations Children's Fund National Committees (UNICEF NATCOMs)	126,746,183	
United Nations Development Programme (UNDP)	1,282,000	
United Nations Fund for International Partnerships (UNFIP)	3,260,000	
World Health Organisation (WHO)	115,000	
NGOs		
American Red Cross	50,000,000	
Arab Gulf Fund	100,000	
Hewlett Foundation	380,952	
International Volley-Ball Federation		3,000,000
Mercy Corps International	20,000	
Oxfam America	496,226	
OXFAM/Community Aid Abroad (OXFAM-Australia)	993,323	
Prem Rawat Foundation	150,000	
Corporate donors		
Rolex	1,000,000	
Private, unspecified	22,009,890	100,000
Total	**1,021,208,655**	**91,527,663**

Channels	Commitments/ contributions (US$)	Uncommitted pledges (US$)
NGOs		
Christian Children's Fund (CCF)	3,643,464	
Cooperation and Relief Everywhere (CARE)	2,202,132	
Foundation for Co-existence	56,503	
Helen Keller International	4,175,347	
International Medical Corps (IMC)	847,940	
International Organization for Migration (IOM)	47,588,215	10,000
International Rescue Committee (IRC)	7,564,729	
Islamic Relief	3,155,000	
Norwegian Refugee Council (NRC)	2,822,399	
OXFAM UK	2,247,552	
Project Concern International	1,282,000	
Save the Children	2,323,269	
World Concern	392,962	
World Vision (WV)	2,142,000	
UN Agencies		
Food and Agriculture Organisation (FAO)	46,673,285	
International Labour Organisation (ILO)	4,037,886	
Office for the Coordination of Humanitarian Affairs (OCHA)	22,284,365	3,250,000
UN Centre for Human Settlements (UN-HABITAT)	6,228,905	
UN Department of Safety and Security (UNDSS)	191,571	
UN International Strategy for Disaster Reduction (UNISDR)	7,126,427	
United Nations Children's Fund (UNICEF)	299,557,122	3,714,924
United Nations Development Fund for Women (UNIFEM)	2,717,286	
United Nations Development Programme (UNDP)	107,913,751	6,880,000
United Nations Educational, Scientific, and Cultural Organisation (UNESCO)	429,326	
United Nations Environmental Programme (UNEP)	3,071,049	
United Nations High Commissioner for Refugees (UNHCR)	48,120,768	1,356,852
United Nations Joint Logistic Centre (UNJLC)	9,077,689	
United Nations Population Fund (UNFPA)	25,102,322	2,212,250
United Nations Volunteers programme (UNV)	7,774,000	
World Food Programme (WFP)	274,568,867	12,000,000
World Health Organisation (WHO)	61,356,484	3,500,000
UN Agencies and NGOs, unspecified	14,534,040	58,603,637
Total	**1,021,208,655**	**91,527,663**

Source: ReliefWeb (http://www.reliefweb.int/fts), Indian Ocean Earthquake-Tsunami Flash Appeal 2005, List of commitments/contributions and pledges, as of 27-May-2005, http://ocha.unog.ch/fts/reports/daily/ocha_R2_A669___05060721.pdf

Source of pledges for Tsunami aid given through the International Federation of Red Cross and Red Crescent Societies

| Type of pledge | Cash | | | | | | | | In kind | | | | | | All pledges | |
| Type of Donor | Government | | Private donors | | Red Cross/Crescent | | Total cash | | Government | | Red Cross/Crescent | | Total In kind | | | |
Place	US$	no. of pledges	US$	no. of pledges	US$	no. of pledges	US$	no. of pledges	US$	no. of pledges	US$	no. of pledges	US$	no. of pledges	US$	no. of pledges
East Asia & Pacific																
Low income economies																
Cambodia	9,534	1	6,654	1			16,188	2							16,188	2
Indonesia			9,534	1			9,534	1							9,534	1
Myanmar			392,891	5			392,891	5							392,891	5
Papua New Guinea			13,020	1	119,723	2	132,743	3							132,743	3
Middle income economies																
China*			3,668	2	17,917,381	18	17,921,048	20			45,647	1	45,647	1	17,966,696	21
Fiji	149,406	1			232,447	1	381,853	2							381,853	2
Malaysia			55,253	3	30,986	2	86,239	5							86,239	5
Micronesia	9,534	1			4,815	1	14,349	2							14,349	2
Philippines			9,519	1			9,519	1							9,519	1
Samoa					29,183	1	29,183	1							29,183	1
Thailand			27,856	3			27,856	3							27,856	3
Tonga					13,106	1	13,106	1							13,106	1
Vanuatu					9,496	1	9,496	1							9,496	1
High income economies																
Australia	3,987,282	2	2,458	1	11,672,976	4	15,662,717	7							15,662,717	7
Brunei			32,304	2			32,304	2							32,304	2
Japan	14,300,556	1	18,551	2	1,635,237	2	15,954,344	5			3,483,458	5	3,483,458	5	19,437,802	10
Korea, Rep.			17,831	2	667,359	2	685,190	4			29,953	1	29,953	1	715,143	5
New Zealand	1,137,593	3	707	1	1,302,547	1	2,440,847	5	95,674	1	10,106	1	105,780	2	2,546,628	7
Singapore	1,176,217	1	28,930	1			1,205,146	2							1,205,146	2
Taiwan					2,860,111	1	2,860,111	1							2,860,111	1
Europe & Central Asia																
Low income economies																
Azerbaijan			86	1			86	1							86	1
Georgia			416	1			416	1							416	1
Kyrgyzstan					494	1	494	1							494	1
Middle income economies																
Albania					123,938	1	123,938	1							123,938	1
Bosnia & Herzegovina					230,840	1	230,840	1							230,840	1

Place	Cash Government US$	no. of pledges	Private donors US$	no. of pledges	Red Cross/Crescent US$	no. of pledges	Total cash US$	no. of pledges	In kind Government US$	no. of pledges	Red Cross/Crescent US$	no. of pledges	Total In kind US$	no. of pledges	All pledges US$	no. of pledges
Bulgaria			12,995	1			12,995	1							12,995	1
Croatia					1,263,300	1	1,263,300	1							1,263,300	1
Czech Republic			4,066	3			4,066	3							4,066	3
Estonia	82,036	1			242,090	1	324,126	2							324,126	2
Hungary			888	1			888	1							888	1
Kazakhstan			8,788	1			8,788	1							8,788	1
Latvia			19,067	1	36,906	1	55,973	2							55,973	2
Lithuania					260,914	1	260,914	1							260,914	1
Macedonia					158,334	1	158,334	1							158,334	1
Poland			260	1			260	1							260	1
Romania			9,534	1	1,148,899	1	1,158,433	2							1,158,433	2
Russia			2,200	1			2,200	1							2,200	1
Slovakia	149,106	1			1,621	1	150,727	2							150,727	2
Turkey			23,834	1	38,135	1	61,969	2							61,969	2
Ukraine			15,143	2	44,538	2	59,681	4							59,681	4
High income economies																
Austria	586,866	1	1,173,280	3	3,043,597	3	4,803,743	7			2,021,238	5	2,021,238	5	6,824,981	12
Belgium	3,907,883	2	36,722	2	1,559,923	3	5,504,528	7			2,200,609	4	2,200,609	4	7,705,137	11
Cyprus					380,069	2	380,069	2							380,069	2
Denmark	1,031,715	2	12,423	2			1,044,139	4			2,804,935	6	2,804,935	6	3,849,074	10
Finland					2,046,735	1	2,046,735	1			721,107	3	721,107	3	2,767,842	4
France			40,685	4	1,299,515	1	1,340,200	5			2,026,663	4	2,026,663	4	3,366,863	9
Germany			41,674	3	1,299,515	1	1,341,188	4			14,089,141	9	14,089,141	9	15,430,329	13
Greece			15,072	4	323,763	2	338,835	6	30,656	1			30,656	1	369,491	7
Iceland	74,114	1			228,405	2	302,518	3	44,805	1			44,805	1	347,323	4
Ireland	973,373	1	25,912	3	3,898,544	1	4,897,828	5	25,940	1			25,940	1	4,923,768	6
Italy	134,228	1	127,833	8	374,574	1	636,635	10							636,635	10
Luxembourg	324,879	1					324,879	1			153,600	1	153,600	1	478,479	2
Malta			18,548	2			18,548	2							18,548	2
Netherlands			162,709	6	1,277,196	1	1,439,905	7			9,074,131	7	9,074,131	7	10,514,037	14
Norway	382,263	2	3,360	1	1,314,674	2	1,700,297	5			3,315,036	7	3,315,036	7	5,015,333	12
Portugal			1,361	1	1,105,282	4	1,106,643	5							1,106,643	5
Slovenia	104,957	1			244,129	2	349,086	3			8,762	1	8,762	1	357,848	4
Spain			37,726	2	1,875,778	4	1,913,505	6			3,114,021	6	3,114,021	6	5,027,526	12

Type of pledge	Cash								In kind						All pledges	
Type of Donor	Government		Private donors		Red Cross/ Crescent		Total cash		Government		Red Cross/ Crescent		Total In kind			
Place	US$	no. of pledges	US$	no. of pledges	US$	no. of pledges	US$	no. of pledges	US$	no. of pledges	US$	no. of pledges	US$	no. of pledges	US$	no. of pledges
Sweden	2,612,926	2	194,927	1	17,621,822	4	20,429,675	7			2,502,982	5	2,502,982	5	22,932,657	12
Switzerland	434,523	3	318,012	14			752,535	17	135,594	1	1,053,157	2	1,188,751	3	1,941,286	20
United Kingdom	147,806	1	1,012,351	9	5,618,321	5	6,778,479	15			6,421,322	11	6,421,322	11	13,199,801	26
Latin America & Caribbean																
Middle income economies																
Belize					23,508	1	23,508	1							23,508	1
Bolivia					5,106	1	5,106	1							5,106	1
Brazil			12,039	2	476,685	3	488,724	5							488,724	5
Chile	19,067	1					19,067	1							19,067	1
Colombia			1,887	1	18,425	1	20,312	2							20,312	2
Ecuador					62,602	1	62,602	1							62,602	1
El Salvador					15,167	1	15,167	1							15,167	1
Grenada					2,267	1	2,267	1							2,267	1
Honduras					4,955	1	4,955	1							4,955	1
Mexico	11,093	2					11,093	2							11,093	2
Panama	4,887	2					4,887	2							4,887	2
Paraguay					4,767	1	4,767	1							4,767	1
Suriname					21,784	1	21,784	1							21,784	1
Trinidad & Tobago	12,570	1					12,570	1							12,570	1
Uruguay	7,608	1					7,608	1							7,608	1
Venezuela	9,534	1					9,534	1							9,534	1
High income economies																
Barbados					112,965	1	112,965	1							112,965	1
Middle East & North Africa																
Middle income economies																
Algeria	2,152	1					2,152	1							2,152	1
Djibouti	4,767	1					4,767	1							4,767	1
Egypt	557	1					557	1							557	1
Iran											133,548	1	133,548	1	133,548	1
Jordan	14,258	1					14,258	1							14,258	1
Lebanon	23,149	2					23,149	2							23,149	2
Libya	477	1			21,055	1	21,532	2							21,532	2
Morocco	65	1			30,597	1	30,662	2							30,662	2
Oman	757	1					757	1							757	1

| Type of pledge | Cash | | | | | | | | In kind | | | | | | All pledges | |
| Type of Donor | Government | | Private donors | | Red Cross/ Crescent | | Total cash | | Government | | Red Cross/ Crescent | | Total In kind | | | |
Place	US$	no. of pledges	US$	no. of pledges	US$	no. of pledges	US$	no. of pledges	US$	no. of pledges	US$	no. of pledges	US$	no. of pledges	US$	no. of pledges
Saudi Arabia	7,648,018	11	28,156	3			7,676,175	14							7,676,175	14
Syria			9,534	1			9,534	1							9,534	1
Tunisia			2,735	1			2,735	1							2,735	1
High income economies																
Bahrain			47,669	1			47,669	1							47,669	1
Kuwait			1,604	1			1,604	1							1,604	1
Qatar			2,002	1			2,002	1			228,519	1	228,519	1	230,521	2
United Arab Emirates			1,417	1	1,775,956	7	1,777,373	8							1,777,373	8
North America																
High income economies																
Canada	3,613,177	2	95,895	2	10,550,745	3	14,259,817	7			11,530,863	10	11,530,863	10	25,790,680	17
United States	5,815,559	2	10,486,074	47	4,862,863	2	21,164,496	51	95,910	1	6,703,328	8	6,799,238	9	27,963,734	60
South Asia																
Low income economies																
Bangladesh					6,969	1	6,969	1							6,969	1
India									8,085	1			8,085	1	8,085	1
Nepal	16,777	1					16,777	1							16,777	1
Pakistan			9,500	1			9,500	1							9,500	1
Middle income economies																
Sri Lanka			72	1			72	1							72	1
Sub-Saharan Africa																
Low income economies																
Ethiopia			97,029	3	23,834	1	120,863	4							120,863	4
Kenya			9,519	1			9,519	1							9,519	1
Madagascar			953	1			953	1							953	1
Mozambique	95,337	1	4,739	1			100,076	2							100,076	2
Nigeria			10,463	2			10,463	2							10,463	2
Tanzania			11,648	1			11,648	1							11,648	1
Uganda					2,998	1	2,998	1							2,998	1
Middle income economies																
Mauritius	47,669	1	14,301	1	95,337	1	157,306	3							157,306	3
Namibia					17,602	1	17,602	1							17,602	1
South Africa			84,041	3	3,352,124	4	3,436,166	7							3,436,166	7
Private On Line Donations			6,683,863	1			6,683,863	1							6,683,863	1

Type of pledge	Cash								In kind						All pledges	
Type of Donor	Government		Private donors		Red Cross/ Crescent		Total cash		Government		Red Cross/ Crescent		Total In kind			
Place	US$	no. of pledges	US$	no. of pledges	US$	no. of pledges	US$	no. of pledges	US$	no. of pledges	US$	no. of pledges	US$	no. of pledges	US$	no. of pledges
Low income	121,647	3	566,454	20	154,018	6	842,119	29	8,085	1			8,085	1	850,204	30
Middle income	8,085,768	16	456,775	52	25,953,868	58	34,496,411	126			179,195	2	179,195	2	34,675,606	128
Low & middle income:																
East Asia & Pacific	168,474	3	518,395	17	18,372,094	28	19,058,963	48			45,647	1	45,647	1	19,104,611	49
Europe & Central Asia	231,142	2	97,277	15	3,550,008	13	3,878,426	30							3,878,426	30
Latin America & Caribbean			78,685	11	635,266	12	713,951	23							713,951	23
Middle East & North Africa	7,648,018	11	86,606	14	51,652	2	7,786,276	27			133,548	1	133,548	1	7,919,824	28
South Asia	16,777	1	9,572	2	6,969	1	33,317	4	8,085	1			8,085	1	41,403	5
Sub-Saharan Africa	143,006	2	232,694	13	3,491,896	8	3,867,595	23							3,867,595	23
High income	40,823,886	30	13,962,237	129	79,097,164	64	133,883,288	223	428,579	6	71,492,933	97	71,921,512	103	205,804,799	326
World	49,031,302	49	21,670,183	203	105,261,504	130	175,962,989	382	436,664	7	71,672,128	99	72,108,792	106	248,071,781	488

Whenever type of donor was Government/RC or was unspecified the pledge was classified as Government.

Pledges by international organisations were attributed to the country of the organisations' secretariat.

Pledge values in source are in Swiss Franks, and were converted into US$ using 26 April 2005 Interbank currency exchange rate.

Totals includes funds committed by countries with population under 100,000 which are not included in the table.

* China includes Hong Kong and Macao.

Source: International Federation of Red Cross and Red Crescent Societies, Operations Update, 3 May 2005: Asia – Earthquake & Tsunamis, East Africa Region; Annex 1: Pledges Recived, 26 April 2005, http://www.ifrc.org/cgi/pdf_appeals.pl?/04/280454.pdf

This record illustrates two aspects of the international philanthropic community – its organisational infrastructure and the international grant-making of philanthropic foundations. The first table offers a snapshot of the latest figures available on international grant making by philanthropic foundations in the US (similar data are not available for European foundations). Besides the 'usual suspects' such as UK and Switzerland, which are home to large international NGOs, some countries stand out as major recipients of US foundations' dollars – Israel, India, South Africa and Armenia.

The second table offers a time series of US philanthropic foundations' international grant-making. The graphs show an increase in grants to international recipients between 1998 and 2000, followed by a slump after 2001 due to the 9/11 attacks and the diversion of US philanthropy to domestic disaster relief. The 2001 decline is more noticeable in the 'share of' chart because the attacks took place in September, when most grants had been finalised. The dip appears to be temporary because the upward trend in international grant-giving reappears in 2003.

The third table presents organisations that provide services to foundations and other grant-making organisations, and are members of the Worldwide Initiatives for Grant-maker Support (WINGS). The WINGS network 'seeks to strengthen the institutional infrastructure of philanthropy worldwide by building a strong, interconnected and collaborative global network of grantmaker associations and support organisations, which, in turn, help grantmaking institutions that support civil society to build a more equitable and just global community' (URL). The table lists the location of WINGS member organisations and the countries where they provide services. The diagram maps the structure of the network, highlighting the US's prominent role and various regional hubs – Germany, Brazil, Philippines and Poland. (See http://wingsweb.org/about/mission_vision.cfm)

US foundation grants to international recipients, 2003

Country	Total grants (US$)	Number of grants	Average grant (US$)
East Asia & Pacific			
Low income economies			
Cambodia	980,820	11	89,165
Indonesia	10,836,304	79	137,168
Laos	989,070	9	109,897
Mongolia	380,000	1	380,000
Myanmar	440,000	2	220,000
Solomon Islands	35,324	3	11,775
Vietnam	6,838,915	110	62,172
Middle income economies			
China*	27,776,579	270	102,876
Fiji	445,000	2	222,500
Malaysia	1,615,880	15	107,725
Philippines	21,129,439	103	205,140
Samoa	30,000	1	30,000
Thailand	7,023,461	48	146,322
Vanuatu	100,000	1	100,000

Country	Total grants (US$)	Number of grants	Average grant (US$)
High income economies			
Australia	2,739,238	53	51,684
Japan	2,302,187	21	109,628
Korea, Rep.	800,000	5	160,000
New Zealand	575,385	8	71,923
Singapore	1,366,397	12	113,866
Europe & Central Asia			
Low income economies			
Moldova	50,667	2	25,334
Uzbekistan	20,000	1	20,000
Middle income economies			
Albania	50,000	1	50,000
Armenia	79,517,242	3	26,505,747
Belarus	390,000	3	130,000
Bosnia & Herzegovina	1,075,316	5	215,063
Bulgaria	450,000	2	225,000
Croatia	470,000	7	67,143
Czech Republic	1,528,244	19	80,434
Hungary	2,832,365	40	70,809
Kazakhstan	44,494	1	44,494
Latvia	64,000	2	32,000
Lithuania	71,351	5	14,270
Poland	18,081,156	53	341,154
Romania	1,220,238	17	71,779
Russia	23,462,485	121	193,905
Serbia & Montenegro	80,000	2	40,000
Slovakia	2,572,000	25	102,880
Turkey	347,420	4	86,855
Ukraine	1,185,000	16	74,063
High income economies			
Austria	6,588,134	16	411,758
Belgium	2,441,583	27	90,429
Denmark	2,457,559	8	307,195
Finland	659,675	3	219,892
France	8,718,764	76	114,721
Germany	10,866,834	61	178,145
Greece	728,629	3	242,876

Country	Total grants (US$)	Number of grants	Average grant (US$)
Iceland	40,000	1	40,000
Ireland	2,693,216	26	103,585
Italy*	4,514,676	62	72,817
Luxembourg	15,025	1	15,025
Malta	50,544	1	50,544
Netherlands	5,192,353	51	101,811
Norway	12,000	1	12,000
Portugal	294,999	4	73,750
Slovenia	115,000	2	57,500
Spain	1,430,784	21	68,133
Sweden	1,718,900	17	101,112
Switzerland	85,831,098	64	1,341,111
United Kingdom*	81,655,113	364	224,327
Latin America & Caribbean			
Low income economies			
Haiti	1,882,673	19	99,088
Nicaragua	1,984,545	15	132,303
Middle income economies			
Argentina	3,799,168	51	74,493
Belize	130,000	4	32,500
Bolivia	1,234,863	9	137,207
Brazil	24,538,146	199	123,307
Chile	5,570,778	60	92,846
Colombia	5,132,248	35	146,636
Costa Rica	2,719,675	12	226,640
Dominican Republic	730,884	7	104,412
Ecuador	2,785,822	15	185,721
El Salvador	1,691,446	13	130,111
Guatemala	1,883,877	30	62,796
Guyana	75,000	1	75,000
Honduras	956,877	7	136,697
Jamaica	427,640	8	53,455
Mexico	30,787,673	265	116,180
Panama	160,000	4	40,000
Paraguay	212,500	2	106,250
Peru	6,742,215	55	122,586
Suriname	138,753	5	27,751

Country	Total grants (US$)	Number of grants	Average grant (US$)
Trinidad & Tobago	120,000	3	40,000
Uruguay	353,400	6	58,900
Venezuela	196,750	3	65,583
High income economies			
Bermuda	1,598,400	10	159,840
Bahamas	95,000	3	31,667
Middle East & North Africa			
Middle income economies			
Egypt	3,507,700	30	116,923
Iran	30,000	1	30,000
Jordan	830,000	4	207,500
Lebanon	1,588,500	11	144,409
Tunisia	110,000	1	110,000
West Bank & Gaza	3,109,000	28	111,036
High income economies			
Israel	45,190,751	252	179,328
North America			
High income economies			
Canada	58,517,645	333	175,729
South Asia			
Low income economies			
Bangladesh	9,874,223	12	822,852
India	38,542,461	223	172,836
Nepal	2,586,888	25	103,476
Pakistan	337,800	2	168,900
Middle income economies			
Sri Lanka	713,878	7	101,983
Sub-Saharan Africa			
Low income economies			
Angola	515,000	2	257,500
Burkina Faso	633,390	4	158,348
Cameroon	45,000	3	15,000
Chad	212,713	2	106,357
Côte d'Ivoire	20,000	2	10,000
Eritrea	35,000	2	17,500
Ethiopia	3,416,461	14	244,033
Gambia	500,000	4	125,000

Country	Total grants (US$)	Number of grants	Average grant (US$)
Ghana	4,013,232	39	102,903
Guinea	40,000	1	40,000
Kenya	19,998,787	109	183,475
Lesotho	301,109	8	37,639
Madagascar	35,000	2	17,500
Malawi	80,010	1	80,010
Mali	618,350	3	206,117
Mozambique	1,290,645	9	143,405
Nigeria	12,511,003	61	205,098
Rwanda	45,000	3	15,000
Senegal	783,630	8	97,954
Somalia	41,000	1	41,000
Sudan	10,691	1	10,691
Tanzania	2,787,136	29	96,108
Togo	11,601	1	11,601
Uganda	8,754,577	57	153,589
Zambia	293,260	4	73,315
Zimbabwe	12,140,517	25	485,621
Middle income economies			
Botswana	415,508	9	46,168
Mauritius	75,000	2	37,500
Namibia	2,175,341	12	181,278
South Africa	40,857,893	263	155,353
Swaziland	545,109	8	68,139

Region	Total grants (US$)	Number of grants	Average grant (US$)
Low income	144,912,802	909	159,420
Middle income	335,907,314	1,936	173,506
Low & middle income:			
East Asia & Pacific	78,620,792	655	120,032
Europe & Central Asia	133,511,978	329	405,811
Latin America & Caribbean	94,254,933	828	113,834
Middle East & North Africa	9,175,200	75	122,336
South Asia	52,055,250	269	193,514
Sub-Saharan Africa	113,201,963	689	164,299
High income	329,209,889	1,506	218,599
World**	810,188,905	4,354	186,079

* China includes grants given to recipients in Hong Kong and Taiwan; Italy includes grants given to the Vatican; United Kingdom includes grants given to recipients in Northern Ireland.

** Figure for World exceeds sum of table, as it includes three grants given to recipients in unspecified countries or in countries with population smaller than 100,000.

Source: Foundation Center, Grants for Foreign & International Programs, 2004/5. Washinton DC: Foundation Center. www.fdncenter.org

US foundation grants to international recipients, 1998-2003*

		1998	1999	2000	2001	2002	2003
International grants, total							
Sum of grants	US$ (1000s)	1,037,245	1,315,035	2,450,716	2,462,013	2,194,975	2,200,077
As share of all grants by US foundations	%	10.7	11.3	16.3	14.7	13.8	15.4
Number of grants	number	8,964	9,593	10,874	11,494	11,396	10,558
As share of all grants by US foundations	%	9.2	8.9	9.1	9.2	8.9	8.7
Grants to overseas recipients							
Sum of grants	US$ (1000s)	416,114	430,100	901,346	770,671	842,767	810,397
As share of all grants by US foundations	%	4.3	3.7	6.0	4.6	5.3	5.7
Number of grants	number	3,796	3,798	4,459	4,703	4,506	4,357
As share of all grants by US foundations	%	3.9	3.5	3.7	3.8	3.5	3.6
Grants to US-based recipients							
Sum of grants	US$ (1000s)	621,131	884,935	1,549,370	1,691,343	1,352,207	1,389,680
As share of all grants by US foundations	%	6.4	7.6	10.3	10.1	8.5	9.7
Number of grants	number	5,168	5,795	6,415	6,791	6,890	6,201
As share of all grants by US foundations	%	5.3	5.4	5.4	5.4	5.4	5.1

*Based on grants of $10,000 or more awarded by a national sample of 1,010 larger U.S. foundations (including 800 of the 1,000 largest ranked by total giving). For community foundations, only discretionary grants are included. Grants to individuals are not included in the file.

Source: The Foundation Center, Foundation Giving Trends, 2005, http://fdncenter.org/fc_stats/index.html

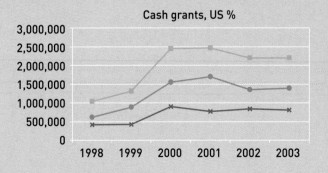

Cash grants, US %

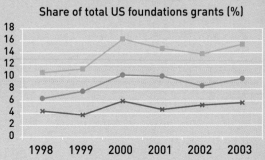

Share of total US foundations grants (%)

- International grants, total
- Grants to overseas recipients
- Grants to US-based recipients

The organisational infrastructure of international philanthropy – WINGS member and service countries

Country	Countries with WINGS member			Countries receiving services from WINGS members	
	Membership serving	Support organisations	Grand Total	Number of providers	Number of providers' countries
East Asia & Pacific					
Low income economies					
Indonesia				2	2
Middle income economies					
China*		1	1	3	3
Philippines	3	1	4	2	2
Thailand		1	1	3	3
High income economies					
Australia	1		1	2	2
Japan	1		1	1	1
Korea, Rep.				1	1
New Zealand	1		1		
Taiwan				1	1
Europe & Central Asia					
Low income economies					
Azerbaijan				1	1
Georgia				1	1
Kyrgyzstan				1	1
Moldova				1	1
Middle income economies					
Albania				2	2
Belarus				2	2
Bosnia & Herzegovina				2	2
Bulgaria	1	1	2	5	5
Croatia				2	2
Czech Republic	1	1	2	3	3
Estonia		2	2	3	2
Hungary				1	1
Kazakhstan				1	1
Latvia		1	1	2	2
Lithuania		1	1	3	3
Macedonia				2	2
Poland	1	2	3	4	3

Country	Countries with WINGS member			Countries receiving services from WINGS members	
	Membership serving	Support organisations	Grand Total	Number of providers	Number of providers' countries
Romania	1		1	2	2
Russian Federation	2	1	3	5	5
Serbia & Montenegro				2	2
Slovakia	2	2	4	4	3
Turkey		1	1	2	2
Ukraine		1	1	3	3
High income economies					
Austria				1	1
Belgium	1	1	2	4	3
Cyprus				1	1
Denmark				1	1
Finland	1		1	1	1
France	1	1	2	2	2
Germany	1	6	7	6	2
Greece				1	1
Iceland				1	1
Ireland	1		1	3	2
Italy*	1	1	2	5	4
Luxembourg				1	1
Malta				1	1
Netherlands	1		1	1	1
Norway				2	2
Portugal	1	1	2	2	2
Spain	3		3	2	2
Sweden				1	1
Switzerland	1		1	1	1
United Kingdom*	2	2	4	5	4
Latin America & Caribbean					
Middle income economies					
Argentina	1		1	1	1
Bolivia				1	1
Brazil	1	1	2	3	3
Chile				1	1

Country	Countries with WINGS member			Countries receiving services from WINGS members	
	Membership serving	Support organisations	Grand Total	Number of providers	Number of providers' countries
Colombia		2	2	3	2
Dominican Republic	1		1		
Ecuador	1	1	2	3	3
El Salvador	1		1		
French Guiana				1	1
Guatemala	1		1		
Guyana				1	1
Jamaica	1		1		
Mexico	1		1	2	2
Paraguay				1	1
Peru				1	1
Suriname				1	1
Uruguay				1	1
Venezuela				1	1
North America					
High income economies					
Canada	3		3	2	1
United States*	24	4	28	5	3
South Asia					
Low income economies					
Bangladesh		1	1	2	2
India		2	2	4	3
Pakistan	1		1	1	1
Sub-Saharan Africa					
Low income economies					
Kenya	1	2	3	2	1
Mozambique				1	1
Zimbabwe				1	1
Middle income economies					
South Africa	3		3	2	2

Region	Countries with WINGS member			Countries receiving services from WINGS members	
	Membership serving	Support organisations	Grand Total	Number of providers	Number of providers' countries
Low income	2	5	7	17	15
Middle income	23	20	43	81	77
Low & middle income:					
East Asia & Pacific	3	3	6	10	10
Europe & Central Asia	8	13	21	54	51
Latin America & Caribbean	9	4	13	21	20
South Asia	1	3	4	7	6
Sub-Saharan Africa	4	2	6	6	5
High income	45	16	61	60	49
World	70	41	111	158	141

* China includes Hong Kong; Italy includes the Vatican; United Kingdom includes Falkland Islands; United States include Puerto Rico.
World total includes countries with population under 100,000 that are not included in the list.

Source: Worldwide Initiatives for Grantmaker Support (WINGS), Participant profiles, http://www.wingsweb.org/network/profiles.cfm

The WINGS global structure

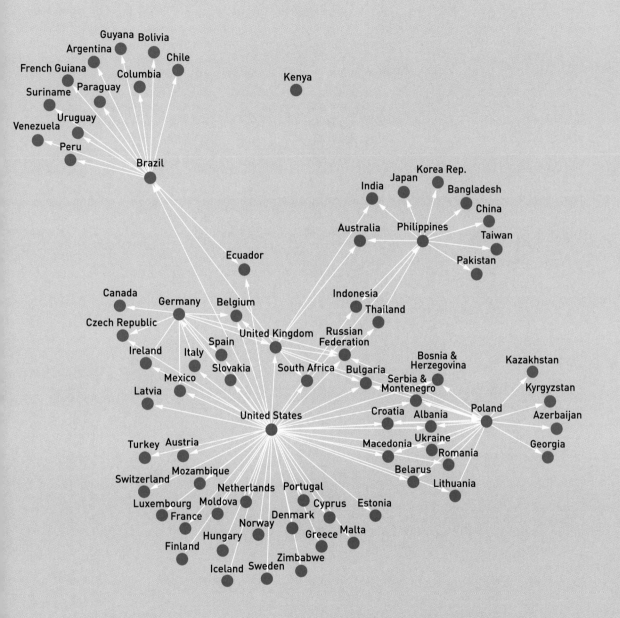

Record 22: **Political rights and civil liberties**

This year we expanded this record to include two additional indicators of democratic polities: freedom of press and religious freedom. Freedom House's index of religious freedom is concerned not with all forms of persecution of religious people but with persecution where the focus or the grounds are themselves religious. The criteria used to construct the index were drawn from international conventions and treaties, including but not limited to the International Covenant on Civil and Political Rights, the United Nations Declaration on the Elimination of All Forms of Intolerance and of Discrimination Based on Religion or Belief, and the European Convention on Human Rights. Freedom House's index of press freedom is likewise based on the Universal Declaration of Human Rights, and analyses the political, legal and economic environment of the press in countries surveyed to develop an index of independence of the media, which is defined as 'the degree to which each country permits the free flow of information'.

This table also updates the index of political rights and civil liberties, which are indicators of the levels of democracy in countries around the world. Freedom House defines these as 'real-world rights and freedoms enjoyed by individuals, as a result of actions by both state and non-governmental actors, and are based on the Universal Declaration of Human Rights' (for details on the methodology used by Freedom House in producing these indices, see http://www.freedomhouse.org/research/survey2005.htm).

For the political rights, civil liberties and religious freedom indices, scores range from 1, the lowest degree of freedom, to 7, the highest, while the press freedom index ranges from zero to 100.

The different indices correlate strongly, high-income European countries scoring the highest, followed by Latin American and Caribbean nations and by the middle-income countries in Europe and Central Asia. The deepest deficits in political rights and civil liberties are found in most Arab nations and in many Sub-Saharan African nations.

Country	Political Rights Index 2004	Civil Liberties Index 2004	Religious freedom rating 2000	Press freedom rating 2004
East Asia & Pacific				
Low income economies				
Cambodia	2	3		38
East Timor	5	5	3	70
Indonesia	5	4	3	42
Korea, Dem. Rep.	1	1	1	3
Laos	1	2		17
Mongolia	6	6	5	65
Myanmar	1	1	1	4
Papua New Guinea	5	5		71
Solomon Islands	5	5		70
Vietnam	1	2	3	18
Middle income economies				
China*	1	2	2	18
Fiji	4	5		70
Malaysia	4	4	4	31
Micronesia	7	7		82
Philippines	6	5	5	65

Country	Political Rights Index 2004	Civil Liberties Index 2004	Religious freedom rating 2000	Press freedom rating 2004
Samoa	6	6		75
Thailand	6	5		58
Tonga	3	5		63
Vanuatu	6	6		76
High income economies				
Australia	7	7		82
Brunei	2	3		25
Korea, Rep.	7	6	6	71
Japan	7	6	6	80
New Zealand	7	7		88
Singapore	3	4	4	34
Taiwan	6	7	6	79
Europe & Central Asia				
Low income economies				
Armenia	3	4	4	36
Azerbaijan	2	3	3	28
Georgia	5	4	4	44
Kyrgyzstan	2	3	4	29
Moldova	5	4	4	35
Tajikistan	2	3		26
Ukraine	4	4	5	41
Uzbekistan	1	2	2	15
Middle income economies				
Albania	5	5		49
Belarus	1	2	3	14
Bosnia & Herzegovina	4	5		55
Bulgaria	7	6	4	65
Croatia	6	6		63
Czech Republic	7	7		78
Estonia	7	7	7	83
Hungary	7	7	5	79
Kazakhstan	2	3	4	25
Latvia	7	6	5	83
Lithuania	6	6	6	82
Macedonia	5	5	4	49
Poland	7	7	6	80

Country	Political Rights Index 2004	Civil Liberties Index 2004	Religious freedom rating 2000	Press freedom rating 2004
Romania	5	6	5	53
Russian Federation	2	3	4	32
Serbia & Montenegro	5	6		60
Slovakia	7	7		79
Slovenia	7	7		81
Turkey	5	5	3	52
Turkmenistan	1	1	1	4
High income economies				
Andorra	7	7		86
Austria	7	7	6	79
Belgium	7	7	5	89
Cyprus	7	7		78
Denmark	7	7		90
Finland	7	7	7	91
France	7	7	5	80
Germany	7	7	5	84
Greece	7	6	4	72
Iceland	7	7		91
Ireland	7	7	7	85
Italy	7	7		65
Luxembourg	7	7		89
Netherlands	7	7	7	89
Norway	7	7	7	90
Portugal	7	7		86
Spain	7	7	5	78
Sweden	7	7	6	91
Switzerland	7	7		89
United Kingdom	7	7	6	82
Latin America & Caribbean				
Low income economies				
Haiti	1	2		34
Nicaragua	5	5		58
Middle income economies				
Argentina	6	6	5	59
Belize	7	6		80
Bolivia	5	5		65

Country	Political Rights Index 2004	Civil Liberties Index 2004	Religious freedom rating 2000	Press freedom rating 2004
Brazil	6	5	6	60
Chile	7	7	5	76
Colombia	4	4	4	37
Costa Rica	7	7		81
Cuba	1	1	2	4
Dominica	7	7		83
Dominican Republic	6	6		62
Ecuador	5	5		59
El Salvador	6	5	5	59
Guatemala	4	4	5	42
Guyana	6	6		77
Honduras	5	5		49
Jamaica	6	5		85
Mexico	6	6	4	58
Panama	7	6		56
Paraguay	5	5		44
Peru	6	5		60
St. Lucia	7	6		84
St. Vincent & the Grenadines	6	7		84
Suriname	7	6		80
Trinidad & Tobago	5	5		76
Uruguay	7	7		71
Venezuela	5	4		28
High income economies				
Antigua & Barbuda	6	6		60
Bahamas	7	7		86
Barbados	7	7		83

Middle East & North Africa

Low income economies

Country	Political Rights Index 2004	Civil Liberties Index 2004	Religious freedom rating 2000	Press freedom rating 2004
Western Sahara	1	2		
Yemen	3	3		24
Middle income economies				
Algeria	2	3		36
Djibouti	3	3		33
Egypt	2	3	3	32
Iran	2	2	1	20

Country	Political Rights Index 2004	Civil Liberties Index 2004	Religious freedom rating 2000	Press freedom rating 2004
Iraq	1	3		30
Jordan	3	4		38
Lebanon	2	3	4	40
Libya	1	1		5
Malta	7	7		82
Morocco	3	4	4	37
Oman	2	3		28
Palestinian Authority	3	2		16
Saudi Arabia	1	1	1	20
Syria	1	1		17
Tunisia	2	3		20
High income economies				
Bahrain	3	3		29
Israel	7	5	5	72
Kuwait	4	3		42
Qatar	2	3		38
United Arab Emirates	2	2		28
North America				
High income economies				
Canada	7	7		83
United States	7	7	7	83
South Asia				
Low income economies				
Afghanistan	3	2		32
Bangladesh	4	4	2	32
Bhutan	2	3	2	34
India	6	5	3	62
Nepal	3	3	3	31
Pakistan	2	3	2	39
Middle income economies				
Maldives	2	3		32
Sri Lanka	5	5	4	44
Sub-Saharan Africa				
Low income economies				
Angola	2	3		34
Benin	6	6		70

Country	Political Rights Index 2004	Civil Liberties Index 2004	Religious freedom rating 2000	Press freedom rating 2004
Burkina Faso	3	4		60
Burundi	3	3		26
Cameroon	2	2		32
Central African Republic	2	3		37
Chad	2	3		27
Comoros	4	4		56
Congo, Dem. Rep.	2	2		19
Congo, Rep.	3	4		49
Côte d'Ivoire				31
Equatorial Guinea	1	2		12
Eritrea	1	2		9
Ethiopia	3	3		32
Gambia	4	4		28
Ghana	6	6		74
Guinea	2	3		27
Guinea-Bissau	4	4		45
Kenya	5	5		39
Lesotho	6	5		58
Liberia	3	4		27
Madagascar	5	5		50
Malawi	4	4		46
Mali	6	6		77
Mauritania	2	3	2	35
Mozambique	5	4		55
Niger	5	5		47
Nigeria	4	4	3	48
Rwanda	2	3		16
São Tomé & Principe	6	6		72
Senegal	6	5		63
Sierra Leone	4	5		41
Somalia	2	1		17
Sudan	1	1	1	14
Tanzania	4	5	4	49
Togo	2	3		27
Uganda	3	4		56
Zambia	4	4		35

Country	Political Rights Index 2004	Civil Liberties Index 2004	Religious freedom rating 2000	Press freedom rating 2004
Zimbabwe	1	2	5	11
Middle income economies				
Botswana	6	6	6	70
Cape Verde	7	7		68
Gabon	3	4		34
Mauritius	7	7		72
Namibia	6	5	6	71
South Africa	7	6	6	74
Swaziland	1	3		21

* China – excludes Tibet and Hong Kong

Note: year of publication is 2005, but data are based on 2004 events (except religious freedom). In Global Civil Society Yearbook 2004/5 data in this table were listed as 2004 when in fact they were from 2003.

Source: Freedom House, 2005. Freedom in the World 2005: Civic Power and Electoral Politics, http://www.freedomhouse.org/research/survey2005.htm; Freedom House, Center for Religious Freedom, 2000. Religious Freedom in the World: A Global Report on Freedom and Persecution, Figure 1, http://www.freedomhouse.org/religion/publications/rfiw/fig1.htm; Freedom House, Freedom of the Press 2005: A Global Survey of Media Independence, http://www.freedomhouse.org/research/pressurvey.htm

Record 23: Attitudes towards the United States

The US has acquired a hegemonic status in world politics and economy, and is a major driver of globalisation. Its policies affect people worldwide, and much of the debate on globalisation is intertwined with the debate on US influence, hegemony, and even imperialism. This record presents attitudes about the role of the US in the world, as expressed in surveys conducted by the Program on International Policy Attitudes and GlobeScan in the first half of 2005. The following survey questions were selected for this table:

- For each of the following possible future trends, please tell me if you would see it as mainly positive or mainly negative...Europe becomes more influential than the United States in world affairs (etc.).

- Please tell me if you think each of the following are having a mainly positive or mainly negative influence in the world...The United States (etc.).

- As you may know George Bush has been reelected as President of the United States. Do you think this is positive or negative for peace and security in the world?

- How does the fact that George Bush has been reelected make you feel toward the American people? Much better, a little better, a little worse, or much worse?*

- How does the fact that George Bush has been reelected make you feel about whether your country should contribute troops to the operation in Iraq?

For each survey question, the shares of respondents reporting positive and negative attitudes are presented. These do not add up to 100 per cent, as varying numbers of respondents in each country did not respond to each question, or responded 'don't know'. For each survey question a ratio was calculated between the shares of respondents reporting positive and negative attitudes, which reveals the overall tendency in each country – ratios exceeding 1 imply more positive attitudes, and ratios below 1 imply mostly negative attitudes. The table demonstrates overall negative attitudes towards US dominance, and favourable attitudes to increasing EU influence, with the exception of China, The Philippines and India. Interestingly, support for the US does not always translate into willingness to send troops to Iraq.

Country	Increased EU influence vs US influence			US influence			Bush re-election			Post re-election feeling towards Americans*			Contributing troops to Iraq		
	Positive %	Negative %	ratio positive/negative	Positive %	Negative %	ratio positive/negative	Positive %	Negative %	ratio positive/negative	Better %	Worse %	ratio better/worse	Favour %	Oppose %	ratio favour/oppose
Argentina	57	16	3.6	19	65	0.3	6	82	0.1	13	54	0.2	3	84	0.0
Australia	62	23	2.7	40	52	0.8	31	61	0.5	20	35	0.6	37	56	0.7
Brazil	53	28	1.9	42	51	0.8	17	78	0.2	28	59	0.5	12	82	0.1
Canada	63	26	2.4	34	60	0.6	26	67	0.4	25	53	0.5	20	76	0.3
Chile	48	17	2.8	29	50	0.6	19	62	0.3	16	40	0.4	9	68	0.1
China	66	16	4.1	40	42	1.0	27	56	0.5	32	33	1.0	19	66	0.3
France	70	22	3.2	38	54	0.7	13	75	0.2	12	65	0.2	9	84	0.1
Germany	79	10	7.9	27	64	0.4	14	77	0.2	12	56	0.2	10	83	0.1
India	35	38	0.9	54	30	1.8	62	27	2.3	65	21	3.1	18	67	0.3
Indonesia	56	22	2.5	38	51	0.7	21	68	0.3	29	55	0.5	14	74	0.2
Italy	76	14	5.4	49	40	1.2	34	54	0.6	22	39	0.6	28	65	0.4
Japan	35	13	2.7	24	31	0.8	15	39	0.4	8	23	0.3	11	35	0.3
Korea, Rep.	53	40	1.3	52	45	1.2	36	54	0.7	32	47	0.7	34	56	0.6
Lebanon	59	14	4.2	33	49	0.7	23	64	0.4	21	42	0.5	9	75	0.1
Mexico	66	8	8.3	11	57	0.2	4	58	0.1	14	49	0.3	0	76	0.0
Philippines	35	54	0.6	88	9	9.8	63	30	2.1	78	15	5.2	36	58	0.6
Poland	58	12	4.8	52	21	2.5	44	27	1.6	22	11	2.0	22	60	0.4
Russian Federation	60	13	4.6	16	63	0.3	16	39	0.4	6	19	0.3	2	89	0.0
South Africa	63	25	2.5	56	35	1.6	35	57	0.6	38	45	0.8	28	63	0.4
Spain	81	9	9.0	29	51	0.6									
Turkey	49	19	2.6	18	62	0.3	6	82	0.1	9	72	0.1	6	88	0.1
United Kingdom**	66	26	2.5	44	50	0.9	29	64	0.5	26	48	0.5	31	63	0.5
United States	34	55	0.6												

Difference of sum of the share of respondents who responded 'positive' or 'negative' from 100% reflects those responding 0 'don't know' or 'depends/either'.

* 'Much' and 'a little' are added together in the table.

**United Kingdom does not include Northern Ireland.

Source: The Program on International Policy Attitudes, Center on Policy Attitudes and the Center for International and Security Studies, University of Maryland: 23 Nation Poll: Evaluating the World Powers, A GlobeScan/PIPA Poll [April 6, 2005], http://www.pipa.org/OnlineReports/europe/040605/Report04_06_05.pdf; 22 Nation Poll on Bush's Reelection: BBC World Service Poll [January 19, 2005], http://www.pipa.org/OnlineReports/BBCworldpoll/html/bbcpoll011905.html

Record 24: Attitudes towards corporate social responsibility

Large businesses are often portrayed as ruthless agents of economic globalisation, drawing opposition from anti-globalisation and anti-capitalist activists alike. Public attitudes towards large companies and their practices can indicate support for or opposition to economic globalisation and global capitalism. The Corporate Social Responsibility Monitor, an annual survey conducted by GlobeScan Inc., allows us to display such attitudes in 22 countries across the globe.

The table below shows the percentages of respondents who said that they 'strongly agree' or 'somewhat agree' with the following statements from the survey:

- Except for a few exceptions, most companies act ethically and responsibly.

- Large companies are doing a good job building a better society for all.

- I would pay 10 percent more for a product if the company donated the extra money to a charity.

- I would pay 10 percent more for a product that was produced in a socially and environmentally responsible way.

- My respect for a charitable or non-governmental organisation would go down if it partnered with a company to accomplish its goals.

- My respect for a company would go up if it partnered with a charitable or non-governmental organisation to help solve social problems.

The data show that trust in large companies is limited across the world, and that many support greater corporate social responsibility practices, environmentally friendly products and collaboration with civil society actors.

in % respondents who 'strongly agree' or 'somewhat agree', per country	Most companies are ethical	Companies build a better society	Would pay more if gains went to charity	Would pay more for socially and environmentally friendly products	Decrease in respect for NGOs if they collaborate with corporations	Increase in respect for companies if they collaborate with NGOs
East Asia & Pacific						
Australia	57	35	64	84	38	86
China	66	59	58	64	46	82
Indonesia	64	90	64	64	41	61
Japan		21	24	52		
Korea, Rep.		31	44	58		
Europe & Central Asia						
France	38	21	49	61	39	69
Germany	39	31	63	84	44	87
Italy	35	27	70	85	49	73
Netherlands	54	48	33	57	37	79
Russian Federation	30	32	26	47	22	74
Spain	38	31	52	49	40	49
Turkey	52	45	62	61	23	74
United Kingdom*	59	40	68	84	46	83
Latin America & Caribbean						
Chile	55	47	58	63	28	62
Mexico	44	32	36	60	48	39
Middle East & North Africa						
Qatar		42	78	73		
North America						
Canada	61	38	66	80	44	84
United States	62	43	61	78	40	77
South Asia						
India	62	61	66	71	47	71
Sub-Saharan Africa						
Nigeria	51	47	48	53	40	62
South Africa	69	66	67	75	54	87
Total (weighted) **	52	41	54	66	40	72

*United Kingdom does not include Northern Ireland.

** the total represents an average of country results weighted by their respective populations.

Figures are based on national samples of adults aged over 18, except Germany (respondents 16 years and above), India and Indonesia (15) and Japan (20). Samples for Chile, China, India, Indonesia, Korea Rep., South Africa and Turkey were taken only from urban populations.

Source: Data from the 2003 Corporate Social Responsibility Monitor, GlobeScan Incorporated Toronto Canada (with permission). See http://www.globescan.com/

Arbitrary detention. Deprivation of liberty imposed arbitrarily, that is, where no final decision has been taken by domestic courts in conformity with domestic law and with the relevant international standards set forth in the Universal Declaration of Human Rights and with the relevant international instruments accepted by the states concerned.

Bribing and corruption. This indicator is taken from the survey of business executives that forms part of the Institute for Management Development's World Competitiveness Yearbook. Respondents are asked to what extent bribing and corruption exist in the economy.

Control of Corruption Index. This measures perceptions of corruption, conventionally defined as the exercise of public power for private gain, and perceived as a failure of governance. A higher score in this index represents better control of corruption. The index is comprised of a range of measures from various sources, from the frequency of 'additional payments to get things done', through the effects of corruption on the business environment, to measuring 'grand corruption' in the political arena or in the tendency of elite forms to engage in 'state capture'.

Corruption Perceptions Index (CPI). This measures corruption in the public sector and defines corruption as the abuse of public office for private gain. The CPI makes no effort to reflect private sector fraud. The index is based on surveys compiled by Transparency International from other organisations that tend to ask questions about the misuse of public power for private benefits, with a focus, for example, on bribing of public officials, taking kickbacks in public procurement, or embezzling public funds, etc. Surveys consulted:

- World Bank and EBRD (Business Environment and Enterprise Performance Survey)
- Columbia University (State Capacity Survey)
- Economist Intelligence Unit (Country Risk Service and Country Forecast)
- Freedom House (Nations in Transit)
- Information International (Survey of Middle Eastern Businesspeople)
- Institute for Management Development (World Competitiveness Yearbook)
- A Multinational Development Bank (Survey)
- Merchant International Group (Grey Area Dynamics)
- Political and Economic Risk Consultancy, Hong Kong (Asian Intelligence Newsletter)
- Gallup International on behalf of Transparency International (Corruption Survey)
- World Markets Research Centre (Risk Ratings)
- World Economic Forum (Global Competitiveness Report)

Discrimination. Any distinction, exclusion, restriction, or preference based on any ground such as race, colour, sex, language, religion, political or other opinion, national or social origin, property, birth, or other status which has the purpose or effect of nullifying or impairing the recognition, enjoyment, or exercise, on an equal footing, of human rights and fundamental freedoms in the political, economic, social, cultural, or any other field of public life.

Emissions. Emissions refer to the release of greenhouse gases and/or their precursors, and aerosols into the atmosphere over a specified area and period of time.

Environmental conservation treaties. Our record includes 220 treaties in the following categories: animal species protection/management; environmental conservation (general); fishing, management/use of harvestable fish; forest conservation, management/exploitation; hunting, management/use of harvestable species; marine resources conservation/management; natural resources and nature conservation; plant species protection/management; renewable energy sources and energy conservation; soil conservation/management; water resources conservation/management.

Extrajudicial executions. Full expression 'extrajudicial, summary, or arbitrary executions': all acts and omissions of state representatives that constitute a violation of the general recognition of the right to life embodied in the Universal Declaration of Human Rights and the International Covenant on Civil and Political Rights.

Foreign direct investment (FDI). Investment to acquire a lasting management interest (10 per cent or more of voting stock) in an enterprise operating in an economy other than that of the investor. It is the sum of equity capital, reinvestment of earnings, other long-term capital, and short-term capital as shown in the balance of payments. FDI stock is the value of the share of capital and reserves (including retained profits) attributable to enterprises based outside the domestic economy, plus the net indebtedness of domestic affiliates to the parent enterprise. UNCTAD FDI stock data are frequently estimated by accumulating FDI *flows* over a period of time or adding flows to an FDI stock that has been obtained for a particular year.

Freedom of association. The right to establish and, subject only to the rules of the organisation concerned, to join organisations of one's own choosing without prior authorisation.

Freedom of expression. Freedom to hold opinions without interference and to seek, receive, and impart information and ideas through any media and regardless of frontiers.

Gross domestic product (GDP). Total domestic expenditure of a country, minus imports, plus exports of goods and services.

GDP per capita, PPP. GDP per capita based on purchasing power parity (PPP). GDP PPP is gross domestic product converted to international dollars using purchasing power parity rates. An international dollar has the same purchasing power over GDP as the US dollar in the United States. Data are in current international dollars.

Gini index. Measures the extent to which the distribution of income (or, in some cases, consumption expenditures) among individuals or households within an economy deviates from a perfectly equal distribution. A Lorenz curve plots the cumulative percentages of total income received against the cumulative number of recipients, starting with the poorest individual or household. The Gini index measures the area between the Lorenz curve and a hypothetical line of absolute equality, expressed as a percentage of the maximum area under the line. Thus, a Gini index of zero represents perfect equality, while an index of 100 implies perfect inequality.

Gross national income (GNI). Formerly known as gross national product or GNP. The sum of value added by all resident producers, plus any product taxes (less subsidies) not included in the valuation of output, plus net receipts of primary income (compensation of employees and property income) from abroad.

Human Development Index (HDI). A composite index based on three indicators: longevity, as measured by life expectancy at birth; educational attainment, as measured by a combination of adult literacy (two-thirds weight) and the combined gross primary, secondary, and tertiary enrolment ratio (one-third weight); and standard of living, as measured by GDP per capita (PPP US$).

Infant mortality rate. The probability of dying between birth and exactly one year of age, expressed per 100 live births.

Internally displaced persons (IDPs). Individuals or groups of people who have been forced to flee their homes to escape armed conflict, generalised violence, human rights abuses, or natural or man-made disasters, *and* have remained within the borders of their home country.

International NGOs. These are currently active, autonomous non-profit making organisations with operations or activities in at least three countries (or members with voting rights in at least three countries), a formal structure with election of governing officers from several member countries and some continuity of activities. Notably excluded are obviously national or bilateral organisations, informal social movements and ad hoc bodies, and international business enterprises, investment houses or cartels and other obvious profit making bodies. Irrelevant are size, importance, degree of activity, financial strength, political or ideological position, field of interest or activity, location of headquarters and language.

International telecom. Outgoing traffic refers to the telephone traffic, measured in minutes per subscriber, either line or cellular mobile, that originated in the country with a destination outside the country.

Life expectancy at birth. The number of years a newborn infant would live if prevailing patterns of age-specific mortality rates at the time of birth were to stay the same throughout the child's life.

Main telephone lines. Telephone lines connecting a customer's equipment to the public switched telephone network.

Merchandise trade. Includes all trade in goods. Trade in services is excluded.

Net primary school enrolment ratio. An indicator of the level of education in countries, listing the number of students enrolled in a level of education that are of official school age for that level, as a percentage of the population of official school age for that level.

Network, nodes and links. A network is comprised of entities such as individuals or organisations (nodes) and the interpersonal or inter-organisational links that connect them, which can reflect structural or legal relations, information flows and other exchanges. In the data represented in Record 4: Students abroad and Record 2: Global trade, the nodes are countries and the links consist of flows of international students (measured by numbers of students), in the former, and flows of trade in US$ in the latter. In record 21: International philanthropy (WINGS members and service countries) the nodes are countries and the link between the two countries exists when one provides services for and/or receives services from the other.

Official development assistance (ODA). Official development assistance and net official aid record the actual international transfer by the donor of financial resources or of goods or services valued at the cost to the donor, minus any repayments of loan principal during the same period. ODA data are comprised of disbursements of loans made on concessional terms (net of repayments of principal) and grants by official agencies of the members of the Development Assistance Committee (DAC) of the OECD, by multilateral institutions, and by certain Arab countries to promote economic development and welfare in recipient economies listed as 'developing' by DAC. Loans with a grant element of at least 25 per cent are included in ODA, as are technical cooperation and assistance.

Passengers carried. Air passengers carried include both domestic and international aircraft passengers.

Peacekeeping forces. Military personnel and civilian police serving in United Nations peacekeeping missions.

Political rights and civil liberties. Indicators of the levels of democracy in countries around the world. Real-world rights and freedoms enjoyed by individuals, as a result of actions by both state and non-governmental actors, based on the Universal Declaration of Human Rights. Political rights are defined as those that 'enable people to participate freely in the political process, including through the right to vote, compete for public office, and elect representatives who have a decisive impact on public policies and are accountable to the electorate'. Civil liberties are defined as those that 'allow for the freedoms of expression and belief, associational and organisational rights, rule of law, and personal autonomy without interference from the state'. These freedoms can be affected by a variety of actors, both governmental and non-governmental. Scores range from one, the lowest degree of freedom, to seven, the highest (for the sake of clarity we modified them from the original index scores which are reversed).

Press freedom. Freedom House's index combines scores on three dimensions: the legal environment (the extent to which this could influence media content and the extent to which governments use this to restrict media), political environment (the degree of political control over news media content), and economic environment (including various factors such as: the structure and nature of media ownership; costs of establishment, production and distribution; advertising and subsidies; impact of corruption or bribery; and impact of the general economic environment on the development of the media). Assessments are made on the basis of a variety of sources, including correspondents overseas, international visitors, human rights and press freedom organisations, various specialists, reports of governments and multilateral bodies, and domestic and international news media. Scores range from zero, the lowest degree of freedom, to 100, the highest (for clarity we modified them from the original index scores which are reversed).

Religious freedom. Freedom House's index rates countries according to the extent of freedom of 'religion or belief'. It therefore includes reference to beliefs that functionally take the place of explicitly religious beliefs, and rather than focusing on the rights of particular religious groups, assesses for *all* people rights explicitly concerned with practising one's religion, and the denial of rights because of the religious beliefs of those who are persecuted and/or those who persecute. The numbers represent ratings of the situation in countries, not of the conduct of governments. Scores range from one, the lowest degree of freedom, to seven, the highest (for clarity we modified them from the original index scores which are reversed).

Refugee. As defined by the UN High Commissioner for Refugees, a person is a refugee if she/he qualifies under the Arrangements of 12 May 1926 and 30 June 1928 or under the Conventions of 28 October 1933 and 10 February 1938, the Protocol of 14 September 1939 or the Constitution of the International Refugee Organisation. For further information see: www.unhcr.ch/cgi-bin/texis/vtx/home

Spring optimisation. Spring graph layouts use optimisation algorithms to represent the structure and strength of ties in a network. Spring optimised network diagrams draw the network as if all its nodes are connected by springs with a resting length proportional to the strength of ties between them. The algorithm alters the graph until an optimal balance between the structures of links in the network and 'spring tension' is achieved. The result is that nodes that have stronger ties and/or shortest paths between them are placed closer together in the graph. Different optimisation algorithms use different measures for strength of ties, eg the Kamada-Kawai (KK) spring optimisation function uses the shortest path distance between nodes.

Torture. Any act by which severe pain or suffering, whether physical or mental, is intentionally inflicted on a person for such purposes as obtaining from him or a third person information or a confession, punishing him for an act he or a third person has committed or is suspected of having committed, or intimidating or coercing him or a third person, or for any reason based on discrimination of any kind, when such pain or suffering is inflicted by or at the instigation of or with the consent or acquiescence of a public official or other person acting in an official capacity. It does not include pain or suffering arising only from, inherent in, or incidental to lawful sanctions.

Transnationality Index (TNI). The average of three ratios: a corporation's foreign assets to total assets, foreign sales to total sales, and foreign employment to total employment.

Transparency of government. This indicator is taken from the survey of business executives which forms part of the Institute for Management Development's World Competitiveness Yearbook. Respondents are asked to what extent their government communicates its policy intentions clearly and publicly.

Total military personnel. Active duty military personnel, including paramilitary forces if those forces resemble regular units in their organisation, equipment, training, or mission.

Total trade. The sum of the market value of imports and exports of goods and services.

Tourists. Visitors who travel to a country other than that where they have their usual residence for a period not exceeding 12 months and whose main purpose in visiting is other than an activity remunerated from within the country visited.

Voice and Accountability. An index comprised of a number of indicators measuring various aspects of the political process, civil liberties and political rights. These indicators measure the extent to which citizens of a country are able to participate in the selection of their government, as well as the independence of the media to monitor those in authority and hold them accountable for their actions.

WINGS Membership associations serving grantmakers. Organisations whose membership includes grantmakers, and provide support services only to their members. These organisations may not all serve grantmakers exclusively; some also serve a broader range of NGOs. WINGS Support organisations serving grantmakers and/or promoting philanthropy. Organisations that provide technical assistance to grantmakers, develop resources for them and/or advocate on behalf of grantmakers or philanthropy as a whole, but do not have a formal membership structure themselves, and whose services are extended to all grantmakers that may apply.

CHRONOLOGY OF GLOBAL CIVIL SOCIETY EVENTS
Compiled by Jill Timms

Contributors: Marcelo Batalha, Baris Gencer Baykan, Andrew Bolgar, Guiseppe Caruso, Joabe Cavalcanti, Hyo-Je Cho, Andrew Davey, Bernard Dreano, Heba Raouf Ezzat, Louise Fraser, Iuliana Gavril, Martin Gurch, Vicky Holland, Stuart Hodkinson, Kadi Jumu, Yung Law, Silke Lechner, Otilia Mihai, Selma Muhic, Richard Nagle, Tim Nagle, Alejandro Natal, Beatriz Martin Nieto, Katarina Sehm Patomaki, Mario Pianta, Oscar Reyes, Asthriesslav Rocuts, Ineke Roose, Thomas Ruddy, Mohamed Said, Kate Townsend, Caroline Watt, Lilian Outtes Wanderley, Sébastien Ziegler.

About the chronology
In this, the fifth, edition of the chronology, we present details of global civil society events that took place between May 2004 and April 2005. The chronology seeks to offer an alternative portrayal of activities around the world, which are often not reported in mainstream media but which involve, or have some significance for, civil society beyond the boundaries of a single country.

We have gathered the information presented here from the contributions of our network of global civil society correspondents. We provide details in the following sections about how you could become part of this team.

The growth of civil society activity beyond the local and national, and our growing awareness of it, mean that it would be impossible to present a comprehensive directory of all events, or even of all events related to a single issue. Therefore, we offer a record that indicates the diverse nature of civil society activity and its significance, and that covers more areas of the globe than conventional chronologies of world news. Our chronology also includes activities that are not easily represented in statistical accounts of civil society: for example, innovative campaigns, spontaneous protests or local gatherings.

With regard to social forums, we have included all the forums – local, thematic and global – that we are aware of, as detailed in Map 6.1 (page 196), because feedback from our correspondents suggests that their proliferation is a significant development that should be monitored. It should be noted that these entries are limited to those forums with active websites or of which correspondents have notified us.

Invitation to contribute to the development of the chronology
We invite our readers to contribute to the evolution of the chronology, which is currently under review, with the aim of developing a database of global civil society that is freely accessible worldwide. The first step of this initiative is to research the usefulness of information contained in the chronology.

We are interested in how the data is used, who uses it, how helpful it is and how we can improve it. To this end we have a designed a short questionnaire, which can be found at: **www.lse.ac.uk/dept/global/chronologyquestionnaire**

Everyone who completes this questionnaire will be entered into a prize draw, the winner of which will be invited to participate in a forthcoming seminar at the London School of Economics to discuss the evolution of the chronology. Details of the conditions can be found on the website.

Since 2000, we have developed a growing network of correspondents in many parts of the world, who regularly update us on events taking place in their locality. We rely on the contributions of each team member for the data in the chronology. Our thanks go to all those who have worked with us on this edition.

We need to increase the scope and range of the network, in terms of both areas of the world covered and the diversity of correspondents. We invite you to join the team, which entails keeping us updated about activities and events in your field or area of the world. Each correspondent who contributes information that is included in the chronology receives an acknowledgement, a complimentary copy of the Global Civil Society Yearbook, and, of course, our thanks. We are exploring innovative ways to develop our collaboration with correspondents. If you are interested in finding out more about becoming a correspondent, or know someone who might be, please visit: **www.lse.ac.uk/depts/global/correspondents.htm**

This is an exciting time for global civil society, and our chronology is one of the ways in which we hope to contribute to, as well as to monitor, these interesting developments.

Global Civil Society events, May 2004–April 2005

May 2004

1 May Celebrations and actions are held throughout the world on Labour Day in support of workers' rights. As ten new member states join the European Union (EU), mostly from Eastern Europe, 10,000 people rally in Brussels as part of the wider global justice demonstrations.

5 May Thousands of Maori protesters march outside Parliament in New Zealand over plans to nationalise the shoreline, which they claim belongs to them. The action is supported by campaigners for the rights of indigenous peoples and environmentalists.

7–8 May The Stockholm Social Forum, Sweden, is held, with nearly 200 events taking place. The forum concludes with a march and rally focusing on the charter of the forum.

19 May In London, UK, the British Prime Minister Tony Blair is hit by four condoms filled with purple flour. These were thrown into the chamber of the House of Commons as part of a public campaign by Fathers4Justice, which lobbies for men divorced or separated from their partners to have greater access to their children. Their protests often involve members dressed as superheroes scaling national monuments.

June 2004

3–5 June The Austrian Social Forum takes place with the participation of secondary school pupils, who discuss issues relevant to them.

4–5 June The Mapuche Social Forum in Villarrica-Pucon, Chile, attracts some 500 participants, mostly indigenous peoples and their organisations.

4–6 June The Midwest Social Forum, also known as the RadFest, takes place at the Lake Geneva Campus of Aurora University, US. The central goal of the forum is to contribute to social movement building by providing organisers, activists, community members, and intellectuals with the opportunity to come together to discuss issues, strengthen networks, and devise strategies for progressive social, economic, and political change.

10 June Indigenous demonstrations are held during the meeting in Quito, Ecuador, of the Organization of American States, with activists demanding the rejection of the Free Trade Agreement of the Americas (FTAA) and the resignation of President Gutierrez.

12 June Some 10,000 protesters from trade unions, farmers' organisations and NGOs converge on the Asian Strategic Insight Roundtable, a regional conference of the World Economic Forum summit, in Seoul, South Korea.

23–25 June The Boston Social Forum hold a one-off parallel event to the Democrat Convention taking place in the city as part of the US presidential campaign.

25–27 June The Triple Frontier Social Forum is held in Puerto Iguazu, Argentina. This regional forum addresses issues concerning Brazil, Argentina and Paraguay, and is held close to where all three borders meet.

July 2004

1 July 500,000 people take part in Hong Kong's biggest ever pro-democracy demonstration against the system whereby the Chief Executive is elected by only 800 people.

9 July Amid much interest from peace activists around the world, the International Court of Justice in the Hague, the Netherlands, rules that the controversial West Bank Barrier, a 425 mile-long wall being constructed by Israel to keep Palestinians out of Jewish settlements in the West Bank, is illegal.

19–21 July In San Salvador, El Salvador, the Central-American Forum is held. Although it is not called a 'social' forum, the event is inspired by the World Social Forum and discusses opposition to the FTAA and Plan Pueblo Panama, which aims to develop trade and tourism links as well as road links across Central America.

25 July 1,500 protesters tear up a field of experimental genetically modified (GM) maize in Toulouse, France. Leading farmers' activist Jose Bove says this represents a new wave of international activism against GM trials.

25–30 July The Americas Social Forum is held in Quito, Ecuador, with some 10,000 participants. There is a strong anti-FTAA and indigenous orientation.

27–29 July The second Moroccan Social Forum draws 1,200 participants from all over the country, and small delegations of Arab, African, American and European NGOs.

29–31 July The third World Education Forum is held and preceded by regional education forums in São Paolo, Brazil, Guadalajara, Mexico and Barcelona, Spain.

August 2004

2 August In Canada, workers at a Wal-Mart store in Jonquière, Quebec, have their right to vote to unionise confirmed by the Quebec Labor Relations Commission. Labour campaigners see this as a significant victory over the company – one of the world's largest retail employers – which until now has not allowed formal union involvement in its labour relations. However, before the contract with the union is finalised, Wal-Mart closes the Jonquière branch. The commission launches legal action against Wal-Mart.

2–4 August The Peru Social Forum takes place in Tambogrande. Although a similar forum was held the previous year, it was called 'Towards a Peru Social Forum'.

14–15 August The first Paraná Medio Social Forum focuses on the theme 'In Defence of Cultural and Biological Diversity'.

18–21 August The inaugural conference of the Globalisation Studies Network (GSN) is held in Warwick, UK.

26–28 August In Buenos Aires, Argentina, the Social Forum of Information, Documentation and Libraries is held, organised by Argentinian and Mexican library associations.

29 August Nearly half a million citizens gather in Manhattan, New York, US, the day before the Republican National Convention to protest against US involvement in Iraq and to oppose the re-election of George W Bush at the forthcoming US presidential election. Leading the protest are members of United for Peace and Justice. Republican New York Mayor Michael Bloomberg, who had sought legal action to stop protestors from gathering in the city, amasses a police force of more than 37,000, including state and federal officers. The protest passes off peacefully.

29 August More than 400 citizens, many from the Industrial Workers of the World union, gather in New York City to protest an appeal by Starbucks Coffee Company against a National Labor Relations Board ruling that would allow individual Starbucks stores to vote on union representation.

September 2004

1 September In Kenya, a campaign is launched by the Masai peoples to win the return of ancestral territory in Laikilia, which was claimed by white farmers under a British colonial treaty of 1904. The campaign is mounted on the expiration of the treaty.

3–7 September The Mineiro Social Forum themed on 'Sovereignty and People's Participation' takes place in Belo Horizonte, Brazil.

8–19 September An international cultural festival, named the World Culture Open, takes place simultaneously in the cities of New York, Seoul, and Pyongyang. Performing groups from 70 different countries and 354 NGOs participate in this 'cultural olympics'.

14 September Representatives of international human rights groups call for the scrapping of the South Korean National Security Law. This follows a gathering of activists from home and abroad before the International Conference for National Human Rights Institutions opens in Seoul to discuss human rights violations related to international conflicts, including war and terrorism in Iraq and Russia.

16–19 September The Uruguay Social Forum is held in Montevideo for the third time. It attracts several thousand participants, and for the first time is held in a decentralised location in Montevideo-West rather than the usual city centre, with discussion of further decentralisation to promote the spread of the forum elsewhere in Uruguay.

17–19 September At an aboriginal reserve near Montreal, Canada, the Montreal Social Forum is held. On two previous occasions it has taken place under the alternative name of the 'Third Citizens' Summit' of Montreal.

17–19 September In Beirut, Lebanon, a meeting 'Where Next for the Global Anti-War and Anti-Globalization Movements?' brings together nearly 250 participants from the Arab region and around the world, including the Stop the War Coalition, Focus on the Global South, Hizbullah, ATTAC, the Muslim Brotherhood in Egypt and the Egyptian Anti-Globalization Group.

17–19 September The Sydney Social Forum, Australia, takes place, with hundreds of participants taking part in more than 70 workshops, many focusing on how peoples' rights and access to basic services have been privatised around the world and how the neoliberal agenda can be reversed. The end of the forum coincides with 'End the Lies' rallies across Australia.

19 September A peace meeting originally planned to be held in Kashmir takes place in the Netherlands before the annual summit between the EU and India. Participants from Kashmir, India and Pakistan share their experiences with peace activists from Kosovo, Palestine, Northern Ireland, France and the Netherlands.

23 September The Pakistan Fisherfolk Forum and the Save Coast Action Committee Badin hold a one-day hunger strike in Karachi to protest against a World Bank-backed drainage project that they claim will damage coastal livelihoods and biodiversity.

23–25 September The Corrientes Social Forum takes place in Argentina, focused on 'Foreign Debt – the Mother of all Ills'.

24–25 September The second Bretagne Social Forum is held in a social centre in Rostronen, Brittany, France. The major themes of the forum are culture, solidarity economy, agriculture/ environment and politics.

25–26 September The Alpes du Sud Social Forum is held in Veynes, France. Participants attempt to re-appropriate the city as a space for debate and collective action. The event includes marching bands and a strong emphasis on the sharing of local food.

25–28 September The Czech Social Forum in Prague attracts about 100 participants.

25 September–2 October The Pays Nantais Social Forum meets in a former cigarette factory in Bayonne, France, under the banner 'Our World is Not for Sale'. Among the many themes discussed are the environment and agriculture, the social forum process, international solidarity and economic alternatives.

29 September–2 October A symposium on 'New Tactics in Human Rights', organised by the Helsinki Citizens' Assembly in Ankara, Turkey, attracts 500 participants from all over the world.

October 2004

1–3 October The Danish Social Forum is held in the Christianshavn neighbourhood of Copenhagen. Approximately 1,000 people take part in a range of activities including marches, discussions, workshops and a cultural programme of film, music and theatre.

2 October Saharawi activists (from Western Sahara) stage protests in southern Morocco and occupied Western Sahara, seeking to create an 'intifada'. The Moroccan government is enraged by South Africa's official recognition of Western Sahara, which is currently pursuing self-determination to gain independence from Morocco.

2–30 October A Monster Tomato Tour takes place in Turkey as part of a European anti-GM campaign, organised by a coalition of 30 Turkish civil society groups, united in the 'No to GMOs Platform'.

8 October The Limousin Social Forum discusses local issues such as agriculture, tourism, and the environment. It contributes to a network of local social forums in France.

8–10 October In various sites in Dublin the Irish Social Forum is held, with the dominant issue being preparation for joining the European Social Forum in London the following week.

9–12 October The Capixaba Social Forum is held in Brazil, and is also run as a regional forum for the state of Espirito Santo.

15–17 October The third European Social Forum (ESF) is held in London. Criticisms about lack of democracy and of inclusiveness in the process leads to several counter-forums in areas designated as autonomous space, meaning that they are self-organised and not part of the official ESF process. These parallel events are collectively referred to as 'Beyond ESF'.

16 October The Lot et Garonne Social Forum is held as a French departmental forum for the people of department 47.

19–22 October The Malawi Social Forum takes place in Lilongwe, Malawi, with the full support of the government.

21–23 October The Southern Cone Social Forum, organised by university lecturers and academics in Rosario, Argentina, explores the theme 'Earth and Food'.

21–24 October In Oslo, the Norway Social Forum adopts a conference format to facilitate discussion of globalisation. It is decided that the national forum should skip a year (the next being held in 2006), and instead efforts will focus on helping develop local social forums.

23 October The first Valparaiso local Social Forum is organised in Chile.

28–29 October The New York City Social Forum focuses on the strengthening of transnational civil society activity in North America. The forum continues to develop its elaborate system of consensus building.

28–30 October In Harare, the second Zimbabwe Social Forum is held, despite an attempt by government to ban it. The focus is largely anti-neoliberal but also anti-government. There is a people's tribunal, a youth tent and faith-based input.

28–30 October The Alpes-Maritimes Departmental Social Forum takes place in Valbonne, France. This is the third time the forum is held and is run in Ariane, a migrant area, after initial problems with local authorities about public buildings being used for the forum are resolved.

30 October 50,000 people in Rome, Italy, demonstrate against the coalition forces in Iraq.

November 2004

4 November The Vietnamese Association of Victims of Agent Orange files a class action law suit in a New York court against Monsanto and 36 other manufacturers of Agent Orange.

5–6 November In São Luis, Maranho, Brazil, the Maranhense Social Forum takes place.

5–6 November In La Serena, Chile, the Coquimbo and La Serena Social Forum is held.

5–7 November The third Argentina Health Social Forum is held in Buenos Aires, Argentina, focusing on local, national and international health policy and links to environmental concerns.

8–9 November An International Forum on Global Democracy is held in Peru.

9–13 November 700 people join together for dis-cussions and cultural events in Makurdi, Nigeria, for the Nigerian Social Forum.

10 November Activists of NGOs working for the rights of overseas Koreans gather in Seoul to discuss ways to improve their rights and strengthen national identity.

11–12 November The Alagoas local Social Forum is held in the Federal University of this Brazilian city.

12–13 November The Basel regional Social Forum takes place in Switzerland, with a strong Roman Catholic input.

12–13 November The Paris-Central Social Forum is held in France, combining local themes such as the new plans for Les Halles, water services and social exclusion, with national themes on wages and social security, and theoretical concerns with democracy.

16–20 November The VIII Annual Meeting of the Global Forum for Health Research takes place in Mexico City, attracting more than 700 participants from governments, civil society and the health profession.

18–20 November 600 people, including 150 leaders of international civil society organisations and social movements, attend a 'Reclaim our UN' international seminar in Padua, Italy, on the future of the UN and the international institutions.

19–28 November The Les Mureaux Val de Seine Social Forum is held in Aubergenville, France. This is the second time the forum has taken place, and plans are already started for the third event, which will have a stronger focus on politics through culture.

20–21 November The Chile Social Forum in Santiago, using the Argentine model, pledges to develop local, regional, and thematic forums in future.

22–28 November In Kiev, mass public protests about vote rigging erupt after the election of Viktor Yanukovychas as Prime Minister of Ukraine. Despite sub-zero temperatures, the protests continue and the 'Orange Revolution' forces a new election to be held that results in the election of the opposition party's Viktor Yushchenko.

24 November More than 200 citizens protest near the Tucson Convention Center, Arizona, US, in a bid to deter some 1,500 South American delegates from signing the Andean Free Trade Agreement. Delegates meet for five days during the sixth round of talks to discuss trade agreements between Colombia, Peru, Ecuador and the US, while Bolivia observes the talks. Protestors include members of the Colombian Network Against Free Trade, human rights groups, labour rights activists, and peace and environmental groups.

24–27 November The regional Nordestino (north-eastern) Brazilian Social Forum is held for the first time.

25 November Students, professors, civil servants, and social movements protest against the 'Labor, Sindical and University Reform', in Brasília, Brazil. More than 20,000 people march through the Esplanada dos Ministérios, calling for more participation in the process of reform to be allowed by students' move-

ments, workers' syndicates and research institutions.

26 November Eleven British activists protest outside the Icelandic embassy in the UK against the building of the Karahnjukar dams.

26–27 November The Kenya Social Forum includes a demonstration and presentation of a memorandum against the meeting of the World Trade Organization (WTO) that will take place in Nairobi in March 2005.

26–27 November The Carioca Social Forum is held in Rio de Janeiro, Brazil.

26–28 November Planned to coincide with Dutch EU presidency, the Netherlands Social Forum facilitates the exchange of ideas and the strengthening of networks to promote social action.

27–28 November The Val de Bièvre local Social Forum takes place in Aubergenville, France, with a total of 26 affiliated organisations.

28 November The Melbourne local Social Forum, Australia, 'A Festival of Possibilities', takes place.

December 2004

3–6 December In the south of Spain, the Malaga Social Forum takes place and nurtures its strong Latin-American connections.

4–5 December A meeting of UK Local Social Forums in Sheffield exchanges experiences in order to promote future support and collaboration.

10–14 December The UK North West Social Forum is held in the city of Manchester, under the theme 'Cross-community and Cross-border'.

10–14 December In Lukasa, Zambia, the third African Social Forum takes place, despite internal struggles that have threatened to stop the event. As well as exploring 'Popular Resistance and Alternatives', there is also discussion about putting Zambia forward as one of World Social Forum venues in 2006, when the event will be decentralised.

11–12 December The Kyoto Social Forum, the first forum in Japan, attracts 300 participants. Topics discussed include trade unions, refugees, environmental issues, the US base in Okinawa, relationships with North Korea, food security, and Japanese war crimes.

12 December In Cairo, Egypt, the newly formed Kefaya, or 'Enough' movement, holds its first protest to demand radical political and constitutional reforms.

16 December Anti-monarchy activists stage demonstrations in the main cities of Saudi Arabia. Six people are arrested.

20–22 December More than 100 activists representing Somali civil society organisations, institutions and individuals gather in Mogadishu for the Somali Social Forum.

24 December In Nunavut, in the Canadian Arctic, 155,000 Inuits agree to file a petition with the Inter-American Commission of Human Rights against the US's lack of action against global warming, which they argue threatens their existence.

26 December International civil society organisations play a key role in bringing emergency relief when a colossal earthquake in the Indian Ocean just west of Sumatra results in a tsunami, devastating coastal populations in Indonesia, Malaysia, Burma and Thailand, as well as in South Asia. The official death toll reaches 125,000 with five million people homeless by the end of 2004. This results in new alliances between international and local organisations, and a general renewed interest and donations to aid organisations internationally.

January 2005

1 January The EU announces that 2005 will be 'The Year of the Mediterranean' and that civil society participation in Euromed policies will be a priority.

1 January The 'Make Poverty History' campaign is launched, mobilising a coalition of development agencies, faith groups, NGOs, trade unions and many others, on issues of trade justice, debt cancellation and better aid for the eradication of global poverty.

5 January In Sierra Leone, a two-day general strike that has brought the capital of Freetown to a virtual standstill ends after the government agrees to increase the minimum wage to the equivalent of US$13 a month and to cut income tax and fuel duty. The result of collaboration between the major trade unions, the protest is seen as a positive sign that the country is returning to normality after the civil war, which ended in 2001.

6 January Thousands of Zambians protest in Lusaka demanding that a new constitution be adopted before presidential and parliamentary elections in 2006.

17 January HIV and AIDS campaigners around the world praise Nelson Mandela for revealing that his son, Makgatho, died of an AIDS-related illness and for highlighting the plight of the millions of people living with HIV and AIDS in Africa.

18–22 January The fourth Pan-Amazonian Social

Forum takes place in Manaus, Brazil, under the banner 'Another Amazon is Possible!'

19 January After more than 40 years of campaigns, Edgar Ray Killen, a former member of the Ku Klux Klan, is charged with the murders of a local black man and two white students who were helping to register black votes in Philadephia, Mississippi, in 1964. The continuous campaigning for his conviction included the making of the 1988 film 'Mississippi Burning'.

20–23 January Hundreds of relatives of the victims of the three-day siege and massacre during 1–3 September 2004 in Beslan, Russia, hold a protest for three days against the lack of progress by the inquiry, blocking a major road in North Ossetia.

26 January Tens of thousands of public schoolteachers in Zambia embark on an illegal strike to press for better wages and housing benefits.

26–31 January The fifth World Social Forum takes place in Porto Alegre, Brazil, with 155,000 participants. The event is organised around several territories, that is, spaces designated for the major themes of the Forum, within which all the events for that theme take place. It attracts the largest number of young people to attend a World Social Forum, with 35,000 registering for the youth camp. It is agreed that for 2006, several forums will be held simultaneously in different parts of the world, replacing the single-location format of the WSF. In 2007, the WSF will again be in a single venue – in Africa – but the country and city have yet to be confirmed.

29 January In Caracas, Venezuela thousands of protesters demonstrate against the abduction of a Columbian rebel leader from Venezuelan territory. This abduction was allegedly a result of provocation by the US.

29–30 January The Ivry Social Forum in France is described as a permanent local open space for the maintenance and development of collective action. The forum takes an unusual form because organisers are responsible for managing a permanent building and have developed as a special association, with open membership and with all action taken in the name of individuals or groups but not the forum itself.

February 2005

6 February Human rights campaigners in Chile and internationally react angrily to the Supreme Court's ruling that investigators looking into the human rights abuses allegedly committed during the era of Augusto Pinochet, the former President, have six months to present their evidence. This means that 365 cases need to be prepared before July.

12 February Activist Sister Dorothy Stang is murdered after more than 30 years working for sustainable development in the Amazon, in particular with the Landless Workers Movement. Dressed in white and carrying candles, her supporters throughout Brazil protest against agro-businesses' destruction of the environment and local farmers' livelihoods. The police suspect Stang's murder was a contract killing by local ranchers, and 2,000 officers are sent to track them down.

14 February After the assassination of former Prime Minister Rafik Hariri in Beirut, a tide of mass demonstrations for and against the Syrian presence in Lebanon shakes the country for weeks. International pressure against the Syrian presence is led predominantly by the US. The campaign leads to an announcement in March 2005 that Syrian troops will be withdrawn.

17–23 February Students protest against increased fees, problems with accommodation, and racist student representative councils in universities across South Africa. Violence breaks out on several campuses where tyres and the South African flag are burned. Police arrest students at the Universities of Limpopo and Pretoria.

19 February In Rome, 500,000 people demonstrate for the liberation of the Italian journalist Giuliana Sgrena, who was kidnapped in Iraq on 4 February.

19 February The European Court of Human Rights rules that two British environmental campaigners were treated unfairly when the British government refused to grant them legal aid for their defence against a libel case brought by McDonald's. Helen Steel and David Morris, who have gained international support from environmentalists and anti-corporate activists, are granted £24,000 compensation and costs. The so-called 'McLibel Two' were sued for handing out leaflets containing allegations about the company's unethical behaviour, including low wages, some of which were proved to be true. The firm's action in response to the leaflets and the resulting trial is described by business analysts as one of the worst public relations failures ever, costing the company £10 million in legal costs.

22 February In what is dubbed the 'Chintz Revolution', 10,000 pensioners in St Petersburg, Russia, hold a rally against economic reforms that are reducing their welfare benefits substantially.

25–27 February The second Alberta Social Forum is held in Calgary, Canada, following its first incarnation in 2003. Strong links are maintained with the Ontario Social Forum.

26 February In Anapu, Brazil, President Lula de Silva creates the world's largest environmental protection area, a ten million-acre forest. This follows international outrage in the wake of the murder of Dorothy Stang, a nun who was fighting for the rights of small landowners.

March 2005

1–7 March Roads and highways throughout South Africa are blockaded by 30,000 truck drivers demanding a wage increase.

3 March In Freetown, Sierra Leone, students, lecturers and their supporters demonstrate against the government as university students have not been paid their grants and lecturers have received no wages for the year so far. Strikes by the lecturers also result in exams being cancelled.

8 March International Women's Day is celebrated around the world.

9 March More than 250 San Francisco State University students and faculty protest against US military recruitment on college campuses across the country. Protestors aim to prohibit recruiters from the US Air Force and the Army Corps of Engineers from campuses. Many activists belong to the group Students Against War.

9 March In Beirut, three weeks of anti-Syrian demonstrations culminate in a massive, Hizbollah-organised rally that fills a central square. Demonstrators support Syria's rejection of a UN resolution calling for the complete and immediate withdrawal of Syrian troops from Lebanon.

11 March Marches are held throughout Spain to mark the first anniversary of the Madrid train bombings. An international summit on terrorism is held in Madrid as part of the remembrance.

12 March–6 April To mark the 75th anniversary of the Salt March, when Gandhi led a march to demonstrate the power of non-violence, events take place in Copenhagen (Denmark) and Stockholm (Sweden), with Committees of the Salt March handing over bags of salt with political messages on them to parliamentarians.

14 March Nearly a million people gather for an opposition rally in Beirut a month after the death of Rafik Hariri. They protest against the presence of Syrian forces in Lebanon.

15–22 March In Niger, the Democratic Coordination Committee of Civil Societies in Niger coordinate a 'dead city' action involving 150,000 protesters to press for the removal of a 19 per cent value added tax imposed by the government on certain basic products. This new financial law is introduced by the government under pressure from the IMF. The leaders of the movement are arrested, then released under judicial control and negotiate with the government to resolve the crisis.

18–20 March The Perth Social Forum, Australia, described as 'the biggest artistic event ever', takes place. A dominant theme is access to and the promotion of artistic forms of resistance.

19–20 March On the second anniversary of the invasion of Iraq, an international day of action against the occupation takes place. Demonstrations include 50,000 protesters in London, a 100,000-strong demonstration in Rome, a march of 4,500 in Tokyo that is coordinated with the arrival of US Secretary of State Condoleeza Rice, and other marches in Stockholm, Istanbul, and some Australian cities. In several US cities, demonstrators march behind mock coffins draped with the country's flag.

22 March World Water Day launches the 'Water for Life' decade, which calls on the global community to strengthen efforts to increase access to water and sanitation for all, in line with the UN Millennium Development Goals.

23 March 70,000 people from Belgium, France, Germany, Italy and the Netherlands march in Brussels against the proposed European Commission Directive on Services in the Internal Market – the so-called 'Bolkestein Directive' – which makes it legal to offer pay and benefits to foreign workers that are similar to levels in their home countries. Campaigners argue that this would lower salaries and benefits for workers generally.

24–27 March The Third Cairo Conference Against War and Globalization is held in Egypt, structured similarly to social forums, as independent, yet relevant, activities are organised under its umbrella. A students' forum and peasants' and workers' forums are organised as part of this, where grassroots activists share experiences and ideas from struggles around the world.

26 March In Osh, Kyrgyzstan, thousands of protesters march on the streets demanding a new election, after alleged vote rigging results in the unpopular Askar Akayev winning the presidential election by a landslide.

28 March 3,000 people flee Baluchistan in Pakistan, in the wake of riots involving local tribes people. The unrest follows the alleged rape of a female doctor by a soldier.

31 March A grassroots Chinese campaign to keep Japan out of the United Nations Security Council has gathered some 22 million signatures, increasing the chances that China will block Japan's bid to join, organisers claim.

April 2005

1–3 April The Ostergotland Social Forum is simultaneously held in Linkoping and Norkoping, Sweden.

2 April The 1.2 billion members of the Roman Catholic Church hold vigils across the world after the death of Pope John Paul II. The Vatican becomes a centre for pilgrims during the Pontiff's final hours, afterwards at his funeral and during the election of his successor. Religious and human rights groups across the world raise awareness of the importance of the new pope's views on issues such as the role of women in the church, homosexuality, and the use of contraception, particularly in the fight against HIV and AIDS.

6 April After four years of coordinated campaigns, the trial begins of 28 Italian police officers for alleged vicious attacks on protesters and for fabricating evidence against them at the 2001 G8 summit in Genoa.

9 April The Libournais Social Forum, a sub-forum of the Gironde regional forum, France, takes place.

9 April Civil rights organisations condemn the creation of a volunteer force, Minuteman Civil Defense Corps, to patrol the Arizona–Mexico border for 'observation purposes' only. Campaigners accuse them of racism, and point out that they endanger official patrols, which do not coordinate with them, and also raise concerns that some of the volunteers carry guns. Although there have been no incidents involving guns, the practice is seen to be threatening and contradictory to the force's ostensible purpose of observation.

9–10 April In Helsinki, the national Finnish Social Forum is held for the third time.

10–16 April The largest ever mobilisation of civil society action on trade issues takes place, as more than ten million people in more than 80 countries take part in a Global Week of Action on Trade, part of the ongoing Make Poverty History and Poverty Zero campaigns. Many diverse initiatives against the WTO, IMF, World Bank, and regional and bilateral trade agreements are organised, under the slogan 'Trade Justice, Not Free Trade'.

12 April In Guatemala City, an Indian activist, supported by indigenous rights campaigners, wins his case against key military officials. Rigoberta Menchu, a Nobel Peace Prize winner, was racially abused during a court hearing to decide whether he could stand as a presidential candidate.

14 April Mass protests are held in China following the publication of eight new textbooks in Japan that are said to play down the country's role in wartime atrocities. Continued public interest, encouraged by the government, later results in the spread of protests throughout China, with rallies and marches in Beijing, Shanghai, Shenzen, Chengdu and Shanyang.

16 April In Baghdad, Iraq, tens of thousands of Shia Muslims loyal to the radical cleric Moqtada al-Sadr demonstrate to mark the second anniversary of the fall of Saddam Hussein and to demand the withdrawal of coalition troops.

18 April In Dongyang, China, thousands of peasants riot in protest at pollution from chemical factories that has ruined crops and been linked to deformities in babies. A news blackout is imposed by the government.

25 April In Togo, there are street protests over alleged vote rigging. The elections had been called only after a public outcry when Faure Gnassingbe, the son of the late president, Gnassinge Eyadema, was sworn in, in defiance of the country's constitution. Faure Gnassingbe went on to win the presidential election but the protests continued.

INDEX

Sudan, 174, 175

Tear Fund, 117
Teivainen, Teivo, 76
telecommunications see communications technology
terrorism, 14–15
    causes, 30
    incidents, 16–17
    targetting NGOs, data, 432–3
Third World Network, 150
Tobin Tax, 174, 184–5
tourism, data, 333–40
trade, data, 314–17
trafficking in persons, data, 328–32
transnational corporations, data, 318–22
Transnational Institute, Carbon Trade Watch, 110, 111
transparency of government (see also governance and
        accountability)
    data, 380–6
transsexuality, 42
Traoré, Aminata, 224
treaties, international, data, 358–65
tsunami, Indian Ocean see Indian Ocean tsunami (26 Dec 2004)
TxtMob, 280

Ukraine, 19, 20
Union of Concerned Scientists, 100
Union of International Associations (UIA), 249
United Kingdom
    discrimination between citizens and aliens, 130–1
    London bombings (7 & 21 July 2005), 15
    migration issues, 134, 136, 139–40, 141
United Nations
    Commission on Human Rights, 166
    Conference on Environment and Development (UNCED), 156
    Conference on Human Settlements, Istanbul, 156
    Conference on Population, Cairo, 156
    Conference on Social Development, Copenhagen, 156
    Conference on the Human Environment, Stockholm, 159
    Conference on Women and Development, Beijing, 156
    conferences and summits, 160–3
    Emergency Peace Service (UNEPS), 184
    Environment Programme, 115–17
    Flash Appeal, 4, 7
    Framework Convention on Climate Change (UNFCCC), 94
    Global Compact, 176, 178–9
    data, 423
    High-level Panel on Security, 159, 168
    High-level Panel on Threats, Challenges and Change,
        28, 159, 172–4
    International Commission on State Sovereignty and
        Intervention, 173
    Millennium Development Goals, 48
    Millennium Project, 29
    Office for the Coordination of Humanitarian Affairs (OCHA), 4
    Office of Constituency Engagement and Partnerships, 176
    organisation, 152–3
    Panel of Eminent Persons on United Nations-Civil Society
        Relations, 25, 28, 159, 176–7

    reform, 150–86
    relationship to civil society, 24–6
    Summit on Sustainable Development, Johannesburg, 156
    Women's Conference, Beijing, 54
United States
    attitudes towards, data, 463–4
    climate change policy, 96, 105, 112
    migration issues, 134–5, 140–1, 142–3
USAID, data, 427
utopian perspective, 71–2

violence, 14–15, 229
voice and accountability index (World Bank), data, 349–57
Voices from Mumbai, 206
volunteering, 126–7

Waterman, Peter, 242
websites, social forums, 195, 206, 238
Western Growers Association (WGA), 141
Whitaker, Chico, 190, 194, 224
Whitaker, Francisco, 76
White Ribbon Campaign, 59
WINGS see Worldwide Initiatives for Grant-maker Support
women, in civil society, 38–63
Women's Caucus for Gender Justice, 46–7
Women's International League for Peace and Freedom
        (WILPF), 151
World Bank, 96
    Climate Change Programme, 105–6, 111
World Development Movement, 11, 135
World Economic Forum, 79
    Davos (1999), 190
    Davos (2005), 30
World Education Forum, 204
World Forum of Liberties, 207
World Heritage Sites, climate change impacts, 112
World Migration Organisation, 133
World Resources Institute, 100
World Social Forum on Health, 204
World Social Forum, organisation and process, 64–86
World Social Forum (WSF), 27, 30, 198–200
    Charter of Principles, 192–3, 194–5
    financial sponsors, 228, 230–1
World Social Thematic Forum on Democracy, Human Rights,
        War and Drug Trafficking, 204
World Summit on the Information Society (WSIS), 252–4
World Trade Centre terrorist attack (11 Sept 2001), effect on
        immigration debate, 140–1, 142
World Trade Organization (WTO), 96
World Wildlife Fund (WWF), 99
WorldWatch Institute, 100
Worldwide Initiatives for Grant-maker Support (WINGS), 444–55
WSF see World Social Forum
WSIS see World Summit on the Information Society

Zhao, Yuezhi, 282